Travel Vision

A Practical Guide for the Travel,
Tourism, and Hospitality Industry

Jeanne Semer-Purzycki

Prentice Hall
Upper Saddle River, NJ 07458

Library of Congress Cataloging-in-Publication Data

Semer-Purzycki, Jeanne

    Travel vision: a practical guide for the travel, tourism, and hospitality industry / Jeanne Semer-Purzycki

      p. cm.

    ISBN 0-13-096089-6

      1. Tourism—Vocational guidance. I. Title.

    G155.5 .S46 2000

    338.4'791'02373—dc21   99-045634

                 CIP

Director of Production and Manufacturing: *Bruce Johnson*
Managing Editor: *Mary Carnis*
Acquisitions Editor: *Neil Marquardt*
Editorial Assistant: *Susan Kegler*
Production Editor: *Denise Brown*
Manufacturing Buyer: *Ed O'Dougherty*
Formatting/page make-up: *Pine Tree Composition, Inc.*
Printer/Binder: *Courier Westford*
Marketing Manager: *Shannon Simonsen*
Creative Director: *Marianne Frasco*
Senior Design Coordinator: *Miguel Ortiz*
Cover Design: *Kiwi Design*

©2000 by Prentice-Hall, Inc.
Upper Saddle River, New Jersey 07458

Printed in the United States of America

10 9 8 7 6 5 4 3 2 1

ISBN 0-13-096089-6

Prentice-Hall International (UK) Limited, *London*
Prentice-Hall of Australia Pty. Limited, *Sydney*
Prentice-Hall Canada Inc., *Toronto*
Prentice-Hall Hispanoamericana, S.A., *Mexico*
Prentice-Hall of India Private Limited, *New Delhi*
Prentice-Hall of Japan, Inc., *Tokyo*
Prentice-Hall (Singapore), Pte Ltd.
Editora Prentice-Hall do Brasil, Ltda., *Rio de Janeiro*

Contents ▼

Travel Vision is a reflection of your future in the travel and hospitality industry.

What Is *Travel Vision?*

Travel Vision: A Practical Guide for the Travel, Tourism, and Hospitality Industry is an all-in-one, comprehensive how-to for those seeking a career in one of the largest industries in the world. The text presents subject matter relevant to what is current in the industry today and, more important, prepares you for travel and hospitality career opportunities into the twenty-first century.

Travel Vision is **relevant and up to date.** The travel and hospitality industry is a volatile one—information changes daily, new products and services are introduced just as rapidly, and challenges such as new technologies and shifting demographics are working to redefine the travel professional. *Travel Vision* is your introduction to this new challenge. But it does much more than that: it goes into a lot more detail than the conventional introductory text. The subject matter reflects the skills and abilities required of the travel professional of the twenty-first century.

Certainly, travel employers are looking for applicants who have traditional skills such as computer technology and airline ticketing. But they are also looking for qualified people who have specialized skills, such as destination geography, group travel, and special-interest tours and cruises. They are also looking for bright and motivated professionals who know how to communicate with their clients and business partners, who go beyond just knowing about the products they sell to knowing how to sell and promote these products successfully.

Travel Vision is **highly interactive.** *Travel Vision* is written in a style to motivate and challenge readers. It is designed to be highly interactive. Spread liberally throughout each chapter are activity icons which alert you to key points, practical exercises, and optional Web activities relevant to the text material. Watch for these icons as you progress through the text.

Fast Forward

At the beginning of each chapter is a list of key points with page number locators. Use *Fast Forward* as your list of learning objectives before starting each chapter. Also use Fast Forward as a study guide to locate quickly one or more specific topics to review.

Web Link

Optional search activities for students connected to the Internet: to provide links to interesting travel sites that reinforce concepts covered in the text and to provide additional study.

✔ *Check Your Understanding*

Written exercises presented in a variety of formats which are scattered liberally throughout each chapter. They serve to reinforce major concepts immediately and to identify areas for further development.

Key Point ➤ Key points or short tidbits of special interest relating to lesson concepts that enable the reader to speculate or reflect on key issues.

Close-Up: At the end of most chapters is a list of subject-related careers in travel and hospitality in addition to a focus on typical entry-level employment opportunities.

Example: Alerts the reader to a detailed, step-by-step demonstration of a particular procedure or process discussed in the text.

➤ **Key Terms** Key terms are boldface when they first appear within the text. These terms are listed at the end of each chapter for quick reference and are defined in the glossary.

Chapter Review End-of-chapter review exercises in a variety of formats which focus on all major concepts and reinforce learning objectives.

Travel Vision is **graphical in nature.** You learn not only by reading and listening, but also by seeing and experiencing. Textbooks must go beyond a presentation of words, and bring the subject matter alive through exciting visuals and graphics. *Travel Vision* contains a variety of stimulating material that helps you understand how the information covered in the text applies to the real world of work. In addition to clear explanations and relevant activities, *Travel Vision* includes many charts, tables, diagrams, pictures, and activity icons to motivate, excite, and involve you in the process of learning about the exciting and challenging travel and hospitality industry.

Who Should Use This Book?

Travel Vision is designed for students enrolled in a degree or short-term certificate program in travel, tourism, and hospitality. It can be used as an introductory textbook since it presents a comprehensive overview of the knowledge and skills required to start a career. Since *Travel Vision* contains more detail than the conventional introductory textbook, it is also recommended as a stand-alone text for short-term travel and tourism training programs.

Travel Vision is also an excellent resource for those already employed in travel. It is filled with current information and helpful tips that can assist the travel professional on a day-to-day basis. Use it as an office resource to review specific subject content or as a training guide for newly hired employees.

Because the textbook is written in a detailed and step-by-step manner, it is an excellent practical guide for independent learners; it is like having a teacher sitting right next to you! The self-teaching format makes it an effective training guide for the general public; specifically for those who wish to become their own travel agent. It can provide most people with the knowledge and skills required to plan and execute their own travel arrangements.

What the Book Is About

The book is divided into twelve chapters, starting with the fundamentals to the more specific and specialized. The chapters can be grouped in major units, as outlined below. A quick synopsis of the content of each chapter follows.

➤ Introduction: The Big Picture

Chapter 1 presents the "big picture" as it traces important benchmarks in the history of tourism development to the present day. It also answers the question "So what is tourism anyway?" by defining the major segments that comprise the industry, how they work together, and an alphabet soup of important regulatory agencies and trade organizations.

➤ Geography: The Fundamental Product

One of the beginning chapters of any introductory travel text should be geography. A knowledge of destinations is of key importance whether you are booking your own airline ticket on your home PC or organizing a group tour through the Far East. Chapter 2 starts out with World Geography 101 by introducing or reviewing basic concepts such as land and water formations, climate, time zones, place-name skills, and other relevant topics. This is followed by a study of *travel* geography, a look at important destinations around the world as seen through the eyes of the travel professional.

➤ Air Transportation: Backbone of the Industry

Chapters 3 and 4 present the fundamentals or backbone of the industry—North American and worldwide air travel, respectively. Learn who the major players are, the alphabet soup of airline terminology and codes used every day, and what you have always wanted to know about air travel from airline clubs and overbooking to agency compensation and air passengers' "Bill of Rights." Technical know-how is detailed with a study of air fares and discounts, electronic rules, and examples of printed and automated resources that travel professionals use to sell and promote airline travel for their customers.

➤ Computer Technology: Much More Than Just Booking Air

Chapter 5 starts with a generic computer "how-to" for the novice (and an excellent review for the not-so-novice) computer user. The balance of the chapter is divided into three major sections.

The first section concentrates on the major airline computer reservations systems (CRSs)—what they do and how they work. Case study demonstrations illustrate how a basic passenger name record is built along with pricing and ticketing capabilities.

The second section focuses on PC (personal computer) applications, with a description of three types of business software, with relevant examples of their uses in the travel workplace: word processing, spreadsheet, and database management.

The third section is devoted to the Internet, with an emphasis on how travel professionals are using this technology as an important resource, communication, and marketing tool.

➤ Product Knowledge: By Land and by Sea

Chapters 6 through 9 detail the land and sea travel products that we sell—from taking an ecotour through the rain forests in Belize, to riding a scenic train through the Alps, to sailing the South Pacific on a tall-masted ship or staying fit at a luxury spa out West. For all of these important leisure products—accommodations, tour packages, cruises, rail and car rentals—the emphasis is placed on product descriptions, client markets, resources, operators, and sales.

➤ Advanced Sales and Specialties: Group Travel, Business Communications, and Sales

Chapters 10 and 11 take the beginner travel professional a step or two further by emphasizing the growing market of group travel for both leisure and business clients, refining sales techniques and skills, and learning how to communicate in business in a professional manner.

➤ Career Development: Plotting Your Course

Chapter 12 serves as an excellent guide to prepare you for a successful career search in the travel and hospitality industry. In addition to the "Career Close-Ups" provided in many individual chapters, additional information about job skills, compensation, and benefits are provided. You are guided step by step through preparing a professional résumé and other related documentation, such as cover letters and interview follow-up correspondence. Typical questions to expect during the interview and what types of questions to ask are explored, with many examples and opportunities to practice your job interview skills. All examples and samples that are provided are geared toward a job search in the travel and hospitality industry.

PREPARING FOR TAP: NATIONAL ACCREDITATION

Travel Vision can help you prepare for the industry's Travel Agent Proficiency (TAP) test. TAP is a basic competency test that measures the basic entry-level knowledge of travel agent professionals and serves as a first step toward occupational professionalism. This test was developed through the efforts of the American Society of Travel Agents (ASTA) and the Institute of Certified Travel Agents (ICTA). In addition, many other national travel industry organizations that represent the airline, cruise, and tour industries made contributions and endorse the test. *Travel Vision* was designed and written to include the relevant topics covered in the TAP examination (subject matter covered in the TAP test may be found in any number of travel and tourism textbooks.)

A unique feature of *Travel Vision* is the inclusion of a practice TAP test at the end of the book. The practice test is presented in the same format as the TAP exam: 100 multiple-choice questions. This is an excellent way for students to review relevant subject matter and identify individual strengths and weaknesses within each content area.

ACKNOWLEDGMENTS

The author wishes to thank the following professionals and educators who reviewed the project as it was developed and whose travel and teaching expertise contributed to this work: Joseph Chen, Virginia Polytechnic Institute and State University; Terence F. McDonough, Erie Community Collete; Yang H. Huo, Roosevelt University; Elizabeth Barber, Temple University; Jan H. van Harssel, Niagara University.

A special thanks to my husband and professional partner, Bob Purzycki, who made major contributions to *Travel Vision* and without whose help and creative ideas this project could not have been written!

About the Author

Jeanne Semer-Purzycki is one of the leading authors in travel and tourism education today. She is the author of four leading textbooks for the travel and tourism industry: *Practical Guide to Fares and Ticketing*, (ITP Publishing), *Guide to SABRE Reservations and Ticketing* (ITP Publishing), *International Travel, Fares and Ticketing* (Prentice Hall), and *Sails for Profit* (Prentice Hall), a comprehensive how-to for cruise travel. Her practical and comprehensive textbooks are being used by travel and tourism educators and students in hundreds of colleges and proprietary schools throughout the world.

During her successful career in travel education, Ms. Semer-Purzycki served as school director for Travel School of America in Boston, Massachusetts, which graduated more than 10,000 people in its 31-year history. Prior to her school directorship, she served as a classroom instructor in all phases of travel on both the college and proprietary school levels. In addition, she served as program director for Lasell College, where she developed a new travel and tourism degree program and served as its lead instructor.

Ms. Semer-Purzycki has also served as contributing author on a contractual basis for the nationally recognized Institute of Certified Travel Agents (ICTA). The author is currently serving as Educational Specialist with the Higher Education Assistance Group based in Boston, Massachusetts. In her role as educational consultant, she assists schools and colleges in all phases of their operation.

She completed her graduate studies at Central Connecticut State University, where she earned the master of science degree in education and instructional media. Her undergraduate work was completed at the University of Vermont, where she earned a bachelor of science in education.

Travel Vision: A Practical Guide for the Travel, Tourism, and Hospitality Industry is the benchmark of this author's writing career. It is the most comprehensive and highly interactive textbook on the market, covering all geographic, sales, product, and technical aspects of this exciting and challenging industry. It also transports the reader into the new millennium with its upbeat tone and style.

Introduction:
The Big Picture

Fast Forward ▼

➤ To be a successful "matchmaker," travel agents need to know who their clients are and what motivates them to travel. . . . 16

➤ According to noted psychologist Abraham Maslow, all people do what they do based on satisfying a pyramid of needs. Where does travel fit? . . . 16

➤ Find out why allocentrics go to places such as Nepal and psychocentrics go to Disneyworld. Where is your place on Plog's destination index? . . . 17

➤ More than 50 percent of leisure travelers have no idea or just a general idea of a destination they would like to visit. For what other services do they seek the advice of their travel agents? . . . 18

The Big Picture

Can you picture yourself escorting a tour through Europe? Planning a corporate meeting for more than 300 participants in Hawaii? Inspecting hotels for your next tour group to Spain? Better yet, planning exciting trip itineraries to romantic and exotic destinations throughout the world? The travel industry needs people to do these types of things and a lot more.

Travel professionals work as travel agents, tour directors, meeting planners, airline ground agents, hotel managers, and corporate specialists—just to name a few opportunities. There are two principal reasons why you should consider a career in travel and tourism: growing demand for top professionals and a variety of career choices.

The travel and hospitality industry is one of the largest industries in the world. It also is one of the fastest growing. In the United States, travel is the second-largest business (see Figure 1.1). According to the U.S. Department of Commerce, travel will evolve into the leading industry by the year 2002. Close to 7 percent of the *gross national product* (*GNP*) is generated by the travel and tourism industry. This remarkable growth certainly affects career opportunities. In fact, America's second-largest employer is travel and tourism (the largest is health services). The travel and hospitality industry employs more than 14.3 million people: 6.3 million people directly and 8 million people indirectly. This means that one out of every three employees works directly or indirectly within travel.

Tourism: What Is It Really?

Tourism: You hear about it, read about it, purchase it, and now think about making it a career. So what is tourism anyway? It's a vast conglomerate of transportation systems, service providers, recreational facilities, accommodations, consumer products, and specialized services—among many others. Practically everything that you see, touch, hear, and taste has something to do with tourism. You visit national parks, you touch animals at the zoo, you hear a symphony, you eat in restaurants—all are related to tourism.

To narrow it down a bit, we can look at tourism in two general categories:

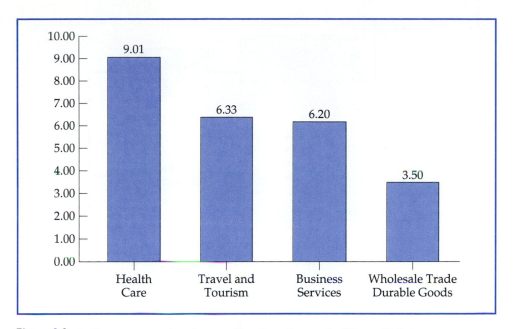

Figure 1.1 *Industry comparison by number of employees (millions of jobs).*
(Data from U.S. Travel Data Center, U.S. Travel and Tourism Administration, and Bureau of Labor Statistics.)

private sector and specialized services. The private sector of tourism includes lodging, restaurants, transportation, entertainment facilities, attractions, travel agencies, and tour operators. These private-sector elements are all supported by specialized services such as research, promotion, advertising, and printing.

All of these companies and services are interrelated and dependent on each other. Let's look at marketing, for example. In terms of tourism, it is a vastly sophisticated and scientific approach to creating tourist products. A good example is the Disney Corporation. Opening a new theme park initiates a vast chain of events that involve the private sector and specialized services of tourism. Marketing research is completed to find out if the site is easily accessible by transportation systems such as air, car, or rail. Consumer feasibility is also determined. Is the site in close proximity to support facilities such as lodging, restaurants, and shops? Is the site close to other attractions? Other factors, such as climate and topography, are also considered.

Tourism is consumer oriented: It is dependent on purchases of travel-related products and services extending from a bottle of suntan oil to a luxury tour through the Orient. To put it in better perspective, we can divide the industry into five major segments: regulatory agencies, trade organizations, transportation, receptive services, and outbound services (see Figure 1.2).

➤ Regulatory Agencies

Regulatory agencies are governmental and private organizations designed to protect the consumer in such areas as pricing and safety. They also ensure that travel companies and organizations that deal with the traveling public are operating within the law. Examples of regulatory organizations are:

1. *Airlines Reporting Corporation* (ARC): consists of the majority of U.S. airline carriers, which are members on a voluntary basis. This independent organization establishes standard practices and procedures regarding airline transportation and the sale of airline tickets. Functions of the ARC are:

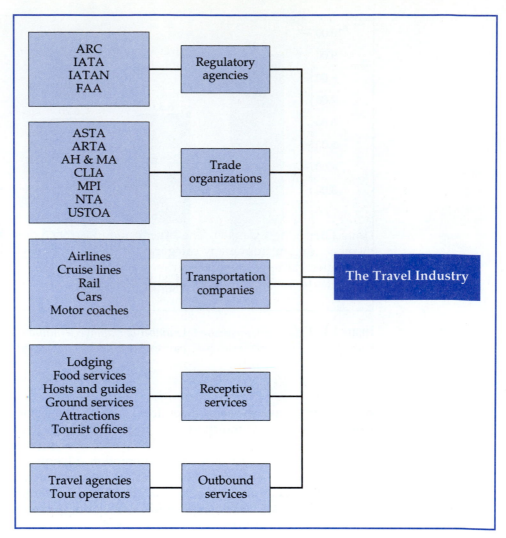

Figure 1.2 *Segments of the tourism industry.*

a. To provide a method of approving authorized travel agencies for the sale of transportation on behalf of member airlines.

b. To print, distribute, and maintain universal airline ticket documents that are used by travel agents.

c. To serve as a clearinghouse to distribute moneys to the airlines for most travel agency ticket sales

2. *International Air Transport Association* **(IATA):** worldwide regulatory agency comprised of the majority of international airline carriers. One of its main functions is to promote a standard and unified system of worldwide air travel by establishing routes and setting safety and service standards.

3. *International Airlines Travel Agent Network* **(IATAN):** not-for-profit corporation that is a subsidiary of the IATA. Its main functions are to appoint and regulate travel agencies to sell airline tickets on international airlines that serve the United States.

4. *Federal Aviation Administration* **(FAA):** agency of the U.S. Department of Transportation (DOT) that is responsible for commercial aviation. The FAA concentrates on issues related to airport regulations, air-traffic control, and aircraft safety and maintenance.

➤ Trade Organizations

Trade organizations are comprised of travel companies and/or individual professional memberships. Trade organizations function to:

1. Promote a particular segment of the travel industry.
2. Legislate changes or new laws in Washington, DC.
3. Educate travel professionals and the traveling public with new products and information relative to the type of travel service it represents.

Examples of trade organizations are:

1. *American Society of Travel Agents (ASTA):* a major travel trade association. Its principal membership is comprised of travel agencies located primarily in the United States and Canada. The organization also includes allied and associate members drawn from many categories of travel suppliers, such as motor coach companies, car rental agencies, airlines, and tour operators.

2. *Association of Retail Travel Agents (ARTA):* a trade association open only to retail travel agents. The primary reason that ARTA became organized is that its sister organization, ASTA, includes airlines, cruise lines, and others in allied membership categories. ARTA leadership has always taken the position that the retail travel agency community cannot be truly represented in the midst of a wide diversity of interests. For example, legislation that benefits an airline or a tour operator may not be in the best interests of the retail travel agent.

3. *American Hotel and Motel Association (AH&MA):* an organization that represents trade associations in the lodging industry throughout the western hemisphere.

4. *Cruise Lines International Association (CLIA):* a trade organization that consists of representative cruise lines and travel agency affiliates. Two main objectives of this association are:

> **a.** To market and promote cruise travel to the traveling public.
> **b.** To offer educational and training support to its member travel agencies.

5. *Meeting Planners International (MPI):* a professional educational association for corporate and association meetings planners.

6. *National Tour Association (NTA):* a trade association of U.S. tour operators and wholesalers. Members operate within the United States and Canada.

7. *United States Tour Operators Association (USTOA):* national organization of more than 600 members, made up of tour operators, hotels, airlines, car rental companies, tourist boards, and other travel service providers worldwide. Like the NTA, its primary goals are to inform the travel industry and the public about tour operators' activities and to maintain a high level of professionalism within the tour operator community.

➤ Transportation

Transportation is one of the most important segments in the tourism industry. It consists of companies that provide air, land, and sea transport for the traveling public. It consists of airlines, rail, motor coach, cruise lines, and car rentals.

➤ Receptive (Inbound Travel) Services

Receptive services are companies that can be considered "hosts" to the traveling public. They provide services and facilities for travelers when they arrive at a destination. Examples of receptive services include:

1. Lodging
2. Food service (restaurants, fast-food outlets, etc.)
3. Meet and greet services (ground arrangements or services that meet and service travelers at the point of arrival, such as at airports and rail stations)
4. Hosts and guides at the destination points
5. Attractions (e.g., theme parks, national parks)
6. Tourist offices, convention and visitor's bureaus

➤ Outbound Services

Outbound service providers are companies that offer travel arrangements and services for travelers who are traveling from the home community to a destination. Examples of outbound service providers include:

1. Travel agencies
2. Tour operators (develop, promote, and sell land tours)

➤ Travel Agencies

The outbound service sector provides many career opportunities in the tourism industry. Companies such as travel agencies also provide a natural springboard for work in all other sectors of the industry. Why? Travel agencies hold a unique position in the industry. They serve as unbiased representatives or agents for all other suppliers, such as airlines, hotels, tour operators, and cruise lines. At the same time, they act as retail customers of these suppliers.

Travel agents receive payment in the form of commission earned from the sale of airline tickets, cruises, and tours on behalf of their suppliers. Figure 1.3 shows how a travel agency acts as a retail outlet for the sale of travel-related services for its clients.

Although most revenue is generated from the commissions earned from the products they sell, some travel agencies charge service fees on certain transactions. One reason to charge a service fee is when the cost of booking exceeds the amount of commission earned. Typical examples are airline tickets, due to a low airline commission structure, and booking a client into a small hotel or inn that does not pay commission.

✓ Check Your Understanding 1-1

1. In addition to regulatory agencies and trade organizations, there are three other major segments that comprise the travel industry. Name them and provide two examples of each.

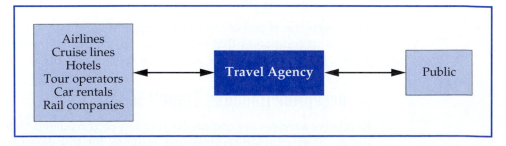

Figure 1.3 *The travel agency as a retail outlet.*

A. _____
   (1) _____ (2) _____
B. _____
   (1) _____ (2) _____
C. _____
   (1) _____ (2) _____

2. The travel industry is broken down into two general categories: private sector and specialized services.

   A. Name three types of companies or services that make up the private sector.

     (1) _____ (3) _____
     (2) _____

   B. Name three elements that make up specialized services.

     (1) _____ (3) _____
     (2) _____

3. Match each major regulatory or trade organization with the correct description.

   A. USTOA   ____   1. Agency of the federal government that oversees aircraft safety and airport regulations.

   B. ARC   ____   2. Trade organization that represents the lodging industry throughout the western hemisphere.

   C. MPI   ____   3. Consists of the majority of international airlines; promotes a standard system of worldwide passenger air travel.

   D. FAA   ____   4. Trade association made up primarily of U.S. travel agencies and associate members, such as tour operators, airlines, and motor coach companies.

   E. IATA   ____   5. Made up primarily of companies that operate tours; maintains professionalism in the tour operator community.

   F. ASTA   ____   6. Consists of the majority of U.S. airlines; oversees standard practices regarding the sale of airline transportation.

   G. CLIA   ____   7. Professional educational association for meeting planners.

   H. AH&MA   ____   8. Association of cruise lines that promotes and markets cruise travel to the general public and serves as a resource to its member travel agencies.

THE PAST IS THE KEY TO THE FUTURE

How did the huge travel and tourism industry develop and evolve into what it is today? Let's take a quick history lesson that outlines some of the most dramatic events that shaped this very important force in today's business economy and even in our personal lives.

Who was the first travel agent? What event actually started what has become a multibillion-dollar global industry today? You'd be surprised to find out that alcohol was at the root of it all! The first "travel agent" was a very modest man in mid-Victorian England who worked as a printer and writer and also happened to be an avid temperance worker. In 1841 he chartered a train that took more than 570 passengers from Leicester to Loughborough for a temperance convention. The man's name was Thomas Cook, and that rail trip was the first round-trip charter in history.

By 1845, Thomas Cook was considered a full-time tour operator and was earning 5 percent commission from the railroads. The familiar saying, "from little acorns mighty oaks grow" applied to Thomas Cook and his son. His success in organizing rail trips in England grew far and wide. Ten years after the historic rail charter, he founded the first travel magazine, *Excursionist*. Cook was an innovator in the travel field. In 1866, Cook's son escorted the first transatlantic group tour. He escorted a group of Europeans to the United States to view Civil War battlefields, where war had only ceased one year prior to the tour.

Cook's dreams extended beyond what was considered to be safe and normal in those days. By 1868, he was escorting groups into the Holy Land, which was very difficult to do under Turkish rule. Cook made his own private treaties with sheiks and rulers for guards and facilities to safeguard the passage of his clients. His Middle East tours were adventurous caravans with sleeping tents, horses, and armed guards through such countries as today's Egypt, Israel, Syria, and Jordan. In fact, Cook was such a success in negotiating on behalf of his group tours that the Egyptian ruler invited him to build deluxe ships to cruise the Nile.

By 1879, Thomas Cook & Son was well established in the United States as a leading tour operator. Cook became more than the innovator of rail tours. The company was to pioneer the first sea cruise and air tour in the twentieth century. In 1892, Thomas Cook & Son chartered a boat to cruise from New York to the West Indies. His company pioneered the first air tours. In the 1920s and 1930s the company booked zeppelins and airplanes, the most famous being a special air charter that flew fans from New York to Chicago to attend the Dempsey–Tunney boxing contest in 1927.

Have you ever heard the expression a "Cook's tour"? It doesn't mean a trip for gourmet food lovers. It means that the traveler who took a Cook's tour enjoyed an exciting and pleasurable trip that included all amenities.

Another Englishman, Thomas Bennett, followed in the footsteps of Thomas Cook as one of the first tour organizers. Bennett worked as a British consular agent in Norway. Part of his job was to give travel advice and assistance to his fellow countrymen during their visit to Scandinavia. In 1850, he began conducting trips into the rugged and scenic interior of Norway by horse and cart. His success as a tour leader grew and he was soon organizing tours using comfortable carriages.

Bennett also developed a voucher program whereby clients would pay in advance for accommodations, meals, and transportation before their tour started. Bennett Tours served for many years as a leading tour wholesaler and can boast of having such notables as Jules Verne, Theodore Roosevelt, Alexander Graham Bell, and Charles Darwin taking its tours.

► The First Travel Agents: Steering the Way

In the United States, the first travel agents were called *steerers*. During the early decades of the twentieth century, most long-distance travel was done by transatlantic steamships. The majority of passengers were European immigrants. Usually, one member of the family would make the trip to the new land, get a job, and save enough money to pay for other family members to make the trip to America.

When these new U.S. residents would show up at the docks to buy steamship passage for their family and relatives, enterprising "salesmen" would "steer" them into certain steamship offices. The steerer would be paid a commission by the steamship offices for the customers he brought to them. Many modern-day travel agencies started this way.

Up until the 1930s, transatlantic steamship travel was the travel agency's bread and butter. Very few traveled across the Pacific at that time. Travel agents would book clients into hotels, but commissions earnings were hit-or-miss. Many travelers went by rail, but few railroad companies paid commission. Tours and cruises were in their infancy. Tourism as an organized and structured industry was just beginning to emerge.

➤ The 1930s: True Beginning of Tourism

In the 1920s, planes carried mail, not passengers, over thousands of miles throughout the country. The beginning of a new era in airline travel started with the first airline passenger in 1926. He was a businessman from Salt Lake City who hitched a ride on a Douglas biplane from Los Angeles, California to Salt Lake City, Utah. He sat on a pile of airmail, with the wind in his face. This was the first passenger of Western Air Express. Later it changed its name to Western Airlines, which is considered to be one of the oldest airlines in the United States (along with United Airlines and TWA).

Regular passenger air service would eventually have a tremendous affect on travel agencies. KLM, the oldest airline in Europe, and other international carriers were on the same course of development at that time.

The year 1935 was a banner year for the fledgling passenger carriers. At that time, Pan Am introduced and put into regular service its Flying Clipper, which carried 50 passengers and was considered enormous in those days. That same year, American Airlines started all-inclusive tours that centered around air travel. These tours were commissionable at 7.5 percent to travel agents.

Soon after, the "flying boats" of Imperial Airways (which became British Overseas Air Corporation) and Pan Am were flying across the Atlantic on an experimental basis. At the same time, Imperial and Pan Am joined forces to offer the first commercial scheduled service between New York and Bermuda.

By the 1930s, travel agents who were in the business to sell travel wanted standards with established practices of sales performance and better commissions from suppliers (i.e., rail companies, airlines, hotels). In 1931, 11 agents formed the first travel industry organization for travel agents, called the American Steamship and Tourist Agents Association. By 1936, membership had grown to more than 450 agencies. Known since 1941 as the American Society of Travel Agents (ASTA), today the organization is one of the leading associations for member travel agencies and employees of travel.

MODERN HISTORY: 1950s TO PRESENT DAY

➤ The Emergence of Jet Travel

If there was one major event that truly revolutionized the tourism industry, it was the one that occurred in 1958—the arrival of commercial jet service. Pan American Airways was one of the first to usher in the jet age, by carrying passengers on its 707 aircraft between New York and Le Bourget airfield in Paris. Other airline companies soon followed. A few weeks later, British Overseas Air Corporation (BOAC) began flying their passengers on scheduled transatlantic flights to London. Up until this time only 10 percent of the U.S. population had ever flown.

The major players in North America included American Airlines, which flew the first passengers on a transcontinental trip, also with a 707. Two other airlines, which are no longer in service, National and Eastern Airlines, started jet service in the eastern United States mainly between New York and Miami. National Airlines had a unique alliance with Pan American. National leased a 707 from Pan Am to fly passengers between New York and Miami. It scheduled its flights during the hours that the Pan Am jet was sitting in New York between transatlantic flights.

At this time travel agencies were appointed through the regulatory agencies of the *Air Traffic Conference (ATC)* and the International Air Transport Association (IATA). These powerful agencies were comprised of the major domestic and international airlines, respectively, and they called all the shots. They not only governed how much commission travel agencies could make but who could open new travel agencies and where they could open up shop. The airlines had the power to allow only a certain number of travel agencies to open in a community based on population and other factors. They also required that agencies be located a minimum number of miles apart.

The few thousand travel agencies that won approval were obviously supportive of the *closed shop* approach, which would restrict competition. However, over protests from many budding travel entrepreneurs, the airlines abolished the "need" clause as a standard for agency approval.

During the late 1950s and the 1960s, travel agents realized their growing dependence on the airlines to make money. The transatlantic trip that once took a week by steamship now could be completed in just a few hours by jet. Most agents did not need a crystal ball to see that the clock was running out on one major source of revenue: luxury transatlantic and transpacific ocean liners.

Agencies' economic dependence on the airlines skyrocketed. More than 70 percent of their earned revenue came from selling air travel. At that time agencies earned 5 percent commission on the sale of air tickets, which barely covered the cost of booking and completing airline ticket transactions.

By 1968 the agencies knew they were in trouble if things stayed the way they were. They appointed an accounting firm to study the economics of travel retailing. The results showed that they were losing money on the average of 3 percent on most airline ticket transactions. This led to the airline regulatory agencies mandating an increase from 5 to 7 percent. This helped but was not the solution.

The solution? One was in the power of numbers. Agencies started banding together in what today are called *cooperatives* and *consortia*. A travel cooperative is an organization that is owned and operated by a number of travel companies which share the benefits derived from the group. In this way, small to medium-sized retailers could have purchasing and economic power that was difficult to achieve as independent outlets.

Another solution was the discovery of alternatives to airline tickets as the retailers' "bread and butter." The great luxury ocean liners of previous decades were giving way to smaller, sleeker vessels built for the new generation of travelers. During the 1960s, the concept of short cruise vacations was born, and it flourished throughout the 1970s. New cruise companies such as Carnival Cruise Line and Royal Caribbean Cruise Line were formed to provide short vacations at sea of a week or less, with destinations of such places as the Caribbean area and Mexico.

Unlike the airlines, cruise companies lacked direct distribution with the general public and thus became solid partners with the retail travel industry. Travel retailers now had a lucrative source of revenue in addition to air travel. Cruise lines were paying commissions at an average of 10 percent. In terms of cost-effectiveness, selling cruises and other types of land leisure products was the way to go. It took the travel retailer a much shorter time to book a cruise at a much higher commission. This close partnership between cruise lines and the travel retailers has remained intact over the years.

➤ Deregulation of the Airline Industry

In 1978 a major benchmark in travel history occurred that would dramatically change the airline and travel agency business forever. The rallying cry for less government control and more competition in business was a major political theme in Washington, DC during the 1970s. Deregulation came closer to becoming a reality during the Carter administration in 1976, and the airline industry was the prime candidate. At the same time that deregulation was rolling through Congress, a glimmer of things to come was being revealed at the **Civil Aeronautics Board (CAB).** Up to this time the CAB had regulated every facet of the commercial airline industry, from establishing airline routes to setting prices for domestic air travel.

When President Carter signed the **Airline Deregulation Act of 1978,** the CAB's power was diminished dramatically. At the same time, the antitrust immunity that allowed the airlines to control every aspect of their operation gradually increased. Each airline was now able to control every aspect of its operations, including travel agency compensation, route establishment, and airline fares. In addition, agency commissions were virtually "open." Airlines could establish their own commission policies.

The complete demise of the CAB also spurred an airline route grab that was as fierce and combative as that experienced in the Old West during the nineteenth-century gold rush. This resulted in a survival-of-the-fittest scenario: A few successful airlines, including, American, United, and Delta, became bigger and more powerful. There were also many casualties.

New upstart airlines such as People Express charged bargain-basement fares but soon fell by the wayside. Many airlines succumbed to bankruptcy only to return later in smaller, scaled-down versions. Other airlines, including Pan American and Braniff, attempted to reorganize themselves financially after a series of bankruptcies, but ultimately failed.

➤ Goodbye ATC, Hello ARC

Another result of deregulation took place in the retail travel agency arena. The regulatory activities of the ATC and IATA as they related to retail travel agency appointments and operations were strict. Many thought that these regulatory agencies placed an unnecessary stranglehold on the agency community. After deregulation the regulatory practices of these agencies were replaced with more cooperative and consultative airline groups.

The Airlines Reporting Corporation (ARC) was formed and resolved to work more closely with travel agency representatives on the domestic front. A subsidiary of IATA called the International Airlines Travel Agent Network (IATAN) was formed to take over the function of appointing U.S. travel agencies to sell travel on international carriers serving the United States. IATAN acted less like a regulatory body and more like a service organization, with its softer and gentler approach to the agency trade.

➤ Agency Technology

During this same period, the agency community was facing dramatic changes that would affect the way they did business. The airlines had maintained their huge seat inventories and processed reservations through the use of their own computer reservation systems since the 1950s. At the same time, travel agents were drowning in paper. Fares and schedules were found buried in huge printed books and tariffs. Travel reservations were conducted on the telephone. Tickets were written by hand. Every booking took a lot of time. So why weren't travel agencies computerized like the airlines?

This became a serious issue in the mid-1970s. It became clear that travel agencies needed computers to deal with the volume of work associated with airline transportation. The airlines tried to create a joint automated reservation system that would enable any travel agent to sell the tickets of any airline. It didn't work. In 1976 the major airlines gave up the idea of a unified system and set out independently. The first two airlines to offer their automated systems to their agency partners were United and American. United Airlines offered an automated reservation system called Apollo, and American soon followed by offering its internal SABRE system to travel agencies.

The advent of agency computers coincided with an upsurge in business travel. A growing number of agencies were now able to handle the large volume of airline sales generated by all types of companies: from the small, neighborhood company to the huge corporate conglomerate generating millions of dollars of business travel each year. A new breed of commercially oriented travel agency emerged. Many of these strong agencies became even more powerful by joining business travel consortia such as Hickory, Woodside, and Travel Trust. The industry began dividing into two major camps: commercial or corporate agencies that concentrate on selling business travel and leisure, and retail agencies that concentrate on promoting discretionary travel.

The majority of small to medium-sized independent agencies probably fall into a third category called *general sales*. General sales outlets provide a mix of corporate and leisure travel products and services for their clients.

► The 1980s: Boom Years

If the 1970s were deemed to be the revolutionary years of the travel industry, the next decade could be called the boom years. Business and leisure travel were booming. The new supersonic *Concorde* was zooming passengers across the Atlantic at twice the speed of sound. Newer and sleeker cruise ships were increasing the number of vacation choices to hundreds of points on the globe: from the traditional Caribbean getaway to adventure cruises to Antarctica. The word *bus* was thrown out of the tour industry lexicon and replaced by terms such as *motorcoach* and *land cruisers* as package tours became far more sophisticated. The baby-boomers were coming of age and had the dollars to spend. This market also demanded and got unique and exciting vacation options. Adventure travel was not only for bungee jumpers and daredevils; ecotourism was not only for botanists; luxury travel was not only for the super-rich.

Not only did the number of customer markets expand but also the number of world destinations. Global politics of the 1980s dramatically changed the world landscape into a virtual *global village*. Countries that were closed to tourists now encouraged vacation and business travelers to their shores. China opened its doors for the first time to tourism. The Berlin Wall in Germany came tumbling down and all travel barriers to that part of Europe followed suit. Communism was doomed in Europe and travel to such places as Russia and the Czech Republic was becoming commonplace.

It was also during this decade that the computer reservation systems continued their march toward faster and more sophisticated technology. More agents became adept at using computers for a wide range of tasks, from booking reservations to back-office accounting. Nonair suppliers joined in the computer systems that enabled agents to book a wide variety of products. Now agents can book a huge inventory of travel products, such as hotels, car rentals, cruises, package tours, rail passes, and theater tickets from their desktop computers.

It was also during this time that airlines were looking for ways to cut costs. Some airlines tried to lower agency commissions from the standard 10 percent. Ironically, it was Delta Airlines that blocked the effort, although a decade later Delta led a group of the major domestic airlines in lowering commissions paid to travel agencies.

► The 1990s: Turbulent Years

The 1990s were marked with some mighty dramatic changes that would revolutionize the travel industry. If you had to point to a particular year when absolutely everything changed, it was 1995: The calamitous commission cap was introduced, service fees in the retail sector strengthened, and some "Net hysteria" among the computer illiterate was produced.

Airlines started experiencing higher costs of doing business. Labor unions were demanding higher wages for airline workers, and a fuel crises here and there contributed to the airlines feeling the cost-cutting squeeze. At the same time, airlines started looking at their ticket distribution costs. In addition to paying travel agencies commission, they were also paying override commissions (higher commissions to their higher-producing agencies), CRS booking fees, costs of cooperative advertising with their agency partners, and so on.

The first shot in the commission war between domestic air carriers and travel agencies was fired in February 1995. Ironically, it was fired by Delta Air Lines, the agents' white knight which had blocked the proposed commission cuts of the 1980s. Delta issued a statement that its domestic commissions would be limited to $50 on a round-trip ticket and $25 on a one-way ticket. Most of the major domestic carriers followed suit. A $200 commission on a $2,000 first-class ticket was now reduced to $50.

Another facet of the travel industry in the 1990s is ticketless travel, the principal advantage of which is to reduce the amount of paperwork. At the same time, passengers do not have to worry about carrying (and losing) tickets on the way to the airport. It is not entirely paperless, as the agent still has to enter the reservation into a computer to generate a receipt coupon for what used to be the actual airline ticket. Electronic or paperless ticketing does not bypass the travel agency altogether, but it does make it easier for the airline to deal directly with consumers. This method is growing and time will tell of its final outcome.

Advancements in computer technology allowed airlines to sell flights directly to the public through such channels as the Internet and interactive kiosks at airports. Travel on the Internet is now commonplace. Back in the early 1990s it produced some Net hysteria among less computer savvy agents. Many predicted that dire things would happen now that users could dial up any airline, cruise line, or other travel provider, make a reservation, and order a ticket right from their home PC.

All of these major occurrences at the end of the twentieth century should have predicted the rapid demise of many travel agencies, especially small to medium-sized independents. How would they survive with lower commissions from the airlines? Won't they be cut out of the distribution loop due to the Internet and such things as paperless transactions?

Some agencies were forced to close their doors. But many more survived and in fact are thriving, not by fighting against these evolutionary changes but by adapting to them. The 1990s did not destroy the retail industry but redefined it. Gone are the days of the travel agent being just an order-taker; anyone can book a simple ticket or hotel room on a home computer or laptop. Agents who continued to function in this way were the first to depart the industry.

The travel professional of the twenty-first century is exactly that: a professional, a consultant, and a specialist in travel planning. Those agencies that have thrived in the face of some of the potential threats of the 1990s are looking in new directions and are using these new technologies to their benefit. Many now require service fees for handling transactions that no longer net a profit. Successful agencies are no longer focused on the sale of airline tickets but are becoming specialists in all sorts of areas: Upscale travel, adventure tours, and independent and group travel planners are all examples of lucrative niche marketing.

The demand for professional travel specialists has never been greater. Travel consumers are presented with a dizzying number of choices wherever they look. Thousands of new destinations, tour products, and discounted air fares are advertised in newspapers, magazines, on television, and over the Internet. Now more than ever, consumers need professional "matchmakers" to research, select, and recommend the best travel product based on their interests and needs.

✓ Check Your Understanding 1-2

Multiple Choice.

Circle the *best* answer.

1. Who became the first "travel agent" when he organized the first round-trip charter by rail in 1841?

   A. Herman Melville

   B. Thomas Cook

   C. Thomas Bennett

   D. Henry Fielding

2. During the early twentieth century the majority of long-distance intercontinental travel was done by what type of transportation?

   A. horse and buggy

   B. wagon train

   C. rail

   D. steamship

3. The first group of travel agents during the early twentieth century were called steerers because:

   A. They organized and led their own tour groups and were paid a commission by transportation companies.

   B. They organized into a large group of agents and so were able to negotiate better prices for their customers.

   C. They would guide people who wanted to buy tickets into certain steamship offices, which would pay them a commission.

   D. They "steered" arriving travelers to particular hotels.

4. Many believe that a new era of air travel for commercial purposes began in the 1930s because of:

   A. the first transatlantic flight that carried passengers

   B. U.S. airlines starting to carry passengers along with the mail

   C. steamships becoming less popular

   D. the inaugural flight of the German zeppelin the *Hindenberg*

5. The event that occurred in 1958 which revolutionized the tourism industry and at the same time spelled doom for luxury transatlantic steamships was:

   A. the emergence of Europe as a popular tourist destination

   B. the airline computer reservations systems

   C. the growing number of European immigrants arriving in the United States

   D. the beginning of commercial jet service

6. What does the term *closed shop* mean when used to describe the travel agency industry during the 1950s?

   A. It provided a method to restrict the number of new travel agencies that could be established in a location.

   B. There were a high number of agency failures due to low commission earnings.

   C. Business was conducted only during the day Monday through Friday, with none conducted evenings and weekends.

   D. Most of the commissions earned by travel agents were for the sale of airline tickets.

7. During the 1960s and 1970s travel agencies realized their growing dependence on what type of product to earn money?

   A. airline travel   C. cruise vacations

   B. escorted tours   D. business trips

8. The primary result of the Airline Deregulation Act of 1978 was:

   A. There were higher commission earnings for travel agencies.

   B. There was no restriction in terms of how many travel agencies could open in a certain location.

   C. There was less government control of U.S. airlines and more competition among carriers.

   D. Previous government restrictions that controlled new travel agency appointments disappeared.

9. The travel agency community was revolutionized in the 1970s when a few of the major U.S. carriers:

   A. introduced standard airline tickets and forms

   B. allowed travelers to fly now and pay later

   C. introduced computer reservations systems

   D. increased the number of reservation offices and phone lines

10. Which event below does not define the dramatic changes that occurred in the 1990s which revolutionized the travel industry?

   A. the establishment by domestic airlines of commission caps

   B. the introduction and rapid growth of the Internet in business

   C. electronic or paperless airline tickets

   D. the decrease in popularity of certain products, such as cruise ships and tours

THE STUDY OF DESTINATIONS: WHO TRAVELS, AND TO WHERE?

As a travel professional you need to be many things to your clients: a counselor, an advisor, a teacher, a geographer, and a computer whiz, just to name a few. Most of what travel professionals do every day is sell and market travel. They serve as matchmakers by recommending the best travel product and destination based on what clients want and need. Product knowledge is of prime importance. Knowing who your clients are and what motivates them to travel are also key factors in matching the traveler successfully with the product.

There are many different ways that we can study the population of travelers. One type of study used frequently is **demographics,** which allow us to categorize people according to such factors as age, marital status, income, family size, and educational background.

► Why People Travel: Hierarchy of Needs

Human needs tell you a lot about selling and marketing travel. If you understand what motivates your clients, you will be able to identify what is best for them. To better understand what motivates people to travel, we should take a look at an important theory of human motivation developed by the distinguished psychologist Abraham Maslow.

According to Maslow, all people do what they do based on fulfilling certain needs. People are motivated to do certain things only after each level of need is satisfied. According to Maslow, these needs are arranged like a pyramid, with the most important and urgent needs at the bottom (see Figure 1.4). The needs near the top motivate people only if the fundamental needs lower on the pyramid have been satisfied. Our basic physical needs for food and water have to be satisfied before we are motivated to seek the next-level needs: safety, establishing a home, securing a job, and so on.

Where does the motivation for travel fit in? Pretty high on the scale. Only after the basics of food, shelter, secure income, and love and affection have been satisfied do people turn toward such needs as self-esteem, respect of others, and self-actualization (realizing your potential).

Leisure travel to destinations unknown and exciting gives people confidence in themselves and their place in the world. It also helps to gain the respect of family, friends, and co-workers to be able to say "I have been there and done that." Certainly, travel belongs to the highest needs of self-actualization, or the desire to become all that you are capable of through adventure, meeting new people, and learning.

Figure 1.4 *Maslow's hierarchy of needs.*

► Where People Travel: Positions of Destinations

Why do people choose a particular destination? Several major factors that affect the choice are weather, shopping, beaches, sightseeing, and attractions. Sounds very straightforward. But it doesn't answer the question of why some people choose to visit Ft. Lauderdale and others choose the beaches on the French Riviera.

One of the first attempts to analyze the behavior of travelers and to answer who travels where was developed in 1972 by a noted social scientist, Stanley C. Plog. He asserts that all travelers can be placed on a scale of psychological types. His model has become very popular and has been mentioned in tourism and sales literature ever since. According to Plog, the choice of a destination is determined by whether a traveler is allocentric or psychocentric.

The **allocentric** is the adventurer who wants to discover the new and exciting. Being in familiar surroundings is not of interest to the allocentric; learning about exotic cultures, developing new friendships in foreign lands, and satisfying a need for freedom and power are most important.

On the other end of the scale is the **psychocentric,** who is less adventurous and more comfortable in familiar surroundings. The psychocentric is more interested in visiting places that are most like home, experiencing comfort and prestige during the trip, and conforming socially.

Most people fall somewhere between these two extremes in three subcategories: *near-allocentric, midcentric,* and *near-psychocentric.* According to the bell curve formed by Plog's model, the majority of people tend to be somewhere in between, in the midcentric range (Figure 1.5). Looking at the scale of destinations, you can now understand why traditional or familiar destinations in North America, such as Miami Beach, Hawaii, or the Caribbean, are preferred by psycho-

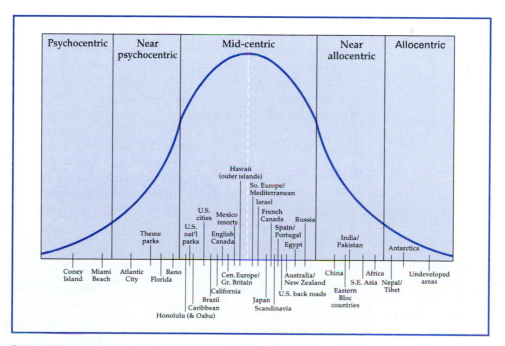

Figure 1.5 *Plog's psychographic positions of destination.*
(*Source: Plog's Research, Inc.*)

centrics and near-psychocentric types, whereas the more exotic and faraway destinations, such as Antarctica, India, Africa, and the Orient, are preferred by the more adventurous allocentric or near-allocentric personality types.

However, people do change their choices of destinations over time. This is due to the buildup of the tourism infrastructure in certain destinations, followed by mass advertising and marketing. A good example of this is the Dominican Republic, a resort island located in the Caribbean. Before the 1990s the Dominican Republic was visited by adventurous allocentrics; hotels and other tourist amenities were not up to the resort standards that many North American travelers have come to expect. But in the past decade the island's tourism infrastructure has improved to include comfortable resorts, restaurants, safe and reliable transportation, and popular recreational facilities such as golf courses and gambling casinos. This once exotic destination has shifted away from being allocentric to being more psychocentric in appeal.

➤ Words from the Wise

In this age of superfast information over the Internet, booking capabilities from your home's personal computer, paperless tickets, ticketing kiosks at airports, and similar technologies, you may wonder why a travel agent is needed at all. In fact, travel experts and trip planners are needed more than ever to help travelers wade through information overload and an overwhelming number of choices. The vast majority of travelers seek the expert advice of travel professionals, especially when planning something more than a simple airline ticket.

Many leisure travelers either have no idea or just a vague idea of where they want to go. According to a recent survey conducted by a major travel trade publication, *Travel Weekly*, about one-sixth (16 percent) of clients seeking an agent's help in planning a trip begin with no particular idea of where they want to go. Approximately 35 percent have only a general or vague idea. A good example is: "We want to go someplace where it is warm—maybe the Caribbean or Mexico?" Of the rest, about 50 percent know precisely where they want to go, but they still seek the advice of an expert to tell them how to get there, what to see, where to stay, and so on.

In fact, most travelers rely on a travel professional's advice. Figure 1.6 is a chart that shows the percentage of clients who ask travel agents' advice relating to individual travel products. From selecting the right tour and cruise ship to the best place to photograph animals in the wild, a travel expert is not only a help but a necessity for most travelers.

Web Link

Interactive Travel Guides: This vast collection of lists and links of travel industry information is designed for both agent and consumer use. It has extensive information and links for all aspects of the industry, including destinations, hotels and resorts, travel news, weather, and maps. For the latest travel news, point your browser to *http://www.travelpage.com.*

➤ Key Terms

- Air Traffic Conference (ATC)
- Airline Deregulation Act of 1978
- Airlines Reporting Corporation (ARC)
- allocentric
- American Hotel and Motel Association (AH&MA)

- American Society of Travel Agents (ASTA)
- Association of Retail Travel Agents (ARTA)
- Civil Aeronautics Board (CAB)

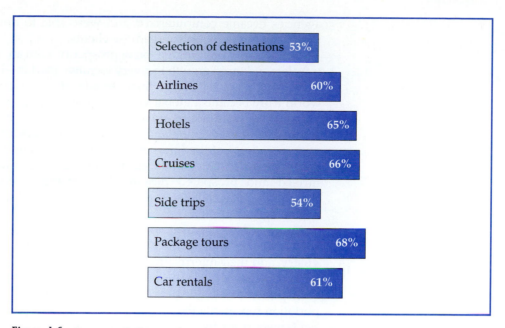

Figure 1.6 *Percent of clients who ask agents' advice relating to individual travel products.* (*From U.S. Travel Agency Survey,* Travel Weekly, August 27, 1998.)

- Cruise Lines International Association (CLIA)
- demographics
- Federal Aviation Administration (FAA)
- International Air Transport Association (IATA)
- International Airlines Travel Agent Network (IATAN)
- Meeting Planners International (MPI)
- National Tour Association (NTA)
- outbound services
- psychocentric
- receptive services
- United States Tour Operators Association (USTOA)

Flashback   Someone once said that to know who we are today and where we are going in the future, we must look to the past. This is certainly true for anyone starting a career in one of the largest industries in the world—travel and tourism. How did it get to be so huge that one out of every three employees in the world works directly or indirectly in travel?

It has not been all smooth sailing! We have traced its beginnings from the first real "travel agent," Thomas Cook, in the mid-1840s, through more than 100 years, including some important events that have truly revolutionized the tourism industry. Modern history in travel started in 1958 with the introduction of commercial passenger jets. Although this spelled doom to the luxury liners of the past, the world's destinations were opened up to more people.

The 1970s was also an eventful decade. The airline industry became deregulated, which resulted in the spectacular growth of some airlines and the ultimate demise of others. For many passengers it meant an explosion of bargain-basement fares and many more choices. The travel agencies became computerized and were able to devote more time to what they did best—sell and advise clients.

The 1980s saw a continuation of prosperity, with an increase in vacation travelers and rapid growth to a very lucrative market—business travel.

With the arrival of the final decade of the twentieth century, the world truly became a global village, signaling unprecedented growth in both business and leisure travel. The last decade of the century also saw some of the most exciting and some of the most devastating events: from widespread use of the Internet and booking engines to paperless tickets and a dramatic decrease in airline commissions. Most travel agencies thrived and prospered despite these changes. Why? Because they learned to change the way they did business and adapted to the new technology.

As a student of travel and a future professional, you should have a solid understanding of the various segments within today's tourism industry, and their interrelationships. Regulatory agencies are designed to protect consumers. Trade organizations help to promote and educate both professionals and travelers on a wide range of products. Transportation represents the largest segment since it provides air, land, and sea transport for the traveling public. Receptive services assist travelers when they arrive, and outbound service companies assist travelers when they depart. All of these segments may have different functions but they all work together to provide a high level of professionalism and excellence of service to travelers worldwide.

Chapter Review

....

True or False?

_____ 1. The tourism industry is the second-largest business in the United States.

_____ 2. USTOA and NTA are examples of associations whose principal membership includes hotels and airlines.

_____ 3. Travel agencies earn most of their revenue by receiving commissions on the products they sell.

_____ 4. Travel agencies never charge service fees for transactions they make on behalf of their clients.

_____ 5. The first airline passenger flew on Western Air Express in 1926.

_____ 6. As a result of the deregulation of the airline industry, the Airlines Reporting Corporation was formed to work closely with the travel agency community.

_____ 7. The first airline computer reservations systems were installed in travel agencies in 1985.

_____ 8. The 1980s were considered boom years in travel, due to new destinations opening up and more dollars being spent on travel by consumers.

_____ 9. India and China are examples of psychocentric destinations.

_____ 10. According to Plog, the motivation for travel ranks high in the pyramid of needs.

Multiple Choice

Circle the *best* answer.

11. Which is not considered to be part of the private sector of the tourism industry?

   A. hotels and resorts
   B. advertising agencies
   C. travel agencies
   D. airlines

12. The government agency that oversees aircraft safety and maintenance is the:

   A. ARC
   B. CAB
   C. IATAN
   D. FAA

13. An organization that is owned and operated by a number of travel agencies that share benefits derived from the group is a:

   A. regulatory agency
   B. tourist office
   C. travel cooperative
   D. trade association

14. Which of the following is considered an outbound service provider?

   A. lodging
   B. tourist offices
   C. restaurants
   D. travel agencies

15. Up until the 1930s, travel agencies earned most of their revenue through the sale of:

   A. transatlantic steamships
   B. air transportation
   C. rail trips
   D. hotels

16. In 1931 the American Steamship and Tourist Agents Association was the first travel industry organization for travel agents. Today this organization is known as the:

   A. Association of Retail Travel Agents
   B. National Tour Association
   C. Meeting Planners International
   D. American Society of Travel Agents

17. During the 1970s a travel product that gained in popularity, becoming a leading source of revenue for travel agencies in addition to air travel, was:

   A. rail
   B. cruises
   C. hotels
   D. escorted tours

18. Which of the following was not a direct result of deregulation?

   A. Some airlines went into bankruptcy due to stiff competition.
   B. Airlines established their own commission policies.
   C. Government maintained control of airline routes.
   D. Many bargain-basement air fares were offered to travelers.

19. The classification and study of consumers by such data as age, income, occupation, and education is called:

   A. geographics
   B. psychographics
   C. demographics
   D. behavioristics

20. According to Maslow, the most fundamental need that must be satisfied before people are motivated to travel is:

   A. respect of others
   B. love and affection
   C. self-esteem
   D. food and shelter

Chapter 2

Tourism Geography

If we are always arriving and departing, it is also true that we are eternally anchored. One's destination is never a place but rather a new way of looking at things.

Henry Miller
(1891–1980)

Fast Forward ▼

INTRODUCTION

Visualize this: You're a professional travel agent planning a trip to the Orient for your clients. In addition to the typical questions about air fares and travel requirements to foreign lands, travelers will also want to know about the weather ("What do we pack?"), types of accommodations ("What type of hotels are there?"), sightseeing and attractions ("What's there to see and do?"), and topography ("Is it mountainous or flat?"). These are typical concerns and questions that travelers have about the places to which they are planning to visit—whether it is a long weekend in the Bahamas or an adventure tour through Nepal.

Product knowledge is the key to selling travel and servicing clients successfully. But product knowledge is not only knowing about tangibles such as airline tickets, cruise vacations, and tour packages. It is also knowing about the intangible products of place: geography and destinations. Remember, for every tangible product that the travel agent sells, a place or destination is also sold. Geographic knowledge is the keystone for every professional working in the travel and tourism industry.

Using maps and other reference tools available in any travel office is helpful. However, you also need a basic knowledge of place-name geography in order to plan trips and service your clients in a professional manner. In the first section of this chapter we concentrate on some basic terms and concepts of world geography. Place-name skill building and other geographic concepts, such as latitude and longitude, time zones, climate, and topography, are introduced. In the second section of the chapter we will take you on a whirlwind tour of the major destinations around the world. Any special or unique features of each region are highlighted along with many maps and visuals.

Remember: This should only be the beginning. A thorough knowledge of your world, its cultures, and major tourism features develops over time and use. Your geography expertise will grow and expand as you work with it every day as a travel professional.

THE CONTINENTS AND OCEANS

Geography involves the study of both land and water surfaces of the world. The earth consists mostly of water; approximately 70 percent of the earth's surface is water; only 30 percent is land. Approximately 90 percent of the world's population lives on six of the world's continents (one is uninhabitable since it is always covered by ice). The other 10 percent live on the habitable islands of the world.

➤ Continents

A *continent* is a major landmass surrounded by water. How many continents are there? The answer is not as clear as you would think. Depending on your perspective of the world, the answer is any number from two to seven! For our purposes as travel professionals, it is best to remember seven continents of the world (see Figure 2.1). They are easy to remember; they all begin with the letter A except for one that starts with another common vowel, E, for Europe. You can remember Europe as an exception to the definition of a continent. Europe is not surrounded entirely by water; it is connected to the continent of Asia (Europe and Asia are sometimes considered to be one continent called Eurasia). The seven continents of the world from the largest to the smallest are:

1. **Asia**   15,776 square miles
2. **Africa**   11,506 square miles
3. **America, North**   9,390 square miles
4. **America, South**   6,795 square miles

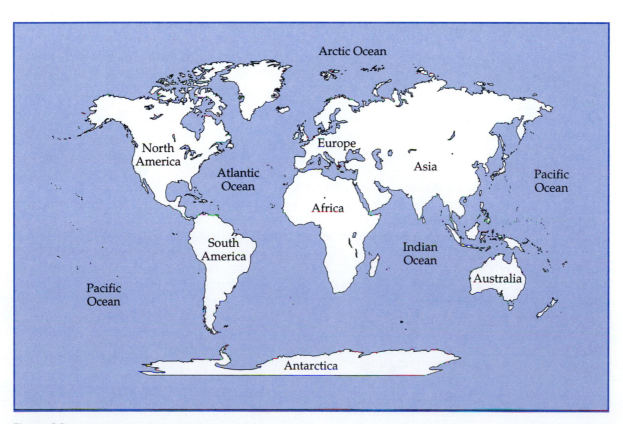

Figure 2.1 *Map of the continents and oceans.*

5. **Antarctica**	5,500 square miles
6. **Europe**	3,616 square miles
7. **Australia**	2,968 square miles

Key Point ➤ Another way of looking at the world's continents is to combine Europe and Asia into one large continent called *Eurasia*. Europe is not an actual continent, because of its unique topography; it consists of thousands of islands and peninsulas. The geographical boundary that separates Europe and Asia is the Ural Mountain range that runs south to the Caspian Sea, along the south side of the Caucasus Mountains to the Black Sea. Check it out on a map.

➤ Oceans

The other 70 percent of the earth's surface is comprised of large and small bodies of water including seas, gulfs, bays, lakes, and rivers. The largest bodies of water on our planet are the four oceans (see Figure 2.1). They are listed from the largest to smallest:

Ocean	*Square Miles*
Pacific Ocean	64,186,300
Atlantic Ocean	33,420,000
Indian Ocean	28,350,500
Arctic Ocean	3,662,200

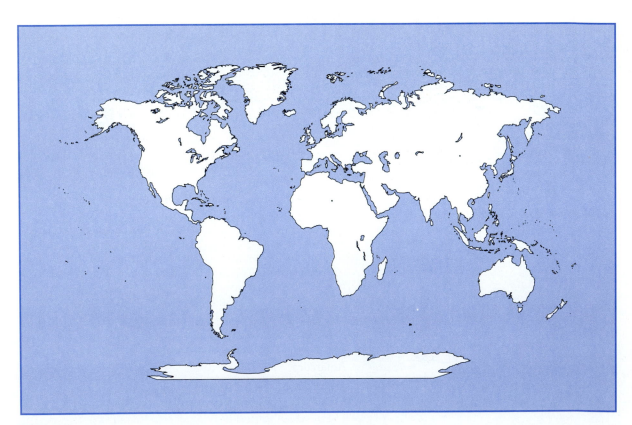

Figure 2.2

✔ Check Your Understanding 2-1

On the map shown in Figure 2.2, label the seven continents and four oceans from memory.

Land and Water Formations

As a travel planner you book clients on ski vacations in *mountain* resorts, cruises through *fjords*, summer vacations by *seas* and *lakes*, resorts on *islands* and *atolls*, "shooting the rapids" on *rivers*, scuba-diving trips to *reefs*, hikes to the rim of dormant *volcanoes*, and archeological tours in *deserts*. You may take such terms as *mountains*, *rivers*, and *lakes* for granted. However, a trip planner does extensive destination research and books travelers to all kinds of land and water formations located worldwide. Table 2.1 provides definitions and tourism examples of key land and water formations.

The Big Three's

Three largest rivers	Nile, Africa	4,145 miles
	Amazon, South America	3,915 miles
	Yangtze, China	3,900 miles
Three largest islands	Greenland	840,000 square miles
	New Guinea	305,000 square miles
	Borneo	290,000 square miles
Three largest lakes	Caspian Sea	143,243 square miles
	Lake Superior	31,820 square miles
	Lake Victoria	26,724 square miles

Table 2.1   Land and Water Formations

Feature	Definition	Key Tourism Destinations
Archipelago	A group of geologically related islands.	Aleutian Islands, Alaska Hawaiian Islands Canary Islands
Bay	Part of a lake, sea, or ocean that is partly surrounded by land.	Bay of Biscay, France Hudson Bay, Canada Chesapeake Bay, Maryland and Virginia
Canyon	A deep, narrow valley having high, steep sides or cliffs.	Grand Canyon, Arizona Copper Canyon, Mexico Bryce Canyon, Utah
Cape	A narrow part of land along a shore that usually curves out into the water.	Cape Cod, Massachusetts Cape Horn, South America Cape Hatteras, North Carolina
Coast	Land along the shore of a sea, ocean, or lake.	Costa del Sol, Spain Algarve, Portugal Turquoise Coast, Turkey
Delta	Land formed by soil deposited at the mouth of a river.	Mississippi Delta, Louisiana Nile River Delta, Egypt

(continued)

TABLE 2.1   LAND & WATER FORMATIONS (CONTINUED)

FEATURE	DEFINITION	KEY TOURISM DESTINATIONS
Desert	A portion of land area in which there is little or no rainfall every year. Can be on land, water, or even in polar regions.	Sahara Desert, Africa Gobi Desert, Asia Mohavi Desert, California
Fjord	A deep, narrow inlet of the sea, between high, steep cliffs.	Norway fjords New Zealand fjords Alaskan fjords
Forest	A large area of land where many trees grow. A rain forest is a dense, green forest that occupies a tropical region and receives abundant rainfall throughout the year.	Rain forests of Costa Rica El Yunque, Puerto Rico Black Forest, Germany
Glacier	A thick, large mass of ice that forms in mountains and is heavy enough to move slowly downhill. Glaciers form over many years in permanent snow fields where more snow falls in winter than can melt in summer.	Glacier Bay, Alaska Perrito Moreno, South America Northwest coast of Norway
Gulf	A large area of the ocean or sea that lies within a curved coastline.	Gulf of Mexico Persian Gulf Gulf of Aqaba (Egypt, Israel, Jordan)
Harbor	A sheltered body of water where ships anchor and are safe from the winds and waves of storms at sea.	New York harbor Hong Kong harbor Sydney harbor (Australia)
Island	Land that is surrounded completely by water and is smaller than a continent.	Bermuda Tahiti Oahu
Isthmus	A narrow piece of land that joins two larger bodies of land.	Isthmus of Panama Isthmus of Corinth, Greece
Lagoon	A pool of shallow water linked to the sea by an inlet.	Certain coastal areas throughout the world
Lake	A body of water, usually fresh water that is surrounded by land.	Lake Victoria, Central Africa Lake Superior, United States and Canada Lake Geneva, Switzerland
Mountain	Land that rises very high, much higher than the land at its base. Mountains are much higher than hills.	Mt. McKinley, Alaska Mt. Everest, Asia Mt. Washington, New Hampshire
Mountain Range	A row of mountains that are joined together. A mountain range makes a giant natural wall.	Ural Mountains, Europe and Asia Rocky Mountains, western United States Alps, Europe Himalayas, Southern Asia

TABLE 2.1   LAND & WATER FORMATIONS (continued)

FEATURE	DEFINITION	KEY TOURISM DESTINATIONS
Oasis	A place in a desert where people can get water. Water in an oasis comes from underground springs or from irrigation.	Palm Springs, California Marrakech, Morocco
Peninsula	A land area with a narrow link to a larger land area. It is *almost* surrounded by water.	Baja, Mexico Florida Italy
Plain	A large, flat land area.	Great Plains, midwest United States La Mancha, central Spain Pompas, South America
Plateau	A large land area that is high and generally very flat.	Central Siberian Plateau Colorado Plateau Ozark Plateau
Reef	A chain of rocks or ridges of sand at or near the surface of the water.	Great Barrier Reef, Australia
River	A large, moving body of fresh water that starts at a source in higher land. The river moves from higher to lower land, and it carries the water to its mouth, where it ends. That mouth is at a lake, ocean, sea, or at another river.	Nile River, Egypt Amazon River, South America Mississippi River, United States
Sea	A large body of salt water nearly or partly surrounded by land. A sea is much smaller than an ocean.	Caribbean Mediterranean Baltic Sea
Strait	A passageway of water that connects two large bodies of water.	Strait of Gilbralter, Spain Straits of Magellan, South America Bering Strait, Alaska and Russia
Tributary	A stream or small river that flows into another river or stream.	Missouri (off Mississippi) Rio Negro (off Amazon) Isar (off the Danube)
Valley	The lower land between hills or mountains.	Shenandoah Valley, Virginia Sun Valley, Idaho Rift Valley, Central East Africa
Volcano	A vent in the earth's crust where molten or hot rock and steam are ejected from the earth's interior. A volcano is active when erupting, dormant during a long period of inactivity, and extinct when all activity has finally ceased.	Mt. Aetna, Sicily (active) Kilauea, Hawaii (active) Mt. Vesuvias, Naples, Italy (dormant) Diamond Head, Oahu, Hawaii (extinct)

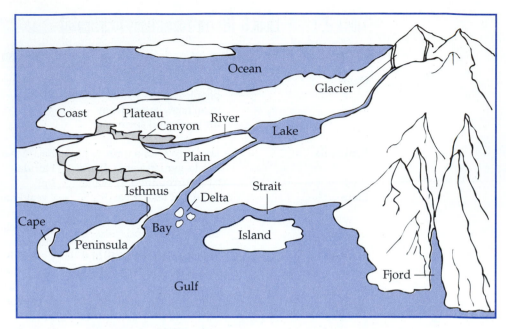

Figure 2.3 *Water and land formations.*

Key Point ➤ *Geography Stumpers:* (1) The North and South polar regions are considered to be *deserts*. Why? Because there is little precipitation in the polar regions; it is so cold that snow that falls there remains for a very long time; (2) What is the tallest mountain in the world? It isn't Mt. Everest or K-2 in Asia, but Mauna Kea in Hawaii. From its base deep in the Pacific Ocean, to its peak over south central Hawaii, measures over 33,000 feet (approximately 4,000 feet higher than Mt. Everest). Mt. Everest is the highest mountain measured from *sea level.*

Key Point ➤ Did you know that the Caspian Sea is really a lake, since it is completely surrounded by land? The Caspian Sea has salt water, due to its vast size and geological age.

✔ Check Your Understanding 2-2

Match each land or water formation with the correct definition.

A. fjord   _____   1. Body of water, usually fresh water, that is surrounded by land.

B. canyon   _____   2. Large area of the ocean or sea that lies within a curved coastline.

C. volcano   _____   3. Portion of land or water area in which there is little or no rain each year.

D. mountain   _____   4. Chain of rocks or ridges of sand at or near the surface of the water.

E. desert   _____   5. Part of a lake, sea, or ocean that is partly surrounded by land.

F. sea

     6. Land that is surrounded completely by water and is smaller than a continent.

G. bay

     7. Land that rises very high, much higher than the land at its base.

H. gulf

     8. Narrow part of land along a shore that usually curves out into the water.

I. glacier

     9. Deep, narrow valley having high, steep sides or cliffs.

J. reef

     10. Deep, narrow inlet of the sea, between high, steep cliffs.

K. peninsula

     11. Sheltered body of water where ships anchor and are safe from high winds and waves from storms at sea.

L. harbor

     12. Lower land between hills or mountains.

M. island

     13. Land area with a narrow link to a larger land area and is *almost* surrounded by water.

N. valley

     14. Thick, large mass of ice that forms over many years and is heavy enough to move slowly downhill.

O. strait

     15. Large body of salt water nearly or partly surrounded by land; much smaller than an ocean.

P. lake

     16. Vent in the earth's crust through which molten rock and other gases are ejected from the interior of the earth.

Q. cape

     17. Passageway of water that connects two large bodies of water.

LATITUDE AND LONGITUDE

The concepts of latitude and longitude are important when studying world geography. These are lines that measure distance on the earth.

➤ Latitude

Latitude is the measurement of distance north and south of the equator. The *equator* is a line of latitude that circles the globe. It runs east and west and is located halfway between the *North* and *South Poles*. The equator is the starting place for measuring latitude on the earth; it is located at zero degrees latitude.

North and south latitude is measured by parallel lines located north and south of the equator, respectively. *North latitude* extends from zero degrees (at the equator) to 90 degrees (North Pole). A point halfway between the equator and the North Pole is at 45 degrees north latitude. *South latitude* extends from zero degrees (at the equator) to 90 degrees (South Pole). A point halfway between the equator and the South Pole is at 45 degrees south latitude (see Figure 2.4). You can describe any place on earth by indicating its latitude (the number of degrees it is located north or south of the equator).

    Example: Use an atlas to find Houston, Texas. It is located 30 degrees north of the equator or at *30 degrees north latitude*. Now locate Cape Town, South Africa. Cape Town is located approximately 32 degrees south of the equator or at *32 degrees south latitude*.

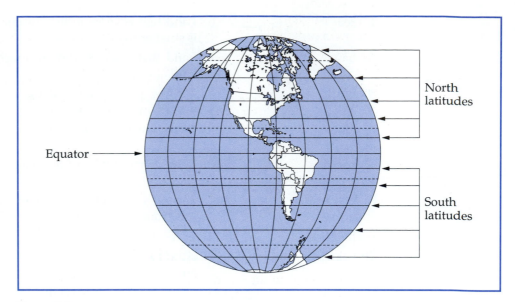

Figure 2.4 *Latitudes.*

▶ Longitude

You have learned that lines of latitude measure distance north and south of the equator. However, in order to measure locations on the earth in more precise terms, another set of lines is required. These lines of measurement are drawn from the North Pole to the South Pole and are called **meridians** or *lines of longitude* (see Figure 2.5).

Longitude is the measurement east and west of the prime meridian. The

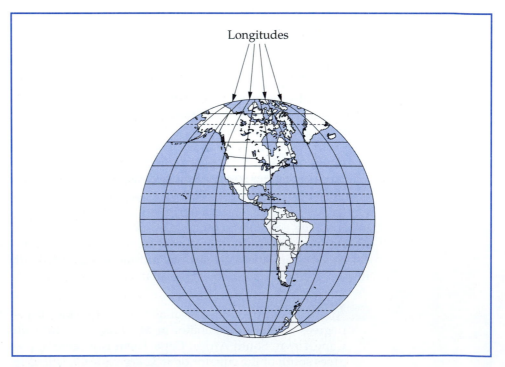

Figure 2.5 *Longitudes.*

prime meridian is the line of longitude that runs through Greenwich, England, and represents zero degrees longitude. Another term for the prime meridian is *zero meridian*. West longitude extends from zero degrees to 180 degrees *west* of the prime meridian. This area includes the Atlantic Ocean and North and South America. East longitude extends from zero degrees to 180 degrees *east* of the prime meridian. This area includes the continents of Europe, Asia, and Africa. You can describe any point on earth by indicating its longitude (the number of degrees it is located east or west of the prime meridian).

> **Example:** Use an atlas to find Philadelphia, Pennsylvania. It is located approximately *75 degrees west longitude*. Now locate Bergen, Norway. It is located east of the prime meridian at approximately *5 degrees east longitude*.

► Absolute Location Measurements

The exact or absolute location of any place on earth is identified by both latitude and longitude.

> **Example:** Use an atlas to find New Orleans, Louisiana. It is located approximately 30 degrees north of the equator and 90 degrees west of the prime meridian. The absolute measurement is *30 degrees north latitude, 90 degrees west longitude. Try this:* Locate Sydney, Australia on a map. It is located approximately 34 degrees _____ of the equator and 152 degrees _____ of the prime meridian, or _____. (Right! *34 degrees south latitude and 152 degrees east longitude*.)

✔ *Check Your Understanding 2-3*

For each city below, circle the most accurate latitude and longitude location. (Use a map or atlas.)

1. Los Angeles, California
   A. 118 degrees north latitude, 34 degrees east longitude
   B. 34 degrees north latitude, 118 degrees west longitude
   C. 118 degrees south latitude, 34 degrees east longitude
   D. 34 degrees south latitude, 118 degrees west longitude
2. Beijing, China
   A. 40 degrees south latitude, 118 degrees west longitude
   B. 116 degrees south latitude, 40 degrees east longitude
   C. 116 degrees north latitude, 40 degrees east longitude
   D. 40 degrees north latitude, 118 degrees east longitude
3. Rio de Janeiro, Brazil
   A. 23 degrees south latitude, 43 degrees west longitude
   B. 43 degrees south latitude, 23 degrees west longitude
   C. 23 degrees north latitude, 43 degrees east longitude
   D. 43 degrees south latitude, 23 degrees east longitude
4. Anchorage, Alaska
   A. 150 degrees north latitude, 60 degrees east longitude
   B. 61 degrees north latitude, 150 degrees west longitude

C. 150 degrees north latitude, 60 degrees west longitude

D. 61 degrees north latitude, 150 degrees east longitude

Name the capital city that is located closest to the following latitudes and longitudes. You will need an atlas or map for this exercise. For example, 47 degrees north latitude, 3 degrees east longitude: Paris, France

5. 41 degrees south latitude, 175 degrees east longitude _____

6. 20 degrees north latitude, 100 degrees west longitude _____

7. 35 degrees south latitude, 58 degrees west longitude _____

8. 40 degrees north latitude, 83 degrees west longitude _____

9. 2 degrees south latitude, 36 degrees east longitude _____

10. 36 degrees north latitude, 140 degrees east longitude _____

11. 60 degrees north latitude, 11 degrees east longitude _____

12. 32 degrees south latitude, 20 degrees east longitude _____

THE EARTH'S HEMISPHERES

Picture our earth reduced to the size of an orange. If you wanted to slice it into two equal sections, there are two ways to do it.

➤ Northern and Southern Hemispheres

You can slice the orange through the middle, from right to left. You would then get a top half and a bottom half. We call these halves of the earth the *northern* and *southern hemispheres*, respectively (see Figure 2.6). The slice through the earth is through zero degrees latitude or through the equator. The top half of the earth, measuring from the equator up to and including the North Pole, is the **northern**

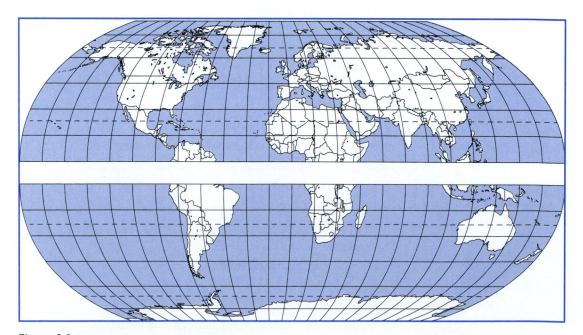

Figure 2.6 *Northern and southern hemispheres.*

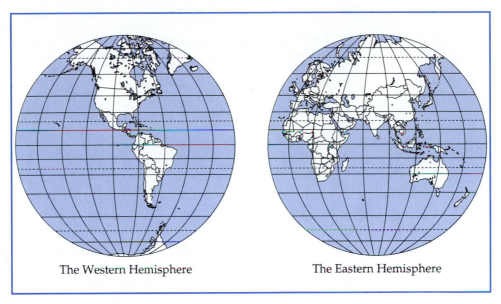

The Western Hemisphere   The Eastern Hemisphere

Figure 2.7 *Western and eastern hemispheres.*

hemisphere. The bottom half of the earth, measuring from the equator down to and including the South Pole, is the **southern hemisphere.**

➤ Western and Eastern Hemispheres

There is another way that we can slice our orange to obtain two half sections or hemispheres. Slice from the top to the bottom (from the North Pole to the South Pole). We call these half sections the eastern and western hemispheres (see Figure 2.7). The **western hemisphere** consists of the North and South American continents, Iceland, one-half of Antarctica, plus all of the adjacent islands, including Hawaii. The **eastern hemisphere** consists of the balance of the world. It includes all of the other continents: Europe, Asia, Africa, Australia, one-half of Antarctica, and the majority of islands in the Pacific Ocean.

✓ *Check Your Understanding 2-4*

For each major city below, write the name of the continent where it is located. Also, identify each city by its hemisphere location. The first has been completed as an example.

| | | HEMISPHERES | | | |
CITY	CONTINENT	NORTH or SOUTH		EAST or WEST	
Example: Paris, France	Europe	×		×	
1. Atlanta, Georgia					
2. Sydney, Australia					
3. Cairo, Egypt					
4. Lima, Peru					
5. Moscow, Russia					
6. Osaka, Japan					
7. Toronto, Canada					

CITY	CONTINENT	HEMISPHERES			
		NORTH *or* SOUTH		EAST *or* WEST	
8. Honolulu, Hawaii					
9. Caracas, Venezuela					
10. Tel Aviv, Israel					
11. San José, Costa Rica					
12. Reykjavik, Iceland					
13. Nassau, Bahamas					
14. Beijing, China					
15. Capetown, S. Africa					

TIME ZONES

Lines of longitude are used not only to measure distance east or west of the prime meridian, but are also used to determine time zones. It takes the earth 24 hours to make one complete rotation on its axis. Since the circumference of the earth is 360 degrees (a circle), the earth turns toward the sun 15 degrees per hour (360 degrees divided by 24 hours). The earth is divided into 24 **time zones** (see Figure 2.8); each time zone is equivalent to approximately 15 degrees of longitude, or is 15 degrees wide.

When the sun is directly over a meridian, the time is 12:00 noon at points located along that meridian. Places located east of that meridian are experiencing afternoon hours, and those located west are experiencing morning hours, with each time zone equivalent to 1 hour.

Greenwich Mean Time (GMT) is the prime meridian; it serves as a basis of all the world's time zones. A time zone that is 15 degrees wide with the prime meridian or GMT running through the center of it was established. The purpose of this was to measure the time at any place on earth and compare it to GMT.

Key Point ➤ The Greenwich Observatory was founded in 1675 by King Charles II to keep accurate tables of the moon's and stars' positions for the calculation of longitude by English ships. In 1750, publication of the tables for ship navigational purposes was begun, and they were published annually after 1838. Up until the late nineteenth century, there was no standard measurement used worldwide for navigation of ships. In 1881, representatives from many countries met in Washington, DC to discuss how to standardize world measurements. Greenwich, England was selected because navigation tables and records from the Greenwich Observatory compiled over several centuries proved to be the most accurate.

➤ East of GMT

Places on earth located east of GMT are a certain number of time zones ahead of GMT, or a certain number of hours *later in time* than GMT. As you move farther east of GMT, times become later at different points on the earth. Refer to Figure 2.8, the time zone map of the world. A place that is located in the first time zone to the east of GMT is at +1, or 1 hour ahead of GMT. A place that is located in the fourth time zone east of GMT is at +4, or 4 hours ahead of GMT. This progression (+1, +2, +3, . . .) continues up to the 180-degree meridian, which is located halfway around the world from GMT.

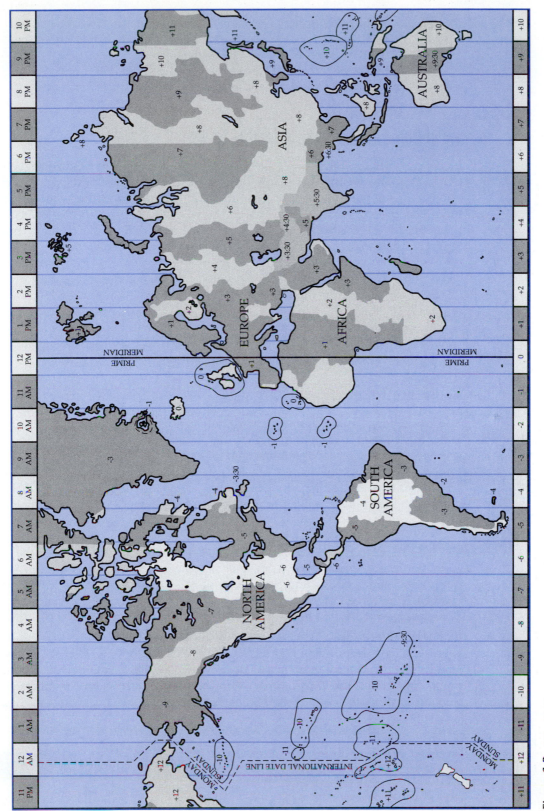

Figure 2.8 *World time zone map.*

Example: Berlin, Germany is located in the first time zone east of GMT or at +1. Berlin is 1 hour ahead of GMT. If it is noontime GMT, it is 1 hour later, or 1:00 P.M., in Berlin.

Nairobi, Kenya, is located three time zones east of GMT, or at +3. If it is 8:00 A.M. GMT, what time is it in Nairobi? (*Right! Three hours later, or 11:00 A.M.*).

➤ West of GMT

Places on earth located west of GMT are a certain number of time zones behind GMT. This also means that places on earth located west of GMT are a certain number of hours *earlier in time* than at GMT. As you go farther west of GMT, times become earlier at different points on the earth. A place that is located five time zones west of GMT is at –5, or 5 hours behind GMT. A place that is located ten time zones west of GMT is at –10, or 10 hours behind GMT.

Example: New York is located five time zones to the west of GMT, or at –5. If the time at GMT is 3:00 P.M., it is 5 hours earlier in New York, 10:00 A.M.

Los Angeles is located eight time zones to the west of GMT, or at –8. If the time at GMT is 6:30 P.M., what time is it in Los Angeles? (*Right! Eight hours earlier, or 10:30 A.M.*)

➤ Determining Time Differences

You can determine the time difference between any two places on earth if you know the location of each in relation to GMT. A time line, as shown in Figure 2.9, is often helpful when determining time differences. Zero on the time line represents GMT. To the right or east of GMT, the numbers +1, +2, +3, . . . refer to the number of time zones or hours later than GMT. To the left or west of GMT, the numbers –1, –2, –3, . . . refer to the number of time zones or hours earlier than GMT.

Example: Refer to Figure 2.9, GMT time line. What is the time difference between New York and San Diego? New York is at –5 (5 hours behind GMT) and San Diego is at –8 (8 hours behind GMT). There are three time zones that separate them, or 3 hours' difference in time. New York is 3 hours ahead of San Diego. When it is 2:00 P.M. in New York, what time is it in San Diego? (*Right! 11:00 A.M.*).

Try another: What is the time difference between Athens and

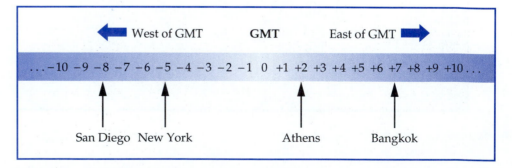

Figure 2.9 *GMT time line.*

Bangkok? (*Right! Five*). If it is 3:00 P.M. in Athens, what time is it in Bangkok? (*Right! 8:00 P.M., since Bangkok is 5 hours ahead of Athens.*)

Try another: What is the time difference between New York (–5) and Bangkok (+7)? Refer to the time line and count the number of time zones. There are twelve time zones or hours that separate these two cities. Bangkok is 12 hours ahead of New York. So, when it is 7:00 A.M. in New York, what time is it in Bangkok? (*Right! 7:00 P.M.*)

✔ Check Your Understanding 2-5

Answer each of the questions below dealing with time differences. The number of hours ahead GMT (+) or behind GMT (–) is given for each city. (Use a time line and atlas, they help in understanding time zones.)

When It Is . . .	*What Time Is It in . . .*	*Answer*
1. 3:00 A.M. in Los Angeles (–8)	GMT (0) ?	_____
2. 8:00 P.M. in Rome (+1)	GMT (0) ?	_____
3. 11:30 A.M. in London (GMT)	Honolulu (–10) ?	_____
4. 9:00 A.M. in Washington, DC (–5)	Madrid (+1) ?	_____
5. 6:00 A.M. in Chicago (–6)	Hong Kong (+8) ?	_____
6. 5:00 P.M. in Anchorage (–9)	Tampa (–5) ?	_____
7. 11:30 A.M. in Copenhagen (+1)	Sydney (+10) ?	_____
8. 5:00 P.M. in Tel Aviv (+3)	Mexico City (–6) ?	_____

9. Your agency is located in Pittsburgh (–5). You need to place a call to a tour company in Paris (+1) at 4:00 P.M. Paris local time. At what time would you place the call from your office?

_____

10. Your agency is located in Chicago (–6), and your office hours are from 8 A.M. to 5 P.M. You need to fax a letter to a company located in Athens (+2) during their office hours. Their office hours are from 9 A.M. to 5 P.M. (Athens time). Between what hours are you able to send the fax from your office in Chicago (your local time)?

_____

INTERNATIONAL DATE LINE

Halfway around the world from the GMT is a time zone that is divided into two parts. The line that divides it into two parts, called the **International Date Line (IDL),** is a boundary that extends from the North to the South Pole across the Pacific Ocean. It closely follows the 180th meridian. Since the International Date Line is at the exact opposite side of the earth from the prime meridian, together they create a connected circle around the world, from pole to pole.

The International Date Line designates a *date change*; when the air traveler crosses it, the date changes to either the day before or the day ahead. The area west of the Date Line (i.e., the Pacific region and Asia) is always one day ahead of the area east of the Date Line (i.e., Hawaii and the continental United States). Refer to Figure 2.10, which shows the location of the International Date Line.

Example: A traveler is on a westbound flight from Los Angeles to Tokyo across the Pacific Ocean, or transpacific. The plane departed on Monday morning. When the plane crosses the International

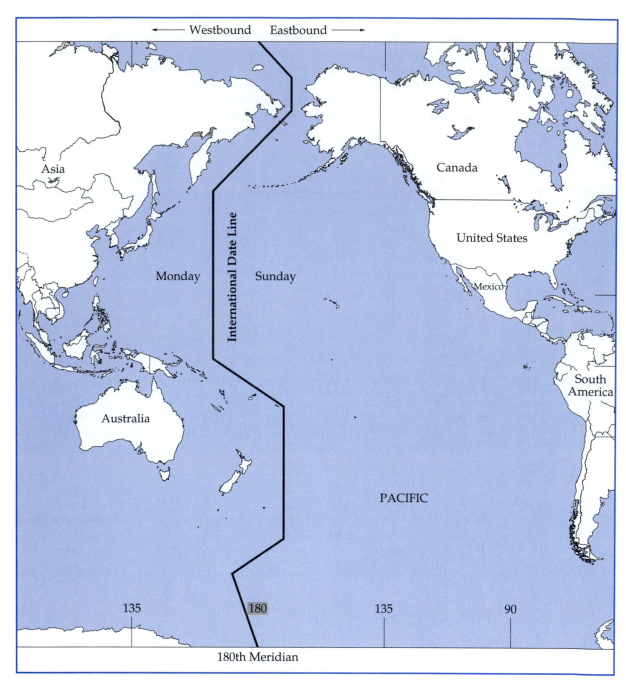

Asia

Canada

International Date Line

United States

Monday   Sunday

Mexico

South
America

Australia

PACIFIC

135   180   135   90

180th Meridian

Figure 2.10 *Location of the International Date Line.*

Date Line, it automatically becomes the same clock time on the next calendar day, or Tuesday.

There is also a calendar change when travel is in the opposite direction, or eastbound transpacific.

Example: A traveler is on an eastbound transpacific flight from Sydney, Australia to Chicago. The flight departed on Wednesday. When the plane crosses the International Date Line, it automatically becomes the same clock time one calendar day earlier, or Tuesday.

➤ Understanding Date Changes

Before reading about it in this book, you had probably heard about the International Date Line (IDL) and the fact that it becomes either a day later or a day earlier when you cross it. But do you really understand how it can happen? Pretend we are in a superfast plane of the future and it takes us only several hours to go completely around the world. Does this mean that if we fly long enough we can "jump" days into the future or back into the past? What prevents us from doing something as crazy-sounding as that if there is a calendar change every time we cross the IDL?

To better understand date changes, you must have an understanding of Greenwich Mean Time (GMT), the International Date Line, plus two "imaginary," constantly shifting lines: the Midday Line and the Midnight Line. The *Midday Line* is a line that is drawn from the North Pole to the South Pole and is *always lined up with the sun*. In other words, the Midday Line always moves with the sun. The *Midnight Line* is a line drawn from the North Pole to the South Pole and located *exactly opposite the Midday Line* on the other side of the earth. It also moves constantly.

Figure 2.11 shows the earth positioned like a globe, with the Midday and Midnight Lines suspended between the North and South Poles. You must imagine both the Midday and Midnight Lines to be suspended in space; they don't touch the surface but follow the curvature of the earth. These imaginary lines re-

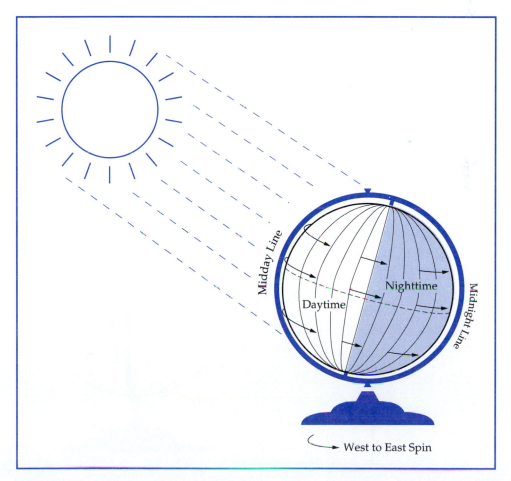

Figure 2.11 *Midday and Midnight Lines.*

main in the same position relative to the sun; they remain in place as the earth spins below.

You must also remember that the earth is spinning, from west to east; Greenwich Mean Time and the International Date Line are drawn along the surface of the earth and therefore spin along with the earth. The Midday and Midnight Lines, however, remain suspended in space and in place as the earth spins below them. Also remember that there are 24 hours in a day; each hour of the day is found somewhere on earth. For example, when it is 12:00 noon GMT it is 7:00 A.M. in New York, 4:00 A.M. in Los Angeles, 2:00 P.M. in Athens, and 8:00 P.M. in Hong Kong.

Figures 2.12 to 2.17 represent a series of illustrations that show how the earth experiences date changes. Each illustration indicates the Midnight Line relative to the earth. You are in space looking down on the earth directly over the Midnight Line in each example. The sun is located on the opposite side of the earth away from the Midnight Line. The sun is hidden from your view. The half of the earth in our view is in dark or nighttime; the opposite side of the earth is in light or daytime.

Figure 2.12 shows the International Date Line, in the Pacific Ocean, lined up with the Midnight Line; therefore, it is midnight on the International Date Line. On the opposite side of the earth, the prime meridian (GMT) is lined up with the Midday Line. It is 12:00 noon GMT. In this position, *all places on earth are experiencing the same day for a split second.* In this position, it is Monday every place on earth.

Figure 2.13 shows the earth's position a couple of hours later. The earth is spinning west to east; the International Date Line has now spun farther east of the Midnight Line. The earth's area that is measured from the stationary Midnight Line to the International Date Line represents an area in the new day, Tuesday. This area is bulge-shaped and is shown shaded in Figure 2.13. Because the earth is spinning, this "bulge" of Tuesday will increase in size as more and more of the earth enters Tuesday. The rest of the earth that has not yet reached the Midnight Line is still experiencing Monday.

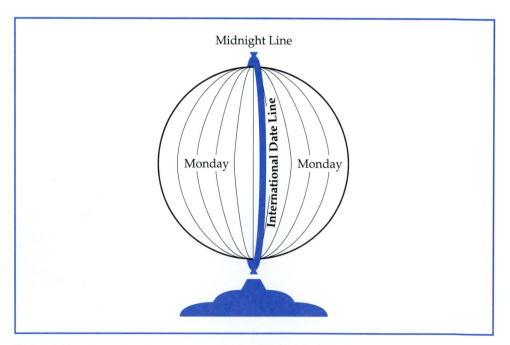

Figure 2.12

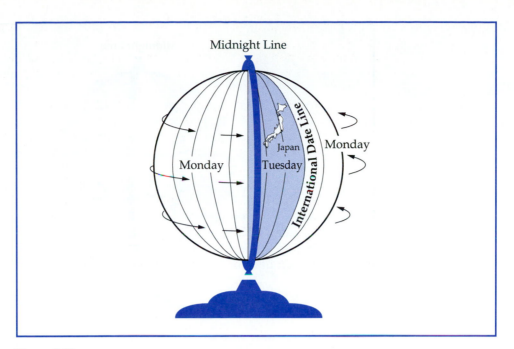

Figure 2.13

Figure 2.14 shows the earth now into the twelfth hour of the new day, Tuesday. The prime meridian (GMT) is now lined up with the Midnight Line (it is 12:00 midnight GMT). On the opposite side of the earth, the International Date Line has reached the Midday Line. It is 12:00 noon along the International Date Line. At this time, half of the earth is experiencing Tuesday (the shaded portion or the entire eastern hemisphere), and the rest of the earth is still experiencing Monday (the unshaded portion, or western hemisphere).

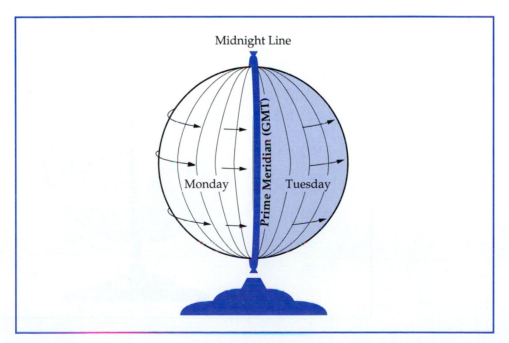

Figure 2.14

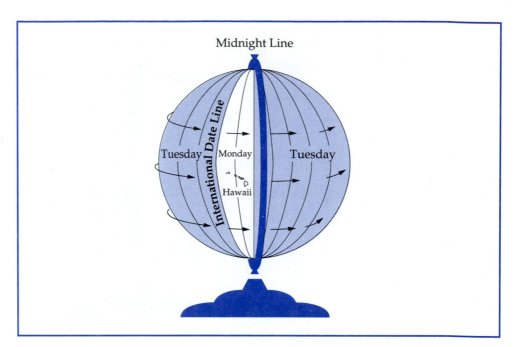

Midnight Line

International Date Line

Tuesday   Monday   Tuesday

Hawaii

Figure 2.15

Figure 2.15 shows the earth several hours later; the International Date Line is spinning closer to the Midnight Line. This is the point where most places on earth are now experiencing Tuesday; a small bulge, containing Hawaii, is still experiencing Monday. One of the last places on earth to reach each new day is the state of Hawaii. The Hawaiian Islands are located immediately east of the International Date Line. In Figure 2.15 the local time in Hawaii is around 10:00 P.M., Monday evening. Hawaii still has a couple of hours left before it reaches Tuesday.

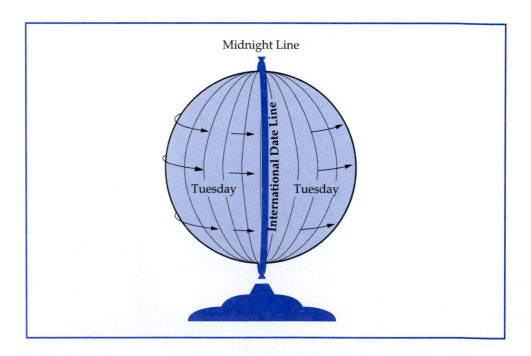

Midnight Line

International Date Line

Tuesday   Tuesday

Figure 2.16

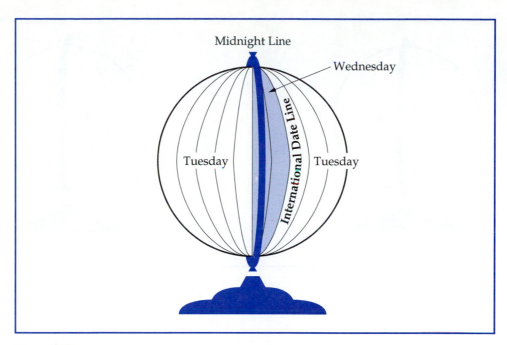

Figure 2.17

Figure 2.16 (Similar to Figure 2.12) shows the earth exactly 24 hours after the time shown in Figure 2.12. The International Date Line has again reached the Midnight Line. For a split second, *it is Tuesday every place on earth.*

Figure 2.17 shows the position of the earth a few hours later. As the earth continues to spin and the International Date Line moves farther and farther east of the Midnight Line, the growing bulge of earth is now experiencing the new day, Wednesday.

Key Point ➤ Japan in the Pacific is located immediately west of the International Date Line. It is one of the first countries to experience each new day. That's why Japan is known as the "Land of the Rising Sun."

✓ *Check Your Understanding 2-6*

Refer to Figure 2.18a and b for these exercises. In both parts, the imaginary Midnight Line is shown and the location of the International Date Line is drawn.

1. In Figure 2.18a, if the point on the earth labeled B is experiencing Thursday, in what day of the week is point A? _____

2. In Figure 2.18b, if the point on the earth labeled A is experiencing Monday, in what day of the week is point B? _____ point C? _____

Round Earth, Paper Maps

There are many different ways of looking at the world. Depending on what book you are reading or what atlas you are using, the world is drawn in various shapes and sizes, with different points of view.

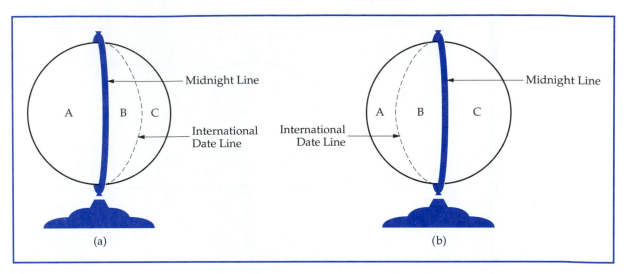

Figure 2.18

A **globe** represents the earth as it really is—nearly spherical in shape. Because of its shape, the entire world cannot be viewed at a glance. Nor are globes very convenient; you can't fold them up and carry them with you like flat maps. Flat maps are more convenient, but they also distort our view of the world. Think of our earth as a rubber ball. Try to flatten the rubber ball and you have an idea of what a problem it is to represent landmasses and bodies of water accurately when you force the round earth onto flat paper. Inevitably, continents, oceans, and seas are stretched, cut off altogether, or otherwise disfigured.

To present the curved surface of the earth as a flat projection is not difficult if you are viewing small areas such as towns and cities; distances between points will be pretty accurate and true. However, if the areas under consideration are huge—entire countries, group of countries, continents, or the whole world—they require a certain type of realistic projection. Dozens of different types of map projections are used for different reasons. The three major types of map projections that are printed in many travel reference books and resources are:

1. *Mercator Projection* (Figure 2.19). The Mercator projection is a very common projection. Land shapes are correct, but their areas are distorted. The farther away from the equator, the greater the area distortion. For example, Greenland looks a lot bigger than the entire continent of South America. In reality, Greenland is smaller than Mexico. The Mercator is used for nautical navigation because a line connecting any two points gives the compass direction between them. This type of map is best used for simple maps of small areas, such as towns, cities, or resort areas.

2. *Goode's Interrupted Projection* (Figure 2.20). This projection interrupts or cuts the globe to minimize distortion of shape. This is commonly used for large world thematic maps. It is also used in atlases to show more accurate relative sizes and shapes of land areas and bodies of water.

3. *Robinson Projection* (Figure 2.21). This is a good compromise projection. It was designed by Rand McNally to present an uninterrupted and visually correct map of the earth. It maintains overall shape and area relationships without extreme distortion. It is widely used in textbooks, atlases, and classrooms.

In addition to types of projections of the earth, there are different types of maps that represent specific types of data. There are maps that show topography,

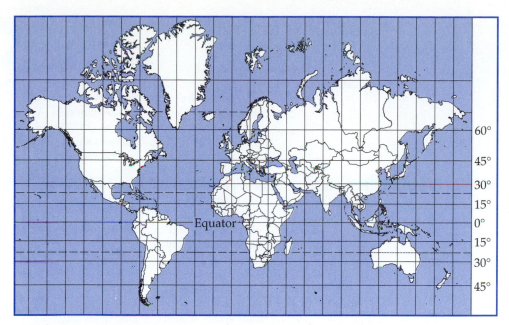

Figure 2.19 *Mercator projection.*

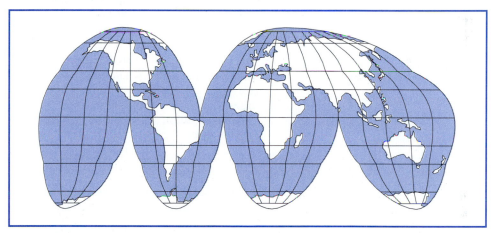

Figure 2.20 *Goode's interrupted projection.*

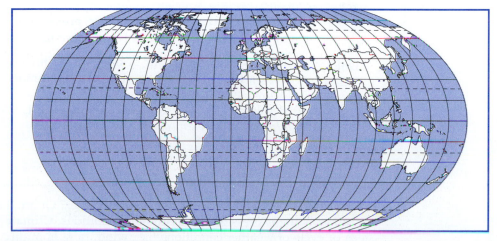

Figure 2.21 *Robinson projection.*

TABLE 2.2   TYPES OF MAPS

TYPE OF MAP	WHAT IT SHOWS	WHERE TO FIND	WHEN TO USE
Political map	Identifies by name, and separates by boundaries, countries, states, cities, provinces, and other geographical regions	General atlases and industry specific reference materials such as *OAG Travel Planners* and tour brochures	Planning itineraries by air, land, and sea; locating a specific city, province, state, or country
Relief map	Shows natural features of the land, including mountains, valleys, rivers, and hills; land elevations and shapes are indicated by different colors and shading	General and travel-specific atlases	Planning self-drive itineraries where major obstacles such as mountains, rivers, etc. are important to know about in advance
Locator map	Identifies location of major hotels, major attractions, and sightseeing areas	Travel industry–specific reference materials, such as *Official Hotel Guide* and *OAG Travel Planners*	Planning business and vacation trips for clients by locating major hotels and key attractions within walking or easy driving distance
Route map	Shows major routes of airlines, trains, and cruise ships through drawn lines and curves on political or relief maps	Travel industry reference materials, such as the *Thomas Cook Timetables for rail travel*, *Official Airline Guides*, cruise resources and brochures	Excellent visual tools when planning itineraries; handy when planning a trip on a preferred airline or planning a vacation itinerary by rail or ship

climate, and world populations. The major types of maps that are used in the travel professions are described in Table 2.2.

Web Link

On a Quest for Maps: There are some pretty nifty Web sites that offer maps, maps, and more maps. Here are two recommended sites:

1. *Mapquest* lets you zoom in on your destination (anywhere in the world), find directions, local hotels, restaurants, and lots more. Go to *http://www.mapquest.com.*
2. *Mapblast* lets you create your own maps of U.S. destinations. Go to *http://www.mapblast.com.*

CLIMATE AND WEATHER

What's the difference between climate and weather? Or are they the same thing? **Weather** is the expression of day-to-day conditions. **Climate** is the general pattern or cycle of weather conditions (i.e., wind, rain, humidity, snowfall, clouds), over a large area, averaged over many years.

Sending travelers to the wrong place at the wrong time of year can ruin vacations and disrupt schedules. Where do you send a client who wants to snow-ski in the middle of August? Would you recommend a Caribbean cruise in September? How about sending someone to the French Riviera for a sunny beach vacation in March?

The climate-savvy travel professional would send clients south of the equator to ski the Andes in Chile or Argentina during summer. Sending someone on a Caribbean cruise in September is real "iffy" since this is right in the middle of hurricane season; and the vacationer looking for a warm resort won't find it at the French Riviera in March—the waters there are still too cold for swimming.

Climate is affected by many factors, such as latitude, prevailing winds, topography, distance from the sea, and ocean currents. Sometimes climate patterns don't make sense. Two places can be close together but experience different climates. Hawaii's northeast slopes are wet, but the southwest regions, located on the other side of mountains, are much drier. On the other hand, two places far apart can have very similar climates. Like eastern China, the southeastern coast of the United States is temperate, humid, has a hot summer, and has no dry season. Chicago and Moscow both have cold winters and hot summers.

Colder climates aren't always close to the North Pole. Great Britain, which is farther north than Newfoundland, has milder weather since it is warmed by the Gulf Stream sweeping up from the equatorial regions.

Let's take a closer look at several factors that affect climate and which subsequently affect tourism.

➤ Land and Sea

Huge mountains can trap heat or cold, and block or alter wind flow. They block clouds that bring warm and moist air. Places located on the side of the mountain facing the wind (*windward*) experience warmer temperatures and more precipitation. The land on the windward side is more green and lush with vegetation. Places located on the other side of mountains or away from the wind (*leeward*) experience cooler and drier weather. Warm air loses moisture and drops in temperature as it rises over mountaintops. The land on the leeward side is more dry and less verdant. Most beach resorts are built on the leeward side of mountains because they experience more sunshine, less rain, and high humidity. However, the trade-off here is a landscape less verdant and lush with natural tropical vegetation.

Key Point ➤ The Leeward and Windward Islands of the Lesser Antilles (part of the West Indies) bear no relationship to the wind. These are merely colloquial names.

Large bodies of water also play a part in climate conditions. Temperatures over the oceans and seas change far less than those over the land because water is a better insulator than soil or rock. Water heats and cools at a much slower rate. Hence coastal temperatures are moderated by the presence of the sea nearby, while the interiors of the continents experience cold winters and hot summers.

➤ Highs and Lows

We all know that *latitude* (where a place is located in regard to the equator) plays an important role in climate; we expect hot temperatures along the equator and much colder conditions at the Poles. It may surprise you to know that the earth's hottest spots are not right along the equator, which is often cloudy, but at about

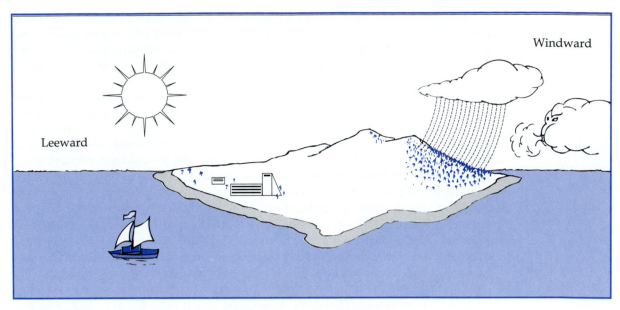

Figure 2.22 *Anatomy of a tropical island (Leeward and Windward).*

20 degrees north and south latitudes. The sky is clearer and the sun remains overhead longer at these slightly higher latitudes.

Altitude, how high a place is elevated, also affects temperature: The higher you are above sea level, the cooler it becomes. The temperature drops approximately 1 degree Fahrenheit with every 985 feet of altitude. A good example is Quito, Ecuador, which is approximately 10,000 feet above sea level. Temperatures in this town average 20 to 25 degrees cooler than what is experienced just several miles away at lower altitudes.

Key Point ➤ A popular tourist destination, Mexico City, is located 7,000 feet above sea level. In past years it used to experience much cooler temperatures because of its high altitude. Due to its rapid growth, the level of pollution over this highly populated region has grown to the point where this city's average temperature has risen and is now equal to that experienced at sea level.

➤ Air Circulation: Bumpy Rides and Hurricanes

Another contributor to climate is the *circulation of the atmosphere*. This ceaseless movement of air, which makes up for the earth's heat imbalances, carries warm, moist air to the polar regions and cool, drier air to the tropics.

It should be noted that both the *jet streams* and *trade winds* are important to climate. However, one has a lot more to do with climate than the other. **Jet streams** are bands of high-altitude winds about 33,000 to 64,000 feet above the earth. Although the jet streams affect weather patterns such as cyclones and monsoons, they have more to do with creating turbulence, giving you a bumpy ride on a jet.

Trade winds are global winds that blow steadily toward the equator from the northeast or southeast. The northern hemisphere trade winds move weather from east to west. That is why the West Indies experience hurricane season in late summer and early autumn. Hurricanes that start near West Africa are pushed across the Atlantic by the trades, where they curve north due to an effect of the earth's rotation. From there, the westerly trade winds continue to push the hurricane farther across the Atlantic into the Caribbean Sea and sometimes even onto the eastern coast of the United States.

➤ Ocean Currents: Warm and Cool Beaches

In addition to air circulation, the circular sweeps of our oceans or *currents* contribute to differences in land and water temperature. How much do you really know about currents and how they affect tourism? Where would you send a client who wants warm beach and comfortable swimming in early June: Daytona Beach, Florida or Santa Monica, California? The answer may surprise you.

Refer to Figure 2.23, a simplified world map showing warm and cold ocean currents. Notice that ocean currents *north of the equator* (northern hemisphere) generally move in a *clockwise* direction; in the *southern hemisphere*, they move generally in a *counterclockwise* direction. Waters sweeping from the polar regions are cold in temperature but become warmer as they approach the equator. Conversely, waters sweeping from the equatorial regions are warm in temperature but become cooler as they approach the polar regions.

Refer to Figure 2.21 again. Can you see a general pattern? In both the northern and southern hemispheres, the *western* coastlines of the continents experience cooler water temperatures, and the eastern coastlines experience warmer temperatures. In North America, the waters along the west coast are much cooler than those along the east coast at the same time of year. In early June, average water temperature in

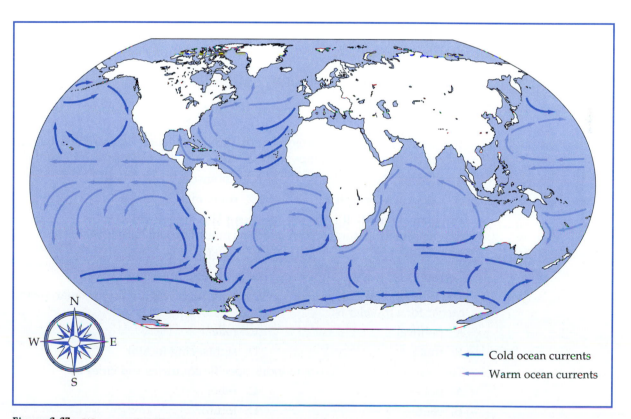

Cold ocean currents
Warm ocean currents

Figure 2.23 *Warm and cold ocean currents.*

sunny San Diego, California is approximately 61 to 63 degrees Fahrenheit—very uncomfortable for swimming. The water temperature in Savannah, Georgia, located the same distance from the equator, is a comfortable 72 to 74 degrees Fahrenheit.

Key Point ➤ The western coastline of Europe is an exception to this general trend. The warm Gulf Stream sweeps north along North America and eastward into the cold North Atlantic. This warm current is responsible for warming western Europe by taking about 10 degrees Fahrenheit off this continent's midwinter chill. This is also why a place like Ireland has a mild climate in which palm trees and other subtropical plants are able to grow. In comparison, parts of northern Québec in Canada, which lie on the same latitude as Ireland, are always cold, with permanently frozen ground.

➤ Climatic Zones of the World

The world's climatic zones are shown in Figure 2.24, with corresponding descriptions given in Table 2.3.

Key Point ➤ The earth receives the greatest amount of solar radiation in the tropics, a zone that lies between the *Tropic of Cancer* (23½ degrees north latitude) and the *Tropic of Capricorn* (23½ degrees south latitude) and is centered along the equator.

✓ Check Your Understanding 2-7

Multiple Choice

Circle the *best* answer.

1. The most accurate representation of the earth is a(n):
   A. map projection
   B. globe
   C. atlas
   D. wall map

2. The most accurate flat projection of the earth since it maintains overall shapes and area relationships without extreme distortion of the continents is:
   A. Mercator
   B. Goode's Interrupted
   C. Robinson
   D. route map

3. The type of map that is best used when planning self-drive tours, in order to compensate for natural features such as mountains, hills, and rivers, is:
   A. political
   B. route
   C. relief
   D. sightseeing locator

4. The type of map that is handy when planning a trip on a particular airline carrier for a traveler is:
   A. political
   B. route
   C. relief
   D. sightseeing locator

5. The best type of map to use to locate specific countries and cities is:
   A. political
   B. route
   C. relief
   D. locator

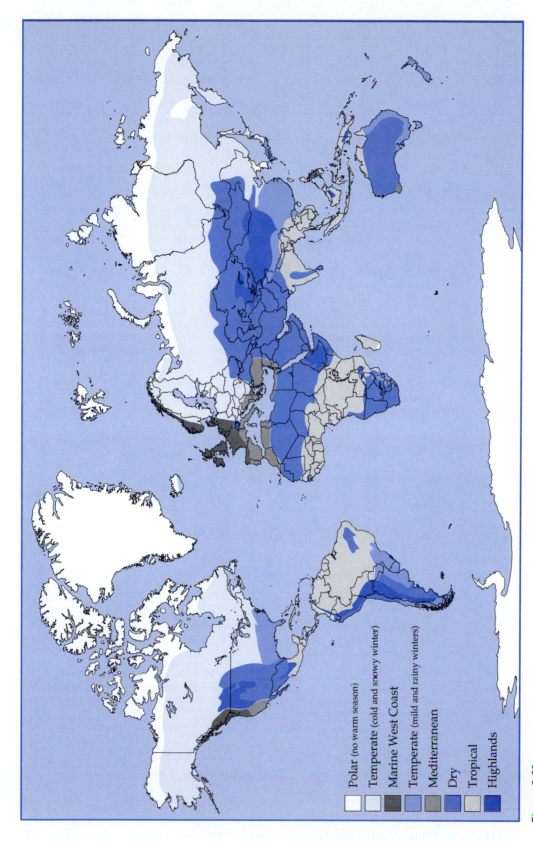

Figure 2.24 *World Climates.*

Polar (no warm season)
Temperate (cold and snowy winter)
Marine West Coast
Temperate (mild and rainy winters)
Mediterranean
Dry
Tropical
Highlands

TABLE 2.3   CLIMATIC ZONES OF THE WORLD

Climate Zone	Description	Average High Temperatures, Jan./June (°F)	Key Tourism Destinations
☐ Polar (no warm season)	*Ice cap* (perpetual frost and temperature never rises over 32°F)	–40/12	Greenland (central region)
	Tundra (land of arctic plains where warmest month never rises above 50°F)	–15/34	Barrow, Alaska
☐ Temperate (cold and snowy winter)	Long, warm, humid summers; cold and snowy winters	32/75	Chicago, Illinois
	Short, warm, humid summer; cold and snowy winters	15/68	Moscow, Russia
	Very short, cool, humid summer; very cold and snowy winter	0/62	Fairbanks, Alaska
■ Marine west coast	Mild and rainy all year	40/62	Dublin, Ireland
■ Temperate (mild and rainy winters)	Warm and humid summer; mild and rainy winter	52/85	Charleston, South Carolina
■ Mediterranean	Hot and dry summer; mild and rainy winter	50/85	Los Angeles Athens, Greece
■ Dry	Desert, no rain	65/95	Aswan, Egypt
	Desert, some rain	60/84	Phoenix, Arizona
☐ Tropical	Hot and rainy all year	82/85	Singapore, Malaysia
	Hot, with rainy and dry seasons	74/80	Caracas, Venezuela
■ Highlands	Varies with height and altitude		Destinations located in following mountain ranges: Andes (South America), Rocky Mountains (western United States), Alps (central Europe), Himalayas (Asia)

6. Which area located in the southern hemisphere would experience the warmest waters for a beach vacation?
   A. Perth, Australia   C. Sydney, Australia
   B. Cape Town, South Africa   D. Valparaiso, Chile

7. Which city below is considered tropical: hot with rain year round?
   A. Auckland, New Zealand   C. Bangkok, Thailand
   B. Geneva, Switzerland   D. Washington, DC

8. Which city in the United States is most like Dublin, Ireland, located in the temperate climate zone (mild and rainy all year)?
   A. Miami, Florida   C. Dallas, Texas
   B. Portland, Maine   D. Seattle, Washington

____ 9. Weather describes day-to-day conditions; climate is the general pattern of conditions such as temperature, rain, wind, and humidity.

____ 10. Colder climates are always close to the North Pole and South Pole.

____ 11. Most beach resorts are built on the windward side of mountains since they experience more sunshine and less rain.

____ 12. Paris, located in the interior, is generally warmer than places located along the same latitude in the coastal regions of France.

____ 13. The higher a place is above sea level, the cooler it becomes.

____ 14. Trade winds have a greater effect on weather conditions than does the jet stream.

____ 15. The earth receives the greatest amount of solar radiation in the tropics, a zone that lies between the Tropic of Cancer and the Tropic of Capricorn.

A Tour of the World

Travel professionals must be geography-savvy (see the world map shown in Figure 2.25). You wouldn't hire a technician who didn't understand about electricity to wire your house or allow a physician who didn't know anatomy to operate on you! Similarly, you cannot expect to be a travel expert and plan itineraries without knowing geography. It is not just understanding where places are on a map, their time zones, and the climate conditions. You have to know what it is really like at a destination: how to get there, the best time to go, what the people are like, and what to see and do once you get there (see Table 2.4 for a summary of popular guidebooks). Learning about the world through the eyes of a travel professional is called *tourism geography*. The world is a pretty big place and you cannot learn it all overnight. Your knowledge of tourism geography grows the more you study and use it in the workplace.

In this section we take you on a whirlwind tour, continent by continent, to some major tourism destination spots. A brief introduction to each area is provided with an at-a-glance list called "Sound Bites" that describes key attractions and facts. A survey of popular travelers' destinations outside the continental United States is shown in Figure 2.26.

➤ North America

North America consists of the following countries and regions:

1. Canada
2. United States (including Hawaii and Alaska)
3. Middle America, includes the following:
   a. Mexico
   b. Central America (consists of Guatemala, Belize, El Salvador, Honduras, Nicaragua, Costa Rica, and Panama)
   c. West Indies (consists of Bermuda, Bahamas, and the Caribbean islands)

The 455 million people who live on this continent produce more goods and consume more resources than those on any other continent. Canada and the United States share a 5,500-mile border, the longest in the world.

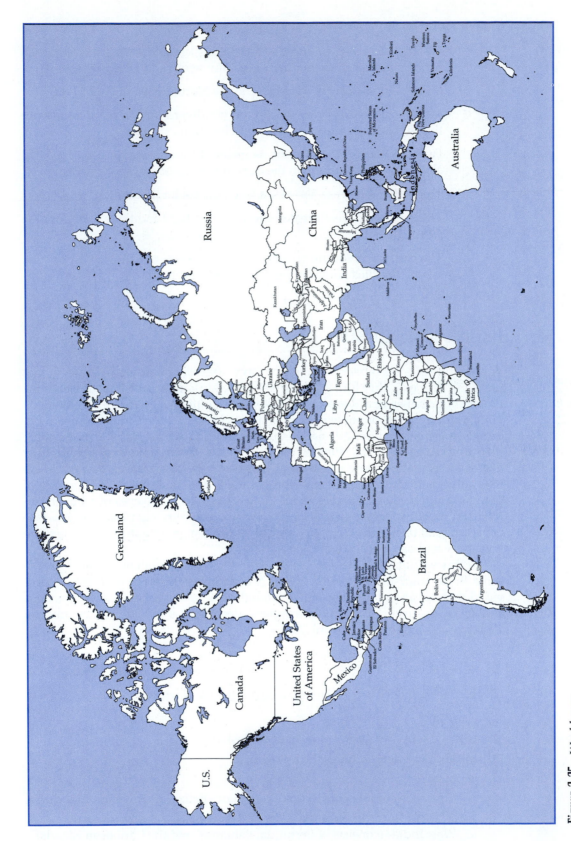

Figure 2.25 *World map.*

TABLE 2.4 GUIDE TO GUIDEBOOKS

Title	General Description	Traveler Type	Key Features	Comments
BAEDECKER	150-year-old classic	Sophisticated	Culture, history, architecture	Color-coding helps you find information, easy A–Z organization
BLUE GUIDE	Encyclopedic guidebook	Sophisticated	History, culture, architecture, the arts, detailed itineraries	Good reference; use with other guidebooks
FIELDINGS	General guide	Upscale adventurer	How to rough it in luxury; trendy take on more civilized destinations	Excellent illustrations of suggested tours; good maps
FODOR'S GOLD GUIDES	In-depth walking and driving itineraries; hotel and restaurant reviews	Families, all	In addition to general destination information, includes restaurant reviews, in-depth travel tips	Fodor's also offers sports guides, pocket guides, and a national parks guide
FODOR'S UP CLOSE	Top sights, hotel and restaurant reviews; great graphics	Young, all	Besides overview of usual sights, includes hip neighborhoods and clubs	Carry this with you on a trip; use more detailed guide for research and planning
FROMMER'S COMPLETE GUIDE	Traditional and off-the-beaten path sightseeing; hotel and restaurant reviews	All	Good photos and maps	Frommer's also offers portable guides, nightlife guides, and a national parks guide
FROMMER'S $-A-DAY	Economy version of Frommer's	Budget		Contains coupons
LET'S GO	Contains essential know-before-you-go information and detailed destination descriptions	Budget, student, all	Lots of B&Bs, pensions, hostels, small hotels, low-cost bistros and ethnic restaurants	Researched, written, and edited by over 200 Harvard students each year
LONELY PLANET	Critical and straightforward guidebook	Budget, all, singles	Casual writing style, quick tips on best places to find inexpensive wine, meet others, etc.	For more upscale information, supplement with other guidebooks or information
MICHELIN	Lots of information; easy-to-understand graphics	All	Comprehensive and straightforward take on political, climate, general sights and history	Slim and easy to carry, perfect if you are going to buy just one book
THE ROUGH RIDE	Straightforward overall guidebook	Budget, all	History, culture, architecture	Easy read, sensible itineraries
TRAVEL & LEISURE	General guide	Upscale and cultural	Highlights what popular sights are run-down or overrun	T&L's sophisticated take combined with Frommer's detail (the two share the same publisher)
			The finer things in life	

Source: Connections, American Express Travel Services Company, Inc.

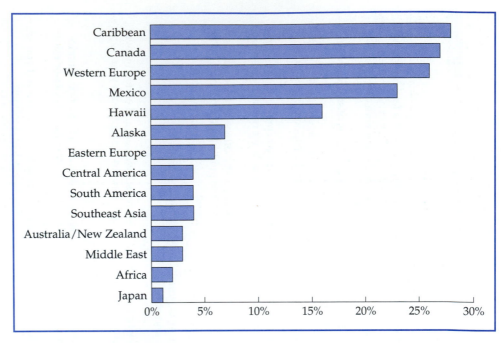

Figure 2.26 *Popularity of travelers' destinations outside the continental United States: percent who said they had traveled there in the past three years. (Source: Data from* Travel Weekly, *Cahners Travel Group.)*

Canada

For people living in the continental United States, Canada is the giant neighbor to the north. The land of Canada extends from the United States to the North Pole (see Figure 2.27). It includes all the islands in the Arctic Ocean from west of Greenland to Alaska. Canada is the second largest country in the world; only Russia is larger. Canada is larger in size than the United States; add another state the size of Texas to the 50 United States and you can get a better idea of Canada's size.

For administrative purposes, Canada is divided into three territories and ten provinces. Don't get too concerned with the difference between these two terms. Both are defined as being an administrative district or division of a country, with less central government control over a territory than over a province. The ten provinces, from east to west are: the Maritimes: *New Foundland & Labrador, Prince Edward Island (PEI), Nova Scotia,* and *New Brunswick;* French Canada: *Québec;* Central Prairie: *Ontario* (the nation's capital of Ottawa is located here), *Manitoba,* and *Saskatchewan;* and Rocky Mountain and West: *Alberta* and *British Columbia.*

It should be noted that the Maritime province of New Foundland is the only one that consists of two distinct land masses: the *island* of New Foundland and mainland Labrador.

The three territories in the far north, from east to west are Nunavut, the Northwest Territories, and the Yukon Territory. Nunavut, the Arctic region that became Canada's newest territory on April 1, 1999, is the homeland of the indigenous Inuit people (Eskimo).

The topography of Canada is extremely varied. The northern parts of this

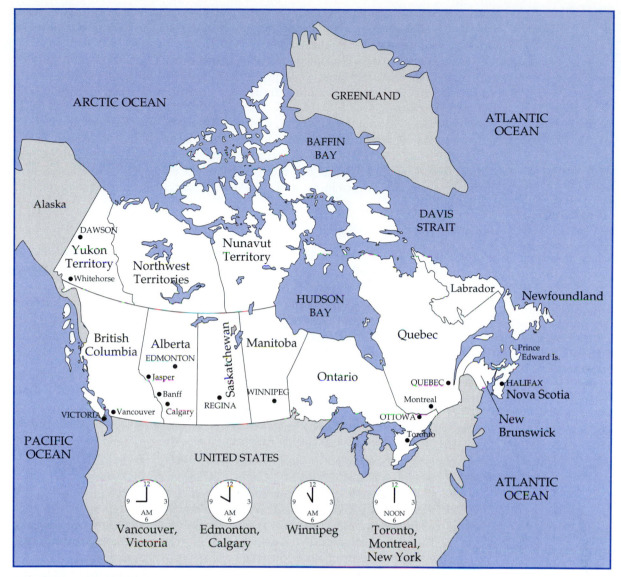

Figure 2.27 *Map of Canada.*

vast country are forbidding: a moss-covered treeless plain with a permanently frozen subsoil. In the southern regions, the land is thickly forested. The eastern and central parts are dominated by rugged plateau of rock. Farther west the land becomes rolling lowlands, where much of this country's agriculture takes place. The far west is home of the majestic Canadian Rockies: a haven for lovers of the outdoors, with beautiful mountain retreats and ski resorts such as Banff (Lake Louise) and Jasper.

Canada is a favorite and convenient vacation destination for people who live in the continental United States since the majority of Canada's major cities and sights are located within 250 miles of the northern U.S. border. Canada is a multicultural nation that has two official languages: English and French. In Québec City, over 90 percent of the population is French-speaking. The citizens of this city also follow many French traditions and customs. In Nova Scotia, the flavor of the area and the lifestyle of its people are in many ways similar to those in Scotland. In contrast, Canadians living in the far western province of British Columbia—especially in the city of Victoria—conduct themselves in the same manner as do their counterparts in Great Britain.

In addition to these European cultures, Canada is also the homeland of two rather distinctive North American cultures: the Inuit (Eskimo) and Indian. Many of them reside in isolated fishing, trapping, and hunting communities in the northern territories.

You can divide the entire country into five general touring regions: French cities and the surrounding areas of Québec and Montreal; the Maritimes in the east; the combination of Ottawa, Toronto, and Niagara Falls around the Great Lakes region; national parks and monuments such as Banff, Lake Louise, and Jasper in the western provinces; and the Pacific coast, including Vancouver and Victoria.

Canada Sound Bites

- *Québec* is the most European of the Canadian cities, with the palatial and world-famous Chateau Frontenac hotel and its lower town, with a French flavor.

- The Maritimes (*Nova Scotia, Prince Edward Island, New Foundland and Labrador,* and *New Brunswick*) are surrounded by water; this region is encircled by rocky and dramatic coastlines with isolated fishing villages and important port cities such as Halifax and St. John.

- History, lighthouses, seafood, rocky and foggy oceanfront cliffs, fishing, hunting, kayaking, whale-watching, and bird-watching are among *New Foundland's* main attractions.

- *Montreal,* the largest French-speaking city in Canada, now boasts a casino that rivals those on the French Riviera.

- *Niagara Falls,* situated in the province of Ontario, is located on the border between the United States and Canada. This natural attraction has been a successful tourist promotion for families and newlyweds for many decades. The dramatic boat ride on the *Maid of the Mist* that takes you "up-close-and-personal" to the falls is one of many ways to view this majestic sight and is recommended. Casino gambling developments on the Canadian side of Niagara Falls add to the region's appeal and vitality.

- Between *Lake Louise* and *Jasper, Alberta* are the Columbia Ice Fields, the largest mass of ice south of the Arctic Circle. Get on a snowmobile and ride up over the glacier to get some of the best views of this glacier phenomenon.

- *Edmonton Shopping Mall* is one of the largest indoor malls in the world.

- Two large cosmopolitan cities, *Calgary* and *Edmonton,* are within driving distance of dramatic glaciers.

- Fjords are found in many places along the coast of *British Columbia;* take a boat tour from Vancouver that visits these natural formations located close to the Alaska border.

- Along the border of British Columbia and Alberta are the beautiful and extensive parks of *Jasper* and *Banff,* both excellent ski and outdoor recreational centers.

- *Calgary* is the eastern gateway to the Rockies and is truly a frontier city. The Calgary Stampede is held here annually and provides everything for rodeo fans.

- *Toronto,* the largest city in Canada, is a thriving, modern, and metropolitan city and also happens to be the major industrial, financial, and commercial center of Canada.

The *Cabot Trail*, on Nova Scotia's Cape Breton Island, is one of the ten best drives in the world. By self-drive car or motorcoach, this beautiful and exciting route winds approximately 180 miles along majestic cliffs and through valleys and rolling hills. The views surpass even the Highlands of old Scotland, and whale sightings are frequent. The trail winds through Cape Breton Highlands National Park, with 28 hiking trails into the park's interior.

✔ *Check Your Understanding 2-8*

Test your place-name geography skills! On Figure 2.28, Canadian provinces are identified by letter, and major cities are identified by number. By memory, write the name of each province and major city beside each letter and number on the lists below.

Canadian Provinces	*Major Cities*
A. _____	1. _____
B. _____	2. _____
C. _____	3. _____
D. _____	4. _____
E. _____	5. _____
F. _____	6. _____
G. _____	7. _____
H. _____	8. _____
I. _____	9. _____
J. _____	

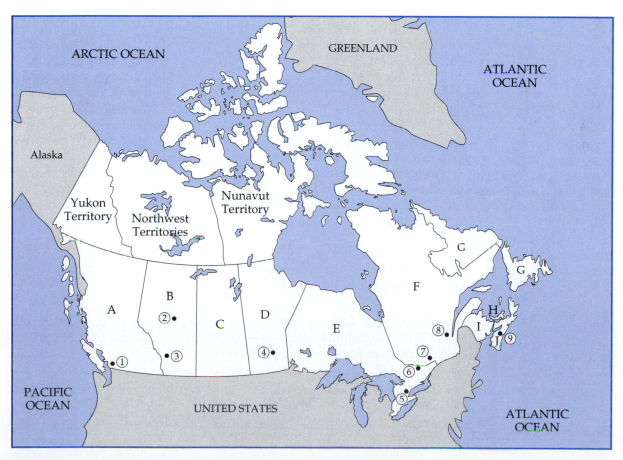

Figure 2.28

United States

The continental United States—the contiguous 48 states—stretches across North America from "sea to shining sea." It borders Canada to the north and Mexico to the south. Alaska juts from northwestern Canada and Hawaii lies 2,000 miles off the western U.S. coast, in the middle of the Pacific Ocean. There are three major mountain ranges: the Appalachians in the east, the Rocky Mountains in the west, and the Sierra Nevada along the border of Nevada and California (see Figure 2.29).

The Atlantic coast is heavily populated where historically rich cities such as Boston, New York, Philadelphia, and Washington, DC are located. Throughout this region, sightseeing and attractions reflect many important events in American history.

The central northeast consists of huge, thriving, industrial centers that are marked by the enormous Great Lakes (Superior, Michigan, Huron, Erie, and Ontario), which occupy an area larger than that of most European countries. Midwestern lake front cities such as Chicago and Detroit are established ports, due to canals and the St. Lawrence Seaway, linking these inland seas to the Atlantic Ocean.

The central area of the United States is considered to be the agricultural center of the nation. This region of flatlands, drained by the mighty Mississippi, Missouri, and Ohio Rivers, is where one can see corn and wheat fields stretching for miles and miles into the horizon.

Farther west, on the Great Plains, are the country's chief grazing areas. Deserts in most areas dominate the southwest, where the climate and poor soil keeps population to a minimum; tumbleweed blowing across the highway is a commonplace sight in these parts.

Next stop are the dramatic and mountainous states of the Rocky Mountains. This is truly the Great West where major ski areas, National Parks and other natural treasures are located. This also includes the arid desert lands of Nevada and Arizona.

Cross the Sierra Nevada and the traveler is on the west coast, the nation's proving ground for new ideas: any innovation, new idea, or new product originating here will soon appear in retail stores, bookstores, menus, shopping malls, or computer screens across the land. The great western cities of Seattle, Portland, San Francisco, Los Angeles, and San Diego have been shaped not only by geography but also by the people who live there. Each resonates with its own character, way of life, interests, and ideas.

The forty-ninth and fiftieth states, Alaska and Hawaii, respectively, are destinations all by themselves. In Alaska, two popular itineraries include the spectacular Inside Passage of Alaska's southeast panhandle, and visits to national parks and national wildlife refuges located in the interior, such as Denali National Park and Preserve.

Hawaii's six islands noted for tourism are (stretching from north to south): Kauai, Oahu, Molokai, Lanai, Maui, and Hawaii. Each one has a different flavor, with its own unique features:

1. *Oahu* (the "main island") is the center of what's happening, with famous Waikiki Beach, nightlife, world-class shopping, and international restaurants balanced by a rich and fascinating history.

2. *Hawaii* (the "big island") is the state's largest island, whose main attraction is the active Kilauea volcano, where visitors can view spectacular eruptions day or night.

3. *Kauai*, known as the Garden Island, is exactly that—a tropical paradise where lush scenery and outdoors activities prevail. Dozens of movies have been shot here, including *Raiders of the Lost Ark, Jurassic Park,* and *South Pacific.*

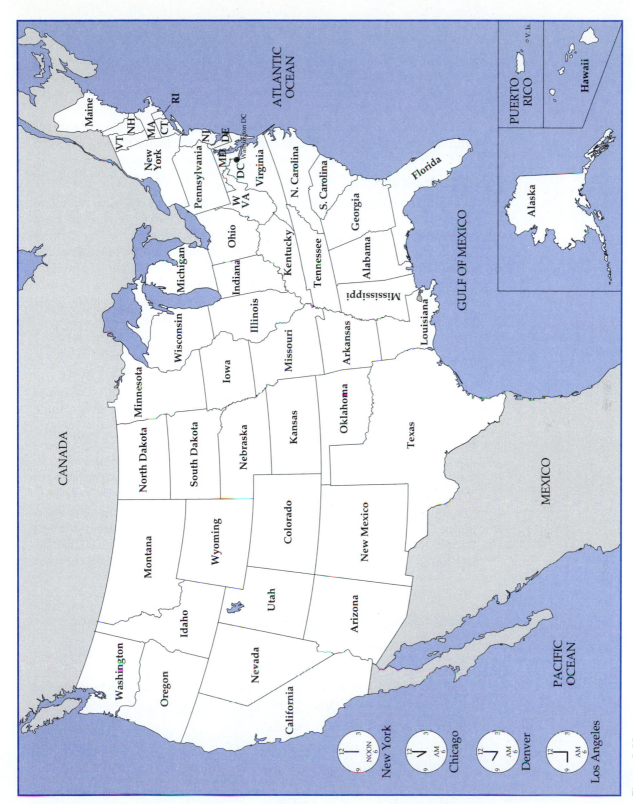

Figure 2.29 *Map of the continental United States.*

4. *Maui* (the "Magic Island") is noted for 42 miles of beautiful beaches and the old whaling town of Lahaina.

5. *Molokai* is considered the most "Hawaiian" of all the islands since it is dedicated to the perpetuation of Hawaiian traditions. A highlight is the Molokai Mule Ride down a 3,000-foot cliff to Kalaupapa Peninsula, home to the ministry of Father Damien.

6. *Lanai* is the most secluded island and attracts those who seek luxury and adventure off the beaten track; the island has only two major resorts, one on a quiet beach and the other amid Norfolk pines in the cool upcountry.

United States Sound Bites

- The traditional American tourist attractions—from Mount Rushmore to the Grand Canyon, from the Statue of Liberty to the Golden Gate—attract a huge number of visitors each year. However, the greatest volume of visitors is seen at "theme" amusement parks that have been modeled after the granddaddy of them all, *Disneyland in California*. More than 170 million travelers visit U.S. theme and amusement parks each year.

- *New York City* is considered the "capital of the world" since the United Nations, Wall Street, and Madison Avenue are located there.

- Civil War landmarks are concentrated in the mid-Atlantic states, with Washington, DC as the gateway: *Manassas, Petersburg, and Richmond, Virginia; Harper's Ferry, West Virginia; Antietam, Maryland; Gettysburg, Pennsylvania.*

- The traditional American landmark of Mt. Rushmore, South Dakota is where the faces of several U.S. presidents have been carved into a huge rock formation.

- Major ski resorts of the west include: in Colorado—*Aspen, Vail,* and *Snowmass;* in Utah—*Snowbird, Alta,* and *Deer Valley;* in Idaho—*Sun Valley;* in California—*Lake Tahoe* and *Squaw Valley.* Those in the east include: in Vermont—*Killington, Stowe, Sugarbush,* and *Mt. Snow;* in Maine—*Sugarloaf.*

- The following attractions in Hawaii are especially suited for families: *Polynesian Cultural Center, Oahu* (experience the cultures of Hawaii and South Pacific), *Kualoa Ranch, Oahu* (4,000 magnificent acres for horseback riding, jet skiing, and dune cycling; served as the backdrop to the blockbuster

Top Twelve U.S. Theme Parks

1.	The Magic Kingdom, Orlando, Florida
2.	Disneyland, Anaheim, California
3.	Epcot, Orlando, Florida
4.	Disney–MGM Studios, Orlando, Florida
5.	Universal Studios, Orlando, Florida
6.	Universal Studios, Los Angeles, California
7.	Sea World of Florida, Orlando
8.	Busch Gardens, Tampa, Florida
9.	Sea World of California, San Diego
10.	Six Flags Great Adventure, Jackson, New Jersey
11.	Knott's Berry Farm, Buena Park, California
12.	Six Flags Magic Mountain, Valencia, California

Source: American Amusements.

movie, *Jurassic Park*); *Waimea Valley* and *Adventure Park, Oahu* (preserves precious archeological sites with adrenaline-pumping activities such as ATV rides, mountain biking, snorkeling, and kayaking); *Maui Ocean Center, Maui* ("walk on water" experience through a 57-foot transparent tunnel through the aquarium).

- The state of *Florida* is the leading vacation destination in the United States. Central Florida is the biggest theme park area in the world, and includes *Disneyworld, Universal Studios, Sea World*, and *Busch Gardens*.

- There are only a few places in the United States that offer *year-round* beach vacations: Major all-year resort regions are *Hawaii* and the southern part of Florida.

- The *Mardi Gras* in New Orleans, Louisiana is the largest and most famous festival in North America. It features jazz, colorful parades, and dancing in the streets, along with exclusive and formal balls by private invitation only. The excitement starts in February five days before Ash Wednesday and officially ends on Ash Wednesday or the beginning of Lent on the Christian calendar.

Top 25 Historical Hot Spots

1. Mesa Verde National Park, Colorado
2. Colonial Williamsburg, Virginia
3. The Freedom Trail, Boston, Massachusetts
4. Independence Hall, Philadelphia, Pennsylvania
5. Monticello, Charlottsville, Virginia
6. The French Quarter, New Orleans, Louisiana
7. Fort Clatsop, Astoria, Oregon
8. Washington, DC
9. Seneca Falls, New York
10. The Alamo, San Antonio, Texas
11. Land of Lincoln, Springfield, Illinois
12. Harper's Ferry, West Virginia
13. Fort Sumter, Charleston, South Carolina
14. Gettysburg, Pennsylvania
15. Mystic Seaport, Mystic, Connecticut
16. Golden Spike, Promontory Summit, Utah
17. Yellowstone National Park, Wyoming
18. Little Bighorn, Hardin, Montana
19. Ellis Island and Statue of Liberty, New York
20. Wright Brothers National Memorial, Kill Devil Hills, North Carolina
21. Hollywood, Los Angeles, California
22. Mount Rushmore, South Dakota
23. USS *Arizona* Memorial, Honolulu, Hawaii
24. Trinity Site, White Sands, New Mexico
25. Montgomery, Alabama

Source: *Historic Traveler*, based in Pittsburgh, PA. Sites were chosen by a group of editors, historians, media figures, and government leaders. As published in Travel Weekly, June, 1998.

- The Mississippi valley region is home to many forms of American music: *Nashville, Tennessee* is home of country music; *Memphis, Tennessee* is home of the rhythm and blues; *New Orleans, Louisiana* is home of its own brand of jazz; and *Branson, Missouri* offers an interesting mix of sounds, from Andy Williams to Box Car Willie.

- *Dude ranch* vacations that provide wild west adventures with all the comforts of home are popular in *Tucson* and *Phoenix, Arizona*.

- Approximately one-third of all visitors to *Alaska* arrive by cruise ship. Alaska cruises feature a week-long itinerary up the Inside Passage visiting such cities as *Ketchikan, Sitka, Juneau,* and *Skagway,* with a day in *Glacier Bay National Park*.

- The majority of gambling resorts are in Nevada: *Las Vegas* (biggest and most popular), *Reno,* and *Lake Tahoe*. Other gambling meccas in the United States are found on *riverboats* sailing up and down the Mississippi River, *Atlantic City, New Jersey,* and Indian casinos found near unlikely places, such as Mystic, Connecticut and Tampa, Florida.

- Visiting national parks is a popular vacation choice for family travel. Many of these natural wonders are located in the west: *Grand Canyon, Arizona; Yellowstone, Wyoming; Glacier National Park, Montana; Yosemite, California; Bryce Canyon* and *Zion National Park* in *Utah*.

- *Kauai's* most popular natural attraction is the "Grand Canyon of the Pacific," called *Waimea Canyon*, which measures 3,600 feet deep and offers spectacular panoramas.

Key Point ➤ The Pacific Coast Drive along the magnificent and dramatic California coastline is a "must-do" for independent travelers. The drive is between San Francisco and Los Angeles along the coastal road, Highway 1. Because of the coastline's easterly curve, it is more spectacular when driving from north to south. The drive takes one day without stops. Of particular beauty is the 17-Mile Drive around the Monterey Peninsula, and a great place to tour along the way is San Simeon, the home of Hearst Castle.

✔ Check Your Understanding 2-9

Test your place-name geography skills. Identify each of the 48 states plus Washington, DC by referring to Figure 2.30.

1. _____	18. _____	35. _____
2. _____	19. _____	36. _____
3. _____	20. _____	37. _____
4. _____	21. _____	38. _____
5. _____	22. _____	39. _____
6. _____	23. _____	40. _____
7. _____	24. _____	41. _____
8. _____	25. _____	42. _____
9. _____	26. _____	43. _____
10. _____	27. _____	44. _____
11. _____	28. _____	45. _____
12. _____	29. _____	46. _____
13. _____	30. _____	47. _____
14. _____	31. _____	48. _____
15. _____	32. _____	49. _____
16. _____	33. _____	
17. _____	34. _____	

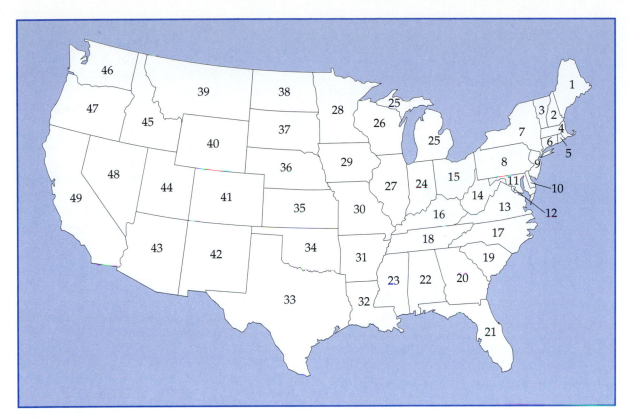

Figure 2.30

Middle America: Mexico and Central America

Mexico and parts of Central America (see Figure 2.31) are perfect destinations for United States and Canadian travelers; they are conveniently close and as exotic and different as countries located continents away. Although these nations share the North American continent, their Latin America heritage and culture are more properly associated with South America located to the south. There are many reasons to visit Mexico and parts of Central America. Ancient cultures of the *Maya, Aztec,* and *Olmec* people can be experienced by visiting more than 155 ancient ruins, out of 10,000 that are known to exist.

The discovery of silver in sixteenth-century Mexico produced much wealth for its mother country of Spain and started what was known as the Colonial Period. The grandeur and enormous prosperity of these times remain in the historically preserved architecture of several cities located near Mexico City: *Morelia, Taxco, Oaxaca* (pronounced "wa-ha-ka"), *Puebla, Tiaxcala,* and of course, *Mexico City* itself.

Mexico offers some of the most scenic coastal resorts in the world since it enjoys a tropical climate with 5,000 miles of coastline. The Pacific coast is known as the Mexican Riviera and boasts such famous resorts as Puerto Vallarta, Mazatlán, Ixtapa/Zihuatanejo, and Acapulco. Along the eastern or Caribbean coast is the Yucatán. This region is a major site of ancient ruins and also offers the government's showcase resort of *Cancún,* and the more informal and laid-back island of *Cozumel.*

Figure 2.31 *Maps of Mexico and Central America.*

Mexico and Central America Sound Bites

- *Los Cabos*, at the very tip of the 750-mile-long Baja, California peninsula (contrary to the name, Baja California is *not* part of the state of California but is part of Mexico), is a haven for sport fishermen, with a wide range of accommodations from budget to upscale.

- Ixtapa/Zihuatanejo is one of Mexico's biggest travel bargains since you get "two resorts for the price of one." The beach resort of *Ixtapa* is ultramodern, with soaring hotels, international dining, and shopping; *Zihuatanejo* is a sleepy fishing village located four miles away where everything is on a much smaller and quieter scale.

- *Acapulco* is world famous for its fast-paced resort amenities that never stop. It is a perfect place to combine beach activities during the day and dazzling shows and recreation at night.

- Some of the world's best areas for diving are around the *Isla de Cozumel*, a small but lively resort island off the Yucatán coast in Mexico.

- To revisit the land of the *Maya*, the most popular ruins are found on the *Yucatán* peninsula in Mexico: *Tulum, Chichén Itzá*, and *Uxmal*. The major gateway to these ruins is the town of *Mérida*. *Cancún* is another jump-off to the ruins but has the added feature of being a popular beach resort.

- To revisit the land of the *Aztecs*, the most popular ruins are found in and around *Mexico City: Tenochtitlan* (the ancient name of Mexico City). To revisit the Olmec culture, visit *Teotihuacan*, which features the famous Pyramid of the Sun and the Pyramid of the Moon.

- In Central America, the greatest Mayan sites are *Tikal* and *Copán*, located in Guatemala and Honduras, respectively.

- Some of the world's greatest whale-watching sites are off *Baja California* in the Sea of Cortez (also called the Gulf of California).

- *Costa Rica* in Central America is known for its grand nature reserves and outdoor attractions: *Volcan Poas National Park*, a crater over five miles across formed by a major volcanic eruption in 1910; *La Amistad International Park*, a biosphere reserve that is one of the world's largest unaltered tropical forests.

Key Point ➤ For lovers of the outdoors and nature, Mexico's Copper Canyon (the Barranca del Cobre) should not be missed. This is a dramatic and breathtaking train ride through mountains and deep canyons between Chihuahua and Los Mochis. The train crosses over 30 bridges that skim over rivers and gorges, and runs through 86 tunnels during the 403-mile ride. The train dips from an 8,000-foot plateau down to sea level for final arrival in the Pacific town of Los Mochis. The main attraction is *Copper Canyon*, which covers 25,000 square miles and plummets more than one-and-a-half times deeper than the Grand Canyon in some places.

✓ Check Your Understanding 2-10

Test your place-name geography skills.

1. Write the name of each major resort area in Mexico identified by number on the map shown in Figure 2.32. Choose from the following: Acapulco, Mazatlán, Cabo San Lucas, Mexico City, Puerto Vallarta, Zihuatanejo, Cancún, Isla de Cozumel, Mérida.

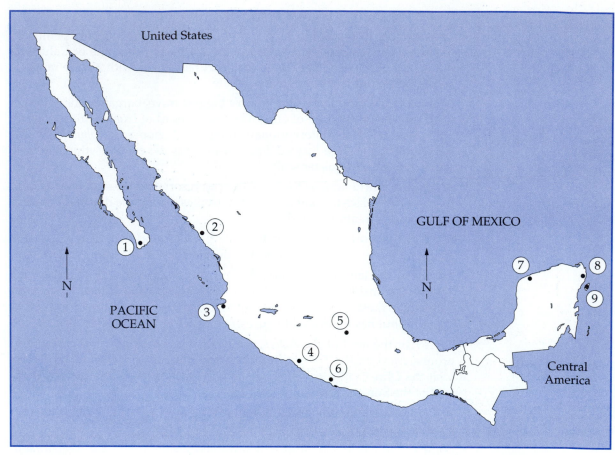

Figure 2.32

1. _____

2. _____

3. _____

4. _____

5. _____

6. _____

7. _____

8. _____

9. _____

2. Write the name of each country in Central America that is identified by number on the map shown in Figure 2.33. Choose from the following: Costa Rica, Belize, El Salvador, Nicaragua, Guatemala, Panama, Honduras.

1. _____

2. _____

3. _____

4. _____

5. _____

6. _____

7. _____

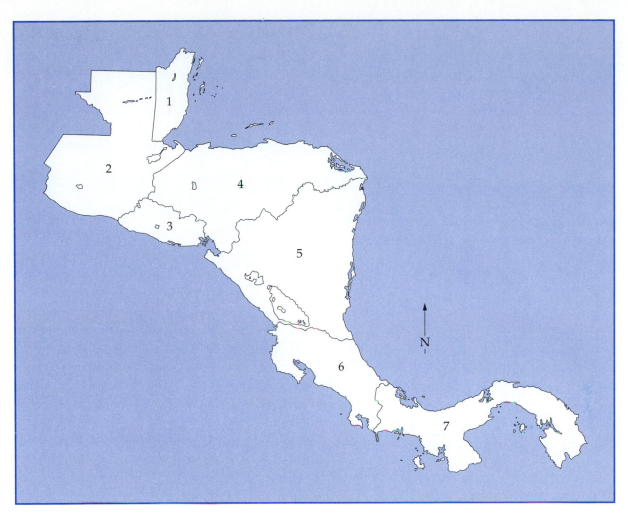

Figure 2.33

Middle America: West Indies (Bermuda, Bahamas, and the Caribbean)

The West Indies is a large group of islands that includes the islands of Bermuda and the Bahamas located in the Atlantic, and the islands located in the Caribbean Sea (see Figure 2.34). Although located in the Atlantic and not in the Caribbean, Bermuda and the Bahamas are often linked with the Caribbean Islands in travel promotional materials and are sold often as a Caribbean destination.

The Caribbean islands are grouped according to these three geographical divisions: Greater Antilles, Lesser Antilles, and southern Caribbean. The *Greater Antilles* are in the northern Caribbean and consist of four large islands located closest to the United States. They are *Cuba, Jamaica, Hispaniola* (divided into *Haiti* and the *Dominican Republic*), and *Puerto Rico*.

The *Lesser Antilles* are greater in number but smaller in size. These are divided into three smaller groups: Leeward and Windward islands in the eastern Caribbean, and the islands in the southern Caribbean. They form an arc that begins with the British and U.S. Virgin Islands in the north to Aruba in the south.

The *southern Caribbean* of the Lesser Antilles chain starts with the ABC islands—Aruba, Bonaire, and Curaçao—which are located off the northern coast of South America, plus Trinidad and Tobago.

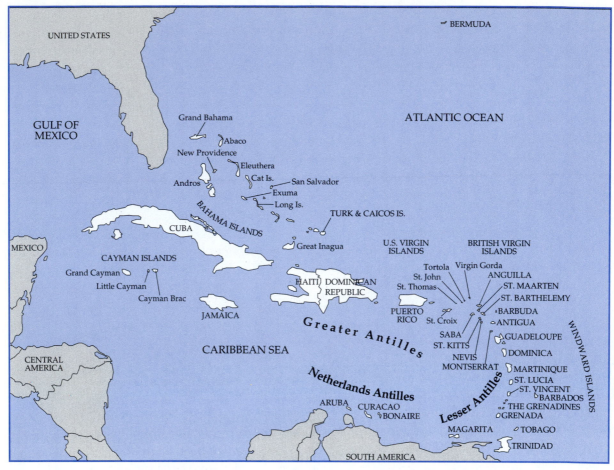

Figure 2.34 *Map of the West Indies.*

What's so special about the West Indies? You have probably heard that "if you've seen one island, you've seen them all." There's a *little* bit of truth in that. All islands provide the same basic elements of a conventional beach vacation: sunbathing, tennis, golf, scuba and snorkeling, nightlife, and shopping, for example. However, each island has its own unique flavor and atmosphere. There is something of interest for practically everyone.

To revisit history and experience different cultures you visit.

- Oriental bazaars in Trinidad
- The oldest synagogue in the western hemisphere, located in Curaçao
- Windmills spinning in St. Maarten
- Hindu temples in Aruba
- Changing of the guard in Bermuda
- Moorish architecture in San Juan
- The home of Ernest Hemingway in Cuba
- The tomb of Columbus in the Dominican Republic

To see exciting natural attractions you can visit:

- Active volcanoes in St. Lucia
- Subterranean caves in Barbados

- Rain forests in Puerto Rico
- Underwater national parks in the U.S. Virgin Islands (U.S.V.I.)
- Waterfalls in Jamaica
- Black sand beaches in St. Vincent

There's more to the West Indies than palm trees and piña coladas!

Key Point ➤ Bermuda is the only island in the West Indies where car rentals are not available. Most tourists either take taxis or rent mopeds (small motor bikes). A driver's license is not required to rent, but people should be cautioned when driving mopeds: Many roads are lined by rocks and have heavy traffic.

West Indies Sound Bites

- High season or the most expensive time to travel to the *Bahamas* and the *Caribbean* islands is during winter and spring—from December 15 through April 15. This is when prices are at their highest in terms of air fares and accommodations. Hotel prices drop anywhere between 20 and 50 percent during low season or summer time.

- Unlike the rest of the West Indies, *Bermuda* is not a year-round *beach* resort. The island is located quite a bit farther in the north, 600 miles off the coast of North Carolina in the Atlantic. Winters are mild but definitely not warm enough for comfortable swimming. High season in Bermuda starts in mid-April and lasts until mid-November.

- The Netherlands Antilles (also called the ABCs) are *Aruba, Bonaire,* and *Curaçao* and are located in the deep southern Caribbean off the coast of Venezuela. They each have something special: Aruba is the "driest" of all West Indies (365 days of sunshine), Bonaire is one of the best diving places in the world, and Curaçao has all the European charm and architecture of the Netherlands.

- *Jamaica* is noted for the concentration of *all-inclusive resorts* where everything is included in one price: meals, drinks, entertainment, tips, and transportation. Many of these resorts target specific clientele, such as singles, couples, families, and sports enthusiasts.

- Puerto Rico has many faces. *Old San Juan* is a quiet oasis that offers a romantic European charm. The *Condado* section of town means action! This area is located directly east of Old San Juan and is a strip of beach lined by high-rise hotels, huge casinos, nightclubs, and restaurants; no low-key "Caribbean-style" atmosphere here. Finally, *Isla Verde,* although located near the airport, offers some of the best beaches in the city, along with many top hotels.

- Two-thirds of *St. John,* the smallest of the U.S. Virgin Islands (U.S.V.I.), is a national park. Accommodations on this small island range from simple campsites to exclusive luxury resorts such as Caneel Bay and Virgin Grand Villas at Hyatt Regency.

- *St. Thomas* is the most developed and populated of the U.S. Virgin Islands. Its deep harbor and duty-free shops make St. Thomas a popular cruise port of call. Nature tourism is also very popular here.

- St. Martin/St. Maarten: Half-French and half-Dutch, this island has two of everything: two ways of spelling the name, two currencies, two distinctive cuisines, and two approaches to life. The French side is slow-paced and casual; the Dutch side is more "Americanized," with busy resorts, restaurants, shopping, and gambling.

- The islands of *St. Kitts* and *Nevis* are the sleepiest islands in the West Indies and together are one of the few countries where agriculture is still a larger part of the economy than tourism.
- The islands with big *casino gambling* are *Aruba, Bahamas, Puerto Rico,* and *St. Maarten.*
- The islands which are best for *camping* include *British Virgin Islands, Guadeloupe, Jamaica, Martinique, Puerto Rico,* and *St. John, U.S.V.I.*
- The very British island of *Barbados* has one of the highest literacy rates in the world. This independent country has remained stable with unbroken British rule from its beginnings.
- The islands known for some of the best *sailing waters* and places to *charter* include *Antigua, British Virgin Islands,* the *Grenadines,* and the *U.S. Virgin Islands.*
- Scuba diving is available on practically every island in the West Indies. Islands known for some of the most spectacular underwater experiences include *Bonaire, Cayman Islands, St. Eustatius,* and *St. John, U.S.V.I.*

Key Point ➤ Can't dive due to poor health or claustrophobia? The latest craze is *snuba,* a combination of scuba diving and snorkeling. The snuba system consists of an inflatable raft that supports a tank of compressed air and a 20-foot hose for one or two people. The raft also has a clear window on the bottom for clear viewing while taking a break. Snuba is available on many islands at a cost of approximately $50 per hour.

✔ *Check Your Understanding 2-11*

Refer to the map of the West Indies in Figure 2.35 to complete the following table. Identify each island that is numbered. A clue is provided to help.

Map Number	Clue	Country
1	The largest of the Greater Antilles, this island has not been a popular tourist destination for U.S. travelers, due to uneasy political relations.	_____
2	This group of 700 islands in the Atlantic offer two major tourism centers, Nassau and Freeport, with fine beaches, shopping, and gambling casinos.	_____
3	Group of islands known for their spectacular diving experiences.	_____
4	This island is divided into Haiti in the west and the Dominican Republic in the east.	_____
5	One of the most popular destinations in the West Indies, this island is known for its all-inclusive resorts and exciting natural wonders, such as climbing the waterfalls at Dunn's River Falls.	_____
6	A little part of the United States in the Caribbean, this multifaceted island offers everything from glitzy nightlife, high-rise resorts and gambling casinos, to lush rain forests and low-key resorts with old European charm.	_____
7	This is the largest and most heavily populated of the three U.S. Virgin Islands, and boasts great shopping and a busy cruise port.	_____
8	This island has two of everything! One half is French, with a casual and informal life-style; the other half is Dutch, with a faster-paced and busy resort atmosphere.	_____
9	This island boasts some of the finest beaches and resorts in the Caribbean. It also has a long history under British rule, which has produced a highly stable political environment.	_____

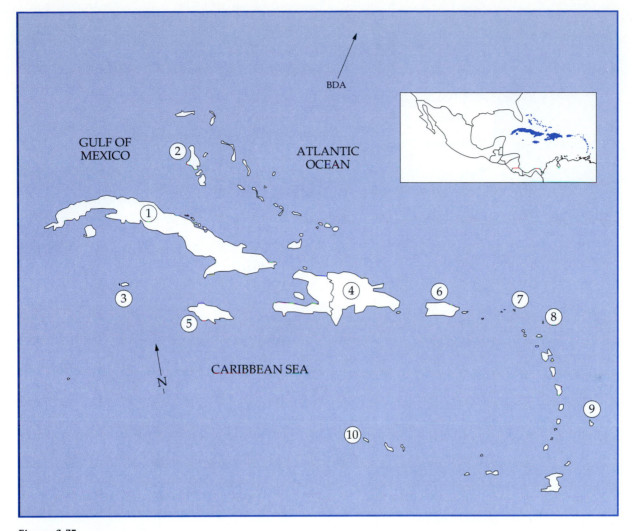

Figure 2.35

Map Number	Clue	Country
10	The westernmost island in the Netherlands Antilles or ABC islands group, this is the driest island in the southern Caribbean and can boast 365 days of sunshine each year.	_____

► South America

South America consists of twelve independent countries and an Overseas Department (French Guiana) (see Figure 2.36). There are three countries that border along the Caribbean (*Venezuela, Suriname,* and *Guyana*), three countries that border the Atlantic (*Brazil, Uruguay,* and *Argentina*), and three that border the Pacific (*Ecuador, Chile,* and *Peru*). The country of *Colombia* borders both the Atlantic and Pacific Oceans. The two inland or landlocked countries are *Paraguay* and *Bolivia*.

Unfortunately, South America is often a hard sell as a tourist destination. Culturally, most North Americans trace their origins to countries in Europe or

Figure 2.36 *Map of South America.*

Asia. Foreign travel for most North American travelers would center on those parts of the world. Educationally, much of South American history is downplayed in world history textbooks, where European and Far Eastern historical developments dominate.

Some travelers may have a limited interest or curiosity to discover South

America. Culturally, the customs, language, and cuisine are very different from what North American travelers are used to. Geographically, the distances between North America and South American cities are nearly twice the distance to cities in western Europe. Even getting around inside South America may present problems. Use of the rail and bus transportation systems is not recommended as they are primitive in regard to equipment, comfort, and frequency of service. Flying from place to place is the traveler's best bet.

Regardless of these perceived negatives, South America is so diverse that there is literally something for every traveler. This continent is especially attractive for those with a romantic and adventurous spirit, willing to sacrifice some creature comforts at times, who will find a land with exciting contrasts, spectacular scenery, rich natural resources, and opportunities for adventurous trips.

Even with its vast size, this continent has a relatively small population of only 319 million. The population of Brazil almost equals that of all other South American countries combined.

Although the major tourist destinations are Brazil, Argentina, Peru, and Chile, there are many interesting and unusual things to see and do in Ecuador, Bolivia, Colombia, and Venezuela.

South America Sound Bites

- The highlight of a trip to *Ecuador* is a visit to the *Galápagos Islands*, twelve volcanic peaks that lie 600 miles directly west of Ecuador in the Pacific Ocean. For the nature lover, these islands are uninhabited reserves for many birds and marine life.

- *Cartegena*, on the north coast fronting the Caribbean Sea, is Colombia's most popular tourist destination. This historic city, which traces its roots back to Columbus, offers contemporary beach resorts with shopping, international restaurants, and gambling casinos.

- The world's highest waterfall, *Angel Falls*, is located in Venezuela, where water drops 3,400 feet down from its summit, along a sheer vertical cliff, to the valley below.

- A vacation in Venezuela is often typified by a half-metropolitan city experience (*Caracas*) and a half-beach resort (*Margarita Island* or *Macuto*).

- *Buenos Aires*, Argentina, is called the "Paris of South America" with its wide boulevards, beautifully landscaped parks, and impressive buildings and shops.

- The *"Land of the Gauchos"* is another name for Argentina because of its vast prairie lands that are worked by gauchos or cowboys. This country is reminiscent of America's Old West in many ways.

- *Patagonia*, at the southern tip of Argentina, is a vast desert plateau that ends in a sharp cliff as it falls to the sea. This area is very remote and sparsely populated, with cold temperatures practically year round. Coastal areas feature seals, penguins, sea elephants, and whales. Glaciers abound within this southern Andean mountain area.

- *Brasilia* is the capital of Brazil and an architectural masterpiece. This unique city is laid out in the shape of an airplane and everything balances; opposite sides of each street have similar buildings. It is the only modern city in the world that was planned with no stoplights.

- For adventurous travelers, an overnight trip from *Manaus* (the capital and gateway to the Amazon) into the jungle to stay at an Amazon Lodge is highly recommended. From these lodges, built on stilts, visitors view exotic flora and fuana that are unique to this area of the world.

- *Iguassu Falls*, the world's largest waterfall, is many times larger and more powerful than Niagara. The falls are bordered by three countries: Brazil, Argentina, and Paraguay (just remember "BAP").

- *Cuzco*, Peru, is the ancient capital of the Incas and is located nearly 12,000 feet above sea level. Cuzco is also the gateway to the most important attraction—the "Lost City of the Incas," *Machu Picchu*. This ancient site is reached by a rustic rail trip that takes approximately four hours each way. What's so special? Machu Picchu was constructed in pre-Columbian times without mortar, with boulders fitting perfectly in place.

- For those who want to snow-ski in July and August, the best places south of the equator are in the Andean mountain resorts of *Barriloche, Argentina* or *Portillo, Chile*.

Web Link

Research global destination information. One of the highly rated sites is the World Travel Guide, which has been a respected geography resource for travel professionals for more than eighteen years. This site provides quick access to concise, up-to-the- minute information on more than 256 countries and more than 2,800 major cities worldwide. Point your browser at *http://www.travel-guide.com/*.

✔ Check Your Understanding 2-12

1. Refer to the map of South America shown in Figure 2.37 to complete the following table. Identify each country that is numbered. A clue is provided to help.

Map Number	Clue	Country
1	This country located in the north offers Cartegena, a busy and contemporary beach resort on the Caribbean coast.	_____
2	This country, in addition to Paraguay, its neighbor to the south, are the only landlocked countries in South America.	_____
3	This is the gateway for nature lovers to visit the Galápagos Islands, which lie 600 miles west of the country.	_____
4	In addition to Argentina, this country offers some of the best snow-skiing during July and August in Portillo, a mountain resort in the Andes.	_____
5	This country's main tourist feature is a visit to Machu Picchu, the ancient site of the Incas.	_____
6	Angel Falls, the world's highest waterfall, is an important natural attraction in this country.	_____
7	This is the counterpart of America's "Old West" in South America. It contains vast prairie lands and local cowboys called gauchos.	_____
8	This is the largest country in square miles and population in South America.	_____

Figure 2.37

Multiple Choice

Circle the *best* answer based on your knowledge of the western hemisphere.

2. To drive the famous Cabot Trail, you would visit the Canadian province of:
    A. Alberta
    B. Québec
    C. British Columbia
    D. Nova Scotia

3. To take a ride on the *Maid of the Mist* in Ontario, you would get a close-up view of what natural phenomena?
    A. Lake Superior
    B. Niagara Falls
    C. Angel Falls
    D. Lake Louise

4. The largest French-speaking city in Canada that boasts a casino that rivals those on the Riviera in Europe is:
    A. Montreal
    B. Victoria
    C. Québec City
    D. Edmonton

5. To visit the active Kilauea volcano on Hawaii's largest island, you would take a trip to the island of:
    A. Maui
    B. Oahu
    C. Molokai
    D. Hawaii

6. The leading U.S. theme park in terms of the number of visitors each year is:
    A. The Magic Kingdom, Orlando, Florida
    B. Sea World of California, San Diego
    C. Disneyland, Anaheim, California
    D. Knott's Berry Farm, California

7. To visit the Grand Canyon, Yosemite, and Bryce Canyon, you would travel to the following states in this order:
    A. Colorado, Arizona, Utah
    B. Arizona, Montana, Utah
    C. Utah, Arizona, Montana
    D. Arizona, California, Utah

8. To vacation in the capital of country music and home of the famous Opryland Theater, you would visit:
    A. Memphis, Tennessee
    B. Nashville, Tennessee
    C. Branson, Missouri
    D. Las Vegas, Nevada

9. To which place below would you not send a traveler who wants a gambling vacation?
    A. Mississippi riverboat
    B. Atlantic City, New Jersey
    C. Honolulu, Oahu
    D. Las Vegas, Nevada

10. You want to ski in the resorts of Aspen and Vail. Where would you go?
    A. Utah
    B. Colorado
    C. South Dakota
    D. California

11. Which of the following is not a year-round beach resort?
    A. Bermuda
    B. San Diego, California
    C. Miami, Florida
    D. Waikiki Beach, Oahu

12. If you were vacationing on the Mexican Riviera, which resort are you visiting?
    A. Mexico City
    B. Cozumel
    C. Puerto Vallarta
    D. Cancún

13. The major site of many Maya ancient ruins such as Tulum and Chichén Itzá is:
    A. Costa Rica, Central America
    B. Yucatán, Mexico
    C. Pacific Coast, Mexico
    D. Mexico City, Mexico

14. Costa Rica in Central America is best known for what type of vacation experience?
    A. beach resorts and nightlife
    B. nature reserves and cloud forests
    C. Maya ruins and ancient wonders
    D. water sports and skydiving

15. Which island is not part of the Caribbean?
    A. Puerto Rico
    B. Grand Bahama, Bahamas
    C. St. Maarten
    D. Aruba

16. The island you would most likely recommend for diving enthusiasts is:
    A. Grand Cayman
    B. Bermuda
    C. Nevis
    D. Puerto Rico

17. The island known to be the driest, with almost 365 days of sunshine each year, is:
    A. Aruba
    B. Bahamas
    C. Puerto Rico
    D. Antigua

18. To visit the action-filled Condado section and stay at a beach resort in Isla Verde, you would be staying on the island of:
    A. Dominican Republic
    B. Jamaica
    C. Cuba
    D. Puerto Rico

19. Two-thirds of what island is a national park and accommodations range from simple campsites to deluxe resorts?
    A. St. Maarten
    B. St. Kitts
    C. St. John, U.S.V.I.
    D. St. Thomas, U.S.V.I.

20. You are visiting Machu Picchu, the "Lost City of the Incas." What country are you in?
    A. Guatemala
    B. Mexico
    C. Peru
    D. Argentina

➤ Europe

Europe is the leading foreign destination outside North America for U.S. and Canadian travelers. More than 10 million North American travelers visit Europe each year, and this number continues to grow. Why? Europe is a source of political ideals, history, art, and culture. The Canadian points to his ethnic origins in Britain and France, the Native American to his Christian beliefs, or a West Indian woman to her democratic principles; they all point to Europe as the source.

Europe is comprised of a collection of peninsulas that make up the western part of the huge landmass that is shared with Asia (see Figure 2.38). Because of its dramatically jagged coastline, Europe has a longer coastline for its size than any other continent. The continent is relatively small; it is about 10 percent larger than the continental United States, including Alaska. In terms of its size, Europe ranks as the second smallest continent in the world, after Australia.

Europe has experienced tremendous political and social changes only within the past few decades. Part of this change has been the development of new countries and political entities within the past fifteen years. As the Soviet Union split

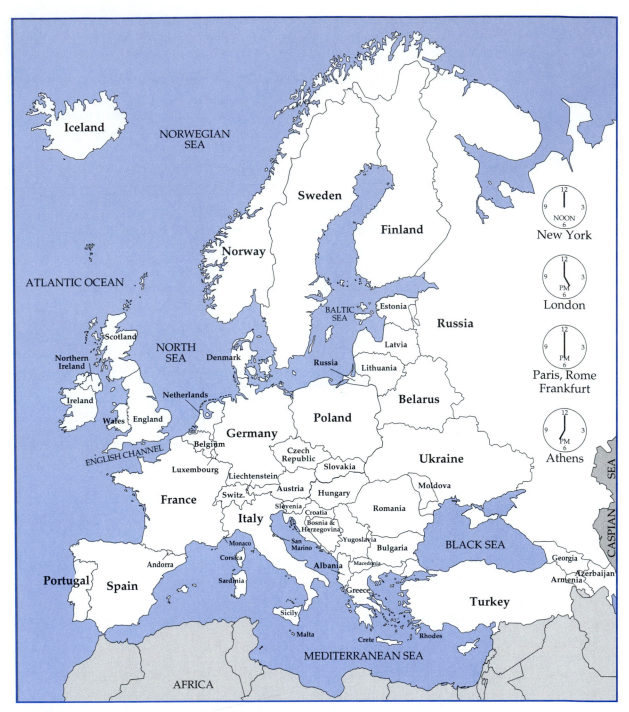

Figure 2.38 *Map of Europe.*

apart in late 1991, fifteen new nations emerged onto the world stage. The breakup of Yugoslavia created five more. In January 1993, Czechoslovakia became two separate nations. All of these dramatic changes followed the collapse of Communism and subsequent rise in nationalism in Europe and parts of Asia.

Today, Europe is comprised of more than 48 political entities that include independent and semi-independent countries and microstates. *Microstates* are tiny political regions from medieval times. Here's an alphabetical list (tiny microstates are noted with the * symbol): Albania, *Andorra, Armenia, Austria, Azerbaijan,

Belarus, Belgium, Bosnia-Herzegovina, Bulgaria, Croatia, Czech Republic, Denmark, Estonia, Finland, France, Georgia, Germany, *Gibraltar, Greece, Hungary, Iceland, Ireland, Italy, Latvia, *Liechtenstein, Lithuania, Luxembourg, Macedonia, Malta, Moldova, *Monaco, The Netherlands, Norway, Poland, Portugal (including the Azores and Madeira Islands in the Atlantic), Romania, Russia (west of the Ural Mountains), *San Marino, Slovakia, Slovenia, Spain (including the Balearic Islands in the Mediterranean and the Canary Islands in the Atlantic Ocean), Sweden, Switzerland, Turkey (the western region), the Ukraine, the United Kingdom (England, Scotland, Northern Ireland, and Wales), *Vatican City, and Yugoslavia.

The traveler to Europe is not like the tourist who wants to visit sun-drenched beaches in the Caribbean or gamble for high stakes in Las Vegas. Although these resort-type activities are available, they do not represent major reasons for European travel. The common profile of the Europe-bound traveler is someone who wants not only to sightsee but to *life-see;* what is important is to visit and experience life as it really is for the Europeans. Another motivation is history. European recorded history can be traced back more than 3,000 years and is reflected in the thousands of museums, architecture, historical sites, and famous landmarks scattered in abundance throughout this continent. To trace one's ethnic roots is also a powerful engine that drives the European tourist machine. Many North Americans can trace their origins to one or more European countries. A personal visit to these lands adds an exciting dimension when tracing one's family tree.

Europe Sound Bites

- London's *Westminster Abbey* is one of the leading attractions for visitors. It is this city's most historic church, with burial places or commemorations of such notables as William Shakespeare, Lord Byron, Sir Winston Churchill, Charles Darwin, and Sir Isaac Newton.

- When in England, visit the *Cotswolds*, a charming and bucolic region located a few hours from downtown London. This is where *Stratford-Upon-Avon* is located, the birthplace of Shakespeare and the site where many of his plays are performed.

- Some excellent reasons why people go to Ireland: (1) The country is particularly inexpensive and a good choice for budget-conscious travelers; (2) many people have retained a close family association to Ireland and want to trace their roots there.

- The famous "Kilometer of Art" in *Madrid* features three famous art museums in a row: *Prado Museum* (one of Spain's premier attractions), *Queen Sophia Museum*, and *Thyssen-Bornemisza*.

- The *Running of the Bulls* (or the Fiesta de San Fermin) takes place early July each year in the town of *Pamplona, Spain*. On this day, courageous people (citizens and visitors alike) try to outrun the bulls which have been let loose in the streets.

- *Vatican City* can be considered the smallest country in the world. Tucked inside the city of Rome, Italy, it is only one-fourth the size of New York's Central Park. This tiny country is the center of world Christianity headed by the Pope.

- In Paris, know your right from your left! The *Left Bank* of Paris (Rive Gauche) is the older part of Paris and is the student quarter centered around the University of Paris. It has an international, and Bohemian flavor, similar to New York City's Greenwich Village. The *Right Bank* (Rive Droite) is the commercial center of Paris, where the majority of attractions, restaurants, shops, and hotels are located.

- The three principal resorts on the French Riviera are *Nice, Cannes,* and the Principality of *Monaco.*
- Italy is generally divided into two touring regions: north and south. Many use Rome as the gateway city to and from Italy. Perfect combination with Rome are visits to *Florence, Milan,* and *Venice* (all located in the north). On longer tours combine Rome with *Naples, Pompeii, Amalfi Drive* (Sorrento), and *Capri,* which are all in the south.
- The *Romantic Road* is a popular driving tour through the heart of Bavaria, Germany. It winds for approximately 200 miles and passes through picture-postcard medieval towns with fairytale castles in the distance.
- *Oktoberfest* is a two-week-long festival featuring Bavarian beer and foods hosted by the city of Munich. Contrary to its name, this festival takes place primarily during the last two weeks in September.
- The famous *Acropolis,* located in the center of Athens, Greece and crowned by the Parthenon, forms the most famous collection of buildings from antiquity.
- The majority of fjords in Europe are found along the western coast of Norway.
- The largest number of lakes in Europe are found in Finland; there is nearly one lake for every Finn!
- The famous *Spanish Riding School* is not located in Spain but in *Vienna, Austria.* This is the home and training center for the world-famous *Lippenzanner* horses and is a major attraction in this elegant European city.
- *Prague,* the capital of the Czech Republic, is considered to be the most beautiful city of central Europe, and was left totally untouched during World War II.
- The most active volcano in Europe is *Mt. Aetna,* located in *Sicily,* which is an island located at the toe of the "boot" of Italy. Visitors can climb all the way to the top and, during winter months, have the choice of skiing on the return.
- That part of Russia west of the *Ural Mountains* is considered Europe. *St. Petersburg,* in European Russia, was founded by Peter the Great as Russia's "Window on the West"; most buildings follow the European Renaissance rather than the Russian style of architecture.
- The *Golden Sands* resort area in *Bulgaria* is the most beautiful and most popular beach resort on the Black Sea.
- The castle called *Neuschwanstein,* located in southern Germany and open for touring, was copied by Disney as Cinderella's castle that has become the trademark of the Disney theme parks.
- *Venice* is not the only city in Europe with canals. Take a trip to any of these cities and take a romantic and leisurely boat ride for two: *Amsterdam, the Netherlands; Brugge, Belgium; Copenhagen, Denmark;* and *St. Petersburg, Russia.*

✓ Check Your Understanding 2-13

How many of the European countries identified on the map shown in Figure 2.39 can you name by memory?

1. _____   6. _____   11. _____
2. _____   7. _____   12. _____
3. _____   8. _____   13. _____
4. _____   9. _____   14. _____
5. _____   10. _____   15. _____

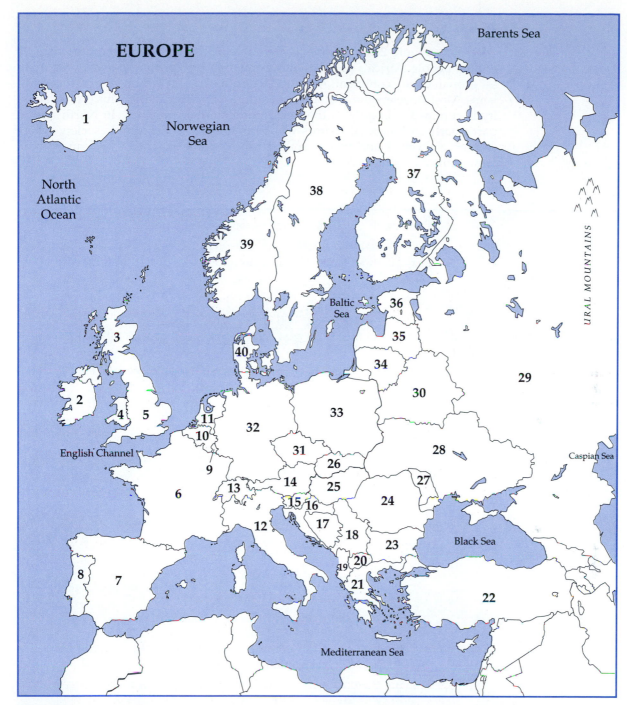

EUROPE

Barents Sea

Norwegian Sea

North Atlantic Ocean

URAL MOUNTAINS

Baltic Sea

English Channel

Caspian Sea

Black Sea

Mediterranean Sea

Figure 2.39

16. _____
17. _____
18. _____
19. _____
20. _____
21. _____
22. _____
23. _____
24. _____

25. _____
26. _____
27. _____
28. _____
29. _____
30. _____
31. _____
32. _____
33. _____

34. _____
35. _____
36. _____
37. _____
38. _____
39. _____
40. _____

➤ Africa

Africa (see Figure 2.40) is home to more than 53 independent countries and 720 million people. Africa's population is expanding by 3 percent per year, the highest growth of any continent. As a tourist destination, the continent of Africa is diverse. Most travelers think of Africa in terms of wildlife safaris. This type of activity is confined primarily to the eastern and southern regions. In North Africa, particularly in Morocco, visitors will be immersed in an Islamic society where women are veiled and where nomad tribes of the Sahara Desert can be seen around the city of Marrakech.

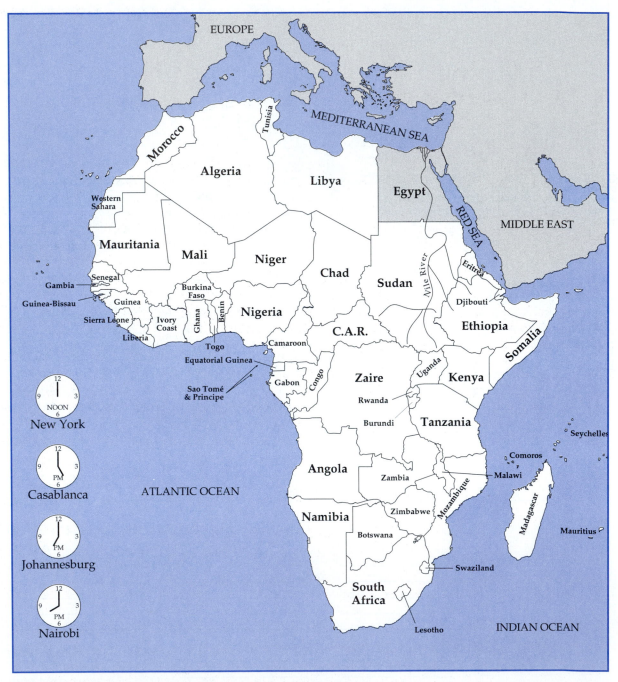

Figure 2.40 *Map of Africa.*

In West Africa, the Ivory Coast offers glimpses of tribal customs and dances plus wonderful beaches, a rain forest and exotic flora. Another part of Africa lies 1,200 miles off the east coast in the Indian Ocean; the Seychelles are a group of coral islands with unspoiled beaches and a quiet lifestyle.

In the northeast corner of this continent is Egypt, which is often considered to be part of the Middle East, due to its Islamic religion and Arab culture. This country also boasts remnants of one of the world's oldest civilizations, with awe-inspiring pyramids, tombs, and colossal monuments of ancient pharaohs.

Web Link

Travel Conditions via the Internet: The U.S. State Department offers a compilation of travel conditions in foreign counties. The site has consular information sheets on every country, as well as travel warnings and public announcements for selected countries based on recent events. If you are concerned with personal safety and security issues, point your browser to *http://travel.state.gov*

Africa Sound Bites

- In *Morocco,* it is not common for women to travel alone or to be out alone at night due to the religion of Islam. Women travelers are advised against traveling alone and to dress conservatively, with long sleeves and hems below the knees.

- *Morocco*—with a visit to Casablanca—is often combined with a tour of southern Europe, due to its close proximity to the European continent: it is only nine miles from the tip of southern Spain.

- The three countries in Africa best known for safaris are *Tanzania* and *Kenya* in East Africa, and *South Africa.*

- *Nairobi,* Kenya is considered to be the gateway or starting place for most African safaris.

- The "Las Vegas" of Africa is *Sun City* in South Africa, only a three-hour drive from Johannesburg, South Africa.

- The more important game reserves for safaris in Kenya are *Masai Mara National Reserve* (northern end of the Serengeti Plain) and *Amboseli National Park* (with glimpses of Mt. Kilimanjaro in nearby Tanzania).

- In South Africa, *Kruger National Park* is the oldest reserve in Africa and can be toured comfortably by self-drive car.

- Egypt, in north Africa, is the home of the *Great Pyramids* of Giza outside *Cairo* and the mighty *Nile River,* the longest river in the world.

- *Victoria Falls* in Zimbabwe, called "The smoke that thunders," is considered one of the seven *natural* wonders of the world. These magnificent waterfalls are on the Zimbabwe and Zambia border, with better viewing from the Zimbabwe side.

- *Johannesburg* is the largest city in South Africa and also considered the cultural and commercial center. Visitors can tour active gold mines that are located right in the heart of the city—highly recommended!

- *The Ivory Coast* is a good destination for travelers who are interested in getting an idea about tribal lifestyles and customs plus a taste of the "bush" with its wildlife.

Key Point ➤ Two unique trips to recommend in South Africa are the "Garden Tour," a dramatic self-drive route along the coastline of South Africa and a ride on either Rovos Rail or the luxurious Blue Train, Africa's answer to Europe's Orient Express.

✓ *Check Your Understanding 2-14*

Check your knowledge on Europe and Africa. Match each tourist region or attraction with the country with which it is associated.

A. Spain	___	1.	Victoria Falls
B. England	___	2.	Amalfi Drive
C. Kenya	___	3.	Acropolis and Parthenon
D. Germany	___	4.	St. Petersburg
E. Italy	___	5.	Safari to Masai Mara and Amboseli
F. Russia	___	6.	Great Pyramids of Giza
G. Austria	___	7.	Casablanca, its major city, is often combined with tours to southern Spain
H. Norway			
I. Morocco	___	8.	Kruger National Park
J. Greece	___	9.	Stratford-Upon-Avon
K. South Africa	___	10.	European fjords
L. Zimbabwe	___	11.	Running of the bulls
M. Egypt	___	12.	Spanish Riding School
	___	13.	Romantic Road

➤ Asia

This vast continent extends from the Ural Mountains in Russia eastward to the Pacific Ocean (see Figure 2.41). In fact, the Ural Mountain range is an important border; it divides the continents of Europe and Asia. Asia consists of more than 40 countries with a total population exceeding 3 billion. This continent has the distinction of having two of the most populous countries in the world, China and India.

The Orient (a.k.a. Far East) is a melting pot: a multiracial mix of Chinese, Japanese, Thais, Malays, Koreans, Indonesians, Indians, and whites; it is also a composite of the world's religions: Buddhist, Hindu, Muslim, Christian, and others. When traveling to this part of the world, the traveler is very conscious of being in a totally different world—unlike anything American or what you might experience in foreign regions of North America or Western Europe.

This is the ancient world of Marco Polo, the Great Khan, sultans, shoguns, and emerald Buddhas. It is also a land reminiscent of the Ming Dynasty, Madame Butterfly, and Suzie Wong. It is gleaming skyscrapers next to exquisite temples centuries old or a ride on a 160-mile-per-hour bullet train, then in a rickshaw.

It is more practical for first-time visitors to this part of the world to go on organized tours. Although English is spoken in this part of the world, there is still difficulty in communicating once you leave major tourist hotels, restaurants, and other tourist centers. Signs are also difficult to read since they are rendered in the country's alphabet, made up of characters different from our own.

The best way to study this vast land mass and its countries is through these four subdivisons: (1) *Southwest Asia* (commonly called the *Middle East*), (2) *Russian Asia and Asiatic Republics*, (3) *Southern and Southeast Asia*, and (4) *East Asia*. In addition, the country of Turkey lies in both Europe and Asia; the western part is in Europe, the eastern is in Asia.

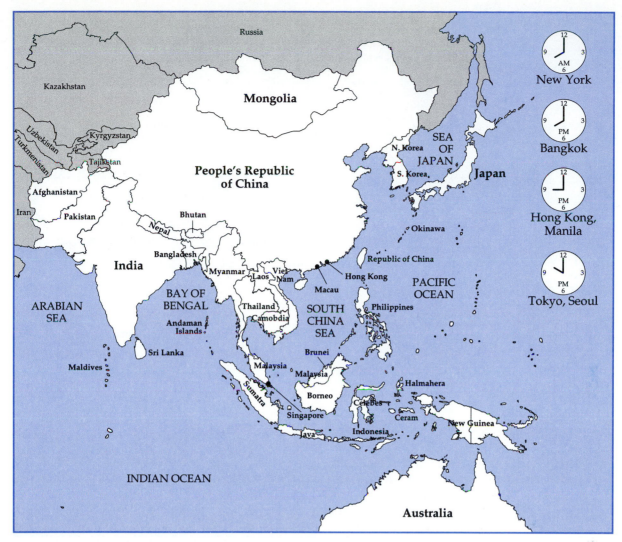

Figure 2.41 *Map of eastern and southern Asia.*

Southwest Asia (the Middle East)

This area, commonly called the Middle East (see Figure 2.42) is a very complex political area. Much of this land is desert occupied by tribes that have paid scant attention to formal political borders. With the exception of the Jewish state of Israel, all of the countries in the area are Islamic. Although Egypt is geographically part of Africa, it is often included in tours to the Middle East due to its cultural and religious ties to the area. There are fifteen independent countries and one disputed territory:

- Pakistan
- Afghanistan
- Iran
- Iraq
- Syria
- Lebanon
- Israel
- Jordan
- Kuwait
- Saudi Arabia
- Bahrain
- Qatar
- United Arab Emirates
- Oman
- Yemen
- Kashmir and Jammu (disputed territories claimed by both India and Pakistan)

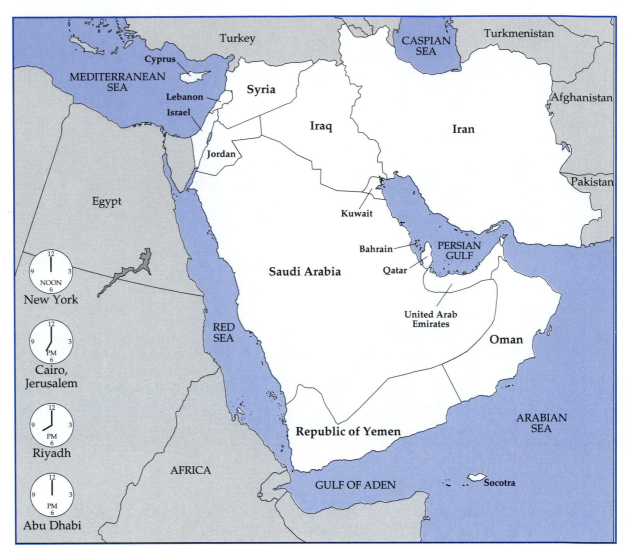

Figure 2.42 *Map of the Middle East.*

Russian Asia and Asiatic Republics

The USSR (Union of Soviet Socialist Republics) ceased to exist at the end of 1991. Before its demise, the USSR was considered a federal state with fifteen political subdivisions called republics. Eleven of these republics have formed an economic union called the *Commonwealth of Independent States* (CIS). In addition to Russia, there are five other CIS republics located in Asia (the others are located on the continent of Europe):

- Russia
- Kazakhstan
- Uzbekistan
- Turkmenistan
- Kyrgyzstan
- Tadjikistan

Key Point ➤ The recurrence of the suffix *-stan* (e.g., Turkmenistan, Uzbekistan, Pakistan, etc.) is because the old Persian word for *stan* means *"home of"* or *"land of."* Therefore, Kazakhstan means land of the Kazakhs.

Southern and Southeast Asia

Similar to the Middle East, this realm is also a complex political region In terms of history, these countries are just emerging. Compare the United States, which was born as an independent country in 1776; it has had hundreds of years of history. Most of these Asian countries were under European colonial administration until recent history—after World War II (mid-1940s). Their independent status is measured only in decades.

Many of the countries in southern Asia—such as India, Nepal, and Sri Lanka—have always appealed to the romantic and adventurous traveler. Whether it is the incredible beauty of the Taj Majal in India, trekking in the majestic Himalayas of Nepal, or visiting the sacred Bhuddist city of Kandy in Sri Lanka, this region of the world has always offered a variety of exotic attractions and experiences.

* India
* Nepal
* Bhutan
* Bangladesh
* Maldives
* Sri Lanka (formerly Ceylon)
* Myanmar (formerly Burma)
* Thailand
* Laos
* Cambodia (Kampuchea)
* Vietnam
* Philippines
* Malaysia
* Singapore
* Indonesia (includes more than 3,000 islands)
* Brunei

East Asia

At least one-fourth of all people on earth live in the area called East Asia. This area is dominated by China and Japan. Study this area by knowing the three countries that are sovereign communist states and three that are noncommunist:

1. Sovereign communist states:
   * People's Republic of China (usually abbreviated PRC; generally called simply "China")
   * Mongolian People's Republic
   * People's Democratic Republic of Korea (North Korea)
2. Sovereign noncommunist states:
   * Japan
   * Republic of China (on the island of Taiwan, or Formosa)
   * Republic of Korea (south Korea)

Key Point ➤ Until very recently, Hong Kong and Macau were a Crown Colony of the United Kingdom and an Overseas Province of Portugal, respectively. They both have returned to China: Hong Kong in 1997 and Macau in 1999.

Asia Sound Bites

* *Jerusalem, Israel* is the home of three religions: Christianity (*Church of the Holy Sepulcher*, site of Christ's death and burial), Judaism (*Western Wall*, last remaining wall of the ancient Temple of Jerusalem), and *Islam* (*Dome of the Rock Mosque*, where Mohammed is said to have ascended into heaven).
* The Taj Majal, located in Agra, India, is a monument of love built by the Shah Jahan as his beloved wife's mausoleum. This graceful structure epitomizes the Moghul architectural style of India.

Top Foreign Leisure Destinations

Region	Percent of International Leisure Sales	Top Three Regional Destinations
Caribbean	28	Jamaica
		The Islands of the Bahamas
		Virgin Islands
Mexico	18	Cancún
		Puerto Vallarta
		Cozumel
Western Europe	17	United Kingdom
		France
		Italy
Canada	6	Toronto
		Montreal
		Vancouver
Asia	5	China/Hong Kong
		Thailand
		Japan
Central America	4	Costa Rica
		Guatemala
		El Salvador
South America	4	Venezuela
		Argentina
		Colombia
Eastern Europe	4	Hungary
		Czech Republic
		Russia
Central/South Pacific	4	Australia
		New Zealand
		French Polynesia/Tahiti
Middle East	2	Israel
		Egypt
		Jordan
Africa	2	Kenya
		South Africa
		Tanzania

Source: *Printed in the U.S. Travel Agency Survey*, Travel Weekly, *August 1998.*

- The highest mountain in the world is Mt. Everest. It measures 29,000 feet and borders the countries of Nepal and China.
- Adventure travelers will love the ten-day *trans-Siberian* railway journey that begins in *Moscow* (European Russia), travels east across the plains of Siberia, and ends in *Vladivostok* on the Pacific Ocean.

- *Hong Kong*, China is a capitalist dynamo financing this huge country's development. Its dual nature is evident in the Central District, where commercial skyscrapers tower over colonial mansions. It is also evident in the Western District, where traditional shopkeepers sell snake meat, pearls, and curative potions. One of the world's most exclusive hotels—*The Peninsula*—is located here.

- *Singapore*, often dubbed as the *"Gibraltar of the East,"* is strategically located at the tip of the Malay Peninsula. This is another multiethnic crossroads devoted to the fine art of making money but with an eastern twist.

- The clouds of war in parts of southeast Asia—*Vietnam*, *Cambodia*, and *Laos*—have lifted, exposing rich cultural and historic experiences for touring. A growing number of overnight sightseeing packages are becoming available to this unknown region of Asia.

- When traveling to China, recommend a three-day stay, with the capital, *Beijing*, as home base: Day 1—*Tiananmen Square* and *Forbidden City*; day 2—*Summer Palace* and *Temple of Heaven*; and day 3—excursion outside the city to the *Great Wall* and *Ming Tombs*.

- An unusual time to visit Japan is during winter, in February, when the annual winter carnival takes place in *Sapporo*, Japan's ski capital.

- One of the most beautiful and palatial complexes on earth is the *Royal Palace* in *Bangkok, Thailand*. This is the home of the current king and his family and is open to the public.

- The most beautiful resort in southern Asia is the island of *Bali, Indonesia*, which combines the modern resort amenities with ancient customs, traditions, and magnificent tropical scenery.

➤ South Pacific: Australia, New Zealand, and the Islands

The South Pacific (see Figure 2.43) has become popular largely due to the friendliness of the Australians and New Zealanders toward tourists. They are quite anxious for foreign visitors to get to know them and are quite proud of how their history runs parallel with that of North America; like the early American settlers, they turned a virtually uninhabitable wilderness into what they believe to be two of the world's most "civilized" countries.

Because of the great travel distances involved, this part of the world is usually a once-in-a-lifetime trip for most North Americans. Ironically, even though the South Pacific is very far away, the culture, traditions, and lifestyles are very similar to those of North America. The European influence felt in the South Pacific region lends a great degree of comfort to most foreign travelers.

Despite the fact that most of the continent of Australia is arid desert, a tremendous variety of landscape exists; tropical jungle and rain forests in the north; spectacular beaches and dive sites in the east; mountains suitable for spectacular skiing in the eastern regions, and even penguins inhabiting islands off the southern coast.

New Zealand, Australia's neighbor toward the southeast, is comprised of two islands which afford rugged mountain scenery, giving way to spectacular outdoor activities. The North Island is more tropical and home to the Maori Polynesian people. The South Island is cooler, more mountainous, and features glaciers and fjords.

To many people, the islands of the South Pacific are the ultimate dream vacation destinations. Think of a South Pacific island and you conjure up palm trees, secluded beaches, friendly locals, and a stress-free lifestyle.

On a map or globe the thousands of Pacific Islands stretch out as tiny dots

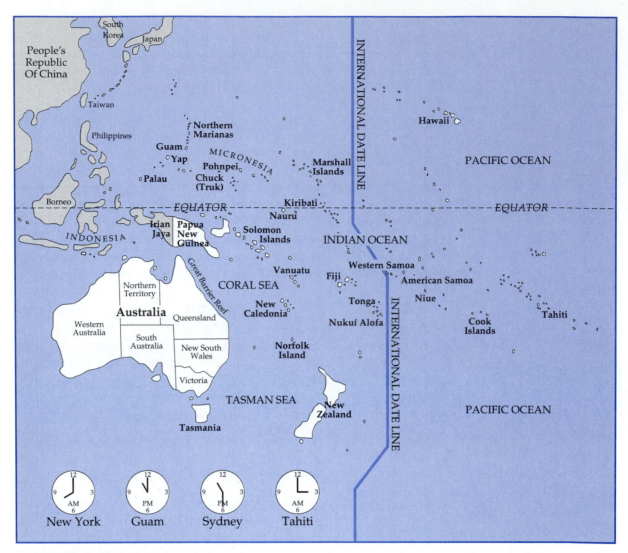

Figure 2.43 *Map of the South Pacific.*

that are confusing to remember and locate. Group them into three major divisons: Polynesia—"many islands" (*poly* means many), Melanesia—"black islands" (*mela* means black or dark-skinned), and Micronesia—"small islands" (*micro* means small). Well-known islands noted for tourism include Tahiti (Polynesia), Guam (Micronesia), and Vanuatu (Melanesia).

South Pacific Sound Bites

- Visit the largest living thing in the world, the *Great Barrier Reef* off the northeast coast of the continent of Australia. The reef stretches approximately 1,500 miles and in many places is only knee-deep, making for some of the best underwater tropical viewing in the world.

- *Sydney, Australia*, with its famous *Opera House* (in the shape of great sails on a giant ship), overlooks the world-famous harbor. An unusual site is the "coat-hanger" bridge that crosses the harbor, so named because of its shape.

- The interior of Australia, called the *Red Center*, is the site of the famous *Ayers Rock*, the largest monolith in the world. This natural phenomenon is

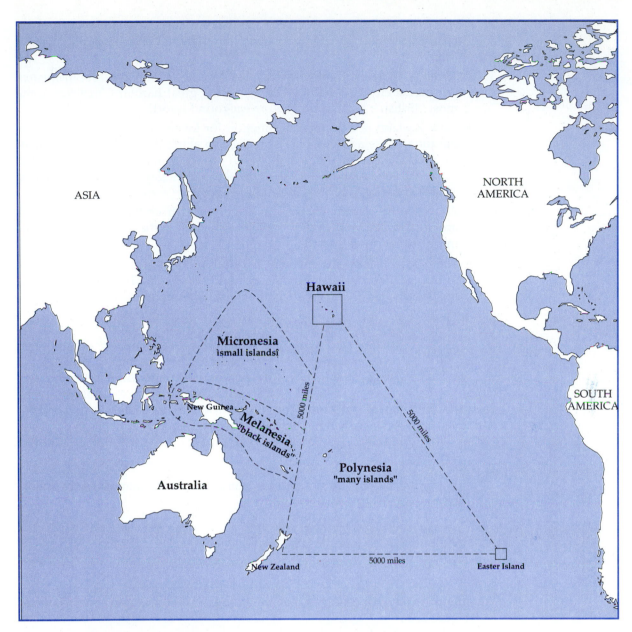

ASIA

NORTH AMERICA

Hawaii

Micronesia
ìsmall islandsî

5000 miles

5000 miles

SOUTH AMERICA

New Guinea

Melanesia "black islands"

Polynesia
"many islands"

Australia

New Zealand

5000 miles

Easter Island

Figure 2.44 *Pacific island divisions.*

1,000 feet high and six miles around its base and the red coloring of the rock changes dramatically from dawn to dusk.

- *Melbourne,* the cultural capital of Australia, is a leader in fashion design and the arts; it is also a beautiful city with many parks, gardens, and tree-lined streets.

- Majestic *Mt. Cook,* in the center of the Southern Alps in New Zealand, has the largest glacier in the world that is outside the polar regions. Adventurous skiers can try skiing after being dropped high on its peaks from a helicopter.

- At *Roturua, New Zealand,* visitors can see up close, thermal geysers and mud pools, feed tame trout, and visit an authentic village of the Maoris (the original natives of New Zealand).

- *Auckland*, the gateway to New Zealand, has the most cosmopolitan and sophisticated flair, with grand hotels, international shopping, and restaurants.

- Three of the most frequently traveled New Zealand cities are *Wellington*, the capital city, in a natural setting with a great harbor; *Christchurch*, the most "British"; and *Queenstown*, a year-round resort.

- New Zealand is a popular destination for lovers of nature and the great outdoors. Take a hiking and camping trip along the *Milford Track*, one of the finest walks in the world, which stretches approximately 35 miles. View glaciers around *Mt. Cook* in the south, visit geysers in the north, and snow-ski during July and August in the *Southern Alps*.

- As in South America, the seasons are reversed from those that most of us are used to, so that the best time or peak season in the South Pacific is during North America's winter.

- Although *Papeete* is the gateway to Tahiti in Polynesia, the real beauty lies in the neighboring islands of *Moorea* and *Bora Bora*. These islands, which are possessions of France, are part of what is termed *French Polynesia*.

Key Point ➤ *Call of the Exotic: The Pacific Rim:* The term *Pacific Rim* is often used in travel literature and geography books to describe the Far East. It includes that part of the Asian continent that borders along the Pacific Ocean. It starts with the Russian Far East, extends down the coast to China, Japan, and Korea, continues through Southeast Asia, and ends in Australia, New Zealand, and nearby islands of the Pacific.

✓ Check Your Understanding 2-15

1. Identify the major countries that are numbered on the map of Africa shown in Figure 2.45.

   1. _____   5. _____
   2. _____   6. _____
   3. _____   7. _____
   4. _____   8. _____

2. Identify the major countries that are numbered on the map of Asia shown in Figure 2.46.

   1. _____   7. _____
   2. _____   8. _____
   3. _____   9. _____
   4. _____   10. _____
   5. _____   11. _____
   6. _____   12. _____

Multiple Choice

Test your general knowledge of Africa and Asia. Circle the *best* answer.

3. The city in Southwest Asia that is the home of the three world religions of Christianity, Judaism, and Islam and such holy sites as the Church of the Holy Sepulcher and the Dome of the Rock is:

   A. Agra, India   C. Cairo, Egypt
   B. Jerusalem, Israel   D. Hong Kong, China

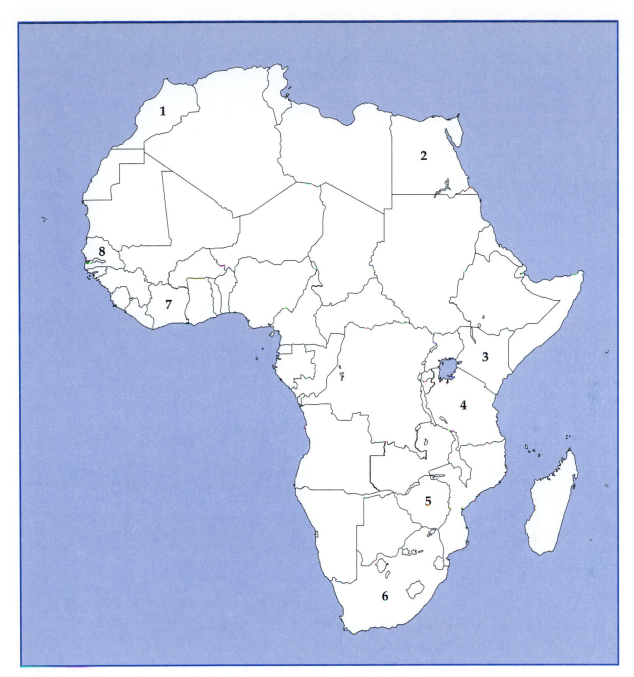

Figure 2.45

4. The suffix *-stan* (as in Pakistan and Afghanistan) means:
   A. province of   C. home of
   B. former name of   D. capital of

5. A sovereign communist country in East Asia is:
   A. Japan   C. Republic of Korea (South Korea)
   B. China   D. India

6. The highest mountain in the world, Mt. Everest, is bordered by these two Asian countries:

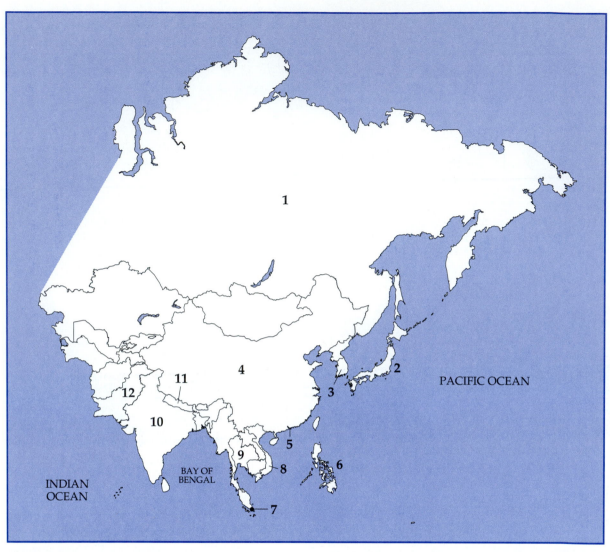

Figure 2.46

A. China and Mongolia   C. Nepal and India

B. Nepal and China   D. India and Pakistan

7. A thriving, westernized city that became part of China in 1997 and considered a financial dynamo is:

   A. Hong Kong   C. Beijing

   B. Singapore   D. Bangkok

8. To visit one of the most beautiful island resorts in the world located in southern Asia you would have to travel to:

   A. Papeete, Tahiti   C. Sydney, Australia

   B. Bali, Indonesia   D. Guam

9. The country that is divided into North and South Islands (the North is tropical and home of the Maori people and the South is cool and mountainous with glaciers) is:

   A. New Zealand   C. Indonesia

   B. Australia   D. Vietnam

10. To visit the dry and arid Red Center and to see Ayers Rock, the largest monolith in the world, you would have to travel to:

    A. New Zealand   C. Australia

    B. Nepal   D. Indonesia

11. Papeete in French Polynesia is the gateway to what island?

    A. Roturua   C. Tahiti

    B. Bora Bora   D. Bali, Indonesia

12. This country lies in both Europe and Asia; the Ural Mountains is the border between the European side on the west and the Asian side on the east.

    A. Turkey   C. Mongolia

    B. Egypt   D. Russia

 Close-Up: Geography-Related Careers

Leisure sales specialist	Tour designer	FIT/DIT specialist
Tourist board representative	Tour director/manager	

The majority of jobs in travel depend on geography knowledge and skills. Those careers that focus on geography include travel agents who specialize in leisure or vacation sales. Since they sell air tickets, cruises, tours, and accommodations to just about everywhere in the world, they must be fully knowledgeable in place-name skills and know something about the culture, way of life, and history of the many world destinations that they book for their clients.

FIT and DIT Specialist

FIT and DIT stand for *foreign independent tour* and *domestic independent tour*, respectively. FIT and DIT specialists create and design unique tours for individual and group clients. They are required to plan day-to-day itineraries, whether for a family visiting the national parks in the western United States or a three-week luxury tour for two through the Orient. They are responsible for booking all air and land arrangements during the tour, including ground transportation, tours and sightseeing tours, rail tickets, cruises, and accommodations. Being an FIT and DIT specialist is one of the most creative and challenging careers in travel.

➤ Key Terms & Phrases

- archipelago
- bay
- canyon
- cape
- climate
- coast
- continent
- delta
- desert
- eastern hemisphere
- equator
- fjord
- forest
- glacier
- globe

- Goode's Interrupted projection
- Greenwich Mean Time (GMT)
- gulf
- harbor
- island
- isthmus
- International Date Line
- Jet Stream
- lake
- lagoon
- latitude
- locator map
- longitude

- Mercator projection
- meridian
- mountain
- mountain range
- northern hemisphere
- oasis
- peninsula
- plain
- plateau
- political map
- Prime Meridian
- reef
- relief map
- river
- Robinson projection

- route map
- sea
- southern hemisphere
- strait
- time zone
- Trade Winds
- tributary
- valley
- volcano
- weather
- western hemisphere

Flashback   Travel professionals are faced with a great number of challenges. Many demands are set upon them to keep current with new information and constant changes that occur. A few of the many tasks that the travel counselor is required to maintain are to fine-tune sales skills, keep pace with computer technology, and expand product knowledge.

One of the most important products that the travel professional deals with is destination geography. People usually don't consider geography itself as a product; they usually think of tangible things such as tours, cruises, and hotels as travel products. But look at it this way: For every tangible product that is sold—whether it is a cruise to the Caribbean, a hotel room in Marrakech, or a tour to China—a destination is always sold along with it.

Firsthand knowledge is obviously the best way to expand destination expertise. However, there are just too many places in the world to visit in one lifetime. The key to increasing geography skills is through learning, research, and using what you have learned everyday in the workplace.

The knowledge that you must have goes beyond traditional concepts such as physical geography and place-name skills. Traditional concepts such as physical, topographical, and climatic characteristics of destinations are important and certainly affect how well we sell and promote travel. Of equal importance is the study of the destinations themselves as seen through the eyes of the travel professional. A growing familiarity of the transportation systems, travel products, history, culture, and traditions of the worldwide destinations that you encounter every day is a useful exercise for all of us who intend to make travel and hospitality a career.

CHAPTER REVIEW

True or False?

____ 1. The term *Eurasia* refers to one large continental mass that includes both Europe and Asia.

____ 2. The Caspian Sea is really a lake since it is completely surrounded by land.

____ 3. Longitude is a measurement north and south of the equator.

____ 4. The prime meridian is another name for the International Date Line.

____ 5. Most island resorts are located on the leeward side of mountains because more sunshine and less rain are experienced there than on the windward side.

____ 6. The higher you are above sea level, the hotter the air temperature.

____ 7. The earth receives the greatest amount of sun in the tropics, a zone that lies between the Tropic of Cancer and Tropic of Capricorn.

____ 8. High or peak season in Bermuda occurs during the winter months.

___ 9. The three major African countries noted for safaris are Tanzania, Kenya, and South Africa.

___ 10. *Pacific Rim* is another term for the Far East that includes China and Japan in the north and Australia, New Zealand, and Pacific islands in the south.

Multiple Choice

Circle the *best* answer.

11. What geographical definition best describes Bermuda, Bahamas, and Puerto Rico?

    A. South America   C. Central America
    B. Caribbean   D. West Indies

12. Kileaua, Hawaii and Mt. Aetna, Sicily are examples of:

    A. valleys   C. volcanoes
    B. ski resorts   D. rain forests

13. Baja, California and the state of Florida are examples of:

    A. peninsulas   C. capes
    B. islands   D. archipelagos

14. What do Alaska and Norway have in common?

    A. penguins   C. fjords
    B. Eskimos   D. deserts

15. If it is 8:00 A.M. in New York (−5, or five time zones west of GMT), what time is it in Rome, Italy (+2, or two time zones east of GMT)?

    A. 1:00 P.M.   C. 3:00 P.M.
    B. 1:00 A.M.   D. 10:00 A.M.

16. You depart on a transpacific flight from Los Angeles at 9:50 A.M., Thursday and arrive in Tokyo, Japan at 1:10 P.M., Tokyo local time. What day is it?

    A. Thursday   C. Wednesday
    B. Friday   D. Tuesday

17. If you are touring Prince Edward Island, Nova Scotia, and New Brunswick in Canada, you are traveling through:

    A. the Prairie provinces C. British Columbia
    B. the Maritime provinces D. the Central provinces

18. The island that offers high-rise beach resorts, international shopping, and nightlife in addition to such popular attractions as the Polynesian Cultural Center and Kualoa Ranch is:

    A. Maui   C. Hawaii
    B. Molokai   D. Oahu

19. If you want to visit Epcot, Sea World, and Busch Gardens theme parks, you have to travel to:

    A. Florida   C. California
    B. Missouri   D. Texas

20. When visiting Paris, France, you are in the:

    A. northern and western   C. northern and eastern hemispheres
       hemispheres
    B. southern and eastern   D. southern and western hemispheres
       hemispheres

21. The *Barranca del Cobre,* a breathtaking and dramatic train ride along Copper Canyon, takes place in:

    A. Central America C. Mexico

    B. West Indies D. South America

22. Which island is not part of the Greater Antilles?

    A. Puerto Rico C. Jamaica

    B. Cuba D. Barbados

23. The most popular destination for American travelers when vacationing outside the continental United States is:

    A. Mexico C. Hawaii

    B. Western Europe D. Caribbean

24. The South American country that borders both the Atlantic and Pacific Oceans is:

    A. Venezuela C. Brazil

    B. Colombia D. Peru

25. When visiting the Galapágos Islands—uninhabited nature reserves in the Pacific—you will most likely depart from:

    A. Peru C. Argentina

    B. Chile D. Ecuador

26. Andorra, Vatican City, San Marino, and Liechtenstein are examples of:

    A. Asian cities C. European capitals

    B. European microstates D. Pacific Islands

27. When visiting Pompeii and Capri, you are traveling in:

    A. France C. Italy

    B. Greece D. Yugoslavia

28. Which country is *not* in Southwest Asia (the Middle East)?

    A. Russia C. Saudi Arabia

    B. Israel D. Pakistan

29. The South Pacific region can be divided into three major geographical divisions. The division that contains the greatest number of islands (or "many" islands) is called:

    A. Melanesia C. Micronesia

    B. Polynesia D. Indonesia

30. The Great Barrier Reef, which stretches more than 1,500 miles and is considered one of the best diving sites in the world, is located off the coast of:

    A. New Zealand C. Bali

    B. Tahiti D. Australia

Short Answers and Fill-ins

31. Name the seven continents. (Can you list them in order from largest to smallest?)

    A. _____ E. _____

    B. _____ F. _____

    C. _____ G. _____

    D. _____

32. Name the four oceans. (Can you list them in order from largest to smallest?)

A. _____ C. _____

B. _____ D. _____

33. The three largest rivers in the world are the Yangtze River in China, the _____ River in South America, and the _____ River in Africa.

34. A place on earth that has the absolute measurement of 35 degrees north latitude, 65 degrees west longitude is located 35 degrees _____ of the _____, and 65 degrees west of the _____.

35. What resource tool provides the most accurate rendering of land and water masses of the earth?

_____.

36. What is the difference between the terms *continental United States* and *United States*?

_____.

37. Of four types of world projections—Globe, Mercator, Robinson, and Goode's interrupted—the _____ features the least amount of distortion of the continents.

38. Name the Hawaiian island for each description.

A. _____ is nicknamed the "Garden Island" since it is a lush tropical paradise.

B. _____ is known for its many beaches and old whaling town of Lahaina.

C. _____ is the most secluded and for those who want to stay off the beaten track.

D. _____ is the most "Hawaiian" since it has retained the old customs and traditions.

39. The island resort off the coast of the Yucatán peninsula of Mexico that is informal with an easy lifestyle is _____.

40. Another name for the prime meridian is _____.

Chapter 3

Domestic Air Travel

In America there are two
classes of travel—
first class and with children.

Robert Benchley
(1889–1945)

Fast Forward ▼

➤ Most commissions earned on domestic tickets are capped, but travel agents can earn higher air ticket commissions through overrides and other incentives through preferred suppliers. . . . 129

➤ "Everything you want to know about domestic air travel . . ." can be found in two major publications used by most professional travel agents: *Official Airline Guide* and *Travel Planners* . . . 137

➤ Learn how to qualify clients by asking the who, what, where, when, and how of air travel. . . . 141

➤ In addition to published discount fares, airlines offer special ticket prices in the form of negotiated fares and discount coupons. . . . 146

➤ Domestic fares include U.S. transportation tax (percentage of base fare) plus any of the following fees and surcharges when applicable: fuel surcharge, passenger facility charge, and segment tax. . . . 152

➤ Travel agents prepare ATB documents for their customers as well as manual tickets when necessary. . . . 154

➤ There are pros and cons of electronic ticketing—the paperless way to travel. . . . 156

➤ The practices of back-to-back and hidden-city ticketing are strictly prohibited by the airlines and should be handled by travel professionals in an ethical and responsible manner. . . . 156

INTRODUCTION

Of all the major events that occurred during the middle years of the twentieth century, the growth of commercial aviation has had the most dramatic effect on everyday living. Commercial aviation got its start in the early 1920s with the first government mail contracts with private airline companies. These early mail carriers didn't carry many passengers; only a few brave travelers decided to use this as a form of transport in those early years of aviation. During the 1930s and into the 1940s, an increasing number of Americans came to accept air transportation as a way to travel faster and in relative comfort.

It wasn't until World War II that flying became almost commonplace. Soldiers were flown courtesy of Uncle Sam and many became sold on the idea of air travel. After the war and throughout the 1950s, the majority of airline passengers were comprised of business travelers. Other passengers flew for emergency reasons or had the time and money for extensive leisure travel.

The airline industry experienced rapid growth during the late 1950s and 1960s. This time period was also a benchmark in aviation because of the introduction and proliferation of commercial jet aircraft. Jets almost tripled the speed of air travel, cut travel time radically, and lowered air fares. Consequently a growing number of travelers chose air travel as their primary mode of transportation, for both business and pleasure. Throughout subsequent decades to the present day, airlines have grown, expanded their routes, and have added more planes and newer aircraft to their fleets.

Today, domestic air travel continues to fuel industry revenue. Domestic bookings are considered to be the backbone of the retail travel agency business. Recent surveys of U.S. travel agencies conducted by major trade publications show that domestic bookings constitute more than 69 percent of total agency revenues. This translates into more than $70 billion of travel agency earnings through domestic air travel.

This chapter begins with some basic codes and terms related to the selling and booking of air travel. Topics such as passenger services and rights, air fares and commission structures, and the methods of airline ticketing will provide you with an overall perspective of the roles of travel agents and airlines in the marketing and selling of airline travel to the traveling public. Also, this information leads to a better understanding of the major airline computer reservations systems that are used by the majority of travel and ticket agents. Travel automation is covered in more detail later in this book.

It is a good idea to begin any course about the travel industry with the subject of airline transportation. You will discover that the terminology and general concepts related to this topic are fundamental to most aspects of the travel and tourism field.

TRANSPORTATION CODES: ALPHABET SOUP OF AIR TRAVEL

➤ City and Airport Codes

Each city that is served by an airport is identified by a unique three-letter code. We call these **city codes.** For example, BOS is the three-letter code for the city of Boston; NYC is the three-letter city code for New York City. These codes are used to identify a passenger's itinerary during the booking process.

The city code usually is enough to identify a specific destination when booking flights. If you are flying to BOS, you know precisely where you are going since Boston has only one major airport. Sometimes the city code is not enough; more information is needed to specify each airport location. For example, New York City (NYC) is served by several airports. The three major airports serving New York City are Kennedy, La Guardia, and Newark. Each airport is identified by a unique three-letter **airport code.** For New York City, Kennedy Airport is *JFK*; La Guardia Airport is *LGA*; and Newark Airport is *EWR*. Other examples of multiairport cities are Chicago (CHI) and Washington, DC (WAS):

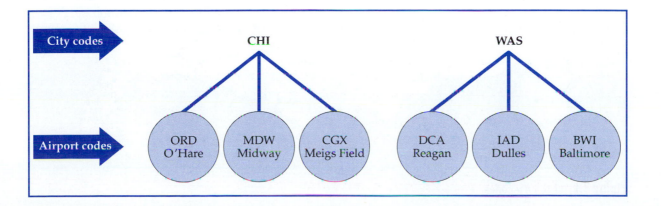

Key Point ➤ Sometimes a city may have the same three-letter code as one of its airports. A good example is DFW: It serves as both the city code for Dallas/Ft. Worth and the airport code for Dallas International Airport. An airport code may also be used as a city code due to the airport's location. Two examples of this are EWR and BWI; each is considered both an airport and a city code. EWR is the airport code for Newark Airport, which serves the greater New York City (NYC) area. EWR is also the city code for Newark, which is a city located in New Jersey. BWI is the airport code for Washington, DC, which serves the greater Washington, DC (WAS) area. BWI is also the city code for Baltimore, which is a city located in Maryland.

Travel consultants and airline ticket agents work with city/airport codes every day. These professionals need to know hundreds of these codes by memory in order to book airline travel efficiently through their computer terminals and over the telephone. Just memorizing them is not enough. It is very important to know where these major cities and airports are located on a map. Travel sales agents must have a mental image of where these places are so that they can plan logical itineraries for their clients.

Figure 3.1 is a map of the United States with selected major city codes identified. Table 3.1 lists major cities and their codes by geographic regions. After studying this section, how many can you name by memory? Can you locate them on a map?

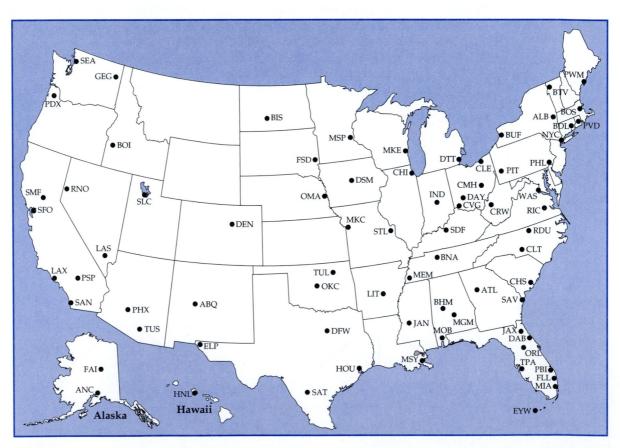

Figure 3.1 *U.S. city codes.*

TABLE 3.1   U.S. City and Airport Codes

City, State	City Code	Airport Code(s) (if applicable)
New England States		
Hartford, Connecticut/ Springfield, Massachusetts	BDL	
Portland, Maine	PWM	
Boston, Massachusetts	BOS	
Providence, Rhode Island	PVD	
Burlington, Vermont	BTV	
Middle Atlantic States		
Baltimore, Maryland	BWI	
Newark, New Jersey	EWR	
Albany, New York	ALB	
Buffalo, New York	BUF	
New York City	NYC	JFK (Kennedy) LGA (La Guardia) EWR (Newark)
Pittsburgh, Pennsylvania	PIT	
Philadelphia, Pennsylvania	PHL	
Washington, DC	WAS	DCA (Ronald Reagan National) IAD (Dulles) BWI (Baltimore)
South Atlantic States		
Charleston, West Virginia	CRW	
Richmond, Virginia	RIC	
Raleigh–Durham, North Carolina	RDU	
Charlotte, North Carolina	CLT	
Charleston, South Carolina	CHS	
Atlanta, Georgia	ATL	
Savannah, Georgia	SAV	
Jacksonville, Florida	JAX	
Daytona Beach, Florida	DAB	
Orlando, Florida	ORL	MCO (International) ORL (Herndon)
Tampa, Florida	TPA	
West Palm Beach, Florida	PBI	
Ft. Lauderdale, Florida	FLL	
Miami, Florida	MIA	
Key West, Florida	EYW	
Tennessee Valley States		
Louisville, Kentucky	SDF	
Nashville, Tennessee	BNA	
Memphis, Tennessee	MEM	
Birmingham, Alabama	BHM	
Montgomery, Alabama	MGM	
Mobile, Alabama	MOB	
Jackson, Mississippi	JAN	
South Central States		
Little Rock, Arkansas	LIT	
New Orleans, Louisiana	MSY	
Tulsa, Oklahoma	TUL	
Oklahoma City, Oklahoma	OKC	
Dallas/Ft. Worth, Texas	DFW	DAL (Love Field) DFW (International)
Houston, Texas	HOU	IAH (Intercontinental) HOU (Hobby)

(continued)

Table 3.1 U.S. City and Airport Codes (continued)

City, State	City Code	Airport Code(s) (if applicable)
San Antonio, Texas	SAT	
El Paso, Texas	ELP	
Great Lakes States		
Chicago, Illinois	CHI	ORD (O'Hare)
		MDW (Midway)
		CGX (Meigs Field)
Indianapolis, Indiana	IND	
Detroit, Michigan	DTT	DTW (Metro Wayne County)
		DET (Detroit City)
Cincinnati, Ohio	CVG	
Cleveland, Ohio	CLE	
Columbus, Ohio	CMH	
Dayton, Ohio	DAY	
Milwaukee, Wisconsin	MKE	
Great Plains States		
Minneapolis/St. Paul, Minnesota	MSP	
Des Moines, Iowa	DSM	
Kansas City, Missouri	MKC	MCI (International)
		MKC (Kansas City Downtown)
St. Louis, Missouri	STL	
Bismarck, North Dakota	BIS	
Sioux Falls, South Dakota	FSD	
Omaha, Nebraska	OMA	
Mountain States		
Boise, Idaho	BOI	
Salt Lake City, Utah	SLC	
Reno, Nevada	RNO	
Las Vegas, Nevada	LAS	
Denver, Colorado	DEN	
Albuquerque, New Mexico	ABQ	
Phoenix, Arizona	PHX	
Tucson, Arizona	TUS	
Pacific States		
Fairbanks, Alaska	FAI	
Anchorage, Alaska	ANC	
Seattle, Washington	SEA	
Spokane, Washington	GEG	
Portland, Oregon	PDX	
Sacramento, California	SMF	
San Francisco, California	SFO	OAK (Oakland)
		SFO (International)
Los Angeles, California	LAX	
Palm Springs, California	PSP	
San Diego, California	SAN	
Honolulu, Hawaii	HNL	

Key Point ➤ Many city codes are easy to remember. They begin with the first three letters of the city (e.g., MIA), or the code is comprised of key letters in the city name (e.g., PSP). However, there are some codes that don't seem to make any sense! For example, how did they come up with the code SDF for Louisville, Kentucky? Some city codes are derived from the

TABLE 3.2   Major Carrier Codes

AA	American Airlines	HP	America West
AC	Air Canada	JI	Midway Airlines
AM	Aeromexico	NW	Northwest Airlines
AQ	Aloha Airlines	WN	Southwest Airlines
AS	Alaska Airlines	TW	Trans World Airlines
CO	Continental Airlines	UA	United Airlines
CP	Canadian Airlines	US	US Airways
DL	Delta Air Lines	YX	Midwest Express
HA	Hawaiian Airlines		

name of their airports; SDF stands for Standiford Field. Other examples are MCO (McCoy Airfield), which serves Orlando, Florida, and BDL (Bradley Airport), which serves Hartford, Connecticut/Springfield, Massachusetts.

➤ Airline Codes

Other important reservation codes are those used to identify airlines. As every major city and airport is identified with a three-letter code, each airline is identified by a unique two-letter or alpha code. The alpha codes are used when booking flights, and they appear on airline tickets and other related transportation documents. In addition to an alpha code, each airline is assigned a three-digit or numeric code. The numeric codes are used generally for airline accounting purposes. Table 3.2 is a list of the major North American airlines and their alpha codes.

Airline Hubs

The **hub** system of airline routes has proven beneficial to both airlines and passengers. Think of a wheel with many spokes radiating from the center or hub. This concept entails designating a major city airport as the hub through which an airline schedules most of its flights to arrive around the same time. The airline then schedules most of its flights to depart about one or two hours later to various destinations on its system. This enables passengers to stay on the same airline or travel *on-line* all the way through to their final destination. They can change planes at the hub airport without the hassle of changing airline carriers and a high risk of lost luggage and missed connecting flights.

A great majority of airline travelers today—approximately 70 percent—travel from their home city to their final destination through a hub city. Hub-and-spoke routings benefit the airlines since they lose fewer of their passengers to other airlines through interline connecting services. An airline is able to provide convenient online connecting service between a greater number of cities—large and small—for a greater number of passengers. In addition to being a major connecting center for passengers, each hub is usually the site where the airline's maintenance facility, administrative offices, and reservation center are located. Figure 3.2 shows a map of the major U.S. hub cities. The major U.S. carriers and the hub airports that they serve are listed in Table 3.3.

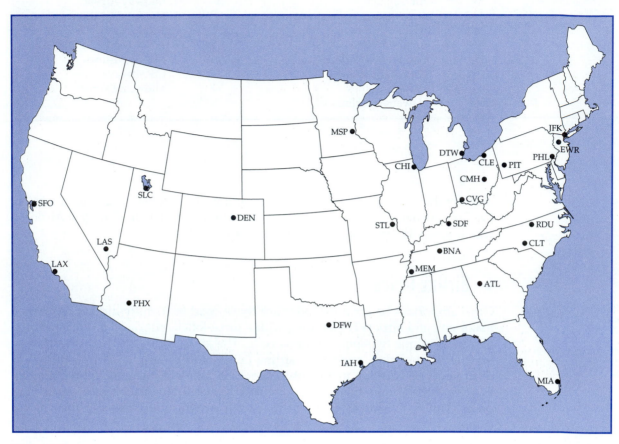

Figure 3.2 *Major U.S. hubs.*

TABLE 3.3   U.S. AIRLINE HUB CITIES

Airline	Hubs		
American Airlines	Chicago	Dallas/Ft. Worth	Nashville
America West	Columbus, Ohio	Phoenix	Las Vegas
Continental	Cleveland	Houston	Newark
Delta	Atlanta	Cincinnati	Salt Lake City
Midway Airlines	Raleigh/Durham		
Northwest	Detroit	Memphis	Minneapolis
TWA	St. Louis		
United Airlines	Chicago	Denver	
US Airways	Charlotte, North Carolina	Philadelphia	Pittsburgh

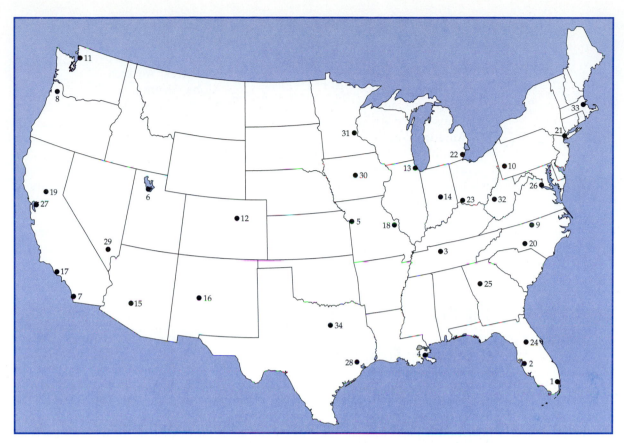

Figure 3.3

✔ *Check Your Understanding 3-1*

1. Identify each code below by writing the city and state name. By referring to the map shown in Figure 3.3, identify by number the location of each city code. The first has been completed as an example.

Code	City Name and State	Map Location	Code	City Name and State	Map Location
MIA	Miami, Florida	1	PIT		
CHI			SMF		
LAS			BNA		
MSY			ATL		
PDX			LAX		
WAS			SFO		
STL			ORL		
TPA			DFW		
DEN			MSP		
BOS			SEA		
RDU			SAN		
CLT			DTT		
CVG			HOU		
NYC			PHX		
MKC			CRW		
IND			DSM		
SLC			ABQ		

2. Write the two-letter code for each airline listed below.

Air Canada	_____	US Airways	_____
Alaska Airlines	_____	Aeromexico	_____
United Airlines	_____	Southwest Airlines	_____
Midway Airlines	_____	Aloha Airlines	_____
Delta Air Lines	_____	Northwest Airlines	_____
Trans World Airlines	_____	American Airlines	_____
America West	_____	Canadian Airlines	_____
Continental Airlines	_____	Hawaiian Airlines	_____
Midwest Express	_____		

3. Explain the hub-and-spoke system. In your answer describe the benefits to the airlines and their passengers.

_____

_____

_____

The Basics: Air Transportation 101

➤ Frequent Flyer Programs

The frequent-flyer concept was conceived by American Airlines in 1981 as a way to make the traveler, especially the frequent business traveler, "brand loyal" to the airline. A **frequent-flyer program** allows travelers to accumulate mileage flown on a particular airline, which can then be traded in for awards such as class-of-service upgrades or free tickets for future travel.

Today, all major airlines offer frequent-flyer programs. In fact, they even have partnerships or tie-ins with noncompeting airlines and other travel suppliers, such as car rental companies and hotel chains. For example, if travelers stay at a designated hotel or rent a car from a designated rental company, they are credited with air mileage. This enables the traveler more ways to accumulate points, and more diversity of awards can be offered.

Travelers must complete frequent-flyer application forms, which are distributed to travel agencies for their clients or given directly to passengers at airport counters. The only role that travel agents play is to track the earned points or mileage for their customers and enter the account number into the passenger's travel record. After the flight, the airline totals the trip miles and sends the traveler a summary of the number of miles flown on the last trip and the accumulated total to date.

The airlines have a limited number of seats on their flights that are used for award travel. Often, the availability of frequent-flyer seats don't appear in the regular availability or flight schedules used by travel agents when booking flights. Often, the traveler claims his or her award directly from the airline through a special number or department.

Web Link

Biztravel: This Internet travel agency keeps track of account balances for frequent travelers on most airlines. Visitors to this site are required to enroll in this service. Go to *http://bizmiles.biztravel.com/*

➤ Airline Clubs

Airport terminals can be pretty busy, hectic, and noisy places. Vacationers jam concourses, families with children in tow waiting in endless lines surrounded by mountains of luggage, and the lines at security check-ins appear endless. In the

Table 3.4   U.S. Airline Clubs

Airline	Clubs Worldwide	First-Year Fee	Alcohol Served	Smoking Area
United	49	$400	Cash bar	Chicago O'Hare, LaGuardia, Miami
Delta	48	300	Free	None
American	45	200	Cash bar	Most international
US Airways	27	350	Cash bar	Most clubs
Northwest	33	295	Free	None
Continental	16	200	Cash bar	None

Source: USA Today *research.*

middle of this chaos, many business travelers look cool and serene as they hustle through the airport process. Why? Because they know that there is an oasis of calm awaiting them—the **airline club.** These havens for the harried are located away from the airport's bustling crowd, down long corridors and hidden around corners. Most people don't even know they are there.

Most major carriers offer airport clubs at selected airports throughout the world. An airline club is a lounge area that is enclosed and private. Hidden behind heavy wooden doors, entering these spacious and carpeted rooms is like sinking into your favorite padded easy chair after a long hard day. Typical amenities at these clubs include beverage and snack services, television, and periodicals. In addition, clubs offer a wide range of informational and booking services for their members: Travelers can check in for their flights, get seat assignments and upgrades, and make future travel arrangements. Business facilities for club members include such services as fax machines, computers, conference rooms, notary and message services, and overnight express pickup. Some clubs at international airports offer posh shower facilities for its members, with heated floors and heated towel racks.

Access to these clubs comes at a price. To join an airline club, travelers pay annual fees that range from $200 to $400, or the cost of a business-class or first-class ticket. Many of the major airlines are forming alliances that include combining their airline clubs for members. Table 3.4 shows approximate fees and services offered by several major carriers.

Table 3.5 shows the names of frequent-flyer programs and airline clubs of ten sample airlines.

Table 3.5   Frequent-Flyer Programs and Airline Clubs

Airline	Frequent-Flyer Program	Airline Club
Air Canada	Aeroplan	Maple Leaf Lounge
Alaska Airlines	Mileage Plan	Board Room
America West	FlightFund	Phoenix Club
American Airlines	Aadvantage	Admirals Club
Continental Airlines	OnePass	Presidents Club
Delta Air Lines	Frequent Flyer	Crown Room
Northwest Airlines	WorldPerks	WorldClubs
Trans World Airlines	Frequent Flight Bonus	Ambassadors Club
United Airlines	Mileage Plus	Red Carpet Club
US Airways	Dividend Miles	US Airways Club

Web Link

QuickAID: This site offers some of the "best airport information on the Web," from BWI to IAD and many overseas airports as well. Go to *http://www.quickaid.com*

➤ Types of Airlines

In the past there used to be three distinctive types of airlines. They were defined relative to the routes they flew and the types of aircraft they operated. The major carriers, called *trunk* or **certified carriers**, flew medium- to long-distance routes. Airlines such as TWA, American, and United are considered trunk carriers.

The domestic local service carriers called **regional** or **feeder airlines** have been in operation since 1945. They provide air service between smaller cities and connect these communities with high-density air traffic centers. They are called regionals because they provide services within defined geographical areas or regions of the United States. Examples of regional carriers of the past include Mohawk and Allegheny Airlines, which served the northeast, and Frontier Airlines, which served the western part of the United States. Most regionals have either merged with larger trunk carriers or have gone out of business. An example of a contemporary regional carrier is Midway Airlines, which operates between the northeast and points in Florida.

The third type, **commuter airlines,** operate short-haul routes of less than 400 miles. Unlike the trunks and regionals that operate jet aircraft, most commuters use smaller propeller or turboprop (aircraft with jet-powered propeller engines) airplanes that seat from twelve to forty people. They are also called *feeder airlines* since they fly passengers from smaller airfields to major airports or hubs served by the major trunk carriers. Today, most commuter airlines don't operate on their own but are affiliated with major carriers. For example, American Eagle operates commuter service under the banner or identification of American Airlines. American Eagle is owned and operated by the AMR Corporation, which also owns and operates American Airlines.

➤ Airline Code Sharing and Alliances

Airline **code sharing** is a cooperative agreement between two or more airlines to share the sale of seats on one airline's aircraft. Since two airlines share the same airline two-letter code designator, they are also called **dual-designated carriers.** Dual-designated carriers are common on international connecting flights.

Code-sharing agreements are beneficial for both airlines and passengers. Airlines benefit because they can transport passengers to and from new destination markets without having to increase their flights. Passengers benefit since they can be checked through from the origin to final destination even though they are actually flying on two different carriers. Also, they can use the total mileage flown toward frequent-flyer mileage on either airline's program.

Delta and United have a code-sharing alliance. This means they will share codes on their domestic route networks. For example, a Delta passenger will be able to fly Savannah, Georgia–Atlanta–Sioux Falls/Rapid City, South Dakota–Green Bay, Wisconsin on a single ticket and earn frequent flyer miles on either carrier.

From the airlines' points of view, code-sharing alliances also means expanding route systems for both carriers involved. Delta and United's route systems don't overlap. Delta has a strong route network in the east, southeast, and southwest; United is stronger in the west and midwest. When two such systems are linked, the number of daily flights to an increased number of city pairs will provide more connecting options for travelers.

The Delta and United alliance is just one example; other domestic and international carriers have formed or are in the process of forming alliances. In addition to sharing routes and frequent-flyer programs, many alliances feature other aspects, such as airline club reciprocity, schedule coordination, and through check-in.

In 1999 the Department of Transportation (DOT) implemented a new rule which requires airlines and travel agents to disclose airline code-sharing arrangements to their travelers. The rules apply for travel to, from or within the United States. Under this ruling, passengers must be told orally before the booking and subsequently in writing.

► Charters

There are two general categories of flights: scheduled and nonscheduled. *Scheduled* or **commercial flights** are those that service airports on a routine basis with published timetables and fares. Most of what travel and ticket agents sell to their customers are scheduled flights.

Nonscheduled or **charter flights** do not travel on any set schedule or have predetermined fare structures. To charter means to hire the exclusive use of any type of vehicle: aircraft, cruise vessel, motorcoach, or rail. In the past, chartered aircraft were called *supplemental carriers* since they offered flights on routes and during times that scheduled carriers did not. A charter can be either private or public. A *private charter* is for the exclusive use of an individual or a particular group of people: a fraternal organization, a school group, or a company, for example. Seats on a *public charter* are sold to the general public.

Today, many tour companies charter aircraft from the airlines for a fixed price. In many cases, they sell public charter seats in conjunction with a land package that they have organized. These charter packages are sold directly to the general public or offered only through travel agencies.

Public charters often save travelers money. However, travel sales agents should explain to their clients the differences between a regularly scheduled flight and a charter. There are some problems that may occur on charter flights such as lengthy delays, rerouting of the aircraft, last-minute changes of flight schedules, and heavy cancellation penalties. A more detailed description of charter tours is covered later in this book.

TYPES OF AIRCRAFT

Types of aircraft vary greatly in terms of seating configuration, passenger capacity, and other technical aspects, such as wing span, velocity, range, and configuration of engines. There are also different types of aircraft categories, such as jet propeller and turboprop (propellers driven by jet engines). There are even amphibian craft used for commercial purposes that land and take off on water. It is not important that travel agents memorize the technical details of every type of aircraft. Basically, what typical travelers want to know are such things as "How big is the plane?," "What meals are served during the flight?," and "What's the movie?."

There are two major categories of aircraft with which the travel professional should be familiar: narrow-body and wide-body. What's the difference? **Narrow-body aircraft** have one walking aisle; **wide-body aircraft** have two walking aisles. Each type of aircraft equipment is identified with a three-character code. These equipment codes are displayed in flight schedules and other air-related information.

Usually, the first character of the code identifies the manufacturer. The four

TABLE 3.6 MAJOR TYPES OF AIRCRAFT AND CODES

CODE	NARROW-BODY AIRCRAFT	CODE	WIDE-BODY AIRCRAFT
727	Boeing 727	747	Boeing jumbo 747
737	Boeing 737	777	Boeing 777
757	Boeing 757 (successor to the 727)	767	Boeing 767
DC9	McDonnell Douglas DC9	D10	McDonnell Douglas DC10
M80	McDonnell Douglas (longer or stretch version of DC9)	M11	McDonnell Douglas (newer version of the D10)
		L10	Lockheed Ten-Eleven
		L11	Lockheed Eleven (newer version of L10)
		AB3	Airbus Industrie Air Bus

major aircraft manufacturers are: Boeing, McDonnell Douglas, Lockheed, and Airbus Industrie. For example, Boeing aircraft will have codes starting with the number 7; McDonnell Douglas aircraft codes begin with either the letter D or M. At the very least, sales agents should be able to identify an aircraft code in the narrow-body or wide-body category. The code 747 identifies the largest type of commercial jet that is manufactured by Boeing Corporation. The 747 is identified by a "second story" or upper deck that extends nearly halfway to the rear of the aircraft. This top section is used for additional passenger seating. Table 3.6 shows the major types of aircraft and their codes.

➤ Aircraft Remodeling

Aircraft manufacturers change equipment into newer and improved models, just like automobiles. However, they don't change as frequently as cars and these improvements may not be visually apparent to travelers. For example, newer versions of aircraft may be built longer or be "stretched" to increase passenger capacity. Others are built smaller and lighter to increase fuel efficiency and fly longer distances without refueling. An example is a newer version of the jumbo 747, which is built with a tilted wing tip. This ensures a smoother ride and results in greater fuel efficiency.

When a new version of an aircraft is rolled out, it is identified by a slightly different equipment code. Usually, the first and second characters remain the same; this helps to identify the family of aircraft to which it belongs. Here are some equipment codes of later versions of the 747:

747	Standard version
74M	Mixed version to carry both cargo and passengers
74L	Special version, longest in range
744	Newest and largest version (with the tilted wing tip)

➤ Classes of Service

The seating arrangement on an aircraft is called **configuration.** The most common configuration divides the aircraft into two main cabins or **classes of service:** first class and coach class. Larger jets that fly medium- to long-range routes may offer a third class of service called business class. Compared to coach class, business-class seating provides at an additional cost a quieter atmosphere and more comfortable seats aimed to attract frequent business travelers. The type of seats and level of service in each class of service differ from airline to airline.

Below is a general description of the three basic classes of service in terms of seating location, level of comfort, and service:

1. *First class.* Seats are located in the forward section of the aircraft. Seats are wider and more comfortable than those in other cabins on the plane. First-class seats are more heavily padded and are set farther away from the seats in front and behind to allow extra legroom. The amount of space between each row of seats is called the **seat pitch.** Seat pitch is widest in first class, averaging between 40 and 55 inches. On the medium- to long-range routes (particularly on international flights), meals are more elaborate, with several courses and more menu choices. Meals are usually served on china with cloth napkins. First-class passengers are served free alcoholic beverages.

2. *Business class.* Seats are considered halfway between first class and coach class in terms of service and comfort. Don't let the name confuse you; this section is not just for business travelers but is intended for those who can't or won't pay the first-class fare and who desire more privacy and comfort than coach class provides. Business-class seats are located directly behind the first-class cabin. On aircraft of the 747 type, the business cabin may be located on the upper deck of the aircraft.

3. *Coach class.* Seats are set closer together and are narrower than those in first- and business-class cabins. The average seat pitch in coach class is between 31 and 34 inches. Beverages and meals are served at no extra charge, although liquor, beer, and wine are usually purchased. On shorter flights, passengers in coach class may be served a lighter snack, whereas passengers in first or business class may be served a full meal. The majority of seats on any aircraft are located in coach class and located behind first- and business-class cabins.

Key Point ➤ Airlines sell many seats in coach class on a **controlled-inventory basis.** This means that the airline designates a certain number of seats for each type of discounted fare it offers. There are many different types of discounted fares. In fact, there may be nine or ten different types of controlled-inventory discount fares available on one flight alone. Each type of discounted fare has certain rules and restrictions of travel—some more than others. For example, a major airline flying from New York to Los Angeles offers coach ticket prices ranging from $250 to $1,600! A major challenge for travel consultants is to qualify their clients for the lowest-possible air fare to their destination. Most discounted fares are based on coach class. First- and business-class discounts are available on selected flights and routes.

➤ Class of Service Codes

Each class of service is designated by a one-letter code:

F	First class
C	Business class
Y	Coach class

These standard class of service codes are very important since they are used to book flights and determine what type of fare is being charged.

In addition to these standard codes, each type of discounted fare is identified with a unique primary letter code:

A	First-class discounted
D	Business-class discounted
B	Coach-class discounted

H	Coach-class discounted
Q	Coach-class discounted
M	Coach-class discounted
K	Coach-class discounted
L	Coach-class discounted
V	Coach-class discounted

The controlled-inventory codes vary and are changed frequently. Some examples are listed above. Notice that the majority of discounted fares are based on coach class. Discounted fares based on first- and business-class travel occur on selected flights and routes.

➤ Seat Maps

Seat maps show the configuration of an aircraft. They are provided to sales agents to assist them in seat selection for their passengers. Seat maps are printed in various industry resource books and are displayed in the airline reservations computer systems. A seat map is a blueprint of the aircraft. Some of the items on a seat map include the number of walking aisles, the number of seats in each row, and the location of the galley (kitchen area), passenger lavatories, and storage closets. Each row is assigned a number (starting with row 1 from the front of the aircraft), and each seat is assigned a letter (starting with A on the right side of the aircraft). When a specific seat is reserved for a passenger, it is called a *seat assignment*. Seat assignments will have the row number and seat letter: 8B is row 8, seat B, for example.

Airline seats are not bolted permanently to the floor of the aircraft; they can be moved. Airlines do it all the time. They may take out rows of seats to increase the pitch or add rows to increase passenger capacity on certain flights That is why seat maps for the same type of aircraft will differ slightly between airlines. Figure 3.4 shows a series of seat maps for various types of aircraft.

Key Point ➤ In the mid-1970s, a revolutionary commercial aircraft was introduced, the supersonic Concorde. Currently, this aircraft is operated by British Airways and Air France between New York and London or Paris. What's so special? It reaches speeds exceeding twice the speed of sound, or approximately 1,400 mph; conventional jets reach between 600 and 650 mph. It takes 3½ hours to fly between the New York and Europe on the Concorde compared to approximately 7 hours by conventional jet. The Concorde cruises more than 60,000 feet high, about twice the cruising altitude of standard jet aircraft. The aircraft is long and narrow, with a maximum passenger capacity of 100. The price tag for a round-trip ticket between New York and Europe is more than $8,000. By the way, there are no discounted fares; it is one class of service.

✓ Check Your Understanding 3-2

1. Name and describe two ways that major airlines establish brand loyalty with frequent travelers.

   A. _____

   B. _____

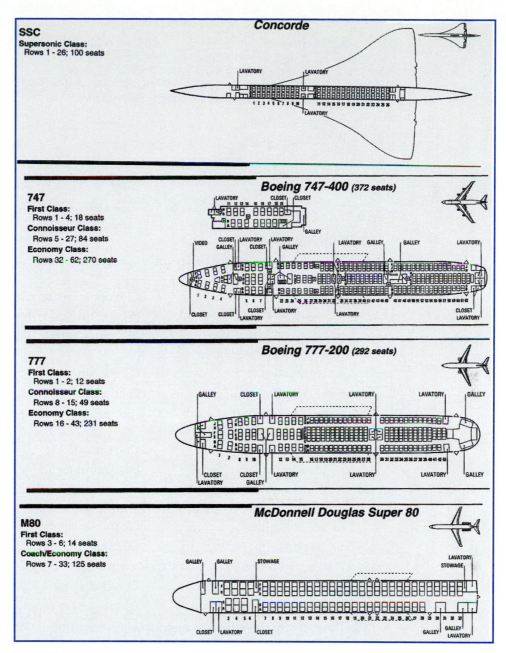

Figure 3.4 *Seat maps.*

2. Next to each code below, write an N if it is a narrow-body aircraft or W if it is a wide-body aircraft.

A. 757 _____   H. M80 _____

B. M11 _____   I. DC9 _____

C. 767 _____   J. D10 _____

D. 747 _____   K. 777 _____

E. L11 _____   L. AB3 _____

F. 727 _____   M. 737 _____

G. L10 _____

3. Write the code for each class of service (nondiscounted).

    A. business class _____   C. coach class _____

    B. first class _____

4. List a minimum of five class of service codes that identify controlled-inventory discount seats in coach-class service.

    A. _____   D. _____

    B. _____   E. _____

    C. _____

Multiple Choice

Circle the *best* answer.

5. The type of airline that flies on short routes of 400 miles or less and uses smaller aircraft is a:

    A. regional carrier   C. supplemental carrier

    B. trunk carrier   D. commuter carrier

6. The type of airline that flies between points within a defined geographical area on a scheduled basis is a:

    A. commuter   C. charter

    B. regional   D. trunk

7. The type of flight that can be either public or private and does not have predetermined schedules or fares is a:

    A. commercial   C. regional

    B. charter   D. commuter

8. A cooperative agreement between two airlines to share the sale of seats on one airline's aircraft on a particular route is (a):

    A. feeder airline   C. public charter

    B. frequent-travel program   D. code sharing

9. The configuration of an aircraft is shown by a:

    A. seat map   C. wing span

    B. pitch   D. passenger capacity

10. The code for the jumbo jet aircraft that has an upper deck for additional passenger seats is:

    A. 777   C. 747

    B. D10   D. 767

PASSENGER SERVICES

➤ Special Meals

Special meals are provided by most airlines and are requested in advance. Such meals as Kosher, vegetarian, low-calorie, low-sodium, Hindu–Moslem, and children platters are a few examples. The travel agent can make special meal requests directly through the agency's computer system at the time of booking or can contact the airline reservations office by telephone.

➤ Infant and Child Travel

Children under the age of 2 are considered infants and travel under a different set of rules from those of their older counterparts between the ages of 2 up to the twelfth birthday. On domestic flights, infants fly free and do not require an airline ticket if they do not occupy a seat. On international routes, infants pay a small charge and must be ticketed even though they do not occupy a seat. The majority of airlines follow this general policy regarding unaccompanied children:

Age of Child	*Unaccompanied General Policy*
Under 5 years of age	Will not be accepted under any circumstances.
Ages 5, 6 and 7	May be accepted on a flight that involves no change of plane.
Ages 8 through 11	May be accepted on non-stop, direct or connecting flights.

Children from 2 years through 11 years of age traveling with an adult pay the full fare or a child discounted fare if applicable. Rules for unaccompanied children vary between airlines. The general rule is that airlines do not accept unaccompanied children under the age of 5 or 6. If a child is accepted by the airline to travel alone, the travel agent must provide the following information at the time of booking: the name(s) of the person(s) bringing the child to the airport for boarding; and the name, relationship, address, and phone contact of the person(s) picking up the child at the arrival airport.

Unaccompanied children are taken care of by flight attendants during the trip. They help children find their seats when boarding, check on their well-being during the flight, and assist them in finding the person who has arranged to meet them upon arrival. Rules and procedures regarding the acceptance and handling of unaccompanied children should be checked with each carrier.

➤ Health Concerns and Assistance

Airlines provide certain types of services and special assistance to those passengers with disabilities or who suffer from medical conditions. Travel agents can reserve wheelchair assistance for their clients by contacting the airline by telephone or directly through the agency computer system. At the airport the traveler advises a sky cap or airline representative that this service has been requested. Airport personnel assist travelers by wheelchair from the ticket counter to the departure gate. If necessary, wheelchair-bound passengers are assisted directly onto the plane. This service is provided free of charge.

Oxygen can also be provided to travelers whose medical conditions warrant it. This service must be prearranged with the airline. This is usually done through a special service coordinator at the airline. There is a charge for the oxygen that costs approximately $50 per tank or unit.

Assistance for the visually impaired can also be requested by the travel agent on behalf of the passenger. If required, the passenger is allowed to bring a guide dog into the aircraft cabin free of charge. This also applies to dogs traveling with the hearing-impaired and those that are trained in search and rescue missions or bomb detection.

➤ Baggage Allowance

Baggage allowances for flights vary from airline to airline. Any baggage carried or checked in by the passenger that is in excess of the free allowance will be subject to charges for excess in number, weight, or size of baggage. Airlines reserve the right to refuse baggage that is not marked with the passenger's name on the outside, that it deems to be unsuitable for transportation, or that the passenger refuses to allow the airline to examine. The following types of special baggage should always be checked with the airline in advance to determine acceptance, special procedures to follow, and/or additional charges:

- Sporting equipment
- Musical instruments
- Live animals or pets
- Firearms and ammunition

Within North America

The piece method is used to determine free baggage allowance when traveling within North America. Baggage allowances will vary from airline to airline. The general rule is to accept up to three checked pieces of baggage, *including* a carry-on. A carry-on must be small enough to fit comfortably under the passenger's seat or in an overhead compartment. Checked baggage cannot exceed a maximum size that is determined by the sum of the outside linear dimensions (length + width + height). The general rule is that a checked bag should not exceed a linear dimension of 80 inches.

Outside North America

Two methods are used to determine the free baggage allowance for international travel: the *piece method* and the *weight method*. The method used depends on the airline(s) involved and the routing. However, the weight method applies for most international flights that do not originate or terminate in the United States. The baggage allowance is determined by the class of service and the maximum weight. The specific weight includes the total number of checked and carry-on bags. The general rules follow:

Class of Service	Checked/Unchecked Baggage
First	88 pounds (40 kilograms)
Business	66 pounds (30 kilograms)
Coach/economy	44 pounds (20 kilograms)

PASSENGER RIGHTS

➤ Delayed and Canceled Flights

Airlines do not guarantee their schedules. If a flight is canceled due to mechanical problems or weather conditions, most airlines will rebook their passengers on the first available flight to their destinations at no extra charge. The first available flight may be within the airline's system or with another carrier. If a flight is delayed, the airline is under no obligation to provide meals, phone calls, or hotel rooms. However, each carrier has its own policies, and these should be checked with the airline staff on a case-by-case basis. In most cases, airlines refuse to pay passengers for any expenses incurred that result from a delayed arrival.

Overbooking & Bumping

Overbooking flights is a common practice by most airlines. This is due to an estimated number of last minute cancellations or "no-shows" at the airport based on historical data. For example, if a particular flight shows a 10 percent average "no-show" rate, that means that ten percent of the seats fly empty; the lost revenue can never be recovered. In order to avoid this loss, airlines will overbook by a projected number of seats.

Voluntary Bumping

As a result, passengers are sometimes left behind or "bumped." The Department of Transportation (DOT) requires airlines to ask passengers to give up their seats on a voluntary basis with compensation. Airlines will negotiate with those passengers who give up their seats voluntarily. Passengers who are bumped voluntarily are compensated usually with a free airline ticket for a future trip or a full refund in addition to receiving transportation on the next available flight to their destination.

Involuntary Bumping

In those cases when the offer of free or reduced travel does not produce enough volunteers to give up their seats, the airline selects passengers to be bumped. Usually they select those passengers who were "last-at-the-gate" to be bumped first. Those passengers who are bumped against their will are also entitled to compensation. If the airline can deliver the passenger to his or her destination within one hour of the scheduled arrival time the airline usually does not compensate. However, if bumped passengers cannot be scheduled within one hour of arrival time then they are entitled to *denied boarding compensation*.

The amount of denied boarding compensation depends on how soon the airline can deliver the passenger to his or her destination. Passengers are usually compensated up to $400 if they arrive between one to two hours of intended arrival time; the compensation doubles to $800 if the arrival is more than two hours.

➤ Damaged, Delayed, or Lost Baggage

If the passenger's baggage is checked and arrives at the destination smashed or torn, the airline will usually pay for the repairs. If the bag is beyond repair, the airline will agree to pay its depreciated value. In the case of damage due to fragile items or carelessness in packing, the airline may decline to pay any compensation. If the passenger's baggage does not arrive at its destination, the passenger is requested to report it to the airline and fill out a form that describes the bag and its contents. The airline will then attempt to trace the bag. In general, airlines will absorb reasonable expenses incurred by the passenger while they look for the lost luggage. In some cases, airlines have a policy whereby a money disbursement is made at the airport for emergency purchases.

Web Link

Rules of the Air: Want to know what your options are if you're bumped from a flight? Or what the airlines' responsibilities are if flights are delayed or your luggage is damaged or lost? Rules of the Air Web site provides plain English answers to dozens of questions like these. Go to *http://www.onetravel.com/rules/rules.cfm*

The *American Society of Travel Agents* (ASTA) is the association of travel professionals to whom the traveling public looks for its travel information and advice. According to ASTA, it has issued these principles of air travelers' rights in the hope that the airline industry will "adopt them in practice as well as in name and thereby restore service and dependability to the traveling public air space."

ASTA's Air Traveler's Bill of Rights

Truth in advertised prices, schedules and seat availability.

Equal access to unbiased, comparative travel information and all fare and service options.

A comfortable seat, reasonable space for carry-on luggage, healthful meals, and clean sanitary facilities, regardless of class of service.

Timely and courteous assistance in making connections.

The right to use all, part or none of the segments on any ticket lawfully purchased.

Timely, complete and truthful information and courteous assistance regarding delays, cancellations, and equipment changes.

Timely and courteous assistance for the disabled and unaccompanied children.

Appropriate in-flight medical emergency assistance.

Access to the courts and state consumer laws to resolve disputes with airlines.

If luggage is officially lost, the passenger fills out another claim form and negotiates a settlement price with the airline. On domestic flights, airlines usually have a ceiling of approximately $2,500 on the amount of money they will pay out for delayed, lost, or damaged baggage. On international flights, liability limits are based on a complex formula that translates into approximately $9.10 per pound. It is important to note that the airline must enter the weight of the passenger's baggage on the airline ticket to take advantage of the liability limit.

Note: A copy of "Flyer Rights" may be obtained for a nominal charge by contacting the U.S. Government Printing Office, Washington, DC 20402.

✓ Check Your Understanding 3-3

True or False?

_____ 1. On domestic flights, infants fly at no charge if they do not occupy a seat.

_____ 2. Most airlines do not accept unaccompanied children under the age of 5 or 6.

_____ 3. Wheelchair assistance for passengers is available at airports at an additional charge.

_____ 4. When travel is within North America the amount of free baggage allowance is based on linear dimensions of each piece of baggage.

_____ 5. Overbooking is a common practice by most airlines.

_____ 6. If passengers are bumped from a flight due to too many passengers and not enough seats, the airlines are required to ask other passengers to give up their seats on a voluntary basis with compensation.

_____ 7. In general, airlines do not take any responsibility for lost or damaged baggage.

_____ 8. If a flight is delayed, the airline is under no obligation to provide meals or accommodations for its passengers.

_____ 9. Airlines do not have the right to refuse passengers' baggage at check-in.

_____ 10. Dogs under special circumstances are allowed into the aircraft cabin free of charge.

AIRLINES REPORTING CORPORATION

The majority of U.S. airline carriers belong to the **Airlines Reporting Corporation (ARC)** on a voluntary basis. This organization establishes standard practices and procedures regarding airline transportation and the sale of airline tickets. The ARC has many functions. Some of these functions as they relate to travel agency operations are:

- To provide a method of approving authorized travel agencies for the sale of transportation on behalf of member airlines.
- To print, distribute, and maintain universal ticket documents that are used exclusively by travel agents for the sale of airline transportation on all airlines.
- To establish standard practices and procedures relating to booking airline transportation, calculating fares, and completing airline tickets.
- To serve as a clearinghouse to distribute moneys to the airlines for all travel agency ticket sales (refer to the area settlement plan later in this chapter).

ARC-approved travel agencies receive the _Industry Agents' Handbook_, which is published and issued by ARC on a monthly basis. The _Handbook_ is the industry's keystone of the rules and procedures as they relate to the selling of air travel. The table of contents includes the following important topics as they relate to travel agency sales: making airline reservations, preparing handwritten and automated airline tickets, processing ticket refund and exchange transactions, accepting credit cards as payment, and applying taxes and fees as they relate to airline ticket sales.

Requirements for Opening a New Travel Agency

Going into business as a travel agent is not as simple as renting office space and hanging out a welcome sign. If the agency intends to sell airline tickets and to make commissions, it must go through an approval process with the ARC in order to sell tickets for domestic travel. It also needs to become appointed by the **International Airlines Travel Agent Network (IATAN)** to sell tickets for international airlines serving the United States.

IATAN is a division of the **International Air Transport Association (IATA),** which is the international counterpart of ARC that oversees international air travel. ARC and IATAN have specific requirements for new agencies seeking approval. Some of these requirements include:

1. *Location.* The agency must be freely accessible to the public and be clearly identified as a travel agency that is engaged primarily in the sale of passenger transportation and related services.

2. *Security.* The agency must provide security for the storage of blank and accountable ticket forms that meets ARC standards. ARC's minimum security requirements dictate that an agency is permitted only a small working supply of tickets at any time. Along with ticket processing equipment, tickets must be stored on premises in a safe that is bolted to the floor. Excess tickets must be stored away from the primary office area, preferably in a bank vault. Stolen and fraudulently used airline tickets cost the airlines millions of dollars each year, so this is a prime issue during the approval process.

3. *Personnel Qualifications.* A new travel agency has the option of having a *Ticket Qualifier* or a *Certified ARC Specialist* or *CAS Qualifier.* To be considered the Ticket Qualifier, either an owner, partner, or manager of the office must have at least two years full-time experience in the selling of travel. If the owner does not have the minimum experience, he or she is required to hire someone who does and put that person in a management position with management responsibilities. The CAS Qualifier candidate must pass a CAS test developed by the ARC. The CAS test is based entirely on the Industry Agents' Handbook. There are additional application procedures and requirements to get into the CAS program. The person who is designated the agency's Ticket Qualifier or CAS Qualifier is also required to complete and submit a complete Personal History form for review by ARC.

4. *Financial requirements.* Airlines are very concerned with any new travel firm that will be handling airline tickets that are negotiable as cash. As a result, the ARC approval process is similar to that of a sophisticated credit application. A current financial statement for the agency must be submitted. In addition, the applicant must submit either a bond or an irrevocable letter of credit in the amount of $20,000. This is increased to a maximum of $70,000 as cash sales of air transportation increase.

➤ Agency and Airline Identification Plates

When a travel agency becomes approved by the ARC, it receives a unique eight-digit identification number. This identification, called the agency's *ARC/IATA number,* is used in transactions involving the airlines and other suppliers. The ARC number serves as verification that the travel agency is a bona fide member of the travel agency community and is permitted to receive commission from sales of airline tickets and related products.

When approved, the agency is issued an identification plate. This is a small metal plate that has the agency's name, location, and ARC/IATA number in raised lettering on its face. It is smaller than a credit card and is used to stamp or endorse airline tickets and related documents that are prepared manually by the agency.

The approved agency also receives an identification plate from each domestic and international airline that is a member of ARC and IATA, respectively. The airline plate is made out of heavy metal and is slightly larger than the agency's identification. On the face of this plate is the carrier name, logo, and three-digit code. These plates are also used to stamp or validate airline tickets and related documents with the airline that is providing transportation or service.

Most airline tickets are issued through the agency's computer reservations system. ARC/IATA approval also authorizes the agency to have its name and the name of the participating carrier imprinted on computer-generated tickets.

➤ Airline Commissions

Travel agencies make money by the commissions they earn from selling airline tickets plus all other products and services they provide. Airlines pay travel agencies commissions on the tickets they sell. Commissions are structured in two ways. Commissions earned on the sale of airline tickets represent a percentage of the base price (before taxes) of the ticket or a fixed dollar amount. The amounts vary from airline to airline. Let's look at how commissions are calculated using both methods.

➤ Commission as a Percentage

The percentage of commission should be checked with each airline. However, the standard percentage on tickets for domestic U.S. travel is 8 percent. The commission is a percentage of the published fare *before taxes*. Airline passengers are required to pay a transportation tax on published air fares. Currently, the *U.S. transportation tax* is 7.5 percent of the published or **base fare** (tax amounts are subject to change).

 **Example:** *How to Calculate Commission as a Percentage:* A ticket is sold to the customer at $300:

Base fare	$279.07
Transportation tax (7.5%)	+ 20.93
Total fare	$300.00

The agency earns 8 percent of the base fare:

Base fare	$279.07
Commission (8%)	× 0.08
Commission earnings	$ 22.33

➤ Commission Caps

Most domestic airlines impose a ceiling or maximum amount that travel agencies can earn on commissions. At the present time, **commission caps** apply to the majority of domestic airline tickets. Many international airlines are applying commission caps but this should be checked on a case-by-case basis.

Under the commission cap policy, the agency earns 8 percent of the fare (without tax) not to exceed *$25.00* for *one-way* tickets and *$50.00* for *round-trip* tickets. You can look at the general rule on commission caps in another way:

For tickets sold:	And if the base fare is equal to or more than:	The maximum commission that can be earned is:
One way	$312.50	$25.00
Round trip	$625.00	$50.00

Key Point ➤ *Remember:* Commission percentages and cap amounts are subject to change and vary among airlines. The majority of carriers follow the 8 percent with cap rule. This should be checked on a frequent basis.

➤ Commission Overrides and Incentives

Travel agencies can earn commissions above the standard levels, as mentioned previously. This is done by selling products from a preferred supplier list. Preferred suppliers can be airlines, cruise lines, car rental companies, and other travel suppliers whose products the agency sells frequently to its clients. These preferred suppliers reward travel agencies with higher commissions to provide them with an incentive to sell their products. These higher commission earnings, called **overrides,** can reach as high as 12 to 15 percent of the retail price of the product sold.

➤ Area Settlement Plan

A major function of the ARC is to provide the basic ticketing and reporting requirements for all ARC-approved travel agency locations. The **area settlement plan** is the process by which agencies report and settle ticket transactions with the ARC carrier participants. The essential elements of the plan include the following:

- Standard or universal traffic documents that can be used for all carriers instead of individual carrier tickets
- One-step imprinting on ticket documents of the issuing carrier's name and the agent's validation at the time the document is issued
- A consolidated weekly sales report and a single-sum remittance for all carriers to a designated area bank
- An area bank, acting as a clearinghouse, to determine the amount due each carrier and transmit the appropriate amounts to the carrier
- Computer-generated sales summaries to each agency and carrier showing their respective sales activity

As part of the plan, agencies are required to complete a sales report on a weekly basis. The report is usually compiled by the agency's bookkeeper or assigned staff member at smaller agencies. The sales report includes all ticket documents that were sold during the previous business week, from Monday through Sunday. The sales report can be completed manually or on the computer. The sales report includes the following:

- A listing of all airline ticket documents by ticket number, amount of sale, and commission earnings
- A copy of each airline ticket as support documentation

The agency tallies the amount of sales from all tickets during that business week. By following a formula, it arrives at the amount of money it owes to the airlines. What is left are the commission earnings for that business week. In simplistic form, the formula looks like this:

total cash sales – agency commission earning = money owed airlines

Example: A travel agency sold $35,000 of airline tickets and related documents during one business week. The agency's total earnings or commission on this amount equals $2,700. What is owed to the airlines?

Total cash sales	$35,000
Commissions earned	– 2,700
Owed to airlines	$32,300

Note: When a ticket is paid by credit or charge card, the airline is paid directly by the credit card company. The agency's commission is kept up front; the commissions earned in the formula above include commission from all ticket sales: cash and credit.

To illustrate the sales report process, refer to Figure 3.5 and the step-by-step explanation that follows.

Step **1.** Agency clients purchase airline tickets and pay the retail sales price to the travel agency.

Step **2.** The travel agency deposits total cash received from the sale of all airline tickets during the business week into its bank account.

Step **3.** At the end of the business week, the travel agency prepares the sales report and sends the report to the ARC Clearing and

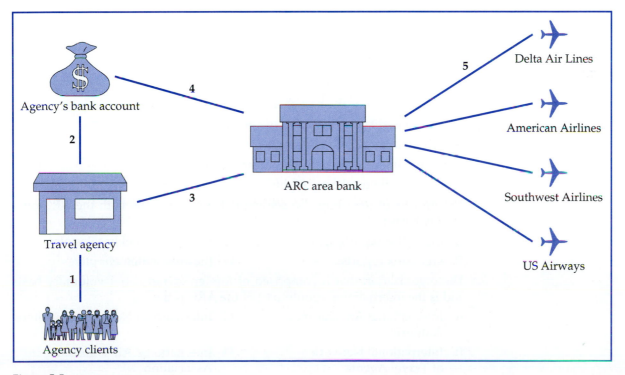

Figure 3.5 *Area settlement plan.*

Processing Center. The clearing center is one of several designated area banks in the United States.

Step **4.** The ARC's area bank has the legal authority to withdraw the total amount due to the airline carriers (cash sales minus agency commission) directly from the agency's bank account.

Step **5.** The ARC area bank remits money to the appropriate airlines.

✓ Check Your Understanding 3-4

Multiple Choice

Circle the *best* answer.

1. ARC stands for:
   A. Airlines Reporting Corporation
   B. Airline Reservation Commission
   C. Aircraft Reporting Commission
   D. Airline Regulation Commission

2. Which of the following is not a function of ARC?
   A. to serve as a clearinghouse to distribute money to individual airlines
   B. to print and distribute airline ticket documents to travel agencies
   C. to oversee passenger safety and aircraft maintenance policies
   D. to establish standard practices in booking and faring domestic air transportation

3. When approved by ARC and IATAN, the travel agency receives what items that allow them to sell airline tickets?
   A. credit cards
   B. agency licenses
   C. airline plates
   D. approval letters

4. The most common type of commission structure for domestic airline travel is:
   A. 7.5 percent of the published fare
   B. 7.5 percent of the published fare with commission caps
   C. 8 percent of the published fare
   D. 8 percent of the published fare with commission caps

5. A travel agency has the best chance to earn commission overrides by:
   A. selling flights that earn mileage points
   B. selling from a preferred supplier list
   C. selling flights on commuter and regional airlines
   D. selling seats on charter flights

6. The process of reporting and settling ticket transactions with the ARC on a weekly basis is:
   A. the airline reporting plan
   B. area bank reports
   C. the airline weekly sales plan
   D. the area settlement plan

7. The organization that is comprised of foreign carriers on a voluntary basis and is the international counterpart of the ARC is the:
   A. International Air Transport Authority
   B. International Network of Travel Agents
   C. International Network of Airlines
   D. International Air Transport Association

FLIGHT RESERVATION TERMINOLOGY

There are some important terms used by sales agents when they plan itineraries, book flights, and calculate ticket prices. These terms are used so often that they become second nature to the travel professional. For example, agents have to know what it means to plan an *open jaw*, know when to calculate a *point-to-point* versus a *through* fare, know when to book a *nonstop* or *direct*, and know the difference between *on-line* and *interline* services. We can categorize these important terms as they relate to air travel in three categories:

1. *Flight itinerary:* terms that describe the types of cities on a flight itinerary
2. *Flight services:* terms that describe how flights operate
3. *Air journeys:* terms that describe different types of routings or itineraries

➤ Flight Itinerary Terminology

To plan flight itineraries, agents need to define the ticketed points of travel on the passenger's ticket. Ticketed points of travel are the cities where the passenger either enplanes (boards the aircraft) or deplanes (gets off the aircraft). Being able to determine such things as the outward destination, connecting cities, stopovers, and outbound and inbound sectors are important when you book air itineraries and price tickets. Refer to the airline trip shown below as you learn about the important flight itinerary terms listed below.

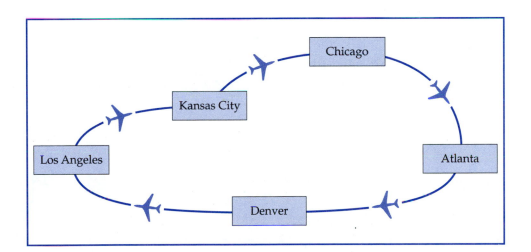

- **Origin:** the city where the trip begins (Los Angeles)
- **Destination:** the final or ultimate stop on the routing (Los Angeles)
- **Outward destination:** the city that is located farthest from the origin (Atlanta)
- **Outbound sector:** the portion of the itinerary measured from the origin to and including the outward destination (Los Angeles–Kansas City–Chicago–Atlanta)
- **Inbound (return) sector:** the portion of the itinerary measured from the outward destination to and including the final destination (Atlanta–Denver–Los Angeles)
- **Intermediate city:** any ticketed point of travel between the origin and the final destination (Kansas City–Chicago–Atlanta–Denver)

- **Stopover city (domestic):** a city on the routing where the passenger makes a deliberate stop for more than four hours [e.g., Kansas City (arrival on Aug 29 at 430P; departure Sep 1 at 2:45P)]
- **Connecting city (domestic):** an intermediate city on the routing where the passenger is required to transfer flights, *with no more than four hours between flights* [e.g., Denver (arrival on Sep 3 at 1:30P, departure same day at 2:45P)] [*Note:* If the passenger is forced to stop for more than four hours involuntarily (e.g., because of flight schedules or delays), the city is still considered a connection as long as the passenger departs on the first available flight to his or her destination.]

► Types of Flight Services

The travel professional must know the difference between direct, nonstop, and connecting flight service when planning flight itineraries for clients. Each type of flight service is defined below and identified on the map shown in Figure 3.6.

- **Non-stop flight (A):** Nonstop flights have no intermediate stops along the route. There is no change of flight number from the origin city to the destination city. *Map example:* AA 1264 nonstop from Denver (DEN) to Dallas/Ft. Worth (DFW).
- **Direct flight (B):** Direct flights contain one or more intermediate stops along the route. Similar to a nonstop flight, there is no change of flight number. *Map example:* UA 2147 direct from Seattle (SEA) to Las Vegas (LAS), with intermediate stops in SFO and LAX.

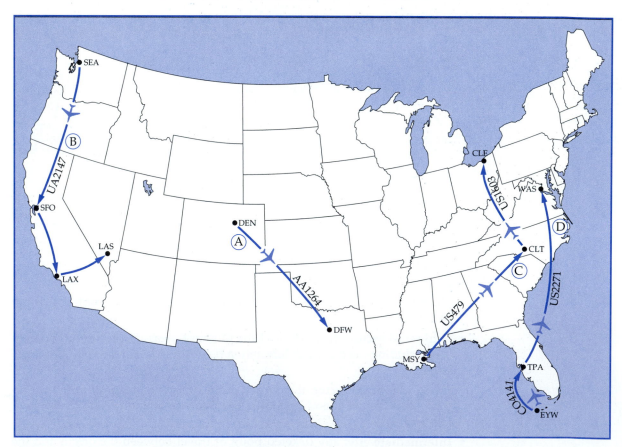

Figure 3.6 *Types of flight service: (A) nonstop; (B) direct; (C) and (D) connecting.*

- **Connecting flight (C and D):** Connecting flights require a physical change of aircraft and a change of flight number at a designated connecting city. A connection can be on-line (a change with the same carrier), off-line, or interline (a change between two different carriers). *Map examples:* On-line connection on US 479 from New Orleans (MSY) to the connecting city of Charlotte (CLT), change planes to US 1603 from CLT to Cleveland (CLE); off-line connection on CO 4141 from Key West (EYW) to connecting city Tampa (TPA), change planes to US 2271 from Tampa to Washington (WAS).

➤ Types of Air Journeys

You have heard the terms *one way* and *round trip*, but how about such things as *circle trips* and *open jaws*? These terms have significance when planning itineraries and calculating air fares. There are four types of air journeys: one way, round trip, circle trip, and open jaw. Each type of air journey is defined below and identified on the map shown in Figure 3.7.

- **One way (A):** a continuous trip from the origin to a different final destination, without a return to the city of origin.

- **Round trip (B):** a journey via a continuously charged air route that returns to the same city as the point of origin. The routing in each direction of travel is exactly the same; the outbound sector is the mirror image of the inbound sector.

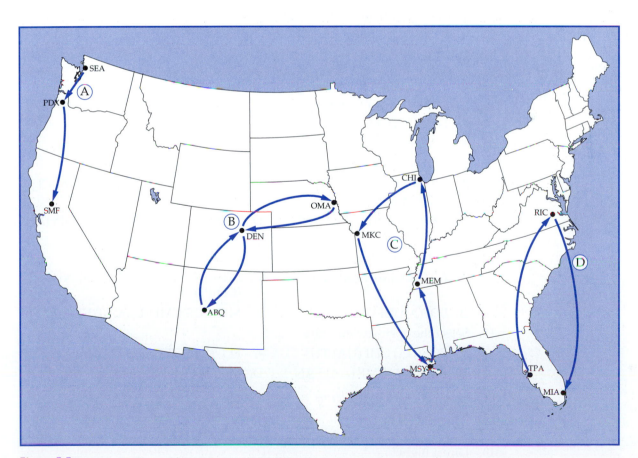

Figure 3.7 *Types of air journeys: (A) one way; (B) round trip; (C) circle trip; (D) open jaw.*

- **Circle trip (C):** a journey via a continuously charged air route that returns to the same city as the point of origin but does not qualify as a round trip (e.g., different routing, airline, and/or fare amounts are charged for each segment of travel).
- **Open jaw (D):** a journey that is an incomplete round or circle trip, which is not completely closed because of a surface (nonair) segment within the itinerary. The two cities between which the passenger surfaces (e.g., self-drives, takes a train, etc.) are called the *terminal points* of the open jaw.

✓ *Check Your Understanding 3-5*

Answer questions 1 to 7 relating to the flight itinerary outlined below. Write out the full city names in your answers.

STL–BNA–CHS–CLT–SDF–STL

1. Name all ticketed points of travel. _____

2. Name all intermediate cities. _____

3. Name the origin city. _____

4. Name the outward destination. _____

5. Name the destination. _____

6. Name the cities in the outbound sector. _____

7. Name the cities in the inbound sector. _____

Multiple Choice

Circle the correct answer.

8. Select the one-way itinerary.
   A. DTT CHI CLE
   B. SEA PDX LAX SFO
   C. JAX TPA SAV
   D. MKC STL CHS

9. Select the round-trip itinerary.
   A. MIA(CO) MSY(CO)ATL (CO) MIA
   B. MSP (NW) STL (TW) MSP
   C. WAS (UA) CHI (UA) SFO (UA) CHI (UA) WAS
   D. LAX(AA)DEN(AA)MKE(AA)PHX (AA)LAX

10. Select the circle-trip itinerary.
    A. NYC(CO)MIA(CO)NYC
    B. SDF(AA)DFW(UA)ELP
    C. PIT(CO)IND(CO)DEN(CO)IND (CO)PIT
    D. MEM(US)CMH(US)CLT(US)MEM

11. Select the open-jaw itinerary.
    A. BOS(UA) CHI (UA) TUS
    B. PDX (UA) SMF (AA) SAN
    C. FLL (DL) DTT (DL) DAB
    D. MSY (CO) DEN (UA) SEA

Define each of the following terms.

12. Nonstop flight

_____

13. Direct flight

_____

14. On-line connection

_____

15. Interline connection

_____

16. An air traveler is flying into Chicago O'Hare on TWA flight 185 arriving at 11:30 A.M. next Thursday. She is departing on TWA flight 446 at 2:45 P.M. the same day. Is Chicago a stopover or a connecting city? Explain your answer.

_____

17. An air traveler is arriving in Charlotte on US Airways flight 442 at 11:45 P.M. next Friday. He is flying on the next available flight on American to his intended destination of Sacramento which departs the next day at 7:35 A.M. Is Charlotte a stopover or a connecting city? Explain your answer.

_____

RESOURCES

Although travel sales agents rely heavily on airline computer reservations systems for flight information and related data, there are a few printed resources that are used generally to supplement the automated systems. This is especially true in the inevitable times when the agent's computer is experiencing downtime and flight information still needs to be furnished to clients in a timely manner. Two major resources are the _Official Airline Guide_ and _Travel Planners_.

➤ Official Airline Guide

The _Official Airline Guide (OAG)_ desktop guide is the printed resource that lists flight schedules and related travel data. There are two editions of the _OAG_. The North American edition includes over 250,000 flight schedules throughout the United States, Canada, Mexico, and the Caribbean. The Worldwide edition contains more than 480,000 flight schedules to destinations within North America and throughout the world. The Worldwide edition is so comprehensive that it can serve as a single source for global flight information.

In addition to flight schedules, which comprise the major portion of this resource, there are several other key sections that are helpful to the travel professional. Some of these key sections and their brief descriptions follow.

- _Airline codes and abbreviations:_ a comprehensive list of airline codes, and other types of reservation codes, such as classes of service and aircraft equipment
- _City and airport codes:_ a list of worldwide three-letter city and airport codes listed alphabetically
- _Airline ticket and baggage agreements:_ contracts among major certified carriers and smaller commuter-type airlines that cover procedures for cooperation in baggage transfer on interline connections
- _Aircraft seat charts:_ seating diagrams for different types of equipment
- _Airport diagrams:_ selected major airport diagrams that show location of terminals and gate areas and other passenger service sections
- _Airport check-in requirements:_ agreements as to the minimum time prior to scheduled departures by which passengers are required to report for check-in
- _Duty-free shops:_ a list of airports that have duty-free shop facilities for international passengers

To	Detroit, Michigan, USA						EDT		DTT
	M - DTW (Metro Wayne County) D - DET (Detroit City)								

From

Seattle/Tacoma, Washington, USA (S-SEA)   SEA

Leave		Arrive		Flight		Class	Eq	MI	S
7:00a	S	3:59p	M	UA	290	FCYBM	M80	S/	1
10:25a	S	5:36p	M	NW	68	FCYBM	D10	B	0
1:30p	S	8:40p	M	NW	264	FYBMH	757	L	0
			CONNECTIONS						
6:10a	S	9:37a	DEN	UA	404	FYBMH	757	B	0
10:15a	DEN	**2:56p**	M	UA	1406	FYBMH	733	S	0
8:11a	S	11:34a	DEN	UA	724	FYBMH	72S	B	0
12:45p	DEN	**5:26p**	M	UA	1790	FYBMH	733	L	0
2:10p	S	8:30p	ORD	UA	1142	FYBMH	757	D	0
9:45p	DEN	**11:50p**	M	UA	698	FYBMH	733		0
11:35p		2:09p	DEN	UA	1224	FYBMH	D10	S/	0
5:45p	DEN	**11:35p**	M	UA	688	FYBMH	733	D	0

Figure 3.8 OAG *flight schedule.*

Flight schedules comprise the major portion of the *OAG*. Refer to Figure 3.8, which is a partial display of a flight schedule from Seattle to Detroit. Headline cities are listed alphabetically; they represent the destination or "to" city. Sub-headline cities are listed alphabetically under each heading; these are the "from" cities. Each flight is broken down into seven columns of information:

1. *Leave:* local departure time
2. *Arrive:* local arrival time (followed by airport letter designator or code)
3. *Flight:* airline and flight number
4. *Class:* class of service codes
5. *Eq:* type of aircraft code
6. *Ml:* meals served (S, snack; L, lunch; D, dinner) [A slash denotes split meal service. Before the slash is the meal for first and business class (if applicable); after the slash is the meal for coach class.]
7. *S:* number of intermediate stops

Nonstops and direct flights are listed first, in order from the earliest to latest departures. Nonstop and direct flights are listed on one line of information. Connecting flights are also listed in chronological order. Connecting flights are listed on two lines of information, one for each flight segment.

► Travel Planners

The *OAG Travel Planners* are all-inclusive guides that include accommodation and destination information in addition to airline-related data. They are issued four times per year on a seasonal basis and are published by the company that issues the *OAGs*. The *Travel Planners* are issued in three editions:

1. *Business Travel Planner* covers North America, Central America, and South America.
2. *Europe Travel Planner* covers Europe, Africa, and the Middle East.
3. *Asia Pacific Travel Planner* includes all of Asia and the Pacific region.

America West Airlines (HP)

FlightFund

FlightFund Service Center, America West Airlines, P.O. Box 20050, Phoenix, AZ 85036-0050
Tel: 800-247-5691

Airlines: Aeromexico • Air France (award partner only) • America West Express • Continental Airlines • Northwest Airlines (award partner only) • SunTrips (award partner only)

Car Rentals: Avis • Dollar • Thrifty

Hotels: Hilton & Conrad International Hotels • Radisson Hotels Worldwide • Westin Hotels and Resorts

Other: FlightFund Visa Card - (Bank of America) • Sprint

Phoenix Club

Phoenix Club, 4000 East Sky Harbor Boulevard, Phoenix, AZ 85034
Tel: 602-693-2994

Locations

USA: Phoenix (2 clubrooms)

Fees: $50 - enrollment fee • $100 - annual dues • $25 - spouse • $225 - three-year membership • $75 - with spouse • $500 - lifetime individual membership • $200 - with spouse

Features: Flight check-in, reservations and seat assignments; complimentary beverages and snacks; conference rooms, free the first two hours; television; personal computer; copier; fax machine; free local calls; credit card phones, check cashing up to $100 at America West ticket counters; two guests or immediate family members per visit. First class passengers are offered complimentary use of lounge facilities. Club locations are non-smoking.

Figure 3.9 *Frequent-flyer and airline club. (From* Business Travel Planner.*)*

Each edition is divided into three general sections: directory, general travel information, and destination index. Here are a few examples taken from the *Business Travel Planner*:

1. *Airline frequent-flyer programs and airline clubs:* a list of domestic and international airlines with details regarding their frequent-flyer programs and airline club services. Figure 3.9 is an example of the listing for America West Airlines.

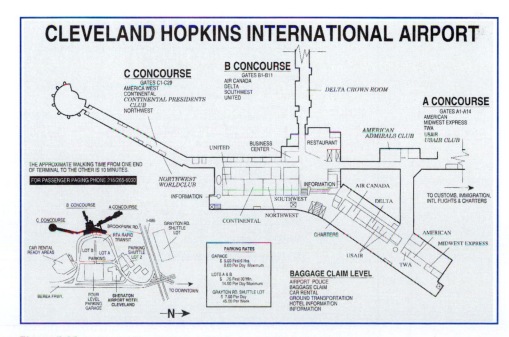

Figure 3.10 *Airport diagram. (From* Business Travel Planner.*)*

2. *Airport diagrams:* diagrams of major airports, including airline ticket/gate positions, facilities, airline club locations, and an overview of the airport area. Figure 3.10 is an example of Cleveland Airport.

3. *Destination facts:* detailed description and facts that include regional maps, city basics, air and ground transportation services, and climate. This section also provides a comprehensive list of accommodations with general descriptions and price ranges. Figure 3.11 is part of the destination facts for San Diego, California.

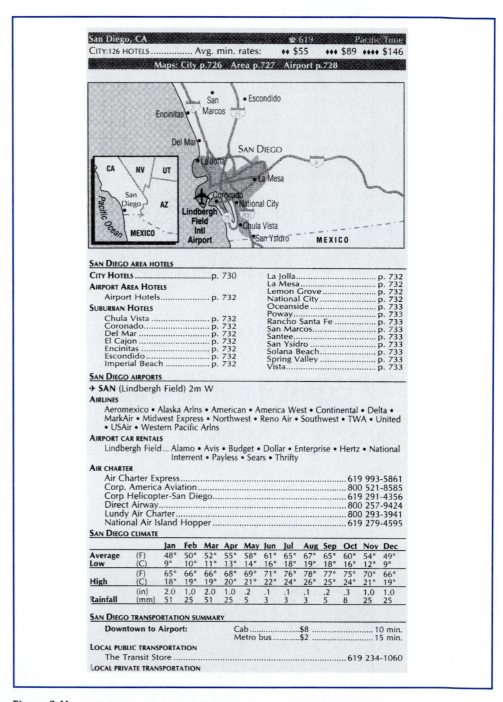

Figure 3.11 *Destination facts. (From* Business Travel Planner.*)*

Making Airline Reservations

Travel agents and airlines communicate with each other continuously. During the normal course of a business day, travel agents contact airlines for a variety of reasons: to book flights, to change or cancel reservations, to make special requests, or to obtain information. Most of this communication is done through the agency's computer reservations system. However, there are situations that still require telephone communications. In this section we study the basics of making airline bookings by this method. Using the airline computer reservations system is covered in detail later in this unit. We walk through a typical airline booking: from qualifying the client, to using your resources, to making the reservation through telephone handling.

➤ Qualifying the Client

The first thing to do is to find out the *who*, *what*, *where*, *when*, and *how* of what your client wants! Finding out exactly what your clients want to do is called *qualifying*. The professional agent knows what questions to ask and the importance of clarifying information, such as desired dates and times of travel. Here are some questions to ask and things to watch out for during the qualifying process:

1. *Who is traveling?* Find out who is traveling and the accurate spelling of everyone's name. If children are traveling, take note of their ages. This may have significance later when searching for air fares. It is also important to write down the name of the person who has contacted your agency for the booking. It may be the passenger or it may be a secretary. This is the person you would always contact for follow-up or additional information needed for the booking.

2. *Where are you going?* Sounds straightforward, doesn't it? Find out the client's desired routing, city to city. Beware of two typical pitfalls: multiple-airport cities and cities with a common name. If the client is traveling to a city with more than one major airport (New York or Washington, DC, for example), he or she will usually have a preference of airports. This preference is based on the ultimate destination point at the arrival city. For example, to attend to business inside the Capital Beltway area, Reagan National Airport is the most convenient. If the passenger is attending a meeting in a northern suburb such as Sterling, Virginia, Dulles Airport would be the better choice. Ask the right questions, know your geography, and use your resources to make the right choice. Another important point is to verify the state location for those cities that have the same name. If the client wants to fly into Columbus, don't assume Ohio. If she wants to go to Portland, don't assume Oregon.

3. *When are you traveling?* Always obtain accurate information from the client regarding exact dates and times of travel. Beware that your client's "next Tuesday" may be different from your "next Tuesday"! Your response should be to confirm with a specific date: "Okay, you would like to fly to Kansas City on Tuesday, April 15." Also, verify the actual length of stay your client desires. A client will often indicate the number of days at the destination. When someone wants to spend four days in Miami, is this counting days or nights? Always verify the date of a continuing flight or return. Your response should include a date verification: "Okay, we have you departing Tuesday April 15 and returning three days later, on Friday, April 18."

4. *How would you like to travel?* The obvious answer to this is the least expensive and most comfortable way possible. However, most travelers have personal preferences. You must consider your clients' requests and make recommendations that would suit them best. Following are some typical preferences shared by travelers:

a. *Airline preference.* Many travelers prefer to travel on a specific carrier. This is due largely to membership in a frequent-flyer program or past experiences with a particular airline that are favorable.

b. *Lowest air fare.* This is probably the primary consideration for most travelers since many of them are budget conscious. This is particularly true for business travelers, whose companies are always looking to save money on travel expenditures.

c. *Type of aircraft.* Some people prefer to fly the "big" jets (i.e., wide-body aircraft); others prefer smaller planes. A major concern for some travelers is flying on small commuter or propeller aircraft—passenger capacity of 30 passengers or less—that are flown on short routes. This should be checked when booking passengers on short-haul routes of less than 400 miles or into small airports that don't support standard jet aircraft.

d. *Connecting city.* If travelers have to take a connecting flight, they often prefer to connect through one airport rather than another if they have a choice. Who wants to connect through Chicago O'Hare in the middle of winter when connecting service through Dallas/Ft. Worth may be available? Or a business traveler may prefer to fly through a particular airport to connect with a business associate or to conduct a quick "meeting" at the airport between flights.

➤ Whom to Contact?

Contact only one airline for a passenger's reservation regardless of the number of airlines involved in the itinerary. If the passenger is using more than one carrier, the agent contacts the first major carrier that participates in the itinerary. For example, the client is requesting the following:

- Chicago to Dallas on TWA
- Dallas to Detroit on American Airlines
- Detroit to Chicago on Northwest Airlines

The travel agent contacts TWA to make the reservation for all flight segments of this booking. Practically all domestic and international carriers are electronically linked and are able to reserve seats on other carriers' flights.

The exception to this is when the first carrier flown is a small commuter or regional carrier. These carriers may not have direct links to the major airlines' computers; instantaneous confirmation of another carrier's flight is not possible. Small carriers send a request to the other airline's computer requesting seat availability. It may take up to two or three days for the request to be received by the other airline and an answer sent back to the commuter carrier's computer system. For example, the client is requesting the following:

- Rochester to Syracuse on Mall Airways (commuter service)
- Syracuse to Chicago on United Airlines

In this case, the agent can simplify this reservation by contacting the *first* major carrier on the itinerary—United Airlines.

➤ Preparing for the Call

The telephone conversation between the travel agent and airline reservation agent should be conducted in an efficient and smooth manner, with little or no chitchat. A typical reservation call should take no more than three minutes to complete. In fact, airline reservation agents are allotted a certain number of phone calls that they are to complete each hour. They are given maximum time limits based on the nature of each call. Before making the call, the travel agent should be prepared with the following information: passenger name(s) and correct spellings, phone contacts, and flight data.

Flight data are entered into the computer in a specific sequence:

1. Airline
2. Flight number
3. Class of service
4. Date of departure
5. From/to cities
6. Number of seats

This sequence of entries is followed by both airline reservation agents and travel agents when selling flights from their office computers. When phoning in reservations, remember to provide the flight information in the correct sequence.

➤ Telephone Reservation Script

Typically, the phone conversation between the airline reservationist (AR) and travel agent (TA) would go something like this:

AR: Hello, my name is John. How can I help you?

TA: Hi, this is Barbara at Worldly Travel in Boston. I would like to make a new reservation.

AR: What flight would you like to book?

TA: On your flight 18, first class, on the "two-one" June, from San Francisco to New York, for a party of two.

AR: Let me check availability. (pause) Yes, I can confirm two first-class seats on our flight 18 on June 21. That departs at 10:15 P.M. and arrives into Kennedy Airport at 6:22 A.M. the next morning. Will this be a one way, or do you need continuing space?

TA: Yes, I need a return on American's flight 23, first class, on the "two-six" June, New York to San Francisco.

AR: Yes, I can also confirm American flight 23 for June 26. That flight departs Kennedy at 8:35 A.M. and arrives into San Francisco at 11:35 A.M. May I have the passengers' names?

TA: Same last name, Jones, Edward and Mary.

AR: May I have the passengers' business and home contacts?

TA: Business phone is 617-555-1556. Home number is 978-555-9022.

AR: Thank you. May I have the name, location, and phone contact of your agency again?

TA: Worldly Travel in Boston, Massachusetts. Our agency phone is 617-555-9000.

AR: Can I help you with any more flight reservations today?

TA: No thanks, that's all for now. Bye!

AR: Thank you for calling United!

1. When making a flight reservation by telephone or in the agency computer, the flight data are entered in a specific sequence. Rearrange the data below into the correct sequence.

Correct Sequence

- From/to   1. _____
- Airline   2. _____
- Class of service   3. _____
- Number in party   4. _____
- Flight number   5. _____
- Date of travel   6. _____

2. Which airline do you contact to make reservations if there is more than one participating in the itinerary? Explain your answer and mention one exception to this rule.

   _____

   _____

   _____

3. List the names of the three editions of the *Travel Planner* resource.

   A. _____

   B. _____

   C. _____

Figure 3.12 is part of the schedule from Denver to Miami from the *Official Airline Guide*. Answer questions 4 to 10 by referring to the schedule.

4. United Airlines flight 1412 departs from Denver at _____ (time) and arrives in Miami at _____ (time).

5. The nonstop dinner flight arrives in Miami at _____ (time).

6. The airline and flight number of the *direct* flight from Denver to Miami is _____.

| To   Miami, Florida, USA | | | EDT | | | MIA | | |
I - MIA (International)			P - MPB (SPB)					
From								
Denver, Colorado, USA						DEN		
Leave		Arrive		Flight		Class	Eq	MI	S
9:45a		3:46p	I	AA	1726	FYBQH	M80	L	0
10:40a		4:23p	I	UA	1412	FYBMH	72S	L	0
2:35p		10:14p	I	CO	1844	FCYBM	M80	L	1
3:30p		9:13p	I	UA	997	FCYBM	757	D	0
		CONNECTIONS							
7:45a		12:28p	ATL	DL	432	FYBMK	767	S	0
1:34p	ATL	**3:20p**	I	DL	1077	FYBMK	M80		0
9:00a		12:19p	ORD	UA	910	FCYBM	777	B/S	0
1:45p	ORD	**5:43p**	I	UA	869	FYBMH	72S	L/S	0
12:55p		5:47p	ATL	DL	178	FYBMK	757	S	0
7:10p	ATL	**9:00p**	I	DL	685	FYBMK	M80	S/	0
3:25p		8:46p	MCO	UA	746	FYBMH	757	D	0
9:30p	MCO	**10:27p**	I	UA	951	FCYBM	757		0

Figure 3.12 OAG *schedule.*

7. Find the early morning on-line Delta connection and fill in. The Delta connection departs from Denver at _____ (time) and arrives in the connecting city of _____ at _____ (time). The first flight segment is on DL _____ (flight number) and a _____ (meal) is served. The second flight segment is on DL _____ (flight number), which departs the connecting city at _____ (time) and arrives in Miami at _____ (time).

8. Find the connection through Orlando and fill in. _____ (airline) operates a connection through Orlando. It departs from Denver at _____ (time) and arrives in Orlando at _____ (time). The five classes of service available on this flight are ____, ____, ____, ____, and ____ (class of service codes). The type of aircraft operated is a narrow-body with the code _____. A _____ (meal) is served on this flight. The second flight segment departs Orlando at _____ (time) and arrives in Miami at _____ (time). The classes of service on this flight are first, coach, _____, and two types of coach discounted seats.

9. Your client prefers a nonstop or direct flight in business class with lunch. What airline and flight number would you suggest? _____

10. Your client will be traveling first class on the connection through Chicago O'Hare. What meal(s) is(are) served in the first class cabin on the first segment? _____ What meal(s) is(are) served on the second segment? _____

DOMESTIC AIR FARES

A typical question from a traveler when planning a trip is: "What will it cost?" Cost is often the primary consideration when planning a trip. In today's deregulated and highly competitive marketplace, the airlines offer a wider selection of specials and discounted fares than ever before. Why? Mainly because of the revolution in airline travel that occurred in 1978. *Deregulation* of the airline industry radically changed the way that airlines and travel agencies do business.

► Deregulation

Prior to 1978, air travel was controlled by the federal government. The airline regulatory agency at that time was called the *Air Traffic Conference (ATC)*. Everything connected to domestic air travel had to be approved by the ATC: from establishing new airline routes to raising or lowering air fares. Consequently, there was little or no competition among the commercial carriers. If the ATC approved a lower air fare between two cities, it was approved for all airlines that flew that route. The number of airlines that were permitted to fly a certain route was also regulated by the ATC.

In 1978, the airline industry became deregulated through an act of Congress. The federal government lost most of its regulatory authority over the airlines. It still maintains authority over issues related to aircraft safety and maintenance under the aegis of the Federal Aviation Administration (FAA). However, today, airlines establish their routes, and raise and lower air fares at will in order to maintain their competitive edge.

The proliferation of discounted fares has been the most dramatic effect of deregulation. If airline X lowers its fares between New York and Los Angeles, airline Y, which also flies that route, will match it or even offer a lower fare to win passengers over. This goes on all the time; fares are introduced into the marketplace, new ones take their place, and so it goes.

Do travelers benefit from all this? In most cases, the answer is yes. There is more choice and a greater amount of discount travel available. This has enabled more people to use air transportation than ever before. That's the upside.

The downside is the effect of deregulation on shorter routes; those that have become monopolized by one or two carriers. It is not economically feasible for major airlines to fly large jet aircraft over short routes of 400 miles or less. As a result, only one or two small commuter or regional airlines may fly a particular route. Because of the lack of competition, air fares between certain cities remain high compared with other heavily traveled routes. That is why the air fare between two cities, such as Boston and Albany, New York (only about 200 miles apart) may be hundreds of dollars more than the fare from Boston to Miami, Florida.

➤ Special Fare Discounts

Before we get into how travel and airline ticket agents price airline tickets on scheduled airlines, we first should mention two types of discount ticketing: negotiated fares and airline coupons.

Negotiated Fares

Airlines offer their best customers—business travelers—the best rates in order to increase business. Special discount rates on air travel can be negotiated either by the corporate account or by the travel agency that handles bookings and other services for their corporate accounts. When a company negotiates directly with an airline for lower ticket prices for its business travelers, we call this *company-negotiated rates*. *Agency-contract rates* are negotiated between the travel agency and one or more airlines. These rates are valid only for business travelers of that agency. Company-negotiated and agency-contract rates represent a discount over standard published normal and special fares.

Discount Coupons

Many domestic carriers use *airline coupons* as a way to offer air fare discounts. These coupons can be found in newspapers, magazines, or mailed and distributed through banks, supermarkets, or credit card companies. In many instances, these coupons target specific passenger markets, such as senior citizens, students, or family travel. All coupons issued by airlines have established rules and restrictions. Some of the common restrictions include blackout dates for travel, length of stay, and controlled inventory (only a certain number of seats on the aircraft allowed to be sold with a coupon discount). There are two general categories of fare coupons:

1. *Discount amount.* This type of coupon allows a certain amount of money off the regular published fare. The amount of discount varies; some allow a percentage discount while others allow a discount of a set dollar amount.

2. *Set rate.* This type of coupon allows a ticket to be issued at a set rate. The rate or amount is usually based on geographical zones or specific routes.

The airlines allow travel agents to issue tickets in connection with their discount coupons. Travel agents tend to deal with airline coupons frequently since travelers must present their coupons at the time of ticketing and they cannot be processed over the telephone. Figure 3.13 is a sample of the front and back cover of a discount coupon issued by Continental Airlines. This is an example of a discount amount since it provides a dollar amount discount based on the price of the ticket.

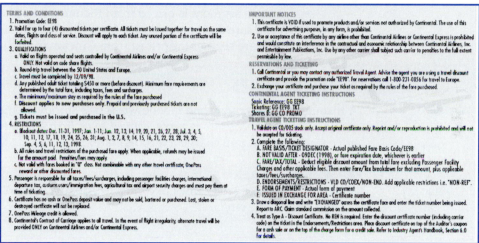

Figure 3.13 *Discount coupon.*

FARE CALCULATION

Domestic airline fares are constructed according to established rules and regulations as prescribed by the Airlines Reporting Corporation (ARC). Travel professionals have to understand the following three terms in order to understand domestic ticket pricing: point to point, through fares, and joint fares.

► Point-to-Point Fares

Point-to-point fare calculation is the basic principle governing domestic air fares. It means that a fare is charged to *each stopover city on a passenger's ticket.*

> **Example:** A passenger is flying on a circle trip from Richmond with stopovers (deliberate stop of more than four hours) in Charlotte and Cincinnati:

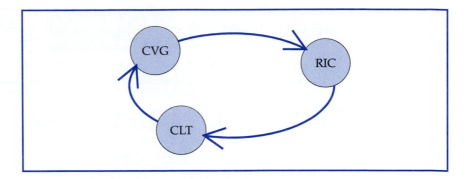

Because each city is a stopover, the agent must charge a point-to-point fare to each stopover city on the routing. This ticket would have three fare segments:

- First fare segment is priced from Richmond to Charlotte.
- Second fare segment is priced from Charlotte to Cincinnati.
- Third fare segment is priced from Cincinnati to Richmond.

➤ Through Fares

A **through fare** is a published fare between two stopover cities over an intermediate connecting city. *A fare is never charged to or from a connecting city.* When you price a connection, you charge a through fare.

Example: A passenger is flying an on-line connection with United Airlines from Salt Lake City to Albany, New York. Chicago is the connecting city:

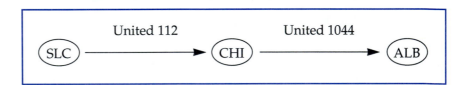

Since Chicago is a connecting city and no fare is ever charged to or from a connecting city, the agent charges a through fare from Salt Lake City to Albany.

➤ Joint Fares

A **joint fare** is charged when the passenger is traveling on an off-line connection. A joint fare is a fare that is agreed to by two airlines via a specific connecting city.

Example: A passenger is flying on an off-line connection from New York to San Diego. The first flight segment is on a United flight from New York to the connecting city of Chicago. The second segment is on an American flight from Chicago to San Diego. Since this is an off-line or interline connection, the fare to charge is a joint fare—agreed to by both United and American. Joint fares are usually more expensive than a through fare for an on-line connection; sometimes they are the same.

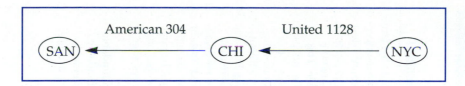

Key Point ➤
Since most connections are scheduled by the same airline through its hub city, the majority of connecting flights are on-line. That also means that through fares are charged more frequently; joint fares may occur from time to time when more convenient on-line service is not scheduled or available to the traveler's destination.

➤ Air Fare Identifiers

Each fare is identified by a unique **fare-type code,** comprised of one or more code elements. A code element can be one character in length or a combination of two characters. A code element identifies a specific condition or restriction of travel.

A fare-type code can be short and simple—only one code element in length. Others can be quite lengthy, with eight or nine code elements. Fare-type codes tell you a lot about a fare. They provide information regarding the class of service or booking code that must be used, what season or days of the week you can travel, how long you can stay, and the type or category of fare you are purchasing. The various code elements are combined in a specific descending order, as follows:

1. Primary/class of service code
2. Part of year (seasonality) code
3. Part of week code
4. Round-trip indicator
5. Advance purchase
6. Fare type

Travel agents need to recognize fare-type codes from fare listings from the CRS or in printed air fare resource books called *air tariffs*. Table 3.7 lists major code elements in the sequence in which they are usually placed. This chart is to be used as a general guide only; there will be exceptions and other types of fare codes not listed here.

➤ Discounted Fares and Rules

Travel sales agents have to qualify travelers for special discounted fares by making sure that all conditions and restrictions of travel are being met. Each fare has a published rule that describes all the requirements and restrictions of that fare. Fare rules are programmed into the airline computer reservations systems. Called **electronic fare rules,** these rules are updated hour by hour by the airlines to provide ticket and travel agents with current information.

Fare rules differ in complexity and length. Just remember, *the less expensive the fare, the more travel restrictions.* The more travel restrictions, the longer the fare rule! Each fare rule is divided into informational categories. Each category describes a particular type of condition or restriction of travel. Shown in Table 3.8 is a quick-at-a-glance list of the general rule categories with examples taken from a major airline computer reservations system that shows the format and wording used. The sample rule shown in the table is for a nonrefundable instant-purchase fare with the fare-type code of ME7NR.

TABLE 3.7 DOMESTIC FARE CODE ELEMENTS

PrimaryClass of Service [Mandatory]	Seasonal Code [Conditional]	Part of Week [Conditional]	Round-Trip Indicator [Conditional]	Advance Purchase [Conditional]	Fare Type [Conditional]
Identify the class of service or booking code. They may appear by themselves or may precede one or more conditional codes.	Place after primary code to indicate time of year (applicable to seasonal destinations such as Caribbean, Bermuda, Europe).	Use to differentiate weekend (high level) and weekday (low level) travel restrictions.	Some discounted fares are valid only for round trips; one-way travel is not permitted. The general name for these types of fares is *excursions*.	Domestic travel: number indicator usually refers to advance purchase restriction if applicable.	Use to identify the fare type or a passenger-type discount. Most discounted domestic fares are non-refundable. This means that no refund is due if the passenger cancels the ticket without rebooking. In many cases, nonrefundable fares are also considered "instant purchase" since the ticket must be purchased within one or two days after booking.
F First class	H High/peak	W Weekend/high	R Round trip		NR Nonrefundable
C Business class	O Mid/shoulder	H Weekend/high	E Excursion		IS Nonrefundable
Y Coach class	K Mid/shoulder	X Weekday/low	(round trip)		N Nonrefundable
	L Low/offpeak	L Weekday/low			IP Instant purchase
Controlled inventory:					
B Discounted					
Q Discounted					
M Discounted					
K Discounted					
L Discounted					
V Discounted					
Examples:	Examples:	Examples:	Examples:	Examples:	Examples:
F	*BH21IP*	KWE14	MXE7	ME7NR	VOE14N
Y26	YLE14N	VXE7IS	VLR21NR	HKW3IP	QE7NR
QXE21NR	VOE7NR				QLR2IP

Ten Most Common Agency Errors

Type of Error	Percent of All Errors
1. Not offering a negotiated air fare	29.1
2. Not offering a lower-cost airline	18.6
3. Not offering an alternative airport	14.9
4. Not offering inventory-controlled discount	10.6
5. Not offering an advance purchase fare	9.2
6. Calculation error by agency	7.5
7. Not offering a lower-cost connecting flight	3.7
8. Not waitlisting a lower fare	3.7
9. Not offering frequent-flyer discount	1.7
10. Not pricing the routing properly	1.0

Source: *Topaz Enterprises, a consulting and business travel ticket-audit firm based in Portland, Oregon. As published in Sept, 1998* Travel Weekly.

TABLE 3.8   FARE RULE CATEGORIES

Informational Category	Fare Rule Example: ME7NR
Booking Code: the class of service or booking code that is required when making reservations for the fare.	01 BK CODE - M -
Penalty: the amount of penalty in the event of ticket cancellation and/or changes to the reservation.	02 PENALTY - TICKETS ARE NON-REFUNDABLE. FOR CONFIRMED CHANGES THE FOLLOWING APPLIES: $50 ADMINSTRATIVE SERVICE FEE WILL BE ASSESSED FOR AN ITINERARY CHANGE.
Reservations/ticketing: the date by which the reservation must be made and the date by which the ticket must be issued.	03 RES/TKT - RES MUST BE MADE NO LATER THAN 7 DAYS BEFORE DEPARTURE FROM ORIGIN. TKT MUST BE PURCHASED NO LATER THAN 7 DAYS BEFORE DEPARTURE FROM ORIGIN OR 1 DAY AFTER RES IS MADE, WHICHEVER COMES FIRST.
Minimum stay: the earliest permissible date the passenger may begin the return trip home.	04 MIN STAY - RETURN TRAVEL IS VALID ON THE 1ST SUN AFTER 12:01A.M.
Maximum stay: the latest permissible date the passenger must begin the return trip home.	05 MAX STAY - RETURN TRAVEL MUST COMMENCE NO LATER THAN 30 DAYS.
Day/Time: the day[s] of the week or time during the day when travel is valid.	06 DAY/TIME - APPLIES DAILY 7:00P.M. - 5:59A.M.
Blackouts: specific date(s) when travel is not allowed. Typical blackout periods occur during holiday or school vacation times.	08 BLACKOUTS - TRAVEL IS NOT VALID 19NOV, 22NOV, 26NOV.
Effective/Expiration: effective date is the earliest and/or latest dates when fare can be sold. Expiration date is the first and/or last date when travel may begin or be completed by the traveler.	09 EFF/EXP - TICKET MUST BE ISSUED BY 15SEP. RETURN TRAVEL AT THIS FARE MUST COMMENCE BY 15DEC.

➤ Domestic Taxes and Surcharges

There are additional taxes and fees that are added to the price of a domestic airline ticket. The major components of any ticket price are:

base fare + U.S. transportation tax = total fare

Base fare is the published fare without taxes. This amount goes to the airline that provides the transportation. The travel agency gets a portion of this as its commission earnings. *Tax* is a percentage amount of the base fare. Currently, the tax is 7.5 percent and is subject to change (all examples in this book are based on 7.5 percent). (See Figure 3.14 in regard to the United States–Canada buffer zone.) *Total fare* or the final selling price is the base fare plus tax plus any other applicable surcharges and fees.

There are three other types of fees associated with domestic travel when applicable: fuel surcharge, passenger facility charge (PFC), and segment tax (Table 3.9). All of them are collected at the time of ticketing and added to the total price. *Remember: These fees are applicable to domestic travel only.*

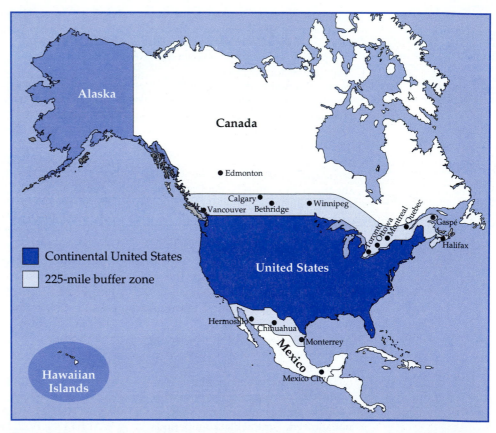

Figure 3.14 *The buffer zone is a 225-mile zone that extends from the northern border of the continental United States into Canada. It also extends 225 miles from the southern border of the United States into Mexico. The buffer zone was established for taxation purposes only. When travel is between any point within the continental United States and any point within the Canadian and Mexican buffer zone, the current U.S. transportation tax is charged.*

TABLE 3.9 DOMESTIC TRAVEL FEES

FEE	TYPE OF CHARGE	DESCRIPTION	CODE	AMOUNT
Fuel surcharge	Not a tax but a surcharge that is added to the base fare amount	Applicable on certain airlines from specified cities of departure.	Q	Varies; they range from $2.00 to $5.00.
Passenger facility charge (PFC)	A federal tax to subsidize airport expansion and improvement projects	Applicable from most major airports. Airports petition the federal government to grant them the right to collect a PFC from each departing passenger. Airports are allowed to collect PFCs for a certain number of years.	XF	Standard PFC is $3.00, but can vary.
Segment tax	A federal tax for each travel segment on an airline ticket	Passenger is charged for each departure from an airport at the beginning of each segment on the airline ticket. Segment taxes do not apply to/from selected rural cities.	ZP	Changes annually. Fee schedule: Year 2000 = $2.50 Year 2001 = $2.75 Year 2002 = $3.00 Year 2003+ = TBA

➤ Fare Displays

The primary resource for air fares is the computer reservations system used by the majority of travel agencies. These systems are explained in more detail later in the book. However, this may be a good time to show you an example of how air fares are displayed on the computer screen. One method is to request fares on all airlines for a given city pair. This is called a *fare scan* or *fare shoppers display*. Figure 3.15 is an example of a fare scan from a major computer reservations system for travel between Boston (BOS) and Charleston, West Virginia (CRW). The first four lines of the display are header lines. They indicate the city pair, travel date, and currency used in the display (USD = U.S. dollar). The airline codes represent the airlines that have published fares for the city pair provided. Each carrier code is followed by a flight service count: number of nonstops/ number of directs / number of connections (e.g., DL 1 / 0 / 4 means that this airline has 1 nonstop flight, zero direct flights, and 4 connections). The balance of the display shows informational columns. The first column lists each fare by line number. The balance of the columns represent the following:

F/B	Fare-basis code
O/W	One-way fare (for fares that can be sold one way)
R/T	Round-trip fare (for fares that can only be sold round trip—will not have a one-way fare shown).
CXRS	Carrier offering the fare
EFF	Effective date (if applicable, the first date that travel may begin from origin city)
EXP	Expiration date (if applicable, the last date that travel may begin from origin city)
TKT	Ticketing date (if applicable, the last date that the ticket may be purchased and issued at that fare)

```
BOSCRW    12 JUN00          USD
DL 1 / 0 / 4      NW  0 / 0 / 4      UA 0 / 0 / 4      US 2 / 0 / 12
PSGR FACILITY CHARGES MAY APPLY
PUBLISHED SELLING CURRENCY USD
```

	F/B	O/W	R/T	CXRS	EFF	EXP	TKT
1	ME21NR		408.00	US	-	-	-
2	ME21NR		408.00	NW	-	-	-
3	QE21NR		408.00	DL	-	-	-
4	HE21NR		408.00	UA	-	15JL	-
5	ME7NR		438.00	DL	01JU	-	-
6	ME7NR		438.00	UA	-	-	-
7	BE7NR		468.00	US	-	-	-
8	ME7NR		468.00	NW	-	-	-
9	Y8	359.00	698.00	US	-	-	-
10	Y06	349.00	698.00	DL	-	-	-
11	Y26	349.00	698.00	NW	-	-	-
12	F8	439.00	878.00	US	-	-	-
13	YUA	439.00	878.00	UA	-	-	15SE
14	F26	449.00	898.00	NW	-	-	-
15	F06	459.00	918.00	DL	-	-	-
16	FUA	519.00	1038.00	UA	-	-	15SE
17	Y	548.00	1096.00	US	-	-	-
18	Y	569.00	1138.00	DL	-	-	-
19	Y	569.00	1138.00	NW	-	-	-
20	Y	569.00	1138.00	UA	-	-	-
21	C	679.00	1358.00	DL	-	-	-
22	F	810.00	1620.00	US	-	-	-
23	F	829.00	1658.00	UA	-	-	-
24	F	839.00	1678.00	DL	-	-	-
25	F	839.00	1678.00	NW	-	-	-

Figure 3.15 *Fare scan display.*

AIRLINE TICKETING

Airline tickets are probably the documents most frequently issued by travel agencies for their customers. Ticket forms are printed and issued to travel agencies by the Airlines Reporting Corporation (ARC). They are called *universal ticket forms* since they can be used for all airlines. There are two general categories of tickets:

1. *Automated tickets.* The most common type of ticket issued to travelers is the **automated ticket/boarding pass (ATB).** This form combines an airline ticket with a boarding pass. The airline section is the left portion and the boarding pass is on the right.

2. *Manual tickets.* Manual forms are used when a handwritten ticket is required. Manual tickets are issued on an infrequent basis, usually when the computer is experiencing downtime and the ticket has to be completed right away for the traveler.

The ATB and manual ticketing form are each comprised of four types of coupons. The same information appears on each coupon; the difference is the distribution channel or to whom the coupon is sent after the ticket is completed:

1. *Auditor's coupon.* Send to the ARC on the weekly sales report.
2. *Agent's coupon.* Keep in agency's files.
3. *Flight coupon(s).* Give to passenger one flight coupon for each flight segment as an exchange for flights.
4. *Passenger's copy.* Give to passenger to use as a personal record or receipt.

To compare both types of ticket forms, Figure 3.16 shows a completed ATB and a manual ticket for the same client, John Roberts. His itinerary is a round trip on Delta Air Lines from Miami to Columbus, Ohio. His fare includes the base fare of $197.21 plus three taxes: U.S. transportation tax of $14.79 (code US), a segment tax in the total amount of $6.00 (code ZP), and a passenger facility charge in the amount of $3.00 (code XF). The fare-basis code is Y26, a discounted coach fare.

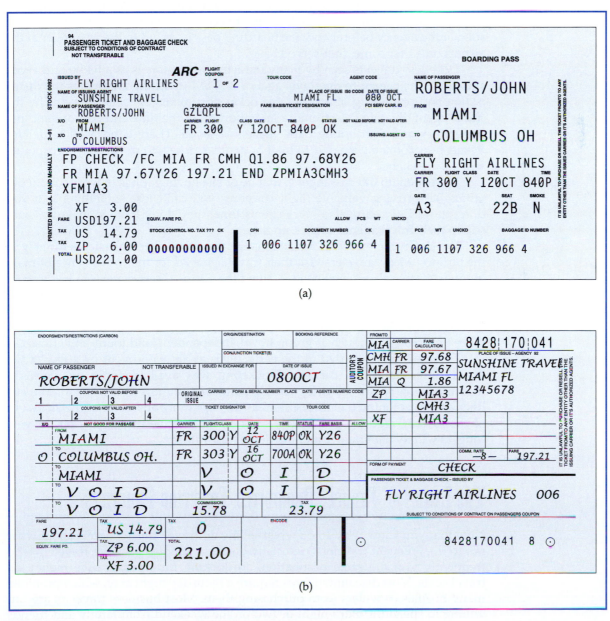

Figure 3.16 *(a) Airline ticket/boarding pass (ATB); (b) manual ticket.*

➤ Electronic Ticketing

Electronic ticketing (E-ticketing) or ticketless travel allows a travel agent to sell air transportation without issuing passenger flight coupons. The travel agent books the air reservation through the agency computer system. The ATB is also printed from the agency's computer but *only the auditor's coupon, agent's coupon, and passenger receipt coupon are generated*. The code ETKT is printed in the upper left corner of each coupon; this identifies it as an electronic ticket. The auditor's coupon is generated for sales reporting purposes, the agent's coupon is generated to maintain a record in the agency, and the passenger's receipt coupon is generated in case the traveler needs a copy of the transaction for his or her records. The agent also prints an automated invoice/itinerary for the passenger for his or her records.

When an agent books a reservation in the computer, it is identified by a unique reservation or confirmation number. When traveling without flight coupons, the passenger checks in at the airport and provides the confirmation number and a photo ID. With electronic ticketing the boarding pass is never issued at the agency beforehand; the boarding pass is issued to the passenger at the airport on a first-come, first-served basis.

Ticketless travel is seen by many industry professionals as a Jekyll and Hyde situation. The benefit to the travel agency is that E-ticketing eliminates the distribution and processing of accountable ticket documents or value coupons by the travel agent. By going electronic, a large portion of the time and cost of handling paperwork and distributing paper tickets is saved. There is no need to deliver tickets to corporate clients or to mail or express tickets to the agency's corporate and leisure clients.

The benefit to the passenger is that he or she no longer has to worry about obtaining or carrying valuable flight coupons; you can't lose something that you don't have! E-ticketing also saves clients time; they don't have to make an extra trip to their travel agency to pick up tickets.

The downside for travel agencies is the fear of losing some clients directly to the airlines. Many travelers visit their travel agencies for the convenience of making inexpensive air arrangements. Calling the airline direct may seem just as convenient with the same results: no need for an airline ticket; just pick up your boarding pass at the airport. The answer for many agents is to reduce dependence on the inexpensive domestic tickets, and work harder to develop and maintain more profitable sales, such as group travel, independent land tours, and cruises.

Ticketless travel started in the early 1990s as an experiment by a few of the major domestic airline carriers. E-ticketing was available only on short- to medium-range routes, allowing simple point-to-point fare construction. The airlines are streamlining the process, and as they get more and more of the kinks out of the system, industry professionals anticipate that the majority of airline passengers will fly paperless sometime in the near future.

THE ETHICS OF TRAVEL: PROHIBITED TICKETING PRACTICES

Now that you know what to do when selling air travel, this section is about what not to do. Frequent travelers, especially business people or leisure travelers who frequently visit the same destination, are looking for ways to save money on travel costs. Most discounted fares require a Saturday night stay, which prohibits many business travelers from purchasing them. Most business travelers are unwilling to spend the extra night or two on the weekend from family and friends just to take advantage of a low-cost advance-purchase ticket.

To avoid paying full-fare prices, travelers discovered a loophole called *back-to-back ticketing*. In the past it was common practice to issue back-to-back tickets for frequent travelers when they requested them. However, times have changed, and although back-to-back and other types of ticketing loopholes are not prohibited by law, *they are strictly banned by the airlines*. Travelers are required to pay the difference between the back-to-back ticket price and the full coach fare when they show up for their flights. Or if the ticket was booked through a travel agency, the agency receives a debit memo or a bill for the additional cost.

Here's how it works. Let's say that a person travels frequently between Los Angeles and New York. A full-fare ticket is around $2,000 round trip. A Saturday-night-stay ticket may be as low as $600 round trip. So the back-to-backer buys the following two tickets, for a total of $1,200 instead of $4,000 for two full-fare tickets:

- Ticket 1:
    a. *First coupon:* Los Angeles to New York, Tuesday March 1
    b. *Second coupon:* New York to Los Angeles, Thursday March 24
- Ticket 2:
    c. *First coupon:* New York to Los Angeles, Thursday, March 3
    d. *Second coupon:* Los Angeles to New York, Tuesday March 22

To make two Los Angeles–New York round-trip tickets requiring no Saturday night stay, you combine part A of ticket 1 with part C of ticket 2; and then combine part D of ticket 2 with part B of ticket 1 to form a second round-trip ticket. In this scenario, the traveler saves about $1,800. Even if he or she made a change and incurred a change fee (approximately $75), the passenger still comes out ahead.

Some passengers may use the *throwaway ticketing* option. The traveler would use only one round-trip ticket (just use parts A and C) and throw out the unused coupons. The airlines also prohibit throwaway ticketing in their rules, which specifically prohibit both back-to-back and throwaway ticketing.

Another loophole is using a *hidden city*. The passenger is ticketed to a city that has a lower fare than that of the intended destination. Here's an example. A passenger wishes to fly from Detroit to Dallas, Texas. The one-way fare is $500. However, the fare to El Paso is less expensive: $350. The passenger is ticketed on a connection from Detroit to El Paso at $350, with a connection through Dallas. When the flight arrives at the connection in Dallas, the passenger deplanes and goes on his or her way; the continuing ticket coupon to El Paso is not used and thrown away. Of course, this works only if there is no baggage checked through to the ticketing city of El Paso. But for business travelers with just carry-on luggage, this was not a problem. Like back-to-back, hidden-city ticketing is prohibited by the airlines; both the passenger and the travel agency are held financially liable if these practices are discovered by the airline.

Often, travel-savvy clients will ask their travel agents to save them money by booking back-to-back or hidden-city tickets. These and similar practices are strictly prohibited by the airlines and should be handled by travel professionals in an ethical and responsible manner.

Close-Up: Airline-Related Careers

Reservation agent	Airport ticket agent	Sales and ticket office agents
Sales representative	Customer service agent	

There are many types of career opportunities with airlines. The majority of entry-level positions are in reservation centers and airports.

Reservation Agent

Reservation agents work in major airline reservation centers; each center may have up to 500 reservation agents employed. Reservation agents primarily receive calls from the general public and from travel agents. They review flight schedules from their computer screens, book flights, and provide travel-related information such as prices and ticketing requirements. Most of their work is over the telephone and on the computer.

Standard requirements for a reservation agent are speed and efficiency on the airline computer system, effective and clear telephone voice, patience, and a genuine willingness to help customers. In many cases, airline agents are evaluated on the number of calls and bookings completed within a period of time.

Since airline reservation centers operate practically 24 hours a day every day of the week throughout the year, there are opportunities for both part-time and full-time work. A workday is divided into day and evening shifts. Beginning reservation agents usually are assigned a shift for the first several months. Only after they have reached a certain level of seniority are they able to bid or select the shift hours they want to work.

Airline reservation agents starting out are compensated at the same level or a little higher than that of entry-level travel agents.

Ticket Agent/Customer Service Agent

Ticket and customer service agents work behind the counter at airports or city ticket offices in downtown areas. They work with the airline's customers and passengers directly, book flights, and write and change tickets. Customer service agents or ground agents work at airports primarily at the gate areas. Their principal duties include announcing flights, completing check-in of flights, and helping with passenger boarding.

Airline Sales Representative

These positions are not typically entry level and require some experience in airline sales, ticketing, or travel agency work. Sales reps are assigned a territory or region of the United States. They are required to make periodic sales calls to the travel agencies that fall within their regions to promote the airline's flight services to their clients. They are also called upon to solve problems, such as clearing space for the agency's VIP clients, or serving as a liaison between the agency and the airline to solve disputes such as refunds. This type of position requires extensive traveling plus excellent selling and customer service skills. The rep must also be thoroughly knowledgeable of the airline, fares, special promotions, schedules, and related services products, such as tours and hotels.

➤ Key Terms

- airline clubs
- airport codes
- Airlines Reporting Corporation (ARC)
- automated ticket/ boarding pass (ATB)
- area settlement plan
- base fare
- bumping
- certified carrier
- charter flights
- circle trip
- city codes
- classes of service
- code sharing
- commercial flight
- commission cap
- commuter airline
- configuration
- connecting city
- connecting flight
- controlled-inventory basis
- denied boarding compensation
- destination
- direct flight
- dual-designated carriers
- electronic fare rules
- electronic ticketing
- fare-type code

- feeder airline
- frequent-flyer program
- hub
- inbound sector
- intermediate city
- International Air Transport Association (IATA)
- International Airlines Travel Agent Network (IATAN)

- joint fare
- narrow-body aircraft
- nonstop flight
- one way
- open jaw
- origin
- outbound sector
- outward destination
- overbooking
- override

- point-to-point fare
- regional airline
- round trip
- seat map
- seat pitch
- stopover city
- through fare
- trunk carrier
- wide-body aircraft

Flashback   Of all the major events that have taken place in the last century, the growth of commercial aviation has had one of the most dramatic impacts on everyday living. Today, air travel is considered the backbone of the retail travel industry. No matter what the travel professional sells—a hotel, land package, or a cruise—an airline ticket is usually sold along with it!

Travel professionals have to learn a different language, the language of airline industry codes and terms that are used when booking air transportation and pricing tickets. Agents need to know, by memory, hundreds of city, airport, and airline codes. They also need to understand terminology that describes the various types of aircraft, flight services, and air journeys.

As a travel professional in training, you need to become acquainted with the many industry resources and how to interpret their information correctly. An understanding of your resources is needed when you qualify clients for the best flights and air fares. In addition to the agency computer reservations systems, two useful airline resources are the *Official Airline Guide* and *Travel Planners*. Along with using these resources, you need to ask clients the right questions: the "who, what, where, when, and how" of air travel.

Deregulation of the domestic airline industry occurred in 1978. The most dramatic effect is the proliferation of air discounts due to the increase in competition among airlines. This has certainly benefited the traveling public because of the many types of discount fares and special programs that are available to them. Two popular methods of discounting tickets are through the use of airline coupons and negotiated fares. Other ways that airlines try to win customer loyalty are through frequent-flyer award programs and airline clubs that provide special services for their frequent travelers.

The last step in the sales process—generating airline tickets—has progressed from the old-fashioned handwritten format to automated documents called the automated ticket/boarding pass (ATB). Although some tickets are still handwritten, the great majority are generated by computer. In fact, the airlines have gone one step further by introducing electronic ticketing (E-ticketing). This enables travel sales agents to make air reservations without requiring the passenger to carry paper flight coupons. E-ticketing started as an experiment on just a few domestic carriers on short point-to-point routes. It is now becoming more frequent. In fact, many industry professionals predict that paperless will be the only way to fly in the future. Time will tell!

CHAPTER REVIEW

1. Decode (write the full city and state name).

   A. SAT _____   I. CVG _____
   B. SDF _____   J. BNA _____
   C. DAB _____   K. MSY _____
   D. PBI _____   L. SLC _____
   E. EWR _____   M. CMH _____
   F. DAY _____   N. FAI _____
   G. DSM _____   O. CLT _____
   H. CRW _____   P. RNO _____

2. Encode (write the city code).

   A. Dallas/Ft. Worth, Texas ____   I. Baltimore, Maryland ____
   B. Las Vegas, Nevada ____   J. Tucson, Arizona ____
   C. New York City ____   K. Honolulu, Hawaii ____
   D. San Diego, California ____   L. Seattle, Washington ____
   E. Washington, DC ____   M. Palm Springs, California ____
   F. Tampa, Florida ____   N. Portland, Oregon ____
   G. San Francisco, California ____   O. Minneapolis/St. Paul ____
   H. Los Angeles, California ____   P. Charleston, South Carolina ____

3. Encode (write the airport code).

   A. New York City–LaGuardia ____   F. Washington–National ____
   B. Washington–Dulles ____   G. Detroit–Wayne County ____
   C. Kansas City–International ____   H. Houston–Intercontinental ____
   D. Orlando–International ____   I. Houston–Hobby ____
   E. New York–Kennedy ____   J. Dallas/Ft. Worth–International ____

4. Encode (write the airline code).

   A. American Airlines ____   G. America West ____
   B. Trans World Airlines ____   H. Continental Airlines ____
   C. US Airways ____   I. Delta Air Lines ____
   D. Midway Airlines ____   J. Air Canada ____
   E. Northwest ____   K. Alaska Airlines ____
   F. Southwest Airlines ____   L. United Airlines ____

Multiple Choice

Circle the *best* answer.

5. Nonscheduled flights that can be sold either publicly or privately are:

   A. certified   D. charter
   B. trunk   E. regional
   C. commuter

6. Which of the following is not a wide-body jet aircraft?

    A. 757   D. 777

    B. 767   E. D10

    C. L11

7. The type of airline that flies short distances and usually operates small aircraft that seat between 12 and 40 passengers is:

    A. supplemental   D. commercial

    B. commuter   E. charter

    C. trunk

8. The class of service code for standard coach seats is:

    A. S   D. B

    B. C   E. F

    C. Y

9. Another name for a number of seats on an aircraft that are set aside by the airline to be sold at discounted prices is:

    A. seat assignments   D. waitlist priority

    B. group discount program   E. controlled inventory

    C. preferred supplier inventory

10. The type of aircraft that is referred to as a "jumbo" jet, which has a second deck for additional passenger seating is:

    A. M80   D. 767

    B. AB3   E. 777

    C. 747

11. The entity that approves new travel agencies to sell domestic airline tickets to the general public is the:

    A. Air Transportation   D. Airlines Reporting Corporation
       Association   E. Department of Transportation

    B. Air Travel Agent
       Network

    C. Federal Aviation Association

12. The process that allows the travel agent to sell air transportation without issuing passenger flight coupons is:

    A. ATB ticketing   D. discount coupon ticketing

    B. manual ticketing   E. frequent-flyer coupons

    C. electronic ticketing

13. The process by which travel agencies report and distribute sales from ticket transactions to ARC participating carriers is:

    A. code-sharing agreements   D. ticket settlement report

    B. airline ticket settlement   E. area settlement plan

    C. airline ticket account

14. The fare-type code that designates a nonrefundable excursion fare to be booked in Q class, for which the ticket must be purchased within 7 days is:

    A. QL7P   D. YQE7

    B. ME7NQ   E. Q7Y

    C. QE7N

True or False?

_____ 15. Free baggage allowance in North America is based on the weight system.

_____ 16. The Department of Transportation (DOT) requires airlines to ask passengers to give up their seats on a voluntary basis with compensation if the airplane is oversold.

_____ 17. A connecting city on a domestic air itinerary is one where the passenger changes planes within four hours.

_____ 18. A direct flight is the most convenient type of air service since it flies direct and nonstop between two cities.

_____ 19. When booking flights the travel agent should contact the first major carrier flown regardless of the number of airlines participating in the itinerary.

_____ 20. Overbooking is a common practice of domestic airlines to avoid lost revenue due to last-minute cancellations and no-shows.

Short-Answers and Fill-ins

21. Answer the questions below based on the following air itinerary:

    ATL–HOU–LAS–MKC–MEM–ATL

    Write the full name(s) of the:
    A. origin city   _____
    B. destination   _____
    C. outward destination _____
    D. outbound sector cities _____
    E. inbound sector cities _____

22. Define each routing below as either R, round trip; C, circle trip; O, one way; J, open jaw.
    A. DEN (AA) CHI (AA) ABQ   ____
    B. PIT (US) DSM (DL) PIT   ____
    C. SEA (UA) PDX (TW) RNO   ____
    D. BOS (UA) NYC (UA) LAX (UA) NYC (UA) BOS   ____

23. When making an airline reservation by either telephone or computer, flight data must be entered in a specific sequence. Unscramble the flight data below into the correct sequence.

    travel date–class of service–flight number–number in party–airline–routing

    1. _____   4. _____
    2. _____   5. _____
    3. _____   6. _____

24. Name the travel publication issued in three editions that includes city maps, airport diagrams, destination facts, and hotel information.

    _____

25. The flight service that entails a change of plane and flight number with the same airline is called a(n) _____ connection.

Chapter 4

International Air Travel

· ·

Fast Forward ▼

➤ Travel professionals advise their foreign-bound clients about required travel documents such as passports, visas, and tourist cards, in addition to health and immunization protection. . . .165

➤ All items purchased or received as gifts while traveling in foreign countries must be declared to the U.S. Customs Service. . . . 172

➤ Questions regarding currency exchange rates, where to change money, and the safest ways to carry money while traveling abroad are major concerns of international travelers. . . . 177

➤ A major responsibility is advising clients, especially first-time international travelers, about foreign airport arrival and departure procedures and recommendations for ground transportation services at the destination. . . . 180

➤ IATA is a worldwide trade organization whose main functions are to promote a standard and unified system of worldwide air travel and through its subsidiary IATAN to appoint and regulate travel agencies to sell international air travel. . . . 183

➤ IATA and the international carriers have divided the world into three traffic conference areas. . . . 184

➤ Travel professionals should know, by memory, the major international flagship carriers, their codes, and their country affiliations. . . . 185

➤ It is important that travel consultants and sales agents identify the major city and airport codes by memory to increase efficiency and maintain accuracy when booking international travel. . . . 187

➤ Two important printed resources when planning international trips are the *Worldwide Official Airline Guide* and the international *Travel Planner* editions. . . . 201

➤ Since a high degree of standardization is required when working with international fares, taxes, and fees, International Standard Organization (ISO) codes are used to identify currencies and countries throughout the world. . . . 205

➤ The two major types of taxes and fees that are applicable to international airline tickets are transportation departure taxes and federal inspection fees. Knowing what they are and when to apply them is important. . . . 206

➤ The best way to organize the maze of international air fares is to categorize them into five general types: normal, restricted normal, standard excursion, advance-purchase excursion, and nonrefundable. . . . 208

➤ Consolidators are companies that contract with the airlines to buy airline seats in bulk and sell them at discount prices. They represent some of the best "deals" in discount travel. . . . 209

➤ All international fares are calculated by one of two methods: mileage or routing. The type of fare determines which system to use. . . . 210

➤ Crazy-sounding things like NUC ("Nuke"), ROE, MPM, TPM, HIP, and CTM all play a part in calculating international air fares. . . . 210

➤ How to read fare displays from printed air tariff publications and the airline computer reservation systems is important when servicing international clients. . . . 216

Introduction

The world is getting smaller. A trip that once took months to undertake with sailing ships and land caravans now takes a matter of several hours in today's high-speed jet travel. What seemed unobtainable a mere century ago is now commonplace; people are able to travel from one day to the next day in a blink of an eye as they cross the International Date Line at more than 650 miles per hour! Nonstop flights between the United States and the far reaches of Asia and beyond are possible with lighter, more fuel-efficient aircraft.

Taking a vacation for a week or two to such places as Europe or Asia was out of reach of most Americans a mere half-century ago. This has changed dramatically, due to the proliferation of airlines, new routes, and discounted fares. New and exciting destinations are now possible to visit due to political and social change. Such places as the former Soviet Union, China, and eastern Germany are now commonplace destinations for vacationers and business travelers alike.

Travel professionals have to provide up-to-date and accurate information for all of their travelers. They have to be able to provide a wide variety of information, ranging from the best air fare between Pittsburgh and Miami to travel requirements in Beijing, China, or health precautions when traveling to Calcutta, India.

The number of international travelers is growing every year. This is due to the relative ease of traveling long distances and the highly competitive airline, tour, and cruise market, which results in more affordable prices for more people.

The travel professional needs to expand his or her knowledge to include transportation and destinations worldwide.

This chapter begins with a description of some of the travel documentation, health precaution measures, and related information necessary when traveling to foreign lands. Then a study of the language of international air travel: the most important codes and terminology used by industry professionals. You will become familiar with some of the printed resources that are used to research international travel information, including flight schedules, destination facts, and air fares.

There is a vast difference between domestic and international ticket pricing. International fare calculation can be quite complex and should be left to the expert rate agents trained and hired by the airlines. However, the sales agent must be familiar with the basics of how an international ticket is priced, to service clients more efficiently. A good understanding of domestic air travel (Chapter 3) makes the process of advising clients traveling worldwide much easier.

INTERNATIONAL TRAVEL REQUIREMENTS

➤ Passports

A **passport** is a federal government document which proves that the bearer is a citizen of that country. It authorizes the bearer to travel outside the country of origin and to return to it. A passport is issued to one person only; for a family traveling together, each member must have his or her own document.

Types of Passports

There are three types of passports, depending on who the traveler is and the purpose of the trip:

1. *Regular passports:* the most common, issued to leisure and business travelers. These passports have a blue cover (the green-cover passports issued up to a few years ago are still valid and do not need to be replaced until the normal expiration date).
2. *Official passports:* issued to government employees traveling on government business only. These passports have a maroon cover.
3. *Diplomatic passports:* issued to members of the diplomatic and consular corps. These passports have a black cover.

How to Apply for a Passport

To obtain a passport you need the following:

- Completed passport application (Figure 4.1)
- Proof of citizenship (any one of the following):
  - Expired passport (if renewal)
  - Certified birth certificate (with official raised seal)
  - Certificate of naturalization
  - Other (if expired passport or certified birth certificate is not available): baptismal certificate, hospital certificate, affidavits of persons with personal knowledge of birth

UNITED STATES DEPARTMENT OF STATE

APPLICATION FOR ☐ PASSPORT ☐ REGISTRATION

SEE INSTRUCTIONS—TYPE OR PRINT IN INK IN WHITE AREAS

1. NAME FIRST NAME   MIDDLE NAME

LAST NAME

2. MAILING ADDRESS

STREET

CITY, STATE, ZIP CODE

COUNTRY   IN CARE OF

☐ 5 Yr.   ☐ 10 Yr.   Issue

R   D   O   DP   Date _____

End.# _____   Exp. _____

3. SEX	4. PLACE OF BIRTH City, State or Province, Country	5. DATE OF BIRTH	6. SEE FEDERAL TAX LAW NOTICE ON REVERSE SIDE	SOCIAL SECURITY NUMBER
Male Female		Mo. Day Year		

7. HEIGHT	8. COLOR OF HAIR	9. COLOR OF EYES	10. (Area Code) HOME PHONE	11. (Area Code) BUSINESS PHONE
Feet Inches	12. PERMANENT ADDRESS (Street, City, State, ZIP Code)			13. OCCUPATION

FOLD

14. FATHER'S NAME	BIRTHPLACE	BIRTH DATE	U.S. CITIZEN ☐ YES ☐ NO	16. TRAVEL PLANS *(Not Mandatory)*
				COUNTRIES DEPARTURE DATE
15. MOTHER'S MAIDEN NAME	BIRTHPLACE	BIRTH DATE	U.S. CITIZEN ☐ YES ☐ NO	LENGTH OF STAY

17. HAVE YOU EVER BEEN ISSUED A U.S. PASSPORT? YES ☐   NO ☐   IF YES, SUBMIT PASSPORT IF AVAILABLE.   ☐ Submitted

IF UNABLE TO SUBMIT MOST RECENT PASSPORT, STATE ITS DISPOSITION: COMPLETE NEXT LINE

NAME IN WHICH ISSUED   PASSPORT NUMBER   ISSUE DATE (Mo., Day, Yr.)   DISPOSITION

SUBMIT TWO RECENT IDENTICAL PHOTOS

FROM 1" TO 1-3/8"

2" × 2"

FOLD

18. HAVE YOU EVER BEEN MARRIED? ☐ YES   ☐ NO   DATE OF MOST RECENT MARRIAGE   Mo. Day Year

WIDOWED/DIVORCED? ☐ YES   ☐ NO   IF YES, GIVE DATE   Mo. Day Year

SPOUSE'S FULL BIRTH NAME   SPOUSE'S BIRTHPLACE

19. IN CASE OF EMERGENCY, NOTIFY *(Person Not Traveling With You)*   RELATIONSHIP
(Not Mandatory)

FULL NAME

ADDRESS   (Area Code) PHONE NUMBER

20. TO BE COMPLETED BY AN APPLICANT WHO BECAME A CITIZEN THROUGH NATURALIZATION

I IMMIGRATED TO THE U.S. (Month, Year)	I RESIDED CONTINUOUSLY IN THE U.S. From (Mo., Yr.) To (Mo., Yr.)	DATE NATURALIZED (Mo., Day, Yr.)
		PLACE

21. DO NOT SIGN APPLICATION UNTIL REQUESTED TO DO SO BY PERSON ADMINISTERING OATH

I have not, since acquiring United States citizenship, performed any of the acts listed under "Acts or Conditions" on the reverse of this application form (unless explanatory statement is attached). I solemnly swear (or affirm) that the statements made on this application are true and the photograph attached is a true likeness of me.

Subscribed and sworn to (affirmed) before me   (SEAL)

Month Day Year

X _____

☐ Clerk of Court or
☐ PASSPORT Agent
☐ Postal Employee
☐ (Vice) Consul USA At _____

(Signature of person authorized to accept application)

(Sign in presence of person authorized to accept application)

22. APPLICANT'S IDENTIFYING DOCUMENTS ☐ PASSPORT ☐ DRIVER'S LICENSE ☐ OTHER (Specify)

ISSUE DATE	EXPIRATION DATE	PLACE OF ISSUE	No.
Month Day Year	Month Day Year		ISSUED IN THE NAME OF

23. FOR ISSUING OFFICE USE ONLY (Applicant's evidence of citizenship)

☐ Birth Cert.   SR   CR   City   Filed/Issued:
☐ Passport   Bearer's Name:
☐ Report of Birth
☐ Naturalization/Citizenship Cert.   No.:
☐ Other:
☐ Seen & Returned
☐ Attached

APPLICATION APPROVAL

Examiner Name

Office, Date

24.

FEE _____ EXEC. _____ POST _____

FORM DSP-11 (12-87)   (SEE INSTRUCTIONS ON REVERSE)   Form Approved OMB No. 1405-0004 (Exp. 8/1/89)

Figure 4.1 *Passport application.*

- Photographs (two identical passport-type photos taken within six months of passport application)
- Proof of Identity (any document with applicant's signature and a physical description or picture)
- Application fee (subject to change)

Applicant	Fee	Validity
Adult (first-time applicant)	$60	10 years
Adult (renewal)	$40	10 years
Child (under 16 yrs)	$40	5 years

Where to Apply

Applications may be obtained at any of the following locations:

- Selected post offices
- Clerk of federal or state courts designated to accept passport applications
- Any one of thirteen passport agencies located in the following cities: Boston, Chicago, Honolulu, Houston, Los Angeles, Miami, New Orleans, New York, Philadelphia, San Francisco, Seattle, Stamford (Connecticut), or Washington, DC

Applying by Mail

To apply for a passport through the mail, the applicant must be in compliance with the following two rules:

1. Applicant must have had a previous passport issued within the past twelve years.
2. Applicant's previous passport must have been issued when applicant was 18 years or older.

➤ Visas

A **visa** is an endorsement or stamp that is placed by a government official or is in the form of a separate document that is usually obtained in advance of a trip. A visa permits the traveler to enter into another country. Some (not all) foreign countries require a visa. Generally speaking, visas are not required of U.S. citizens traveling to most western European countries for a short period of time. They are required for some countries located in Africa, the Middle East, Asia, and the Pacific region.

A visa does not bear the traveler's name but will indicate the conditions under which the traveler may enter the country. For example, visas will indicate the period of time that the traveler may stay in the country. If travelers wish to extend their stay, visas can often be renewed without leaving the foreign country.

In addition to a tourist visa for the vacation traveler, students who travel to a foreign country to study for a semester or a full academic year usually need a student visa. Business travelers visiting for the sole purpose of conducting business may require a business visa.

It is important to remember that not all foreign countries require a visa. These requirements should be checked on a client-by-client basis.

How to Apply for a Visa

As a separate document, a visa may be obtained from a consular representative either directly or through a visa service agency in the United States before trip departure. A visa service should be used when obtaining two or more visas. Visa service agencies are located in major cities throughout the Untied States. The U.S. cities that offer visa service locations include New York, Atlanta, Boston, Chicago, Denver, Dallas, Los Angeles, San Francisco, Seattle, and Washington, DC. Visas usually take from two to six weeks to process. The following items are required when obtaining a visa as a separate document:

- Valid passport
- Visa application
- Photo(s) (only if required)
- Visa fee (varies by country)

➤ Tourist Cards

A **tourist card** is similar to a visa because it serves as permission to enter a foreign country. The tourist card shows the name of the traveler and the purpose of traveling to that country. The information on tourist cards is generally used by governments to study travel patterns and statistics of foreign travelers into that country.

The following items are required to obtain a tourist card:

- Application form
- Proof of citizenship
- Fee (amount varies and is not required by some countries)

The following agencies/locations can provide application forms and process tourist cards:

- Airline providing transportation
- Tourist office
- Consulate
- Embassy

Key Point ➤ Mexico is the country for which U.S. travel agents are most likely to issue tourist cards.

✓ Check Your Understanding 4-1

1. What is the purpose of a passport?

   _____

2. How many people can be included on one U.S. passport? _____
3. State the passport fee for:
   A. an adult (first-time applicant) _____
   B. a child (under 16) _____
   C. an adult (renewal) _____

4. In addition to the application fee, list four other documents or items required to obtain a U.S. passport.

    A. _____

    B. _____

    C. _____

    D. _____

5. State the validity or period (years) before expiration for:

    A. an adult passport (first time)   _____

    B. an adult passport (renewal)   _____

    C. a child passport (under 16)   _____

6. Which of the following is not considered to be proof of citizenship?

    A. expired passport   C. driver's license

    B. baptismal certificate   D. certified birth certificate

7. What two conditions must be met when applying for a passport through the mail?

    A. _____

    B. _____

8. Name the three types of U.S. passports. Can you also remember the color of each for identification purposes?

    A. _____   Color? _____

    B. _____   Color? _____

    C. _____   Color? _____

9. Name the four items that are required when one is applying for a visa.

    A. _____

    B. _____

    C. _____

    D. _____

10. When should a visa service or agency be used?

    _____

11. Name three types of visas.

    A. _____

    B. _____

    C. _____

12. What is a tourist card?

    _____

13. To which country that requires tourist cards is a U.S. travel agent most likely to send clients?

    _____

14. Name four places where you can obtain a tourist card.

    A. _____

    B. _____

    C. _____

    D. _____

➤ Health and Immunization Documents

The issue of health and protection against certain diseases becomes very important when traveling to certain parts of the world. Many diseases, such as cholera and yellow fever, have been controlled completely in the United States. However, when visiting destinations where these diseases are still active, international travelers may endanger their health and the health of their fellow citizens upon their return home. These diseases can be prevented by vaccination. Therefore, the **World Health Organization (WHO)** has established regulations regarding immunization for travelers to certain countries and areas that are still threatened by cholera or yellow fever. In addition, WHO may suggest preventive measures against malaria when traveling to areas that are still threatened by this disease.

International travelers required to have immunizations must record vaccination(s) or other preventive measures taken in a document called the **international certificate of vaccination** (Figure 4.2). This document is issued by the World Health Organization and is accepted as the approved format by all members of the United Nations. These yellow booklets, called *shot cards*, become valid only with a doctor's signature or public health stamp. Some travel agencies keep their own supply on hand for their clients.

Generally speaking, U.S. travelers visiting destinations within Canada, the

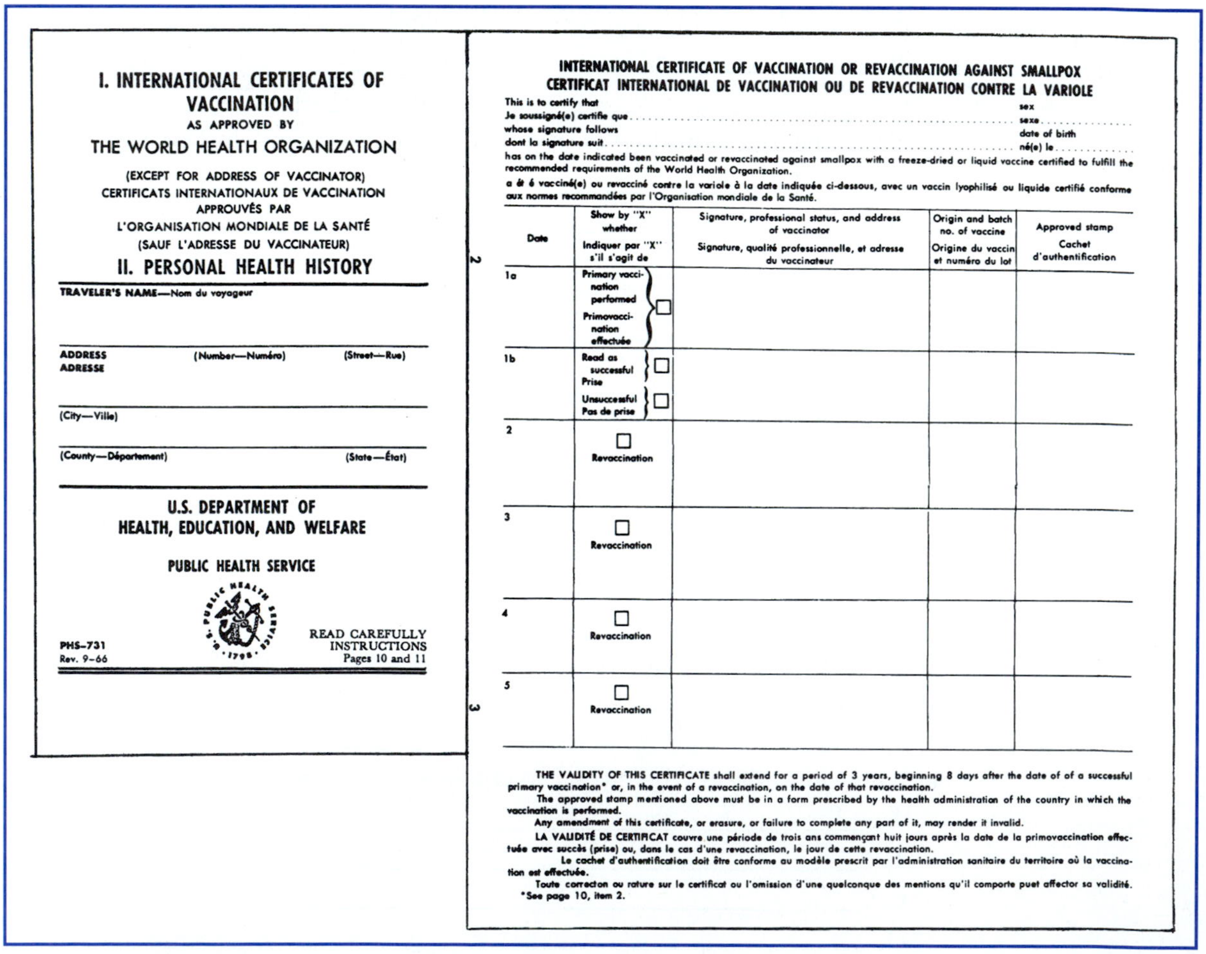

I. INTERNATIONAL CERTIFICATES OF VACCINATION
AS APPROVED BY
THE WORLD HEALTH ORGANIZATION
(EXCEPT FOR ADDRESS OF VACCINATOR)
CERTIFICATS INTERNATIONAUX DE VACCINATION
APPROUVÉS PAR
L'ORGANISATION MONDIALE DE LA SANTÉ
(SAUF L'ADRESSE DU VACCINATEUR)

II. PERSONAL HEALTH HISTORY

TRAVELER'S NAME—Nom du voyageur

ADDRESS / ADRESSE (Number—Numéro) (Street—Rue)

(City—Ville)

(County—Département) (State—État)

U.S. DEPARTMENT OF HEALTH, EDUCATION, AND WELFARE

PUBLIC HEALTH SERVICE

PHS-731
Rev. 9-66

READ CAREFULLY INSTRUCTIONS Pages 10 and 11

INTERNATIONAL CERTIFICATE OF VACCINATION OR REVACCINATION AGAINST SMALLPOX
CERTIFICAT INTERNATIONAL DE VACCINATION OU DE REVACCINATION CONTRE LA VARIOLE

This is to certify that / Je soussigné(e) certifie que .... sex / sexe ....
whose signature follows / dont la signature suit .... date of birth / né(e) le ....
has on the date indicated been vaccinated or revaccinated against smallpox with a freeze-dried or liquid vaccine certified to fulfill the recommended requirements of the World Health Organization.
a ét é vacciné(e) ou revacciné contre la variole à la date indiquée ci-dessous, avec un vaccin lyophilisé ou liquide certifié conforme aux normes recommandées par l'Organisation mondiale de la Santé.

Date	Show by "X" whether / Indiquer par "X" s'il s'agit de	Signature, professional status, and address of vaccinator / Signature, qualité professionnelle, et adresse du vaccinateur	Origin and batch no. of vaccine / Origine du vaccin et numéro du lot	Approved stamp / Cachet d'authentification
1a	Primary vaccination performed / Primovaccination effectuée ☐			
1b	Read as successful / Prise ☐ Unsuccessful / Pas de prise ☐			
2	☐ Revaccination			
3	☐ Revaccination			
4	☐ Revaccination			
5	☐ Revaccination			

THE VALIDITY OF THIS CERTIFICATE shall extend for a period of 3 years, beginning 8 days after the date of of a successful primary vaccination* or, in the event of a revaccination, on the date of that revaccination.
The approved stamp mentioned above must be in a form prescribed by the health administration of the country in which the vaccination is performed.
Any amendment of this certificate, or erasure, or failure to complete any part of it, may render it invalid.
LA VALIDITÉ DE CERTIFICAT couvre une période de trois ans commençant huit jours après la date de la primovaccination effectuée avec succès (prise) ou, dans le cas d'une revaccination, le jour de cette revaccination.
Le cachet d'authentification doit être conforme au modèle prescrit par l'administration sanitaire du territoire où la vaccination est effectuée.
Toute correcton ou rature sur le certificat ou l'omission d'une quelconque des mentions qu'il comporte puet affector sa validité.
*See page 10, item 2.

Figure 4.2 *International certificate of vaccination.*

West Indies, or western Europe are not required to receive vaccinations for these diseases. Travelers visiting countries outside these areas should check with the Department of State regarding their itinerary. Vaccination and other health requirements are contingent on the countries the traveler will visit, and these requirements are subject to change.

As of this writing, specific countries in Central America, South America, Africa, and the Pacific areas are considered to be infected areas. Some examples of infected countries are: in Central America: El Salvador, Guatemala, and Panama; in South America: Bolivia, Colombia, and Peru; in Africa: Tanzania, Kenya, and Nigeria; and in the Pacific: China, India, and Vietnam.

Key Point ➤ Travel agents and other industry professionals are not medical doctors! They should never offer advice to their clients regarding preventive measures such as drugs or other medical aids. They always recommend that their clients seek health and medical advice from a physician.

➤ International Driver's Permit

Any person who rents and drives an automobile in another country is required to have a valid driver's license. However, many countries either recommend or require visitors to obtain an **international driver's permit (IDP).** This document, written in nine languages and recognized internationally, is valid for one full year from the date of issue. The purpose of the IDP is to facilitate official procedures in case of an automobile accident or other emergency while abroad.

Travel professionals usually recommend that their clients obtain an IDP, even if the countries they are visiting do not require it. An IDP can be obtained on the spot at any American Automobile Association (AAA) agency. The requirements are:

- Valid U.S. driver's license
- Two passport-sized photos
- $10 fee

Key Point ➤ The IDP is not valid in the country of issue; that is, it is not valid in the United States itself if issued here.

✓ Check Your Understanding 4-2

1. Name the organization that provides regulations regarding vaccination and other health requirements for international travelers.

   _____

2. Name the two serious diseases that are still active in certain parts of the world for which vaccinations are required.

   A. _____   B. _____

3. The document used to record required vaccination(s) for international travelers is called a shot card or _____.

4. Shot cards become valid with either of these two items. Name them:

   A. _____   B. _____

5. Name three international areas or regions where a shot card is not ordinarily required for U.S. travelers.

   A. _____   B. _____

   C. _____

6. What does IDP stand for?

   _____

7. Where is an IDP obtained?

   _____

8. List the three items required to obtain an IDP:

   A. _____   B. _____

   C. _____

9. A U.S. tourist can use an IDP anywhere in the world except in _____.

CUSTOMS REGULATIONS

You've heard the old saying "nothing in life is free;" well, that certainly applies to purchases that you bring home from abroad. All items either purchased or received as gifts while traveling abroad must be declared to the U.S. Customs Service upon return home. Every country in the world, including the United States, limits the value and kinds of items and goods that can be brought back into the country. If the traveler exceeds these limits, a duty or tax is charged based on the amount that exceeds the allowance; up to the limits, the goods are *duty-free*. In addition to a dollar limitation on all items purchased or received as gifts, the U.S. Customs Service also limits the amount of tobacco and liquor products that can be brought into the country.

► Customs Allowances

Customs allowances or limits are different when returning from different parts of the world. Travel agents advise their clients of these allowances so there won't be any nasty surprises upon their return. U.S. citizens are required to pass through customs and immigration clearance at the first point of entry into the United States. For example, a returning traveler is flying home on a connecting flight from Madrid to the final destination of Houston, Texas. He is making a connection in New York. Where does the traveler pass through customs and immigration? The first point of entry, New York, in this example.

Web Link

What's in that Suitcase? How do you make sure travelers aren't asked to pay duty on that new Japanese camera they brought from home? Or, how can salespeople travel with merchandise samples? Can you bring Cuban cigars into the United States if purchased outside Cuba? These answers, and more, are at this U.S. Treasury site. Point your browser at *http://www.customs.treas.gov*

► What Must Be Declared

International travelers must declare the following when passing through customs and immigration:

- All items purchased or acquired abroad
- Items brought home at another person's request
- Gifts presented to the traveler while abroad

TABLE 4.1   CUSTOM ALLOWANCE CHART

AMOUNT THAT IS DUTY FREE	RETURNING TO THE UNITED STATES FROM THESE AREAS:			
	Puerto Rico	*U.S. Virgin Islands, American Samoa, Guam*	*Foreign West Indies/ Central America*	*Balance of the World*
Value of goods	Unlimited	$1,200	$600	$400
Liquor	Unlimited	5 liters (plus 1 if produced in U.S.V.I.)	1 liter	1 liter
Tobacco	Unlimited	Standard: 1 carton of cigarettes and 1 box of cigars		

Articles totaling $400, $600, or $1,200, depending on your trip destinations, may be entered free of duty, subject to the limitations on alcoholic beverages, cigarette, and cigars. Table 4.1 is a reference chart showing the duty-free allowances when returning from these four areas: (1) Puerto Rico, (2) U.S. Virgin Islands and all U.S. possessions throughout the world (e.g., American Samoa, Guam), (3) the foreign West Indies (Bermuda, Bahamas, and the balance of the Caribbean Islands) plus Central America, and (4) the rest of the world. These custom allowances are per person, and children and infants are entitled to the the same allowances (except for alcoholic beverages).

Key Point ➤ *North American Free Trade Agreement (NAFTA): NAFTA was implemented on January 1, 1994. U.S. residents returning from Canada or Mexico are eligible for free or reduced duty rates on certain goods (as defined by NAFTA) in either country. For more information about NAFTA-originating goods, contact the NAFTA center at (972) 574-4061.*

➤ How the Traveler Declares

Before landing or arriving back in the United States, all passengers complete a customs declaration form. These forms are distributed to all passengers on planes or ships and completed in advance of arrival into the first point of entry in the United States (Figure 4.3). If two or more members of a family are traveling together, only one form is required per family. The front side of the customs declaration form is for general information, which includes name, arriving airline and flight number, citizenship, and so on. The reverse side of the form is used to list all items that are being brought into the United States, including their cost, or if gifts, their value. An itemized list is required only if the total allowance for the traveler or family is exceeded. If the total value does not exceed the allowance limitation, an itemized list on the form is not required. The passenger may make an oral declaration to the customs agent of the total amount.

If the traveler exceeds the allowance, he or she pays the U.S. customs fee directly to the Customs Service located at the airport. The following are acceptable forms of payment:

- Personal check
- U.S. currency
- Traveler's check/government check/money order
- Credit card

WELCOME TO THE UNITED STATES

APHIS/FWS USE ONLY | CUSTOMS USE ONLY

DEPARTMENT OF THE TREASURY
UNITED STATES CUSTOMS SERVICE

FORM APPROVED
OMB NO. 1515-0041

CUSTOMS DECLARATION

19 CFR 122.27, 148.12, 148.13, 148.110, 148.111

Each arriving traveler or responsible family member must provide the following information (only **ONE** written declaration per family is required):

1. Family Name

2. First (Given) Name   3. Middle Initial(s)   4. Birth Date (day/mo/yr)

5. Airline/Flight No. or Vessel Name or Vehicle License No.   6. Number of Family Members Traveling With You

7. (a) Country of Citizenship   7. (b) Country of Residence

8. (a) U.S. Address (Street Number/Hotel/Mailing Address in U.S.)

8. (b) U.S. Address (City)   8. (c) U.S Address (State)

9. Countries visited on this trip prior to U.S. arrival

a.   b.

c.   d.

10. The purpose of my (our) trip is or was: (Check one or both boxes, if applicable)   ☐ Business   ☐ Personal

11. I am (We are) bringing fruits, plants, meats, food, soil, birds, snails, other live animals, wildlife products, farm products; or, have been on a farm or ranch outside the U.S.:   ☐ Yes   ☐ No

12. I am (We are) carrying currency or monetary instruments over $10,000 U.S., or foreign equivalent: ☐ Yes   ☐ No

13. I have (We have) commercial merchandise, U.S. or foreign: (Check one box only)   ☐ Yes   ☐ No

14. The total value of all goods, including commercial merchandise, I/we purchased or acquired abroad and am/are bringing to the U.S. is: $ _____ (U.S. Dollars)

(See the instructions on the back of this form under "MERCHANDISE" and use the space provided there to list all the items you must declare. If you have nothing to declare, write "- 0 -" in the space provided above.)

SIGN BELOW AFTER YOU READ NOTICE ON REVERSE

I have read the notice on the reverse and have made a truthful declaration.

X _____

Signature   Date (day/month/year)

U.S. Customs use only -- Do not write below this line -- U.S. Customs use only

INSPECTOR'S BADGE NUMBER   STAMP AREA

TIME COMPLETED

Customs Form 6059B (013194)

NOTICE

ALL PERSONS ARE SUBJECT TO FURTHER QUESTIONING AND THEIR PERSONS, BELONGINGS, AND CONVEYANCE ARE SUBJECT TO SEARCH. (19 CFR 162.3 - 162.8)

The unlawful importation of controlled substances (narcotics, chemicals, prescription medicines if not accompanied by a prescription, etc.) regardless of amount is a violation of U.S. law.

AGRICULTURAL AND WILDLIFE PRODUCTS

To prevent the entry of dangerous agricultural pests and prohibited wildlife, the following are restricted: Fruits, vegetables, plants, plant products, soil, meats, meat products, birds, snails, and other live animals or animal products, wildlife and wildlife products. Failure to declare all such items to a Customs/Agricultural/Wildlife officer can result in penalties and the items may be subject to seizure.

CURRENCY AND MONETARY INSTRUMENTS

The transportation of currency or monetary instruments, REGARDLESS OF AMOUNT IS LEGAL; however, if you take out of or bring into the United States more than $10,000 (U.S. or foreign equivalent, or a combination of the two) in coin, currency, traveler's checks or bearer instruments such as money orders, personal or cashier's checks, stocks or bonds, you are required BY LAW to FILE a report on Form 4790 with the U.S. Customs Service. If you have someone else carry the currency or instruments for you, you must also file the report. FAILURE TO FILE THE REQUIRED REPORT OR FAILURE TO REPORT THE TOTAL AMOUNT YOU ARE CARRYING MAY LEAD TO THE SEIZURE OF ALL THE CURRENCY OR INSTRUMENTS, AND MAY SUBJECT YOU TO CIVIL PENALTIES AND/OR CRIMINAL PROSECUTION.

MERCHANDISE

VISITORS (NON-RESIDENTS) must declare in item 14 the total value of all articles intended for others and all items intended to be sold or left in the U.S. This includes all gifts and commercial items or samples. (EXCEPTION: Your own personal effects, such as clothing, personal jewelry and camera equipment, luggage, etc., need not be declared.)

U.S. RESIDENTS must declare in item 14 the total value of ALL articles, including commercial goods and samples, they acquired abroad (whether new or used; dutiable or not; and whether obtained by purchase, received as a gift, or otherwise), including those articles purchased in DUTY FREE STORES IN THE U.S. OR ABROAD, which are in their possession at the time of arrival. Articles which you acquired on this trip mailed from abroad, (other than articles acquired in insular possessions and various Caribbean Basin countries) are dutiable upon their arrival in the U.S.

THE AMOUNT OF DUTY TO BE PAID will be determined by a Customs officer. U.S. residents are normally entitled to a duty free exemption of $400 on those items accompanying them; non-residents are normally entitled to an exemption of $100. Duty is normally a flat rate of 10% on the first $1000 above the exemption. If the value of goods declared in Item 14 EXCEEDS $1400 PER PERSON, then list ALL articles below and show price paid in U.S. dollars or, for gifts, fair retail value. Please describe all articles by their common names and material. For example: MAN'S WOOL KNIT SWEATER; DIAMOND AND GOLD RING; etc. Also, please have all your receipts ready to present to the Customs officer, if requested. This will help to facilitate the inspection process.

COMMERCIAL MERCHANDISE can be defined as articles for sale, for soliciting orders, or other goods not considered personal effects of the traveler.

IF YOU HAVE ANY QUESTIONS ABOUT WHAT MUST BE REPORTED OR DECLARED ASK A CUSTOMS OFFICER

DESCRIPTION OF ARTICLES (List may be continued on another Form 6059B)	VALUE	CUSTOMS USE
TOTAL ▷		

Paperwork Reduction Act Notice: The information collected on this form is needed to carry out the Customs, Agriculture, and Currency laws of the United States. We need it to insure that travelers are complying with these laws and to allow us to figure and collect the right amount of duty and taxes. Your response is mandatory. Statement required by 5 CFR 1320.21: The estimated average burden associated with this collection of information is 3 minutes per respondent or recordkeeper depending on individual circumstances. Comments concerning the accuracy of this burden estimate and suggestions for reducing this burden should be directed to U.S. Customs Service, Paperwork Management Branch, Washington DC 20029 and to the Office of Management and Budget, Paperwork Reduction Project (1515-0041), Washington DC 20503.

☆ U.S.G.P.O.: 1994—748-767   **Customs Form 6059B (013194)(Back)**

Figure 4.3 *Customs declaration form.*

Key Point ➤ Customs Service officials cite the following exemptions to standard custom allowances as examples of those that often confuse travelers:

- No customs duties are collected on goods of any amount purchased in San Juan, Puerto Rico.
- The duty rate of goods in excess of $1,200 purchased in the U.S. Virgin Islands is not 10 percent, but 5 percent.
- There is no duty on U.S.-made products, but items such as cigarettes and bourbon are subject to collection of Internal Revenue Service excise taxes.
- Many products made in Mexico are duty-free, but others are dutiable at 5 percent.

- Goods purchased in any of the 26 Caribbean Basin countries are exempt up to $600, but only if the passenger's last port of call is one of those countries.
- Works of fine art, such as oil paintings, and antiques proven to be at least 100 years old are exempt from all duty.
- Four types of precious stones are unconditionally duty-free: diamonds, rubies, sapphires, and emeralds.
- Items such as pre-Columbian artifacts and items made of endangered animal parts, such as ivory and leather, are prohibited.

➤ Resources

The travel professional uses several types of printed and automated reference material to research the most current information regarding passport and visa requirements, health precautions, travel advisories, and customs. Two resources that are frequently used in the industry are the *TIM Guide* (*Travel Information Manual*) and the "Know Before You Go" brochure, published and distributed by the U.S. Customs Service.

TIM Guide

The *TIM Guide*, published monthly, provides detailed information regarding entry requirements for nearly 200 countries. It is controlled by 14 airlines, which contribute, monitor, and update the contents. There is also an automated version of the *TIM Guide* in the airline computer reservations systems. Figure 4.4 is a sample page from the *TIM Guide* that shows travel requirements and restrictions when traveling to Peru.

"Know Before You Go" Brochure

This brochure is published for the traveling public and distributed by the U.S. Customs Service. Travel agencies can obtain a bulk supply of these brochures and will often distribute them to their international travelers. Figure 4.5 shows sample sections from the brochure.

■ PERU

1. **Passport:** Required, except for holders of:
   1. Laissez-Passer (travelling on duty) issued by the United Nations;
   2. Seaman Book (travelling on duty) issued by any country.

2. **Visa: Warning**
   If passengers arrive without a visa (if required) they will be deported and the delivering carrier must pay a fine of USD 500.00 per passenger, which will be doubled in case of recurrence.
   Visa required, except for:
   1. nationals of Peru;
   2. diplomats accredited to Peru (they must hold à red card issued by the Peruvian Protocol or a diplomatic passport provided with a special stamp from a consulate abroad);
   3. those holding diplomatic or official passports, (nationals of Israel also if holding service passports), for a stay not exceeding 15 days (unless a longer period is granted according to their nationality elsewhere in the Visa section);
   4. nationals **21** of:
      Argentina, Austria, Belgium, Bolivia, Brazil, Canada, Denmark, Ecuador, Finland, France, Germany Fed. Rep. (West), Greece, Honduras, Ireland, Italy, Japan, Korea Rep. (South), Liechtenstein, Luxembourg, Netherlands, Norway, Portugal (for a stay not exceeding 60 days), Spain, Sweden, Switzerland, United Kingdom, Uruguay, U.S.A.;
   5. those holding a "Laissez-Passer" issued by the United Nations and travelling on duty;
   (TWOV)
   6. merchant seamen (travelling on duty) arriving by air to join a ship in Peru, whether holding a passport or seaman book.
      The Shipping Agent in Peru should submit a guarantee to Immigration. He must be present on arrival to accompany the seaman to his ship;
   7. provided not leaving the transit area at the airport —: those holding tickets **with reserved seats** and other documents to continue their journey to a third country by same or connecting aircraft: up to six hours stay in Lima allowed.
   Re-entry permit: Required for returning alien residents:
   1. a re-entry permit "Ficha de Reingreso" to be obtained before leaving Peru: or
   2. a "Permiso Especial de Salida y Reingreso "A" ("Special Permit for Exit and Re-entry") (Green Card) issued for several "Exits and Returns" within 6 months, or
   3. a visa to be obtained from a Peruvian consulate abroad.
      Returning alien residents are entitled to only one entry within the period of validity of the "Ficha de Reingreso".
   Exempt are those holding a "Laissez-Passer" issued by the United Nations and travelling on duty.
   Additional Information:
   1. Tourists **22** from any country must hold tickets and other documents for their onward or return journey. Immigration officers are very strict on this regulation; if passengers arrive without a return or onward ticket they must buy a ticket or they will be deported on first available flight.
   2. Those coming to Peru for business purposes and artists have to report to the Immigration authorities within 15 days after their arrival. In case above groups of passengers fail to report, they will not be allowed to depart.
   Notes:
   21 Generally, visa exemptions are for a stay of 30, 60 or 90 days (up to the discretion of the Immigration authorities) unless otherwise specified and provided holding tickets and other documents for their return or onward travel.
   22 The obligation for tourists to hold onward or return tickets is not applicable to those holding diplomatic or official passports and to nationals of Israel also if holding Service passports.

3. **Health:** Required — except for transit passengers not leaving the airport — vaccination against:
   yellow fever, if arriving within 6 days after leaving or transiting **31** infected areas (see General Health Information).
   Exempt are children under six months.

   Recommended:
   1. vaccination against:
      yellow fever for all passengers visiting any areas outside the main cities in Peru, except children under 6 months;

Figure 4.4 *Sample page from the* TIM *Guide.*

KNOW BEFORE YOU GO

customs hints for returning residents

CUSTOMS POINTERS

Traveling Back and Forth Across the Border

After you have crossed the United States boundary at one point and you swing back into the United States to travel to another point in the foreign country, you run the risk of losing your customs exemption unless you meet certain requirements. If you make a "swing back," don't risk your exemptions—ask the nearest customs officer about these requirements.

"Duty-Free" Shops

Articles bought in "duty-free" shops in foreign countries are subject to U.S. customs duty and restrictions but may be included in your personal exemption.

Articles purchased in U.S. "duty-free" shops are subject to U.S. customs duty if reentered into the U.S. Example: Liquor bought in a "duty-free" shop before entering Canada and brought back into the United States will be subject to duty and internal revenue tax.

Keep Your Sales Slips

You will find your sales slips, invoices, or other evidence of purchase not only helpful when making out your declaration but necessary if you have unaccompanied articles being sent from the U.S. Virgin Islands, American Samoa, or Guam.

Packing Your Baggage

Pack your baggage in a manner that will make inspection easy. Do your best to pack separately the articles you have acquired abroad. When the Customs officer asks you to open your luggage or the trunk of your car, please do so without hesitation.

Photographic Film

All imported photographic films, which accompany a traveler, if not for commercial purpose, may be released without examination by Customs unless there is reason to believe they contain objectionable matter.

Figure 4.5 *Sections from the "Know Before You Go" brochure.*

Money Matters

Travelers to foreign countries will have many questions regarding local currencies and exchange rates. Travel agents and booking agents should be familiar with this information and be able to advise their clients on how, where, and when to exchange their U.S. dollars into currencies of countries they are visiting.

➤ Market Exchange Rates

The value of U.S. currency and all other foreign currencies changes and fluctuates periodically. Currency values are greatly influenced by social, economic, and political factors affecting each country. Also, each currency changes in relation to others; this is not easy to predict.

Oanda Currency Converter: This site offers daily currency conversions for more than 100 countries. Go to *http://www.oanda.com*

Web Link

If a country is experiencing inflation, this means that the prices of local goods and services are increasing. When this happens, the purchasing power of its currency decreases and it loses value in comparison with other currencies on the world market. In other words, you need more local dollars to buy or exchange for other currencies. The amount of local dollars needed to exchange for other currencies is called the **market exchange rate.** Market exchange rates don't necessarily change each day, but they do change periodically. As far as the traveler is concerned, the exchange rate of currencies may very well change between the time a trip is booked and actual departure.

The travel professional can find current exchange rates in various resources. The system most commonly used is the airline computer reservations system (CRS). Airlines maintain a current list of market exchange rates in their systems. In fact, the CRSs can perform the actual exchange calculations for you. Another resource is the *Wall Street Journal* or a local major bank that has a foreign currency department. Any of these resources can provide you with current exchange rates.

Table 4.2 shows market exchange rates that were current at the time of publication and are to be used as examples only. As you can see, the table provides an alphabetical list of countries, followed by the name of its currency and a three-letter currency code. Currency codes are used in international fare tariffs and displays and are also entered on airline tickets. The market rate provides the amount of foreign currency that is equivalent to one unit of U.S. currency, or one U.S. dollar. To exchange U.S. currency into a foreign currency, the *amount of U.S. dollars being exchanged is multiplied by the market exchange rate.*

Example: You wish to exchange USD250.00 into Danish krone. If the market exchange rate is 6.88, how many Danish krone will you receive? *Answer:* USD250 × 6.88 = DKK 1720.

➤ Where to Exchange Money

When currencies are exchanged, a loss occurs. Banks offer the best method of exchanging money; the loss is minimal. Travel agents advise their clients to exchange money before their departure at a local bank. They will get the best rate this way. If that isn't possible, exchange bureaus at airports can provide this ser-

TABLE 4.2	SAMPLE EXCHANGE RATES		
Britain	pound	GBP	0.6129
Denmark	krone	DKK	6.88
Greece	drachma	GRD	307.87
Hong Kong	dollar	HKD	7.75
Japan	yen	JPY	144.1100
United States	dollar	USD	1.0000

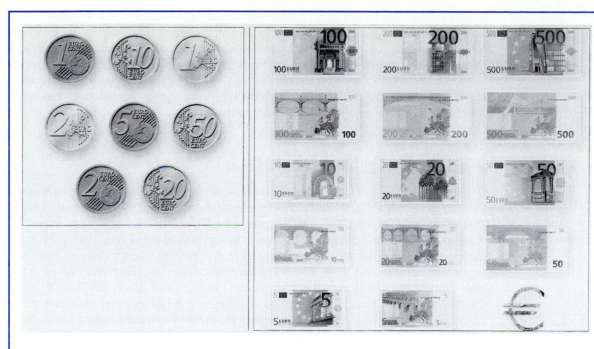

Euro Currency

Eleven countries that are part of the European Union have adopted the same currency, called the *Euro*. They are: Austria, Belgium, Finland, France, Germany, Ireland, Italy, Luxembourg, Netherlands, Portugal, and Spain. All other countries have maintained their original currencies, but some may join the Euro at a later time. Between January 1, 2002 and July 1, 2002, Euro bank notes and Euro coins go into circulation. *By July 1, 2002, notes and coins of all national currencies will be withdrawn from circulation; the Euro will be the only currency used in the countries affected.*

Source: Travel Weekly, *November 1998.*

vice, although the rates are not favorable. The last resort would be to exchange money at hotels or retail shops, which offer the least desirable rates of exchange.

► Ways to Carry Money

Traveler's Checks

Traveler's checks are probably the best and safest way to carry money. If they are lost or stolen, they can easily be replaced. Also, they are secure monetary instruments, since a duplicate signature is required to cash them. Traveler's checks can be purchased through local banks or through travel companies such as American Express or AAA ("Triple A"). There is sometimes a minimal charge to purchase them.

Credit Cards

Major credit cards, such as American Express, MasterCard, and Visa, are accepted in hotels and major shops and restaurants throughout the world. Many of the major credit cards are part of the worldwide system of *automated teller machines (ATMs)*. This enables the cardholder to obtain instant cash issued in the local currency at any of these machines. However, using a credit card for purchases abroad can be either an advantage or a disadvantage to the traveler. Why? When a credit card is used in a foreign country, it sometimes takes weeks, if not months, for it to be posted on the traveler's credit card account. The exchange rate that is used to obtain the U.S. currency equivalency to charge is the one in effect at the time the charge is posted, that is, the time when the paperwork reaches the United States, not when the purchase was made. Since a long time can separate these two time periods, the exchange rate in effect at the time of purchase can be quite different at the time of posting.

▶ ATMs: The Cashless Way to Travel

Cashless is how many travelers are going these days. The major credit cards, such as Visa and MasterCard, are part of the worldwide system of automated teller machines (ATMs). This enables the cardholder to obtain instant cash at any of these machines worldwide. There are overseas withdrawal fees that vary from bank to bank ($1.75 to $5.00 per transaction). The two main overseas cash networks are Cirrus and Plus. Travelers can obtain a comprehensive list of ATM sites around the world in two ways: printed booklets and Web sites. Both MasterCard/Cirrus and Visa/PLUS print comprehensive ATM location directories that are available from the companies themselves and some major banks.

A word of caution: Most ATMs will withdraw money from the user's primary account (usually checking), but some cannot locate money in a savings account. If that is the case, the traveler can call his or her bank from overseas to make the change. Also, users may need a different four-digit PIN (personal identification number) if traveling to Europe; this should be checked before the trip.

▶ Don't Leave Your VAT Behind!

In an average year, American tourists lose about $50 million in Europe, and most of them don't even know it. Most travelers don't realize that they can claim **value-added tax** (**VAT**) refunds on the purchases they make overseas. Here's how it works. The VAT is usually built into the purchase price and varies from country to country; this is why many travelers don't even know they are paying a VAT, much less the amount of tax they are paying! It can range from 2.9 percent of the purchase price in Singapore to as high as 20 percent in Sweden.

One way of getting the VAT refund is to stop at a VAT refund location at the airport of departure and present purchase receipts. The refund is either mailed in a check or credited to a credit or debit card, which usually takes several weeks to process. A company called Global Refund has sought to simplify the process. This company is affiliated with more than 126,000 stores in Europe, Canada, and Singapore. The shops display the tax-free shopping logo in their windows. Affiliated stores will provide the customer with a Global Refund Cheque. The check must be stamped by a customs official at the airport of departure and cashed at a cash refund office, usually located nearby.

The VAT refund is a privilege extended to U.S. residents shopping in certain countries. Table 4.3 is a list of the countries in which Global Refund operates and the percentage of the purchase price that is VAT (amounts are subject to change).

INTERNATIONAL ARRIVAL AND DEPARTURE PROCEDURES

From the passenger's point of view, flying from Albany, New York to Pittsburgh is a simple matter. Go to the ticket counter, check in, get a boarding pass (if you don't already have one), pass through security, and away you go! Traveling from Chicago to Paris, for example, may be a little more complicated; especially for the

TABLE 4.3   How Much VAT? (%)

Austria	16.7
Belgium	17
Croatia	4.8–16.7
Denmark	20
Finland	18
France	17.1
Germany	13
Greece	11.5–15.3
Hungary	9.1–20
Ireland	17.4
Italy	13.8–16
Liechtenstein	6.1
Luxembourg	13
Netherlands	14.9
Norway	18.7
Portugal	14.5
Slovenia	4.8–24.2
Spain	13.8
Sweden	20
Switzerland	6.1
United Kingdom	14.9

first-time international traveler. Travel agency clients have questions and concerns regarding perceived language and cultural barriers when traveling abroad. It is an important part of a travel professional's job to inform clients of what they will be expected to do when they arrive at their foreign destination. Concerns regarding how to check in for their flight, immigration checks, and transportation once they get there are often expressed. What follows is a sequence of events that the international traveler can expect from the time of flight check-in at departure to arrival at the final destination.

➤ Airport Check-in

At international check-in, the airline ticket agent requests to see the passenger's ticket, along with the required travel documentation. In most cases this is a valid U.S. passport. The agent will cross-check the name on the passenger ticket with the one identified in the passport. This is why it is required to enter the passenger's full name on the ticket as it appears on the passport or other required travel document. After check-in, the passenger proceeds through the security check. All carry-on baggage and other items being hand-held are screened.

➤ Immigration Card

Right before landing, the airline distributes to all passengers an *immigration card* that everyone must complete. This card includes the name of the traveler, address, destination abroad, and purpose of the visit.

➤ Arrival at Destination Airport

The passenger deplanes and proceeds through the immigration check. At this point the immigration card is surrendered to officials at the immigration checkpoint. The passenger's passport is also checked and stamped. The passenger then retrieves his/her luggage at the baggage claim and proceeds through the customs check or inspection area. Either an oral or a written declaration is given.

➤ Arrival at a Connecting Airport (in Transit)

If the passenger is only connecting (not leaving the airport), he or she is said to be *in transit*. A transit passenger does not proceed through immigration or customs checks, but proceeds directly to the gate area for the connecting flight.

➤ Ground Transportation Services

Arriving passengers require ground transportation from the airport to downtown or city center locations. Four basic types of ground transportation services are available at most international airports around the world:

1. *Public taxi*. These are available at all airports; prices vary. When possible, the travel agent should provide advice regarding standard rates and tipping policies.
2. *Bus or motorcoach service*. There is scheduled service between most airports and the downtown airport terminal and/or major hotels. Usually, it is less expensive than public taxi service.
3. *Car rentals*. Car rental facilities are either located on the airport premises or at off-airport locations. If the latter, the car rental agencies usually provide their clients with complimentary shuttle service to their off-airport facilities.
4. *Private transfer*. This service is sometimes recommended for international travelers who are not sure of the language or customs of the country they are visiting for the first time. This is also the recommended service for deluxe clients, since this is the most expensive method of ground transportation. Private transfers are always arranged in advance and prepaid through the travel agency. Private transfers include:

- Meeting and interpreter service upon arrival
- Baggage handling
- Transportation directly to the hotel or arrival point by private car or van

Key Point ➤ Many foreign cities have *downtown airport terminals*. These locations contain airline ticket offices and reservation centers for one or more airlines that provide service to or from the area. Surface transportation is available between the airport and the downtown terminal locations, either free or at a minimal charge.

✔ *Check Your Understanding 4-3*

1. A returning passenger is flying from Rome to Chicago with a connection through New York. In what city does the person proceed through customs and immigration clearance?

   _____

2. What is the duty-free allowance for a U.S. citizen when returning to the United States from each of these countries or islands?
   A. England _____
   B. St. John, U.S. Virgin Islands _____
   C. Barbados (Caribbean) _____
   D. Puerto Rico _____

3. List four acceptable forms of payment when a traveler is required to pay duty at an airport.

A. _____   C. _____

B. _____   D. _____

4. What is the safest and easiest way to carry money when traveling abroad, and why?

_____

5. A traveler charged his hotel in Italy on his Visa card during a recent trip. The total charge in U.S. dollars appeared on his Visa statement several months after his return. When was the hotel charge in Italian lire actually converted to U.S. dollars?

_____

6 What does *in transit* mean?

_____

7. In addition to private transfers, name three other types of ground transportation that arriving international air passengers can take between the airport and downtown locations.

A. _____   B. _____

C. _____

8. List three features that private transfer services include.

A. _____   B. _____

C. _____

9. Why is it good policy to enter the international passenger's full name on his or her airline ticket and other travel documents?

_____

10. What does VAT stand for? _____

INTERNATIONAL AIR TRANSPORT ASSOCIATION

The **International Air Transport Association (IATA)** is a worldwide trade organization comprised of the majority of international airline carriers. It is commonly referred to as IATA. One of the main functions of IATA is to promote a standard and unified system of worldwide air travel by establishing routes and setting safety and service standards. IATA also develops rules and standards for international faring and ticketing. Another major function of IATA is to appoint and regulate travel agencies to sell international air travel. This function, however, is handled by a subsidiary of IATA called **International Airlines Travel Agency Network (IATAN).**

► IATA Geography

As noted, one of the major functions of IATA is to standardize international faring and ticketing procedures for ticket agents around the world. The travel agent in Chicago and the travel agent in Rome, Italy are required to follow the same fare construction principles and airline ticket formats for their international travelers. These standards and formats are in accordance with IATA regulations.

International air fares often are described and categorized geographically. For example, a certain type of air fare offered by an airline may be available only when travel is between North America and Scandinavia. Another type of fare may be available when travel is between the Middle East and the North/Central Pacific region. Travel and ticket agents are required to have a working knowledge of these geographical categories as they relate to air travel in order to select the correct fare for their clients. We call the geographical terms used for international faring and ticketing purposes *IATA geography*.

Many IATA geographical terms will not be new to you. Terms such as *Europe*, *Middle East*, and *Asia* are used in both IATA and traditional geography. However, some of the IATA definitions are slightly different from those in traditional geography. For example, IATA's definition of Europe includes three countries located on the African continent that are not traditionally considered Europe: Algeria, Morocco, and Tunisia.

➤ IATA Areas

IATA and its international carriers have divided the world into three areas. Each area is called an *IATA area* or **traffic conference area.** Each IATA area is identified by a number: 1,2, or 3. Figure 4.6 represents how the world is divided into the three IATA areas. Here is a brief description:

- Traffic conference area 1 consists of the North and South American continents, including the adjacent islands: Bermuda, Bahamas, all Caribbean islands, and Greenland; and the following islands in the Pacific: Hawaiian Islands and Palmyra and Midway Islands.

- Traffic conference area 2 consists of the continents of Europe (including Iceland) and Africa and the islands adjacent. It also includes that part of Asia west of and including Iran; and that part of Russia west of the Ural Mountains.

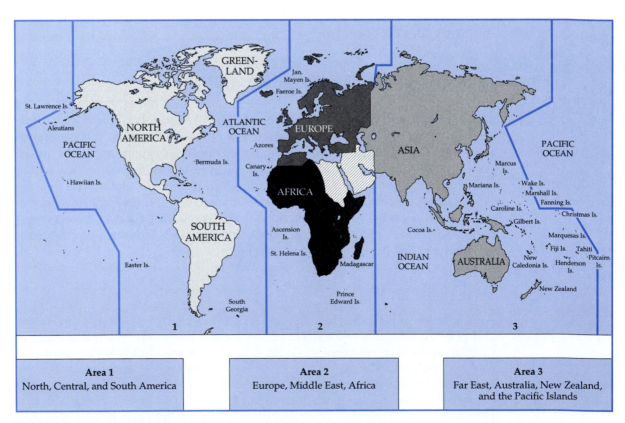

Area 1	Area 2	Area 3
North, Central, and South America	Europe, Middle East, Africa	Far East, Australia, New Zealand, and the Pacific Islands

Figure 4.6 *Traffic conference areas.*

- Traffic conference area 3 consists of the balance of the world. It includes the rest of Asia and the adjacent islands, the East Indies, Australia and New Zealand, and all islands in the Pacific except those located in traffic conference area 1.

✔ *Check Your Understanding 4-4*

Identify each city below with its IATA area location (1, 2, or 3). Use a map if needed.

City	*IATA Area*
1. Chicago, Illinois	_____
2. Johannesburg, South Africa	_____
3. Kiev, Ukraine	_____
4. Buenos Aires, Argentina	_____
5. Delhi, India	_____
6. Bermuda	_____
7. Manila, Philippines	_____
8. Stockholm, Sweden	_____
9. Honolulu, Oahu	_____
10. Auckland, New Zealand	_____
11. London, England	_____
12. Toronto, Canada	_____
13. Reykjavik, Iceland	_____
14. Acapulco, Mexico	_____
15. Kabul, Afghanistan	_____
16. San José, Costa Rica	_____
17. Nairobi, Kenya	_____
18. Jakarta, Indonesia	_____
19. Minsk, Belarus	_____
20. Tehran, Iran	_____

INTERNATIONAL AIRLINE AND CITY CODES

It is important that travel agents know, by memory, the abbreviations and codes that are used when booking international travel. These reservation codes are recognized internationally to identify cities, airports, and airlines throughout the world. Table 4.4 shows a sample list of major international airlines. Each airline represented is a flagship carrier of a particular country. A *flagship carrier* is owned privately or by the government of a particular country. They are called flagships because the government has given rights to the airline to represent the country's flag all over the world. The United States has several international flagship carriers. They include American Airlines, Continental Airlines, Delta, Northwest Airlines, Trans World Airlines, and United Airlines.

✔ *Check Your Understanding 4-5*

Fill in the chart below. Try to do it by memory.

CODE	COUNTRY	FLAGSHIP CARRIER
AF	France	_____
_____	Switzerland	_____
_____	_____	Aeromexico
_____	Finland	_____

TABLE 4.4   MAJOR INTERNATIONAL FLAGSHIP CARRIERS AND CODES

Code	Country	Flagship Carrier
AC	Canada	Air Canada
AF	France	Air France
AI	India	Air India
AM	Mexico	Aeromexico
AV	Colombia	Avianca
AY	Finland	Finnair
AZ	Italy	Alitalia
BA	Britain	British Airways
CI	China	China Airlines
CX	Hong Kong, China	Cathay Pacific Airways
EI	Ireland	Aer Lingus
FI	Iceland	Icelandair
IB	Spain	Iberia
JL	Japan	Japan Airlines
KE	South Korea	Korean Air
KL	Netherlands	KLM–Royal Dutch Airlines
LH	Germany	Lufthansa German Airlines
LO	Poland	LOT–Polish Airlines
LY	Israel	El Al Israel Airlines
MH	Malaysia	Malaysia Airlines
NH	Japan	All Nippon Airways
NZ	New Zealand	Air New Zealand
OA	Greece	Olympic Airways
OK	Czech Republic	Czech Airlines
OS	Austria	Austrian Airlines
QF	Australia	Qantas Airways
RG	Brazil	Varig
SA	South Africa	South African Airways
SK	Scandinavia	SAS–Scandinavian Airline
SN	Belgium	Sabena–Belgian World Airlines
SQ	Singapore	Singapore Airlines
SR	Switzerland	Swissair
SU	Russia	Aeroflot–Russian International Airlines
TG	Thailand	Thai Airways International
TP	Portugal	TAP Air Portugal
VA	Venezuela	Viasa
VS	Britain	Virgin Atlantic Airways

CX	Hong Kong, China	_____
_____	Italy	Alitalia
	Portugal	_____
UA	_____	_____
_____	Colombia	Avianca
_____	Japan	All Nippon Airways
JL	Japan	_____
QF	_____	Qantas Airways
_____	Austria	_____
	_____	Trans World Airlines
OK	Czech Republic	_____
_____	Israel	_____
CO	Poland	_____
_____	_____	_____
EI	Iceland	Lufthansa German Airlines
_____	_____	Aer Lingus
KE	_____	Iberia
_____	_____	Olympic Airlines
DL	_____	Northwest Airlines
_____	_____	_____
AC	_____	Thai Airways International
KL	_____	_____
SN	_____	Sabena–Belgian World Airlines
RG	Brazil	_____
_____	Britain	Virgin Atlantic Airways
_____	India	_____
AA	_____	Malaysia Airlines
_____	_____	China Airlines
_____	_____	British Airways
SQ	New Zealand	_____
SA	_____	_____
_____	_____	SAS–Scandinavian Airlines
VA	Russia	_____

International City Codes

Other important booking identifiers are city and airport codes. It is important that travel consultants and sales agents identify the major city and airport codes by memory in order to increase efficiency and maintain accuracy when booking international travel. In this section you will discover the major international city codes and their locations on maps. This is a good way to reinforce geography skills.

► Major Airport and City Codes of the Western Hemisphere
Canada (see Figure 4.7)

YEA	Edmonton, Alberta	YTO	Toronto, Ontario
YHZ	Halifax, Nova Scotia	YVR	Vancouver, British Columbia
YMQ	Montreal, Quebec	YWG	Winnipeg, Manitoba
YOW	Ottawa, Ontario	YXE	Saskatoon, Saskatchewan
YQB	Quebec City, Quebec	YYC	Calgary, Alberta
YQR	Regina, Saskatchewan	YYT	St. Johns, Newfoundland

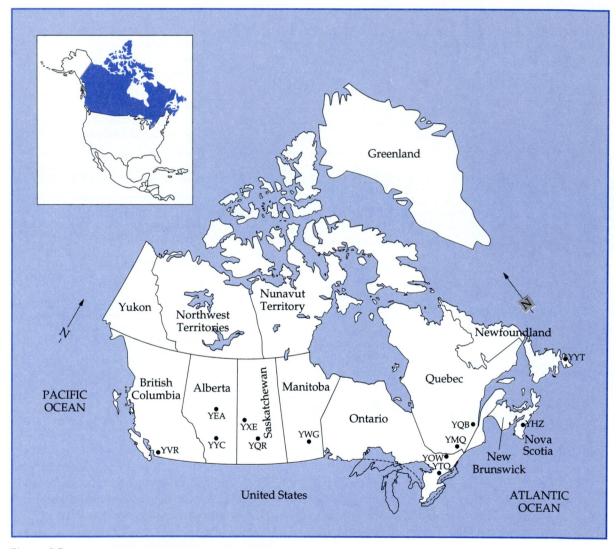

Figure 4.7 *City codes for Canada.*

Mexico (see Figure 4.8)

ACA	Acapulco	MZT	Mazatlán
CUN	Cancún	PVR	Puerto Vallarta
GDL	Guadalajara	ZIH	Ixtapa/Zihuatenejo
MEX	Mexico City	ZLO	Manzanillo
MID	Mérida		

Figure 4.8 *City codes for Mexico.*

Central and South America (see Figure 4.9a and b)

ASU	Asunción, Paraguay, S.A.	MVD	Montevideo, Uruguay, S.A.
BOG	Bogotá, Colombia, S.A.	PTY	Panama City, Panama, C.A.
BUE	Buenos Aires, Argentina, S.A.	RIO	Rio de Janeiro, Brazil, S.A.
BZE	Belize City, Belize, C.A.	SAL	San Salvador, El Salvador, C.A.
CCS	Caracas, Venezuela, S.A.	SAO	São Paulo, Brazil, S.A.
CTG	Cartagena, Colombia, S.A.	SCL	Santiago, Chile, S.A.
GUA	Guatemala City, Guatemala, C.A.	SJO	San José, Costa Rica, C.A.
LIM	Lima, Peru, S.A.	UIO	Quito, Ecuador, S.A.
MGA	Managua, Nicaragua, C.A.		

Figure 4.9a *City codes for Central America.*

Figure 4.9b *City codes for South America.*

West Indies (see Figure 4.10)

ANU	Antigua	PAP	Port-au-Prince, Haiti
AUA	Aruba	POS	Port of Spain, Trinidad and Tobago
BDA	Bermuda		
BGI	Barbados	PTP	Pointe-à-Pitre, Guadeloupe
CUR	Curaçao	SDQ	Santo Domingo, Dominican Republic
FDF	Fort-de-France, Martinique		
FPO	Freeport, Bahamas	SJU	San Juan, Puerto Rico
GCM	Grand Cayman	SLU	St. Lucia
GND	Grenada	STT	St. Thomas, U.S. Virgin Islands
KIN	Kingston, Jamaica	STX	St. Croix, U.S. Virgin Islands
MBJ	Montego Bay, Jamaica	SXM	St. Maarten
NAS	Nassau, Bahamas		

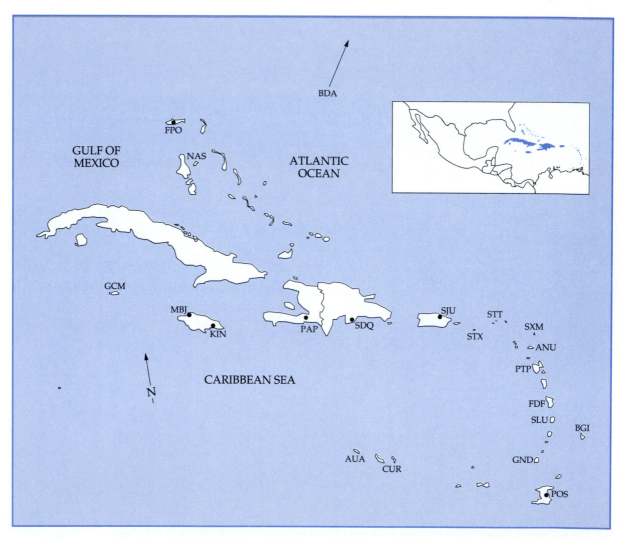

Figure 4.10 *City codes for the West Indies.*

✓ *Check Your Understanding 4-6*

For each geographical region, decode or encode according to the directions.

1. Circle the correct code for each city listed.

A.	Ottawa, Canada	YOT	OTT	YWO	YOW
B.	Mexico City, Mexico	MEC	MEX	EXC	MCY
C.	Vancouver, Canada	YVR	VCR	YRV	YYV
D.	Acapulco, Mexico	ACP	APO	ACM	ACA
E.	Montreal, Canada	MON	YDV	YMQ	YOL
F.	Puerto Vallarta, Mexico	PRV	PVR	PVA	PVT
G.	Québec City, Canada	YQB	YBQ	YQC	QEC
H.	Mérida, Mexico	MER	MID	MDA	MIA
I.	Toronto, Canada	YYP	YYT	YTO	YTP
J.	Cancún, Mexico	CUN	CAN	CAD	CUA
K.	Calgary, Canada	YCA	YCC	YYC	YCG
L.	Guadalajara, Mexico	GUA	GDA	GDJ	GDL

2. Match each code with the correct island/city name.

A. PTP	_____	1.	St. Croix
B. CUR	_____	2.	Freeport
C. STX	_____	3.	Fort-de-France, Martinique
D. AUA	_____	4.	Bermuda
E. SXM	_____	5.	Montego Bay, Jamaica
F. SJU	_____	6.	Grenada
G. MBJ	_____	7.	Port of Spain, Trinidad and Tobago
H. GND	_____	8.	Antigua
I. ANU	_____	9.	Santo Domingo
J. SLU	_____	10.	Grand Cayman
K. KIN	_____	11.	Aruba
L. STT	_____	12.	Pointe-à-Pitre, Guadeloupe
M. FDF	_____	13.	San Juan, Puerto Rico
N. PAP	_____	14.	Nassau, Bahamas
O. BDA	_____	15.	Kingston, Jamaica
P. NAS	_____	16.	Port-au-Prince, Haiti
Q. FPO	_____	17.	Curaçao
R. SDQ	_____	18.	St. Lucia
S. GCM	_____	19.	St. Thomas
T. BGI	_____	20.	St. Maarten
U. POS	_____	21.	Barbados

3. Decode each below. The name of the country in either Central or South America is given for each as a clue.

	Code	Country	City
A.	GUA	Guatemala	_____
B.	LIM	Peru	_____
C.	MVD	Uruguay	_____
D.	SAO	Brazil	_____
E.	ASU	Paraguay	_____
F.	PTY	Panama	_____
G.	BOG	Colombia	_____
H.	BUE	Argentina	_____
I.	RIO	Brazil	_____
J.	CCS	Venezuela	_____
K.	UIO	Ecuador	_____
L.	SCL	Chile	_____
M.	SJO	Costa Rica	_____
N.	SAL	El Salvador	_____
O.	BZE	Belize	_____
P.	CTG	Colombia	_____
Q.	MGA	Nicaragua	_____

➤ Major Airport and City Codes of the Eastern Hemisphere

Europe (see Figure 4.11)

AMS	Amsterdam, The Netherlands	LIS	Lisbon, Portugal
ANK	Ankara, Turkey	LON	London, England, UK
ATH	Athens, Greece	LUX	Luxembourg, Luxembourg
BCN	Barcelona, Spain	MAD	Madrid, Spain
BER	Berlin, Germany	MIL	Milan, Italy
BRU	Brussels, Belgium	MOW	Moscow, Russia
BUD	Budapest, Hungary	MUC	Munich, Germany
BUH	Bucharest, Romania	NCE	Nice, France
CPH	Copenhagen, Denmark	OSL	Oslo, Norway
DBV	Dubrovnik, Croatia	PAR	Paris, France
DUB	Dublin, Republic of Ireland	PRG	Prague, Czech Republic
EDI	Edinburgh, Scotland, UK	REK	Reykjavik, Iceland
FRA	Frankfurt, Germany	ROM	Rome, Italy
GLA	Glasgow, Scotland, UK	SNN	Shannon, Republic of Ireland
GVA	Geneva, Switzerland	STO	Stockholm, Sweden
HAM	Hamburg, Germany	VCE	Venice, Italy
HEL	Helsinki, Finland	VIE	Vienna, Austria
IEV	Kiev, Ukraine	WAW	Warsaw, Poland
IST	Istanbul, Turkey	ZRH	Zurich, Switzerland

Figure 4.11 *City codes for Europe.*

Middle East (see Figure 4.12)

AMM	Amman, Jordan	KRT	Khartoum, Sudan
AUH	Abu Dhabi, United Arab Emirates	KWI	Kuwait
		LCA	Larnaca, Cyprus
BAH	Bahrain, Bahrain	MCT	Muscat, Oman
BEY	Beirut, Lebanon	RUH	Riyadh, Saudi Arabia
CAI	Cairo, Egypt	THR	Tehran, Iran
DHA	Dhahran, Saudi Arabia	TLV	Tel Aviv, Israel

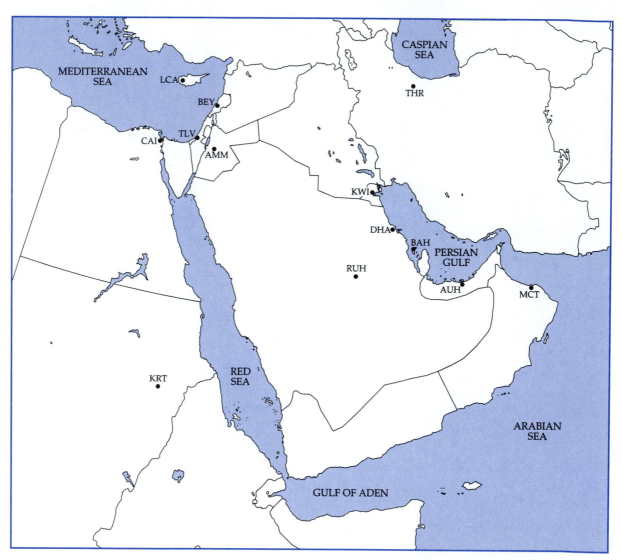

Figure 4.12 *City codes for the Middle East.*

Africa (see Figure 4.13)

ABJ	Abidjan, Côte d'Ivoire	DKR	Dakar, Senegal
ACC	Accra, Ghana	JNB	Johannesburg, South Africa
ADD	Addis Ababa, Ethiopia	LOS	Lagos, Nigeria
ALG	Algiers, Algeria	NBO	Nairobi, Kenya
CAS	Casablanca, Morocco	TUN	Tunis, Tunisia
CPT	Cape Town, South Africa		

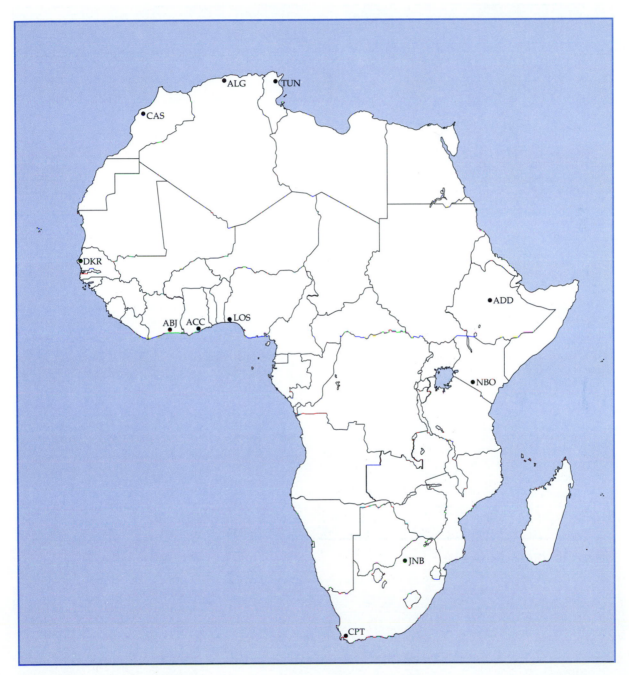

Figure 4.13 *City codes for Africa.*

Asia (see Figure 4.14)

BJS	Beijing, China	HKG	Hong Kong, China
BKK	Bangkok, Thailand	RGN	Yangon, Myanmar
BOM	Bombay, India	SEL	Seoul, Republic of Korea
CCU	Calcutta, India	SGN	Ho Chi Minh, Vietnam
DEL	Delhi, India	SIN	Singapore, Singapore

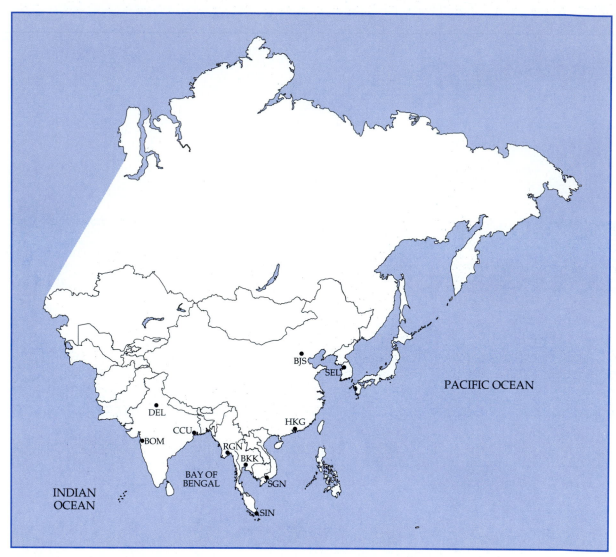

Figure 4.14 *City codes for Asia.*

Pacific Rim [see Figure 4.15]

AKL	Auckland, New Zealand	PER	Perth, Australia
GUM	Guam, Guam	PPG	Pago Pago, American Samoa
JKT	Jakarta, Indonesia	PPT	Papeete, French Polynesia
MEL	Melbourne, Australia	SYD	Sydney, Australia
MNL	Manila, Philippines	TPE	Taipei, Taiwan
OSA	Osaka, Japan	TYO	Tokyo, Japan

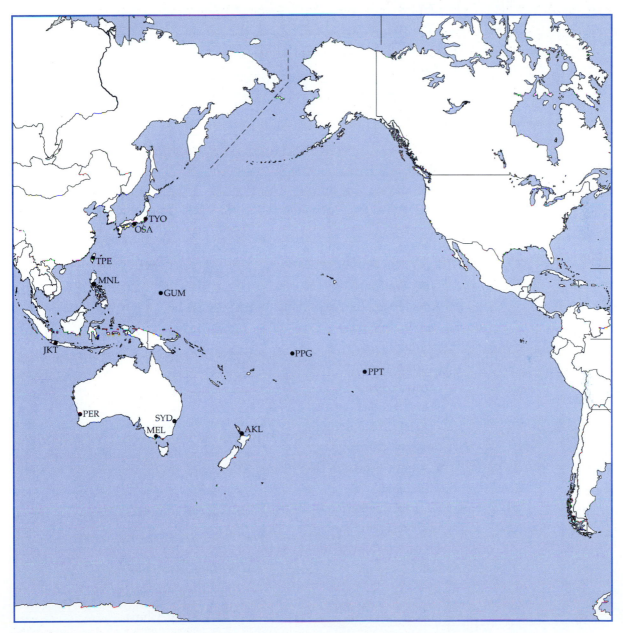

Figure 4.15 *City codes for the Pacific Rim.*

1. Decode: Write the full city name and country for each major European city code below.

   A. ROM   _____   _____

   B. STO   _____   _____

   C. PAR   _____   _____

   D. ATH   _____   _____

   E. FRA   _____   _____

   F. OSL   _____   _____

   G. CPH   _____   _____

   H. LON   _____   _____

   I. ZRH   _____   _____

   J. VIE   _____   _____

   K. IEV   _____   _____

   L. BRU   _____   _____

   M. VCE   _____   _____

   N. MAD   _____   _____

   O. LIS   _____   _____

2. Encode: Write the three-letter code for each major European city listed below.

   A. Geneva, Switzerland   _____

   B. Barcelona, Spain   _____

   C. Nice, France   _____

   D. Amsterdam, the Netherlands   _____

   E. Dublin, Ireland   _____

   F. Istanbul, Turkey   _____

   G. Munich, Germany   _____

   H. Moscow, Russia   _____

   I. Warsaw, Poland   _____

   J. Prague, Czech Republic   _____

   K. Reykjavik, Iceland   _____

   L. Glasgow, Scotland, UK   _____

   M. Milan, Italy   _____

   N. Geneva, Switzerland   _____

   O. Budapest, Hungary   _____

3. Match each code with the correct city name.

   A. NBO   _____   1. Sydney, Australia

   B. BEY   _____   2. Johannesburg, South Africa

   C. HKG   _____   3. Hong Kong, China

   D. BOM   _____   4. Cairo, Egypt

   E. CAS   _____   5. Delhi, India

   F. BKK   _____   6. Osaka, Japan

   G. TYO   _____   7. Nairobi, Kenya

H. SGN	_____	8. Tokyo, Japan
I. SYD	_____	9. Bombay, India
J. BJS	_____	10. Beirut, Lebanon
K. DEL	_____	11. Tel Aviv, Israel
L. JNB	_____	12. Ho Chi Minh, Vietnam
M. CAI	_____	13. Casablanca, Morocco
N. TLV	_____	14. Beijing, China
O. OSA	_____	15. Bangkok, Thailand

INTERNATIONAL FLIGHT RESOURCES

Picture yourself working as a travel agent. You are now in the process of planning a business trip to Europe for a corporate client. There are many details of the trip that you have to organize. In addition to typical questions regarding flight schedules and air fares, you also have to answer questions about visas, currency exchange rates, weather conditions, what clothes to bring, hotels, and sightseeing. Typical questions from clients range from a simple, "How much will it cost?" to "Will my hairdryer work in Bulgaria?" Sound difficult? It really isn't as long as you know your resources: where to find the information, and how to communicate this information clearly to your clients. In addition to the CRS in your office, there are two primary resources that are helpful when planning international trips: the *Worldwide Official Airline Guide (OAG)* for flight schedules and other information, and the *OAG Travel Planner* for accommodation and destination data.

➤ Twenty-Four-Hour Clock

Before you can study international timetables and schedules, you should have a working knowledge of the *24-hour clock*. This way of telling time is used in the military and that is why it is also called *military time*. All international time-tables—airlines, trains, buses, and ships—are published in the 24-hour clock. It is easy to understand and it makes sense.

There are 24 hours in one day. For each hour a different number is used, beginning with "00" and on through "24." Time on the 24-hour clock is indicated with four numbers; the A.M. and P.M. designators are not used. The first two numbers designate the *hour of the day* (from 00 to 24). The last two numbers designate the *number of minutes past the hour*. In international airline and rail schedules the numbers 0000 and 2400 designate the same time—midnight. The number 2400 indicates an *arrival* time at midnight; the number 0000 indicates a *departure* time at midnight.

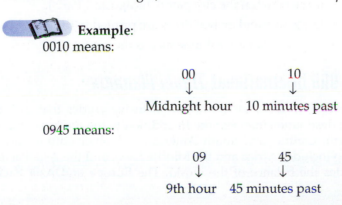

Example:
0010 means:

$$00 \qquad\qquad 10$$
$$\downarrow \qquad\qquad\quad \downarrow$$
Midnight hour   10 minutes past

0945 means:

$$09 \qquad\qquad 45$$
$$\downarrow \qquad\qquad\quad \downarrow$$
9th hour   45 minutes past

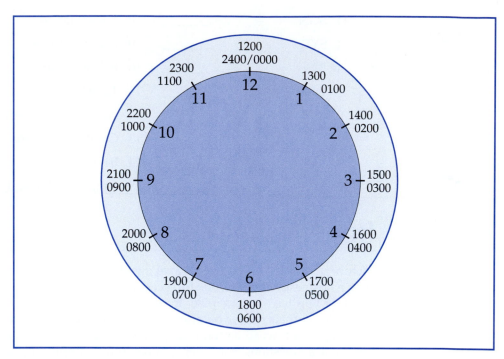

Figure 4.16 *24-hour clock.*

The designations A.M. and P.M. are not used or necessary since each hour of the day uses a different number, from 00 to 24. Converting mentally is easy: If the 24-hour time is 1300 or over, just think "P.M." and subtract 12 from the hours, and you will have the traditional time (e.g., 1855 – 12 = 6:55 P.M.). Figure 4.16 shows a 24-hour clock superimposed on a traditional clock for your reference.

➤ The *Worldwide Official Airline Guide*

The Worldwide edition of the *OAG* contains flight information and schedules for *both* domestic and international routings. The Worldwide edition is similar in format and content to the North American edition. Figure 4.17 is a cutaway sample showing flights from Chicago to Paris, France. Here are some key points about the Worldwide schedules (refer to Figure 4.17):

- *+2:00* on the first line indicates the number of time zones ahead (+) or behind (–) the destination city (Paris) is located from GMT.
- *4150 Mi* shows the number of direct air miles or the shortest operated distance between the city pair (Chicago and Paris).
- Departure and arrival times are printed in the 24-hour-clock time.
- *+1* next to an arrival time means the next day.

➤ OAG International *Travel Planners*

The *OAG Travel Planners* are all-inclusive guides that include accommodations and destination information. In addition to the *Business Travel Planner* that covers North, Central, and South America, two other editions are the Europe edition (also includes Africa and the Middle East), and the Asia Pacific edition, which includes the balance of the world. The Europe and Asia Pacific editions contain

To	PARIS, FRANCE					+2:00			PAR

C-CDG (CHARLES DE GAULLE)

O-ORY (ORLY)

CHICAGO, ILLINOIS, USA (O-ORD)						4150Mi		CHI	
	1555	O	0915+1	O	DL	6164	FCYB	AB3	D	1
	1730	O	0835+1	C	UA	942	FCYBM	777	DB	0
X4	1805	O	0900+1	C	AF	055	FCYMQ	74M	D	0

CONNECTIONS

	1330	O	1626	IAD	UA	910	FCYBM	777	S	0
	1810	IAD	0735+1	C	UA	914	FCYBM	777	DB	0
	1435	O	1655	JFK	TW	804	FYBQK	72S	L/	0
X25	1930	JFK	0850+1	C	TW	800	FCYBQ	767	DS	0
	1945	O	2125	YYZ	AC	818	CYMBQ	767	D	0
	2330	YYZ	1045+1	O	AC	880	FCYBQ	767	DB	0

Figure 4.17 *Worldwide OAG schedule.*

many of the same sections as the *Business Travel Planner,* such as airport diagrams, destination facts, city and regional maps, and frequent flyer information. Other important sections include the following to assist the international traveler: passport and visa procedures, clothing size conversion charts, international airport and road signs, and medical and health organizations designed to assist the traveler abroad (Figure 4.18).

✓ *Check Your Understanding 4-8*

1. Convert each time below into 24-hour-clock format.

   A. 12:10 A.M. _____   H. 3:55 P.M. _____

   B. 2:45 A.M. _____   I. 4:04 P.M. _____

   C. 6:00 A.M. _____   J. 6:00 P.M. _____

   D. 11:05 A.M. _____   K. 7:35 P.M. _____

   E. 12:15 P.M. _____   L. 9:30 P.M. _____

   F. 1:25 P.M. _____   M. 11:50 P.M. _____

   G. 2:35 P.M. _____   N. 12:00 mid _____

2. Part of schedule from the *Worldwide OAG* for flights from Chicago to Paris is shown in Figure 4.17. Answer the fill-in questions by referring to this schedule.

   A. Paris is _____ hours ahead of GMT.

   B. There are two airports for Paris. Charles de Gaulle (CDG) is indicated with the letter _____ for flight arrival times into that airport. Orly (ORY) is indicated with the letter _____ for flight arrival times into that airport.

   C. The only direct flight shown is on _____ (carrier) flight number _____. This flight makes ____ intermediate stop(s) between Chicago and Paris.

   D. The nonstop flight on Air France departs Chicago at _____ (show time in A.M./P.M.). This flight arrives at the airport _____ (name airport) in Paris at _____ (show time in A.M./P.M.). If the passenger departed Chicago on Thursday, he or she will arrive in Paris on _____.

   E. The flight departing at 5:30 P.M. from Chicago operates every day except _____.

VISA SERVICES

Visa Services offices will provide one or more of the following services to assist travelers in obtaining a passport and/or visa: expedite services, passport amendments and application forms.

ATLANTA, GA
   International Visa Service, 278 Hilderbrand Dr. NE. Box 720715, 30358. TEL: 404/843-0005, U.S., Caribbean 800-627-1112. Hours: 9 AM - 7:30 PM (Mon.-Fri.); 9 AM - Noon (Sat.).

BALTIMORE, MD
   Visa Adventure, Inc., 205 Hillendale Ave., 21227. TEL: 410/242-5602. Hours: 8:30 AM - 4 PM (Mon.-Fri.).

BOSTON, MA
   Visa Service, Inc., 581 Boylston St., 02116. TEL: 617/266-7646. FAX: 617/262-9829. Hours: 9 AM - 5 PM (Mon.-Fri.).

CHICAGO, IL
   Adventure Seekers Tours, 36 W. Randolph, 60601. TEL: 312/346-9100. Hours: 9:30 AM - 5:30 PM (Mon.-Fri.).
   American Visa Service, Inc., 53 W. Jackson, Ste. 1457, 60604. TEL: 312/922-8860. Hours: 9 AM - 4:30 PM (Mon.-Fri.).
   Center For International Business & Travel (CIBT), 20 N. Michigan Ave., Ste. 525, 60602. TEL: 312/629-9500, U.S. 800-394-2428. FAX: 312/629-2906. Hours: 8 AM - 6 PM (Mon.-Fri.).
   Chicago Visa Service, 201 N. Wells, Rm. 430, 60606. TEL: 312/332-7211. FAX: 312/332-3811. Hours: 9 AM - 5 PM (Mon.-Fri.); 9 AM - 1 PM (Sat.).
   Perry International Inc., 100 W. Monroe St., 60603. TEL: 312/372-2703. Hours: 9 AM - 5 PM (Mon.-Fri.).

(a)

INTERNATIONAL AIRPORT SIGNS

Immigration

Customs

Security Check

Hotel Reservations

(b)

UNITED STATES PASSPORTS

WHERE TO OBTAIN A PASSPORT?

(1) Clerk or Deputy Clerk of a Federal or State Court of Record which exercises their authority to accept passport applications.

(2) Certain Post Offices have been designated by the Postmaster General to accept Passport applications in the same fashion as the Clerks of Court. Inquire at your local Post Office in advance to ascertain whether they accept Passport applications.

(3) Applications accepted by mail or in person at the following Passport Agencies:
   Boston, MA 02222, Thomas P. O'Neil Fed. Bldg., 10 Causeway St., Rm. 247. TEL: 617/565-6998/90.
   Chicago, IL 60604, Kluczynski Federal Office Bldg., 230 S. Dearborn, Ste. 380. TEL: 312/353-5426 or 312/353-7155.

(c)

Falling rocks

Swing bridge

Use of horn prohibited

Stop: Customs

(d)

Figure 4.18 *Sections from the* OAG Travel Planner: *(a) visa services; (b) international airport signs; (c) passport procedure; (d) international road signs. (Reproduced with permission from Reed Travel Group, © 1996 Reed Elsevier, Inc.)*

F. The passenger is flying on the Air Canada connecting service. This flight departs Chicago at _____ (show time in A.M./P.M.). The connecting city is _____ (full name of city). The flight number on the first segment is Air Canada _____. The flight from the connecting airport departs at _____ (A.M./P.M.) and arrives at _____ Airport in Paris at _____(A.M./P.M.) the next day.

G. _____ Airlines offers connecting service through Washington, DC. This connection arrives in Paris at _____ (A.M./P.M.). The meals that are served on the transatlantic segment are _____ and _____.

TABLE 4.5   ISO Codes

Country	Country Code	Currency	Currency Code
Australia	AU	dollar	AUD
Canada	CA	dollar	CAD
Denmark	DK	krone	DKK
Germany	DE	mark	DEM
Hong Kong	HK	dollar	HKD
Japan	JP	yen	JPY
Mexico	MX	peso	MXN
United States	US	dollar	USD

International Country and Currency Codes

A high degree of standardization is required when travel professionals work with international fares, taxes, and related fees. This information is the same whether the agent is selling air fares in Mexico, Europe, Asia, or the United States. The airline ticket agent in Bangkok, for example, must be able to interpret the ticket that was issued by a travel agent in Dubuque, Iowa. That is why IATA has created standard codes that are used to identify countries, local currencies, and taxes. These codes are called **International Standards Organization (ISO) codes**.

The first type of ISO code is the currency code. Each currency is identified by a three-letter code. For example, when a fare is displayed in a foreign country's currency, the currency code is placed either in front of or following the fare amount, to identify it. In addition to currency codes, other ISO identifications include two-letter country codes. A complete list of ISO codes is found in the airline computer reservations systems as well as printed resources such as the *Worldwide OAG* and *Travel Planners*. Table 4.5 is a partial list of ISO codes.

International Taxes and Surcharges

➤ Taxes

There are many differences between domestic and international air fares and tickets. One difference is the higher number of taxes and fees that are associated with international air travel. Remember the three types of taxes associated with domestic travel? They are the following: (1) U.S. transportation tax (currently at 7.5 percent), (2) passenger facility charge (PFC), and (3) segment tax (ZP).

An international ticket may have five or more types of taxes and fees included. Each type of tax is identified by a two-letter code. The tax codes are placed either before or after the tax amounts when they are displayed on a computer screen and when entered on a passenger's ticket.

Two general types of taxes and fees are applicable to international routings: transportation departure taxes and federal inspection fees. *Transportation departure taxes* apply to international passengers *departing* from airports in the United States to foreign countries. *Federal inspection fees* apply to international passengers *returning* to the United States from foreign countries. All of these taxes and fees are normally collected at the time of ticket purchase and included as part of the fare. An exception are local airport departure and arrival taxes, which are collected by some foreign governments. The international passenger pays local taxes upon arrival or departure from the foreign airport. The majority of local taxes are paid upon departure. If applicable, the passenger checks in for the flight and is required to pay the local tax before boarding the aircraft.

Table 4.6 is a reference chart of international taxes and fees with routing examples. Remember that all tax amounts are subject to change.

➤ Surcharges

Surcharges are amounts that are added to the price of an airline ticket. They are not taxes and are not to be treated like taxes when pricing tickets. Surcharges are added to the fare amount before taxes. They become part of the base fare and are also commissionable. There are two major types of surcharges:

TABLE 4.6   INTERNATIONAL TAXES AND FEES

Tax Code	Name of Tax	Amount	When Applicable	Routing Examples
Transportation Departure Taxes				

US	U.S. domestic	7.5%	Between points within the continental United States, Hawaii, and Alaska
			Between points within the continental United States and points in Canada and Mexico located inside the buffer zone[a]
				Chicago–Miami
				Honolulu–Kona–
				  Honolulu
				Fairbanks–
				  Anchorage
				Boston–Montreal

US	U.S. international departure tax	USD12.10 (one-way)
		
		USD24.20 (round trip)
			From the United States to foreign countries, including to Puerto Rico, U.S. Virgin Islands, and U.S. possessions (charge in each direction)
			Departure from the United States to points in Canada and Mexico located outside the buffer zone[a]
				New York–Paris
				Miami–Rio
				  de Janeiro
				Atlanta–Nassau
				Denver–San Juan
				Chicago–
				  Edmonton,
				  Canada

XF	Passenger facility charge	USD1.00 USD2.00 USD3.00	From United States airports authorized to collect this fee	
ISO code	Foreign local departure tax	Varies	From specific countries	Bermuda–New York Tel Aviv–Rome
Federal Inspection Fees				
YC	U.S. Customs fee	USD5.00	Return to the United States *except* from Canada, Mexico, and Caribbean	Tokyo–Los Angeles Rio de Janero– Miami Athens–Chicago
XY	Immigration and Naturalization (INS) fee	USD6.00	Return to the United States *except* from Puerto Rico, U.S. Virgin Islands, Guam, and other U.S. possessions	
XA	United States animal and plant health inspection fee (APHIS)	USD2.10	Return to the United States *except* from Canada and Puerto Rico	London–Los Angeles Bermuda–Boston Tokyo–Denver Mexico City–Miami

[a]*Buffer zone includes all cities in Canada and Mexico located within 225 miles of continental U.S. borders.*

1. *Fuel surcharges:* applicable from certain cities in the United States plus Puerto Rico and the U.S. Virgin Islands. Fuel surcharges are not applicable from foreign countries. Therefore, they are more common on domestic tickets.

2. *Security surcharges:* apply to or from specific international points; they never apply when travel is wholly within the United States. Security surcharges are to help subsidize security operations at international airports. They apply *on U.S. flagship carriers on transatlantic flight segments only*. They also apply between points in the United States and specific airports in the West Indies. The standard amount of security surcharge is USD5.00 per passenger for each applicable flight segment. Like the fuel surcharge, the security surcharge is identified with the code Q on the passenger's airline ticket.

> **Example:** A passenger is traveling round trip between New York and London. American Airlines is the transatlantic carrier outbound to London, and British Airways is the transatlantic carrier inbound. What is the amount of security surcharge that is applied to this ticket? Right, the New York to London segment on the U.S. flagship American Airlines will have a security surcharge of $5. There is no surcharge applicable on the return since British Airways is not a U.S. flagship carrier.

✓ Check Your Understanding 4-9

1. Match each tax code with the correct name.

   A. XA   _____ 1. U.S. animal and plant health inspection fee

   B. YC   _____ 2. U.S. international departure tax

   C. XF   _____ 3. Passenger facility charge

   D. US   _____ 4. Immigration and Naturalization Service fee

   E. XY   _____ 5. U.S. Customs fee

2. An international security surcharge applies under what two conditions of travel?

   A. _____

   B. _____

3. For each routing below, list each type of tax that is applicable by writing the tax code and the amount (refer to Table 4.6 for help). The first has been completed as an example. Select from the following tax codes: US, YC, XY, XA. For example,

Atlanta–Bermuda–Atlanta	Taxes = US24.20
	XY6.00
	XA2.10

   A. Tampa–San Juan–Tampa   Tax(es) = _____
   B. St. Louis–St. Thomas–St. Louis   Tax(es) = _____
   C. San Diego–Acapulco–San Diego   Tax(es) = _____
   D. New York–Rome, Italy– New York   Tax(es) = _____
   E. Seattle–Tokyo (one way)   Tax(es) = _____

INTERNATIONAL FARES

The number of air fares available between any two cities in the world is mind-boggling. It wasn't always the case. A couple of decades ago there were three types of international air fares no matter where and when you were traveling:

first class, economy class, and excursion. Today, there can be hundreds of different air fares between a city pair. For example, there are more than 400 air fares to choose from if you are traveling between New York and Paris. They range from as low as $400 to approximately $6,000 round trip! Why is there such a difference? The ticket prices will be lower for passengers who are flexible, don't mind a lot of restrictions, and are willing to pay in advance. For passengers who aren't so lucky, who must depart and return on specified dates, and who are paying the last minute, ticket prices will be a lot higher.

➤ International Fare Categories

To make some sense out of this air fare maze, it is best to keep in mind the general types or categories of international fares. Table 4.7 is a reference chart that lists the general fare categories. Keep in mind that this is a general guide only; there will be exceptions to the restrictions shown. They are listed from the most expensive ($$$$$) to the least expensive ($). Notice that the number of travel restrictions increase as the price decreases.

- *Normal.* These fares have no restrictions. The passenger is allowed to make an unlimited number of stopovers between the origin and outward destination cities without a fare charged to each stopover city. Normal fares are also called all-year fares since the ticket is valid for one year from the date of issue.
- *Restricted normal.* These fares are similar to normal fares except that the passenger is not allowed unlimited stopovers at no extra charge. Usually, these fares permit one or two stopovers in each direction of travel either free or at an additional charge. Like normal fares, the tickets are valid for one year and there are no other restrictions.
- *Standard excursion.* Three types of restrictions are usually associated with standard excursion fares: (1) Travel must be round trip—one-way journeys are not allowed; (2) additional stopovers between the origin and outward destination are not allowed or are severely limited, usually at a charge per stopover; and (3) there is a minimum stay and a maximum stay. No other restrictions apply.
- *Advance-purchase excursion (APEX).* These fares are very restrictive. They have all of the restrictions of standard excursions, plus four: (1) The reservation must be made a certain number of days or weeks prior to departure; (2) the ticket must be issued a certain number of days prior to departure;

Table 4.7   International Fare Categories Reference Chart

| | | Travel Restrictions | | | |
Fare Category	Stopovers	Validity Min./Max.	Advance Ticket	Change Penalty	Cancellation Penalty
Normal ($$$$$)	Unlimited	No	No	No	No
Restricted normal ($$$$)	Limited	No	No	No	No
Standard excursion ($$$)	Limited	Yes	No	No	No
Advance-purchase excursion ($$)	Limited or none	Yes	Yes	Yes	Yes
Nonrefundables ($)	None	Yes	Yes	Yes	Yes (100%)

(3) there is a fee penalty for changes to the reservation after the ticket has been issued; and (4) there is a fee penalty if the ticket is canceled.

- *Nonrefundable.* These fares are the least expensive but are the most restrictive of all categories. They contain the same restrictions as the APEX fares, except stopovers are never allowed and there is no refund if the passenger cancels the ticket. These fares are also considered to be "instant-purchase" to certain markets since the ticket must be issued within a day or two after booking.

➤ Consolidators and Discounted Fares

Would you believe a $500 fare from Los Angeles to Hong Kong with no advance purchase at a 20 percent travel agency commission? It is possible by using consolidators. **Consolidators** are companies that contract with the airlines to buy airline seats in bulk and sell them at discount prices. They get these contracts because of a proven ability to deliver a very high volume of sales.

There are two types of companies: consolidators and tour operators who sell air only. Both have high-volume contracts with airlines that offer either net fares (without commission built in) or high-commission bulk fares. The majority of consolidators sell net, allowing the travel agent to mark up the ticket to arrive at a fair commission and a fair price for the client.

What are the advantages for travel agencies to use their services? Consolidators offer unique opportunities for higher commissions (over the standard 8 percent) and lower fares. Also some tickets sold through consolidators do not have the same restrictions as tickets sold directly by the airlines, such as Saturday night stays and advance purchase. Most consolidators can also offer the same frequent-flyer credits for travelers and sales credit for the agency with the airline on which the ticket was written.

Some of the disadvantages to travel agencies is determining which consolidators are reliable and which are not. There are some marginal operators that advertise themselves as consolidators but are not true consolidators. Fortunately, the majority are operated professionally. Travel agents can verify the stability of consolidators by checking two trade publications: *Jax Fax*, which is the primary advertising medium for most consolidators, and *The Index of Air Travel Consolidators*, which is used to evaluate consolidator reliability and publishes travel agency ratings of each firm. Another method is to use consolidators that are ASTA (American Society of Travel Agents) members or members of a recognized consumer protection program.

Another disadvantage is that many consolidators do not accept credit cards but want payment in advance. Also, many consolidator fares are not accessed through the airline computer reservations systems; the travel agent must rely on phone calls to obtain seat availability and fare quotes. Most consolidator fares are available only on international flights. However, it is certain that there will be a growing availability of consolidator fares for domestic routes.

Web Link

Many consolidators are selling their wares on-line. In some cases, the sites are exclusively for travel agents. Others allow the traveler to make his or her arrangements on-line. The reservation is then sent to the travel agency for ticketing. Here are a few consolidator sites:

1. *Airline Discount Store:* includes more than 5 million international fares, no domestic. Go to *www.airvalues.com*
2. *UniTravel OnLine Reservation System:* consolidator air fares exclusively for travel agents; approximate $200 annual fee.

International Fare Calculations

Calculating fares for international routings can be quite complex. All major carriers have a staff of international rate agents that calculate fares for passengers and travel agents. Rate agents train for their job for several years. What makes international faring so complex is that there may be several different ways to calculate one ticket; each method is correct. The rate agent has to make sure that every possible way to calculate the ticket has been tried in order to give the passenger the best price. Some tickets, such as simple round- or circle-trip routings, are very straightforward. Others can be very complex, with multiple stopovers and surface segments.

Travel agents are not international rate experts, nor are they expected to be. However, clients have questions regarding the price on their ticket, so agents must have a basic knowledge of how the ticket was priced. Studying about how to calculate international fares is like studying an alphabet soup of crazy-sounding things like NUCs, ROEs, MPMs, TPMs, and HIPs—they all play a part!

➤ Neutral Units of Construction

International fares are displayed in both the currency of the country of origin and in counting units called **neutral units of construction (NUCs;** pronounced "nukes"). For example, fares from Los Angeles to Tokyo will be displayed in both U.S. dollars and NUCs. Fares from Rome to New York will be displayed in Italian lira and NUCs.

What exactly are NUCs? They are just counting units and are not equivalent to any particular currency until they are adjusted mathematically. How much is a NUC worth? Nothing until they are adjusted mathematically. When an air fare is published in NUCs, it is multiplied by a certain number or factor. Once it is multiplied by a set factor, it becomes equivalent to a real currency value.

We call the number or factor that is used to change a NUC value to a currency value the IATA rate of exchange (ROE). The ROE is adjusted four times per year to keep current with realistic currency values on the world market. Current ROE values are updated in the CRSs. Table 4.8 shows a partial display of ROEs displayed from an airline computer reservations system. These rates were accurate at the time of publication and are to be used for illustration and training purposes only.

IATA selected the U.S. dollar currency to serve as the basis of the rates of exchange for NUCs. Since ROEs are based on the value of the U.S. dollar, the formula to convert a NUC into U.S. currency is easy! Just remember that 1USD = 1NUC. This means that NUCs have a *par* or one-to-one relationship with U.S. currency. This makes it easy for travel agents in the United States, where ticket transactions are made in U.S. currency.

In many cases, fares on international tickets are listed in NUC values, then converted to the currency of payment by the correct rate of exchange. Neutral

Table 4.8   Rates of Exchange

Country	Currency/ISO Code	ROE
Austria	shilling/AUS	13.24153
Canada	dollar/CAD	1.22805
Denmark	Danish krone/DKK	7.24743
Thailand	baht/THB	26.53500
United States	dollar/USD	1.0000

units of construction amounts are identified by the code NUC. The applicable ISO or currency code identifies the currency of payment on the airline ticket.

✓ Check Your Understanding 4-10

Multiple Choice

Circle the *best* answer.

1. The fare category that provides unlimited stopovers and for which there are no advance purchase or cancellation penalty restrictions is:

   A. standard excursion
   B. nonrefundable
   C. APEX
   D. unrestricted normal

2. The most restrictive (and therefore the least expensive) fare category below is:

   A. APEX
   B. nonrefundable
   C. standard excursion
   D. restricted normal

3. APEX stands for:

   A. all-penalty excursion
   B. all-passenger excursion
   C. advance-purchase exception
   D. advance-purchase excursion

4. NUC stands for:

   A. neutral unit of calculation
   B. normal unit of construction
   C. neutral unit of construction
   D. normal unit of calculation

5. The IATA rates of exchange (ROEs) change:

   A. one time per year
   B. twice each year
   C. monthly
   D. four times per year

6. The ROE is used to:

   A. exchange airline tickets
   B. change a fare from a NUC value to a specific currency amount
   C. change a fare from a specific currency amount to a NUC value
   D. exchange one currency for another at airports and banks

7. NUCS are par with U.S. currency. This means that:

   A. NUCs and USD are equivalent: 1NUC = 1USD.
   B. The ROE for U.S. currency is 1.0000.
   C. Only A is true.
   D. Both A and B are false.
   E. Both A and B are true.

8. Companies that buy airline seats in bulk and sell them at discount prices are:

   A. cooperatives
   B. value shops
   C. consolidators
   D. discount houses

MILEAGE AND ROUTING

International air fares are calculated by one of two methods: the *mileage system* or the *routing system*. The type of fare that is being charged will determine which system is used. The mileage system is based on the number of air miles the passenger flies between the origin and the outward destination or farthest point on the trip. The more expensive fare categories, such as normal first class, business class, and economy, are based on the mileage system. The routing system restricts the passenger to travel on specific carriers or combinations of carriers through specific connecting or stopover cities. In general, the least expensive fare categories, such as APEX and nonrefundables, are usually based on the routing system.

➤ Mileage System

The mileage system of fare construction makes sense. It allows the passenger to travel up to a certain maximum number of air miles between the origin and outward destination cities on the routing. There are six basic elements of the mileage system:

1. *MPM:* **maximum permitted mileage**
2. *TPM:* **ticketed point mileage**
3. *EMA:* extra mileage allowance
4. *EMS:* extra mileage surcharges
5. *HIP:* higher intermediate point
6. *CTM:* circle-trip minimum

MPM

When constructing fares based on mileage, the through fare is charged from the origin to the outward destination. We call the two cities between which a through fare is charged the *fare breakpoints.* The types of fares that are based on mileage, such as normal and restricted normal fares, will allow either an unlimited or certain number of stopovers between the fare breakpoints at the published through fare. These stopovers are allowed as long as the passenger *does not exceed a maximum number of air miles between the fare breakpoints.* The maximum number of air miles that is allowed between the fare breakpoints is called the *maximum permitted mileage (MPM).* Every city pair that has published fares will also have a published MPM.

MPMs are established by IATA and are never calculated by the sales agent. An MPM is determined by taking the shortest operated air distance between two cities and increasing that number by approximately 20 to 25 percent. The MPM that results is higher than the actual mileage between two cities and allows the passenger to make stopovers and connections along the way without an increase of air fare.

> **Example:** You are planning a one-way trip from Chicago to Rome for a business traveler. He must also stop in Madrid and Zurich along the way for meetings. You are charging a normal economy fare that allows additional stopovers. The through fare between Chicago and Rome is USD950.00. The fare is based on mileage. The through fare of USD950.00 can be charged as long as the actual flown mileage between each ticketed point of travel (Chicago–Madrid–Zurich–Rome) does not exceed the MPM, which is 5,779.

TPM

To determine if the passenger's itinerary of Chicago–Madrid–Zurich–Rome is equal to or less than the MPM, the actual mileage flown between each city must be totaled. The actual mileage flown is called the *ticketed point mileage (TPM).* A TPM represents the shortest air distance operated between two cities. Like MPMs, TPMs are established by IATA and can be obtained in printed tariffs and are calculated automatically in the airline computer reservations systems. The TPMs have been calculated for our example as follows:

	TPMs
Chicago	
Madrid	4,189
Zurich	771
Rome	435
	5,395

TPM between Chicago and Rome = 5,395; MPM between Chicago and Rome = 5,779. Since the total air mileage flown (TPM of 5,395) is less than or equal to the maximum permitted mileage (MPM = 5,779), the through fare of USD950 can be charged with the two stopovers. If the passenger's TPM in any one direction exceeds the MPM, a fare surcharge may be required.

EMA

The *extra mileage allowance (EMA)* is designed to help the airline passenger if the total flown mileage (total TPM) in any direction *exceeds* the maximum permitted mileage (MPM). If applicable, the EMA permits you to deduct a certain number of miles from the TPM calculated. This gives you an *adjusted TPM*. If the adjusted TPM is equal to or less than the permitted mileage, no fare surcharge is required. EMAs are valid between some destinations when traveling on specified routings. A list of EMAs is published in the international air tariffs and CRSs. Table 4.9 shows a few examples of EMAs when travel is between North America and destinations abroad.

EMS

If the TPM (or the adjusted TPM after an allowance is applied) exceeds the MPM in one direction of travel, the one-way fare is increased by either 5, 10, 15, 20, or 25 percent. This is called the *excess mileage surcharge (EMS)*. The amount of surcharge or percentage increase is determined by the number of TPMs that ex-

TABLE 4.9   EMA Table

When Travel Is Between:	And:	Applicable Routing Is:	The EMA Is (deduct from the TPM if required):
Continental U.S.	IATA 3	Honolulu, across the North or Central Pacific on any carrier	800 miles
Portland, Oregon and Seattle, Washington	Austria, Belgium, Finland, France, Germany, Greece, Ireland, Italy, Netherlands, Norway, or the United Kingdom	TWA	200 miles
United States/ Mexico	South Africa	Tel Aviv	210 miles
Canada	Seoul, Korea	Via Hong Kong when CX is the transpacific carrier	390 miles

ceeds the MPM. The higher the passenger travels over the MPM, the higher the percentage increase that is charged. The amount of surcharge is determined by a formula and is calculated by the computer reservations systems. In addition, there is an excess mileage percentage table that is used to determine the percentage increase. This table is printed in various international tariff resources that some travel agencies use in combination with the computer reservations system.

HIP

If the passenger is on a round- or circle-trip routing, there is an additional step called the *higher intermediate point (HIP)* check. A higher intermediate point is defined as any ticketed point of travel on the itinerary that has a higher fare than the established fare between the origin and outward destination cities. The outward destination (or the city on the routing to where the through fare is charged) is determined by the city that is located farthest from the origin. This is done so that passengers can take advantage of the highest MPM. However, it is not always true that air fares are determined by the distance you travel; the city that is located farthest from the origin point may not have the highest fare!

Example: The passenger is traveling from New York to Athens with a stopover in London in each direction: New York–London–Athens–London–New York. The passenger is traveling on Delta Air Lines, standard economy class, which permits one free stopover in each direction of travel. The outward destination is Athens, since it is located farthest from New York. The MPM and fare are based between New York and Athens:

MPM (each direction) = 5,912   one-way Y fare = $1,040

However, the one-way Delta economy fare from New York to *London* (intermediate stopover city) is $1,100. London is called the higher intermediate point since it has a higher fare than the established through fare to the outward destination of Athens.

Remember, the "Golden Rule" of international fare calculation is that the passenger must be charged the *highest fare between any two cities on the itinerary*. Therefore, this passenger must pay the New York–London higher fare of $1,100. We call this the *higher intermediate fare (HIF)*. Since this passenger is on a round trip (same routing in each direction of travel), he is charged $1,100 (HIF) on the outbound journey and $1,100 (HIF) on the inbound journey.

CTM

The circle-trip minimum check is the final step when calculating circle-trip itineraries. The *circle-trip minimum (CTM)* is defined as the highest round-trip fare between any two cities on the routing. The passenger must be charged, at the minimum, the highest round-trip fare or CTM. In the example above for the round trip New York–London–Athens–London–New York, the passenger is automatically paying the highest round-trip fare between any two cities on the routing; he is paying the higher intermediate fare of $1,100 in each direction or $2,200 round trip. That is the highest round-trip fare or CTM. What if the passenger is on a circle trip (i.e., a different routing and fare in each direction of travel)? The passenger must still pay the highest round-trip fare between any two cities on the entire itinerary.

Interior view of the Coliseum in Rome, Italy

Grand Canal—Venice, Italy

Ancient amphitheater of Taormina, Sicily, Italy

Dubrovnik, Croatia

Milford Sound, South Island, New Zealand

Entering the Gatun Locks by cruise ship, Panama Canal

Glacier Express, Alpine region of Switzerland

Royal Palace, Bangkok, Thailand

Skyline of Istanbul, Turkey

Air New Zealand over the Pacific

Cruise ship sailing the Geiranger Fjord, western Norway

Example: Our passenger is traveling on the circle trip below (notice a different stopover city in each direction of travel). He is traveling on TWA, business class that allows unlimited number of stopovers in either direction of travel: New York–Geneva–Warsaw–Vienna–New York. The outward destination is Warsaw since it is located farthest from New York (and it has the highest MPM). The MPM and fare between New York and Warsaw in each direction are

$$MPM = 5{,}110 \qquad \text{fare business class} = \$1{,}125$$

Let's compare New York to Warsaw with the business-class fare from New York to Geneva (stopover) and New York to Vienna (stopover):

$$\text{New York–Geneva} = \$1{,}250$$
$$\text{New York–Vienna} = \$1{,}350$$

In this case we have a different higher intermediate fare in each direction of travel. On the outbound trip, you will charge the HIF of $1,250 (New York and Geneva). On the return trip, you will charge the HIF of $1,350 (Vienna and New York). To satisfy the CTM rule, determine the two cities that have the highest fare. In this example, the highest fare is between *New York* and *Vienna* at $1,350 one way, or $2,700 round trip. *The CTM is $2,700 in this example.*

So when you add the HIF fare outbound ($1,250) and the HIF return ($1,350), the calculated fare equals $2,600. However, the CTM (the highest round-trip fare) is $2,700. An additional $100 ($2,700 – $2,600) must be added to increase the calculated total to the CTM.

➤ Routing System

Since most discounted fares such as nonrefundables and APEX fares usually do not allow additional stopovers, these types of fares are based not on mileage but on the *routing* system. An air fare that is based on routing may contain any one or more of the following travel restrictions:

- *Type of flight service* (e.g., some discounted fares allow travel on connecting flights only)
- *Permitted connecting cities* (e.g., if a passenger is flying on a discounted fare from Boston to Nice, France, the routing may allow only Paris as a connecting city)
- *On-line service only* (e.g., if a passenger is buying a nonrefundable fare on American Airlines between Chicago and Athens, Greece, the fare may restrict the passenger to fly each segment on American Airlines)

Routings are usually displayed like diagrams in printed air tariffs and in computer systems.

Example: A typical routing diagram looks like the one below. This example shows the routing that is permitted for a discounted fare on American Airlines, Chicago to Brussels, Belgium. As you can see, city and airport codes are used. In the example below, the slash (/) means *or*. The dash (–) means *through* or *to*.

$$\text{CHI–AA/DL/UA–NYC/EWR/BOS–AA–BRU}$$

Explanation: The passenger is restricted to the following cities as connecting points: NYC, EWR, or BOS. The passenger is restricted to fly either AA, DL, or UA on the domestic segment (from Chicago to the connecting city) and AA on the transatlantic segment to Brussels.

International Fare Resources

There are three types of resources that travel agents use to help them search for fares and to do necessary mileage or routing calculations: (1) airline rate agents, (2) printed air tariffs, and (3) computer reservations systems. The best resource to use depends on what is available to the agent and the complexity of the itinerary that is to be priced.

➤ Tariffs

What is a tariff in the travel industry? A **tariff** is a compilation of fares, rules, and related information of one or more transportation carriers in a published volume. There are rail tariffs for train prices, car rental tariffs for rental rates, and airline tariffs for fares. Since air tariffs can become rather cumbersome and bulky for daily use, many carriers publish short tariff memoranda that consist of a few pages or updated fare information. The memoranda are mailed periodically to travel agencies for easy reference.

Two tariff publications are used by travel agents: the *Airline Passenger Tariff* (APT) and the *Air Tariff*. The APT represents fares for many European carriers (in addition to some of the American flagships) and is used more widely throughout Europe. The *Air Tariff* represents fares for most U.S. and Canadian flagship carriers, so it is used more frequently in North America.

Figure 4.19 is a cutaway from the *Air Tariff* that shows a partial list of fares from New York to Frankfurt, Germany. The tariff identifies each fare by a fare-type code and carrier. The fare is shown in both the headline city's currency (U.S. dollars in this example) and NUCs. Rule number identifiers are provided which direct the agent to a detailed description of the conditions and restrictions of travel for each fare. The MPM is provided in the upper right corner of the page. A

FARE TYPE	CARRIER CODE	HEADLINE CITY CURRENCY	NUC	RULES	GI MPM RTE REF
NEW YORK CITY (NYC) N.Y., USA To Frankfurt				U.S.	$(USD) MPM AT 4621
Y	AA	1184.00	1184.00	N0300	AT
C	AA	1386.00	1386.00	N0300	AT
F	AA	2503.00	2503.00	N0300	AT
HLXAPNR	AA	736.00	736.00	N3691	AT r95
HLWAPNR	AA	796.00	796.00	N3691	AT r95
HHXAPNR	AA	900.00	900.00	N3691	AT r95
HHWAPNR	AA	960.00	960.00	N3691	AT r95
BLXE3	AA	1063.00	1063.00	N1300	AT r105
BLXE3	AA	1233.00	1233.00	N1300	AT r105
Y11	TW	1184.00	1184.00	N0890	AT
C	TW	1386.00	1386.00	N0305	AT
F	TW	2503.00	2503.00	N0305	AT

Figure 4.19 *Fare display from the* Air Tariff.

global indicator code (GI) of AT indicates the direction of travel that is required—via the Atlantic. The "r" plus a number opposite a fare indicates that the fare is based on routing (e.g., r95, r105). If an "r" reference is not present, the fare is based on mileage. Fares in lightface print are one way; fares in **boldface** print are round trip.

► Computer Fare Displays

The computer reservations systems that are used by travel agencies and other booking companies have become the most important resource for fare and related airline information. International fares in the systems can be displayed in a variety of ways. The first method is to display all possible fares on *all* carriers for a given city pair and travel date. Another method is to display fares for one or more specified carriers only. This method is effective when the travel agent knows in advance which carrier will be used for transportation.

Figure 4.20 is a sample display from a major airline computer reservation system. It is called a fare scan or fare quote since it is displaying fares for a given car-

ORG - CHI   DST - BRU   TRIP-OUTBOUND   CXR - AA   11AUG00   USD
** BA   CO   DL   NW   TW   UA   US
   INTL TAXES/FEES/US PFC - NOT INCL IN TOTAL

QTE	F/B	BK	FARE	EFF	EXP	TKT	AP	MIN/MAX	RTG
1-	F	F X	3092.00	-	-	-	-	-/ -	4001
2-	C	C X	1680.00	-	-	-	-	-/ -	4001
3-	Y	Y X	1343.00	-	-	-	-	-/ -	4001
4-	KLWAN	K R	658.00	28JN	-	-	##	7/ 1M	96
5-	KLXAN	K R	608.00	28JN	-	-	##	7/ 1M	96
6-	KKWAN	K R	788.00	-	-	-	##	7/ 1M	96
7-	KKXAN	K R	728.00	-	-	-	##	7/ 1M	96
8-	HLWAPNR	H R	758.00	-	-	-	##	7/ 2M	96
9-	HLXAPNR	H R	708.00	-	-	-	##	7/ 2M	96
10-	HHWAPNR	H R	988.00	-	-	-	##	7/ 2M	96
11-	HHXAPNR	H R	928.00	-	-	-	##	7/ 2M	96
12-	HKWAPNR	H R	888.00	-	-	-	##	7/ 2M	96
13-	HKXAPNR	H R	828.00	-	-	-	##	7/ 2M	96
14-	ML2	M X	769.00	-	-	30AU	1	-/ -	97
15-	MH2	M X	787.00	-	-	30AU	1	-/ -	97
16-	BL16	B X	849.00	-	-	-	-	-/ -	104
17-	BH16	B X	932.00	-	-	-	-	-/ -	104
18-	BLEE3	B R	1270.00	-	-	-	-	-/ 180	104
19-	BHEE3	B R	1342.00	-	-	-	-	-/ 180	104
20 -	MLWAPS6	M R	858.00	28JN	-	-	##	SUN/6M	201
21-	MLXAPS6	M R	808.00	28JN	-	-	##	SUN/6M	201

ROUTINGS →

96	AT - AA - BOS - AA - LON - AA/BD
	AT - AA - NYC/EWR/BOS - AA - LON - AA/BD
97	AT - AA
	AT - AA - NYC - AA
104	AT - AA - NYC/EWR/BOS - AA
	AT - AA - NYC/EWR/BOS - AA - LON/MAD - YY
	AT - AA
201	AT - AA - NYC/EWR/BOS - AA
	AT - AA - RDU/NYC/EWR/BOS - AA

MPM →

4001   MPM - 4976 - VIA THE ATLANTIC

Figure 4.20 *Computer fare display.*

rier and travel date. In this example, the travel agent knows that the passenger will be traveling on American Airlines sometime in mid-August and wishes to see a list of fares in effect at that time from Chicago to Brussels. The fare-scan format for international fares is the same as that for domestic U.S. fares (as discussed in Chapter 3). In Figure 4.21, note that the last column—RTG—rovides a route reference number. These route reference numbers reference the routing descriptions printed on the bottom of the display. Note that the fares based on mileage are referenced with the number 4001 under the RTG column. Reference number 4001 on the bottom of the display indicates the maximum mileage permitted between the city pair.

✓ Check Your Understanding 4-11

Multiple Choice

Circle the *best* answer.

1. The maximum number of air miles allowed between the origin and outward destination (also the first element of the mileage system) is the:
   A. ticketed point mileage (TPM)
   B. extra mileage allowance (EMA)
   C. higher intermediate point (HIP)
   D. maximum permitted mileage (MPM)

2. The shortest operated distance between two points (also the second element of the mileage system) is the:
   A. ticketed point mileage (TPM)
   B. circle-trip minimum (CTM)
   C. maximum permitted mileage (MPM)
   D. extra mileage surcharge (EMS)

3. This is designed to help the airline passenger if the total mileage flown exceeds the permitted mileage. It permits you to deduct a certain number of miles when applicable. This is the third element of the mileage system.
   A. extra mileage allowance (EMA)
   B. circle-trip minimum (CTM)
   C. extra mileage surcharge (EMS)
   D. higher intermediate point (HIP)

4. If the total mileage flown exceeds the permitted mileage, the fare is increased by either 5, 10, 15, 20, or 25 percent. This is the fourth element of the mileage system.
   A. circle-trip minimum (CTM)
   B. ticketed point mileage (TPM)
   C. extra mileage allowance (EMA)
   D. excess mileage surcharge (EMS)

5. This is the check you do in each direction of travel to see if there is a city that has a higher fare than the fare between the origin and outward destination cities. If so, this fare is charged. This is the fifth element of the mileage system.
   A. higher intermediate point (HIP)
   B. extra mileage surcharge (EMS)
   C. ticketed point mileage (TPM)
   D. circle-trip minimum (CTM)

6. This final step is to determine the highest round trip fare between any two cities on the routing. The round-trip fare charged on the ticket cannot be less than this highest fare. This is the sixth element of the mileage system.
   A. extra mileage surcharge (EMS)
   B. circle-trip minimum (CTM)
   C. higher intermediate point (HIP)
   D. extra mileage allowance (EMA)

Refer to Figure 4.20: Fares from New York to Frankfurt as displayed in the *Air Tariff* publication.

7. The maximum permitted mileage, one way, between New York and Frank-furt is _____.

8. The one-way first-class fare on American Airlines in U.S. dollars is _____.

9. The round-trip economy-class (Y) fare on American Airlines in U.S. dollars is _____.

10. The round-trip nonrefundable fare with the code HLWAPNR in U.S. dollars is _____.

Refer to Figure 4.21, a sample of a computer display of air fares.

11. The one-way business class [C] fare from Chicago to Brussels in U.S. dollars is _____.

12. The round-trip fare for the fare that must be booked in K class, during low (L) season, during midweek (X), and is nonrefundable (AN) is _____.

13. The passenger is paying the round-trip nonrefundable fare with the code HKXAPNR.

    A. The minimum number of days that he is required to stay before returning home is _____.

    B. The maximum number of days, weeks, or months that he is allowed to stay is _____.

14. Your passenger is paying the $769 one-way fare in M class. He is flying from Chicago to Brussels connecting in New York. He is flying American Airlines on both segments. Is this routing allowed? (*Hint:* Find the routing indicator under the RTG column. Find that same routing indicator below the fare display. Is NYC allowed as a connecting city? What airline is he required to fly?) _____ (yes or no)

15. The passenger is flying standard economy class from Chicago to Brussels.

    A. What is the one-way fare? _____

    B. Is this fare based on routing or mileage? _____

    C. If the fare is based on mileage, what is the maximum permitted mileage in each direction of travel? _____

Close-Up: International Air-Related Careers

Rate specialist	Airport ticket agent	Sales and ticket office agents
Sales representative	Customer service agent	Reservation agent

The same types of positions that are available with domestic airline carriers are also available with foreign carriers. However, the employee of a foreign carrier is usually required to speak the language of the country.

International Air Specialist/Airline Rate Agent

Each major carrier offers a department called the *rate desk*. Rate desk agents are specially trained and expert in calculating air fares for complex routings such as circle trips and around-the-world fare constructions. Rate agents who work for the airlines go through years of training to be the best in their field.

Travel agents rely on this valuable resource to obtain the best or lowest possible fare for their clients. Agents submit their booked itineraries to the airline rate desk for pricing either by telephone or through the agency's CRS. It takes approximately 24 to 48 hours for the airline rate agent to respond back to the travel agency with the fare breakdown. Remember that this method is to be used only for complex itineraries; travel agents rely on other resources for the more simple one-way and round-trip itineraries.

➤ Key Terms

- consolidators
- customs allowance
- International Air Transport Association (IATA)
- International Airlines Travel Agency Network (IATAN)
- international certificate of vaccination

- international driver's permit (IDP)
- International Standards Organization (ISO)
- market exchange rate
- maximum permitted mileage (MPM)
- neutral unit of construction (NUC)
- passport

- tariff
- ticketed point mileage (TPM)
- tourist card
- traffic conference area
- value-added tax (VAT)
- visa
- World Health Organization (WHO)

 Flashback The number of international travelers is growing every year. This is due to more affordable air fares, new destination markets opening due to political changes, and ease of long-distance travel. The travel professional needs to expand his or her knowledge to include transportation systems and destinations worldwide.

This knowledge starts with learning the basics of international codes and air travel terminology. Knowing the major codes that identify world cities, airports, and flagship carriers is necessary to plan itineraries to anywhere in the world.

In addition, professionals need to be able to advise their clients on important requirements when traveling abroad. Information on how to obtain documentation such as passports, visas, tourist cards, and the IDP in addition to health precaution measures are relevant to the role of the travel agent as an advisor and counselor.

The questions "How much will it cost?" and "Can I get there cheaper?" are often posed by travelers. The travel agent must be able to identify the various types of fares and their restrictions on travel to qualify clients for the best product. Pricing complicated international tickets is best left to the experts—airline rate agents. However, the travel professional should have a working knowledge of the basic systems of international fare calculation. This knowledge is required to interpret prices and related entries on the passenger's ticket. Also, knowing how the routing and mileage systems work may result in revising a passenger's itinerary to reduce the price of the ticket substantially.

Although the travel professional relies heavily on the airline computer system to schedule international flights and price airline tickets, there are other important printed resources that are used in the travel workplace. When printed resources such as the *Worldwide Official Airline Guide* and the international *Travel Planner* editions are used to supplement the computer system, travel counselors are able to qualify their clients for the best product, plan itineraries to practically any point on the globe, and provide professional advice in a professional and efficient manner.

CHAPTER REVIEW

Multiple Choice

Circle the *best* answer.

1. Which of the following is not a true statement?

    A. Some visas are just stamps or endorsements that are placed in the passport upon entry into a foreign country.

    B. All visas must be applied for in advance of a trip through either a visa service or consulate.

    C. Visa requirements vary from country to country and should be checked on an individual basis.

    D. There is sometimes a fee required when applying for a visa as a separate document.

2. Which country below is the one where U.S. travel agents are most likely to need to issue tourist cards?

    A. Greece

    B. Kenya

    C. Mexico

    D. Caribbean

3. Your clients plan to visit and drive through the countries of France and Germany. You have found out that neither country requires an international driver's permit (IDP). Circle what you consider to be the best advice for this client.

    A. Since it is not required and the client is leaving in two days, you recommend that she not bother getting one.

    B. You don't recommend it since the traveler already has a valid U.S. driver's license.

    C. You advise her to get the IDP in case of accident or other road emergency during the trip.

    D. You recommend it only if another person will be driving the automobile.

4. Circle the destination that has a $1,200 customs allowance for returning U.S. citizens.

    A. Bermuda

    B. U.S. Virgin Islands

    C. Bahamas

    D. Canada

5. Circle the destination that has an unlimited allowance for returning U.S. citizens.

    A. U.S. Virgin Islands

    B. American Samoa

    C. Canada

    D. Puerto Rico

6. Name the federal agency that establishes regulations regarding immunizations for travelers in certain regions in the world.

    A. Department of Transportation (DOT)

    B. International Air Transport Association (IATA)

    C. U.S. Department of Health, Education, and Welfare (HEW)

    D. World Health Organization (WHO)

7. If the traveler exceeds the customs allowance when returning to the United States, which of the following is not an acceptable form of payment?

    A. credit card

    B. personal check

    C. U.S. currency

    D. They are all acceptable.

8. Which method of carrying money is safest when traveling abroad?
   - A. credit cards
   - B. foreign currency of the country
   - C. U.S. dollars
   - D. traveler's checks

9. Which major city below belongs in IATA area 3?
   - A. Bombay, India
   - B. Nairobi, Kenya
   - C. Montreal, Canada
   - D. Moscow, Russia

10. Which major city below belongs in IATA area 2?
    - A. Tel Aviv, Israel
    - B. Kabul, Afghanistan
    - C. Honolulu, Hawaii
    - D. Caracas, Venezuela

11. A flight's arrival time is midnight. How would this arrival time appear in an international flight schedule?
    - A. 12M
    - B. 1200
    - C. 0000
    - D. 2400

12. A passenger's ticket is round trip from Atlanta to Rome, Italy. Circle the type(s) of taxes below that would apply to this ticket. (There may be more than one answer.)
    - A. Immigration and Naturalization fee (XY)
    - B. U.S. Customs fee (YC)
    - C. U.S. domestic tax
    - D. U.S. animal and plant health inspection fee (APHIS)

13. A passenger's ticket is round trip from Miami to St. Thomas, U.S. Virgin Islands. Circle the type(s) of tax that would apply to this ticket. (There may be more than one answer.)
    - A. U.S. Customs fee (YC)
    - B. Immigration and Naturalization fee (XY)
    - C. U.S. animal and plant health inspection fee (APHIS)
    - D. U.S. international departure tax

14. A passenger's ticket is one way from Denver to London, England. Circle the type(s) of tax(es) that would apply to this ticket (there may be more than one answer).
    - A. U.S. international departure tax
    - B. U.S. animal and plant health inspection fee (APHIS)
    - C. U.S. Customs fee (YC)
    - D. Immigration and Naturalization fee (INS)

15. Which category below represents the least expensive and the most restrictive type of international fare?
    - A. advance-purchase excursion (APEX)
    - B. restricted normal
    - C. nonrefundable
    - D. standard excursion

16. Decode the following international flagship carrier codes.
    - A. SN _____
    - B. LH _____
    - C. BA _____
    - D. JL _____
    - E. RG _____
    - F. AZ _____
    - G. VS _____
    - H. SR _____
    - I. QF _____
    - J. CX _____

17. Encode the following international flagship carrier names.

A. Singapore Airlines _____   F. TAP Air Portugal _____

B. Aer Lingus _____   G. Olympic Airways _____

C. Finnair _____   H. Air New Zealand _____

D. El Al Israel Airlines _____   I. Iberia _____

E. Aeromexico _____   J. Viasa _____

18. For each city/airport name below, circle the correct code.

A. Cancún, Mexico	CNC	CCU	CUN	CAN
B. Toronto, Ontario, Canada	YTO	YTR	YTC	YOR
C. Buenos Aires, Argentina	BAA	BUA	BUE	BUR
D. Montego Bay, Jamaica	MBY	MBJ	MTJ	MON
E. Panama City, Panama	PTY	PAN	PCP	PTP
F. Zurich, Switzerland	ZUR	ZRS	ZRC	ZRH
G. London, UK	LGW	LHU	LON	LHO
H. Cairo, Egypt	CRO	CAI	CRE	CIR
I. Nairobi, Kenya, Africa	KEN	NAI	KYA	NBO
J. Hong Kong, China	HKG	HKK	HGK	HKC
K. Sydney, Australia	SID	SYN	SIA	SYD
L. Ho Chi Minh, Vietnam	HCM	SNG	HCV	SGN

Short Answers and Fill-ins

19. Your clients, Mr. and Mrs. Thomas and their son Jim (15 years old), are traveling to Europe for the first time. They are also applying for passports for the first time. Answer the following questions.

A. _____ (how many) passport applications are required to be completed.

B. In addition to the passport application, list the four items required.

(1) _____   (3) _____

(2) _____   (4) _____

C. Circle the document(s) below that are acceptable proofs of citizenship when applying for a passport.

(1) hospital certificate   (4) expired passport

(2) credit card   (5) social security card

(3) driver's license   (6) certified birth certificate

D. The fee for either Mr. or Mrs. Thomas's passport application is _____, and each passport will be valid for _____ years.

E. The fee for Jim's passport application is _____, and the passport will be valid for _____ years.

20. A flight is shown departing Los Angeles at 1810 next Monday. It arrives in Berlin at 1430+1. Using standard A.M./P.M. times,

A. What time did this flight depart Los Angeles? _____

B. What time did this flight arrive in Berlin? _____

C. What day did this flight arrive in Berlin? _____

21. International fares are displayed in two ways: in the currency of the country of origin, and in counting units called _____ (write out full name).

22. A traveler is flying from New York to Paris first class. He is allowed an unlimited number of stopovers as long as his trip doesn't exceed the _____ mileage.

23. The shortest operated flying distance between two points is called the _____ mileage.

24. The client is traveling from Dallas to Amsterdam. She is flying from Dallas to New York–Kennedy on Delta and connecting to Trans World Airlines from New York to Amsterdam. She is on a nonrefundable fare that permits any one of the routings below. Does she qualify? If your answer is no, explain your answer. If your answer is yes, indicate the routing by number that confirms your answer. _____

    1. DFW–DL/US–ATL–TW–AMS

    2. DFW–TW–AMS

    3. DFW–AA/DL/US–BOS/NYC/WAS–TW–AMS

25. Name three resources that the travel agent can use when researching international air fares.

    A. _____   B. _____

    C. _____

Chapter 5

Computer Technology

• •

Fast Forward ▼

➤ The two essential parts of any computer system are hardware and software. . . . 227

➤ The typical travel agent's workstation consists of four major types of computer hardware: a cathode ray tube (CRT), a central processing unit (CPU), a keyboard, and a mouse device. . . . 227

➤ Other important types of hardware that every computer user should know about are RAM, modem, printers, and scanners. . . . 228

➤ The four basic types of software programs that have direct applications in the travel workplace are word processing, database management, spreadsheet, and communication. . . . 229

➤ Today, more than 95 percent of U.S. travel agencies are computerized with one or more of the four leading computer reservations systems: SABRE, Apollo, Worldspan, and Amadeus/System One. . . . 233

➤ To understand how powerful the CRS is, we must look at these systems as being both interactive and dynamic. They are also used as storage and communication devices. . . . 238

➤ Today, travel agency computers link up with many major airlines systems through direct connections and not through the intermediary computer called ARINC. . . . 241

➤ All required and important information regarding each passenger's reservation is stored in the passenger name record (PNR). . . . 243

➤ The five mandatory fields of a PNR can be remembered through P.R.I.N.T. . . . 244

➤ A case study is an effective way to understand some of the ways that travel agents use the CRSs: request flight availability, sell from availability, enter passenger data, and display the price and completed PNR. . . . 245

➤ Today, personal computers and off-the-shelf software programs are becoming as commonplace as the telephone and calculator in the business world, especially in the travel office. . . . 255

➤ Technically, the Internet is the world's largest network of computers, a huge internetwork of computers. . . . 256

➤ To understand how the Internet works, an understanding of such things as servers and browsers is necessary: One serves as a gatekeeper and the other helps you navigate on the Web. . . . 257

➤ The four major reasons and benefits for travel professionals to access the Internet are communications, marketing, informational services, and product sales. . . . 260

➤ How does a travel company decide whether or not designing a Web site is a wise investment? What things should be considered in order to make a decision with confidence? . . . 264

➤ Professional Web travel site designers offer the important ten commandments for a successful Web site. . . . 266

Introduction

Computer technology has a tremendous effect on how a travel agency handles and services its business and leisure clients. The effect is beneficial since computer technology enables the travel professional to work faster, more accurately, and to present highly professional documentation for clients and colleagues.

Travel agents and other industry professionals use their office computers for more than the traditional tasks of booking flights, hotels, and car rentals for their clients. According to a recent survey conducted by *Travel Weekly* trade magazine, approximately 80 percent of travel agencies use their terminals for word processing, database management, and spreadsheets. They use these important business applications to do a wide variety of tasks, such as write letters to clients and suppliers, maintain customer profiles for mass mailings, and create professional-looking newsletters and brochures to market new programs.

In addition to the traditional personal computer applications, on-line technology is forcing travel professionals to take a fresh look at how they do business. More than 20 percent of travel agency computers are on-line and agents use the Internet for a wide variety of functions such as destination research, marketing, and long-distance and interoffice communications.

Since the use of computers is vital to the growth and success of most travel companies, we should first examine what computers are and what they do. In the first section of this chapter we present a basic overview of basic terminology and some general functions of computers. If you consider yourself a technowizard, you may want to glance quickly over this beginning section. However, the ABCs of computers tie in with later sections of this chapter that focus on the three major functions of automation in the travel workplace: airline computer reservations systems, personal computer applications, and Internet technology.

COMPUTER 101: OF MICE AND MONITORS

The two essential parts of any computer system are hardware and software. *Hardware* refers to the mechanical components of the computer, such as the display monitor and keyboard. With basic and peripheral (additional) hardware devices, you can do things like print airline tickets, scan pictures to use in a presentation, or create a slide presentation with animation and sound effects.

Software refers to the programs or applications that run on your computer's hardware. Some software is already built into the computer that you use; other software programs are purchased off-the-shelf. With software you can do things like book airline tickets, create brochures, send electronic mail, and create colorful three-dimensional charts for presentations. Sophisticated and creative software give your computer the power to meet your ever-widening needs in the travel workplace.

➤ What Makes It Tick: Hardware

The types and quantity of computer equipment differs between travel companies. However, the standard travel agent's workstation consists of four major types of computer hardware: a cathode ray tube (CRT), a central processing unit (CPU), a keyboard, and a mouse device. Four other types of hardware—RAM, modems, printers, and scanners—are used frequently to enhance efficiency and productivity in the workplace.

The Agent's Workstation

Let's first take a look at a typical agent's workstation (Figure 5.1):

1. The **cathode ray tube (CRT)** is the display monitor. It is a color monitor that looks like a television screen. The information entered by the user and the responses from airlines, suppliers, and other recipients are displayed on the CRT.
2. The **central processing unit (CPU)** is the "brain" of the computer. It resides inside your computer and is roughly the size of a postage stamp. It is also called a *microprocessor* because this is where most processing takes place; interpreting data, performing calculations, and storing and receiving information all happen here. The CPU is like an airport control tower since it directs the flow of data traffic in and out of the computer system.
3. The **keyboard** is the primary input device of the computer. The keyboard panel of any airline or personal computer resembles a standard typewriter keyboard. The center section is similar to a standard typewriter with letter and numeric keys. Special function, editing, and operational keys are located along the top row and along the sides of the keyboard panel. You type data in special formats when you use the computer for travel-related functions such as booking airline seats or displaying air fares. For non-travel-related tasks such as word processing, you type data as free text (no special formats or entries are required).
4. The **mouse** is an optional device that is used along with the keyboard to communicate with the computer. It is a rounded plastic instrument that is moved across the flat surface of the desk (usually on a protective pad). The mouse provides a "point-and-click" method of communication. You make on-screen selections by pointing to a word or object on the screen and clicking a button located

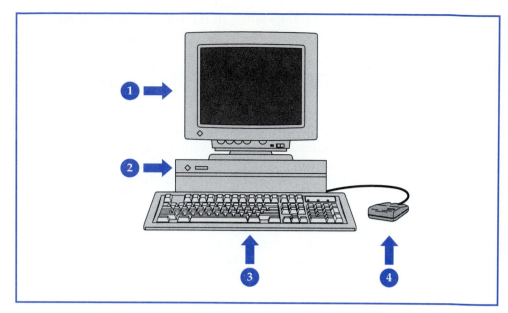

Figure 5.1 *Computer workstation.*

on top of the mouse device. Some computers, especially the small and portable versions, have mouse pads or a similar device built into the keyboard.

Random Access Memory

Random access memory (RAM) is a temporary storage area located inside the CPU that holds the programs and files with which you are currently working. RAM is also called *read/write memory* since you can retrieve or *read* information stored there and also record or *write* information to it. This is for temporary storage only; if you turn your computer off in the middle of creating a letter without saving it, the document is lost!

Modem

The **modem** is an optional device that allows computers to talk to each other by transmitting data through telephone lines. *Modem* stands for *modulator–demodulator*. The modem serves as a *translator* because it changes the data you enter into your computer into a form that can be transmitted over telephone lines. When the information transmitted reaches the destination, the modem changes it back to a form or language that is understood by the computer on the receiving end. A modem that can send messages to fax machines all over the world is a *fax/modem*. Many can receive faxes also. In addition to sending and/or receiving faxes, a modem allows you to send electronic mail (E-mail) and tap into the Internet.

Printer

Almost every computer system is hooked up to one or more **printers** that generate hard copies of documents, reports, charts, and anything else you create. In the travel office, printers also generate passenger and travel documents, such as airline tickets, invoices, and trip itineraries. There are different types of printers; they differ in quality, price, and color versus black-and-white reproduction. The major types of printers in order of average to best in print quality are dot matrix, ink jet, and laser. Most ticket and boarding pass printers used by travel agencies and airlines are dot-matrix printers; characters are printed as a series of dots on the ticket or page. However, since many agency computers are used with word processing programs, the use of laser printers is becoming more common.

Scanner

A **scanner** lets you store pictures in your computer. It works like a copy machine since it takes an electronic image of practically anything you give it: a picture, text, illustration, or drawing. In fact, you can scan any object that you put in the scanner's view field. It is unlike a copy machine in that it isn't used to print multiple copies. You use a scanner to store the image in your computer to use in a document or slide show, to send it by electronic mail or fax to a colleague or client, or to save it like any other document for use at a future time. Scanners can be small and compact, like a windshield wiper that is hand held and "swiped" over the image; these are called *hand-held scanners*. The type most common in business offices is the *flatbed scanner*, about the size of a standard typewriter.

➤ What Makes It Run: Software

When you write a proposal, send a letter to over a hundred group tour participants, or create a statistical chart about your business, you are using different software programs. The available variety of software programs makes the use of a *personal computer* (PC) productive and efficient. The word *applications* is also used to describe software programs.

Four basic types of software programs or applications are used in the home and business workplace:

1. *Word processing* lets you compose letters, memos, reports, proposals, or any other text document. Because of the advance in computer memory and speed plus more "user-friendly" graphic-art software, travel sales agents can produce colorful and professional-looking brochures and newsletters right from their own computers. Examples of word processing software programs include Microsoft's *Word* and Corel's *WordPerfect. Word processing programs are efficient secretaries.*

2. *Database* applications allow you to manage data and produce reports from that data. You also use a database to sort and access lists of information, such as names, addresses, phone numbers, date of trip departure, or payments from clients. Database programs allow you to view this type of data in a variety of ways: alphabetically, by trip departure date, or by payment status, for example. You can also select certain types of data and create reports and charts directly from this information. An example of a database software program is Microsoft's *Access. Database programs are efficient office managers.*

3. *Spreadsheet* applications are the electronic equivalent of large sheets of accounting paper divided into rows and columns for numerical data (see Figure 5.2). You enter numbers and formulas to instruct the computer to make a variety of calculations. Spreadsheet programs can add, subtract, multiply, and divide, and obtain averages and percentages. Similar to an accountant keeping a running total of balances in accounts, spreadsheet applications make the same calculations automatically. They also have built-in graphic capability, which allows you to create a variety of charts and graphs based on your numerical data. An example of a spreadsheet software program is Microsoft's *Excel. Spreadsheet programs are efficient accountants.*

4. *Communications software* enables computers located anywhere in the world to "talk" to each other through phone lines via a modem. This type of software al-

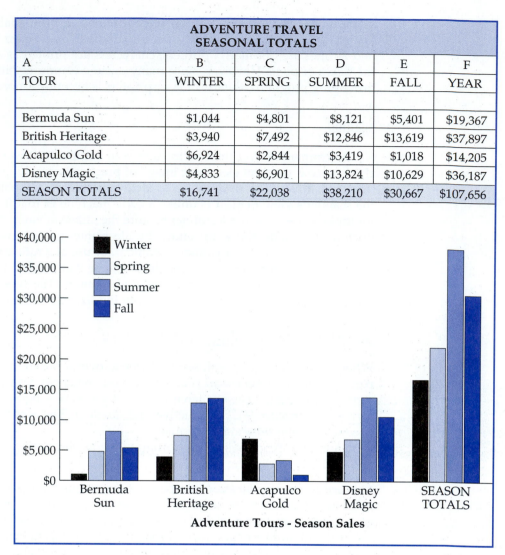

ADVENTURE TRAVEL SEASONAL TOTALS					
A	B	C	D	E	F
TOUR	WINTER	SPRING	SUMMER	FALL	YEAR
Bermuda Sun	$1,044	$4,801	$8,121	$5,401	$19,367
British Heritage	$3,940	$7,492	$12,846	$13,619	$37,897
Acapulco Gold	$6,924	$2,844	$3,419	$1,018	$14,205
Disney Magic	$4,833	$6,901	$13,824	$10,629	$36,187
SEASON TOTALS	$16,741	$22,038	$38,210	$30,667	$107,656

Figure 5.2 *Example of spreadsheet and chart programs at work in the travel workplace.*

lows you to send faxes and E-mail to virtually anyone who has a PC and modem. You can send a message to a client who lives on the other side of town, or to a tour company located halfway around the world. Another major feature of communications software is access to an on-line service that serves as a gateway to the Internet.

► Data Storage Devices

There are three methods of storing data into computers:

1. Floppy disk. This is a portable storage device that is a thin, rounded piece of plastic on which information is stored magnetically. The disk is inside a covering or jacket that protects it from dust, scratches, and liquid. Most floppy disks are 3½ inches in diameter. The thin slit that is built into the front of your computer is called the *disk drive.* You insert a floppy disk into the disk drive to copy the information on the disk to your computer's storage area (called the *hard drive*) or to copy from your hard drive to the floppy disk for portability.
2. Hard drive. The hard drive is built right into you computer. In many ways it is a better storage device than the floppy disk. It holds hundreds of times more

information, and it works faster when reading and copying information. Whereas a floppy disk can get lost or destroyed, anything you copy on a hard drive is better protected because it is built into your computer.

3. Compact disk (CD-ROM). A compact disk (CD) can hold more information than a floppy disk or hard drive. In fact, one CD can store more information than hundreds of floppy disks. CD-ROMs are different from floppy disks or hard drives because they can produce multimedia presentations. In addition to text and graphics, they can also play video, animation, and sound presentations. Another difference is that you can only read or play from compact discs; you can't write or record on them. That's where the ROM in CD-ROM comes in; ROM stands for *read-only memory*.

Key Point ➤ You should know what computers can do and what they *cannot* do. Computers don't think for themselves, they aren't smart, and they can't read your mind! What makes computers brilliant thinking machines that work at lightening speed are the instructions written by programmers. They use the language of numbers that computers understand. Through the use of programs and software, you communicate with the computer in a "user-friendly" way. But the computer is only as smart as the person who is using it. If the computer gives you the "wrong" answer or no answer at all, don't blame the machine. It only acts on the information and commands you provide it. It you give it faulty or wrong information, it will give it right back to you. Remember: *Garbage in, garbage out!*

➤ Cool Operators: DOS and Windows

Most personal computers used in business are either IBM PCs and IBM-compatibles or Macintosh computers ("Macs"). The major differences between the two computer camps are how the hardware is manufactured and the types of programs they run.

An IBM-compatible or IBM-clone has components similar to those of an IBM-manufactured computer and thus can use the same programs as those used by IBM computers. Macintoshes are generally more expensive but are faster to set up and are generally friendlier to use. Macs are also known for their quality in graphics. Nearly all of the computers used in travel agencies are IBM PCs or IBM-compatibles.

Today, most computers in the workplace and PCs for home use are run on a Windows operating system. To understand what this means, you should have an understanding of the basic operating system that runs computers. The **disk operating system (DOS)** is the keystone of almost every computer. Simply put, DOS is the "technician" inside the computer. DOS handles all the computer mechanics, such as starting your computer, regulating all the hardware components (e.g., the monitor), and shuffling information to and from different parts of the equipment.

Before Windows, DOS was the operating system of most PCs. At that time, computers pretty much worked and looked the same way. With a DOS, computers used a *character-based user interface (CUI)*. This means that you typed commands and pressed special keys on the keyboard to tell the computer where you wanted to go and what you wanted to do. In a CUI environment, there are no visual cues or pictures displayed on the screen to help you manage your work. You had to know exactly how to type in information and what special keys to use for certain functions.

The computer software powerhouse Microsoft introduced a whole new look and feel in personal computers when they introduced *Windows* software, which revolutionized how we communicate and interact with computers. What is Windows? It is a program that relies on pictures and graphics rather than text to help you manage your programs and data. It is called a *menu-driven environment* because rather than typing in commands, Windows allows you to click pictures or bold text on the screen or select from a menu of functions and tasks you want to do.

Windows-based operating systems are beneficial to professionals in the travel workplace because of these three major advantages:

1. *Windows provides a graphical user interface (GUI).* This means that you communicate with the computer through icons (pictures or graphic symbols), menu choices, and buttons that can be clicked by the mouse device or selected by pressing a key or two. Another key element of the GUI environment is the use of frames or rectangles in which programs and data are displayed—hence the name Windows. Both the keyboard and mouse are used together in the Windows environment.

2. *Windows allows for multitasking.* Before Windows, if you were working in one program (e.g., typing a letter to a client) and needed to check some information located in another (e.g., statistical information from a spreadsheet program), you had to save and close the letter you were working on and open the spreadsheet program. Windows allows you to work in two or more programs at the same time. The program that you are working on currently is displayed in the window that is displayed on the top; the second program is still running in the background. By clicking the mouse, you can jump from one program to another by opening up each Window.

3. *Windows allows you to share information from one program or document to another.* By using three simple commands with the mouse or keyboard, you can cut, copy, and paste any text, numbers, or pictures from one document to another. For example, you can grab the flight itinerary you have booked for your client from one program, copy it, and paste it into the letter you are writing in a word processing program without having to exit either program.

✓ Check Your Understanding 5-1

1. What is the major difference between computer hardware and software?

   _____

2. What are the two devices that you can use to communicate with your computer?

   _____   _____

3. Why is the CPU also called a microprocessor?

   _____

4. Name the method of storing data that:
   A. Is portable and allows you to copy data to and from other computers.   _____
   B. Resides safely inside a computer.   _____
   C. Is capable of storing and projecting video and sound presentations.   _____

5. Why is a modem also called a translator?

   _____

6. What does RAM stand for, and why is it called a read/write system?

   _____

7. Name the three major types of printers used in the workplace. Which one would you recommend using for formal letters, proposals, or presentations being sent to clients?

   A. _____   B. _____

   C. _____

8. Name the type of software application that enables you to:

   A. Write a business letter.   _____

   B. Maintain a running account of the total deposits that   _____
   have been received for a group tour.

   C. Maintain a directory of client names, addresses, and   _____
   telephone numbers.

   D. Send E-mail and faxes to business colleagues.   _____

AIRLINE COMPUTER RESERVATIONS SYSTEMS

Before computers entered the travel scene, reservations for airlines and other transportation companies were maintained in separate books and on huge boards. When a booking was made, the transaction was recorded manually on the board or in the book. The airlines needed computer systems to maintain their huge inventory of airline seats on thousands of flights operating each day. The major airlines developed computer systems for their own use to manage the huge databases of travel-related information, such as fares, flight numbers, airline schedules, seat numbers, and special meals.

Computer reservations system (CRS) is the term used in the travel industry for the main computer database of a company. Each airline's computer reservations system has one central database where all the information is kept. A CRS will have a number of central processing units (CPUs) in one area for the storage and retrieval of all information in the database.

Like the airline industry, the travel agency business runs on computers. Today, practically everything a travel professional does—booking reservations, communicating with suppliers, generating airline tickets and other travel documents—is through the CRS. This was not always the case. In fact, the advent of travel agency computers is a fairly recent event. Just go back about 25 years and things were a lot different!

After the airlines became automated in the 1950s, there were many attempts to develop one universal computer system that could be used by all travel agencies. All attempts failed. It wasn't until 1976 that travel agencies became automated.

Before 1976 you could get rich quick by going into the printing business; travel agency business ran on paper. What was it like? All communications were transacted on the telephone. Travel agents called suppliers and other service companies to get availability, make bookings, change reservations, and conduct research on travel products and destinations. This resulted in hundreds of telephone calls per week being placed by an average-sized agency. Multiply this by the tens of thousands of agencies throughout the United States and you can imagine the amount of time spent on hold!

Each travel agency maintained a virtual library of printed manuals, tariffs, and resource books to research everything from airfares to Pittsburgh, the cheapest hotel on Maui, to entry requirements into Pakistan. There were so many printed books and manuals that the travel agent's desk would virtually sag with all the weight. Travel industry information is also time sensitive; news such as

The SABRE Story

From a "Lazy Susan" to an Electronic Travel Supermarket

American Airlines' first pioneering effort with reservations was the "request and reply" system used in the 1930s. A reservations agent would telephone the central control point where inventory was maintained to inquire about space available on a flight, and a response would be returned via teletype.

Through the mid-1940s reservations were recorded manually with a pencil on different-colored index cards, nicknamed "Tiffany" cards after the lamps with the colored glass shades. These cards were arranged as a "lazy Susan," and flights were controlled by half a dozen employees sitting around a table spinning the lazy Susan for index cards that would correspond to particular flights. By counting the pencil marks on each card, a clerk at the reservations center could give a "yes" or "no" to a request for a seat.

Using the Tiffany system to complete one booking for a round-trip reservation from New York City to Buffalo required twelve people performing more than a dozen separate steps during a three-hour period—longer than the flight itself!

Source: *"The SABRE Story," The SABRE Group home page, Microsoft Internet Explorer.*

discounted air fares, vacation package deals, and resort and cruise specials change daily. It was quite a task to keep resources current with all these changes.

All travel documents were either handwritten or typed. This included airline tickets, hotel and car rental vouchers, invoices, and itineraries. If one agent completed an average of fifteen bookings per day, think of the number of handwritten airline tickets, typed vouchers, itineraries, and invoices that were required to be prepared by hand. The process took a lot of time and the potential for error was enormous.

In 1976, events took a turn for the better. This is when major airline carriers such as American, United, and TWA began offering their computer reservations systems to travel agencies. Why was it important for the airlines to share this technology with travel agents? Travel agents were considered an important sales force for airlines. The great majority of airline seats were booked through travel agencies and not directly with airlines. Members of the travel agency community were considered to be partners with the airlines.

➤ The Major Players

Today, more than 97 percent of U.S. travel agencies are computerized. The 5 percent that are not include new agencies or companies that are very small and may not have the financial resources. Other types of travel companies that are not automated may have found a travel niche or specialize in nonair products such as motor coach tours and cruises.

U.S. travel agencies use four major computer reservations systems. The airline that owns a computer reservations system (CRS) and offers it to the travel agency is called the *host* or *host system*. They are also considered *vendors* since they sell their computer systems. Table 5.1 lists four major CRSs and their hosts.

The travel agency that buys and uses the CRS is called the *subscriber*. Each system is capable of displaying flight information and seat availability for all other airlines, so a travel agency needs only one system. Many airlines and other suppliers, such as hotels and car rental companies, do not have their own computer reservations system, so rely heavily on the CRS to sell their inventory of airline seats or hotel rooms. They are called *co-hosts* or *participants* of a CRS.

TABLE 5.1 Major CRSs

CRS	Major Host	CRS Owners	Background
SABRE	American Airlines	AMR (American Airlines) Corp., 82.8% Public–NYSE, 17.8%	A chance meeting between two Mr. Smith's on an American flight from Los Angeles to New York in 1953 resulted in the development of a data processing system for American. The chance meeting between C. R. Smith, American Airlines' president, and R. Blair Smith, senior sales representative for IBM, led to the 1959 announcement of a *Semi-Automated Business Research Environment*, better known today as SABRE. Today, SABRE is the world's largest privately owned, real-time computer network. SABRE handles approximately 25 percent of the world's airline reservations, 20 percent of the world's hotel bookings, and 80% of U.S. car rental bookings. SABRE serves approximately 28,000 travel agencies in more than 70 countries worldwide. SABRE's central computer is in Tulsa, Oklahoma.
Apollo (Galileo International)	United Airlines	Public, 35.11% United Airlines, 31.9% KLM, 10.15% British Airways, 6.68% Swissair, 6.68% Alitalia, 1.52% Olympic, 0.86% Air Canada, 0.15% Aer Lingus, 0.08% Austrian Airlines, 0.08% TAP Air Portugal, 0.08%	Apollo is owned by Galileo International, a major European reservations system that is owned by Aer Lingus, Air Canada, Alitalia, Austrian Airlines, British Airways, KLM, Olympic Airways, Swissair, TAP Air Portugal, and USAirways. Galileo International (including Apollo) has a global market share of about 30 percent, measured by locations. The company serves over 36,000 automated travel agencies worldwide in more than 58 countries. Apollo's central computer is located in Denver, Colorado.
Worldspan	Delta Air Lines Northwest Airlines, Trans World Airlines	Delta Air Lines, 38% Northwest Airlines, 32% Trans World Airlines, 25% Abacus, 5%	CRS is jointly owned by affiliates of Delta Air Lines, Northwest Airlines, Trans World Airlines, and Abacus Distribution Systems, a leading CRS operating in Asia. In 1990, agreement was reached to merge Delta Air Line's DATAS II and TWA's and Northwest's PARS systems in Worldspan. In the same year, Worldspan and Abacus reached equity-sharing agreement and an alliance between the two systems was born. Today, the Worldspan unified system serves more than 15,000 travel agencies in over 40 countries to access information for 365 airlines, 26,000 hotel properties, 40 car rental companies, and other special travel service providers. The Worldspan International division operates in 31 countries throughout Europe, the Middle East, and Africa.

(continued)

TABLE 5.1 Major CRSs (continued)

CRS	Major Host	CRS Owners	Background
Amadeus (SystemOne)	Continental Airlines	Continental Airlines, 33.3% EDS, 33.3% Amadeus (includes Air France, Iberia, and Lufthansa), 33.3%	System One was founded by Eastern Airlines (no longer in operation) and taken over by Continental Airlines. Amadeus Global Travel Distribution, began operating in 1992, and held more than 50% of the travel agency market share in Europe and South America. In 1995, Amadeus acquired Continental Airlines' assets of its System One subsidiary. Today, System One's travel agent customer base and other assets are part of a company named System One Information Management, owned equally by EDS (Electronic Data Systems Corp.) and Amadeus. More than 700 airlines, 29,000 hotel properties, and 41 car companies now contract with System One and Amadeus that are available over a single network to approximately 41,000 travel agencies worldwide. In addition to Continental Airlines, the three other owners of Amadeus Global Travel Distribution Network are Air France, Iberia Airlines, and Lufthansa, each retaining 29.2 percent interest in the central Amadeus organization.

Source: Business Travel News/BTN Automation Directory, September 29, 1997, as published in ASTA Agency Management, Vol. 66, No. 12, December 1997.

Remember, the owners of the computer reservations systems operate a profit-making business. They generate revenue by charging fees to their subscribers and co-hosts or participants. The amounts of these fees vary from vendor to vendor.

Travel agencies (subscribers) usually are charged for leasing the required hardware, such as computer terminals and printers. In addition, there is often a monthly usage fee plus a charge for each transaction made. Rates are negotiated between each travel agency and vendor. In some cases, vendors offer substantial discounts to high-volume producers such as corporate mega-agencies that generate millions of dollars of airline sales each year.

In addition to standard usage and transactions charges, productivity-pricing formulas are built into most U.S. agency–CRS vendor contracts. The travel agency is required to pay a penalty when its productivity in air and nonair sales drops below a booking quota that is identified in the contract. In some cases the CRS contract can be renegotiated to reduce the quota and subsequent penalty charges.

Co-hosts or participants of a CRS are charged a booking fee for each transaction. For example, the average airline booking fee is between $2 and $3 for each flight segment booked through another airline's CRS. The average fee for a hotel or car rental is approximately $5 per booking.

How does a travel agency select the CRS? It depends on many factors. The major reasons to select one CRS over another include the following:

- The host carrier maintains dominant air service in the agency's area.
- Price and service contracts are within the agency's budget.
- Special or unique features of the CRS meet the needs of the agency's clientele.
- Booking capabilities fit the needs of the agency.

A travel agency needs only one CRS since each system displays information for other airlines and suppliers, handles both domestic and international travel, and offers similar booking capabilities. Most small to medium-sized agencies have only one CRS. The exceptions to this are large corporate agencies that handle a huge amount of airline bookings on a daily basis. For example, a large corporate agency that handles a mix of domestic and international bookings may require a CRS to handle the domestic bookings, and another that offers stronger booking capabilities for international routes. Figure 5.3 shows the travel agency market share in the United States for each CRS.

➤ The CRS Keyboard

The keyboard panel of each CRS looks similar to a standard typewriter keyboard (see Figure 5.4). Depending on the model of the computer, there are three general groups of keys:

1. *Alpha keys,* located in the main section, contain the alphabet. Number and punctuation keys are located along the upper portion of the keyboard. These keys are identical to the keyboard of a standard typewriter.

2. *Numeric keys,* located to the right of the main section, serve as a built-in calculator for high-speed entry of numbers.

3. *Special function keys,* usually located along the top rows, are identified by the letter *F.* They are also called *programmable keys,* as lengthy formats can be programmed into one keystroke to save valuable time.

Some of the keys have a dual function. *Dual-function keys* have a character or number etched on the top of the key, and another character, number, or term

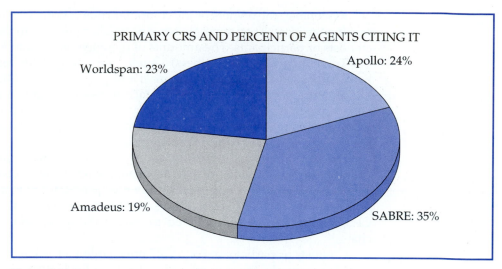

PRIMARY CRS AND PERCENT OF AGENTS CITING IT

Worldspan: 23%

Apollo: 24%

Amadeus: 19%

SABRE: 35%

Figure 5.3 *Results of ASTA poll showing CRS market share among agents (primary CRS and percent of agents citing it). Based on a survey of nearly 600 mostly smaller agencies. Total does not equal 100 percent because of rounding.*
(From 1998 ASTA Agency Automation Report, Travel Weekly, September 1998.)

etched on the front of the key. For example, on the SABRE system, the number one (1) key is used both as a numeric entry and the key that identifies flight availability requests. The computer figures out the function of these dual-function keys by their location in the entry.

➤ What the CRSs Can Do

Travel professionals use the computer reservations systems for many different tasks. There are an increasing number of other suppliers, such as hotels, car rental companies, tour operators, and cruise lines, that use CRSs to display their product availability and offer booking capabilities for travel agencies. This is only the tip of the "iceberg;" there is a lot more information than just the price of airline seats and hotel rooms. To understand how powerful the CRS is, we must look at these systems as being both *interactive* and *dynamic*. They are also used as a *storage* and *communication* device.

Interactive and Dynamic Systems

The computer reservations systems are *interactive* because of their "request and reply" system, which is a communication device between the travel agent and each system's vast storage of airline and travel data. The CRS user asks for information by typing a request on a keyboard that looks similar to a standard typewriter or word processor. The travel agent enters each request in a specific format. A format consists of a series of keystrokes that combine letters, numbers, and special symbols. When keying in a format, the computer user has to get it right every time. The CRS is very sensitive to errors and missed keystrokes; an error message is displayed on the screen after each mistake. The bottom line? You have to know your formats—many of them by memory—to be able to communicate with the CRS quickly and efficiently.

The CRS is also *dynamic*; the data stored in the CRS are constantly changing. These systems are constantly being programmed—24 hours a day, seven days a week—with updated information. For example, the CRS SABRE stores more than

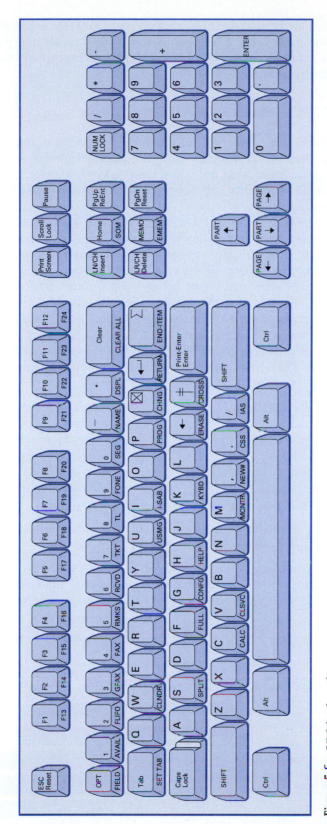

Figure 5.4 *CRS keyboard*

50 million air fares and makes, on average, 10,000 fare changes per day. It tracks 80 million passengers, 4,400 flights, and 200,000 meals every day. A typical CRS handles 2,000 messages and processes 3 million passenger bookings files per day through its central computer site.

Storage and Communication Devices

The computer reservations systems serve as both storage and communication devices. They maintain a vast storage of information. For example, SABRE maintains flight schedules for more that 650 worldwide carriers. This is in addition to seat-by-seat availability and airline fares on any given day for more than 285,000 city pairs.

The great majority of travel agency airline bookings are done on the CRS. However, an increasing number of other travel products, such as hotels, car rentals, tour packages, and cruises, are being booked through the computer reservations systems. Figure 5.5 shows a recent survey that elicited the percentage of each travel product that travel agents book through their CRS (and not over the telephone, sending faxes or telex, or by other means).

The variety of travel information stored in CRSs is mind-boggling. The travel agent can request weather conditions for practically any city on earth, find out what documents are needed to travel to Pakistan, or order tickets for a hit Broadway show. The CRSs contain an impressive amount of travel-related data, which include:

- Cruise ship availability and deck plans
- Travel advisory warnings
- Ski conditions
- Customs and immigration policies
- Currency conversions
- Yacht vacations
- Calculator functions
- Las Vgas shows
- Golf and tennis tours bookings
- In-flight movies and meals
- International rail schedules and tickets
- Destination maps and sightseeing tips

➤ Putting It All Together

When all computer hardware and systems are working properly, everything happens in a matter of seconds. The average response time to any request you make on the CRS is about 3 seconds. A lot happens in such a short time. Figure 5.6 is a

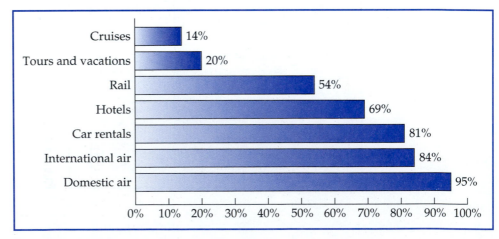

Figure 5.5 *Travel products booked through CRSs.*
(From U.S. Travel Agency Survey, Travel Weekly, *September 1998.)*

simplified diagram, and a step-by-step description of how it all works follows. In the example, an agent located in Any City, USA is communicating with American Airline's SABRE central computer located in Tulsa, Oklahoma.

Step 1. The travel agent enters a request for a list of air fares between Miami and Chicago on Delta Air Lines. The request is entered in a specific format.

Step 2. The request travels into the agency's modem. The modem then translates or changes the request from "computer language" to a form that can be transmitted over telephone lines.

Step 3. The request hurtles through thousands of miles of telephone lines to SABRE's central computer located in Tulsa, Oklahoma.

Step 4. The request travels into the modem in Tulsa, which then translates it back into language that the computer can understand.

Step 5. SABRE searches and finds the air fares within its huge data bank.

Step 6. The information goes back into the modem in Tulsa, which translates it into a form for transmission back to the agency.

Step 7. The information hurtles back through thousands of miles of telephone lines to the travel agency.

Step 8. The agency modem translates it back into computer language.

Step 9. A listing of air fares between Miami and Chicago is displayed on the agent's monitor.

Count to three and that's how long it takes!

➤ ARINC or Direct?

Until very recently, the computer systems of all airlines and suppliers communicated with each other through an intermediary computer called the **ARINC (Aeronautical Radio Incorporated) computer.** This was necessary since each computer system spoke a "different language."

Think of ARINC as an interpreter in the United Nations. Each "delegate" or computer system would tune in to the interpreter to communicate with other computer systems. In travel terms, let's say that a travel agent sells a TWA flight

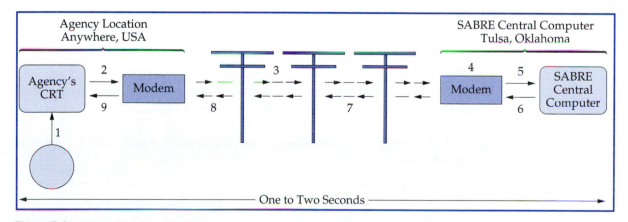

Figure 5.6 *How the CRS works.*
(Reprinted with special permission from ITP Publishing, from Practical Guide to SABRE Reservations and Ticketing, by J. Semer-Purzycki.)

on American Airlines' SABRE system. Since TWA and American's computer systems use different identification codes and formats, they can't "speak" with each other directly. They need an interpreter, or ARINC, to put their requests and responses in a common language that both computer systems can understand.

The downside of this process is that the sales agent is not receiving "real-time" seat availability. This is due to the amount of time it takes for each CRS to reprogram its database to show current information. It is difficult for each CRS to maintain up-to-the-minute seat availability for other airlines, due to the thousands of flight departures and changes in seat inventories that occur every hour of the day. Flight availability is in constant flux: Airline seats are confirmed, they are changed, and they are canceled minute to minute. For example, United Airlines has four seats available on its morning flight from Chicago to New York next Thursday. United sells these four seats through its own computer system Apollo. A couple of hours later, a travel agent who uses SABRE sells these same seats, since they show on her monitor as being available. Why? United did not have time to reprogram availability for SABRE, Amadeus, or Worldspan users in time. It may take up to 24 hours for these other systems to receive the updated information.

The reverse can also happen. A particular flight may show on the travel agent's computer screen as being sold out, but a number of seats may actually be available. This is due to last-minute cancellations not yet programmed back into inventory.

Today, the travel agent is able to communicate *directly* with other airline computer reservations systems through the agency's CRS. In other words, rather than going through the ARINC switching station, the agent is actually able to "move" into a participating carrier's computer to see accurate data. This "direct connection" results in more accurate and timely information from the other carrier's database. This is *last seat availability*, or up-to-the minute inventory of airline seats on any flight and practically any other airline.

✓ Check Your Understanding 5-2

1. *CRS* stands for _____.

2. Name the CRS that is hosted by each airline or group of airlines below.

    A. United _____   C. American _____

    B. Delta, Northwest,   D. Continental _____
       TWA _____

3. When did travel agencies start becoming automated?

    _____

4. The travel agency that buys and uses the CRS is called the _____ to that system.

5. Other airlines and suppliers that contract with a CRS to display their information and availability are called the co-hosts or _____ of that system.

6. List at least three factors used when determining which CRS to use in a travel office:

    A. _____

    B. _____

    C. _____

7. Why would a travel agency use more than one CRS?

    _____

8. Name the CRS that has the largest travel agency market share in the United States.

   _____

9. The great majority of airline bookings are done through the travel agency's CRS. But an increasing number of other travel products can be booked through a CRS. Identify at least four types of travel suppliers that display their information on the CRS for booking purposes.

   A. _____

   B. _____

   C. _____

   D. _____

10. The variety of travel-related information that an agent can access through a CRS is impressive. List at least five types of travel-related data that can be found. (Many answers are possible here.)

    A. _____

    B. _____

    C. _____

    D. _____

    E. _____

11. ARINC used to be the way that all CRSs communicated with each other. What does ARINC stand for?

    _____

12. What does *last seat availability* mean? How does it benefit the travel agent?

    _____

The Passenger Name Record

The primary function of the CRS is to provide booking capabilities for airline flights, accommodations, and car rentals, but other types of reservations, such as cruise vacations, tour packages, rail tickets, and theater tickets, can also be booked through the CRS. The travel agent can use the CRS to send passenger requests, such as for special in-flight meals or for wheelchair assistance at the airport. All required and important information regarding each passenger's reservation is stored in the **passenger name record (PNR).** All booked flight, hotel, and car rental segments are recorded and stored in the PNR. Other passenger data, such as names, phone contacts, mailing address, form of payment, and special requests, are also included.

➤ Fields and Items

Think of a client's PNR as a drawer in a file cabinet. When opened, the PNR drawer will contain separate files of information. Each file represents a specific type of information pertaining to that passenger's trip. One file is for the passenger's name, another for the flight reservations, another for the phone number, and so on. Depending on the complexity of the trip, a PNR can contain five or more "files" of information.

When building a PNR for a passenger, we don't call these files of information; we call them *fields*. A PNR field contains a specific type of information pertaining to the passenger's record. A PNR may include any number of fields; it all depends on the complexity of the booking.

Each PNR field can contain one or more separate entries. For example, the name field can contain two or more passenger names (as long as they are traveling together every step of the way), or the phone field can contain three phone contacts: passenger's business, passenger's home, and agency's contact. Each separate entry in a field is called an *item*.

A PNR contains numerous single-item fields, fields that can have only one item, such as the remarks and ticketing fields. You can record only one person who has contacted the agency and one ticketing instruction at a time. There are also multi-item fields, fields that can contain more than one item, such as the passenger name and phone fields. These fields can contain more than one passenger name and phone contact.

➤ PNR Mandatory Fields

A PNR must contain a minimum of five specific fields. If any one of these five fields is omitted, the PNR cannot be completed and sent to the system's central computer for processing. We call this not being able to "end the record." To remember the five mandatory PNR fields, think of the acronym P.R.I.N.T.

P   Phone contacts (passenger and agency number)
R   Received from (name of person who contacted the agency)
I   Itinerary (at least one booked itinerary segment)
N   Name of passenger(s) (one or more if traveling together)
T   Ticketing (when and how ticket is to be issued)

➤ PNR Optional Fields

In addition to the five mandatory fields, there are optional types of information that can be entered into a PNR. There are four general types of optional entries:

1. *General information.* These types of remarks serve as an electronic "notepad" for the travel agent. The agent can enter any type of useful information that will assist him or her when servicing a customer. Some examples of general remarks are:

- PAX SPEAKS SPANISH ONLY
- PREFERS WINDOW SEAT
- MARK 4 YRS OLD
- TENTH WEDDING ANNIVERSARY
- DR WILLIAMS VIP
- WHEELCHAIR NEEDED
- NAME PRONOUCED TOMBS
- CLIENT HARD OF HEARING
- LOW SALT MEALS REQUIRED

2. *Printed information.* When typed into the PNR in a special format, these optional entries will be printed on a document generated from the printer, such as the airline ticket, invoice, or itinerary. Some examples of printed information are:

- CHECK *(form of payment on ticket)*
- REMEMBER TO BRING PASSPORTS *(reminder on passenger's itinerary)*
- CALL OUR HOT LINE 800-555-1212 FOR ASSISTANCE *(notice on invoice)*

3. *Reminders.* These remarks are reminders for the travel agent to take some action concerning the passenger's booking. These types of remarks are not printed on the passenger's documentation but are for the travel agent's eyes only. Some examples of reminders are:

- CAR RENTAL BY 15JUL
- HOTEL IN MIAMI 1ST NIGHT
- RESERVE AISLE SEAT
- DELIVER TIX 1 WK PRIOR
- ORDER VEGETARIAN MEAL
- SEND CRUISE DEP BY 10OC

4. *Historical remarks.* These entries to a PNR are important information that are retained in the PNR after the passenger's return date (everything else is purged about 24 hours after the return date). Usually, this information represents critical information that was communicated to the passenger before the trip. This is done just in case the passenger encounters a problem and blames the agent for not advising him or her of a particular aspect of the trip. Some examples of historical remarks are:

- ADVISED PASSPORT/VISA REQUIREMENTS
- ADVISED PAX OF CANCELLATION PENALTY
- FARE QUOTED LOWEST AT TIME OF BOOKING—$290.00
- ADVISED PAX TO OBTAIN INTL DRIVERS LICENSE

➤ Displaying a PNR

When the agent is building the PNR, he or she is entering all requests and information in specific formats or entries: passenger name, phone numbers, special meal requests, flight segments, and ticket information, for example. The separate fields of a PNR can be entered in any sequence; it does not matter. Depending on the circumstances, the agent may decide first to confirm flights, then to enter the passenger data. With another booking, the agent may enter passenger data such as the name and phone fields before confirming flights. It doesn't matter. The CRS accepts entries in any sequence.

The PNR can be displayed at any point of the process; during or after completion. When the PNR is displayed, the CRS "descrambles" the fields and displays them in an organized and structured way. Every displayed PNR will look the same in format no matter what sequence was used to enter the fields of information.

Let's take a look at Figure 5.7, which shows a completed PNR for a traveler. All the entries have been made by the travel agent. This PNR is for two passengers, Paul Smith and Lillian Perez. Can you identify the five mandatory fields of this PNR? Can you identify optional fields of this PNR? A brief explanation of each field is shown to the right.

➤ Case Study: Building a PNR

This case study shows an airline booking step by step. Our agent is Bob from City Loop Travel in Chicago. His client, Susan Hill, is traveling with her friend, Mary Jones, to New Orleans next June on a short vacation to visit friends. Bob has to check seat availability, book flights, and process airline tickets—all in his computer. His agency uses the SABRE system.

Step 1: Checking Flight Availability

One of the most important functions of the CRSs is to display flight availability for all airlines that operate between a given city pair. Availability can be obtained for domestic and international flights for a period of approximately 330 days into the future.

The travel agent requests flight availability by specifying each of the following: desired travel date, city pair, and time of departure or arrival. In response to this request, the computer shows a **city pair availability (CPA) display,** so called because the computer displays flights for a given city pair such as Chicago and New Orleans. The CPA displays flights that it considers to be the "best" according to these factors: (1) desired time of departure or arrival, (2) elapsed flying

```
1.1SMITH/PAUL   2.1PEREZ/LILLIAN              ←→ Passenger name field
    1AA  103F  24OCT   F  BOSLAX  HK2 545P 851P   ←→ Flight itinerary (HK2 - holding confirmed 2 seats)
    2UA  174F  03NOV  M  LAXBOS  HK2 750A 417P
TKT/TIME LIMIT -                              ←→ Ticketing field (TAW12 OCT = ticketing arrangement
    1.TAW12OCT/-                                  will be made on 12 OCT)
PHONES -
    1.BOS617-555-8755-A PAUL REVERE TRAVEL DIANE  ←→ Phone field (A-agency; B-passenger's business;
    2.BOS617-555-8988-B SMITH                     H-passenger's home)
    3.BOS617-555-9833-H SMITH UNLISTED
ADDRESS -                                     ←→ Agency's mailing address
    PAUL REVERE TRAVEL
    1776 CONSTITUTION AVENUE
    BOSTON MA 12345
AA FACTS -                                    ←→ Special information and requests sent to host
    1.OSI PEREZ SPEAKS SPANISH ONLY               airline - American Airlines.
    2.SSR VGML AA103F24OCT/BOS NN2
GENERAL FACTS -                               ←→ Special information and requests sent to other
    2.SSR WCHR UA NN1 LAXBOS0174F03NOV            airline participating in itinerary (United)
REMARKS -                                     ←→ Other helpful remarks such as -
    1.AX0000123456789#9/0                         form of payment
    2.CARDHOLDER PAUL SMITH                        credit card information
    3./MR. PAUL SMITH                             passenger's billing address
    4./1334 BOYLSTON STREET                       helpful reminders for travel agent
    5./BOSTON MA 01234                            printed notice on passenger document
    6.H#MAKE HOTEL RES IN LAX BY 10OCT
    7.H-PSGRS ADVD NON-REFUNDABLE FARE
    8.#HAVE A WONDERFUL TRIP
RECEIVED FROM - PAUL SMITH                    ←→ Received from (who contacted agency)
```

Figure 5.7 *Sample PNR*
(SABRE).

time, and (3) types of flight service available (nonstop being the most favorable, then direct, and finally, connecting flights).

Susan and Mary want a flight from Chicago to New Orleans on June 21. They would like to leave anytime after 12 noon. Bob's first step is to display flight availability for that day. On the SABRE system, the identification or command key used to request availability is the number 1 key; this is a dual-function key that also serves as the availability segment key. The format to request city pair availability is 121JUNCHIMSY12P. *Format explanation:* /availability command/ travel date/city pair codes/time desired.

Refer to Figure 5.8, the CPA in response to Bob's request. Each screen of the CPA shows a maximum of six flights. Additional flight availability for the same city pair can be displayed by entering the format MD (Move Down). The first line of the city pair availability is a repetition of the availability format. The second line shows the following: (1) travel date requested, (2) day of the week, (3) the origin and destination cities with the time zone location for each (CDT = central daylight time), and (4) the time difference between the two cities (zero in this case). The balance of the CPA displays flights by segment number (1 through 6). An explanation of each informational column follows:

1. Carrier code.

2. Flight number.

3. Seat availability for each class of service.

4. City pair in code.

5. Dependability factor (e.g., 8 means that that the flight arrives/departs within 15 minutes of the published schedule between 80 and 89 percent of the time).

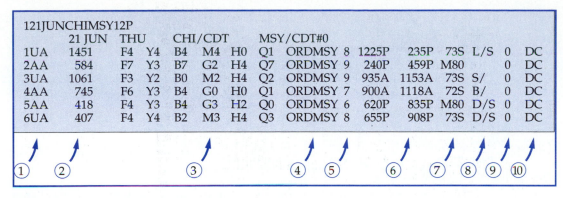

Figure 5.8 *CPA display*
(SABRE).

6. Departure and arrival times.

7. Type of aircraft in code.

8. Meals served on board in first and business class, followed by coach service. Meal codes used in SABRE include: B, breakfast; R, brunch; L, lunch; S, snack; D, dinner.

9. Number of intermediate stops.

10. Direct-connect participants (the agent is connecting directly into the carrier's computer to view availability).

Step 2: Selling Seats

A common method of selling airline seats is from a CPA. The client usually contacts the travel agent to request availability of flights for a certain date, city pair, and time. The agent displays the CPA and discusses them with the client. When the client selects a flight, the agent can sell one or more seats by referring to the segment number from the CPA display. The identification key that is used when selling a flight is the zero (0) key. This key is a dual-function key since it also serves as the sell identification key.

Bob's clients prefer American Airlines flight 584. Refer to Figure 5.8. Notice that this flight is line 2 on the CPA. They will be traveling in coach class (Y). Bob sells two coach-class seats on the flight that appears on line 2 on the CPA. This is the format that is used to sell from availability: 02Y2. *Format explanation:* /Sell command/# of seats/class of service/line number from CPA.

Step 3: Selling Response

After the agent makes the sell entry, the computer responds with a repitition of the flight data and the status of the flight. The status of the flight is displayed with a status code. The most commons status code is *SS* followed by a number. This means that the agent has sold that number of seats on the flight. After Bob has sold the American flight, SABRE responds:

1AA   584Y   21JUN   Q   ORDMSY   SS2   240P   459P

Description of sell response:

1	Segment number in passenger's itinerary
AA	Airline booked
584	Flight number

Y	Class of service
21JUN	Travel date
Q	Day-of-the-week code (*M*, Mon.; *T*, Tues.; *W*, Wed.; *Q*, Thurs.; *F*, Fri.; *J*, Sat.; *S*, Sun.)
ORDMSY	From/to cities
SS2	Status code and number of seats sold
240P	Departure time
459P	Arrival time

Step 3: Requesting Return Flight Availability

To request return availability, the agent can use the same format. Bob's clients want to return from New Orleans to Chicago on June 30, departing around 8 A.M. The availability entry is: 130JUNMSYORD8A.

Since most passengers request a return after the initial flight, the CRS has a shorter way to request return availability. In the short version, the city pair is omitted and the letter R for return is used. The *R* assumes a reverse of the city pair (i.e., from New Orleans to Chicago). The short version for return availability is: 1R30JUN8A. *Format explanation:* /Availability command/R for return/travel date/time desired. Figure 5.9 is the CPA in response to the return availability from New Orleans to Chicago.

After discussing the flight availability, Susan and Mary decide on the 9:35 A.M. departure (line segment 3). What is the format to sell two coach-class seats on this flight? The format is: 02Y3. The response to the sell entry appears below. The return flight is the second segment in the passenger's itinerary. What else can you tell from this display?

2AA   1572Y   30JUN   J   MSYORD   SS2   935A   1153A

Step 4: Entering Passenger Data Fields

Remember the five required fields of a PNR? In addition to the itinerary, four required passenger data fields are required. Without them, the PNR cannot be completed and sent to the CRS main computer for final processing. Bob needs to enter the following mandatory passenger fields:

- Passenger name
- Phone contact
- Received from (contact name)
- Ticketing

The mandatory passenger data and the optional data that Bob enters into this PNR are listed in Table 5.2, which shows each PNR field and the format used to

```
130JUNMSYCHI
         30 JUN  SAT      MSY/CDT      CHI/CDT#0
1AA     1508    F5  Y5  B3  G2  H0  Q0  MSYORD 9    750A   1004P  S80  B/V  0  DC
2UA      570    F6  Y5  B2  M2  H4  Q7  MSYORD 8    845A   1110A  73S  B/S  0  DC
3AA     1572    F3  Y2  B0  M2  H4  Q2  MSYORD 6    935A   1153A  73S  S/   0  DC
4UA      412    F6  Y3  B4  G0  H0  Q1  MSYORD 6   1100A   218P   72S  L/S  0  DC
5AA     1390    F4  Y3  B4  G3  H2  Q0  MSYORD 9    220P   505P   S80  S/   0  DC
6UA     1654    F3  Y4  B2  M3  H4  Q3  MSYORD 7    310P   555P   73S  S/   0  DC
```

Figure 5.9 *Return CPA display*
(SABRE).

TABLE 5.2   FORMATS FOR PASSENGER AND OPTIONAL DATA (based on SABRE)

DATA TO ENTER	FORMAT	TIPS, HINTS, AND SHORTCUTS
Passenger names are Susan Hill and Mary Jones.	-HILL/SUSAN MS -JONES/MARY MS	For multiple passengers: -2JONES/PAUL MR/LUCILLE MRS A slash (/) separates each passenger's name. The number in the party must equal the number of slashes.

Agency's number is 312-555-6000; Susan Hill's home number is 312-555-8933 and business number is 312-555-7844, extension 756.	9312-555-6000-A
	9312-555-8933-H SUSAN HILL
	9312-555-7844X756-B SUSAN HILL
		Additional information can be added to phone field:
		  Agency/agent's name:
		    9312-555-6000-A CITY LOOP TRAVEL BOB
		  Identify unlisted number
		    9312-555-8933-H UNLISTED
		  Fax identifier:
		    9312-555-0909-FAX

Susan Hill's secretary, Amy, contacted the agency.	6AMY/SECRETARY	If passenger is the contact: 6P or 6PASSENGER. If multiple passengers in PNR, identify contact by name: 6PJOHN ROBERTS.
Ticket on June 15.	7TAW15JUN/	Specify ticket date in entry (for future ticket). Walk-in, immediate ticketing: 7T-A.
Form of payment is by check.	5-CHECK	Identifier is number 5 key. Form of payment by credit card: 5-*AX0000123456#9/03.

Bob needs a reminder to rent a car.	5C#CAR RENTAL NEEDED	Identifier is number 5 key.
		Other reminders may include:
		  5H#HOTEL NEEDED
		  5S#SEAT ASSIGNMENT
		  5M#SPECIAL MEAL

enter each field item (using SABRE as the example). For those readers more technically inclined, the third column displays some tips, hints, and shortcut entries.

Remember that a specific key identifier is used when entering a field item. This key identifier is always the first entry in the format. Some of the key identifiers differ among CRS systems. For example, in SABRE the identification key entered before a passenger name is - (hyphen), phone number is *9;* received from is *6;* and the ticketing field is *7.* In Apollo the identification key for passenger name is *N:,* phone number is *P:,* received from is *R:,* and the ticketing field is *T:.*

Step 5: Displaying the PNR

Figure 5.10 is the completed PNR displayed on Bob's monitor. Changes can be made at any time by redisplaying the PNR by passenger name, flight number, and travel date. As you can see, the CRS displays all fields in a certain sequence and format.

Step 6: Pricing the PNR

The next step in this booking is to request the CRS to price the itinerary. The travel professional can display a fare for a PNR that is displayed on the monitor. The computer "reads" various elements of the itinerary and displays the price.

```
    1.1HILL/SUSAN MRS   2.1JONES/MARY MRS
      1AA    584Y  21JUN Q  ORDMSY SS2  240P    459P
      2AA  1572Y  30JUN J   MSYORD SS2  935A  1153A
    TKT/TIME LIMIT -
      1.TAW15JUN/
    PHONES -
      1.CHI312-555-6000-A
      2.CHI312-555-8933-H HILL
      3.CHI312-555-7844X756-B HILL
    REMARKS -
      1.—CHECK
      2.C#CAR RENTAL NEEDED
    RECEIVED FROM - AMY SECRETARY
```

Figure 5.10 *Completed PNR for case study.*

The price is based on the city pair (routing), travel dates, length of stay, and class of service booked.

In our example, Bob requests the coach fare for the PNR itinerary: round trip between Chicago and New Orleans. In SABRE, the basic entry to request a price is *WP* (Will Price). Figure 5.11 is the itinerary price display for this PNR. A more detailed explanation of the price display follows.

1. This line shows the round-trip base, tax, and total fare breakdown, *per passenger,* based on the adult (*ADT*) fare:

USD795.35	68.65XT	USD864.00ADT
Base fare (without tax)	Combined tax	Total fare (base fare + combined tax)

2. This line shows the combined tax breakdown ($68.65) per passenger

59.65US	6.00ZP	3.00XF
U.S. transportation tax	Segment tax (ZP)	Passenger facility charge (XF)

3. This line shows the base, tax, and total fare breakdown for the total (TTL) number of passengers (two in this example).

1590.70	137.30	1728.00TTL
Base fare for two	Combined tax for two	Total fare for two

4. This line indicates the passenger type, number of passengers, and the type of fare charged:

ADT-02	YX26
Adult passengers (two)	Fare-type code (coach discounted)

```
WP
            BASE FARE                 TAXES              TOTAL
1-          USD795.35                 68.65XT            USD864.00ADT       ↔ ①
              59.65US   6.00ZP   3.00XF                                     ↔ ②
              1590.70                  137.30            1728.00TTL         ↔ ③
ADT-02    YX26                                                              ↔ ④
  CHI AA MSY Q4.65 395.35YX26 AA CHI 395.35YX26 795.35 END                  ↔ ⑤
  ZPORD3MSY3   XFMSY3                                                       ↔ ⑥
```

Figure 5.11 *Itinerary price display*
(SABRE).

5. This fare calculation line displays the base fare and applicable fuel surcharge for each segment of the itinerary, per passenger. City and airline codes are used in this display.

CHI AA MSY
Q4.65 395.35YX26

Segment 1: From Chicago on AA to New Orleans = $4.65 fuel surcharge + $395.35 YX26 base fare	**Segment 2:** Return on AA to Chicago = $395.35 YX26 base fare	**Total** base fares plus applicable fuel surcharges. END = end of itinerary
	AA CHI 395.35YX26	795.35 END

6. Breakdown of segment (ZP) and passenger facility (XF) taxes, if applicable. The airport code is followed by the amount of tax charged.

ZPORD3MSY3
Segment taxes: O'Hare (ORD) @ $3.00
New Orleans (MSY) @ $3.00

XFMSY3
Passenger facility charges
New Orleans @ $3.00

Step 7: Issuing the Ticket

After the PNR is completed and priced, Bob is now ready to print tickets through his computer terminal. Ticketing is the most common function of the CRS. The agent enters electronically all required ticketing data—passenger name, reservation information, price—and issues an automated ticket for the PNR.

The type of tickets generated from the computer is the **automated ticket/ boarding pass (ATB).** The Airlines Reporting Corporation (ARC) issues ATB ticket stock to travel agencies. The ATB issued to agencies is universal in nature; the same ticket form is used for any CRS and carrier participating in the itinerary. Figure 5.12 is the completed ticket for passenger Susan Hill.

➤ Queues

When you hear the word *queue* you probably picture a line of people waiting for something. A queue is used not only to describe people waiting in line but also is a very helpful and efficient method of sending and receiving messages through a CRS.

Figure 5.12 *Completed ticket.*

The travel agent frequently sends requests to airlines and other suppliers through the computer. These requests usually require a response. An answer from a supplier could be in the form of a change in a passenger's reservation or in the form of a flight confirmation. Here are some typical examples of computer-generated messages that are sent periodically to travel agencies or maintained in the computer:

- The passenger's name was put on a waiting list for a flight that was booked. The airline is now confirming that the flight is available and sends a message to the travel agent advising of the confirmed status.
- An airline has changed the departure time of one of its flights. The flight change affects a travel agent's passenger name record (PNR). The airline sends a message to alert the agent of the schedule change, so that the agent can advise the passenger.
- An airline wants to send a broadcast message to all travel agencies promoting a new air fare or tour product.
- The travel agent needs to issue tickets for various passenger records on specific dates. A reminder is required at the beginning of each day in regard to which records need to be ticketed.

All of these types of transactions require an efficient and organized method of identifying to the travel agent what PNRs require attention or work each day. This method of communication, called a queue, consists of a line-up of messages in an agency's computer that require attention.

Think of each type of queue as being a "mailbox" inside the computer. There are more than 220 different types of queues. The first thirty or so queues are used for messages coming in from airlines and other vendors. All other queues are devoted to the travel agency's own use, such as sending messages to another agent in a branch office. At the beginning of each day one or more travel agents are assigned to conduct a queue count. This tells the agent how many PNRs require attention for each different queue or mailbox.

✓ Check Your Understanding 5-3

1. The electronic record of a traveler in the computer is called a PNR or
   _____.

2. The five mandatory fields of a PNR that are necessary to end or complete a booking are remembered by the acronym P.R.I.N.T. List the five mandatory fields of a PNR:

   P _____

   R _____

   I _____

   N _____

   T _____

3. Name two types of single-item fields.

   A. _____   B. _____

4. Name two types of multi-item fields.

   A. _____   B. _____

Figure 5.13 shows the flight availability display on a monitor. Answer questions 5 to 15 from this display.

5. This shows flight availability from (city name) to _____ (city name).

6. The departure date is _____.

```
128FEBBOSDEN7A
    28 FEB    FRI        BOS/EST           DEN/MST-2
1 UA   201    F4  Y4  B3  M4  Q4  H3  BOSDEN 7  838A  1110A  M11   B  0  XS
2 CO   129    F5  Y0  Q7  H1  K7  B7  BOSDEN 5  855A  1140A  737   B  0
3 CO   215    F5  Y7  Q7  H2  K7  B3  BOSDEN 7  125P   432P  737   S  0
4 UA   281    F3  Y4  B4  M4  Q4  H4  BOSDEN 6  520P   749P  D8S   D  0
5 CO   765    F5  Y7  Q7  H4  K7  B7  BOSDEN 9  640P   933P  M80   D  0  XJ
6 UA   445    F4  Y3  B2  M4  Q3  H1  BOSDEN 8  915A   205P  733   BL 1
```

Figure 5.13

7. There are _____ hours difference in time between the two cities.

8. Continental flight 129 departs Boston at _____ (time).

9. The same flight—Continental 129—arrives into Denver at _____ (time).

10. The airline and flight number that serves a snack only is _____.

11. United flight 201 operates every day except _____ (name the day).

12. The airline/flight number that is a direct flight is _____.

13. There are _____ first-class seats available on the 5:20 P.M. departure.

14. The airline and flight number that shows sold out in standard coach (Y) class is _____.

15. You are booking a party of three who want the earliest departure on Continental Airlines in H class service (for a discounted fare). The flight number that shows as being available is _____.

Figure 5.14 shows a displayed PNR. Answer questions 16 to 30 by referring to this display.

16. The passenger is _____ (name).

17. _____ contacted the travel agency to make this booking.

```
1.1PAGE/KEVIN MR
  1US  460Q 22AUG   F  TPABWI HK1 720A  914A
  2US  501Q 25AUG   M  BWITPA HK1 135P  315P
TKT/TIME LIMIT -
  1TAW20AUG/
PHONES -
  1.TPA813-555-8996-A SUNSHINE TRAVEL SUSAN
  2.TPA813-555-3100-B
  3.TPA813-555-7834-H AFTER 5P
ADDRESS -
  SUNSHINE TRAVEL
  786 BLUEBIRD AVENUE
  TAMPA FL 12345
REMARKS -
  1.-CHECK
  2./MR KEVIN PAGE
  3./576 NORTH MAIN STREET
  4./TAMPA FLORIDA 34288
  5.H#HOTEL NEEDED 1ST NIGHT
  6.VIP BUSINESS CLIENT
  7.PREFER AISLE SEAT
RECEIVED FROM - AMY/SECY
```

Figure 5.14

18. The traveler is flying from the city of _____ to the city of _____ on the first segment.

19. This booking is a _____ (one-way, round-trip, circle trip).

20. The flight departs on August 22 at _____ (time). It arrives at the destination at _____ (time).

21. The date of the passenger's return is _____. The day of the week of his return is _____.

22. The passenger is booked in _____ (first, business, coach) class.

23. The travel agent added a reminder to book an additional service in this PNR. What is it? _____

24. This passenger prefers a(n) _____ seat assignment.

25. The ticket will be paid by _____.

26. The name of the travel agency that completed this booking is _____.

27. The passenger's business phone contact is _____.

28. The name of the travel agent who made this booking is _____.

29. The airline and flight number on the return are _____.

30. The ticket will be issued by _____ (date).

Figure 5.15 shows the itinerary price display for the PNR in this example. Answer questions 31 to 38 by referring to the price display.

31. The round-trip base fare is _____.

32. The total tax amount is _____.

33. The total fare is _____.

34. The one-way fare from Tampa to Baltimore includes a fuel surcharge (code Q). The fuel surcharge amount is _____.

35. The one-way *base* fare from Tampa to Baltimore (not including the fuel surcharge) is _____.

36. The one-way *base* fare on the return—Baltimore to Tampa—is _____.

37. The total tax amount is comprised of three types of taxes.

    A. The U.S. transportation tax amount is _____.

    B. The segment tax (ZP) is _____.

    C. The passenger tax (XF) is _____.

38. The fare-type code is _____.

```
WP
           BASE FARE              TAXES                TOTAL
1-         USD283.72            30.28XT           USD314.00ADT
           21.28US    6.00ZP     3.00XF
           283.72                30.28                314.00TTL
ADT-01     QE7NR
  TPA US BWI Q1.86 140.93QE7NR US TPA 140.93QE7NR 283.72 END
  ZPTPA3BWI3   XFTPA3
```

Figure 5.15

PC Applications in the Travel Workplace

The retail travel industry has become dependent on automation technology to perform tasks in every aspect of operations. Today, personal computers and off-the-shelf software programs are becoming as commonplace as the telephone and calculator in the business world, especially in the travel office.

Up until the early 1990s, travel agencies used CRS hardware for CRS functions only: booking flights, hotels, and car rentals, for example. The CRS was closed to non-CRS tasks. If a letter had to be typed or a report produced for the next staff meeting, the travel professional relied on a standard typewriter. In rare cases, a travel agency may have had a personal computer installed for these types of tasks.

To make their systems more versatile for travel agents, the major CRSs started to design their own proprietary software programs that were compatible with their systems only. For example, American Airlines' SABRE offered personal computer software called SABREWORKS that offered four PC-based applications for the travel community: word processing, database, spreadsheet, and communications. SABREWORKS allowed the travel agent to work on both standard booking-related and personal computer tasks from the same computer. Unfortunately, CRS vendors are not in business to develop cutting-edge business applications on their own. The sophistication of the CRS proprietary software fails in comparison with other off-the-shelf products.

Today, using CRS proprietary software is the exception and not the rule. In 1992, the Department of Transportation (DOT) required the CRSs to develop open platforms in order to be compatible with third-party software vendors. This means that computer experts from outside the industry—and travel professionals, too—are developing specialized software for travel agencies. This also means that off-the-shelf software such as Microsoft Office and desktop publishing products are used for a wide spectrum of tasks that were otherwise impossible for the average travel office to complete: publishing client newsletters, generating computerized mailing lists, or any number of desktop publishing applications.

The CRSs are rolling out Windows platforms for travel agency users with PCs so that they can perform standard airline reservation tasks along with other kinds of software applications. Specific examples of CRS software that travel professionals are using to increase efficiency are:

1. *SABREmail Res and SABREmail Fax:* programs offered to commercial agencies that allow their business travelers to fill in specifics of their travel plans on-screen, then transmit the data by modem to the travel agency, where internal software prepares the order for quick handling by office agents. This does not require any telephone handling, which results in increased productivity.
2. *Worldspan's electronic Weissman Travel Reports (WTR):* a comprehensive destination-information database that covers approximately 7,600 cities and towns worldwide. Travel agencies that subscribe to this software have the option of cutting and pasting sections from the WTR to print out the information for their clients.
3. *Apollo Spectrum:* provides mapping capability through hundreds of detailed city maps, which include such locations as office and manufacturing facilities and their proximity to hotels.
4. *Personal Apollo:* a tool designed for the travel agency's frequent travelers who are on the road and wish to access a database to make changes in their itineraries, do bookings, and so on. The agency will still fulfill the travelers' ticketing requirements.
5. *System One HomePro:* a way for retail travel agents to plug into the system when they are not in the office. This software allows any IBM-compatible,

modem-equipped computer or laptop to become a SystemOne CRS workstation over a phone line.

6. *Worldspan's TourSource:* an electronic tour and package booking system geared for leisure agencies.

In addition to CRS-supplied equipment and basics such as fax machines, telephone answering machines, and VCRs, modems and PCs are in use at an impressive number of agencies: 79 and 75 percent, respectively. According to a recent survey conducted by the American Society of Travel Agents, approximately 92 percent of automated agencies use off-the-shelf software, and 82 percent reported that they use the Microsoft Windows operating system.

Personal computers are the "jacks of all trades" for travel agencies today. They handle a wide variety of tasks, from general word processing to viewing the hottest destinations on a CD-ROM. Figure 5.16 shows the results of a recent Louis Harris survey of agencies with access to PCs. The leading tasks are general word processing, database management (for mailing lists), and various accounting tasks.

Getting Connected: Travel on the Net

Hundreds of travel companies, tourist boards, and publications have taken their products and services on-line. There are hundreds of travel sites on the Internet: Airlines, tour companies, cruise lines, tourist boards, and travel publications are

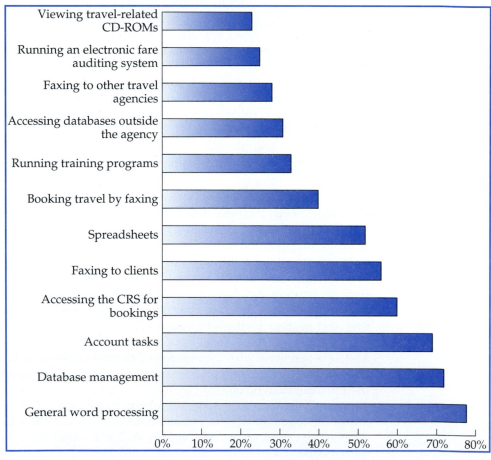

Figure 5.16 *Louis Harris survey, "What Agents Use Pcs For."*
Based on agencies with access to PCs.

just several examples. The Internet is not only a source of global information and research, but presents a platform for electronic commerce and new strategies in direct consumer marketing. Internet technology and the World Wide Web are designed to deliver not only text but also photos, sounds, and video presentations. Let's begin with what the Internet is and how it works.

➤ An Internet Primer

The **Internet:** You hear about it, read about it, and probably use it every day, but what is the Internet? And what's the difference between the Internet and the World Wide Web, or are they the same thing?

Technically, the Internet is the world's largest network of computers; you could call it a huge *internetwork* of computers. Picture yourself thousands of miles out in space looking down at our tiny planet Earth. Now picture a huge network of lines drawn all over the globe, in every direction; thousands crisscrossing, intersecting, and linking one to another. It looks like a giant spider web spread across the surface of our planet. All intersecting points on this "web" are connected; you can get from one point to another anywhere in the world by traveling on hundreds of thousands of connected lines. Located at each connection or intersection on this web is one or more computers that link the entire network. A part of the structure of each computer or network of linked computers is called a *server*, a gatekeeper through which information travels to get from one computer to another on the vast Internet system. This weblike structure and the servers that act as gatekeepers enable all connected computers to talk to each other as if they were all linked directly, which they aren't.

The **World Wide Web (WWW)** makes the Internet readable and more user-friendly to most PC users. The WWW is a menu-based software program (like Windows) that links millions of information and research resources on the Internet. The WWW turns the Internet into "virtual stores" where the user can browse through pictures, graphics, and information in the same layout as that of a Windows-based computer. Because the WWW creates a user-friendly interface with the Internet, it allows companies to advertise via Web sites, consisting of Web pages of information. A Web *browser* is a software program that allows you to access information and move around or navigate on the Web. Three common browsers are *Netscape, Microsoft Explorer,* and *Netcruiser.*

➤ Search Directories

The Internet can be a pretty intimidating place. There are over 40 million total pages of information on the Web and approximately 5 million articles posted. The decentralized design of the Net means that it is relatively easy to add new computers and smaller networks all the time, making it impossible to track its growth. On the other side, computers and entire subnetworks are added or removed from the Internet without notice or fanfare.

Individuals as well as companies are adding their own Web sites at a phenomenal pace—some come and some go. It is virtually impossible to keep track of what's out there and what's been removed. Anyone can find practically anything on the Internet. **Search engines** and other collectors of information not only make it possible but also make it easy.

A search engine is a type of index for Web sites. It helps you to find Web sites when you type in key words, just as you would look up a topic in a book using an index. Some examples of popular search engines are Yahoo!, Webcrawler, AltaVista, and InfoSeek (see Table 5.3). They vary from one another in how they index the information.

TABLE 5.3   SEARCH ENGINES FOR TRAVEL INFORMATION

SEARCH ENGINE	ADDRESS HTTP://	KEY POINTS
AltaVista	www.altavista.digital.com	Works in tandem with one of the most popular search engines, Yahoo! Has excellent destination links and a long list of travel agents.
Atevo	www.atevo.com	Offers a collection of travel-related information, including general travel news, air fares, travel advisories, currency converters, driving directions and guide-books.
Crossroads	www.twcrossroads.com	Designed for travel professionals, includes searchable database of industry news plus other information from the industry publication *Travel Weekly*, along with agency polls and forums
Dogpile	www.dogpile.com	Searches with 26 engines at once. Search results are presented engine by engine, but if you click on MetaFind, you can display results as if they all were from one source. Only drawback: Some searches generate a huge quantity of information.
Excite	www.excite.com	One of the top-rated travel sites, it includes links with airline, hotel, cruise, and other major industry databases.
HotBot	www.hotbot.com	Not your average search engine. You can search by geographic region and by time: within the past week or past month or year, for example. Extensive lists, with links, of travel suppliers and other travel entities, all categorized for easy reference.
Snap!	www.home.snap.com	Some good collections are located here, including worldwide tourism offices, guidebooks, CityNet destinations, international chambers of commerce, festivals, and other scheduled events around the world.
TGIF Directory	www.tgifdirectory.com	Specializes in lists—more than 50 of them—which range from the very short to the very long (airlines, resorts, agencies, tour operators, etc.)

Source: *Compiled from Travel Technology Report*, Travel Weekly, *July 1998.*

► Service Providers

Since there is no central management group that oversees the Internet, anyone with a little knowhow and the proper computer connections can retrieve and provide information on the system through Internet service providers. These are mostly for-profit companies that are like telephone companies. They offer you a pipeline for sending and receiving information to and from other computers linked to the Internet.

There are different types of Internet service providers. There are local providers that offer local telephone links to the Internet. There are also national Internet access providers, such as AT&T and Netcom. However, the best known and most popular are the commercial on-line service providers, such as *America Online, Prodigy, CompuServe*, and *Microsoft Net*.

A major reason for the explosive popularity of using the Internet is the Web's easy-to-use and easy-to-read graphical system. For example, the Web uses highlighted text and graphics called *hyperlinks* that transport you to other areas on the Internet when you click on them. For example, you may be reading an article about European capital cities. You come to the highlighted word *Paris* in the article. Click on Paris and you are transported to enough information about Paris to fill a book! Information such as climate, history, city maps, sightseeing, culture, and even where to go to book trips to the destination are displayed in detail. These new sites may have their own hyperlinks, which lead you to more and more information. It could be a dozen or so "jumps" later that you decide to return to the article that started it all.

➤ Intranet: A Matter of Privacy

Remember that the Internet is a global network of computers all linked together. You can just as easily communicate with other computers as far away as China as long as they are linked up on-line. An **intranet** is an internal, private communication link within a company or other organization that uses Internet and Web technologies. Unlike the Internet, which is accessible by *anyone* with the proper on-line link, the intranet is accessible only to people within the organization and other authorized people.

Two major advantages that intranets offer to travel agencies and their clients are booking capabilities and research tools. Many large corporations offer their business travelers and in-house travel arrangers a rich variety of reservation capabilities via an intranet linked to an outside travel agency. All bookings are queued to the agency for final processing, delivery, and follow-up. This enables travelers to link to the agency's private-label Web site with direct access to airline reservations and booking capabilities. The booking is routed directly back to the agency's office for ticketing and servicing. Many experts believe that the use of travel agencies will remain essential since on-line reservation capabilities aren't robust enough to handle some important tasks that only an expert agent can manage. Such things as last-seat flight availability, upgrades, and lowest fare checks are still best handled by the professional travel agent in the field (see Figure 5.17).

Another benefit of an intranet to large agencies is the ability to communicate easily with branch offices and to share data and files across different platforms—IBM PCs to Macs, for example. In fact, agencies can design more Web-like or user-friendly screens with color and graphics that would fit right over the traditional CRS displays, thus reducing the time and money spent on training new agents.

Some travel agencies are also using intranet technology as a research tool to share industry-related information with other travel agencies. Travel agencies subscribe to a company's intranet by paying a fee. They are given a user name and password that provide direct links to airlines, cruise lines, tour companies, and destination Web sites that are selected to be the most valuable and informative for leisure or corporate travel agencies. How does it benefit travel agents? It provides a faster and more convenient way for travel professionals to access vital information in a short period of time in order to service their clients better.

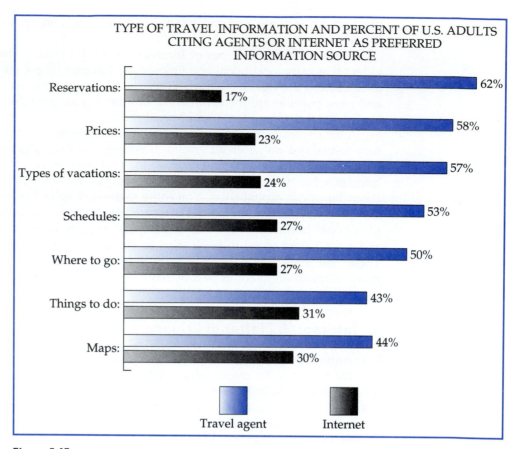

Figure 5.17 *Travel agents versus the Internet: Americans strongly prefer retailers as a travel information source. Study based on a survey of 1,200 U.S. adults. Percentages of respondents citing other information sources are not included.*
(From Washington-based Travel Association of America as published in Travel Weekly, *July 1998.)*

Travel Agents on the Net

There are many benefits to a travel office going on-line. A major benefit and a steadily growing necessity is the ability to access the same information as the agency's clients who are Net users themselves. Information about discounted air fares, new cruise ships, group tours, and exotic destinations are published on the Net for all to see. Net-savvy travel professionals use this shared information to generate sales with their equally savvy clients. The four major reasons and benefits for travel professionals to access the Internet are *communications, marketing, informational services,* and *product sales* (see Figure 5.18).

► Communications On-line

In addition to being the world's storehouse of information and research, the Internet also allows computers to send and receive messages to each other instantaneously around the world. The two methods of communication that are possible between any on-line computers are electronic mail (E-mail) and fax transmissions.

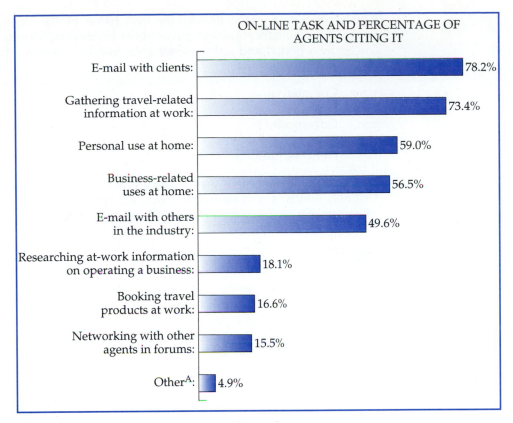

ON-LINE TASK AND PERCENTAGE OF
AGENTS CITING IT

Task	Percentage
E-mail with clients:	78.2%
Gathering travel-related information at work:	73.4%
Personal use at home:	59.0%
Business-related uses at home:	56.5%
E-mail with others in the industry:	49.6%
Researching at-work information on operating a business:	18.1%
Booking travel products at work:	16.6%
Networking with other agents in forums:	15.5%
Other[A]:	4.9%

Figure 5.18 *Most-common ways in which agents are using the Internet, based on a survey of 349 mostly smaller agents who have access to the Internet.* (*[A]Includes communicating with outside agents and research for personal financial investments.*)
(From 1998 ASTA Agency Automation Report, Travel Weekly, September 1998.)

E-Mail

Electronic mail (E-mail) is a method of sending messages from your computer to the computer of another person or group of people. What you need is a computer, the proper communications software, and a modem. What you also need is a link-up with other computers. This link can be in the form of a commercial or on-line service company such as America Online, a local **service provider**, or as part of a **local-area network (LAN).** A LAN connects computers in a limited or small area such as within an office or building.

More than 89 percent of travel agents use E-mail every day for communicating with customers, suppliers, and other agencies. There are two reasons why E-mail is the main method of communications in today's travel companies: It is fast and inexpensive. When you compose and send a message by E-mail, it travels along telephone lines and "drops" into the receiver's electronic mailbox a few seconds or minutes later. You can send E-mail at any time, and you don't pay long-distance phone charges. Unlike postal mail; messages cost fractions of pennies, even those sent overseas.

Key Point ➤ **Basics of E-mail Addressing:** The typical E-mail address consists of two parts, separated by the @ (for "at") symbol. The first part is the user's name (e.g., the author's user name is jpurz).

The second part is the domain or host name of the organization, network provider, or an educational or government institution. Most host names are followed by a period and a three-letter code that identifies the type of entity they are. *Common identifiers are:*

com   Commercial
edu   Education
gov   Government
org   Nonprofit organization
net   Network resource

For example, the author's user name is jpurz, and the domain is aol (American Online), which is a commercial (com) entity. The author's E-mail address is *jpurz@aol.com.*

Facsimile

Facsimile (fax) transmission is one of the most dramatic inventions for both personal and business use in the last couple of decades. As a society, we depend more and more on this type of instant communication.

Fax machines scan and transmit anything on paper, such as text, graphics, or photos. You can send a fax through a dedicated fax machine or through your office PC equipped with a fax/modem. The fax/modem permits transmission through telephone lines to fax machines or to other computers that have the same device. The older modems don't contain fax capabilities; the newer modems do. A hard copy of the transmission is generated at the receiving fax station. It takes only seconds to transmit and receive a fax, whether it is sent to an office located across the street or to a company located halfway around the world.

Broadcast (burst) faxing is used frequently in the travel industry. This enables the sender to program any number of fax numbers into his or her fax machine and transmit to all designated recipients at once. Many travel companies use this method of multiple and high-speed faxing to promote new products and services. A good example of broadcast or burst faxing is when a cruise line or tour operator sends information regarding new services, products, or discount prices to thousands of travel agencies at once. Fax transmissions are similar to E-mail in being faster and less expensive than other forms of communication, such as overnight mail or telegrams.

► Customer Marketing

The Net is proving to be an effective way to market a company's product; especially a well-defined specialty such as adventure tours, cruise-only, and discount airline tickets. The ability to communicate instantaneously with prospects who live in other regions or countries makes marketing a company's products and services convenient, cheaper, and more effective.

The majority of travel agencies have a Web site, and the numbers increase every year. The majority of these sites are used to attract new business and to display travel promotions. Figure 5.19 shows a survey of the number of retailers that have a Web site. Also shown are several types of functions and the percentage of agencies that feature each type in their Web sites.

Using the Net is especially effective if a company's prospective customers fit the typical profile of users who are likely to book on the Internet: 35 plus years old, well educated, upper-middle to high income level. A powerful marketing tool is to merge or marry the agency's client profiles to E-mail. For example, if the travel agency knows that a group of repeat clients are interested in a Caribbean

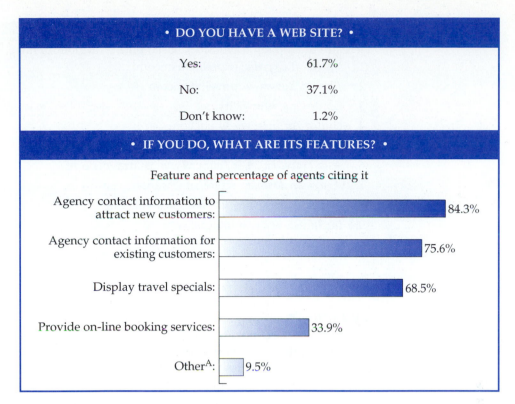

• DO YOU HAVE A WEB SITE? •

Yes:	61.7%
No:	37.1%
Don't know:	1.2%

• IF YOU DO, WHAT ARE ITS FEATURES? •

Feature and percentage of agents citing it

Agency contact information to attract new customers: 84.3%

Agency contact information for existing customers: 75.6%

Display travel specials: 68.5%

Provide on-line booking services: 33.9%

Other[A]: 9.5%

Figure 5.19 *Survey of agents' use of Web pages, based on responses from 577 primarily smaller agencies.* ([A]*Includes E-mail, links to other sites, photo gallery, franchise information, and staff photos.*)
(From 1998 ASTA Agency Automation Report, Travel Weekly, August 1998.)

cruise next winter, the company can E-mail special offers and promotions as they get them. Using E-mail as part of a company marketing strategy can also save money. Sending a company newsletter to corporate accounts and other customers via E-mail would cut postage or fax costs.

► Information Resources

Net agents can provide their clients with a wide variety of travel information such as detailed maps, electronic brochures, and destination information as part of their sales and promotion efforts. Another benefit of the Net to travel agents is to share information with other travel professionals through *on-line bulletin boards*, also called *newsgroups* and *forums*. These are a large collection of bulletin boards, each on a particular subject. There are thousands of them on the Net, ranging from current affairs, swapping recipes, to technical discussions about multimedia computing. You can post a question on a bulletin board and receive responses and comments from other subscribers over a period of time.

There are a number of travel-related newsgroups on the Net. An example is the "travel professionals forum" through America Online, which is part of its larger "travel forum" area. Another site, called *ASTAnet*, sponsored by the American Society of Travel Agents, provides a members-only area.

Chat rooms offer another way to communicate with others on a particular subject. These are active, real-time, on-line interchanges that are hosted by people who act as facilitators for the discussions.

Ten Top Travel Sites on the Net

Here are the top ten travel sites, based on the number of hits.

1. *Microsoft Expedia:* expedia.msn.com
2. *Travelocity:* www.travelocity.com
3. *Excite City:* www.city.net
4. *United Airlines:* www.ual.com
5. *MapQuest:* www.mapquest.com
6. *Asia Travel Hotel & Tours:* www.asiatravel.com
7. *American Airlines:* www.americanair.com
8. *Carnival Cruise Lines:* www.carnival.com
9. *Intellicast:* www.intellicast.com
10. *Preview Travel:* previewtravel.com

Key Point ➤ Travel agents are not able to market or promote aggressively through newsgroups or chat rooms; they are supposed to be "commercial free." However, travel professionals can make initial contact with prospective clients just by mentioning the name of their travel companies and specialties in a newsgroup posting or chat room discussion. If the reader shows an interest, he or she can send an E-mail message.

➤ Product Sales

The Net is an effective way to sell your own product inventory to other travel agencies or directly to the public. This is especially true if your company's product is simple enough and at a low enough price that it can be booked easily without speaking to a travel agent. A growing number of travel agencies and other service companies are designing their own Web sites and offering direct bookings for their customers.

Is selling on the Net right for every travel company? The answer is no. To decide if the Net is the way to go, a company must examine how they do business, what they sell, and their customer base. Imagine that you are an owner or manager of your own travel agency and must decide whether or not to design a Web site for your company. What things should you consider to make your decision with confidence? Here are some questions to ask and things to consider from a *Seminar in Print* by Greg Merkley, an industry professional and expert in the field of Internet technology.

1. Are your customers on-line, and if so, how are they using the Internet? Have they or would they consider buying travel on the Net, and would they be willing to buy from your Web site? If your existing customers are already accessing the Web and using E-mail, you may need to make your business accessible in this environment, too. How often are you asked for your E-mail and Web site addresses?

2. If your agency doesn't have a presence on the Net, will your company lose customers and revenues to those companies offering their services on the Web? On the other hand, if you do create a Web site, will you be able to keep your customer base? Look at the Web and its on-line services as competition. If you feel that the Web is, or will be, eroding your customer base, it is probably time to use the Internet as an economical way for you to advertise your company's range of knowledge and services. If you decide not to go on-line in some way, plan how to keep those of your customers who are inclined to buy on the Net.

3. What impact will the Web have on the current technology that exists in your office? Research to find out what additional hardware is required and how much you will need to invest. There are two general ways to approach this issue. Most technology is tied in with the agency's CRS. Many CRSs will allow an agency to "private label" their reservation programs on its own Web site. This means that a customer can purchase flights and other related services directly at the agency's site. The agency still maintains "credit" for these bookings and receives commissions. This raises the agency's cost to thousands of dollars of additional charges paid to the CRS. Another method is to buy and install a stand-alone computer that serves the agency's on-line needs. The cost for a computer to handle Web marketing and E-mail can be less than $1,800, including a printer. Add to this approximately $250 for on-line access fees.

> *Key Point* ➤ According to a recent survey from the Travel Industry Association air tickets dominate on-line sales. The airlines' share is approximately 75 percent, followed by hotel and car rental bookings.

➤ How to Build a Successful Travel Web Site

Once a travel agency decides to build its own Web site, two major considerations loom: How much does it cost, and who can design it? Pricing for a private Web site is based on how many graphics and how much text appears on the screen. Some Web publishers charge by the month for a fixed size; others count the number of pages and graphics. Additional services or special features, such as on-line booking engines, customer forms, and updates, all cost extra. Experts say that for a small to midsized company creating a multipage site with client services and sales features, the approximate "publishing" cost is $500 to $1,200 for the first year. It is recommended that there be an agency staffer who works at least part-time on E-mail and Web marketing programs.

There are thousands of Web publishers and designers; however, there are obvious advantages to finding those that understand the travel business. Resources such as the major CRSs and trade organizations such as ASTA work with preferred Web publishers for their travel agency members. Professional Web site designers Tom and Mary Kay Aufrance offer ten commandments for a successful Web site (see Table 5.4).

> *Key Point* ➤ Internet travel is dominated by several megatravel Web sites that account for approximately 75 percent of Internet revenue in the travel industry. As of this writing they are: (1) Easy SABRE/Travelocity, (2) Internet Travel Network, (3) Preview Travel, (4) American Express Interactive, (5) TravelWeb, and (6) Microsoft Expedia.

✓ Check Your Understanding 5-4

Multiple Choice

Circle the *best* answer.

1. Airline computer reservation systems first became installed in U.S. travel agencies in the mid:

    A. 1950s   C. 1970s

    B. 1960s   D. 1980s

TABLE 5.4 TEN COMMANDMENTS FOR A SUCCESSFUL WEB SITE

1. *Prominent identification.* The site should prominently identify the travel company, services, and how to make contact with you (such as your company's 800-number).

2. *A picture is worth a thousand words.* Right on top, you need an attractive photo that allows the reader to imagine, "That's me there in that exotic place! Where do I sign up?"

3. *Call to action:* Make sure your call to action is interspersed throughout the text ("Click here to make your reservation request, now!"). This "click here" button should lead to a reservation request form that includes all the information you need to replace that first phone call, such as name, address, phone number, E-mail address, desired service, and arrival/departure times. You need to get all the information you can, in order to respond and close the sale on each lead.

4. *Quick response.* Your request form should send you an E-mail message (which means that you need your own E-mail account) so that you or your staff can respond within 24 hours, before the lead goes stale. If you don't, some other travel site will respond quicker and get that lead instead of you.

5. *Get compatible.* Ideally, your request form will not only send you an E-mail message, your requests should also go into a Microsoft Office–compatible database, which you can use later for promotional mailings or marketing analysis. Why Microsoft Office–compatible? Because it is what most office staffs know how to use for mail merges or other marketing programs.

6. *Variety is the spice of life.* You should be able to make changes to your own Web site so that you can add specials or try experimenting with new offers for your Internet customers. You should not have to wait for your Web designer to get around to it.

7. *User interaction is key.* A "search" on your site is like a magnet for readers. You will get more readership on those pages that are titled "Search for Your Dream Vacation" or something like that. People love the interactivity, and also the ability to customize their search criteria to fit their personal desires. And if you can fill someone's desire for that "two-bedroom condo near Heavenly Valley ski area over Christmas," you've made a sale.

8. *Sell the sizzle.* Sell the sizzle of your vacation area! For example, create a clickable map of area golf courses and intersperse your call-to-action all over it, for example, "Click here to make reservations near this golf course."

9. *Make bookings possible.* As soon as you can, get Internet commerce to work on your site. Take credit cards and make reservations. (If you have to, include a disclaimer that your confirmation will follow within 24 hours, by phone or E-mail.) Get ready to let your Web site actually make those sales for you!

10. *Make it easy to find you.* Probably the most important commandment is to make it easy to find your site on the Net. Register your site with the various major Internet search directories, such as Yahoo! and Alta Vista. Try to get your link to come up on the first few pages of each directory. If it doesn't, hire a Web developer to work on improving your position.

Source: *Reprinted by special permission from* NetTravel: How Travelers Use the Net, *co-published by Songline Studios, Inc. and O'Reilly & Associates Inc.*

2. In 1992, the Department of Transportation required the CRSs to be:
   A. available to the general public to book their own flights
   B. compatible with off-the-shelf and third-party software applications
   C. linked to one another by ARINC
   D. installed in any travel agency that required them

3. The device that links computers within a small area such as a building or an office is the:

A. Intranet
C. modem
B. electronic mail
D. local-area network (LAN)

4. America Online, Prodigy, and Microsoft Net are examples of:

A. search engines
C. browsers
B. on-line service providers
D. hyperlinks

5. Yahoo!, Webcrawler, and AltaVista are examples of:

A. search engines
C. servers
B. on-line service providers
D. browsers

6. Windows uses a GUI environment. GUI stands for:

A. graphic user interaction
C. graphical user interface
B. graphical user interactivity
D. graphical user insert

7. The product that dominates on-line travel sales in terms of revenue generated is:

A. car rentals
C. cruises
B. tours
D. airline tickets

8. Which of the following would not be a reason for a travel agent to use newsgroups, forums, or bulletin boards on the Internet?

A. to market and promote the agency's products and services aggressively
B. to exchange information and communicate with peers and prospective clients
C. to ask or post a question related to the travel industry
D. to find out what other travel agents think of a particular cruise line or destination

9. The leading non-CRS task for which the majority of U.S. travel agencies use their personal computers in the workplace is:

A. database management
C. word processing
B. spreadsheets
D. viewing travel-related CD-ROMs

10. A software program that allows the user to access information and navigate on the World Wide Web is a:

A. server
C. browser
B. service provider
D. hyperlink

11. One or more computers which serves as a gatekeeper through which information travels between computers on the Internet, is a:

A. browser
C. hyperlink
B. search engine
D. server

12. An internal, private communication link within a company or a group of companies that use Internet and Web technologies is a(n):

A. intranet
C. intracommunication link
B. Internet hyperlink
D. local internet network

13. The main method of communication between on-line companies that is fast and inexpensive is:

A. express mail
C. electronic mail
B. telephone
D. telex

14. An electronic method to transmit anything on paper—text, photos, or graphics—instantly to another person or company is:

    A. telex   C. priority mail

    B. facsimile   D. telegram

15. A method of sending an electronic message, graphic, or photo to a number of designated recipients at once is called:

    A. hyperlink transmission   C. broadcast faxing

    B. priority E-mail   D. express telegram

➤ Key Terms and Phrases

- Aeronautical Radio Incorporated (ARINC) computer
- automated ticket/boarding pass (ATB)
- broadcast (burst) faxing
- cathode ray tube (CRT)
- central processing unit (CPU)
- city pair availability (CPA) display
- compact disk (CD-ROM)
- computer reservations system (CRS)
- database
- disk operating system (DOS)
- electronic mail (E-mail)
- facsimile (FAX)
- floppy disk
- hard drive
- Internet
- intranet
- keyboard
- local-area network (LAN)
- modem
- mouse
- passenger name record (PNR)
- printer
- random access memory (RAM)
- scanner
- search engine
- service provider
- spreadsheet
- word processing
- World Wide Web (WWW)

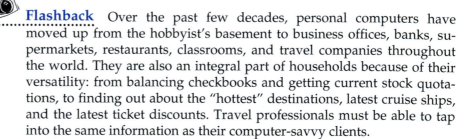

Flashback Over the past few decades, personal computers have moved up from the hobbyist's basement to business offices, banks, supermarkets, restaurants, classrooms, and travel companies throughout the world. They are also an integral part of households because of their versatility: from balancing checkbooks and getting current stock quotations, to finding out about the "hottest" destinations, latest cruise ships, and the latest ticket discounts. Travel professionals must be able to tap into the same information as their computer-savvy clients.

How to begin? Travel professionals should first learn computer basics. Just as a physician needs to understand anatomy in order to treat patients, or the auto mechanic must know the parts of an engine, travel professionals must understand how computers work and how to use them effectively and efficiently in their offices.

Computer technology serves the travel workplace in three ways: computer reservations systems (CRSs), personal computer applications, and on-line or Internet access.

The great majority of travel agencies use one or more computer reservations systems (CRSs). Agents use these systems for a wide variety of traditional tasks, such as booking airline flights, making hotel reservations, and generating airline tickets for their clients. In addition to their booking capabilities, the CRSs serve as immense storage and retrieval systems for a huge amount of travel-related information.

Travel professionals also use their office computers to complete more traditional PC-oriented tasks. These tasks that have direct applications in the travel workplace are word processing, database management, spreadsheets, and communications. Third-party and off-the-shelf software programs allow agents to generate mass mailings, create colorful brochures and newsletters, manage huge amounts of data, produce reports and charts, and communicate with on-line companies and people located anywhere in the world in an instant.

The Internet has had a major impact on how travel agencies do business. The four major benefits to travel agencies using the Internet are communications, marketing, informational services, and product sales. The number of on-line consumers is growing each year. Their preferred method of communication is through a keyboard and modem, so travel agents have to remain in the electronic loop. For example, on-line clients can book their own travel arrangements, then E-mail the information to their agents, who ticket their bookings. In this way, travel agencies continue to be the service providers and earn commission on bookings that might have been lost to them.

CHAPTER REVIEW

Multiple Choice

Circle the *best* answer.

1. That part of the computer that serves as the "brain" because it processes and directs all incoming and outgoing data is the:
   A. CRT
   B. RAM
   C. CPU
   D. GUI

2. A translator that allows computers to send and receive information over telephone lines is the:
   A. monitor
   B. modem
   C. CD-ROM
   D. hard-disk drive

3. Which application would you use to maintain the names and addresses of over 200 clients participating in a group tour with your agency next year?
   A. word processing
   B. database management
   C. spreadsheet
   D. communications

4. Which application would you use to track commissions your agency has earned for different cruise lines over a period of a year?
   A. word processing
   B. database management
   C. spreadsheet
   D. communications

5. The storage medium that can provide multimedia presentations and stores more information than any other type of storage device is the:
   A. CD-ROM
   B. RAM
   C. floppy disk
   D. hard disk

6. The keystone of practically every computer that serves as a "technician" handling all mechanical operations and regulating hardware is the:
   A. hard drive
   B. software application
   C. graphical user interface
   D. disk operating system

7. Software that uses a graphical user interface and relies more on pictures and graphics than on text only to help manage programs and data is the:
   - A. disk operating system
   - B. Windows application
   - C. intranet
   - D. local graphical interface

8. A computer system that allows the user to run two or more programs or applications at the same time is:
   - A. graphical user interface
   - B. utility management
   - C. multitasking
   - D. on-line access

9. The display monitor of the computer is the:
   - A. central processing unit (CPU)
   - B. cathode ray tube (CRT)
   - C. microprocessor
   - D. random access memory (RAM)

10. Hardware that takes an electronic image of text, a picture, an illustration, or a drawing and either stores it in the computer or sends it to another computer by electronic mail or fax is a:
    - A. laser printer
    - B. microprocessor
    - C. scanner
    - D. mouse

Short Answers and Fill-ins

11. The two types of communication devices of a computer are a keyboard and an optional device called a(n) _____.

12. A _____ is a portable storage device that can be used to copy information to or from other computers.

13. LAN stands for _____, which links computers within a small area like a building or an office.

14. If a computer is being used to send a fax (rather then a fax machine), what other type of hardware is required? _____

15. The two major manufacturers of PC hardware are _____ and _____.

16. List four major uses or benefits of the Internet for travel agencies.
    - A. _____
    - B. _____
    - C. _____
    - D. _____

17. List the names of the four CRSs used in U.S. travel agencies and the major airline host(s) for each.

CRS:	Host(s)
A. _____	_____
B. _____	_____
C. _____	_____
D. _____	_____

18. The travel agency that uses a CRS is called a _____ to that system.

19. Other airlines and travel suppliers that use a particular CRS to market and sell their products and services are called co-hosts or _____.

20. To complete a passenger name record (PNR) in any system, five fields are required. Name them.
    - A. _____
    - B. _____
    - C. _____
    - D. _____
    - E. _____

21. You have been selected to create a new Web site for your travel agency office. Write a minimum of six key "commandments" to follow.

A. _____

B. _____

C. _____

D. _____

E. _____

F. _____

22. Your agency is considering creating a Web site on the Internet. It is up to you, the manager, to decide whether or not this is a good idea for your company. List at least three questions or issues that you need to investigate in order to make your decision with confidence.

A. _____

B. _____

C. _____

Chapter 6

Accommodations

This hotel is renowned for its peace and solitude. In fact, crowds from all over the world flock here to enjoy its solitude.

Excerpt from an Italian hotel brochure

Fast Forward ▼

➤ There has been a boom in the hotel business in recent years and the industry has responded by creating a wide variety of hotel properties. We can simplify by categorizing accommodations into three general types: transient, resort, and residential. . . . 275

➤ There are four examples of transient properties: city commercial, airport, all-suite, and motels or motor inns. . . . 276

➤ Resorts are destinations by themselves. Popular types of resorts include all-inclusives, B&Bs, and spas. . . . 276

➤ Club Med pioneered the all-inclusive resort concept nearly 50 years ago. Today many all-inclusive properties offer luxurious surroundings, gourmet restaurants, and other posh amenities. . . . 277

➤ Some unique and romantic accommodations that reflect the history, culture, and traditions of the host country include Japanese ryokans, Spanish paradores, French Relais & Chateaux, and the Romantik Hotels of Germany. . . . 278

➤ Accommodations can be classified by the type of ownership and management control, such as independent, affiliation, franchise, and chain organizations. . . . 284

➤ Hotels determine their price structure based on several components: room size, number of beds, meal plans, and other miscellaneous items. Travel professionals are required to know basic room and meal plan terms and codes. . . . 286

➤ Hotels are classified by formal rating systems. Most members of the World Tourism Organization adhere to five classifications. . . . 289

➤ There are four basic factors that affect the price of a hotel and rooms: hotel location, room location, room size and decor, and length and time of stay. . . . 290

➤ Most travelers don't pay the "sticker" price or the rack rate at a hotel. Why? There are many types of discounts available, including corporate rates and frequent-stay programs. . . . 292

➤ How to select the right hotel for your clients? Know your *resources*. In addition to the agency CRS, the four major printed hotel references are the *Official Hotel Guide* (OHG), *Hotel & Travel Index*, the *STAR Service*, and the *Travel Planners*. . . . 295

➤ There are two general types of travelers: business and leisure. The business and leisure traveler look for different things when picking a hotel. . . . 307

➤ Three major methods of guaranteeing a hotel reservation are deposit/prepayment, credit card, or travel agency. . . . 308

➤ The computer reservations systems are the dominant means of booking hotels, followed by toll-free numbers and direct phone calls to the property. . . . 309

➤ Calculate the cost of a hotel reservation by including room price, tax, and other supplemental charges, such as optional meal plans and each additional person costs. . . . 311

➤ Travel agencies provide any of three types of hotel documentation for clients: hotel confirmation notice, automated itinerary/invoice form, and/or personalized agency voucher. . . . 315

Introduction

A good choice of a hotel can make a vacation; a poor choice can break it. If the traveler is accustomed to first-class travel, it is likely that he won't be happy at a bargain hotel located blocks from where he wants to be, with few comforts and amenities. A hotel like that is no bargain at any price.

Selecting the right accommodations for your clients may sound easy and rather routine. But it isn't. The travel professional must consider many factors in making the right choice: Price, location, facilities, and service are only a few examples of what business and leisure travelers look for when they select accommodations.

Accommodations account for the second-largest number of bookings for travel agents after air transportation. The question "Can I make a hotel reservation for you?" should go hand-in-hand with the air booking—chances are that travelers will need a place to stay once they get to their destination. Sales agents who forget to ask or just don't bother to ask for the business are doing a disservice to the client and ignoring a potential for increased agency revenue. The average commission earnings on hotel bookings range from 10 to 15 percent.

What type of traveler books hotels most frequently? Vacationers book the most often followed by business travelers. Figure 6.1 shows the results of a recent

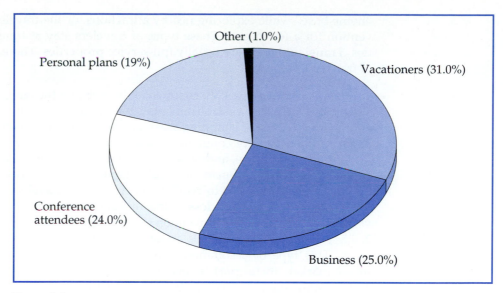

Figure 6.1 *Breakdown of lodging customers.*
(From Travel Weekly, *September 1998.)*

survey conducted by *Travel Weekly* that shows the breakdown of lodging customers.

In this chapter we first explore the various kinds of hotels according to the level of services, amenities, and organization structure. Included is a study of the factors that affect the price of a room, including some important accommodation and meal plan terminology. You will become familiar with the major hotel resources used by travel professionals—those in print and those accessed through the computer reservations systems. Finally, you will learn how professionals book hotels by telephone and the computer, what it means to guarantee a reservation, how to transmit advance payments, and other important booking procedures.

TYPES OF PROPERTIES

There are many different ways to classify hotels. One way is to classify according to the type of property. Depending on who you talk to or what book you read on this subject, there could be between two and a dozen types of accommodations. There has been a boom in the hotel business in recent years and the industry has responded by creating a wide variety of specialized types of accommodations. To simplify this hodgepodge of classifications, we can divide all accommodations into three general types: transient, resorts, and residential. Depending on how technical you want to get, you can further divide each major type into subcategories. For our purposes here, we define the standard types of accommodations that are booked frequently for business, leisure, and group travelers.

▶ Transient Properties

Transient accommodations are designed for short-term stays of one or two nights. This type of property appeals to a broad spectrum of travelers: a business traveler stopping overnight for a meeting, a family on vacation using the hotel as "home base" while exploring nearby attractions, or the traveler attending a convention for a few nights. These types of travelers stay at transient-style properties. **Transient hotels** are usually full-service properties. There are four examples of transient properties:

1. *City commercial hotels.* City commercial is probably the largest category of transient properties. These establishments are located close to their markets: business and financial districts, shopping areas, and entertainment centers. There are three major markets for city commercial hotels: business travelers, vacation travelers (individual and group), and people attending conventions, meetings, and conferences. For example, a business traveler staying in New York City may prefer a downtown location close to Wall Street. A vacation traveler may prefer the midtown, Times Square area, close to theaters and shops. For those attending a convention, proximity to the convention site and restaurants is an important factor.

2. *Airport hotels.* Airport hotels are exactly that—they are located in or near airports. This type of accommodation is selected by travelers by necessity. The major markets for airport hotels are business travelers, honeymoon packages, and meeting sites. A major feature of airport properties is the convenience for early morning departures or late evening arrivals. Another selling point is the avoidance of traffic. All airport hotels offer guests courtesy ground transportation to and from the airport.

3. *All-suite hotels.* This type of accommodation is a fairly recent phenomenon. It began in the early 1980s and has grown to be a large and important segment of the hospitality industry. All-suite hotels appeal to relocating executives, the employee on a long-term project, or the leisure traveler who wants cooking facilities and more space than is available in a traditional bedroom. A typical all-suite unit incorporates a living room, sleeping area, and kitchenette.

4. *Motels.* These accommodations, also called *motor inns,* are located on or near major roads and highways. Major markets are those traveling by automobile: salespeople who are meeting customers and suppliers, vacation travelers on an independent driving tour, and people who are traveling for personal reasons—to visit family and friends. Many motels or motor hotels have more than 300 rooms and others have less than 25. Today, it is difficult to distinguish some motels from full-service hotels The level of service and number of amenities differ depending on the location and price of the property. Some motels have minimal services, such as a small diner or restaurant; others may offer full dining service plus recreational facilities such as pool or tennis.

➤ Resorts

Resort properties are considered to be destinations by themselves. They offer a full range of services and amenities for their guests. The major markets for resorts are vacation travelers and those attending meetings and conventions. Resorts come in all sizes and the variety and sophistication of guest services and facilities differ from one property to the next. Typical features of resorts include restaurants, shops, water and land sports, pools, spas, and sometimes casinos. Resort properties want to attract guests for longer stays. That is why many resorts, especially during the high season of travel, require a minimum number of nights stay. A good example is the Caribbean, where the standard required stay is a minimum of two or three nights.

In addition to the large resort property catering to a wide cross section of travelers, there are many different types of resorts. The three major resort categories booked frequently by travel professionals for their clients are all-inclusives, bed & breakfasts (B&Bs), and spas.

All-Inclusives

All-inclusive resorts offer complete vacation packages at one all-inclusive price. The price includes accommodations, all meals (American plan), full use of the resort's sport and recreation facilities, entertainment, and transfers to and from the airport. In a true all-inclusive vacation there should be no hidden surprises. Club Med pioneered the all-inclusive concept nearly 50 years ago. In the early days, all-inclusive properties offered bare-bones facilities with a "let's have a party" atmosphere aimed at young couples. These earlier properties offered basic accommodations, long lines at the buffet tables, and standard amenities. Today, many all-inclusives offer luxurious accommodations, several gourmet restaurants with à la carte dining, and other posh amenities, such as fitness centers, spa treatments, and suites with full bars. Some properties even offer flower petals sprinkled on guests' pillows and in-room compact disk players. In addition to Club Med properties, which have locations worldwide, other examples of all-inclusives are Super Clubs, Sandals, and Couples in the Caribbean (see Table 6.1).

Web Link

Resorts Online: This site provides links to more than 1,300 resorts and includes a search feature that makes it easy to find properties that suit a traveler's needs. For starters, you can search by any of ten factors, such as scuba, skiing, meeting facilities, spa and golf. Go to *http://www.resortsonline.com*

Bed & Breakfasts

Bed & breakfast (B&B) establishments have increased rapidly in the United States. The concept started in Europe with British B&Bs and Italian pensiones. In the United States during the Depression years of the 1930s, many people converted their homes into rooming houses to supplement their income.

Today, innkeepers of bed & breakfast establishments do it not only for financial reasons but as a hobby or adventure. Guests pay for a room, including break-

---

TABLE 6.1   EXAMPLES OF ALL-INCLUSIVE RESORTS IN THE BAHAMAS, BERMUDA, AND THE CARIBBEAN

Antigua
    Curtain Bluff
    Pineapple Beach Club–Antigua
    Sandals Antigua at the Anchorage
Guadeloupe
    Club Med–Caravelle
Jamaica
  Montego Bay
    Sandals Inn
    Sandals Montego Bay
  Negril
    Grand Lido
    Hedonism II
    Negril Inn
  Ocho Rios
    Boscobel Beach Hotel
    Couples Jamaica
    Sandals Ocho Rios

Runaway Bay
    Franklyn D. Resort
    Jamaica Jamaica
St. Kitts
    Jack Tar Village
    Sandals Resort
Martinique
    Club Med–Buccaneer's Club
St. Lucia
    Club Med
    Le Sport
    Sandals St. Lucia
St. Maarten
    Great Bay Beach Hotel & Casino
St. Thomas, U.S. Virgin Islands
    Bolongo Elysian Beach Resort

fast with the host family. There is a level of intimacy between hosts and guests since there is sometimes a lack of privacy that is not found in the more traditional establishments: two or more guest rooms may share a bath, and innkeepers and guests often share conversation around the breakfast table.

Most B& Bs in the United States are small, eight rooms or less. There is an upscale version called a country B&B that has its routes in New England. These establishments usually serve all meals, not just breakfast.

Web Link

The Bed and Breakfast Channel This Web site offers extensive directories of bed & breakfasts, country inns, and small hotels all over the world, with photos, descriptions, and nearby attractions. Interested? Point your browser at *http://www.bbchannel.com*

Spas

Spas are health resorts that specialize in diet and fitness programs. Spas had their beginnings in ancient Rome and hit their stride during the eighteenth century throughout Britain and the European continent. In those days, resorts were built around inland mineral springs and later along the seacoast for the waters' health benefits and curative aspects. During this era, spas became so fashionable that they became centers for social events, recreation, dancing, games, and even gambling.

Today, spa resorts are located near inland mineral springs or along coastal areas in many countries throughout the world. They include all standard resort services and amenities, with the emphasis on health, fitness, and diet.

➤ Residential Hotels

In contrast to transient and resort properties, residential guests sign on for long-term stays. Travel agents and other retailers do not usually get involved in booking this type of accommodation. Guests at some *residential hotels* may take up permanent residence; others may be more transient. Sometimes a long-term lease is involved. A popular type of residential property is the *apartment hotel.* They offer fewer hotel services than residential hotels and usually provide kitchen facilities. Extended stays for the transient guest may be as short as a few weeks and as long as several months. This type of property is marketed to business travelers who have long-term projects and commitments.

➤ Unique Properties Worldwide

In addition to the more traditional types of accommodations, there are some very unique and traditional accommodations throughout the world that reflect the history, culture, and traditions of each country and its people. Some of these unique accommodations are privately owned; others are owned and operated by governments. One thing that they all have in common is their uniqueness and their ability to reflect the peoples and culture of the country they represent. Following are descriptions of some of these unique lodgings by country or region.

British Isles and Mediterranean Europe

Bed & Breakfasts (B&Bs). The bed & breakfast concept had its start in Great Britain. Today, the European version of B&Bs are located throughout Britain and parts of the European continent. They are situated in both city and countryside settings. B&Bs are comfortable accommodations which may be in a private resi-

America's Ten Best Spas

Travel & Leisure readers rate their favorite reviving facilities:

Facility	Score (%)
Sea Island Spa at the Cloister, Sea Island, Georgia	83.7
The Greenbrier, White Sulphur Springs, West Virginia	83.5
The Phoenician, Scottsdale, Arizona	83.1
Grand Wailea Resort & Spa, Wailea, Maui, Hawaii	82.5
Golden Door, Escondido, California	82.3
Hyatt Regency Kauai Resort & Spa, Koloa, Kauai, Hawaii	81.9
Canyon Ranch Health Resort, Tucson, Arizona	81.6
Miraval Life in Balance, Catalina, Arizona	80.8
American Club, Kohler, Wisconsin	80.6
Lodge & Spa at Cordillera, Edward, Colorado	80.2

Best spas for value:

- Sea Island Spa at the Cloister
- Miraval Life in Balance
- Hyatt Regency Kauai Resort & Spa

Best spas for service:

- The Greenbrier
- Sea Island Spa at the Cloister
- The Phoenician

Best spas for food:

- The Greenbrier
- Sea Island at the Cloister
- Golden Door

Best spas for treatments:

- Golden Door
- Canyon Ranch Health Resort, Tucson
- Grand Wailea Resort & Spa

Source: Travel & Leisure *in association with Yankelovich Partners. As published in* Travel Weekly, *Nov., 1998.*

dence, a country pub, or a bungalow by the sea. These accommodations are known to provide the traveler with both the warmth that one gets when staying with family or friends and an "up-close-and-personal" glimpse of the people, their traditions, and day-to-day lifestyle.

A slightly more sophisticated version of the B&B are guest houses, which are larger and a little more expensive. Guest houses are generally situated in seaside locations and other heavily populated areas. Guest houses have more rooms than B&Bs, room size is larger on average, and there is a higher percentage of rooms with private bath facilities.

Family Stays: Bungalows and Working Farms. Visitors to such countries as Ireland and Britain can stay with local families in their homes in the city or countryside.

Accommodations can range from a modern bungalow, to a cozy rose-trellised cottage, to a Georgian mansion.

Working farm accommodations are a version of the B&B and guest house concepts. This type of experience allows the visitor to become "part" of the host family during the visit. Guests rent accommodations in anything from a private working farm to modest homes. The fun is in participating with the family in various recreational and sports activities, such as hiking, horseback riding, playing golf or tennis at nearby facilities, or fishing and swimming in local streams and lakes. A special sign usually identifies farmhouses and homes approved by local tourist boards.

Castles and Manors. These types of romantic accommodations abound throughout Great Britain and the rest of Europe. Former country manors and medieval castles have been restored to their former glory and now accept guests to subsidize the costs incurred to renovate and maintain these architectural treasures (see Figure 6.2). Romantic castles and major homes are situated in dramatic settings such as rolling farmland, along river banks and lake shores, along rugged seacoasts, or in forest settings. Some can be rented for as short a period as a week, up to a full season.

Figure 6.2 *Main entrance to the majestic Glamis Castle, a medieval and romantic hotel in the highlands of Scotland.*

Spain and Portugal

Paradores.   Unique to Spain, **paradores** comprise a vast network of government-owned lodgings that have been converted from old buildings such as castles, convents, and monasteries. These historic buildings were renovated with modern-day amenities and converted into charming and unique lodgings. The renovation work on these beautiful buildings has not destroyed their atmosphere and natural charm. Paradores are also available in Puerto Rico but are limited in number.

Portugal has its own version of the Spanish paradores called **pousadas.** These accommodations are also situated in beautiful settings in historic buildings such as restored palaces and castles. Since the number of paradores and pousadas are limited and in high demand, especially during the tourist season (May through October), advance reservations are required.

South America

Estancias.   **Estancia** means ranch in Spanish, and that is exactly what this type of lodging represents. Travelers can stay at privately owned cattle ranches located in the *pampas* or grasslands of Argentina. Guests participate in many of the recreational activities, such as horseback riding and hiking. Best of all, the price of the room includes home-cooked meals featuring fresh beef from cattle raised on the ranch. Accommodations are moderately priced.

France

Relais & Chateaux.   A hospitality group called *Relais & Chateaux* offers a remarkable variety of upscale and charming lodging facilities: historic city hotels, seaside resorts, mountain chalets, turreted castles, ancient abbeys, country estates, and manor houses. Most member hotels are family-owned and managed and are predominately small, averaging 25 rooms or less.

These upscale accommodations have banded together into a network of more than 400 elegant hotels and charming restaurants that are located in approximately 40 countries worldwide. France is the headquarters of the Relais & Chateaux organization and the country where a great number of these special accommodations and restaurants are located.

Germany

Romantik Hotels.   *Romantik Hotels* are special accommodations in Germany. They comprise a network of privately owned hotels that are located in historic settings with a lot of atmosphere. The emphasis is on quality in both food and accommodations. Prices vary in relation to the guest services and amenities offered, but offer excellent value for guests who wish to stay in charming and unusual accommodations with a lot of atmosphere.

There is also the *Gast im Schloss* ("Guest in Castle") program, which is similar to Romantik Hotels. These are castles that have been transformed by their owners into palatial and luxurious hotels.

Japan

Ryokans.   **Ryokans** (pronounced "roy-khans") are typical Japanese inns that offer all facilities and amenities in traditional Japanese style. Guests sleep on tatami mats, which are thin reed mattresses placed on the floor, covered by large pillows or futons. Other services include Japanese-style baths and food served in the traditional way—guests sit on the floor with costumed attendants serving them. Ryokans are surrounded by beautiful garden settings and can be found near major cities and throughout the countryside. These accommodations can be quite expensive and are sometimes included on specialized tours of Japan.

Key Point ➤ The **American Hotel & Motel Association (AH&MA)** is the trade association that represents the lodging industry in the United States. It is the umbrella organization for local and state chapters and is located at 1201 New York Avenue, N.W., Washington, DC 20005-3931.

Hotel Organization

Depending on the size and complexity of the property, there are differences in job titles and functions and in how working relationships are assigned. In its most simple form, the organization structure of a small bed & breakfast may consist of two or three people: the manager, front desk manager, and general assistant. In a full-service establishment there may be more than thirty position titles identified; many representing dozens of employees fulfilling the responsibilities of a position.

In any type or size of hotel property there are operating departments that make sure that everything runs smoothly. Some of these departments have direct contact with guests and are referred to as *front of the house*. Other departments provide indirect services or operate "behind the scenes" and are referred to as *back of the house*. Table 6.2 is a breakdown of a typical hotel's front- and back-of-the-house organization.

The basic organization pyramid in major hotels is structured around a management team comprising a general manager and a resident manger or executive assistant manager. The general manager (GM) is in charge of the entire property and is responsible for the overall performance of the hotel and all employees.

The resident manager ensures that the policies established by the GM are carried out by all departments on a day-to-day basis. This person is highly visible to the staff and takes an active role in supervising other managers and in the functioning of their departments.

The next management layer that reports directly to the general manager and/or resident manager consists of the controller, director of marketing and sales, food and beverage manager, rooms division (or front office) manager, executive housekeeper, human resource director, and chief engineer. Figure 6.3 shows a typical organizational structure of a medium-sized to large hotel.

Table 6.2 Hotel's Front and Back of the House

Front of the House	Back of the House
Front office	Food preparation
Front service (door, bell, and valet attendants)	Food and beverage purchasing, receiving, storage
Guest services	Accounting
Switchboard	Security
Reservations	Engineering/maintenance
Housekeeping	Laundry
Dining room and bar service	Personnel and training
Banquet functions	Sales and promotion
Meeting rooms	
Recreational and entertainment facilities	

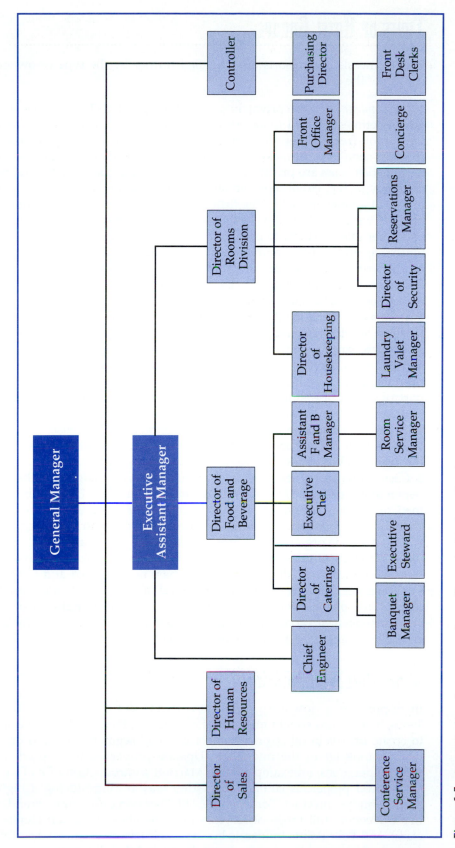

Figure 6.3 *Organizational structure of a medium-sized to large hotel.*

TYPES OF HOTEL GROUPS

Hotels, motels, and resorts are classified further by the type of ownership and control of the property:

1. *Independent hotels* are privately owned and operated. These types of properties are sometimes referred to as "Mom-and-Pop." Many of these properties do not have a toll-free number for reservations. That means that the travel agent needs to write, send a fax, or make a long-distance phone call to make the reservation.

2. *Affiliation hotels* are privately owned but have contracted with a representative company or rep. Hotel representative companies can be viewed as branch sales offices of a hotel or motel. One firm will represent any number of noncompeting hotels. Two major functions of reps are to supply travel agencies with literature and other sales aids and to provide a reservation service for their member hotels. Since they offer toll-free numbers, the travel agent saves time and money not having to write a request, fax, or place a long-distance call to make a reservation. Representative companies also provide marketing and advertising services for their client hotels. Some examples of major hotel representatives are Utell International, International Travel & Resorts, Forte Hotels North America, and Jarvinen Worldwide Hotels.

3. *Franchise hotels* are also independently owned and operated but are guided and serviced by a franchise group. Franchising means selling the right to a name, a product, and a system, along with exclusivity for a specific area. Hotels that are part of a franchise still have independent control but are required to conform with standards mandated by the franchise organization. The properties operate under the franchise group's name. An example of a franchise operation is Best Western Hotels. They are advertised as Best Western, and reservations are made through Best Western's toll-free service.

4. *Chain hotels* are owned, operated, and managed by a company; they are not independently owned. The largest hotel/motel chains are Holiday Inn, the Sheraton Corporation, Hilton Hotel Corporation, and Marriott. A hotel that is part of a chain usually receives direction and control from the central management organization. All chain organizations provide toll-free numbers and a wide range of services to the travel sales agent. A main advantage of booking chain accommodations is *predictability:* All properties in a chain are operated and managed in the same manner. You can expect the same level of service and amenities in each location. The combination of brand recognition and the strengths of size and powerful management account for chains' popularity and growth. In fact, chain-controlled hotels now dominate the U.S. hotel industry.

▶ Market Segmentation

In response to a downturn in business trends during the late 1970s and early 1980s, hotel chains sought methods of broadening their markets. One answer was to create brands in other price categories; hotel segmentation and brand identification took off in the mid-1980s. Upscale properties introduced moderately priced operations, an example being Marriott's introduction of its Fairfield Inns. Mid-priced properties could move either way by introducing a higher-priced and/or budget product. For example, ITT Sheraton offers three brands: the Luxury Collection (full range of services and amenities), Sheraton Hotels (superior class), and Four Points (midscale business and leisure markets). See Table 6.3 for several other examples of major hotel chains and their brand names.

Web Link

Virtual Hotel Tours: This Web site promises "tours" of select properties if you download a RealPlayer plug-in. Check it out at *http://www. hotelview.com*

✓ *Check Your Understanding 6-1*

1. Match each hotel type with the correct definition.

A. resort _____ 1. Especially popular for travelers who have early morning flights.

B. motel _____ 2. Unique to Spain, a vast network of government-owned lodgings that are converted historic buildings such as castles, convents, and monasteries.

C. all-inclusives _____ 3. Traditional inns that offer all facilities and amenities in traditional Japanese style.

D. residential _____ 4. Considered to be destinations themselves since they offer a full range of amenities and facilities for both leisure and business travelers.

E. ryokan _____ 5. Network of privately owned hotels in Germany that are located in historic settings that emphasize quality in both food and accommodations.

F. airport _____ 6. Accommodations include a living room, sleeping area, and kitchenette; cater to business travelers on long-term projects.

G. transient _____ 7. Price includes room, all meals, use of sports and recreational facilities.

H. spa _____ 8. Health resorts that specialize in diet and fitness programs.

I. paradores _____ 9. Hospitality group based in France that offers a variety of upscale and charming lodging facilities and restaurants.

J. bed & breakfast _____ 10. The apartment hotel is an example of this type of property, which caters to long-term guests and may or may not involve a lease arrangement.

K. all-suite _____ 11. Major category of hotel that is designed for short-term stays of one or two nights. City commercial hotels and motels are examples.

L. Relais & Chateaux _____ 12. Located on or near major roads and highways that cater to vacation and business clients traveling by car.

M. Romantik Hotels _____ 13. Small, privately owned establishments where the guest pays for room and breakfast with the host family.

TABLE 6.3   MAJOR HOTEL CHAINS AND BRANDS

	Holiday Inn Worldwide	Hyatt	Marriott International	Choice Hotels International
Low-end	Crowne Plaza	Hawthorne Inns	Fairfield Inn	Comfort Inns, EconoLodge, Friendship Inns, Rodeway Inns, Sleep Inn
Midscale	Holiday Inns		Courtyard, Residence Inn	Quality Inns
Upscale	Crowne Plaza Resorts	Regency Park Hyatts	Marriott Hotels and Resorts, Ritz-Carlton	Clarion
Suites	Holiday Inn Hotels and Suites	Hyatt Suites, Hawthorne Suites	Marriott Suites	Comfort Suites, Quality Suites, Clarion Suites

2. Fill-in the blanks with the correct type of hotel group.

   A. _____ hotels are privately owned and operated. Some have a toll-free number to make reservations; others do not. Sometimes referred to as "Mom-and-Pop."

   B. _____ hotels are owned, operated, and managed by an outside company; they are not independently owned. Holiday Inns, Sheratons, and Hiltons are examples of this type of property. This type of hotel group dominates the U.S. hotel industry.

   C. _____ hotels are privately owned and operated but are required to conform with standards mandated by a business organization. These properties also have to operate under the other organization's name. An example of this type of operation is Best Western Hotels.

   D. _____ hotels are privately owned but have contracted with a representative company. These companies offer sales, marketing, and reservation services for their client hotels.

Hotel Terminology

Hotels determine their room price structure based on several components: room size, number of beds, meal plans, and other miscellaneous items. Before we get into the pricing and booking aspects of hotels, you should know some basic room and meal plan terms and their codes.

➤ Room and Accommodation Terms

Here are some important terms and their codes that are used to describe types of rooms. Rooms are defined by the number of occupants:

- *Single:* room occupied by one person
- *Double:* room occupied by two people
- *Twin:* room occupied by two people
- *Triple:* room occupied by three people
- *Quad:* room occupied by four people

Codes are used to define rooms by the number/type of bed(s):

- *SWB:* single with bath, single bed
- *DWB:* double with bath, one double bed
- *DDWB:* double-double with bath, two double beds
- *TWB:* twin with bath, two twin beds

In addition to standard rooms, special types of accommodations are available at selected hotels:

- *Cabana:* hotel room located on the beach or pool area, usually separated from the main building
- *Lanai:* room with a balcony or patio overlooking water or garden, usually in a resort hotel
- *Efficiency:* hotel room with housekeeping facilities, usually including a stove, refrigerator, and sink
- *Studio:* room with couches for daytime use that convert into beds for sleeping
- *Suite:* separate sitting area connected to one or more bedrooms
- *Junior Suite:* large hotel room with a partitioned sitting area and bedroom
- *Hospitality Suite:* room in a hotel used for entertaining, usually at conventions or meetings
- *Duplex:* two-story suite connected by a private stairway

Key Point ➤ There is a major difference between adjoining and connecting rooms. **Adjoining rooms** are two or more rooms located side by side but without private connecting doors; access between rooms is through the outside hall. **Connecting rooms** are located side by side and are connected by a private door that enables guests to move between the rooms without going through the outside hall area.

➤ Meal Plans and Codes

The price of a hotel room is sometimes determined by what meal(s) is/are included in the cost of the room. There are six general types of meal plans: American, modified American, Bermuda, continental, bed & breakfast, and European. These meal plans, their codes, and definitions are:

- *American plan or full American* (AP/FAP). Room rate includes three meals per day; also called full board or **full-pension** in Europe.
- *Modified American plan* (MAP). Room rate includes two meals per day (breakfast and lunch or dinner); also called **demi-pension** in Europe.
- *Bermuda plan* (BP). Room rate includes a full American-style breakfast.
- *Continental plan* (CP). Room rate includes a small breakfast consisting of coffee, tea, juice, and rolls.

- *Bed & breakfast plan* (BB). Room rate (usually in a guest house or inn accommodation) includes a full American-style breakfast.
- *European plan* (EP). Room rate includes no meals.

✓ *Check Your Understanding 6-2*

1. Match each accommodation term with the correct definition.

   A. duplex   _____ 1. Hotel room used for entertaining.

   B. studio   _____ 2. Hotel room in pool or beach area usually away from the main building.

   C. twin   _____ 3. Sitting room with separate bedrooms.

   D. double   _____ 4. Hotel room with couches that convert into beds for sleeping.

   E. lanai   _____ 5. Room occupied by two guests with two beds.

   F. cabana   _____ 6. Room occupied by one guest.

   G. adjoining rooms   _____ 7. Room with balcony overlooking pool or garden area.

   H. connecting rooms   _____ 8. Room occupied by two guests with one bed.

   I. junior suite   _____ 9. Rooms side by side with no common door.

   J. efficiency   _____ 10. Room occupied by four guests.

   K. suite   _____ 11. Large room with sitting area and partitioned bedroom.

   L. quad   _____ 12. Room with cooking facilities.

   M. single   _____ 13. Two-story accommodation.

   N. hospitality   _____ 14. Rooms side by side with a common door.

   O. triple   _____ 15. Room occupied by three guests.

2. For each meal plan definition below, write the name and the code.

Room Rate Includes:	Code	Meal Plan Name
A. breakfast and lunch or dinner (demi-pension)	_____	_____
B. no meals	_____	_____
C. small breakfast of coffee, tea, and rolls	_____	_____
D. three meals per day (full board or full-pension)	_____	_____
E. full American-style breakfast (in a standard hotel)	_____	_____
F. full American-style breakfast (in a small inn or guest house accommodation)	_____	_____

TABLE 6.4   GENERAL HOTEL RATING GUIDE

RATING	DESCRIPTION
Deluxe/luxury (◆◆◆◆◆)	Top of the line; exclusive and expensive property offering elegant and luxurious public rooms and the highest standards of service. Usually located at a prestige address. For discriminating travelers.
First class (◆◆◆◆)	Above-average hotel; may be an exceptionally well-maintained older hotel or a modern hotel designed for first-class market. Accommodations and public areas tastefully furnished and very comfortable. For average clients and may satisfy many discriminating travelers if the best in its category (i.e., superior first class).
Limited-service first class (midprice) (◆◆◆)	A hotel offering many first-class accommodations but limited public areas, food service, and facilities. Properties tend to be moderate in size and many offer complimentary breakfast or evening cocktails in the lobby or small restaurant. For individual business or vacation traveler.
Tourist/economy class (◆◆)	Budget property that offers functional but clean accommodations; public rooms and "frills" are limited or nonexistent. Often, these establishments are only for a place to sleep. Good value but use with caution.
Third/fourth class (◆)	Low-budget operation, usually old facility and not well kept; international properties may not have private baths, centralized heat, or even carpeting. Recommend only if others are not available, and clients should be cautioned what to expect.

HOTEL RATING SYSTEMS

Hotels are classified by formal rating systems. Most members of the World Tourism Organization adhere to five classifications: deluxe or luxury, first class, tourist class, third class, and fourth class. It should be noted that inspectors from individual countries can be quite subjective in their ratings. For example, if the hotel has all first-class amenities, the property will be categorized as such whether or not the pool is clean or the elevators work!

Because the individual country ratings often are subjective and vague, it is difficult to maintain one standard rating system throughout the world. This is why a first-class-rated hotel in one country may qualify as deluxe in another. For example, first-class properties in many parts of Western Europe are comparable to deluxe-rated hotels in some parts of Africa or the Middle East.

In the United States, hotels are rated by private organizations such as the American Automobile Association (AAA) and Mobile Travel Service. Mobile uses stars and AAA uses crown symbols in their rating systems. Table 6.4 shows a general hotel rating guide that uses both the traditional system of deluxe–first class–tourist class system and the AAA ("Triple A") rating systems.

Poll Ranks Top Hotel Chains

Hotel, a trade magazine reporting on the lodging industry, recently sponsored a written survey of more than 2,800 U.S. households, asking participants to name their favorite hotel chains in four price categories:

- Top luxury:
    1. Ritz-Carlton
    2. Four Seasons
    3. Nikko
- Top five first class:
    1. Marriott
    2. Hilton
    3. Hyatt
    4. Sheraton
    5. Embassy Suites
- Top five midpriced:
    1. Holiday Inn
    2. Best Western
    3. Ramada
    4. Courtyard by Marriott
    5. Quality Inns/Hotels/Suites
- Top five economy:
    1. Days Inn
    2. Comfort Inns/Suites
    3. Motel 6
    4. Econo Lodge
    5. Hampton Inn

What Affects Price

A big challenge is to select the right hotel for the right client. In fact, selling hotels can be more of a challenge than selling air tickets. When selecting flights, seat A is pretty much the same as seat B no matter on which airline you are traveling. Hotel A is rarely like hotel B. Hotels and rooms vary greatly according to size, location, services, and amenities. However, no matter where a hotel is located, or how many rooms it has, or what types of guest services it offers, there are some constant factors that affect the price of any hotel room. The experienced travel professional knows how to evaluate these factors each time a selection is made for a client.

➤ Factor 1: Hotel Location

Where the hotel is located is probably the most important factor influencing the cost of rooms. Resorts that are located directly on the beach or those that have a commanding view of the ski slopes are top price. Similarly, a city commercial hotel located in the heart of the downtown business district and close to convention facilities will also command top prices.

A hotel will also command top prices due to the lack of competition in the area; if you are the only game in town, you can call the shots. A good example of this is the *Four Seasons Resort Nevis*. This is the only major resort property on the small island of Nevis in the Caribbean. There are other types of lodging available, but mainly small properties. Four Seasons adds uniqueness to its striking location on this tiny island and is one of the most expensive accommodations in the Caribbean.

Another factor related to location is a hotel located in a foreign country. The price of the room to U.S. visitors will vary with fluctuations in the currency exchange rate at the time. U.S. dollar prices are not firm unless guaranteed. For clients who pay the hotel bill in U.S. currency or traveler's checks, the exchange rate will be the rate in effect that day and not the day of booking. For those who pay their hotel bill by credit card, the exchange rate is the rate in effect when the bill is posted and not the day of booking. This can work either to the advantage or disadvantage of the traveler.

Key Point ➤ Normally, currencies do not fluctuate greatly from day to day or week to week. However, it does well to remember that if you see a price for a foreign hotel quoted in U.S. currency, treat it as an *approximation* only. The actual price is fixed on the day of payment.

➤ Factor 2: Room Location

The second major factor affecting hotel prices is room location. In resort-style hotels, the most expensive rooms are those that command the best view (i.e., oceanfront, poolside lanai, mountain view, etc.). Less desirable rooms, such as those overlooking the parking lot or the back lots of other buildings, will be priced lower. Proximity to noise and foot traffic also affects price. Rooms located close to noisy stairwells or elevator doors are usually less expensive. Rooms on lower floors overlooking busy and noisy traffic may be less expensive than those located on higher floors.

➤ Factor 3: Fixtures and Size of Room

Many American travelers take for granted that the room in which they are staying will contain standard amenities: private bathroom, air-conditioning, and a bathtub and shower. In some foreign countries these fixtures may only be available in the more expensive rooms or may not be available at all. The travel professional cannot take for granted that things that are considered standard in one country will necessarily be the same in others.

In the United States and Canada, higher-priced rooms will contain all of these standard features as well as some extras, such as hair shampoo, sewing kits, exotic soaps, and even bathrobes and slippers. All of these extras or "fluff" items are added to the cost of the room. Room size is also a consideration. Some hotels are planned so that all the rooms are about equal in size; this factor would not matter in these cases. However, many hotels have rooms of different sizes and layouts. Luxury and upscale establishments usually offer suite or junior suite accommodations that are more like small apartments in size and layout.

Key Point ➤ Many hotel chains are adding *corporate rooms* or entire floors for business travelers. These special rooms located on designated floors are higher in price because they offer additional amenities, such as enhanced computer workstations, free local phone calls, spacious desks, in-room fax machines, and complimentary breakfast or use of the health facilities. For example, Sheraton Hotels call this floor *Club Level* and Hyatt Hotels call this floor *Regency Club*.

➤ Factor 4: Length and Time of Stay

Sometimes the time of year, the day of the week, or even the time of day will affect the room price. In resort areas that are subject to seasonal demand, hotel rates will rise and fall with the seasons.

To stay in the Caribbean during the high or peak period—the winter months—is more expensive than staying during the low or basic season—the summer months. Some resorts areas even have a third season that is more expensive than low season but less expensive than high. This third season is called *shoulder*. Shoulder seasons are "wedged" between the end of one season (high, for example) and the beginning of the other (low, for example). Bermuda is a good example of a three-season resort destination. Table 6.5 shows some popular resort destinations with the approximate high- and low-season periods.

Time of week also affects the price of rooms in certain types of hotels. For example, city commercial properties cater to business travelers during the work-week; weekends are generally slow. To boost revenue during the weekend, many commercial hotels offer lower room rates or special package deals during Friday, Saturday, and Sunday.

The time of day may affect how much you pay for a room. Special rates exist for stays of less than overnight. These are called *day rates* or *part-day rates*. Day-rate guests arrive and depart on the same day. A small group of business travelers may prefer to meet in a day-rate room to take advantage of room service rather than a more impersonal meeting room. Day-room rates are also popular for those who want to take a nap and a hot shower during a lengthy layover between connecting flights.

Rack Rates and Discounts

The quoted, published room rate that is charged to full-paying customers is called the **rack rate**. In other words, the rack rate is the full retail rate. However, just as people don't pay the sticker price on a brand-new car, most travelers don't pay the "sticker" price or the rack rate at a hotel. Why? There are many types of discount rates and programs available. Below are some examples of discount rates that most hotels offer.

Table 6.5   Seasonal Destinations

Destination	High Season	Low Season
Florida	Dec. 15–Apr. 15	Apr. 16–Dec. 14
Caribbean	Dec. 15–Apr. 15	Apr. 16–Dec. 14
Bermuda	May. 1–Nov. 30	Dec. 1–Apr. 30
Mexico	Dec. 15–Apr. 15	Apr. 16–Dec. 14
Colorado Rockies	Thanksgiving–Easter	Balance of the year
Europe	Apr. 1–Oct. 30	Nov. 1–Mar. 30

Corporate Discounts

Even who you are can affect the price of a room: Most hotels offer reduced rates to their most frequent customers, business travelers. These discounted rates for business travelers are called corporate rates. There are four general types of corporate rates:

1. *Standard corporate rates.* Standard corporate rates are published and found in the travel agency's computer reservations system. These rates do not represent a dramatic discount over rack rates. Hotels set aside a certain number of rooms to be sold at its standard corporate rate. Virtually any client of the agency—business and leisure—can be sold a standard corporate rate as long as it is available.

2. *Company-negotiated rates.* Company-negotiated rates represent a larger discount over the rack and standard corporate rates. These rates are negotiated and pre-arranged between a specific company and the hotel. When a company has a pre-arranged rate with a hotel, it is assigned a *corporate discount identification code* or number. This discount code must be provided when you make the reservation and when the guest checks in at the front desk. The company-negotiated rate, therefore, *is valid only for that company's travelers.* In most cases, company-negotiated rates are not commissionable to travel agencies.

3. *Agency-contract rates.* Agency-contract rates are negotiated between the travel agency and the hotel. These rates are valid only for clients of that agency. Similar to company-negotiated rates, the agency is assigned a special identification code that needs to be provided when booking the agency rate. These rates are fully commissionable to travel agencies.

4. *Convention/meeting rates.* The largest discounted rate is for guests renting rooms while attending conventions or meetings. Any organization or association that arranges a convention or large meeting can expect a substantial room discount. Competition for this type of business is at a high pitch since groups provide the host hotels with many opportunities to make money. Convention and meeting guests are guaranteed to use many services on the property during their stay, such as the bar and lounges, shops, and health facilities.

Other Discount Rates

Other types of special discount rates apply to senior citizens, "Triple A" members, and people traveling on government business. Many hotels will also offer family rates where children can stay free or at a reduced cost in the same room. Rooms are also discounted for tour groups. The company who is putting the tour together blocks a number of rooms in advance for the anticipated number of tour participants. Because of this commitment and guarantee of future business, hotels offer lower rates for tour participants.

Frequent-Stay Programs

Major hotel chains offer *frequent-stay programs* to encourage brand loyalty. For example:

Best Western	Gold Crown Club
Embassy Suites	Diplomat
Hilton	Hhonors
Holiday Inn	Priority Club
Hyatt	Gold Passport
Marriott	Honored Guest Awards

Ramada	Business Card
Sheraton	Club International
Westin	Premier

Similar to the frequent-flyer programs offered by airlines, members of frequent-stay programs earn points based on the amount of money they spend on rooms, along with other expenses, such as meals. Points can be redeemed for upgrades to more expensive rooms, free stays at a later date, and in some cases, merchandise.

Often, hotels link their frequent-stay programs with airline and car rental companies. Most chains offer free membership. A simple application is available at travel agencies, hotel front desks, or by calling the chain's toll-free number. Each hotel chain's program has a different name. In addition to room upgrades, other features for members may include early check-in and late checkout privileges.

Key Point ➤ **Run-of-the-house (ROH)** is another type of discount and automatic upgrade program that is growing in popularity. The traveler pays a flat minimum room rate that the hotel guarantees regardless of the quality of accommodations provided. The guest receives the best available room at no extra charge when he or she checks in.

✓ Check Your Understanding 6-3

1. Many factors affect the price of a hotel room. Describe two ways in which each factor below affects the price.

   A. Hotel location

      (1) _____

      (2) _____

   B. Room location

      (1) _____

      (2) _____

2. Describe three factors that relate to time of stay that may affect the price of accommodations.

   A. _____

   B. _____

   C. _____

3. Identify the type of hotel rate for each description below. Select from *standard corporate, company-negotiated, convention/meeting, agency-contract, rack rate,* and *run-of-the-house.*

   A. _____ is a discount rate that is prearranged between a business concern and a hotel and where an identification code must be used by the travelers from that business concern. These rates are not generally commissionable to travel agents.

   B. _____ is the published retail and nondiscounted rate.

   C. _____ is a discount rate where the guest pays the standard minimum room rate and is upgraded to the best available room at check-in.

   D. _____ is a rate negotiated between the travel agency and a hotel that is valid only for business clients of that agency.

E. _____ is a discounted rate that is published in the agency's computer reservations system and is available virtually to any traveler.

F. _____ represents the largest discount of all for those attending group events at the hotel.

RESOURCES

When choosing the best hotel for your clients, you must do so with great care! The selection of hotels is more complex than choosing an airline. Airlines offer similar services and amenities. Let's face it, if the flight departs on time, offers frequent-flyer bonus points, and the passenger's checked luggage ends up where it should be, you probably selected the right flight for the traveler. However, hotels vary dramatically in size, atmosphere, level of service, rates, decor, and much more.

How to make the right choice? Start with knowing your *resources*. There are many hotel resources available to travel agencies and other service companies. The four major printed reference guides are the *Official Hotel Guide (OHG), Hotel & Travel Index,* the *STAR Service,* and the *Travel Planners.* The fifth major resource for hotel descriptions and prices is the airline computer reservations systems. Each of these resources generally offers the same type of information. The differences are the amount of informational detail and the format. In this section we give you examples from each of these resources and how best to utilize each one in the travel workplace.

➤ Official Hotel Guide

The *Official Hotel Guide (OHG)* is probably the most detailed printed resource for worldwide hotel information. The *OHG* is issued in three volumes. The first two volumes cover North America: the United States, Canada, Mexico, Caribbean, and Latin America. The third volume covers the balance of the world: Europe, Asia, the Middle East, Africa, and the Pacific region. Travel agencies subscribe to this publication, which costs approximately $400 per year.

Hotels are listed in geo-alpha order, alphabetically by state or region. Depending on the size of the hotel, some descriptions are more lengthy and given in more detail than others. An excellent feature is the separate list of city and airport hotels. This is certainly helpful when searching for city-center versus airport locations.

Agents Pick Their Favorite Hotels

- *Best health spa:* La Costa Resort, Carlsbad, California
- *Best bed & breakfast:* Green Gables Inn, Pacific Grove, California
- *Best dude ranch:* Lone Mountain Ranch, Big Sky, Montana
- *Best casino hotel:* The Mirage, Las Vegas, Nevada
- *Best golf resort:* The Boulders, Carefree, Arizona
- *Best tennis resort:* The Colony Resort, Sarasota, Florida
- *Best for children's programs:* Boscobel Beach Hotel, Ocho Rios, Jamaica
- *Best for seniors' programs:* The Disney Institute, Orlando, Florida

Source: *Annual survey of hundreds of agents conducted by* Official Hotel Guide, *a sister company of* Travel Weekly. *As published in* Travel Weekly, *Aug., 1998.*

In addition to hotel descriptions and prices, this resource also includes destination maps that provide a geographic overview highlighting destination locations and topographical features. Also included are city maps for selected areas that identify the locations of major hotels and city landmarks.

Refer to Figure 6.4, a sample list for the Four Seasons Vancouver. The elements that are included in all hotel listings include:

1. Booking information (top of the listing)
   - Name, address, phone, fax, and telex numbers
   - Toll-free reservation number(s)
   - Travel agency commission (R-10 means 10 percent of the room rate)
   - Number of rooms
   - Credit cards accepted
2. Additional reservation data (bottom of listing)
   - Hotel representatives through which reservations can be made
   - Computer reservations system(s) where the property is listed
3. Description of location, facilities, and services
   - Classification of hotel (i.e., first, superior, or deluxe class)
   - Date hotel was opened
   - General descriptive information

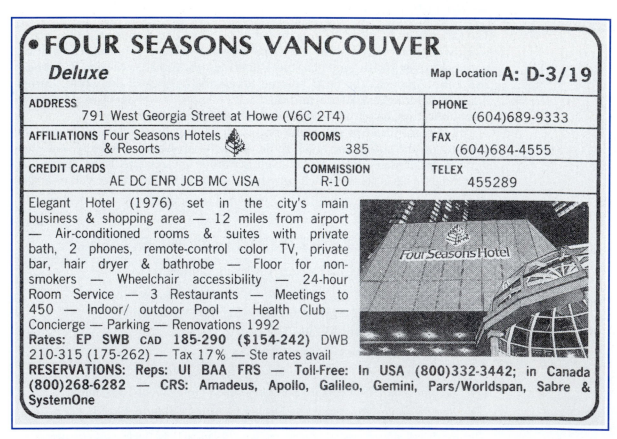

Figure 6.4 OHG *listing.*

4. Rates

- Approximate room rates by room type [e.g., EP SWB means that the room rate is based on European plan (no meals), single with bath]
- Rates printed in the country's currency (rates shown in parentheses represent U.S. dollars)
- Service charge and tax (if applicable, to be added to room rates shown)

Figures 6.5 and 6.6 show additional examples from the *OHG*. Figure 6.5 shows a list for the all-inclusive Sandals St. Lucia. Note that the rates shown are based on AP (American plan) and for seven nights. Figure 6.6 is a partial list of the airport hotels at Seattle International Airport.

• SANDALS ST. LUCIA
All-Inclusive Resort Hotel   Map Location **B-2/12**

ADDRESS	PHONE
PO Box 399, La Toc Road, Castries	(809)452-3081

AFFILIATIONS	UNITS	FAX
Sandals Resorts	260	(809)452-1012

CREDIT CARDS	COMMISSION	TELEX
AE MC VISA	R-10	— — —

Description/Location: Sophisticated All-Inclusive Couples-Only Resort (1993), situated on a 110-acre tropical estate, sloping down a hillside to a golden beach — 2 miles from airport — Formerly La Toc Hotel and Suites

Accommodations: Stylish rooms with air conditioning, satelite color TV, direct-dial phone, clock radio, in-room safe and private bath with hair dryer; some with terrace or balcony; most with oceanview — 54 tastefully-appointed suites with separate air-conditioned bedroom, living room and stocked bars; some with plunge pool

Facilities/Services: Bayside Restaurant featuring continental and Caribbean cuisine — Kimono Restaurant offering Oriental Cuisine — Les Titons Gourmet Restuarant serving continental and nouvelle cuisine — 7 Bars including swim-up pool bar, pub-style nightclub and piano bar — Nightly Entertainment — Meeting Facilities — 2 Freshwater Swimming Pools — 3 Whirlpools — Saunas — 5 Tennis Courts — 9-hole Golf Course — Table Tennis — Volleyball — Shuffleboard, Horseshoes and Croquet — Fitness Center — Water Sports including scuba diving, snorkeling, waterskiing, windsurfing and Hobie Cat sailing —½-mile white sand beach — Roundtrip airport transfer included in rates

Rates: American Plan
7 Nights
Double with Bath ....($2770-3785)
Suite .... (3960-4650)
SC & Tax incl — Trade Discount: Inquire direct

RESERVATIONS:
Reps: $SDC_{1,3}$ — Toll-Free: (800)SANDALS

Figure 6.5 OHG: *all-inclusive resort.*

SEATTLE INT'L AIRPORT/ SEA-TAC

☎ Country Code: 1

Refer to Seattle map, page 413.

● **Airport Plaza Hotel**   102 Rooms   Map B: E-1

18601 International Blvd, Seattle POST CODE: 98188 PHONE: (206)433-0400 TELEX: 470580 FAX: (206)241-2222
Moderate First Class - Comfortable Hotel (1964) located ¼ mile from airport (24-hour courtesy car) - 10 miles from Amtrak station - Air-conditioned rooms with full baths (shower massage), king or queen beds, phone, radio & color satellite TV (CNN) - Restaurant & Lounge - Bar - Meeting facilities to 300 - Business Services - Sauna - Hair Salon - Laundry - Free Parking - Golf & lake activities nearby
RATES: EP S/DWB from $44 - Tax 10.8% COMM: R-10 CREDIT CARDS: AE CB DC DIS MC VISA
RESERVATIONS: REPS: UI ISA₃ Toll-Free: (800)356-1000 CRS: Apollo, Pars, ReserVec, Sabre, SystemOne

● **Best Western
   Pony Soldier Motor Inn**   86 Rooms

1233 N Central, Kent POST CODE: 98032 PHONE: (206)852-7224 FAX: (206)854-9631
Superior Tourist Class - Motel (1978) in Kent, situated 5 miles from airport & convenient to industrial area - Air-conditioned rooms with TV (CNN/HN, movies) - Rooms for nonsmokers - Wheelchair accessibility - Complimentary continental breakfast - Meeting Room to 15 - Heated Pool - Therapy Pool (in season) & Sauna - Guest Laundry - Restaurant & lounge adjacent
RATES: CP SWB $60-75/662-77 DWB 63-78/65-80 EAP 5 - Max rates May 16-Dec 31 - Tax 10.6% COMM: R-10 (CA$H) CREDIT CARDS: AE CB DC DIS ENR MC VISA
RESERVATIONS: REPS: BW Toll-Free: (800)528-1234

● **Best Western Airport Executel**   138 Rooms   Map B: E-1

20717 Internaional Blvd, Seattle POST CODE: 98198 PHONE: (206)878-3300 FAX: (206)824-9000
Moderate First Class - Airport Motor Inn (1981) located off I-5 near 200th St Exit, 1 mile from airport (courtesy van) - Rooms with TV (movies); some with Jacuzzi - 8 Suites - Rooms for nonsmokers - Wheelchair accessibility - Full-service Restaurant & Lounge - Meeting Facilities to 150 - Indoor Pool - Whirlpool, Sauna & Exercise Room - Car rental - Free Parking - Water sports nearby - Renovations in 1992
RATES: EP SWB $65-99 DWB 75-109 - Tax 10.6% - Corp & ste rates avail COMM: R-10 (CA$H) CREDIT CARDS: AE CB DC DIS MC VISA TD: 50%
RESERVATIONS: REPS: BW Toll-Free: (800)648-3311 CRS: Apollo, Galileo, Gemini, Sabre, SystemOne, Worldspan

Figure 6.6 OHG: *airport hotels.*

✔ *Check Your Understanding 6-4*

Refer to Figure 6.4 or 6.6 (samples from the *Official Hotel Guide*) as noted to answer the questions below.

1. Your clients are interested in staying at the Four Seasons Vancouver (see Figure 6.4). Answer these typical questions.

    A. What is the local telephone number for this hotel? _____

    B. What number would you call to make reservations? (Your office is located in the United States.) _____

    C. How many rooms does this hotel have? _____

    D. What is the rating of this hotel? _____

    E. What commission does this hotel pay travel agencies? _____

F. When was the hotel built? _____

G. How many miles is this city hotel located from the airport? _____

H. Does this hotel have meeting facilities? _____

I. In what year did this hotel undergo renovations? _____

J. What is the room rate range in U.S. dollars for a double room? _____

K. The room rate is based on what meal plan? (Write out the full name.) _____

2. Your client, a business traveler, is attending a one-day meeting in Seattle. The client prefers to stay at a hotel located on or near the airport because of an early morning departure the next day. Answer the following questions (see Figure 6.6.)

A. Of the three hotels in the sample listing, which one is closest to the airport? _____

B. Your client is not renting a car and wants to stay at a hotel that offers courtesy transportation to and from the airport. Which hotel would you recommend: Best Western Pony Soldier Motor Inn or the Best Western Airport Executel? _____

C. What is the highest rate for a single room at the Best Western Airport Executel? _____

D. Which hotel offers complimentary continental breakfast? _____

E. Two room rate ranges are shown for the Best Western Pony Soldier Motor Inn. The higher or maximum rate range for a double room—$65 to $80—applies at what time of the year? _____

➤ Hotel & Travel Index

The *Hotel & Travel Index* is a comprehensive guide of worldwide hotels that is published quarterly. Travel agencies subscribe to this resource for approximately $100 per year. Like the *OHG*, it contains thousands of hotel properties throughout the world. This resource also has multicolored regional, area, and specific city maps of major destinations. Unlike the *OHG*, all hotels are contained in one volume. A major difference between this resource and the *OHG* is that the *Hotel & Travel Index* does not contain as much detail. The *Hotel & Travel Index* is best utilized for quick and easy reference when you do not require extensive information regarding the hotel property.

Figure 6.7 is a partial listing at the beginning of the Florida section. In addition to general maps of the state, useful information such as time zone information and area codes are listed. Data provided for each hotel are general in nature: hotel name, mailing address, and local telephone and toll-free numbers are provided. General rate ranges are also shown, along with a brief description of the general location of the property (i.e., oceanfront, near airport, etc.). In Figure 6.10, to the right of the hotel listings are some of the codes and symbols that this resource uses to show such items as commission, number of rooms, meal plans, accommodations, and rates.

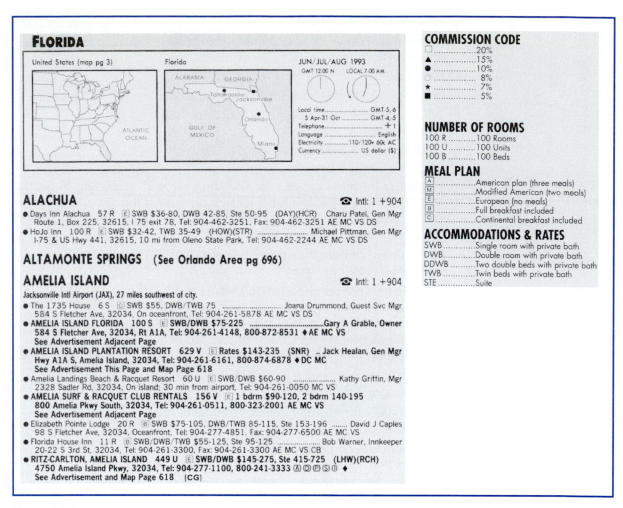

Figure 6.7 Hotel & Travel Index.

✓ *Check Your Understanding 6-5*

Refer to Figure 6.7 (sample from the *Hotel & Travel Index*) to answer the following questions. Your clients are planning to vacation on Amelia Island, Florida. You are looking at the beginning listing of Florida hotels in the *Hotel & Travel Index*.

1. What is the area code for Amelia Island in Florida? _____

2. Into which airport would you book your clients who want to stay on Amelia Island? _____

3. How far is the airport from Amelia Island? _____

4. What is the rate range for the Ritz-Carlton, Amelia Island, for double occupancy? _____

5. What is the least expensive suite at the Elizabeth Point Lodge? _____

6. Is the 1735 House on the oceanfront? _____

7. What number would you call to make reservations at the Amelia Island Plantation Resort if your agency is located in Dallas, Texas?

8. How much commission does the Florida House Inn _____
   pay travel agencies?

9. How many room's does the Elizabeth Point Lodge _____
   have?

10. Name the two hotels on this list that include a full   A. _____
    breakfast with the price of the room.   B. _____

➤ The *Travel Planners*

In addition to being useful resources for airline-related information (as covered in Chapter 3), the *Travel Planners* also are valuable hotel resource guides. As a reminder, *Travel Planners* are published as a series of three volumes: *Business Travel Planner* (for North America), *Europe*, and *Pacific* editions.

As a hotel resource, the *Travel Planner* is similar to the *Hotel & Travel Index*. Descriptions are not detailed and only general information such as hotel name, address, telephone numbers, rate ranges, and booking information is provided. Hotels are also shown separately under city and airport listings. This is an excellent resource to use as a quick reference. Figure 6.8 shows an example of the hotel section from the *Business Travel Planner*. It includes a city/hotel locator map and a partial listing of the city hotels for New Orleans. Also included is a key to some of the abbreviations and symbols used in this resource.

✓ *Check Your Understanding 6-6*

Refer to Figure 6.8 (sample listing from the *Business Travel Planner*) to answer the following questions. A major feature of the *Travel Planner* as a hotel resource are hotel locator maps of major cities. Hotels represented are listed alphabetically and coded by number. A map grid letter and number are also noted to help you locate the hotel on the map.

1. Number 37 on the map represents what hotel? _____

2. The Lafayette Hotel is located on the corner of _____
   Lafayette and what street?

3. Which of the following three hotels is located closest _____
   to the Superdome: Radisson, Le Pavillon Hotel, or
   Hyatt Regency?

4. Name the hotel that is located closest (within _____
   walking distance) to the Riverwalk Marketplace.

5. Your client wants to stay right in the heart of the _____
   French Quarter. By just looking at the map, which
   of the following hotels would you recommend:
   Avenue Plaza Suite Hotel, Maison Dupuy, or
   Doubletree Hotel New Orleans?

6. Your client is staying at the Place D'Armes. How _____
   many blocks would you say this hotel is from the
   French Market (choose one): eight blocks, ten blocks,
   one block, or six blocks?

7. Your client is attending meetings at a major corpora- _____
   tion in New Orleans called Freeport-McMoran. He
   wants to stay at a hotel located close to this place of
   business. Which hotel from the following would you
   recommend: Ramada Garden District, Quality Inn
   Midtown, or Westin Canal Place?

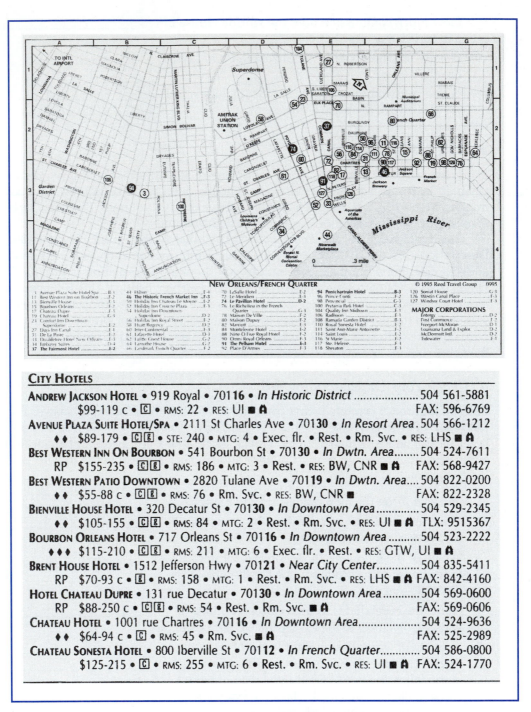

Figure 6.8 Business Travel Planner: *hotel section.*

Answer the following questions from the hotel description listings (Figure 6.8).

8. In which location is the Bourbon Orleans Hotel located (choose one): city center, resort area, historic district, or downtown?

9. Which hotel shown on the sample list does *not* offer a corporate rate?

HOTEL LISTINGS ABBREVIATIONS AND SYMBOLS

⚐	American Hotel & Motel Association member
■	8% or more commission paid to travel agents
a	American Plan (breakfast, lunch and dinner)
b	Full breakfast
c	Continental breakfast
⟦c⟧	Corporate rate available
DWB	Double with bath
Exec. flr.	Executive floor, Club Floor or VIP Level
FAX	Facsimile number
⟦g⟧	Government rate available
m	Modified American Plan (breakfast and lunch or dinner)

MTG	Total number of meeting rooms
NP	New property
RMS	Number of rooms
Rm. svc.	Room service
RES	Hotel Companies and Representatives
Rest.	Restaurant on premises
RP	Renovated property
STE	Number of suites
TLX	Telex number
WK	Weekly

Figure 6.8 Business Travel Planner: *hotel section. (Continued)*

10. Which hotel shown on the sample list has the most rooms? _____

11. What is the least expensive double room rate at the Bienville House Hotel? _____

12. The *Business Travel Planner* uses the "Triple A" rating system. Would you say that the Chateau Hotel is rated deluxe, first class, tourist class, or fourth class? _____

13. How many meeting rooms does the Chateau Sonesta Hotel have? _____

14 Which hotel listed includes continental breakfast in the room rate: Best Western Inn On Bourbon, Bienville House Hotel, Brent House Hotel, or Chateau Sonesta Hotel? _____

➤ The *STAR Service*

The *STAR Service* is probably the most detailed and objective compilation of hotel reports and descriptions. The *STAR Service*'s subtitle is *The Critical Guide to Hotels and Cruise Ships*. This resource began as a collection of reports submitted by travel agents and other industry professionals regarding the hotels they visited. Today, it is a major publication that lists over 7,500 hotels and resorts worldwide. Pages are bound in a three-ring binder notebook format for easy removal and updating. Revision pages are sent when there are major changes to report.

What is so special about this resource? The hotels themselves do not submit the descriptions of their properties for publication as they do for the other hotel resource guides such as the *Official Hotel Guide* and *Hotel & Travel Index*; hotels pay these publications to have their properties included. The descriptions published in the *STAR Service* are submitted by objective travel professionals who have no affiliation with the hotels. That is why the information in the *STAR Service* is very detailed, comprehensive, and sometimes quite critical in its evaluation of the properties and ships listed. This "tell-it-like-it-is" reference is widely used for this reason. Figure 6.9 is a sample from the *STAR Service* for a hotel in Dallas, Texas. Read through it and notice how it describes the facilities and accommodations in great detail.

WYNDHAM ANATOLE HOTEL, 2201 Stemmons Fwy., MARKET CENTER, opposite Market Center, three mi NW of downtown, is a world unto itself, the largest hotel in Dallas and its premier convention hotel. Given the staggering array of facilities and relatively moderate rates, the poor level of individual service is not surprising but rather inevitable. This hotel is scaled for conventions, and those here on their own will find themselves endlessly sandwiched in lines when not endlessly waiting for sandwiches from restaurants and room service. The hotel directs its energies towards expansion rather than refinement, most recently breaking ground for a state-of-the-art conference center to add onto the existing exhibition hall. The modern architecture of this high-profile 45-acre property is stunning, and the elaborate interiors of the 12-, 14-, and 27-story brick towers are impressive. Gallery-quality art—Coromandel screens, 10 Picasso prints, a Louis XIV bronze, and carved rhinoceros horns—commands attention, while whimsical, lamplit London-style "streets" and pseudo-pagodas put a theme-park spin on public rooms. The six restaurants and eight bars are gathered around the two glass-capped atriums and perched on the 27th floor. The food ranges from Mediterranean to Tex-Mex to heart-smart spa fare. The signature restaurant, atop the tallest tower, is an American grill ranked among the best in Dallas. A central kiosk dispenses cappuccino and snacks 24 hours a day, jazz swings in the rooftop bar, and the garden lounge, disco, TV lounge, and poolside bar also pour forth refreshment. An outdoor pool, indoor-outdoor pool, whirlpool, pair of squash courts, and handball courts are on the premises, and for a fee, guests can use one of the largest fitness centers in the US, which includes a health club, exercise room, glassed-in pool, adjacent whirlpool, eight racquetball courts, six lighted tennis courts, sauna, and steam room. The seven-acre park separating the health center from the hotel features a cushioned jogging track and a croquet lawn. The four ballrooms, along with the squadron of meeting rooms and the exhibition hall, reel in plenty of business. Conference capacity exceeds 5000, and business services are offered round the clock. Parking is free in the vast, unsecured lot. Guest rooms fill the upper floors in the main tower and the two atrium buildings. They vary in the quality of their appointments. The large, well-designed period-style quarters hold to traditional standards, with roomy sitting areas, hardwood desks, phones with voice mail, TVs, safes, coffeemakers, irons and ironing boards, minibars, and marble baths with double vanities, second phones, and fine toiletries. Most rooms have two double beds, while the remainder have kings. Some beds are canopied. More expensive tower rooms offer excellant views and seem larger only because they lack the love seats and chairs that cramp the atrium rooms. When completed, the new *Adam's Mark* may steal some convention business from the lower end here, but this hotel continues to offer the best meeting venue in the Southwest. Upscale individuals—especially those here on business—will find the adjacent *Renaissance* better suited to their needs. 1620 rooms. $149-$235 single or double. Patrick Lupsha, mgr. (C-10) Utell, Wyndham. Phone (214) 748-1200. Fax (214) 761-7520. ★★★★

Figure 6.9 STAR Service: *hotel listing.*

➤ Hotels in the CRSs

In addition to the printed resources, the airline computer reservations systems provide travel sales agents with hotel descriptions in addition to availability and booking capabilities. A unique feature of the CRS as a hotel resource is its sophisticated search capability. Travel agents can enter a number of specific requests— location, maximum room rate, availability of courtesy transportation for example—and the CRS responds with a list of only those hotels that satisfy the requests.

Figure 6.10 is a partial display from the SABRE system for the Hyatt Regency New Orleans Hotel. The agent had requested availability for this hotel for arrival April 23 for a seven-night stay for two people. In addition to room rates, four major sections are displayed: (I) policy requirements, (II) property information, (III) room descriptions, and (IV) location and area information.

✔ Check Your Understanding 6-7

Your clients want to stay at the Hyatt Regency New Orleans. To answer their questions regarding this property, you have displayed the hotel index from your computer terminal (refer to Figure 6.10).

1. What is the street address for this hotel?   _____

2. What is the fax number?   _____

3. What is the standard rack (RAC) rate for a deluxe   _____
    double room (code A2D)?

4. What is the run-of-the-house (ROH) rack rate?   _____

5. What is the run-of-the-house (ROH) corporate rate?   _____

6. This hotel has a Regency Club floor, which offers   _____
    continental breakfast in addition to other amenities.
    What is the standard rack rate for a room on this
    floor? (*Hint:* look under "Room Descriptions" in the
    display to get the room code.)

7. The Hyatt Regency New Orleans is located near   _____
    which major landmark?

8. What number are you required to call to make reser-   _____
    vations at this hotel for December 30–31?

9. A family of three (two adults plus a child 11 years   _____
    of age) will share a room. Is there a charge for the
    child?

10. By what time does your client have to cancel his   _____
    guaranteed reservation at the hotel to avoid being
    charged for the room?

11. What time is checkout?   _____

12. What is the name of this hotel's full-service   _____
    restaurant?

```
                    HYATT REGENCY NEW ORLEANS              AIRPORT - MSY
                    500 POYDRAS AT LOYOLA AVE              ***23APR-7NT2***
                    NEW ORLEANS LA 70113
                    FONE  504-561-1234
                    FAX   504-587-4141
                    *** RATES QUOTED IN USD ***
                    BUS-*     A2D-*      RGC-*      ROH-*
RAC                 285.00    $270.00    $305.00    $270.00
                    BUS-*     ROH-*      RGC-*
COR                 219.00    204.00     254.00
LOCATION - NEXT TO SUPERDOME
I.  POLICY REQUIREMENTS
                    * RESERVATIONS MUST BE BOOKED THRU THE HOTEL DIRECT FOR THE
                       FOLLOWING DATES -  NOV 28-30 AND DEC 30-31
                    * FAMILY PLAN/CHILDREN UNDER 18 YEARS ARE FREE IN PARENT*S ROOM
                    * MAXIMUM 4 PER ROOM - ONLY 1 ROLL-AWAY PER ROOM
                    * CANCELLATION / 6PM DAY OF ARRIVAL
                    * CHECK IN  3 PM    *CHECK OUT  12NOON
                    * PETS/SEEING EYE ONLY.
II.                 PROPERTY INFORMATION
PROPERTY TYPE-
    FIRST CLASS
*DESCRIPTION
  AN ULTRA MODERN 33 STORY HIGHRISE BUILT AROUND A 27 STORY ATRIUM, FEATURING LANAI
  UNITS AND 8 LIGHTED GLASS CAPSULE ELEVATORS. HOTEL IS CONNECTED TO THE SUPERDOME AND
  OFFERS 1184 ELEGANTLY APPOINTED GUEST ROOMS.

* FACILITIES -
          HEATED OUTDOOR POOL               FITNESS CENTER
          JOGING TRACK/AROUND SUPERDOME     GOLF/4 MILES
          TENNIS/11 BLOCKS                  NON-SMOKING ROOMS
          BUSINESS CENTER                   CITY TOUR COUNTER
          HANDICAP ROOMS                    ATM MONEY MACHINE
          JACUZZI                           POOL DECK


* SERVICES -
          BABYSITTING                       IN-HOUSE MOVIES
          CABLE TV                          PARKING/SELF AND VALET
          VALET/LAUNDRY                     ROOM SERVICE
* DINING
          TOP OF THE DOME STEAKHOUSE        DINNER/COCKTAILS
          COURTYARD RESTAURANT              FULL-SERVICE
          SARAH*S COFFEE                    COFFEE AND PASTRY

III.  ROOM DESCRIPTIONS
      *A*   LOCATED ON FLOORS 6 - 26, OFFERING VIEWS OF THE CITY AND SUPERDOME
      *RGC*        REGENCY CLUB, A PRIVATE FLOOR WHICH INCLUDES COMPLIMENTARY BREAKFAST
                   DAILY AMONG OTHER AMENITIES
      *ROH         RUN-OF-HOUSE ROOMS. SPECIFIC ROOM TYPE ASSIGNED AT CHECK-IN.

IV.   LOCATION AND AREA INFORMATION
* LOCATION - NEXT TO SUPERDOME
  OVERLOOKING THE FRENCH QUARTER IN THE HEART OF THE
  BUSINESS DISTRICT, ATTACHED TO MACY*S, LORD AND TAYLOR
  AND THE SUPERDOME - NEXT TO CITY HALL, MOBIL, EXXON AND
  AMOCO OIL.
  DRIVING INSTRUCTIONS - TAKE I-10 EAST TO DOWNTOWN. FOLLOW SIGNS
  FOR I-10 EAST. STAY IN RIGHT LANE WHEN YOU GET CLOSER TO
  CITY. EXIT AT 234-B POYDRAS/SUPERDOME. THE EXIT IS ON THE
  LEFT, WHICH RUNS INTO POYDRAS STREET. FOLLOW STRAIGHT ON
  POYDRAS TO THE FOURTH LIGHT. AT LIGHT TURN RIGHT INTO HOTEL.
* TRANSPORTATION -
  SHUTTLE      LIMO    TAXI    CAR RENTAL
  INDEXES              C       14W         L  MSY
               LA      C       0           O  NEW ORLEANS
               LA      C       0           O  SUPERDOME
               LA      C       1S          H  FRENCH QUARTER
                       S       60W         O  BTR
               LA      C       8E          O  METAIRE
               LA      C       8W          O  UNIV OF NEW ORLEANS
               LA      C       6N          O  TULANE UNIV
               MS      C       75NE        O  BILOXI
               LA      C       1W          O  NEW ORLEANS CONV CTR
               LA      C       1W          O  RIVERWALK
               LA      C       5E          O  LOYOLA UNIV
               LA      C       1S          O  BOURBON STREET
               LA      C       6W          O  AUDUBON ZOO
```

Figure 6.10 *Hotel index display in SABRE.*

13. Your clients want to play golf during their stay. How far from the hotel is the nearest golf course?   _____

14. Your clients will be renting a car during their stay. Does this hotel have parking facilities?   _____

15. You're giving directions to someone driving to the hotel. What is the exit number off I-10?   _____

16. Does this hotel offer courtesy shuttle service to/from the airport?   _____

17. How many miles is the airport (MSY) from the hotel?   _____

18. Your clients wish to visit Tulane University during their stay. The hotel is located how many miles north of this school?   _____

SELECTING THE HOTEL

Selecting the right hotel for a traveler requires knowing your resources. It also requires knowing who your clients are and what they want: the who, what, when, where, and why they are traveling. There are two general types of travelers: the corporate or business traveler and the vacation or leisure traveler. Each type will have different needs and requirements when selecting the right accommodations. Below are some typical requirements that both markets look for when selecting hotels.

For the business traveler:

- *Location.* Business travelers look for convenience, due to their hectic travel schedules. If the client's meetings or appointments are in the downtown district, this is where the hotel should be! If the traveler is on a quick overnight business trip with an early morning departure, perhaps staying at an airport location is more convenient.

- *Parking and Garage.* If your business client is renting a car, he or she will require a downtown location that offers parking and garage facilities. This should be checked, especially when booking smaller downtown properties.

- *Room type.* The client may prefer suite accommodations if staying for a lengthy period of time or by personal preference. If the client needs access to a computer, fax machine, secretarial services, or other business-related services, perhaps a room situated on a special floor for business travelers would be more suitable (i.e., Sheraton Hotels' *Club Level*).

- *Dining.* Many business travelers require a hotel with both a coffee shop with popular-priced menus and a dining room with more formal atmosphere and a higher standard of service.

For the vacation traveler:

- *Availability of family plan.* This may be the most important factor for families traveling on vacation. Most hotel chains offer family plans (i.e., child under a certain age occupying the same room at no extra charge with existing beds). Cots or rollaway beds may be available at no charge or a minimal fee. Most hotel chains, especially in resort areas, offer family plans.

- *Meals.* For those vacationers who are staying at a resort located a distance from downtown or restaurants, a meal plan may become more of a requirement than a preference. In some areas, purchasing a meal plan may be more economical.

Table 6.6　Picking a Hotel: What's Important

Business Travelers	Leisure Travelers
1. Location	1. Price/discounts
2. Service	2. Location
3. Nonsmoking rooms	3. Security
4. Security	4. Service
5. Price/discounts	5. Nonsmoking rooms
6. Reputation	6. Reputation
7. Express checkout	7. Swimming pool
8. Airline mileage tie-in	8. Family-oriented
9. Frequent guest program	9. Fine restaurant
10. Fitness center	10. Express checkout

- *Location.* Unlike the business traveler, for whom a hotel's proximity to business centers or the airport takes top priority, the leisure traveler prefers a beachfront or ocean view and/or a hotel that is located close to sightseeing attractions, sports facilities, golf courses, etc. Finding out your clients' interests and the reasons for traveling will play a large part in locating the right hotel.

- *Sports and recreational facilities.* Vacation travelers want to relax and enjoy some amenities and services that they do not usually receive at home. When selecting accommodations they may look for a pool, exercise room, Jacuzzi, or saunas. For sports enthusiasts, they may want tennis and or golf facilities on the premises or located nearby.

Table 6.6 shows the results of a recent survey conducted by the Newspaper Association of America. It was based on a questionnaire of more than 6,200 business and leisure travelers who had been on a trip recently. The eight most important factors when picking a hotel are listed in order of importance for each group of travelers.

Guaranteeing the Reservation

To **guarantee** a room is an important concept when booking accommodations. To guarantee a room reservation is to "promise" the hotel that payment for the room will be provided even if the guest fails to arrive or cancel in time. Remember, a hotel room—like an airline seat—is a "perishable" product; revenue lost due to an unoccupied seat on an airplane or an empty hotel room is lost forever.

Most hotels will hold a room reservation until 6 P.M. (or 4 P.M. in many resort areas). This is called the **hold time.** If the client expects to check in after the hold time, you will need to guarantee the reservation.

Sending a deposit or full *prepayment guarantee* can hold the reservation. Some

Four Ways to Guarantee

- Send a deposit.
- Send full prepayment.
- Provide a credit card number.
- Provide the travel agency name and address.

hotels, especially those located in resort areas during peak travel periods, require a deposit sent to them for two or more nights. This is sent before the client's arrival. Or in some cases, travelers may prefer to fully prepay the entire hotel stay because of the convenience and comfort of knowing that the room charge has been paid. A deposit or full prepayment can be put on a credit card. If a credit card is used, it will be debited at that time.

When guaranteeing by deposit or full prepayment, the procedure is as follows:

1. After confirmation, the travel agency invoices the client for the deposit or prepayment amount. The client pays the travel agency this amount.

2. The client's payment (by cash or check) is deposited in the agency's bank account. The client's personal check is never sent to the hotel. The booking agency issues a company check and sends it to the hotel. This is done immediately after receiving payment from the client.

3. The payment is usually sent with a copy of an agency's hotel voucher (fully explained in the next section). The voucher shows the client's name, reservation data, confirmed room rate, arrival and departure dates, and confirmation number.

If there is not enough time to mail a deposit payment, most hotels accept a major credit card number to guarantee the reservation. When the room is guaranteed, the reservation is assured. No matter what time the guest checks in—even at 3:00 A.M.—the room is ready.

When you use a credit card to guarantee, the reservation agent needs the credit card number, expiration date, and the name of the cardholder. Make sure that you have this information before making the reservation. The hotel will charge the room to the credit card if the client fails to check in and does not cancel the guaranteed reservation in time (generally by 4 P.M. or 6 P.M. of the day of arrival). Since their schedules are so unpredictable, business travelers like to guarantee their hotel reservations.

If the client does not have a major credit card, the agent can use the name and address of the travel agency as a guarantee. This means that the travel agency is billed should the client be a no-show. Many agencies will not handle that liability unless the client is a VIP or a repeat customer. Others will not provide an agency guarantee under any circumstances. It is best to check the agency's policy on this.

Key Point ➤ Travel agencies earn a standard 10 percent on hotel bookings; the commission amount is included in the room price (just like airline fares). Some hotels pay commission on the room rate only; others pay commission on the room rate plus any meal plan options, such as AP or MAP if applicable. This must be checked with each hotel. The standard commission payment policy is to send the agency a commission check after the client checks out, *not before*. So, when sending a prepayment, the commission amount is usually not deducted upfront.

BOOKING THE RESERVATION

The computer reservations systems are the dominant means of booking hotels, followed by toll-free numbers and direct phone calls to the property. In this book we emphasize those major aspects of making a hotel reservation through the computer and telephone handling.

Before you place the call or book the property in the computer, make sure that you have:

- The client's name and the number in the party
- The type of accommodations desired (i.e., double, twin, etc.)
- The number of rooms
- The type of service, if applicable (i.e., MAP, AP, etc.)
- The arrival and departure dates (number of nights)
- Arrival information (airline flight number and expected time of arrival)
- If guaranteed by credit card, the card number and expiration date
- Special requests (i.e., king-size bed, oceanfront room, lower floor, etc.)

If booking on the telephone, make sure that you provide the hotel representative/reservation agent with the following information:

- The agency's name and address
- The agency's ARC/IATA number (some hotels/reps will ask)
- Your name as the booking agent
- All reservation information as listed above

Before completing the call (or ending the record in your computer) make sure that you get the following information:

- A confirmation or reservation number
- The name of the reservation agent/date of call
- A confirmed rate (what is/is not included)
- The cancellation policy
- The procedure for advance payments (e.g., deposit), if applicable
- The option date (date when payment is due), if applicable

➤ Hotel Reservation Script

The following is a model script that illustrates a typical hotel reservation booking between a travel agent (TA) and a hotel representative (HR) company. In this example, the hotel rep is Hilton Hotels Corp. and the hotel being booked is the Boston Back Bay Hilton.

Introduction

HR: Hilton Reservations, this is Judy, may I help you?

TA: Hello, my name is Susan from Pioneer Travel in Boston. I would like to book one double room at the Boston Back Bay Hilton for two people, four nights. Arrival date is June 10 and departure is June 14.

Status

HR: I have checked those dates and can confirm the following rates: $180, $195, or $210 per night. Which rate would your clients prefer?

Confirm Rate and Place Special Request(s)

TA: They want deluxe accommodations—the best that you have at $210 per night. They would like a room that overlooks the courtyard; would it be available?

Request Made/Name of Client

HR: Well, not all deluxe rooms overlook the courtyard. I will put in a request that will be confirmed upon their arrival. What is the name of the party?

TA: Mr. & Mrs. John Sullivan.

Provide Arrival Time

HR: What time is their arrival on the tenth?

TA: Around 8 P.M. I would like to send a deposit to secure the room—what is the hotel's policy?

Payment Procedure/Recap

HR: One night's deposit is required to hold the room for late arrival. Please send it directly to the hotel. Okay. Let me recap this reservation. I am holding one deluxe double room for arrival June 10, departure June 14, four nights at the rate of $210 per night. The reservation is booked in the name of Sullivan, John at the Back Bay Hilton in Boston. To send the confirmation, may I have your agency's address or ARC number and your telephone number?

Agency Address/Phone

TA: Agency address is 1344 Berkeley Street, Boston MA 02215. Agency's telephone number is 617-555-0400.

Confirmation Number

HR: We will mail you the written confirmation. Your confirmation number for this booking is H134456. Be sure to send one night's deposit in the amount of $210 to Back Bay Hilton, 40 Dalton Street, Boston, MA 02218. Deposit to be received by June 3. Is there anything else I can do for you today?

TA: No, thank you, goodbye.

Web Link *Vision for Hotels:* This Web site was designed with the multicultural aspects of Web users in mind, offering hotel reservation services in 12 languages. *Parlez-vouz* hotel reservations? Check out *http://www.ehotel.de*

PRICING THE HOTEL

When calculating the total hotel cost for clients, remember that prices are published *per accommodation*, not per person. There may be some exceptions to this rule, but they will always be noted in whatever reference you are using. For example, when calculating the total cost for two people in a double room, the room rate is shown for the room, per night, based on two people. If the hotel offers one or more meal plan options, the meal plan charges are published *per person*.

Let's look at three examples of hotel costing. The first example is booking a room rate only. The second example includes a charge for an additional person in the same room. The third example includes a meal plan supplement. These examples will also show how to calculate room tax and commission earnings. We will use Figure 6.11, a sample hotel listing from the *Official Hotel Guide* resource.

● GROTTO BAY BEACH HOTEL & TENNIS CLUB

Superior First Class

Map Location B-6/13

ADDRESS 11 Blue Hole Hill, Hamilton Parish	**PHONE** (809)293-8333

AFFILIATIONS — — —	**ROOMS** 201	**FAX** (809)293-2306

CREDIT CARDS — — —	**COMMISSION** P-10	**TELEX** — — —

Description/Location: Casual and Charming Beach Hotel and Tennis Club in hillside setting overlooking a secluded cove — Located in the vicinity of 2 million-year-old caverns and 5 grottos — Renovations 1988

Accommodations: Eleven 3-story lodges in a town house setting on 21 acres of beautiful grounds — All rooms with a double or king-size bed, balcony with oceanview, air conditioning, hair dryer, color TV, coffee maker, radio and other amenities

Facilities/Services: Main building houses Hibiscus Restaurant, Rum House, and Lounge with live entertainment (seasonal) — Terrace Cafe for breakfast, lunch, dinner and outdoor barbecues (seasonal) — Unique, outdoor freshwater swim-up Pool Bar with "in the water" bar stools — Unusual Discotheque located in 1,000,000-year-old cavern — Meetings to 200 — 4 Tennis Courts (2 lighted) and Tennis Pro Shop with resident pro — Large Indoor Pool set in one million-year-old cave — 3 Private Beaches — Exotic Gardens — Mopeds — Water Sports — Honeymoon Beach with outdoor hot tub — Summer Children's Program — Golf nearby

Rates: EP S/DWB ($110-130/158-198) Each Additional Adult (50) Each Additional Person 6-16 yrs (25) Each Additional Child under 6 yrs free — Max rates Apr 1-Oct 31 — SC (6.30) — Tax 6% — PP-BB +(12) MAP +(40) — Variety of pkgs avail — TD: Inquire direct

RESERVATIONS:
Toll-Free: (800)582-3190
CRS: Sabre

Figure 6.11 OHG: *hotel listing.*

Examples: You have confirmed your clients—a party of two—into the Grotto Bay Beach Hotel at the confirmed rate of $175 per night (refer to Figure 6.11).

1. What is the total room cost for a party of two, arrival September 10 and departure September 15, no meals included (European plan)? First, obtain the *total per night* charge for both occupants:

$175

Then, multiply by the number of nights' stay:

$175 \times 5 = \$875$

2. What is the total tax on this booking? Room taxes are not usually prepaid but are paid at checkout. Refer to Figure 6.11 under the rates section. The tax is 6 percent of the room total:

$$\$875 \times 6\% = \$52.50$$

3. What is the total room charge, including tax, for this booking? Add the room charge plus tax:

$$\$875 + \$52.50 = \$927.50$$

4. What commission is earned on this booking? The listing for this hotel shows the commission code P10. This means that the travel agency earns 10 percent commission on all meal plans. Remember: *Commission is never calculated with room tax.* Multiply the room rate (exclusive of tax) by the appropriate percentage:

$$\$875 \times 10\% = \$87.50$$

Examples: You have confirmed your clients—a party of three adults—into the Grotto Bay Beach Hotel, at the confirmed rate of $120, based on a double room.

1. What is the total room cost for a party of three, arrival December 12 and departure September 14, no meals included (European plan)? First obtain the *total per night* charge based on double occupancy plus the additional charge for an extra person. Notice that the hotel charges $50 per night for each additional adult:

$$\$120 + \$50 = \$170$$

Then multiply the total per night charge by the number of night's stay:

$$\$170 \times 2 \text{ (nights)} = \$340$$

2. What is the total tax on this booking? Multiply the total room charge by the appropriate percentage:

$$\$340 \times 6\% = \$20.40$$

3. What is the total room charge plus tax for this booking?

$$\$340 + \$20.40 \text{ (tax)} = \$360.40$$

4. What commission is earned on this booking? (*Remember:* Calculate the commission without the room tax.)

$$\$340 \text{ (room rate)} \times 10\% = \$34$$

Examples: You have confirmed your clients—a party of two adults—into the Grotto Bay Beach Hotel, at the confirmed room rate of $185. They also want MAP. The MAP supplement is $40 per person per day (see rates).

1. What is the total room cost for a party of two, arrival June 3 and departure June 10 , with two meals per day (modified American plan)? First obtain the *total cost per night including the room and MAP supplement for both guests.* (*Remember:* Room rates are *per accommodation;* meal plan supplement rates are *per person.*)

$185 per night room rate (double occupancy)
$40 per person, MAP supplement
+ $40 per person, MAP supplement
$265 per night for room plus MAP supplement for two

Now multiply by the total number of nights:

$$\$265 \times 7 = \$1,855$$

2. What is the total room tax on this booking? The tax is applicable to the room rate only (not the meal plan supplement charges). First determine the total room rate for seven nights (exclusive of the meal plan):

$$\$185 \times 7 \text{ (nights)} = \$1,295$$

Then multiply the total room rate by the tax percentage:

$$\$1,295 \times 6\% = \$77.70$$

3. What commission is earned on this booking? Be careful with this one! Some hotels pay commission on the *room rate only*; others will pay for all plans (room plus applicable meal plan supplements). The commission code *R-10* means commission on room rate only; the commission code *P-10* means commission on all plans. The commission for this hotel is P-10: commission on both total room and meal plan rates. What is the total commission earned on this booking?

$$\$1,855 \times 10\% = \$185.50$$

✓ Check Your Understanding 6-8

Refer to Figure 6.11, the sample listing for the Grotto Bay Beach Hotel from the *Official Hotel Guide*, to calculate the costs for each client case study below.

1. Client: Mr. George Tenney (single traveler). Confirmed rate at $145 per night. No meals. Arrival: June 20. Departure: June 26.

   A. What is the total room charge *per night*? _____

   B. What is the total room charge for the *entire stay* (six nights)? _____

   C. What is the total amount of tax that he will pay upon checkout? _____

   D. What is the agency's commission? _____

2. Clients: Mr. & Mrs. Jeffrey Stone. Confirmed rate at $210. Two meals per day (use the MAP rate shown in the sample). Arrival: November 2. Departure: November 5.

   A. What is the *per night* total, including room and MAP supplement, for both clients? _____

   B. What is the total cost for both clients, including room and MAP supplement, for the entire stay (three nights)? _____

   C. What is the total room tax for the entire stay? (*Remember*: The tax is on the room rate only.) _____

   D. What is the agency's commission? _____

3. Clients: Johnson family of two adults and child (12 years) sharing the same room. Confirmed room rate at $175. Bed & Breakfast (BB) Plan. Arrival: August 18. Departure: August 23.

   A. What is the *per night* total, including room, BB, and additional person charge (EAP) for three clients? _____

   B. What is the total cost for three clients, including room, BB, and additional person supplement for the entire stay? _____

C. What is the total room tax?   _____

D. What is the agency's commission?   _____

Hotel Documentation and Vouchers

When making hotel reservations for travelers, the travel agent usually issues the traveler an "official" document that shows important reservation data such as the hotel name, arrival and departure dates, confirmed room type and rate, and confirmation number. Travel agencies provide any one of three types of hotel documentation for their clients: hotel confirmation notice, automated itinerary/invoice form, or personalized agency voucher.

➤ Hotel Confirmation Notice

After a reservation has been made, the hotel representative or reservation service mails a *hotel confirmation notice* to the travel agency. This document shows pertinent information regarding the reservation, including the name and address of the hotel, arrival and departure dates, confirmed room rate, confirmation or reservation number, and the name and address of the agency that made the booking on behalf of the client. The traveler usually hand-carries the hotel confirmation notice and presents it when checking in at the hotel's front desk. The confirmation notice serves as a backup document to the reservation. Figure 6.12 is a sample confirmation notice.

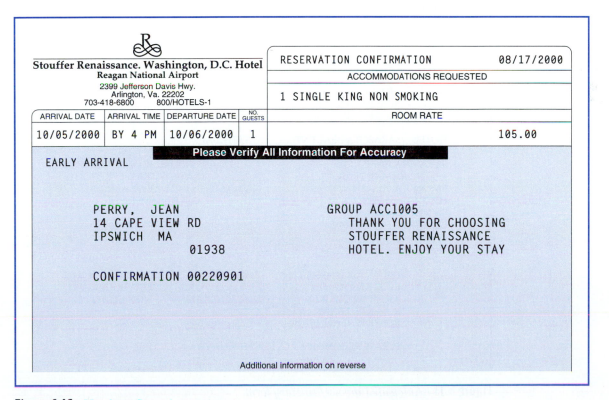

Figure 6.12 *Hotel confirmation notice.*

➤ Automated Invoice/Itinerary Form

If the hotel reservation is made through the agency's computer reservations system, the hotel reservation data are printed on an automated form that serves as both an invoice and an itinerary form. Figure 6.13 is a sample automated invoice/itinerary form that shows the client's flight and hotel confirmation data on one form.

Key Point ➤ The printed confirmation notice or automated invoice form is *not required* by hotels. However, it is good policy to provide clients with either the hotel's confirmation notice or the computer-generated invoice form in case there may be a question regarding the reservation when the traveler checks in.

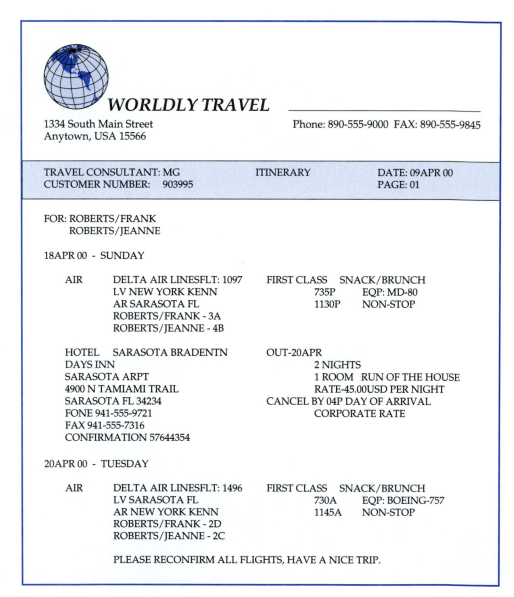

| TRAVEL CONSULTANT: MG | ITINERARY | DATE: 09APR 00 |
| CUSTOMER NUMBER: 903995 | | PAGE: 01 |

FOR: ROBERTS/FRANK
     ROBERTS/JEANNE

18APR 00 - SUNDAY

    AIR   DELTA AIR LINESFLT: 1097   FIRST CLASS   SNACK/BRUNCH
          LV NEW YORK KENN   735P   EQP: MD-80
          AR SARASOTA FL   1130P   NON-STOP
          ROBERTS/FRANK - 3A
          ROBERTS/JEANNE - 4B

    HOTEL   SARASOTA BRADENTN   OUT-20APR
    DAYS INN   2 NIGHTS
    SARASOTA ARPT   1 ROOM   RUN OF THE HOUSE
    4900 N TAMIAMI TRAIL   RATE-45.00USD PER NIGHT
    SARASOTA FL 34234   CANCEL BY 04P DAY OF ARRIVAL
    FONE 941-555-9721   CORPORATE RATE
    FAX 941-555-7316
    CONFIRMATION 57644354

20APR 00 - TUESDAY

    AIR   DELTA AIR LINESFLT: 1496   FIRST CLASS   SNACK/BRUNCH
          LV SARASOTA FL   730A   EQP: BOEING-757
          AR NEW YORK KENN   1145A   NON-STOP
          ROBERTS/FRANK - 2D
          ROBERTS/JEANNE - 2C

      PLEASE RECONFIRM ALL FLIGHTS, HAVE A NICE TRIP.

Figure 6.13 *Automated invoice/itinerary form.*

➤ Agency Voucher

Some agencies provide their clients with their own printed *hotel vouchers* or *coupons*. Agency vouchers are not standardized forms; they are stylized by each agency and will have the agency's name and address preprinted on them. An agency may issue a hotel voucher—rather than just a confirmation notice or automated itinerary—for any of the following reasons:

- Hotel confirmation notice not sent in time
- Extra service provided for leisure clients taking deluxe personalized independent tours
- For a deposit or full prepayment guarantee reservation

Usually, the agency hotel voucher form is in booklet form with multiple coupon copies. The coupons are carbonized so that appropriate entries that are handwritten or typed on the voucher will imprint on all subsequent coupons. Each coupon is then distributed to the appropriate channels as shown below:

- *Coupon 1: Client copy.* This is issued to the client to hand-carry.
- *Coupon 2: Commission copy.* A notice of commission is sent to the hotel if the agency's commission is not received in a timely manner.
- *Coupon 3: Reconfirmation notice and advice.* This coupon is sent to the hotel along with a deposit or prepayment check if applicable. The reconfirmation coupon can be retained by the hotel for its records.
- *Coupon 4: File copy.* This is attached to the client's file and maintained as the agency's copy of the transaction.
- *Coupon 5: Bookkeeping copy.* This is sent to the agency's bookkeeping department (if applicable) for accounting and commission tracking purposes.

Figure 6.14 is an example of an agency's hotel voucher.

FULL PREPAYMENT VOUCHER
GLOBAL TRAVEL VOUCHER   NO. 39766

CLIENT'S NAME   Dr. George Baylor (party of one)
PRESENT TO   The Barclay, Chicago (312-555-0877)
                       166 S. Superior Street, Chicago Il 60644
FOR   One standard-rated suite with private bath
                       for two nights at $155.00 per night, including
                       Continental Breakfast. Tax (12.4%) and
                       service charges not included. Full prepayment.

ARRIVAL: July 20, 2000. UA133, 8PM   **VALUE**
DEPARTURE: July 22, 2000 $310.00
CONFIRMED BY: John at Berkley Hotel Inc.
CONFIRMATION NO. 344589H

AGENT: Susan Brown   **DATE OF RESERVATION:** July 2, 2000

GLOBAL TRAVEL SERVICE, INC. 1448 DUNCAN ROAD, ST. LOUIS, MO. 34552

Figure 6.14   *Agency hotel voucher.*

Reservation agent	Concierge	Food and beverage director
Front-desk clerk	Executive housekeeper	Night auditor
Restaurant manager	Sales and marketing	Rooms division manager
Convention coordinator	Human resource director	General manager

Hospitality operations are found not only in traditional hotel and resort properties but in other areas of travel, such as cruise ships, parks, camps, casinos, and riverboats.

Front-Desk Clerk

Since the front desk has a high degree of interaction with other major departments, such as housekeeping, sales and marketing, and accounting, it is probably one of the best places to learn about the hospitality industry. A job at the front desk is considered to be an essential steppingstone to just about any supervisory or management position. This is a key area since the first representative that an arriving guest meets is standing behind the front desk at check-in. Front-desk clerks receive guests as they check in, service them throughout their stay, and handle their departures at checkout. Front-desk clerks (1) handle reservations, (2) quote room rates and select and block rooms for arriving guests, (3) maintain an inventory of vacant and occupied rooms, (4) coordinate activities between the front service staff and housekeeping, (5) receive and act on guests' complaints, (6) respond to guests' inquiries regarding hotel services and location, and (7) handle cash or credit payments upon guest checkout.

Concierge

The word *concierge* is from the Latin *conservus,* meaning "fellow slave." This position got its start in high-class lodging establishments in Europe and other parts of the world. The concierge is now recognized in the United States as being a valuable employee who serves the needs of the guests. The concierge assists guests at the concierge desk (usually situated in the hotel lobby area) and over the telephone during the entire guest cycle: prior to arrival, at check-in, during the stay, and after departure. No task is too difficult or complicated for an experienced concierge. The concierge arranges any thing from baby-sitting services to booking onward travel arrangements for guests. The concierge (1) keeps current on all city attractions, sightseeing tours, transportation schedules, entertainment, and related services for guests; (2) arranges and books tours, theater tickets, and special attractions in the local area; and (3) maintains contact with businesses in the area, including restaurants, theaters, airlines, ground transportation, clubs, and so on.

Sales and Marketing

The sales and marketing team of a traditional hotel includes a director of marketing who oversees a group of sales managers. Entry-level positions are titled *account executives* or *sales associates.* Other entry-level titles may be *sales and marketing assistant* or *researcher.* Entry-level personnel (1) plan and develop promotional campaigns that include advertising, public relations, and publicity; (2) generate group and convention business for the hotel; (3) conduct tours of the property; and (4) correspond with travel agencies worldwide concerning planned tours to the area.

Convention Coordinator

A convention coordinator's main function is to complete follow-up and to coordinate all conventions, meetings, and other group functions that are booked through the sales office. The coordinator takes care of all details after the group has been booked by the sales office. A coordinator (1) sets up meeting dates, times, and the required number of meeting rooms and accommodations during the group stay; (2) assists with the selection of banquet menus; (3) works with other departments to ensure smooth operations of all groups using the hotel at the same time; and (4) services the group while in attendance and assists in such things as changes in schedules, arrival times, rental equipment needed, time of registration, and so on.

➤ Key Terms

- adjoining rooms
- American Plan (AP)
- all-inclusive resorts
- American Hotel & Motel Association (AH&MA)
- bed & breakfast (B&B)
- Bermuda Plan (BP)
- cabana
- connecting rooms
- Continental Plan (CP)
- demi-pension
- double
- duplex

- efficiency
- estancias
- European Plan (EP)
- full-pension
- guarantee
- hold time
- hospitality suite
- junior suite
- lanai
- Modified American Plan (MAP)
- paradores
- pousadas

- quad
- rack rate
- resort
- run-of-the-house (ROH)
- ryokans
- single
- spas
- studio
- suite
- transient hotel
- triple
- twin

Flashback   Travel professionals today must be very attentive to details when booking trips for their clients. This not only includes the obvious airline ticket, but also includes selling a hotel with every airline ticket. Due to many U.S. airlines imposing a maximum or cap to the amount of commissions that agents can earn on the sale of airline tickets, agencies must turn to other products and sources to contribute to their bread-and-butter earnings. Hotel sales fit the bill. Why? Most travelers will need a place to stay once they arrive at their destination. Also, centralized commission payment offerings such as Hotel Clearing Corp. (HCC), an electronic commission collection service, have made it easier for agencies to collect commissions on their hotel bookings.

The lodging industry is made up of many different types of properties: everything from small, intimate bed & breakfasts, to luxurious all-inclusive beach resorts, to huge city-commercial properties. As a professional you must be able to match your clients with the correct type of lodging. When booking accommodations for the business traveler, such things as location, level of service, and type of corporate discounts are of prime concern. For the vacation traveler, other factors, such as availability of family plan, sports and recreational facilities, and proximity to beaches and golf courses, become more important.

A major part of this matchmaking process is knowing your resources. In addition to the computer reservations systems, which is the leading method of booking hotels, there are many useful and informative printed reference guides that are used on a frequent basis. Such resources, such as the *Official Hotel Guide (OHG)*, *Hotel & Travel Index*, the

STAR Service, and the *Travel Planner* series, are standard in any travel office's resource library.

The hotel and lodging industry has its own language of terms, codes, and abbreviations. This unique language, which describes such things as meal plans, room types, and occupancy, must be understood by any professional when selling and booking hotels. Along with other parts of the industry lexicon, such as airline and city codes, hotel "lingo" is an integral part of any travel professional's vocabulary.

Finally, the travel professional knows how to guarantee room reservations and how to book accommodations on the computer and by telephone. The agent also is familiar with three types of forms that are used to document a hotel booking: the hotel confirmation notice (generated by the hotel or hotel representative), agency vouchers (completed by the agency), and automated invoice/itinerary forms (generated by the travel agency's CRS).

CHAPTER REVIEW

True or False?

_____ 1. Most airport hotel properties offer courtesy ground transportation to and from the airport.

_____ 2. Travel agents usually do not get involved in booking residential properties.

_____ 3. Vacation travelers book hotels more often than business travelers do.

_____ 4. Hotel security, fitness center facilities, and reputation are the three top concerns when business travelers select hotels.

_____ 5. The printed hotel confirmation notice or an agency hotel voucher is required at hotel check-in.

_____ 6. The *STAR Service* is a printed resource that contains detailed descriptions and objective evaluations of hotels around the world.

_____ 7. Toll-free numbers are the dominant means of booking hotel reservations in most travel agencies.

_____ 8. Standard corporate room rates are less expensive than group and convention rates at hotels.

_____ 9. Ryokans are lodgings in traditional Japanese style.

_____ 10. The most popular method of guaranteeing a hotel reservation is by providing the travel agency name and address.

Multiple Choice

Circle the *best* answer.

11. The largest category of transient hotels is:

    A. resorts   C. city-commercial

    B. motels   D. residential

12. *Super Clubs, Sandals,* and *Couples* are examples of what type of accommodation?

    A. spas   C. bed & breakfasts

    B. all-inclusives   D. motor inns

13. Accommodations that specialize in diet and fitness programs are:
    A. bed & breakfasts
    C. spas
    B. dude ranches
    D. all-inclusives

14. Government-owned lodgings in Spain that are converted castles, convents, and monasteries are:
    A. paradores
    C. pousadas
    B. Romantik Hotels
    D. farm stays

15. The type of corporate rate that represents the least amount of discount that is available to virtually any traveler of the travel agency, leisure or business, is:
    A. company-negotiated
    C. standard corporate
    B. rack rate
    D. agency-contract

16. The type of discount that is usually not commissionable to travel agencies is:
    A. agency-contract
    C. frequent-stay
    B. company-negotiated
    D. convention/meeting

17. The type of discount program where the guest pays the standard minimum rate and gets the best room available at check-in is:
    A. senior citizen
    C. run-of-the-house
    B. family plan
    D. agency-contract

18. Hyatt's Gold Passport and Sheraton's Club International are examples of:
    A. senior citizen discounts
    C. run-of-the-house programs
    B. executive floors
    D. frequent-stay programs

19. The type of property where guests can expect the same level of service and amenities at each location since they are owned by the same managing company is a(n):
    A. franchise
    C. affiliation
    B. chain
    D. all-inclusive

20. The type of accommodation that contains a separate sitting area connected to one or more bedrooms is a(n):
    A. suite
    C. studio
    B. efficiency
    D. cabana

Short Answers and Fill-ins

21. What is the difference between a double and a twin room?

    _____

22. Define the difference between adjoining and connecting rooms.

    _____

23. You can group major hotel chain properties into four general categories: luxury, first class, midprice, and economy/budget. Name at least two chains in each category:
    A. luxury
        (1) _____ (2) _____
    B. first class
        (1) _____ (2) _____
    C. midprice
        (1) _____ (2) _____

D. economy

   (1) _____ (2) _____

24. List four major factors that affect the price of a hotel or room.

   A. _____ C. _____

   B. _____ D. _____

25. The standard published rate of a hotel is the: _____.

26. Name the hotel resource.

   A. _____ is published in three volumes (volumes 1 and 2 cover North America and volume 3 covers the balance of the world) and is noted for detailed hotel descriptions in addition to destination maps.

   B. _____ is considered "tell-it-like-it-is" since it contains a compilation of reports submitted by travel agents and other professionals on the hotels they visit.

   C. _____ is a comprehensive guide of worldwide hotels in one heavy volume and is best utilized as a quick and easy reference when you do not require detailed property information.

   D. _____ is a popular resource that combines airline-related data, destination maps, and hotel information for all cities listed in three volumes.

27. In addition to providing the travel agency name and address, list three other methods that are used frequently by travel agents to guarantee hotel reservations.

   A. _____

   B. _____

   C. _____

28. Accommodation rates are usually printed per _____, and meal plan supplement charges are published per _____.

29. The average commission for travel agencies when booking hotel accommodations is _____.

30. You have a party of two sharing a room at the Sonesta Beach in Bermuda. The rates shown in the printed resource are:

   DWB $95.00–$185.00   MAP $35.00

   They will arrive on October 10 and depart on October 15. They would like to purchase the meal plan option. Assuming that you have confirmed the highest rate for a double room, the total cost for the room and meal supplement for their entire stay is _____.

Tours and Vacation Packages

Fast Forward ▼

➤ The *Jax Fax* is a popular resource for tour packages, air charters, and scheduled air discounts to worldwide destinations. . . . 345

➤ Sending an agency check to a tour operator is probably the most prevalent method used when booking vacation packages. . . . 350

➤ An ARC document called a miscellaneous charges order (MCO) is one way of transmitting payment for a tour package, and it has many other functions as well. . . . 354

➤ Unlike the MCO, which has many functions, the tour order can only be used to process payments for land packages. . . . 355

INTRODUCTION

What if someone suggested that you should take a package tour during your next vacation. Does your first reaction sound something like this: "Tours are too regimented; I want to see things on my schedule and not on someone else's"? Or how about, "Tours are just for old people—I want to be active and do things, not just stare through a window of a tour bus all day"? Do these types of reactions sound familiar?

It must be one of the travel industry's most enduring images: a whirlwind, see twenty-countries-in-fifteen-days type of bus tour where cities, museums, churches, and other attractions become a hazy blur through the window of a tour bus. It is long past due to put the old "If it's Tuesday, it must be Belgium" frantic tour to a well-deserved rest!

Today, packaged tours are not as regimented or frantic as they sound. In the past, these misconceptions obscured the value and benefits of taking a vacation package, one of which is independence. That may sound like a contradiction in terms, but it really isn't. Many packages, even escorted tours, which are the most structured of all, have enough independent components built in even to satisfy the most freewheeling and experienced traveler. In fact, there are independent packages for those who want minimal guidance and the flexibility to see what they want to see, when they want to see it, at their own pace.

Escorting tours really had their start way back in the 1920s, when the first reliable multipassenger motorcoaches hit the roads. During the early days, touring was a local affair. At first, tour companies offered short tours of one day or less, stopping to visit one or two attractions along the way. Soon after they started adding hotel overnights to their packages. This continued until World War I, when virtually all leisure travel came to a stop.

After World War II, people were eager to have some fun and to see the world. The war brought major breakthroughs in automotive engineering that produced safe, reliable, and comfortable sightseeing motorcoaches. At this time most tours were domestic. International travel was mostly for those who could afford expensive foreign independent tours (FITs). Companies who created these unique tours for individual travelers began to organize trips for affinity groups, a group of travelers who share a common interest or reason for travel. An affinity group could be a group of war veterans wanting to revisit Europe's World War II battlefields, or doctors combining a convention in Paris with some sightseeing in Europe.

By sharing the cost of transportation, accommodations, and meals, members of affinity groups were able to benefit from discount bulk rates that were a fraction of FIT prices. Soon, enterprising FIT operators expanded their markets by passing along group rates to the general public. In the 1950s such tour operators as Caravan, American Express, Globus, and Thomas Cook began distributing international tour brochures to travel agencies to sell to their clients. The concept of group tour travel really took off in the late 1950s when the Boeing 707 made transatlantic travel faster and more economical than sea journeys had been. Long-range jet travel opened up other international destinations, such as Africa and the Orient, putting such locales within the reach of adventurous travelers. With the advent of the Boeing 747, the first wide-body, large-capacity commercial jet, air travel for international tourism became affordable for an even larger portion of North Americans.

Today, tour packages have become highly sophisticated and within the reach of practically every type of traveler. The tour package product continues to evolve while new destinations emerge, such as Antarctica and the once-forbidden countries of China and Vietnam. Creative packaging methods continue to attract a growing number of travelers, with special interests from hot-air ballooning over the Masai Mara to a pampered wine-tasting picnic through Burgundy, France. There are adventure tours for those who want excitement and action, and there are nature tours (or ecotours) for those who wish to enjoy the environment and help to preserve it.

In this chapter we introduce the reader to the various types of tours—who takes them and who puts them together—and the resources and selling process of this very important and dynamic travel and leisure product.

Definition and Components

What's a tour? It is the opportunity to buy two or more different travel components that otherwise would be purchased separately from different tour and transportation companies. Buying a packaged tour is like buying a computer; you purchase all of the components, such as the monitor, modem, and mouse, as one unit in one store. With a **tour package,** the traveler is purchasing different elements, such as accommodations, sightseeing, and ground transportation, as one unit from one travel company.

The alternative is to go the independent route. If nothing on the assembled market appeals to you, you may prefer to buy components from different suppliers or companies, whether it is a computer for your home or a vacation when you travel. It may take a little longer to put together and cost a little more, but the result will be exactly what you want. A tour package that is put together to suit an individual traveler's tastes and needs is called a **domestic independent tour (DIT)** or a **foreign independent tour (FIT).**

Whether it is a package, a DIT, or an FIT, a tour is a combination of elements that are sold and coordinated for a group or independent travelers. These elements are put together by a travel or tour planner, planned for specific dates, and sold at one price. The six basic elements of any type of tour are as follows:

1. Transportation
   - Motorcoach
   - Minicoach or van
   - Small, local bus
   - Air (scheduled or charter)

- Train
- Limousine
- Ship or ferry

2. Accommodations
- Resort
- Hotel
- Motel
- Lodge
- Cruise ship
- Camping
- Special/unique

3. Meals
- Breakfast only
- Two meals per day (MAP or demi-pension)
- Three meals per day (AP or full-pension)

4. Sightseeing/guide services
- Natural sites/parks
- Scenic roads
- Guided city tours
- Countryside excursions

5. Attractions
- Museums
- Art galleries
- Theme parks
- Historical
- Educational/cultural

6. Activities
- Walking, hiking
- Sports (golf, tennis, scuba diving)
- Photography
- Special interests
- Adventure
- Special events

Who Operates Tours

➤ Tour Operators

There are many types of companies and individuals who operate tours. You have heard the term **tour operator** many times, but what is a tour operator? According to the **United States Tour Operators Association (USTOA)**, it is a broad term that describes companies whose primary purposes are to plan, arrange, and market tour packages to a variety of domestic and/or worldwide destinations. The cost of such packages includes the use of transportation by air or land, ground

Travel agents select tour operators based on their reputation and past booking experiences with them. It is very important to protect their clients' travel payments by directing them toward tour operators who are financially secure and dependable. To ensure the stability of tour operators, many agents check to see if the company is a member of the United States Tour Operators Association (USTOA). The USTOA is a national organization of wholesale tour operators of more than 600 members, comprised of tour operators, hotels, airlines, car rental companies, tourist boards, and other travel service providers worldwide. USTOA's primary goals are to inform the travel industry and the public about tour operators' activities and to maintain a high level of professionalism within the tour operator community. In addition, each member of the USTOA is required to post $1 million in security, held by the USTOA, for the sole purpose of reimbursing consumers for tour payments or deposits in the event of company bankruptcy, ceasing operations, or failure to return consumer deposits or payments within a certain period of time if the tour company fails to complete performance.

arrangements such as hotels, restaurants, local guides, and other related services. Most tour operators sell directly to the public and through travel agencies. Packages are commissionable to travel agents, who, in turn, sell the product to their customers.

These companies may actually operate specific aspects of a tour. They may own their own facilities or vehicles and employ personnel such as drivers and tour escorts. Examples of tour operators are American Express, Brendan Tours, Globus & Cosmos, Pacific Delight Tours, Inc., Rail Europe, TNT, and Trafalgar Tours.

➤ Tour Wholesalers

Tour wholesalers are companies that usually create and market inclusive tours and FITs through travel agencies. Wholesalers put packages together and market them. They research destinations, purchasing tour elements in bulk from suppliers in those destinations while receiving volume discounts. They develop tours to selected destinations departing on scheduled dates, then market these tours in creative and attractive ways.

The term *tour wholesaler* is often used interchangeably with *tour operator,* but several distinctions can be drawn: (1) A wholesaler presumably sells nothing at retail (directly to the general public); a tour operator often does both; (2) a wholesaler does not always create its own products, whereas a tour operator virtually always does; and (3) a wholesaler usually leaves the operations of the tour to the individual suppliers or to coordinating companies at the destination known as local **ground operators.**

Wholesale companies offer commissions to travel agents just as airlines, hotels, and cruise companies do. The standard commission for selling a tour package is 10 percent. Incentive commissions at a higher percentage are also offered from time to time to increase sales of a particular tour product and/or departure date.

➤ Travel Agencies and Other Suppliers

Some large travel agencies operate and sell their own tour packages. Some of the tours that they develop are designed for certain types of groups that are offered continually or on selected departure dates. Other tours may be intended for marketing to the general public with regular or frequent departures. Other travel suppliers that organize and market tour products are airlines, hotels, and motor-coach companies.

Airlines work closely with tour operators and wholesalers in terms of advertising and marketing of destinations. The airlines themselves print their own brochures listing tours in destinations to which they operate. Hotels market their own packages to the general public, such as long weekends or golf and tennis get-a-ways. Hotel packages generally include a minimum number of features, such as accommodations and one or two meals.

Motorcoach tour operators generate revenue from the rental or charter of their major assets, the motorcoaches. Major operators such as Tauck Tours have their own internal systems to develop exciting and interesting itineraries, utilizing the services of tour operators and receptive operators. One of the most popular motorcoach itineraries is the fall foliage tour through New England, which includes ground transportation, sightseeing, guide service, and meals.

TYPES OF TOURS

Tours are marketed and sold either to the general public or to *affinity groups*. An affinity group is comprised of members who share a common interest, goal, or reason for travel. A tour may be organized and developed to suit the unique needs of the particular group. Some examples of affinity markets are school groups, civic organizations, or social clubs. Group travel is covered in more detail later in the book. In this chapter we concentrate on the various types of tours that are sold to the general public.

Tours come in varying degrees of structure and regimentation. From the least structured to the most structured in format, the four general categories of tours are: independent, hosted, escorted, and custom-designed tours called DITs and FITs.

➤ Independent Tours

Independent tours offer the minimum amount of structure and prepaid features. Usually, accommodations plus one other feature (such as ground transfers, car rental, or one-half day of sightseeing) are the only elements included. Passengers on independent tours do not travel to and from the destination as a group; passengers arrive on any day and have the option of extending their stay.

The independent tour products are more versatile, more relaxed, and customer-driven. In fact, this type of package allows travelers to virtually design their own tours. A typical independent tour is a *hotel package*. Such a package contains the minimum number of prepaid features: round-trip transfers between the airport and hotel, accommodations, meal plan (usually breakfast only), and a one-half-day sightseeing tour. Independent hotel packages are popular in resort destinations such as the Caribbean or Florida and in major tourism cities such as Washington, DC, San Francisco, and New York.

Another popular type of independent tour is the *fly & drive*. Most packages contain only two features: accommodations and a car rental for the length of the trip. Passengers depart and return on any day—there are no preset arrival/

departure dates—and they decide on where to go. They also select from a list of accommodations along their desired itinerary and routing. Most tour operators of fly & drive packages offer different categories of accommodations based on services, location, and amenities offered. Hotel vouchers are purchased in advance and are presented upon check-in during the trip.

A car rental is also included in fly & drive packages. In some cases the traveler may have the option of substituting a self-drive car with rail travel. This is especially popular in Europe, where train service is frequent and efficient. Figure 7.1 is a sample fly & drive package operated by American Airlines Vacations. It includes a list of hotels from which to choose and the car rental options.

➤ Hosted Tours

Hosted tours are a little more structured than independent tours but still allow travelers to pace themselves for much of the time. Like independent tours, travelers can arrive any day of their choice, and the length of stay can be adjusted. There may be more inclusive features on a hosted tour: transfers, accommodations, some meals (usually breakfast), a half-day city sightseeing tour, and discount coupons to shops and attractions.

The main difference is that this type of package offers the services of a *local host* who helps passengers plan activities, book theater and other special events, and recommends sightseeing and excursion trips. The host desk is usually located in the lobby area of the hotel with scheduled hours of operation.

Figure 7.2 is an example of a hosted package in Paris.

➤ Escorted Tours

Escorted tours are the most structured and organized packages and have the least flexibility. They begin and end on fixed dates; some tours may allow for extended stays by adding on at the beginning or end of the tour. Escorted tours include round-trip transfers, sightseeing, and most meals. Usually, all taxes and service charges are also included.

The most popular method of transporting tour passengers is the motorcoach. The motorcoach industry has become very sophisticated, with an emphasis on comfort and amenities. Many long-distance operators use coaches with fully equipped rest rooms, cocktail bar, large windows and observation areas, video display units, and the like. Most motorcoaches can seat up to 48 adults comfortably.

Depending on the size of the tour, minicoach vehicles may be used. They hold between 20 and 25 people and have the same amenities as the large coaches. They are preferred for small groups, especially small corporate groups, because they are comfortable, highly maneuverable, and afford more privacy.

These tours feature a **tour escort** or **tour manager** who stays with the passengers for the duration of the trip. In addition, experienced local guides who are specialists in certain areas or cities may conduct narrated tours of a particular area. These local specialist guides are called *step-on guides* and may relieve the escort from being on stage for a few hours or a number of days during the tour.

Other types of transportation may be used on an escorted tour: short air trips, ferry crossings, river cruises, or train trips, for example. When several types of transportation are combined in a tour, it is called an **intermodal tour.**

Many travelers prefer to take escorted tours when visiting exotic and foreign destinations where language and social customs present a barrier. Escorted tours are popular in destinations such as Africa, the Middle East, and the Orient. They are also popular in Europe for travelers visiting multiple countries over large dis-

Figure 7.1 *Fly & drive package.*

Figure 7.2 *Hosted package.*

tances who don't want the hassle of border crossings, customs, changing languages, and different currencies at every turn.

Figure 7.3 is an example of a fully escorted motorcoach tour of the highlights of Asia. It is an intermodal tour since it includes more than one form of transportation. What are they?

► Custom-Designed Tours: DITs and FITs

Purchasing a packaged tour and a custom-made independent tour is the difference between buying a suit off the rack and having one tailormade. The customer who walks into a travel agency and doesn't find the packaged tour that suits his or her interest is like the shopper who can't find the right suit among the hundreds displayed in a store.

We use the term *FIT* (foreign independent tour) or *DIT* (domestic independent tour) to mean any tour program that is custom designed and planned for a particular client. The FIT/DIT contains something more than just adding a sightseeing trip to an airline ticket booking. Thus FITs and DITs run the gamut from minor specialization to a complete, personalized, unrestricted tour that is tailormade to the exact specifications of the client.

At the not-so-personalized end of the FIT/DIT scale, very little is demanded of the travel planner. In these cases, the agent arranges basic transportation and adds one, two, or three easy-to-book services, such as a hotel and car rental in Florida, with a few suggestions for sightseeing in the area. Make the airline booking, send the reservation form to the hotel, secure the car rental, contact the

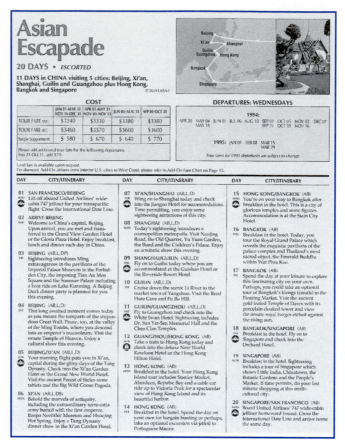

Figure 7.3 *Fully escorted motorcoach tour.*

tourist bureau for road maps and tourist information of the area, and you have completed a simple DIT.

At the other end of the scale, a fully personalized and detailed FIT to such places as Europe or the Orient takes a great deal of skill, knowledge, and time on the part of the travel planner. Such complex personalized tours include a number of prepaid services, such as air transportation, ground transfers, cruises and ferry crossings, rail trips, meet-and-greet assistance at each arrival point, private guides and drivers, meals at specialty restaurants, tickets to theater and special events, plus a detailed day-by-day itinerary with suggested sightseeing and attractions, for example. This type of detailed planning is done by experienced specialists. Some large travel agencies may have a specialized DIT/FIT department that specializes in domestic and foreign custom-made trip planning for their clients.

When pricing an FIT, the agent costs many of the individual features and services in net prices—without commission. A commission is earned by applying a **markup** or by increasing the net total by a certain percentage. The amount of markup depends on many factors. It is designed to absorb expenses incurred for booking, making reservations, and the time involved in putting it together. In addition, a profit is built into the markup to reflect the amount of specialized service and expertise of the planner. Markup percentages can range anywhere between 25 and 50 percent.

Many retail travel agencies are not set up to handle major FIT/DITs in an economical manner. For such tours it may be best to use the services of a wholesale operator that offers FIT/DIT service. When wholesalers are used, the retail travel agent prepares a basic outline of the itinerary in consultation with the client. This basic outline includes hard data such as number in party, ages of children, date of departure, length of trip, type of accommodations, desired sightseeing, special requests of the client, and so on. The wholesaler prepares a tentative itinerary with a quote. The retail agent then consults with the client, presents the itinerary and quotation, makes any changes, and sends it back to the wholesaler for revision. The wholesaler returns a final itinerary and the sale is completed.

When a wholesaler is used, the retail travel agent usually receives a standard tour commission. In some cases the wholesaler may quote a net total price and the retailer determines his or her own markup. The markup is less when a wholesaler is used and averages between 15 and 25 percent.

Web Link

Tour Director is a worldwide directory of city guides and tour managers, enabling travel agents and tour managers to find qualified guided staff for every purpose, from short city tours to multiweek escorted trips. Check it out at *http://www.tourdirector.com*

Check Your Understanding 7-1

Multiple Choice

Circle the *best* answer.

1. This type of company arranges tour packages and may operate certain aspects of the tour at the destination. It also can sell directly to the general public or through travel agencies.
   A. tour wholesaler
   B. airline
   C. tour operator
   D. motorcoach guide service

2. An international tour that is custom designed by the travel agent to suit a particular traveler's needs and interests is:
   A. the DIT
   B. hosted
   C. fly & drive
   D. the FIT

3. A type of tour that allows travelers to arrive on any day and offers the assistance of a local "helper," usually stationed at the hotel, to assist tour members with such things as sightseeing recommendations, theater tickets, and so on, is a(n):
   A. hosted tour
   B. escorted tour
   C. independent tour
   D. hotel package

4. A guide who joins an escorted tour for a day or two as a tour narrator and who specializes in the destination and attractions being visited is a:
   A. step-on guide
   B. tour escort
   C. local operator
   D. ground coordinator

5. The term used to describe a tour that contains more than one type of transportation is:
   A. multifeature
   B. intermodal
   C. multitransfer
   D. intertransportation

6. A company that develops and markets tour packages but does not, as a rule, sell directly to the general public is a:
   A. ground operator
   B. tour operator
   C. tour wholesaler
   D. retail travel agency

7. The percentage by which the travel agency increases the cost of an FIT or a DIT to cover direct expenses and commission earnings for this type of service is the:

   A. selling price   C. net cost

   B. markup   D. incentive increase

Short Answers

8. Meals are one of six basic elements of a tour package. Name the other five elements and provide two specific examples of each.

   A. _____

   B. _____

   C. _____

   D. _____

   E. _____

BENEFITS OF A TOUR PACKAGE

Purchasing a tour package is not going to be the right choice for every traveler on every trip. There are some destinations or special interests of the traveler that make purchasing a tour package the right thing to do. When selling this type of product, the advantages should be considered—for both the traveler and the travel counselor.

The benefits for the traveler are:

1. *Peace of mind.* All travel details, such as tipping, baggage handling, and ground transportation, are handled by someone else.

2. *Pay one price.* The cost of the trip is known in advance. One price includes any number of the following features: air, hotels, transportation, transfers, meals, sightseeing, baggage handling, and tips.

3. *Volume discounts.* Costs for hotels and transportation are discounted, due to volume bookings.

4. *Assured entrances.* All tickets to attractions and events are planned and purchased in advance; there is no chance of being turned away because an attraction or event is sold out.

5. *Preferential treatment.* Tour groups rarely wait in long lines; they either skip to the front of the line or are admitted through special entranceways into major attractions such as museums, art galleries, or archeological sites.

6. *Reliable sightseeing.* Itineraries are planned by tour specialists who have both researched and acquired firsthand knowledge of major sights, attractions, events, and the cultural experiences unique to the countries or regions being visited. Tour operators keep sightseeing itineraries that have proven track records with the traveling public.

The benefits for the retail travel agent are:

1. *Time savings.* One phone call books all the elements of a tour, including such elements as accommodations, transportation, meals, sightseeing, and transfers.

2. *Cost-effective.* The time it takes to book a tour package is certainly less than if the agent had to book each component separately. The average commission on a tour package is 10 percent but can go as high as 15 percent due to incen-

tive commission programs with certain tour operators. The agent may take about one-half hour with clients to select a tour, and book it in one phone call to the tour operator. For a party of two, if the tour costs $2,000 per person, at an average commission of 10 percent, the agency's earnings for this booking is $400; this amount is certainly cost-effective for the time spent.

3. *Client satisfaction.* If the *right* tour was sold to the *right* person at the *right* price, the chances are pretty high that the traveler will come home satisfied. The professional travel agent should only book with reliable and reputable tour operators. In addition, if the traveler knows exactly what he or she is buying (e.g., the traveler paying economy tour prices is not expecting deluxe hotels), and most services are prepaid, there is less chance of things going haywire during the trip. For example, being told that you don't have a reservation when checking in to your hotel doesn't usually happen when the tour is booked through a reliable operator.

Adventure Tours

Some travelers may be quite content to view new and exotic destinations through the tinted windows of an air-conditioned motorcoach. About 100 million Americans—more than one-third of the adult population—don't agree; this is why many people take adventure-related vacations each year (see Figure 7.4). **Adventure tours** are more strenuous and active than traditional vacation packages. Some are marketed as *soft adventures,* such as camping, bird-watching, wildlife safaris, and cultural programs. Others, sold as *hard adventures,* are for those looking for more physical challenge. These include such activities as white-water rafting, rock climbing, camel treks, and cave exploration.

Who is the typical adventure traveler? You probably picture a young man or woman in the 20-something range. In fact, adventure travelers range across a broad spectrum. The average profile of the adventure traveler is a person 40 to 45+, good income, and well educated. According to a recent survey conducted by the World Congress, the majority of adventure travelers are women who average in the late 40s.

Figure 7.5 is an example of a hard-adventure tour, "Golden Ring by Snowmobile," which includes traditional sightseeing by motorcoach plus touring by your own snowmobile through the Russian countryside.

Web Link

America Outdoors, an association of more than 550 adventure companies, provides more than 50 different adventure options in more than 40 states and 50 countries. The major feature is to search for a vacation by a particular activity, state, region, or country. Planning you next adventure? Point your browser at *http://www.americaoutdoors.org*

Ecotourism

What has become important to an increasing number of travelers is how to enjoy the outdoors without destroying it. **Ecotourism** combines people's interest in nature along with their concern about the environment in such forms as recycling, energy, conservation, and the like. This growing awareness and appreciation of a clean environment have created a booming market for nature tourism: trips to sight birds, watch whales, photograph animals in the wild, and hike the nature trails, for example. Nature tours or ecotourism is one of the fastest-growing segments in the travel industry. Some of the most popular ecotourism destinations are shown in Figure 7.6.

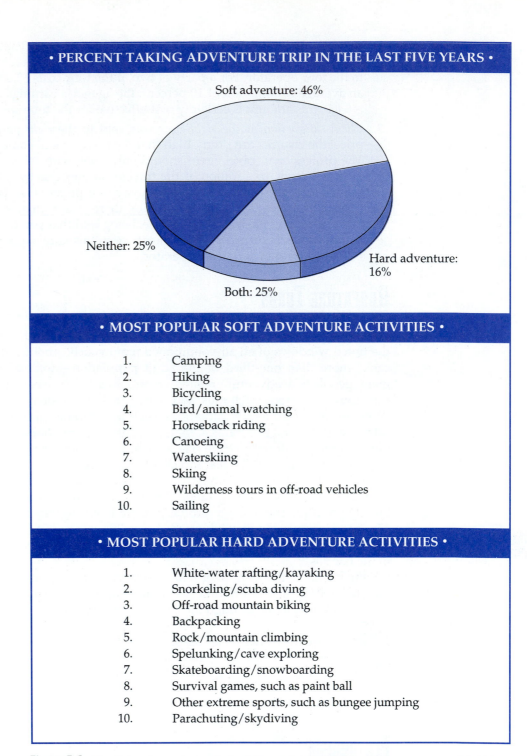

Figure 7.4 *Participation survey of adventure-related vacations, from a survey of 1,200 adults conducted by the Travel Association of America, based in Washington, DC. (From* Travel Weekly, *August 1998.)*

An Adventure Trip That's Just Out of This World

For all jaded travelers who have been there, done that, relief is in sight. The next era of travel will take you literally out of this world. The World Tourism Organization predicts that by the year 2020, space travel will be commonplace for just about anyone. Confidence is so high that there are already several tour companies that have begun accepting reservations for suborbital flights scheduled sometime in the early twenty-first century. Many adventure travelers have already plunked down deposits between $5,000 and $6,000 to reserve a spot on the next commercial space voyage. The full price of the space tour, which is *two hours long,* is set at approximately $100,000 plus tax! Here's what's included:

1. Transportation in a reusable space vehicle that holds six passengers 62 miles above sea level.

2. The two-hour flight will include two and one-half minutes of weightlessness.

3. Awe-inspiring views right out of *Star Trek*: blue curvature of the entire earth below, and the starry black void above.

First launch is scheduled some time during the next several years. Anyone interested?

Golden Ring by Snowmobile

1997 Group Rates
7 days / 6 nights

DEPARTURES INTERNATIONAL
1793 Union Street
San Francisco, CA 94123
Phone (415) 563-5959
Fax (415) 563-5935
Toll Free (800) 509-5959

Day One   Arrival in Moscow with immediate transfer to Suzdal. Hotel check-in followed by Welcome dinner and general briefing of the tour.

Day Two   After breakfast today, you will be given instruction and special clothing for use on your snowmobile. You will tour the area of Suzdal by snowmobile-along the Kamenka river and the hunting regions. After a tavern lunch, you will visit the "Gostiny Dvor" shopping rows, the museum of the Spasso-Yefimiyevsky Monastery (the Monastery of the Saviour and St. Euthimius) and the Museum of Wooden Architecture.

Day Three   Breakfast at hotel. Depart today for Bogolubovo-founded in 1165 by Prince Andrei Bogolubsky. The oldest monuments include: Sviatye Vorota (Holy Gates), the Bell Tower (1841) and the two-story building of the Monks Cells (early 19th century). The huge five-domed Cathedral of the Nativity of the Mother of God (1866) is a perfect example of Russo-Byzantine style. Lunch today will be a traditional "Samovar and Russian pies" meal. Return to Suzdal for dinner and overnight.

Day Four   After breakfast today, you depart for the ancient town of Vladimir. Vladimir was founded in the year of 1108 by Prince Vladimir Monomakh of Pereslavl who was very effective in the unification of Russian lands. The town is located on the high left bank of the Kliazma river, affording wonderful views and great sight-seeing. Lunch today at "Russian Village" restaurant. After lunch, a tour of Vladimir, then return to Suzdal. Tonight you will enjoy a Farewell dinner served in a Russian bath house.

Day Five   Breakfast at hotel. Today you will tour Suzdal by snowmobile "Ski-Doo". Visit the Kremlin, the Cathedral of the Nativity, the Archbishop's Palace which contains the local museum with exhibits of icons, decorative religious arts and the history of architecture in this area of Russia. Return your "Ski-Doo" and sportsgear. After lunch departure for Moscow. Arrival in Moscow and transfer to the hotel "Belgrade". Hotel check-in.

Day Six   After breakfast you will enjoy a city tour which includes the center of Moscow, Red square, the former headquarters of the KGB, Moscow University, the Russian White House, etc. After lunch, a tour of the former Novodevichy convent which was associated with the Royal family and for several centuries played a role in important historical events.

Day Seven   After breakfast transfer to the airport.

Price per person based on Double Occupancy:
1 passenger per snowmobile.............................900.00

2 passengers per snowmobile..........................780.00

Single supplement.......................................180.00

The price includes: Moscow/Suzdal/Moscow transfers, double accommodations at the hotels: "Belgarde" in Moscow, "Pokrovsky Monastery" in Suzdal, full board, all sight-seeing including entrance fees, guides, rent of "Ski-Doo" (Scandic-503), instruction and porterage.

The price does not include: Maximum liability for damage to a snowmobile of $250.00.
Minimum group of 6 passengers required.

Figure 7.5   *Hard-adventure tour.*

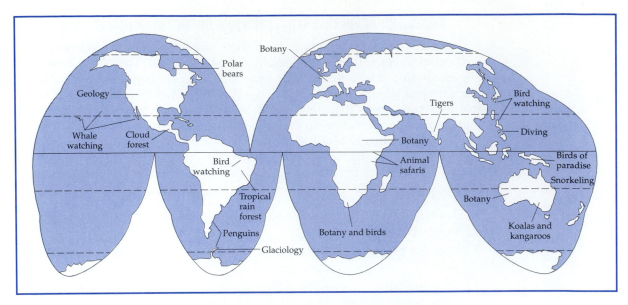

Figure 7.6 *Ecotourism hot spots around the world.*

Why is it so popular? Not only has ecotourism opened exciting opportunities for travel and learning, but it also helps developing countries prosper through increased tourism while keeping the environment intact. Ecotourism helps countries and regions because of the following:

1. Trips are educational and fun at the same time; they serve to increase people's awareness of natural beauty, different habitats, and the peril of endangered species. Because of this awareness, people become more willing to support conservation efforts.

2. Many entrance fees to nature parks and reserves help to finance environmental programs and organizations and to fight against animal poaching in certain areas of the world.

However, the exploding growth of ecotourism is a double-edged sword. Although it is clearly a benefit to increase people's awareness of the world's fragile environments, there has been an increase in the number of tourists to some ecologically sensitive regions. How to balance the two? Many feel that the answer lies in stricter controls. For example, there are so many sightseeing boats to the Galàpagos Islands that the government now restricts the number of visitors to these nature preserves. Some U.S. national parks are literally overrun by tourists during certain times of the year, so limitations on the number of accommodations have been imposed. It might also be useful to promote ecotourism to places that are less well known.

There are two general varieties of ecotourism or nature tours. There are *general interest tours,* which take an overall look at all natural elements in a particular destination, such as birds, trees, flowers, animals, and geological structures. Usually, these types of tours include an adventure component, such as white-water rafting, hiking over rugged terrain, or canoeing.

Other nature tours offer a specific aspect of the environment at one or more destinations. These include guides who are specialists in a particular field and include detailed and informative narratives about such things as birds, botany and wildflowers, animal safaris, whale-watching, and geology.

Figure 7.7 *Ecotour package.*

Figure 7.7 is a sample tour called "Ecoadventure Costa Rica." It is a perfect example of both an ecotour (a trip to a cloud forest, volcano, wildlife spotting, etc.) and an adventure tour (hiking, kayaking, river floating, mountain biking, and snorkeling).

Web Link

Here is a useful guide to the ecotourism marketplace and tour information worldwide. Point your browser at this ecotourism site *http://www. ecosourcenetwork.com*

Special-Interest Tours

In addition to adventure and ecotourism, there are other specialty trips, called **niche tours** because they target a specific segment of the traveling population, that focus on just about any type of hobby or interest. The list of activities and interests that can be fulfilled through vacation packages is too lengthy to put here. Table 7.1 is a list of a variety of specialized markets—from A to Z—that travel professionals book frequently. Most of these specialized tours are available in just about every major country or region in the world. However, a few examples of key destinations for each specialty are provided in the table as reference.

TABLE 7.1   SPECIAL-INTEREST TOURS FROM A TO Z

Aerobics	United States, Caribbean, South America	Jewish tours	New Mexico, Britain, Eastern Europe, Russia
Anthropology	Africa, Amazon, Ecuador, New Guinea	Kite flying	North Carolina
		Language study	Asia, Baltic, Latin America, central Europe, Uzbekistan
Antiques	Britain, Egypt, Greece, Spain		
Art history	Central Europe, Iceland, Mexico, Indonesia	Music/dance	Austria, California, Portugal, Trinidad
Ballooning	France, Kenya, Switzerland, western United States	Mystery tours	Britain
		Opera	Australia, Germany, Italy, New York
Cave art	Australia, India, Turkey, Utah	People over 50	England, Himalayas, Latin America, Thailand
Chocolate tours	Belgium, England, Europe, Scandinavia	Religion/spirituality	Belgium, China, Florida, Israel, Mongolia
Cooking school	Austria, France, India, Italy	Seniors/retired people	Canada, East Africa, India, Vietnam
Cultural expeditions	Bali, Belize, Japan, mid east	Single travelers	Asia, Caribbean, Philippines, western Europe
Desert expeditions	Australia, Egypt, Israel, western United States	Stress management	Arizona, Hawaii, Nepal, New Zealand
Dogsledding	Arctic, Canada, Norway, Siberia	Teachers' tours	Amazon, Ecuador, France, Mexico
Elephant rides	Asia, Indonesia, Nepal, Vietnam	Treasure hunting	Arizona, Colorado, Montana, New Mexico
Fashion tours	England, Europe, Greece, Italy	University tours	Argentina, England, Morocco, Peru
Film/film history	England	Vegetarian tours	Baja, Belize, Ecuador, Peru
Garden tours	Australia, British Columbia, Ireland	Vintage cars	Alabama, Germany, Hungary, Monaco
Genealogy	Britain, Ireland, Italy, Poland	Wild horse watching	Oregon
Ghost towns	Arkansas, California, Montana, Wyoming	Wine tasting	Argentina, California, central Europe, South Africa
Gourmet	Belgium, Britain, Iceland, Japan	Yoga/meditation	Hawaii, Mexico, Nepal, Utah
Historic houses	Britain, Holland, New England, Turkey	Zoology	Amazon, Australia, Chile, Virgin Islands
Investments	Belize, Europe, New Zealand, Panama		

✔ Check Your Understanding 7-2

Multiple Choice

Circle the *best* answer.

1. A trip to the Philippines for bird-watching and a trip to the rain forests in Central America are two examples of a(n):

   A. soft adventure   C. hard adventure

   B. hosted tour   D. ecotour

2. White river rafting on the Colorado and trekking through the Himalayas are two examples of:
   A. soft adventure
   B. ecotours
   C. hard adventure
   D. escorted tours

3. A popular destination for an ecotour to view penguins and glaciers is:
   A. Alaska
   B. South America
   C. Africa
   D. Russia

4. A popular destination to go whale-watching is:
   A. Australia
   B. England
   C. Baja California
   D. Miami, Florida

5. Specialty group tours that focus on a specific hobby or interest are also called:
   A. natural tours
   B. target tours
   C. foreign independent tours (FITs)
   D. niche tours

Short Answers

6. List five reasons for travelers to take tour packages.
   A. _____
   B. _____
   C. _____
   D. _____
   E. _____

7. List three reasons for the travel agent to sell tour packages.
   A. _____
   B. _____
   C. _____

SELLING TOUR PACKAGES

It is difficult to pigeonhole people as tour-takers or independent travelers. Below is a list of typical travel client markets. Which ones do you think would prefer to take a tour package rather than to travel independently?

- All-inclusive clients
- Groups
- Singles
- Seasoned travelers
- Cruise enthusiasts
- Adventure travelers
- Working couples
- History and culture buffs
- Teachers
- Corporate travelers
- Families
- Honeymooners
- First timers
- Ecotourists
- Seniors
- Professionals
- Students
- Independent travelers

You are right if you said that all these markets are potential tour buyers. For example, *business travelers* often enjoy travel on their off time, such as tacking on leisure activity after meetings or having their spouses or family meet them to go touring together. Even the most *independent* and *seasoned travelers* prefer a structured tour to parts unknown. For example, a seasoned traveler may feel comfortable touring independently through Europe, but may prefer to take an escorted tour during a first visit to the Far East.

First-timers enjoy covering a lot in a little time and prefer multicountry, multi-state, or regional tours that offer a good overview of a destination. For *singles,* taking a tour provides the security and companionship of a group. *Working couples* and DINKS (dual income, no kids) have the discretionary income to spend money on travel and a strong desire to see the world before raising a family. Members of this market want stress-free travel, convenience, comfort, and quality. Finally, *professionals* who live in a fast-paced and busy world much of the time want convenience and stress-free travel when they vacation. Not to make decisions regarding where to stay, what to see, and how to get there all make taking all-inclusive vacation packages an excellent option.

It is up to the travel agent to determine if the client is a tour buyer or strictly an independent. Counseling in tour planning is a *nondirective* process. That means that at first, the client does all the talking and the agent listens to determine the client's wishes and general feelings about travel. As the counseling session progresses, a shift takes place to a *directive process* where the counselor starts directing the client to make the right decisions. Whether the client suits an already designed vacation package or requires a custom-designed DIT or FIT, the agent needs to know the following in order to match the client with the right product:

1. *Purpose of the trip.* Determine the client's basic motives for taking the trip: Is it to meet other people? To expand his or her cultural outlook? To become educated? Is the trip partially for business or totally for relaxation? Looking for new experiences? Satisfying a lifelong curiosity?

2. *Time requirements.* How long is the trip? Is one week the absolute limit, or can they tack on an extra few days? Are they very restricted in terms of time, or can they travel for any length of time?

3. *Financial ability.* Are we talking about a shoestring budget to tour Europe under $600 or a deluxe trip for $4,000? How firm is the maximum price the client has set for the vacation?

4. *Physical ability.* Are there any special health concerns that may affect how far the client can walk? Any special food requirements? This is critical for those who want to take an adventure or nature tour that requires a degree of strength and agility.

5. *Travel background.* Is the client a first-time traveler, or does he or she "know the ropes" of travel? Where has he or she been before, and what did he or she particularly like and dislike about past vacation experiences?

6. *The "independence quotient."* How self-sufficient is the client? Does he or she prefer a group environment with an escort for a totally worry-free experience, or does the person want no timetables, no schedules, or have a personal agenda of his or her own?

7. *Special interests.* What are the client's primary interests? Nature lover? City-life dweller? Music, art, theater? Bungee jumping, rock climbing, mountain biking? Cultural buff? Party and nightlife?

These are some of the questions that need to be answered for travel counselors to serve as vacation matchmakers for their clients. Once the client's interests, background, motivations, and budget requirements are considered, the agent can determine if the client is a candidate for a tour package, and if so, which one. The next step is to research the tour products that are on the market; the agent needs to know his or her resources.

TOUR PACKAGE RESOURCES

Many resources are used by travel professionals to research tours, prices, and other important information related to the selling and booking of vacation packages. In this section you are introduced to a sample of references that are used frequently.

➤ *Official Tour Directory*

The *Official Tour Directory* (see Figure 7.8) is a large, soft-bound book that is subscribed to by travel agencies. There are two annual editions: fall–winter, and spring–summer. It has a wealth of information that includes the following sections:

- *General information:* comprehensive list, by type of business, of companies and toll-free numbers that travel agents use frequently. Some of the companies include air consolidators, hotels and rep firms, insurance services, limousine/private van services, motorcoach companies, railroads, theater services, travel guidebooks, travel publications, and associations. *Key feature:* Also included is a calendar of upcoming travel industry events (see Figure 7.9).

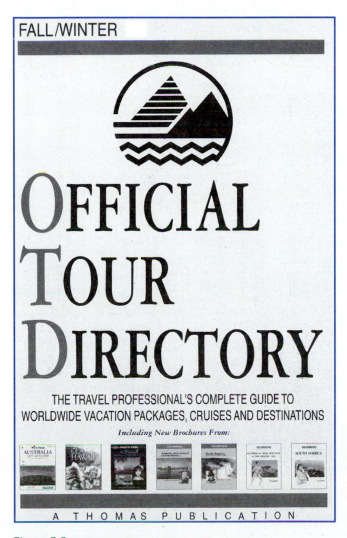

Figure 7.8 Official Tour Directory *cover.*

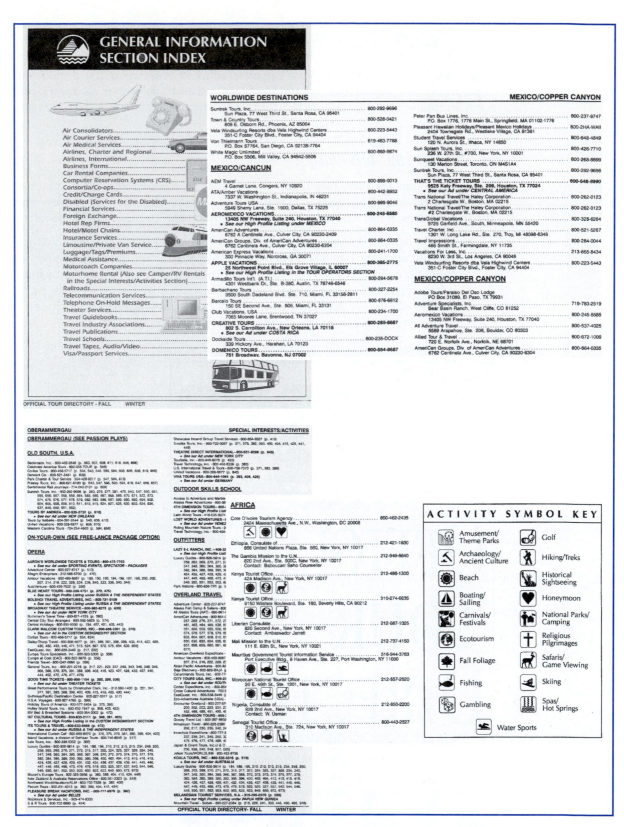

Figure 7.9 *Sample content of the* Official Tour Directory.

- *Domestic and international tourist offices:* listing, by region, of toll-free numbers and contacts for more than 900 tourist information offices. Domestic and International offices are listed separately, and each is further subdivided by state or region. *Key feature:* Graphic symbols are incorporated into the listings, indicating the most popular activities for that destination (see Figure 7.9).

- *Tour operators/company profiles:* alphabetical list of U.S.- and Canadian-based tour operators that offer worldwide packages. All companies list mailing addresses, E-mail addresses, and telephone numbers. *Key feature:* Many companies include high profile listings (HPLs) with key information such as company background, airline and association affiliations, booking policies, and commission rates for travel agencies.

- *Custom designed/FIT tour operators:* identifies those operators specializing in custom-designed/FIT tour packages.

- *Worldwide destinations section:* organizes tour operators under the destinations they serve. More than 750 destinations are arranged by broad regions (Africa, Asia, Canada, Caribbean, Europe, South America, etc.). *Key feature:* This section features key information on a variety of destinations and a brochure order hotline (see Figure 7.9).

- *Special interests/activities:* used when clients want a particular type of tour or vacation package (e.g., botany tours, golf packages, river rafting, safaris, wine tasting, etc.). *Key feature:* This section includes more than 200 types of specialty tours located conveniently in one resource (see Figure 7.9).

➤ Jax Fax Travel Marketing Magazine

Jax Fax (see Figure 7.10) is a monthly magazine publication that is subscribed to by travel agencies. Its key function is to provide a listing of tour packages, air charters, and scheduled air discounts to worldwide destinations. Figure 7.11 is a cutaway section from a *Jax Fax* listing. A description of each part of the listing follows:

1. *Departing*
   - Specific dates of departure
   - Departure on numbered days of the week (1, Mon.; 2, Tues.; 3, Wed.; 4, Thurs.; 5, Fri.; 6, Sat.; 7, Sun.)
   - Generic terms (DAILY, MNTHL)

2. *Trip type*
   - SKED AIR: round-trip air only via scheduled airline
   - CHTR AIR: round-trip air only via charter airline
   - SKED TUR: round-trip air and land package via scheduled airline
   - TOUR PKG: motorcoach package; air additional
   - SPCL INT: special-interest tour

3. *Airline:* official two-letter airline codes.

4. *Number of days:* number of days for tours, flights, or hotel packages with specific duration.

5. *Minimum price:* lowest quoted price; restrictions may apply and availability of seats is limited. If flights are included, the fare is round trip. If accommodations are included, the price is per person/double occupancy.

6. *Net:* indicates that travel agents pay the supplier the full displayed or agreed fare and add whatever they feel their commission should be when billing clients.

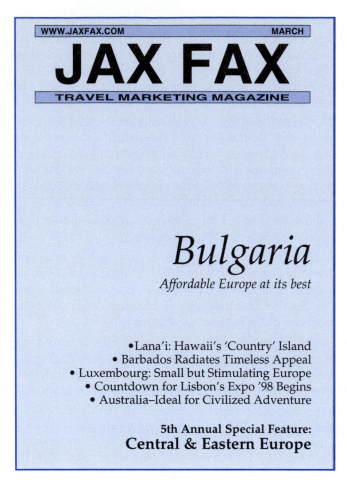

Figure 7.10 Jax Fax *cover.*

7. *Maximum price:* highest quoted price during validity period.
8. *Supplier:* contact information. Toll-free and/or local numbers of all suppliers are listed in a separate section of this resource.
9. *Validity:* time span for quoted prices.
10. *Additional:* details from supplier.

➤ Tour Brochures

Travel agencies receive hundreds of tour package brochures and associated materials each year from tour operators, airlines, hotels, and other suppliers of vacation packages. This is probably the most important resource, since brochures are designed with both the consumer and the travel agent in mind. They contain exciting and enticing descriptions of the tour vacations to *motivate* the consumer to buy the product. They also contain important pricing, booking, and travel conditions information to *inform* the travel sales agent.

Figure 7.12 is a reproduction of a brochure from an operator called Adventure Tours. The brochure offers several vacation packages in Florida. In our sam-

DEPARTING	TRIP TYPE	AIR LINE	# DAYS	ROUND TRIP PRICE MIN	MAX	SUPPLIER	VALIDITY PERIOD	ADDITIONAL INFORMATION
PERU								
						To:CUZCO RETURN FROM: MACHU PICCHU		
DAILY	TOUR PKG		5	$ 370	$ 780	INKA'S EMPIRE TOURS	TO 3/31/98	CUZCO 3N; MACHU PICCHU 1N; 212-875-0370
MIAMI						**To:CUZCO RETURN FROM: MACHU PICCHU**		
DAILY	SKED TUR		8	$1799	$2160	TOURS INTERNATIONAL	1/1/98-12/15/98	MYSTICAL EXPERIENCE
67123	SKED TUR		8	$1090	$1390	TOURS INTERNATIONAL	1/1/98-12/15/98	FROM THE INCAS TO THE AMAZON
67123	SKED TUR		5	$ 890	$1070	TOURS INTERNATIONAL	1/1/98-12/15/98	INCA VALLEY; OVERNITE MP; MEALS; EXCUR.
FIXED	SKED TUR		5	$ 850	$ 900	TOURS INTERNATIONAL	4/14/98-11/10/98	INCA TRAIL; TREKKING; FB
						To:HUARAZ		
DAILY	TOUR PKG		8	$ 800	$1200	INKA'S EMPIRE TOURS	TO 3/31/98	MTN CAMPING 7N; 212-875-0370
MIAMI						**To:IQUITOS RETURN FROM: AMAZON**		
6	SKED TUR		8	$1599	$1899	TOURS INTERNATIONAL	1/1/98-12/15/98	7D CRUISE; FB; JUNGLE EXC; EXTENSIONS
						To:LIMA RETURN FROM: LA PAZ		
DAILY	TOUR PKG		10	$ 790	$1100	INKA'S EMPIRE TOURS	TO 3/31/98	LIMA 2N; CUZCO 3N; PUNO 2N: LA PAZ 2N
						To:LIMA RETURN FROM: MACHU PICCHU		
DAILY	TOUR PKG		6	$ 520	$ 950	INKA'S EMPIRE TOURS	TO 3/31/98	LIMA 2N; CUZCO 3N; WWW.INKAS.COM
						To:LIMA RETURN FROM: PARACAS		
DAILY	TOUR PKG		13	$1380	$1491	INKA'S EMPIRE TOURS	TO 3/31/98	W/TAMBOPATA,CUZCO,PUNO,NAZCA,PARACAS
						To:LIMA RETURN FROM: PUNO		
DAILY	TOUR PKG		8	$ 650	$ 883	INKA'S EMPIRE TOURS	TO 3/31/98	LIMA 2N; CUZCO 3N; MACHU P; PUNO 2N
ATLANTA						**To:LIMA**		
DAILY	SKED AIR			$ 535 Net		AGENTS ADVANTAGE	TO 5/31/98	800-816-2211; OTHER CITIES AVBL.
DAILY	SKED AIR			$ 455 Net	$ 500	P & F INTERNATIONAL	ALL YEAR	(800)444-6666 OR (718)937-1998
BOSTON						**To:LIMA**		
DAILY	SKED AIR			$ 535 Net		AGENTS ADVANTAGE	TO 5/31/98	800-816-2211; OTHER CITIES AVBL.
DAILY	SKED AIR			$ 455 Net	$ 500	P & F INTERNATIONAL	ALL YEAR	(800)444-6666 OR (718)937-1998
CHICAGO						**To:LIMA**		
DAILY	SKED AIR			$ 513 Net		J & O AIR	3/1/98-3/31/98	800-877-8111; FAX:619-282-4164
DAILY	SKED AIR			$ 530 Net	$ 549	P & F INTERNATIONAL	ALL YEAR	(800)444-6666 OR (718)937-1998
DAILY	SKED AIR			$ 634		SOLAR TOURS	TO 3/31/98	800-388-7652; 800-727-7652; NO ADV.
DALLAS						**To:LIMA**		
DAILY	SKED AIR			$ 428 Net		PRIME TRAVEL	TO 4/15/98	US A/L; ALL C/S AMERICA; 800-447-4013
DENVER						**To:LIMA**		
DAILY	SKED AIR			$ 645 Net		AGENTS ADVANTAGE	TO 5/31/98	800-816-2211; OTHER CITIES AVBL.
DAILY	SKED AIR			$ 513 Net		J & O AIR	3/1/98-3/31/98	800-877-8111; FAX:619-282-4164
DAILY	SKED AIR			$ 530 Net	$ 549	P & F INTERNATIONAL	ALL YEAR	(800)444-6666 OR (718)937-1998
DAILY	SKED AIR			$ 634		SOLAR TOURS	TO 3/31/98	800-388-7652; 800-727-7652; NO ADV.
DAILY	SKED AIR			$ 662 Net		TRANS AM TRAVEL INC.	TO 3/31/98	800-822-7600; OTHR CITIES AVBL; NO ADV
DETROIT						**To:LIMA**		
DAILY	SKED AIR			$ 645 Net		AGENTS ADVANTAGE	TO 5/31/98	800-816-2211; OTHER CITIES AVBL.
DAILY	SKED AIR			$ 513 Net		J & O AIR	3/1/98-3/31/98	800-877-8111; FAX:619-282-4164
DAILY	SKED AIR			$ 530 Net	$ 549	P & F INTERNATIONAL	ALL YEAR	(800)444-6666 OR (718)937-1998
LOS ANGELES						**To:LIMA**		
DAILY	SKED AIR			$ 560 Net		J & O AIR	3/1/98-3/31/98	800-877-8111; FAX:619-282-4164
MIAMI						**To:LIMA**		
DAILY	SKED AIR			$ 495 Net		BRAZILIAN WAVE TOURS	ALL YEAR	BUSINESS CLASS AVBL; (800)6B2-3315
DAILY	SKED AIR			$ 450	$ 495	S.A.C.T.T.	TO 3/30/98	800-327-8554; **TOUR PKGS,1ST,BIZ AVBL.**
DAILY	SKED AIR			$ 437		SOLAR TOURS	TO 3/31/98	800-388-7652; 800-727-7652; NO ADV.
MINNEAPOLIS/ST.PAUL						**To:LIMA**		
DAILY	SKED AIR			$ 634		SOLAR TOURS	TO 3/31/98	800-388-7652; 800-727-7652; NO ADV.

Figure 7.11 *Sample content of* Jax Fax.

ple, the package "Disney's Resort Magic" is featured. Read through this sample brochure and highlight these important sections:

- *Inclusive features.* This is a list of all inclusive features of a tour, including such elements as accommodations, transfers, and other items, such as an unlimited "magic" pass to theme parks, WDW transportation, and early admission.

- *Prices.* Some brochures present prices for different accommodations and trip duration in chart format. This package is three, five, or seven nights in length. Important: Tour package prices are *per person* (unless otherwise noted). Also notice that prices are for land package only or for air-inclusive packages. The agent would contact the tour operator for more information related to air transportation.

- *General or travel conditions.* This is a very important part of any tour brochure. It includes booking information relative to deposit and final payments, cancellation policies, refunds, flight schedules, tour documentation, and responsibility and liability of the tour operator in the case of personal injury, loss of personal items while traveling, etc.

FLORIDA

AIR INCLUSIVE AND LAND ONLY PACKAGES

■ Exciting, fun-filled vacations to: WALT DISNEY WORLD® Resort · Orlando · Florida

■ INTRODUCING: Affordably priced 2 night cruise vacations aboard Cape Canaveral Cruise Line.

■ Fabulous bonus offers from Planet Hollywood, Church Street Station, Hard Rock Cafe and more.

■ Save hundreds of $$ with discount coupons to Orlando Area Attractions and Restaurants.

www.adventurevacations.com

More Than A Reservation. An Adventure Vacation.

WALT DISNEY WORLD® Resort

What's the only thing better than visiting the WALT DISNEY WORLD® Resort? Staying there!

Resort Magic — Your selection of a WALT DISNEY WORLD® Resort property represents a wise choice in enhancing your visit to Orlando and ensuring a memorable vacation experience. The on-site resorts offer many exclusive benefits available only to their guests, including:

◆ 24-Hour Disney Magic.
◆ Preferred on-site dining/priority seating.
◆ Early admission to selected theme park on selected days.
◆ Unlimited Walt Disney World transportation.
◆ Child care services and Disney's Learning Programs.
◆ Assistance and guidebooks for the disabled.

Disney's Resort Magic

PACKAGE CODE: WDW98

3, 5 or 7 nights include:
◆ Round-trip airport transfers via **Mears Motor Shuttle**.
◆ Accommodations at selected WALT DISNEY WORLD® Resort property, including hotel tax.
◆ UNLIMITED MAGIC PASS with DISNEY'S FLEX FEATURE. (See page 6.)

Air-inclusive packages also include:
◆ Round-trip off-peak published air via scheduled service on selected airline from **Philadelphia, PA**.* Additional cities also available.
◆ $20.00 Planet Hollywood Gift Certificate which can be applied towards food, beverage or merchandise.
* See footnotes page 17.

Rates are per person/double occupancy.

	3 Nights Air Inclusive	3 Nights Land Package	5 Nights Air Inclusive	5 Nights Land Package	7 Nights Air Inclusive	7 Nights Land Package
Disney's All-Star Music Resort						
Disney's All-Star Sports Resort						
1/1-2/12 Standard	522	357	662	497	793	628
2/13-4/25	546	381	702	537	849	684
4/26-5/5	537	372	687	522	828	663
5/6-8/22	556	391	708	543	853	688
8/23-12/22	541	376	683	518	818	653
Disney's Caribbean Beach Resort						
Disney's Port Orleans Resort						
Disney's Dixie Landings Resort						
Disney's Coronado Springs Resort						
1/1-2/12 Standard	603	438	797	632	982	817
2/13-4/25	639	474	857	692	1066	901
4/26-5/5	621	456	827	662	1024	859
5/6-8/22	702	475	848	683	1049	884
8/23-12/22	622	457	873	708	1007	842
Disney's Wilderness Lodge						
1/1-2/12 Woods View	732	567	1012	847	1283	1118
2/13-4/25	789	624	1107	942	1416	1251
4/26-5/5	765	600	1067	902	1360	1195
5/6-7/4	784	619	1088	923	1385	1220
7/5-12/22	751	586	1033	868	1308	1143
Disney's Fort Wilderness Resort and Campground						
1/1-2/12 Cabin	738	573	1022	857	1297	1132
2/13-4/25	798	633	1122	957	1437	1272
4/26-5/5	771	606	1077	912	1374	1209
5/6-7/4	790	625	1098	933	1399	1234
7/5-12/22	757	592	1043	878	1322	1157
The Villas at the Disney Institute						
1/1-2/12 Bungalow	738	573	1022	857	1297	1132
2/13-4/25	798	633	1122	957	1437	1272
4/26-5/5	771	606	1077	912	1374	1209
5/6-7/4	790	625	1098	933	1399	1234
7/5-12/22	757	592	1043	878	1322	1157
Disney's Contemporary Resort						
1/1-2/12 Garden-Standard View	756	591	1052	887	1339	1174
2/13-4/25	816	651	1152	987	1479	1314
4/26-5/5	789	624	1107	942	1416	1251
5/6-7/4	808	643	1128	963	1441	1276
7/5-12/22	775	610	1073	908	1364	1199

	3 Nights Air Inclusive	3 Nights Land Package	5 Nights Air Inclusive	5 Nights Land Package	7 Nights Air Inclusive	7 Nights Land Package
Disney's Old Key West Resort						
1/1-2/12 Studio	780	615	1092	927	1395	1230
2/13-4/25	831	666	1177	1012	1514	1349
4/26-5/5	807	642	1137	972	1458	1293
5/6-7/4	826	661	1158	993	1483	1318
7/5-12/22	799	634	1113	948	1420	1255
Disney's BoardWalk Inn						
1/1-2/12 Standard	822	657	1162	997	1493	1328
2/13-4/25	873	708	1247	1082	1612	1447
4/26-5/5	849	684	1207	1042	1556	1391
5/6-7/4	868	703	1228	1063	1581	1416
7/5-12/22	841	676	1183	1018	1518	1353
Walt Disney World Dolphin Resort						
Walt Disney World Swan Resort						
1/5-1/15 Run of House	839	674	1190	1025	1386	1221
1/16-5/5	903	738	1297	1132	1682	1517
5/6-5/15	922	757	1211	1046	1707	1542
5/16-12/19	858	693	1318	1153	1411	1246
Bonus: Kids 12 & under eat free from children's menu (restrictions apply), in-room coffee, daily newspaper, unlimited use of Health Club, seventh (7) night free already reflected in rates (1/5-1/15 & 5/16-12/19).						
Disney's Yacht and Beach Club Resorts						
1/1-2/12 Standard	843	678	1197	1032	1542	1377
2/13-4/25	900	735	1292	1127	1675	1510
4/26-5/5	876	711	1252	1087	1619	1454
5/6-7/4	895	730	1273	1108	1644	1479
7/5-12/22	862	697	1218	1053	1567	1402
Disney's Polynesian Resort						
1/1-2/12 Gardenview	858	693	1222	1057	1577	1412
2/13-4/25	918	753	1322	1157	1717	1552
4/26-5/5	891	726	1277	1112	1654	1489
5/6-7/4	910	745	1298	1133	1679	1514
7/5-12/22	877	712	1243	1078	1602	1437
Disney's Grand Floridian Resort & Spa						
1/1-2/12 Gardenview	900	735	1292	1127	1675	1510
2/13-4/25	1017	852	1387	1222	1808	1643
4/26-5/5	933	768	1347	1182	1752	1587
5/6-7/4	948	783	1368	1203	1777	1612
7/5-12/22	919	754	1313	1148	1700	1535

Children's Package Rates

		3 Nights Air Inclusive	3 Nights Land Package	5 Nights Air Inclusive	5 Nights Land Package	7 Nights Air Inclusive	7 Nights Land Package
Child (Ages 3-9)	1/1-5/5	358	193	406	241	446	281
	5/6-12/31	373	208	423	258	466	301
Junior (Ages 10-17)	1/1-5/5	402	237	462	297	513	348
	5/6-12/31	421	256	483	318	538	373

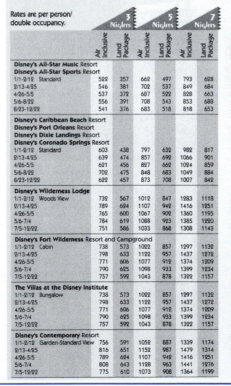

Figure 7.12 *Vacation package brochure.*

GENERAL CONDITIONS

IMPORTANT INFORMATION IN REGARDS TO YOUR VACATION PACKAGE.

Tour Operator: Adventure Vacations, 10612 Beaver Dam Road, Hunt Valley, MD 21030-2205. Package rates include our service charge for planning and arrangement.

Deposit Required: $100.00 per person is due within 7 calendar days after booking is made. Full payment due 45 days prior to travel date. Payment policies may be required earlier due to airline restrictions and special events.

Insurance: Adventure Vacations strongly recommends Travel Waiver which can be arranged at time of booking through Adventure Vacations.

Late booking fee: There will be a $15.00 fee assessed for bookings made 14 days or less prior to travel.

Revisions/changes: There will be no charge for the first revision unless documents have been issued. There will be a $20.00 per booking fee for each additional revision, plus any hotel penalties. If any airline tickets need to be reissued, an additional $75.00 per person fee will apply.

Cancellation: There will be a $50 fee per booking once deposit is received. On all air packages, there will be a $50 fee per booking outside 35 days and a $75 fee per booking inside 35 days; plus any applicable air, hotel or feature charges. Hotel penalties differ based on destination but usually charge a 1 night penalty for Domestic destinations. Different cancellation policies may apply over holiday periods, please check with your travel agent.

48 hour cancellation: On land only reservations, there will be a $100 fee per booking. Air-inclusive reservations will incur a fee of $150 per booking plus any vendor fees if applicable.

Refunds: For refundable unused services, written request must reach Adventure Vacations within 30 days of termination of travel with unused coupons and/or hotel and car rental receipts. Further, refunds are contingent upon Adventure Vacations receipt of invoices from hotels, car companies, and/or ground operators. Unused hotel nights are refunded only if they cover a minimum of two consecutive nights. There will be a $50.00 refund fee per booking for any unused features.

Restrictions: 5 days in advance ticketing, 2 night minimum stay/30 days maximum.

Flight schedule: Adventure Vacations does not guarantee any specific flight schedules. In the event the air carrier with whom Adventure Vacations has a contract to perform the air transportation described is delayed in performance or unable to perform with such aircraft, the provisions of the air carrier's tariff shall govern the rights and obligations of both parties. Any additional expenses incurred due to airline scheduling will be the responsibility of the passenger(s).

Airport check-in time: We recommend check in 2 hours prior to departure time. Passenger's reservation will be cancelled no earlier than 30 minutes before departure time of the flight on which the reservation was made.

Tour Documents: will be mailed approximately three weeks before departure, but not before receipt of final payment.

Tour Packages: These tour packages are designed for vacation travelers and the rates shown do not apply to individuals attending a convention at the hotel. In the event that a conventioneer purchases one of these packages utilizing a hotel at which he is attending a convention, he will be liable for the room rate designated by his convention committee. Name changes may not be accepted for a confirmed reservation during certain periods.

Responsibility & Liability: As a tour operator, Adventure Vacations organizes, promotes and sells tour programs consisting of hotel accommodations, transportation and other travel services which it purchases or reserves from certain suppliers.

The hotels, carriers, and other suppliers which provide services in connection with these tours are independent contractors and are not agents of Adventure Vacations. Adventure Vacations does not have control over them. Accordingly, Adventure Vacations is not responsible if any of them fail to deliver services or commit any other negligent or willful act or omission.

All coupons, receipts, passes, and tickets issued by the hotels, carriers and other suppliers are issued on the terms and conditions specified by the suppliers. Adventure Vacations does not have the authority to vary those terms.

Adventure Vacations is not responsible for personal injury, loss or damage to property, inconvenience, or expense resulting from matters beyond its control, such as acts of terrorism, defects in vehicles, breakdowns in equipment, government actions, strikes, theft, changes in itinerary or schedules, inclement weather, and Acts of God.

Participants are responsible for obtaining valid travel documents, for following travel instructions, for complying with customs regulations, for procuring any insurance they desire, and for complying with the laws of the place to which they are traveling.

Certain activities (including, but not limited to, white water rafting, scuba diving, horseback riding, parasailing, parachuting, hang gliding, jet skiing, water skiing, snow skiing, water slides, water rides, hot air ballooning, climbing, hiking) included by Adventure Vacations in the tour programs, or otherwise available through the carriers, hotels, tour operators or other suppliers, or generally available at or near the participants destination, may carry a higher than ordinary risk of injury. Participation in any sport or activity regardless of whether the sport or activity is included in the tour program, is strictly at the participants risk. You, therefore, release, and exonerate and discharge Adventure Vacations and its agents and successors from all claims, causes of action, damages, losses and liabilities of any nature arising out of your participation in any sports or activities except as may result from the gross negligence or willful misconduct of Adventure Vacations.

Adventure Vacations is not responsible for personal injury, loss or damage incurred by a participant, except as may result from the gross negligence or willful misconduct of Adventure Vacations. If Adventure Vacations is liable for any matter, its liability is strictly limited to a refund of the money paid by the participant.

Adventure Vacations may decline to accept or retain a person as a participant on any tour whenever, in its sole judgment, circumstances so require. If a person's participation on a tour is discontinued after the tour has commenced, Adventure Vacations will refund that portion of the money paid by the participant which it, Adventure Vacations, in its sole judgment, reasonably attributes to the uncompleted portion of the tour.

Adventure Vacations may, in its sole judgment, make any changes and cancellations to tour programs and schedules that it believes are necessary.

Adventure Vacations ASSUMES NO LIABILITY WHATSOEVER IN CONNECTION WITH ANY TOUR EXCEPT AS SPECIFICALLY SET FORTH IN THESE GENERAL CONDITIONS. THE WARRANTIES HEREIN ARE IN LIEU OF ANY EXPRESS, IMPLIED OR STATUTORY WARRANTIES, INCLUDING, BUT NOT LIMITED TO, ANY WARRANTIES OR MERCHANTABILITY OR FITNESS FOR A PARTICULAR PURPOSE.

Payment of the required deposit or any partial or full payment for a reservation constitutes your consent to these conditions.

These conditions and the terms of your tour cannot be changed except by a writing signed by an authorized agent of Adventure Vacations.

Rates- are quoted in U.S. currency, effective at time of printing, and subject to change without notice. Rates are guaranteed upon receipt of full payment. We reserve the right to reinvoice you in case of an error made in computing your price.

ALL BROCHURE CONTENTS ARE SUBJECT TO CHANGE WITHOUT NOTICE.

Adventure Vacations strongly suggests the purchase of our Travel Protection Plan.
For details, see below.

TRAVEL PROTECTION PLAN

PLEASE TAKE A MOMENT TO REVIEW AND CONSIDER THIS VALUABLE ADDITION TO YOUR VACATION PACKAGE.
Sometimes, unforeseen circumstances do occur. Because of this, Adventure Vacations strongly recommends the following Travel Protection Plan. For a very reasonable fee, you can rest assured that both yourself and your vacation investment are well protected.

TRIP CANCELLATION WAIVER/INTERRUPTION

TRIP COST The Trip Cancellation Waiver protects you for any cancellation penalties and administrative fees if you cancel your trip for any reason up to 48 hours prior to departure. The Trip Interruption coverage protects your non-refundable payments (not including administrative fees) if you must cancel your trip in the 48 hour period prior to departure or after your trip begins for a covered reason such as injury, sickness, death or a covered unforeseen circumstance.

TRIP DELAY

$500 Provides up to $100 per day for reasonable accommodations and traveling expenses until travel becomes possible if you are delayed for more than 12 hours due to a covered reason such as air carrier delay; Injury, Sickness or death of you or your Traveling Companion; quarantine; loss of passport, travel documents or money; or natural disaster.

ACCIDENTAL DEATH & DISMEMBERMENT

$25,000 Covers loss which occurs from a covered injury during your trip.

MEDICAL EXPENSE/ EMERGENCY ASSISTANCE

$25,000 Provides reimbursement for reasonable and customary medical expenses incurred within 365 days of a covered sickness or injury which occurs while on your trip, emergency dental treatment received during your trip; the costs for emergency transport to home or an appropriate hospital, including escort expense (both, if deemed necessary by the attending physician) for a covered injury or sickness which occurs while on your trip.

BAGGAGE/TRAVEL DOCUMENTS

$1,000 Coverage for direct physical loss or damage to your baggage, passports or visas while on your trip. A $500 maximum limit applies to jewelry, gems, watches, cameras and camera equipment and furs - a $250 per article limit applies to all other items. If, while on your trip, your baggage is delayed for 24 hours or more, we will pay up to $100 for the purchase of necessary additional clothing and personal articles.

ONLY $19 Per Person Domestic Land-Only Pkgs.

ONLY $29 Per Person Domestic Air-Inclusive Pkgs.

ONLY $99 Per Family Domestic Air-Inclusive Pkgs.

Certain exclusions and limitations apply and are detailed in the Description of Coverage Brochure. For example, coverage does not apply to: any sickness or condition that existed during the 90 days prior to the effective date of the coverages, suicide, normal pregnancy, war or any act or war, mental or nervous disorders. Unforeseen Circumstances include only those specified reasons that are defined in the policy, such as: carrier delay due to organized labor strikes, jury duty, or destruction of your residence from a natural disaster. A Traveling Companion means a person booked to share accommodations with you in the same room during your tour. Sickness means an illness or disease of the body which requires treatment by a Physician - sickness of you, Traveling Companion, or immediate Family Member must commence while your insurance is in force.

Program Administrator: Trip Mate Insurance Agency, Inc. • 9225 Ward Parkway, 2nd Floor • Kansas City, MO 64114 • 1-800-888-7292

SEE YOUR TRAVEL AGENT

Printed on Recyclable Paper

ORLANDO You Never Outgrow It.
Member of the Orlando/Orange County Convention & Visitors Bureau, Inc.

Discover America

ASTA

Second Printing
Printed in the U.S.A.

Visit us on the world wide web at http://www.adventurevacations.com

Figure 7.12 *Vacation package brochure. (continued)*

1. Write the name of the tour resource you would use to find each of the following. Choose from *Official Tour Directory*, *Jax Fax*, and tour brochure.

   A. a list of domestic and international tour offices _____

   B. a list of tour operators offering packages by special interest or activity _____

   C. a list of operators offering motorcoach tours or air and land packages to Paris, including departure dates and minimum costs _____

   D. information pertinent to a particular tour package that contains inclusive features, prices, booking, and cancellation policies _____

2. Refer to Figure 7.9 to answer the following questions.

   A. Circle the tour operator listed below that offers packages to Cancún, Mexico.

(1) Armadillo Tours	(3) Funjet Vacations
(2) Allied Tour & Travel	(4) Friends Travel

   B. The number you would call to make a reservation on a Mexico Copper Canyon tour with Aeromexico Vacations is _____.

   C. You can find out more about this activity found in Senegai through the Senegai Tourist Office.

(1) ancient culture	(3) historical sightseeing
(2) festivals	(4) all of the above

   D. You want to obtain tourist information, maps, and guides for your client who is traveling to Morocco. The number you would call is _____.

   E. The Kenya Tourist Office has information on three activities that are popular at that destination. What are they?

   (1) _____ (3) _____

   (2) _____

3. Refer to Figure 7.11 to answer the following questions.

   A. The U.S. city that offers daily motorcoach packages to Lima, Peru is _____.

   B. The tour operator that offers round-trip air and land packages from Miami to Cuzco is _____.

   C. This tour operator schedules round-trip air and land packages to Iquitos on _____ day(s) of the week.

   D. To book round-trip scheduled air between Denver and Lima with Solar Tours, the number you would call is _____.

   E. The tour operator that offers scheduled air between Detroit and Lima all year long is _____.

   F. The minimum price on Inka's Empire Tours' package from Miami to Lima that returns from Machu Picchu is _____. The maximum price is _____.

4. Refer to Figure 7.12 to answer the following questions.

   A. The price, per person, for the Disney Resort Magic five-night land package at the Disney's Wilderness Lodge, arrival date March 3, double occupancy, is _____.

B. Which feature below is not included in the Disney Resort Magic land package?

    (1) accommodations   (3) airport transfers

    (2) breakfast and dinner daily   (4) Walt Disney World transportation

C. The total amount of deposit you need to send for a party of two traveling on the Disney Resort Magic package is _____.

D. Final payment is due _____ (how soon) before departure.

E. Two people are booked on the air package departing August 30. They cancel two weeks prior to departure. In addition to any applicable air, hotel, or feature charges, the cancellation fee for this booking is _____.

F. The tour operator will mail documents to the travel agency _____ (how soon) before departure.

Transmitting Payments and Documentation

After the tour package is booked, there are three general methods of land package payment and documentation. The method that the travel professional uses depends on the requirements of the tour operator. It also depends on the form of payment used to pay for the deposit and/or final payment of the tour. The three methods are by agency check, miscellaneous charges order (MCO), or tour order.

➤ Agency Check Transmittal

This is probably the most prevalent method used when booking vacation packages—and the easiest! Here is a typical example of what happens when payment is made by agency check:

1. The travel agency contacts the tour operator, makes a reservation on behalf of the traveler, and receives written confirmation from the tour operator which confirms the tour by name, travel dates, cost, and other booking details.

2. The tour operator requires a deposit (if the tour is booked far in advance) and requires a deposit to be sent to secure the booking. This is usually done if the tour is booked more than two months prior to departure. If the tour is booked closer to the departure date, full payment is usually required.

3. The travel agency invoices the client for the deposit or final payment. The client transmits payment (either check or cash) to the agency for the invoiced amount.

4. After receiving payment from the client, the agency sends payment to the tour operator drawn on the agency's check; the client's check is never sent to the tour operator. If a deposit is being sent, the full amount of the deposit is sent to the tour operator (the agency does not deduct its commission at this point). If the final payment is sent, the agency sends the net amount (i.e., the total cost of the package minus the agency's commission) to the tour operator.

Example: Your clients, Mr. & Mrs. Pierson, are purchasing a two-week escorted tour through China with Aberdeen Tours, the tour operator. The agency booked the tour four months before departure. The total land cost for the tour is $2,400 per person. Aberdeen requires a $100 per person deposit within ten days of the booking date. Final payment is due no later than 45 days before departure. The agency commission is 10 percent. The payment transaction for this booking looks like this:

Deposit is sent:

$4,800	Total tour cost for two
− 200	Deposit sent to Aberdeen Tours within 10 days after booking
$4,600	Final payment due from clients to the travel agency 45 days before departure

Agency commission is calculated:

$4,800	Tour cost
× 10%	Percentage of commission
$ 480	Agency commission amount

Final payment is sent:

$4,600	Final payment due
− $ 480	Agency commission
$4,120	Final net amount sent to Aberdeen Tours

5. After receiving the final payment, the tour operator prepares tour package documents and sends them to the travel agency. The amount and types of tour documents vary and depend on the type of tour and other details. However, the typical tour documentation package consists of the following:

- Land vouchers for all prepaid land services: transfers, accommodations, sightseeing, etc. In some cases, one voucher is provided to the traveler which identifies all prepaid land features (see Figure 7.13).

- Baggage tags.

- Personalized itinerary (see Figure 7.14).

- "Extras" such as maps and guidebooks.

Sometimes the tour operator also prepares airline tickets if special group or charter flights are included in the package. In most cases, the tour operator handles the land package only; the travel agency books the air flights and prepares the airline ticket documents. However, for organized excursions such as escorted tours, the travel agency checks with the tour operator with regard to airline ticketing procedures.

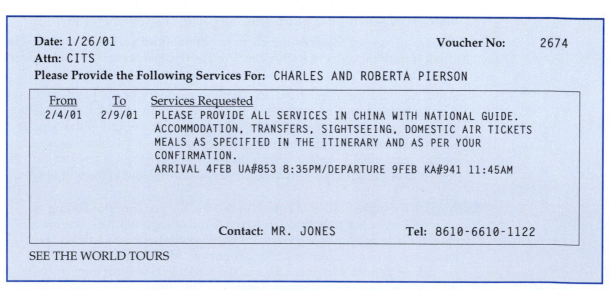

Figure 7.13 *Land package voucher for tour to China.*

Your Personal Itinerary
China Escapade

For: *Mr. & Mrs. Charles Pierson*

February 3/Tuesday   United States/Tokyo

Board your United Airlines flight to Beijing.
Cross the International Date Line and lose a day.

February 4/Wednesday   Beijing

8:35PM   Arrive at the Peking Capital Airport

Welcome to Beijing! This city reigns as both an ancient capital of Imperial China and as the capital of the present-day China. Nowhere else can you get a more concentrated impression of the old and the new China. Upon arrival, you will be transferred to your hotel.

Kempinski Hotel

February 5/Thursday   Beijing

Begin the day of sightseeing with a visit to the heart of Beijing - Tiananmen Square and the Forbidden City. Explore the chambers and view the priceless treasures of China's past, where emperors resided and common people were forbidden entry. This 250-acre palace contains more than 9,000 rooms and has only been open to the public since 1949. From the bustling energy of the city we move on to the tranquil retreat of the Summer Palace with its shimmering lakes. Explore the Summer Palace, a rest and recreation area of the Royal Families for more than a thousand years. Tonight, enjoy an acrobatic show.
Breakfast/Lunch/Dinner

February 6/Friday   Beijing

We continue touring Beijing with a visit to the historical Ming Tombs, where you will travel along the Sacred Way, stopping to photograph the stone animals that guard the route once forbidden to all, except the emporer's funeral cortege. The next stop is the Great Wall. As you walk atop China's most famous attraction, it is hard to believe this structure built some 2,300 years ago, extends 3,750 miles, and was one of the only landmarks on earth clearly recognizable to the Apollo astronauts. Enjoy the breathtaking view! Lunch will be served en-route. This evening, rest up and join us for dinner hosted by the Kempinski Hotel.
Breakfast/Lunch/Dinner

February 7/Saturday   Beijing/Xian

This morning, you will enjoy the behind the scenes view of Hutong, the old city of Beijing. With our guide on a three-wheel cycle, visit the 15th century Drum Tower for an overview of the intricate labyrinth comprising the district, then walk along its ancient alleyways and visit typical quadrangles where ordinary citizens live. In the afternoon, board a flight to Xian. Upon arrival, you will be met and transferred to your hotel. Xian is the largest city in northwest China. As one of China's seven ancient national capitals, it was the capital of twelve dynasties for over a thousand years. Tonight enjoy a dumpling Banquet and Tang Dynasty show.
Breakfast/Lunch/Dinner

Sheraton Xian Hotel

February 8/Sunday   Xian

This morning, visit the burial place of Emperor Qin Shihuang. This emperor unified the country and completed construction of the Great Wall over 2,200 years ago. This archaeological site displays the life-like army of Terra-Cotta Warriors and Horses that guard the tomb. Experience the thrill and awe of seeing the individually sculptured faces of the warriors. After lunch visit the Banpo Museum. The Banpo people settled in this area about 6,000 years ago. This Neolithic villa was uncovered in 1953. In addition to living quarters, there are many artifacts depicitng living conditions of that time. Final stop is at the Wild Goose Pagoda. This seven-story structure has offered a spectacular view of the ancient walled city since its construction in 652 A.D.
Breakfast/Lunch/Dinner

February 9/Monday   Xian/Hong Kong

After breakfast, transfer to the airport and board your flight to Hong Kong.

11:45AM   Board Dragonair flight KA#941
2:30PM   Arrive in Hong Kong

Hong Kong is an Oriental world of teeming lanes, crooked alleyways, and ladder streets, which strongly contrast with the western-style business center, and the elegance of the hill-climbing residential quarters. Upon, arrival, transfer to your hotel.
Breakfast

Hong Kong Renaissance Hotel

February 10/Tuesday   Hong Kong

An orientation tour this morning will start with a drive up to Victoria Peak for a panoramic view of Hong Kong island, Kowloon and the surrounding islands. Visit picturesque Repulse Bay. Proceed next to the well-known fishing village of Aberdeen to see the "floating community", it is still very much a part of Hong Kong's society.
Breakfast

February 11/Wednesday   Hong Kong

A day on your own to explore Hong Kong and all it has to offer. Wander around your own and do some shopping. We will be happy to recommend and book any of our one-half or full-day sightseeing tours for you - Hong Kong Island Tour, Ocean Park Tour, City & Harbor By Night Dinner Cruise, or Macau Day Tour with Lunch. Your Aberdeen guide will be happy to help you plan an exciting day in Hong Kong.
Breakfast/Lunch/Dinner

Figure 7.14 *Personalized itinerary.*

➤ Miscellaneous Charges Orders

Another method of transmitting payment is by the **miscellaneous charges order (MCO)** document. The MCO is an accountable ticket document issued by the Airlines Reporting Corporation (ARC). The MCO looks similar to an airline ticket: It has a ten-digit ticket number and the MCO is validated on the airline carrier used for transportation. Unlike an airline ticket, an MCO can be used for multiple passengers as long as they are traveling together on the trip.

This document is called *miscellaneous* because it has many uses in the travel industry. In addition to transmitting payments for land tours, an MCO is also used for any of the following transactions:

- Car rentals
- Hotel accommodations
- Surface transportation
- Cruise deposits

The MCO can be used for either a deposit payment or full payment of a land package. It is important to remember that an MCO is used only when requested by the tour operator. Below are two examples of when an MCO is usually issued:

1. When the tour is booked through an airline
2. When a deposit is required and a credit card is used as payment

The MCO is shaped like an airline ticket and is in booklet form. It consists of multiple coupons. One of the coupons, called the *exchange coupon*, can be handled in one of two ways: (1) the MCO coupon is hand-carried by the passenger to the destination and is then exchanged for tour documents, or (2) an MCO coupon is mailed to the airline/tour operator in exchange for tour documents. These documents are then mailed to the travel agency in advance of the traveler's departure date. Like an airline ticket, the MCO is processed on the ARC weekly sales report and the airline/tour operator is paid through the area settlement plan.

The tour operator/airline provides instructions to the travel agency on the entries to use when completing the MCO. Figure 7.15 is an example of an MCO used to transmit a deposit for the American Airlines' tour "Las Vegas" for two

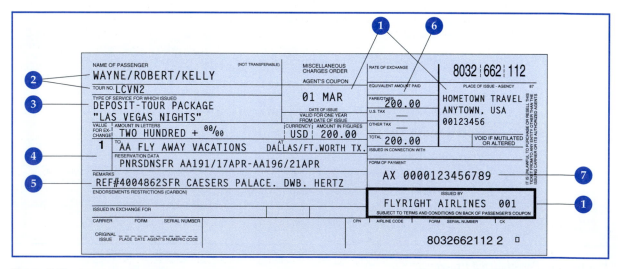

Figure 7.15 *Miscellaneous charges order.*

passengers. The amount of deposit transmitted is $100 per person, or $200 total. The clients paid with an American Express credit card. Descriptions of the parts of the MCO shown in Figure 7.15 are as follows:

1. *Validation:* issue date, agency name and location, and airline.
2. *Passenger data and tour number:* passenger name(s) and tour code for identification.
3. *Tour name and type of service:* type of service (deposit or full payment) and tour package name.
4. *Tour details:* name and location of tour operator, reservation data (such as flight number, dates of travel).
5. *Remarks:* additional information such as confirmation or reference number of tour, name of hotel, and other land features.
6. *Deposit/final payment:* amount being transmitted on MCO.
7. *Form of payment:* identify how passenger paid for MCO (if credit card, enter card type and account number). For check or cash transactions, enter CHECK or CASH, respectively.

➤ Tour Orders

Like the MCO, the **tour order** is an accountable ticket document issued by the Airlines Reporting Corporation. The tour order document can also be used for multiple passengers. It has a ten-digit ticket number and is validated on the airline carrier used as transportation. Unlike the MCO, which has many functions, the tour order can only be used to process land packages. Also, the tour order is used to *transmit final payments only;* it is not used for deposits.

The tour order is shaped like an airline ticket and has multiple coupons. It consists of four *service coupons* which are hand-carried by the passenger and serve as actual travel vouchers for various land services included in the tour: airport transfer or car rental, hotel or tour operator, sightseeing or other land features. Like an airline ticket and MCO, the tour order is processed on the ARC weekly sales report and the airline/tour operator is paid through the area settlement plan.

The tour operator/airline provides instructions to the travel agent in regard to the entries to use when completing the tour order. Figure 7.16 is an example of a tour order to transmit payment for a British Airways tour, "Flavors of London." This document is valid for two people and is transmitting the total package price of $942 for both travelers. Descriptions of the parts of the tour order shown in Figure 7.16 are as follows:

1. *Validation:* issue date, agency name and location, and airline
2. *Name of tour operator*
3. *Tour name and passenger(s) name(s)*
4. *Service coupons:* to be presented to (1) London Regional Transport for round-trip transfers, (2) Blakemore Hotel in London, (3) British Overland Tours for sightseeing; (4) void
5. *Tour details:* list of prepaid features; type of hotel accommodations on tour, arrival and departure dates
6. *Cost column:* total tour cost ($942) transmitted by tour order
7. *Form of payment*

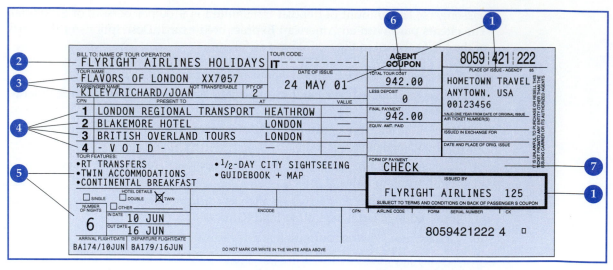

Figure 7.16 *Tour order.*

✓ Check Your Understanding 7-4

1. Of the three methods of transmitting tour payments—agency check, MCO, or tour order— _____ is used most frequently.

2. You have booked a ten-day "Pacific Delight" tour for two clients. The cost of the land package is $1,400 per person. The tour operator requires a $200 per person deposit within ten days of booking; the final payment is due 45 days prior to departure. The agency can earn 12 percent commission on this booking since the tour operator, Aberdeen Tours, is a preferred supplier. Answer the following.

   A. What is the total cost for the land package? _____

   B. What is the agency's commission? _____

   C. What is the total amount of deposit you will send? _____

   D. After you sent the deposit, the final payment is due 45 days prior to departure. What is the final payment amount you would send to Aberdeen Tours? _____

3. The ARC documents—miscellaneous charges order (MCO) and tour order— are sometimes used to transmit payment for tour packages if requested by the tour operator.

   A. Which document can be used for either a deposit _____ or full payment?

   B. Which document can be hand-carried by the _____ traveler and contains up to four service coupons (for transfers, hotel, etc.)?

🔍 Close-Up: Tour-Related Careers

Reservations agent   Sales representative   Group coordinator
Tour designer   Negotiator   Tour manager/escort

Typical staff positions outlined here can apply to both operators and wholesalers. However, remember that not all positions are available with each company since staffing requirements and descriptions depend on the size and internal organization. Similar positions can also be found in specialized group tour departments of large travel agencies.

Tour Reservations Agent

Tour reservations agent is similar to any reservations position with airlines, car rental, and other travel providers. The tour reservations agent handles telephone calls from travel agents, airlines, or the general public (if the company handles retail sales). After checking availability, they either confirm a reservation or suggest alternative date(s) or package(s).

Reservations agents must also be highly knowledgeable about all the tour products being offered. They are asked direct questions about the components of each tour, such as prices, schedules, hotels, and meals. They are also asked to provide destinations information, such as sightseeing, attractions, weather, and society of the places visited.

Sales Representative

Just like the airlines and other travel suppliers, tour sales reps are responsible for a region of travel agencies and other customers. Their primary concern is to encourage them to sell the company's tours and packages through educating them about the various products. They are often called upon to help travel agencies with their marketing efforts to sell the tour products by giving a talk and by showing a video or film to the agency's potential group and individual clients.

Group Coordinator

Group coordinators are involved in a variety of functions, depending on the size and type of company in which they are working. Typically, they are involved in all processing of group movements: selling special tours, taking reservations, maintaining an inventory of airline seats and hotel rooms sold, and completing travel documentation. This type of position is also available in large travel agencies that operate a group or tour division. In many cases group coordinators may also serve as group escorts.

Tour Designer

Tour designer is usually not an entry-level position and requires in-depth destination knowledge and research and writing skills. This person may be a retail travel agency employee, a tour operator, or a consultant or independent contractor with these specialized skills. The tour designer puts together all of the elements of a tour: airline transportation, planning the day-to-day itinerary, sightseeing and attractions, special events, hotels, land and/water transportation, meals, and so on.

Many tour designers are hired as DIT or FIT specialists with large travel agencies that specialize in this type of travel. They are usually experienced travel professionals who bring to the table a knowledge of the company's clients, travel industry skills, good business sense, marketing, and costing of travel products.

Tour Manager/Escort

A tour manager is also called a tour escort or a tour conductor. The tour manager is many things rolled into one. Tour managers must be very versatile since they have multiple functions during a tour: They serve as "housemothers," business managers, social directors, psychologists, and teachers. The tour manager provides continuity from city to city and country to country but does not serve as a tour narrator at each destination. This is handled by local city guides who join the group for any length of time. They may be with the group for just a few hours for a narrated city sightseeing tour or two or more days for a guided tour of a broader region.

Negotiator

The primary function of negotiators is to bargain or negotiate special rates with hotels, car rental companies, airlines, cruise ships, railways, and local tourist boards to develop tour packages. Negotiators work with any company or supplier that develops and markets tours such as tour operators, wholesalers, and travel agencies. Negotiators are often hired based on previous experience in sales and tour consulting. They are also required to have detailed knowledge of pricing and tour package development.

➤ Key Terms

- adventure tour
- domestic independent tour (DIT)
- ecotourism
- escorted tour
- foreign independent tour (FIT)
- ground operator
- hosted tours

- independent tour
- intermodal tour
- markup
- miscellaneous charges order (MCO)
- niche tour
- step-on guide
- tour escort

- tour manager
- tour operator
- tour order
- tour package
- tour wholesaler
- United States Tour Operators Association (USTOA)

Flashback The concept of a group tour encapsulated in the old saying, *"If it's Tuesday, it must be Belgium"* has finally been laid to rest! The image of a group of senior citizens being herded like sheep from museum to museum on a whirlwind tour has been replaced by today's reality in tour marketing: from hot-air ballooning over the Serengeti Plains to a homestay with Berber tribesmen in the Atlas Mountains. There is something for just about every traveler.

There are many different types of companies that develop and market tour packages: tour operators and wholesalers who specialized in this type of trip planning, as well as travel agencies, airlines, hotels, and cruise and rail companies. There are highly structured and organized packages called escorted tours where literally everything is included in one price. Or, for the "been there, done that" independent traveler, travel agents—with or without the help of wholesale companies—can create custom-made tours called DITs or FITs. These specialized packages can range from an extension trip of a few days with the bare minimum of elements, to a fully-organized and complex three-week trip through the Orient.

Tour packages are an easy sell because there are many benefits to the traveler: Worry-free travel, volume discounts, preferential treatment, and reliable sightseeing and professional guide service are a few examples. The primary benefit to the travel agent is the cost-effectiveness of tours. The amount of commission earned is high compared to the short period of time spent booking the tour—usually one phone call to book all elements of the tour package.

The travel agent has many resources on hand to help find out who is operating tours, when they are scheduled, where they are going, and how much they cost. Printed manuals such as the *Official Tour Directory* and *Jax Fax* are primary examples. The tour brochure itself is the most influential marketing piece when selling tours; they contain the information the client needs to make a decision and conditions of travel the counselor needs to book the tour.

Once the trip is booked, there are several methods of transmitting payment and receiving tour documentation for tours. The most common method is by agency check transmittal directly to the tour operator. The tour operator then packages the traveler's tour documents and mails them to the travel agency. Two other methods are through two ARC traffic documents: the miscellaneous charges order (MCO) and tour order. These documents are generally used to transmit payment for air and land packages.

CHAPTER REVIEW

···

True or False?

_____ 1. Business travelers represent a market for vacation packages.

_____ 2. When travel agencies develop custom-made tours for their clients, they are still paid the standard 10 percent commission from each supplier.

_____ 3. The typical adventure traveler is a young man or woman in the age range 25 to 30.

_____ 4. To maintain ecotourism, stricter controls on the number of tourists in environmentally sensitive destinations are required.

_____ 5. A mystery tour through Britain's manor houses is an example of a special-interest tour.

_____ 6. Camping, bird-watching, and wildlife safaris are all examples of hard-adventure travel.

_____ 7. An MCO can be used to transmit either a deposit or the final tour payment.

_____ 8. The *Official Tour Directory* and *Jax Fax* resources list prices for specific tours along with important booking information such as deposits and cancellation penalties.

_____ 9. A tour order can only be used for full or final payment of a tour.

_____ 10. Tour packages are only for people who do not want to travel independently.

11. Match each tour package term with the correct definition.

   A. tour operator _____ 1. Guide who is with an organized tour group throughout the entire duration of the trip.

   B. intermodal _____ 2. Company that put packages together and sells them to travel agents; they rarely sell directly to the general public.

   C. ecotour _____ 3. Popular resource for travel agencies that lists motorcoach tours and air transportation by destination.

D. ground operator _____ 4. Local specialist who joins an escorted tour group for a short time at a particular destination or region.

E. host _____ 5. Company that specializes in selling tours directly to the public or through travel agencies.

F. tour escort _____ 6. National organization of more than 600 wholesale tour operator members that promotes vacation packages within the industry.

G. tour wholesaler _____ 7. Local suppliers or coordinating companies that help operate a tour at the destination.

H. step-on guide _____ 8. Term that describes a tour that contains more than one type of transportation.

I. USTOA _____ 9. Tour that combines people's interest in nature and concern about the environment.

J. *Jax Fax* _____ 10. Person who is usually set up in the hotel lobby during scheduled hours to assist tour members with special requests, recommendations, etc.

12. Complete the MCO shown in Figure 7.17 for full payment based on the following tour and client information. Below is a cutaway section from a tour brochure featuring hotel packages in Washington, DC. Prices shown are per person, based on double occupancy. The tour operator is United Airlines.

	2 Nights	3 Nights	4 Nights
WASHINGTON, DC (BWI) UAVWAS98			
Holiday Inn Downtown			
6/15–7/4 & 9/14–10/31	475	558	641
7/5–9/13	451	522	593
11/1–12/31	423	480	537

Clients, Mr. & Mrs. Charles and Judith Smythe; hotel used on package, Holiday Inn Downtown; arrival date, September 18; departure date, September 21; tour name; "Capital Delights." United Airlines requires full payment by MCO. They have instructed you—the travel agent—to complete the MCO as follows:

- *Clients' names:* Smythe/Charles/Judith.
- *Tour no.:* UAVWAS98.
- *Type of service:* Full payment, tour package, "Capital Delights."
- *Amount boxes:* Show total cost for two.
- *To box:* United Airlines, Denver, Colorado.
- *Reservation data:* Arrival: UA (United Airlines) #124 on Sep 18.
  Departure: UA #335 on Sep 21.
- *Remarks:* Enter the confirmation number, 45578; the name of the hotel, double room with private bath (DWB), plus round-trip transfers included.

Figure 7.17

Figure 7.18 *London Package.*
TWA and Getaway are registered trademarks of Trans World Airlines, Inc.

- *"Fare/Other" and "Total" boxes:* Show full cost of land package for two.
- *Form of payment:* Check.

13. Complete a tour order based on TWA's "Majestic London" vacation package as shown in Figure 7.18, given the following passenger and reservation data:

- *Passengers:* Mr. & Mrs. Robert Woods.
- *Arrival:* Mar 10 on TWA # 115.
- *Departure:* Mar 13 on TWA # 330.
- *Tour operator:* TWA Getaway Vacations.
- *Tour code:* IT7TW16070.
- *Tour cost:* Price basic air/land package from New York. Include all fees, charges, and taxes as shown in brochure sample (Figure 7.18). The tour order is for the full price of the air/land package for two passengers.

TWA's tour reservation desk has given the following instructions to assist you in the completion of the tour order:

- Include the name "Majestic London" in the "Tour Name" box.
- Include the tour reference number in the "Tour Code" box: IT7TW16070.
- List the following tour features by completing the service coupons as follows:

  Coupon 1: London Regional Transport, London, Heathrow

  Coupon 2: (*note:* name hotel on package) London

  Coupon 3: Brit Tours and Sightseeing, London

  Coupon 4: Void

14. Complete the tour order shown in Figure 7.19.

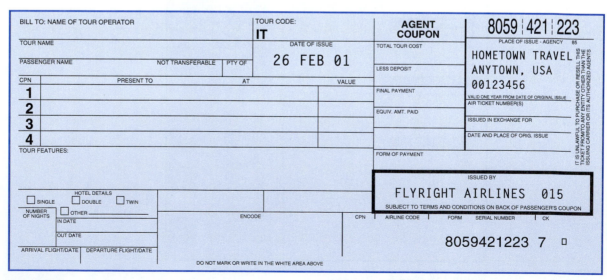

Figure 7.19

Chapter 8

Cruise Travel

Ships at a distance have every man's wish on board.

Zora Neale Hurston
(1907–1960)

Fast Forward ▼

➤ The cruise industry generates the second largest source of revenue for U.S. travel agencies after airline ticket sales. . . . 364

➤ The demographics of cruise clients in terms of age, gross income, cruise length selected, and average cruise cost may surprise you. . . . 365

➤ Believe it or not, cruises have been around for thousands of years, since the Romans crossed the Mediterranean Sea by ship to view the ancient pyramids in Egypt. . . . 366

➤ The drawing boards for cruise ships of the twenty-first century reveal some of the most fantastic and imaginative vessels ever created. Cruise industry forecasters predict that these new luxury cruise vessels will be in the 250,000-ton 5,200-passenger range. . . . 368

➤ When selling cruises you should know your bow from your stern. Know the basics of nautical talk. . . . 371

➤ Cruise travel specialists classify the majority of cruise vessels into eight categories: traditional, small luxury, masted sailing, adventure/expedition, river, barge, steamboat, and passenger freighter. . . . 374

➤ Who's cruising? People from all walks of life. We can categorize them broadly into four markets: mass, budget, upscale, and luxury. . . . 380

➤ The most appealing feature of a cruise is that it is sold as an inclusive package; but not everything is included. Find out what is and is not included in the price. . . . 383

➤ Cruise ships have anywhere between 250 and 500 crew and staff members. Some charge for their services, others do not. Some have frequent contact with passengers, others do not. Find out who's who. . . . 387

➤ The price of a cruise depends largely on where your cabin or stateroom is located, its size, and other important considerations. . . . 388

➤ Find out about what it is like to take a cruise—from dining to port lectures; swimming laps to wedding ceremonies; ice skating to rock climbing—by taking a ship tour. . . . 392

➤ The identity of the ports of call is one of the top reasons why travelers pick a cruise. You can cruise around the world, take an ice-breaker adventure in Antarctica, or sail on a luxury barge up the Thames River. There are lots of choices. . . . 397

➤ The cruise brochure is probably the leading sales tool when booking cruises. Get to know what the cruise lines are trying to say in their sales materials. . . . 408

➤ Travel sales specialists rely on a variety of resources when selling and booking cruises: the Internet, along with a variety of publications such as the *Official Steamship Guide International, Official Cruise Guide,* and the *CLIA Manual.* . . . 413

INTRODUCTION

The cruise industry is a gold mine that is virtually untapped! It's a gold mine because the cruise experience ranks highest in customer satisfaction. According to a recent travel industry survey, more than 90 percent of those people who have sailed on a cruise vacation came back totally satisfied with the experience; they would consider taking another cruise in the future. The potential for repeat cruise customers is very high compared with other types of vacation products. This gold mine is untapped because only *10 percent* of vacation travelers have taken a cruise; this leaves more than *90 percent of vacation travelers as potential cruise customers.*

Even with only 10 percent of the market share, the cruise industry generates the *second-largest source of revenue for U.S. travel agencies* after airline ticket sales. According to a survey conducted by *Travel Weekly* (Figure 8.1), cruise sales account for approximately 14 percent of total travel agency revenue; this translates into

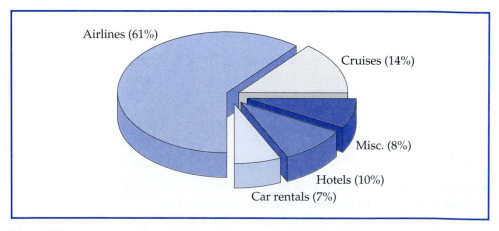

Figure 8.1 *Shares of travel agency revenues.*
(Data from Travel Weekly.*)*

more than $ .5 billion (airlines account for 61 percent of total agency revenue, with $61.2 billion). Cruises are the second-largest source of revenue right after airline sales.

Another interesting statistic shows that the majority of cruises are booked through travel agencies and not by passengers directly through the cruise lines. Figure 8.2 shows the percentage of each of four leisure products—air, accommodations, cruises, and car rentals—that is booked through travel agencies. Compared to all other products, the majority of cruises, approximately 95 percent, are booked through travel professionals. Because of the wide variety of different types of cruises, itineraries, and prices, people need to rely on professionals for guidance and recommendations when selecting cruises.

Who takes cruises? The answer may surprise you. Many people think that a cruise vacation is only for the very old and very rich; nothing can be further from the truth. The demographics or standard profiles of cruise clients and what they buy appear below:

- *Age*
    | 18–34 | 37% |
    | 34–54 | 25% |
    | 55+ | 38% |

- *Gross household income*
    | Under $15K | 20% |
    | $15K–28K | 28% |
    | $28K + | 52% |

- *Cruise length selected*
    | 1–5 days | 23% |
    | 6–8 days | 61% |
    | 9–17 days | 15% |
    | 18+ days | 1% |

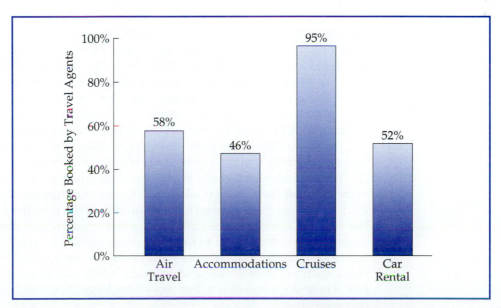

Figure 8.2 *Percentage of four leisure products booked through travel agencies.*

- *Average cruise cost*

  Low $100 per day
  High $800 + per day
  Average $200–250 per day

More than one-third of all cruise clients are under 34 years of age; the great majority of them, approximately 64 percent, are under 54 years of age. Approximately half of all cruise clients have a gross household income of under $28,000, and the average cruise cost is between $200 and $250 per passenger per day. The majority of cruise vacations taken, 61 percent, are one week in length.

So take a vacation product that is the second-leading revenue generator for travel agencies, coupled with a vast untapped market, and you have a very important vacation product that plays a major role in the huge travel and tourism industry. In this chapter we familiarize you with all of the important aspects of selling cruise vacations: from basic nautical terminology to shipboard life, world itineraries, and key resources that can help you market and sell cruises effectively to future clients.

A Look Back

How long have cruise vacations been around? Did they have cruises a hundred years ago? Two hundred or more? Believe it or not, cruises have been around for thousands of years, since the Romans crossed the Mediterranean Sea by ship to view the ancient pyramids in Egypt.

But don't imagine that sea voyages have always been luxurious and carefree. Since ancient times, sea travel had been dangerous, perilous, and something that people didn't look forward to. Passenger travel by ship started in earnest during the late eighteenth and early nineteenth centuries. During this era, millions of people left Europe to settle in such places as the United States, Canada, and Australia. During the same period, a growing number of people made the same journeys for business and trading. It was also at this time that wealthy people took similar journeys for pleasure.

The advent of the steam engine in the early nineteenth century made sea travel safer, faster, and more comfortable. This era spawned such famous ship companies as Cunard, which is still operating today, making it one of the longest-operating passenger ship companies in the world. This period in sailing history witnessed a race for supremacy of the seas. The year 1897 marked the beginning of a race to build the biggest, fastest, and most elegant passenger vessels afloat. The starting gun of this race resounded when the ship *Kaiser Wilhelm der Grosse*, built in Germany, became the world's most modern and luxurious ship. Competitors from England, France, and the United States followed with fast, luxurious liners: notably Great Britain's *Lusitania*, *Mauretania*, and the doomed *Titanic*, which sank on its maiden voyage after hitting an iceberg.

With the advent of World War I, these beautiful passenger ships were stripped of their luxuries and configured to carry troops and supplies. Practically all transatlantic passenger traffic ceased for the duration of the war, from 1914 to 1918. After the war the United States curtailed foreign immigration dramatically, and the transatlantic steamers had to find new passengers. The late 1920s and throughout the 1930s heralded not only the most luxurious but also the biggest transatlantic ships, such as the *Ile de France* and Cunard's famous *Queen Mary* and *Queen Elizabeth*. These ships and others like them were large, fast, and luxurious, with no expenses spared.

During World War II, many of these superliners, such as the *Queen Elizabeth*,

Cruise Travel Milestones

1819	*Savannah:* Advent of steam travel to transatlantic liners.
1840	Samuel Cunard begins transatlantic passenger service.
1858	Largest passenger ship built as a steam and sailing vessel: SS *Great Eastern,* with five smokestacks, six sailing masts, and measuring nearly 700 feet long.
1897	*Kaiser Wilhelm der Grosse:* most modern steamship of the day and most luxurious.
1907	Two passenger liners, *Lusitania* and *Mauretania,* launched first use of steam turbine engines, which heralds the great age of transatlantic luxury crossing.
1927	Luxury liner, *Ile de France,* launched: the largest and fastest ship to date.
1931	*Normandie* built as the most elegant transatlantic liner of the era.
1940	*Queen Elizabeth I* launched as largest transatlantic liner of all time.
1948	*Caronia* is the first ocean liner built for cruising.
1958	For the first time, more people cross the Atlantic by air than by ship.
1965	The *Oceanic* is the first ship to be launched as a cruise ship. At 1,600 maximum berths, she is the largest for cruising.
1966	Norwegian Caribbean Line begins service with the futuristic *Sunward* to the Bahamas, the true beginning of modern-day cruises.
1988	*Sovereign of the Seas,* largest cruise ship ever built—2,600 passengers at 73,200 tons—does one-week cruises in Caribbean.
1996	Carnival Cruise Line's *Destiny* begins service. At 101,000 tons, she is the largest passenger cruise ship breaking the 100,000-ton barrier.
1998	Princess Cruises launches the *Grand Princess,* 109,000 tons with a 2,600-passenger capacity.
1999	Royal Caribbean International launches the first of its enormous Eagle-class ships, called *Voyager of the Seas,* at more than 142,000 tons with a capacity of approximately 3,200 passengers.

spent their early years as camouflaged war ships. They didn't start transatlantic service until after the war. Up until 1948, all passenger vessels were designed primarily for transatlantic crossings. A transatlantic crossing was designed to do just that—to get passengers from point A to point B as quickly and comfortably as possible. These early liners were based on a strict on-board class system. The price you paid for your ticket determined where you were allowed to eat, sleep, and walk on deck and which passenger facilities and services were available.

A cruise is a different experience from a transatlantic trip. It is not only a form of transportation but a way to see new destinations and do some sightseeing along the way. Also, cruise ships are truly a classless society—they offer just one class of service. All passengers, from the least expensive to the most expensive cruise fare, share the same passenger facilities and services.

The first ship that was actually designed to operate cruises was the *Caronia,* which offered lengthy cruises around the world. Other ships soon followed, offering both shorter and longer cruises to worldwide ports of call.

The death knell of the luxurious transatlantic liners was the advent of the jet age. People were now able to cross the Atlantic in seven hours rather than seven days and at a fraction of the cost. In 1958, for the first time, more people crossed the Atlantic by air than by ship. Most shipline companies had to renovate their current ships or build new vessels for the emerging cruise market.

In 1966, Norwegian Caribbean Cruise Line [the name has been changed to Norwegian Cruise Line (NCL)] was formed as the first company that offered cruises exclusively. NCL began service with the futuristic *Sunward,* which sailed three- and four-day cruises to the Bahamas; this was another milestone in the development of the cruise vacation as we know it today.

Throughout the 1960s and 1970s, cruise travel flourished. New cruise line companies, such as the Royal Caribbean Cruise Line (the name has been changed to Royal Caribbean International) and Carnival Cruise Line, were formed and operated regularly scheduled cruises to such places as the Caribbean and Mexico.

An important benchmark in cruise travel occurred in 1988 when Royal Caribbean International (RCI) introduced the first megaship, *Sovereign of the Seas.* This was the first ship of what were later to be called Sovereign-class ships. Nothing like it had been built since the *Queen Mary* and *Queen Elizabeth* of the 1930s. The ship was enormous; it was more than 73,000 gross registered tons and carried 2,600 passengers on one-week cruises through the Caribbean. This was the beginning of the megaship era: ships that top more than 65,000 tons.

After the 1980s, cruise vessels just got bigger and bigger. During the 1990s the 100,000-ton barrier was broken by the three largest cruise companies: Carnival Cruise Lines, Princess Cruises, and Royal Caribbean International. Carnival was the first to top the 100,000-ton record with the inauguration of the *Destiny* in 1996. In 1998, Princess Cruises introduced the *Grand Princess* at approximately 105,000 tons. This ship is so big that the entire *Pacific Princess,* the original Love Boat itself, can fit inside the *Grand Princess*'s dining and lido deck areas!

In 1999, Royal Caribbean International broke all records with the *Voyager of the Seas,* the largest cruise ship in the world. The first of three 3,200-passenger Eagle-class ships, the *Voyager* weighs more than 142,000 tons.

As you can see, the sayings "Less is more" and "Good things come in small packages" do not apply to cruise travel today.

Web Link *Floating Palaces of the Past:* From the ill-fated *Normandie* to the experiences of a young child aboard the legendary *Queen Mary,* revisit the great Atlantic liners—find out about their history, art, and the people who made them great. Additional links to discussion groups, photographic archives and ports of call. Go to *http://www.uncommonjourneys. com/pages/.*

Sailing into the New Millennium

The drawing boards for cruise ships of the twenty-first century reveal some of the most fantastic and imaginative vessels ever created. Cruise industry forecasters predict that these new luxury cruise vessels will be in the 250,000-ton 5,200-passenger range. They are so large that they are more like floating resort islands that move through the water than ships. There are two very interesting projects on the drawing boards for the near future: *Phoenix–World City* and *SWATH.*

➤ Phoenix World City

The *World City* (originally called the *Phoenix;* see Figure 8.3) initiated by Norwegian Caribbean Cruise Line, has since been spun off. If it is ever built, this futuristic vessel will be almost a quarter of a mile long and 100 yards wide, with three separate hotel-like towers supported by a catamaran-style hull. Each resort tower

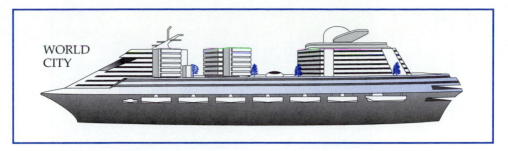

Figure 8.3 *Futuristic vessel* World City.

would house tropical gardens, parks, promenades, cafes, and a four-pool lagoon with palm trees and a real sand beach.

➤ The SWATH Project

Some futuristic designers think that the *SWATH* (small waterplane area twin hull) design shows great promise. A SWATH vessel will be very fast and ultra-stable, built on a platform lifted above the water by struts attached to two submerged pontoons that provide the vessel's buoyancy (see Figure 8.4). The Swath design is not new. In 1992, Radisson Seven Seas Cruises introduced the *Radisson Diamond*, a small luxury cruise ship of approximately 350 passengers of unique double-hulled catamaran construction.

The SWATH cruise ship of the future is projected to be approximately 500 feet long and 200 feet wide, to accommodate a minimum of 2,000 passengers. A key feature of the futuristic SWATH vessel is a huge central recreational area of over 30,000 square feet. This outdoor court would be sheltered on three sides by 1,000 passenger cabins, many of which would have private balconies facing the central recreational area and the ocean. The center area would house cafés, gardens, a large swimming pool, a surfing beach, squash courts, escalators, and a water slide. Also in the plans are underwater and celestial observatories. A detachable surfing platform would be linked to the stern or back of the vessel by twin towing rods. This platform can be used for sailboating and for small launch services (see Figure 8.5).

Figure 8.4 *Today's SWATH design: Radisson Seven Seas Cruises'* Radisson Diamond, *20,295 tons, 350 passengers.*

Figure 8.5 *Extending the principle, future SWATHs might include separate deployable harbors.*

Will futuristic floating resorts such as *World City*, SWATH, or similar projects become a reality? Industry forecasters say yes, and probably in the not-too-distant future.

✓ Check Your Understanding 8-1

1. Briefly discuss two reasons why cruise travel is one of the highest sources of revenue for travel agencies.

    A. _____

    B. _____

2. Briefly discuss the demographics or standard profiles of typical cruise travelers in terms of age, gross income, cruise length selected, and average daily cost.

    _____

    _____

3. Name one of the oldest passenger ship companies in the world that still operates cruises and transatlantic crossings.

    _____

4. The majority of passengers on early transatlantic crossings in the late nineteenth and early twentieth centuries were _____.

5. The late 1920s and the 1930s saw the birth of not only the most luxurious but also the biggest transatlantic ships. Name two luxurious transatlantic liners that operated during this period.

    A. _____   B. _____

6. What event in the mid-twentieth century doomed many large transatlantic liners?

    _____

7. Explain the major difference between a cruise experience and a transatlantic crossing:

    _____

8. What did all newly built cruise ships have in common during the 1990s?

_____

9. Cruise ships of today are truly a classless society. Explain what that means.

_____

10. SWATH is an example of a futuristic design in cruise ships. A version of it exists today. Name the cruise company and the ship that it operates that has a double-hull design.

_____

Ahoy There: Do You Know Your Port from Your Aft?

When you visit a foreign country it's nice to be able to speak the language of that country. If you don't, the next best thing is to know a few key words and phrases in order to make yourself understood. This also applies when you sell cruises to clients and even when you are on a cruise as a passenger. It sounds so much more professional to tell your clients that their cabin is located **starboard amidships** rather than on the right side of the ship toward the middle. Or that the dining room is located in the *stern* rather than in the back end of the ship. Here are some basics in nautical talk that people who *sell* cruises and people who *take* cruises should know!

➤ Deck and Location Terms [Figure 8.6]

1. *Hull:* the frame and body of the ship; that part of the vessel that rests in the water.
2. *Superstructure:* the part of the ship above the hull.
3. *Main deck:* the longest deck on the ship; separates the hull and the superstructure.
4. *Weather deck:* any deck open to the outside.
5. *Boat deck:* the deck where the lifeboats are located.
6. *Bridge:* navigational and command center of the ship.
7. *Center of gravity:* the fulcrum or balancing point in the ship; located at the point where a vertical and a horizontal line are each drawn through the middle of the ship.

➤ Directional Terms [Figure 8.7]

1. *Bow:* the front part of the ship. Example: *"Cabin 602 is located in the bow."*
2. *Forward:* toward or in the front (bow) of the ship. Example: *"The passenger cabins are located forward of the lobby."*

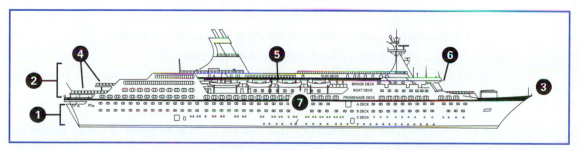

Figure 8.6

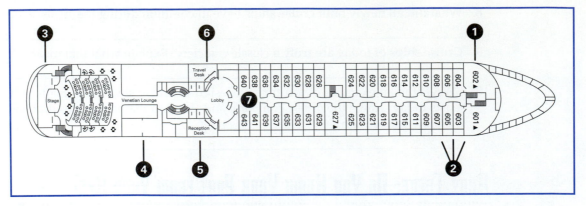

Figure 8.7

3. **Stern:** the back end of the ship. Example: *"The stage is located in the stern."*

4. **Aft:** toward or in the rear (stern) of the ship. Example: *"The Venetian Lounge is located aft of the lobby."*

5. **Starboard:** the right side of the ship when facing toward the bow. Example: *"The reception desk is located on the starboard side on the ocean deck."*

6. **Port:** the left side of the ship when facing the bow. Example: *"The travel desk is located on the portside on the ocean deck."*

7. **Amidships (or midships):** in or toward the middle of the ship. Example: *"The lobby is located amidships on the ocean deck."*

➤ More Nautical Terms

- **Berth:** (1) a bed in a ship's cabin; (2) the location at the pier where a ship docks.
- **Cabin** (*stateroom*): a passenger's accommodation on board ship.
- **Debark** (*disembark*): to get off or exit a ship.
- **Deck:** any floor on a ship, inside or out.
- **Deck plan:** a blueprint or a floor plan of a ship's design.
- **Embark:** to get on board a ship.
- **Galley:** a ship's kitchen.
- **Hold:** interior space below a ship's main deck for storage or cargo, where passengers are not allowed.
- **Leeward:** the side of a ship facing away from the wind.
- **Manifest:** a list or invoice of a ship's passengers, crew, and cargo.
- **Pitch:** the front-to-back (bow-to-stern) motion of a ship.
- **Porthole:** round window or opening on the side of a ship.
- **Quay** (*pronounced key*): a berth, dock, or pier.
- **Registry:** the country with whose laws a ship and its crew are obliged to comply.
- **Roll:** the side-to-side motion of a ship.
- **Stabilizers:** finlike devices that extend from both sides of a ship below the waterline to provide a more stable ride.

- *Tender:* a small vessel, sometimes a ship's lifeboat, used to ferry passengers to shore when the ship is at anchor.
- *Windward:* the side of a ship facing into the wind.

✓ Check Your Understanding 8-2

1. The deck plan of a ship is shown in Figure 8.8 (front of vessel facing right). It shows cabin numbers and other passenger areas. Describe the location of the cabins and facilities listed below by filling in the blanks. Choose from the following terms: aft, amidships, port, bow, stern, starboard, forward.

   A. Cabin 5010 is located _____ or in the _____ section.

   B. The Oklahoma Lounge is located _____ or in the _____.

   C. The Photo Gallery is located _____ of the Can Can Lounge.

   D. The Schooner Bar is located on the _____ side of the ship.

   E. The Can Can Lounge is located in the middle of the ship or _____.

   F. Cabins 5078 and 5076 are located on the _____ side of the ship.

   G. You just rode the elevator (or lift) and are now facing the back of the Can Can Lounge. To find the Conference Center located on this deck, you walk _____ (forward or aft).

2. Match each nautical term with the correct definition on the right.

   A. deck _____   1. To get on board a ship.

   B. stabilizers _____   2. Navigational and command center of a ship.

   C. bridge _____   3. Any floor on a ship.

   D. center of gravity _____   4. Country with whose laws a ship and crew are obliged to comply.

   E. debark _____   5. Side-to-side motion of a ship.

   F. registry _____   6. To get off or exit a ship.

   G. quay _____   7. The fulcrum or balancing point in the middle of a ship.

   H. galley _____   8. Ship's kitchen.

   I. tender _____   9. Blueprint of a ship's design.

   J. pitch _____   10. Longest deck on a ship; separates the hull and superstructure.

   K. leeward _____   11. Small vessel that transports passengers between ship and shore.

   L. roll _____   12. Berth, dock, or pier.

   M. windward _____   13. Front-to-back motion of a ship.

   N. embark _____   14. Side of a ship opposite the direction from which the wind blows.

   O. main deck _____   15. Finlike devices mounted on a ship's hull that provide a smooth ride.

   P. deck plan _____   16. Side of a ship facing the direction from which the wind blows.

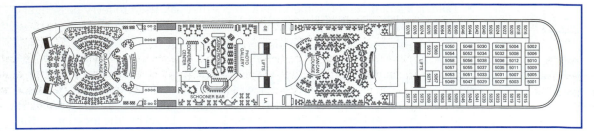

Figure 8.8

Who's Who

There are many different kinds of cruise experiences; from the conventional cruise ship that is like a floating resort to a much smaller, intimate, and slow-moving passenger barge meandering through Europe's inland waterways. There are ships that cater to every income level and interest. Some appeal to the mass market—people representing a wide spectrum of tastes, styles, interests, and income levels. Others target a specific type of traveler, called a niche market.

Ships come in all sizes and shapes. Many of today's newly built ships are so big that they are called *super megaships*. They average between 100,000 and 142,000 tons and can accommodate up to 3,800 passengers. Others are small and yachtlike in appearance and hold no more than a few dozen people. Some cruises last a day or two only, others last for months.

Ships are designed differently. Some ships resemble floating cities with multitiered shopping malls, pools, and health spas, and some even have a mini-golf course on the top deck! Others are tall-masted schooners where passengers can help sail the vessel, or small, intimate luxury barges that offer gourmet food and the best wines.

With all these choices, how do you match the client with the best cruise? To make a successful match, you need to know as much as you can about your clients: who is traveling—a single person, a couple, a family? What are their ages? Where do they want to go? What do they want to do? Have they cruised before? Next, you need to know as much as you can about the various cruise ships: What are they like? What do they offer? How much do they cost?

In this section we first take a look at *what's sailing*—a sampling of the various types of cruise experiences or cruise categories from which to choose. Then we study *who's cruising*—the types of people who go on cruises.

➤ What's Sailing

A destination visited by two different types of ships can result in two dramatically different cruise experiences. Leading cruise resources have classified the majority of cruises into eight categories:

1. *Traditional cruise ships.* Traditional cruise vessels are categorized by their size, accommodations, passenger facilities, and services. On-board characteristics vary from ship to ship. These voyages are vessel-oriented trips in which the ship and all the amenities it provides are the main focus of the cruise experience. Standard cruise ships are designed to be resorts at sea with all the amenities found in any deluxe land-based resort. The great majority of passenger ships belong to this category. Vessel tonnages range from 15,000 to 142,000 tons, with passenger capacities from 300 to 3,800. Traditional cruises appeal to a broad range of passengers and average four to ten days in length; the most popular is the one-week cruise. The atmosphere on board varies from ship to ship. Some stress a lot of activity and nonstop entertainment; others offer a more quiet and relaxing mood.

Examples: *Carnival Cruise Lines, Celebrity Cruises, Costa Cruise Lines, Cunard, Disney Cruise Line, Holland America Line, Norwegian Cruise Line, Princess Cruises, Royal Caribbean International* (see Figure 8.9).

2. *Small luxury ships.* Yacht-style vessels are smaller versions of larger cruise ships. They are designed to carry fewer passengers and provide a more intimate and pampered experience. They have the same facilities and amenities as their larger counterparts but on a smaller and more intimate scale. Typically, all cabins are outside accommodations with windows; many have private verandahs. Passengers who select this style of cruising expect spacious and elegant staterooms, gourmet food and wines, and top-notch service. Vessel tonnage is less than 15,000, with cabins for 50 to 300 passengers.

Examples: *Cunard Sea Goddess, Seabourn Cruise Line, Radisson Seven Seas Cruises, Silversea Cruises* (see Figure 8.10).

3. *Masted sailing ships.* This type of vessel is for those who want to recreate what sailing was all about in earlier times—to feel the wind in their faces and the roll of the sea under their feet. Modern-day sailing offers diverse experiences, encompassing everything from large, super-deluxe ships with computerized sails to small, privately owned schooners. Popular sailing experiences called *barefoot windjammers* allow passengers to participate actively in sailing the ship if they

Figure 8.9 *Traditional cruise ship: Princess Cruises'* Grand Princess.

Figure 8.10 *Luxury small cruise ship: Seabourn Cruise Line's* Seabourn Pride.

want to. Masted sailing ships range in size from 65 to 620 feet and range in service from very basic to the very luxurious. Capacities range from 12 to 430 passengers.

   Examples: *Star Clippers, Windjammer Barefoot Cruises, Windstar Cruises* (see Figure 8.11).

4. *Adventure/expedition cruises.* Travelers choose these types of cruises on the basis of ports of call visited rather than the ship itself; they don't usually provide the wide range of passenger amenities and entertainment that traditional cruises offer. Adventure and expedition cruises visit out-of-the-way and more exotic destinations such as the continent of Antarctica or the Galápagos Islands, a wildlife refuge located hundreds of miles off the coast of South America. People who take these types of cruises are part of the "been there, done that" crowd—looking for new and exciting experiences and learning about the places visited. That is why

Figure 8.11 *Masted sailing ship: Windstar Cruises'* Windsong.

Figure 8.12 *Adventure/expedition ship: Clipper Cruise Line's Clipper Adventurer.*

these cruises will have a naturalist, historian, or other expert on board to provide lectures and lead field trips: The emphasis is on education rather than recreation.

Examples: *Clipper Cruise Line, Special Expeditions* (see Figure 8.12).

5. *River ships.* River vessels are small ships designed to sail the world's inland waterways of rivers and canals. River boats are probably the most diverse of small ships. Passengers consider river ships as a means of transportation rather than a floating resort. Although comfortable, river ships do not have the wide range of resortlike amenities and features that other standard cruise ships offer. Passenger capacities range from 22 to 175 passengers. A river cruise can be on a modern, streamlined vessel meandering slowly along the Rhine River in Germany, passing by romantic castles and medieval towns. It can also be an adventure trip up the Nile River in a floating hotel to discover the mysteries of ancient Egypt. River cruises have widespread appeal, but generally target those who are looking for a more culturally enriching and educational trip at a leisurely pace.

Examples: *Abercrombie & Kent, EuroCruises, KD River Cruises of Europe* (see Figure 8.13).

Figure 8.13 *Peter Dielmann American River Cruises' MV Mozart.*

Figure 8.14 *Deluxe luxury passenger barge docked in Amsterdam, the Netherlands.*

6. *Barges.* Passenger barges are very small flat-bottom, narrow-beam vessels designed to slowly cruise inland waterways and canals of the world. A canal cruise can be on a luxury barge that highlights gourmet cuisine and a wide assortment of wines while traveling through the wine-and-chateaux region of France. Another popular itinerary is a historical but leisurely venture up and down the Thames River in England. Barge cruises can be as short as overnight or up to ten days in length. Capacity ranges from four to twelve passengers.

Examples: *Abercrombie & Kent, European Waterways, French Country Waterways, Ltd.* (see Figure 8.14).

7. *Steamboats.* A unique and nostalgic type of river boat, steamboats evoke the days of Mark Twain and the old paddlewheelers. These vessels are designed with shallow bottoms and high ceilings. Many are appointed with a Victorian-like ambiance complete with chandeliers, polished wood interiors, plush carpeting, and gleaming brass fixtures. Steamboats are generally used for scenery and historic tours. Some of the smaller steamboat companies offer gambling on inland waterways. Many paddlewheel ships offer full on-board facilities and amenities that a standard cruise ship offers. Capacity is up to 450 passengers.

Example: *Delta Queen Steamboat Company* (see Figure 8.15).

8. *Passenger freighters.* Some cargo vessels offer accommodations for cruise passengers. These vessels have some—if not all—resortlike amenities that are found on traditional ships and many offer surprisingly high levels of passenger comfort. The atmosphere is unstructured and flexible, with a lot of passenger space. The average passenger capacity is twelve but can range from as few as four to a maximum of sixty passengers. Trips on passenger freighters are longer in length than a typical cruise; they average between 18 and 21 days. Since accommodations are limited on these vessels, reservations are required far in advance.

Examples: *Ivaran Lines* (deluxe passenger freighter), *Freighter World Cruises Incorporated* (represents various lines) (see Figure 8.16).

Key Point ➤ *How Big Is Big?* A ship's size is measured in **gross registered tons (GRT)**. Regardless of what the name implies, GRT is not a measurement of weight. It is a measurement of interior space available and accessible to passengers on board the ship: *1 GRT is 100 cubic feet of enclosed revenue space within a ship.* The best way to measure the amount of

Figure 8.15 *Steamboat cruise: Delta Queen Steamboat Company's* Mississippi Queen *(foreground) and* Delta Queen.

Figure 8.16 *Passenger freighter: Ivaran Lines' MV* Americana.

elbowroom or passenger space is to calculate the ship's *space ratio*. This will tell you how much space is occupied by one passenger if a full complement of passengers is sailing:

$$\text{space ratio} = \text{GRT} \div \text{standard passenger capacity}$$

For example, Carnival Cruise Line's *Destiny* has a GRT of 101,000; standard passenger capacity is 2,642.

$$\text{Space ratio} = 101,000 \div 2,642 = 38$$

A Space Ratio of:	Is:
Below 20	Below average (very crowded)
21–28	Average
29–38	Spacious
38 +	Yachtlike

➤ Who's Sailing?

The best way to put this all in perspective is to find out what type of traveler is attracted to what type of cruise. To be a matchmaker, you not only have to identify different categories of cruise ships but also to categorize people. We do this through demographics—the statistical study of populations with reference to such things as age, budgets, marital status, special interests, and hobbies, for example.

One word of caution: It is difficult to categorize people, their likes and dislikes, let alone all of the different types of cruise ships available to sell. Practically every ship can satisfy passengers fitting every demographic profile. Also, people can't be neatly pigeonholed; we all have contradictory tastes and interests. It is not unusual to enjoy both contemporary rock music and classical music at the same time or to find bungy jumping and bird-watching equally satisfying.

Who's cruising? Cruise passengers are people from all walks of life: lawyers, software programmers, doctors, corporate executives, engineers, actors, farmers, and college students—traveling as singles, couples, families, and in groups.

Where does each one fit? To simplify matters, you can divide all potential cruise passengers into four general demographic groups: budget, mass market, upscale, and luxury. Each category is briefly described with an average cost per day per person, along with a sample of cruise line companies that target that particular market. It should be noted here that money is not the only criterion when selecting a cruise. Some clients would spend many thousands of dollars to go on a once-in-a-lifetime adventure cruise to Antarctica but would never dream of spending the same amount of money for a traditional cruise through the Caribbean.

1. *Mass market.* These are the traditional ships that cater to a broad range of passenger types: couples, singles, families, and seniors looking for a typical cruise vacation. In general, these travelers work and have the traditional two weeks vacation per year. They have saved up for a vacation and are looking for value for their money. They are somewhere within the middle-class income level.

- Average cruise cost per day per person: $200–250
- Cruise line examples: *Carnival Cruise Lines, Costa Cruise Lines, Royal Caribbean International, Norwegian Cruise Line (NCL)*

2. *Budget market.* These ships cater to those who want to take a cruise but at the same price they would pay on a discounted land-based hotel package. Usually, these people are first-time cruisers looking to spend one week or less on their vacation.

- Average cruise cost per day per person: $100–150
- Cruise line examples: *Premier Cruise Lines, Windjammer Barefoot Cruises*

3. *Upscale market.* These ships target those who travel frequently and have sophisticated tastes and judgment as to what to expect. Money is not a primary concern as long as these travelers receive good value for the money spent. Generally in the upper-middle-class income level.

- Average cost per day per person: $300–500
- Cruise line examples: *Princess Cruises, Holland America Line, Celebrity, Cunard QEII*

4. *Luxury market.* These ships cater to those travelers who want the very best and where price is no object. They expect excellent service, gourmet food, the very best wine selections, and individual pampering.

- Average cost per day per person: $500+
- Cruise line examples: *Radisson Seven Seas Cruises, Crystal Cruises, Silversea Cruises, Seabourn Cruise Line, Cunard Sea Goddess, Windstar Cruises*

Table 8.1 is an at-a-glance reference chart that lists representative cruise lines with the following descriptive categories: cruise category, price range, passenger category, and type. A word of caution: *This chart is a general guide only.* For example, every cruise line company listed will certainly attract a broad range of passenger types (e.g., singles, families, couples, etc.). If one or more target groups are checked, that means that the cruise line markets and wants to attract that specific type of passenger. If a cruise line markets evenly for all types of passengers, no target group is indicated on the chart.

✓ Check Your Understanding 8-3

1. For each cruise company listed below, indicate the classification by letter: T, traditional cruise ship; L, luxury small ship; A, adventure/expedition; R, river or canal ship; S, steamboat; M, masted sailing ship; P, passenger freighter.

A. Carnival Cruise Line	____	H. Norwegian Cruise Line	____
B. Delta Queen Steamboat Co.	____	I. Abercrombie & Kent	____
C. Seabourn Cruise Line	____	J. Special Expeditions	____
D. Star Clipper	____	K. Royal Caribbean International	____
E. Ivaran Lines	____		
F. Clipper Cruise Line	____	L. Cunard Sea Goddess	____
G. Windstar Cruises	____		

Company Mergers: Who Owns Whom?

We live in an era where consolidations and company mergers are commonplace, and the cruise industry is no exception. A prime example is *Carnival Corporation*, the parent company of Carnival Cruise Lines, which has acquired over the past years *Holland America Line, Costa Cruise Lines, Windstar Cruises, Cunard Line,* and a 50 percent share of *Seabourn Cruise Line.* Another big player in the merger arena is *Royal Caribbean International,* which recently bought *Celebrity Cruises.* However, these mergers are virtually "invisible" to the consumer; each cruise line that was acquired by a larger one keeps its name, identity, level of service, and target market. For example, the Carnival Cruise ships are mass market, while the *Windstar* and *Seabourn* ships that it owns continue to be identified and sold to the upscale and luxury markets, respectively.

TABLE 8.1 CRUISE LINES SUMMARY

CRUISE LINE	SHIP CATEGORY	PRICE[a]	PASSENGER CATEGORY	Singles	Families	Seniors	Adventurers
Abercrombie & Kent	River and canal	$$$	Upscale				●
American Hawaii Cruises	Traditional	$$	Mass market			●	
Carnival Cruise Line	Traditional	$$	Mass market	●			
Celebrity Cruises	Traditional	$$$	Upscale				
Clipper Cruise Line	Adventure and expedition	$$$	Upscale				●
Costa Cruise Lines	Traditional	$$–$$$	Mass market				
Crystal Cruises	Traditional	$$$$	Upscale to luxury			●	
Cunard: *Queen Elizabeth II*	Traditional	$$$$	Upscale			●	
Cunard Royal Viking	Traditional	$$$$	Upscale			●	
Cunard Sea Goddess	Traditional	$$$$$	Luxury			●	
Delta Queen Steamboat Co.	River/steamboat	$$$	Mass market to upscale				●
Disney Cruise Line	Traditional	$–$$	Budget to mass market		●		
Holland America Line	Traditional	$$$	Upscale			●	
KD River Cruises of Europe	River and canal	$–$$	Budget to mass market				
Norwegian Cruise Line (NCL)	Traditional	$$–$$$	Mass market		●		
Premier Cruise Lines	Traditional	$	Budget market		●		
Princess Cruises	Traditional	$$$–$$$$	Upscale				
Radisson Seven Seas Cruises	Traditional and expedition	$$$$–$$$$$	Upscale to luxury				
Renaissance Cruises	Traditional	$$$$–$$$$$	Upscale to luxury				
Royal Caribbean International (RCI)	Traditional	$$–$$$	Mass market				
Seabourn Cruise Line	Traditional	$$$$$	Luxury				
Silversea Cruises	Traditional	$$$$–$$$$$	Upscale to luxury				
Special Expeditions	Expedition	$$$$	Upscale				●
Star Clippers	Masted schooner	$$$	Upscale				●
Windjammer Barefoot Cruises	Masted schooner	$–$$	Budget to mass market	●			●
Windstar Cruises	Masted schooner	$$$$	Upscale				●

[a]*Price key (average cost per person per day): $, = under $200; $$, = $201–$300; $$$, = $301–$400; $$$$, = $401–$600; $$$$$, = $600+.*

2. For each client description, which of the following types of cruises or vessels would you suggest: traditional cruise, river or canal cruise, adventure/expedition, masted sailing ship?

A. a young couple who have never cruised before and aren't sure if cruising is for them   _____

B. a well-traveled retired couple, who want to travel off the beaten path and to learn about new places and cultures at a leisurely pace   _____

C. a young couple who want an informal cruise experience to more exotic ports and where they can even help to sail the ship   _____

D. a well-traveled, "done that, been there" sort of person who is looking for excitement and something totally different   _____

3. Name one cruise line company that targets for:

A. family-oriented travel   _____

B. luxury where price is no object   _____

C. river cruises within the United States   _____

D. tall masted schooners in the upscale or luxury range   _____

E. traditional cruises for a wide cross section of travelers   _____

F. strictly budget   _____

CRUISE PRICES AND DISCOUNTS

There are aspects of cruising that are totally different from any other type of vacation. The most appealing feature of a cruise is that the vessel itself provides practically everything that a land-based vacation offers: accommodations, dining, entertainment, recreation, sports, and a full range of passenger services. The travel professional must be able to clarify to clients what features are included and what features are not included in the price of the cruise package.

► Air/Sea Packages: Becoming the Exception and Not the Rule?

Until recently, most cruise companies offered "free air" as part of the all-inclusive cruise vacation. They called these combination cruise vacations **air/sea packages**. Air/sea packages include round-trip air, transportation by motorcoach between the airport and ship, and transfer of luggage to and from the ship. Of course, nothing is actually *free*. Cruise companies were able to bundle air costs into their cruise fares at drastically discounted rates since they provided airlines with large volumes of business.

A growing number of cruise lines no longer offer the traditional air/sea package. Due to the increasing difficulty of getting rock-bottom prices from the airlines, many cruise lines have stopped including air transportation costs in the total price of an air/sea package. Many now charge "cruise-only" prices and sell air transportation as **air add-ons**. Passengers have a choice of purchasing the air transportation from the cruise line or on their own.

The price of the air add-on is calculated from the passenger's gateway city and printed in the cruise line's brochure. If the passenger buys the air add-on, transfers and baggage handling are included. If the passenger purchases air independently, he or she can usually buy airport transfers directly from the cruise lines. The availability of inclusive air/sea packages or air add-ons should be checked ship to ship.

➤ What Is and Is Not Included

An attractive feature of a cruise vacation is that practically everything is paid for up-front. This is a major reason why cruise travel has the highest percentage of customer satisfaction among all types of vacation experiences. With the exception of airline add-ons, **pre- and postcruise land tours,** port charges (taxes levied by each **port of call** or destination where the ship visits), and other items, practically everything is prepaid, so the client knows exactly how much money to bring for the extras; there will be no unhappy surprises such as money running out midway through the vacation because of expenses the traveler did not anticipate.

Here's a quick synopsis of what is and is not included in the price of the cruise package:

Included	*Not Included*
• Accommodations	• Liquor/soft drinks
• Meals (on board)	• Shore excursions
• Entertainment	• On-board shops
• Recreational facilities	• Beauty parlor/barbershop
• Tips (included on some ships)	• On-board spa: massage, etc.
• Soft drinks at meals	• Laundry/dry cleaning
	• Medical services
	• Port charges or taxes
	• Tips (most ships do not include)

➤ A Superior Value

Cruise vacations have the highest percentage of customer satisfaction because they are totally inclusive. The average cost for a cruise **per diem** (per day) is between $200 and $250 per person. This may seem expensive, but when you consider all that is included—accommodations, meals, and entertainment—a cruise vacation offers high value for the money.

To illustrate the value of a cruise vacation to clients, cruise specialists often compare a typical seven-day Caribbean cruise vacation with a comparable seven-day Caribbean land-based resort vacation. The prices used in the comparison shown in Table 8.2 are based on average prices between a mass-market ship and a comparable land resort located on the island of St. Maarten. Prices are based on two adults traveling from St. Louis for seven nights during winter (peak), the most expensive time of year.

➤ Cruise Prices: Who Pays Sticker Prices Anymore?

The full advertised cost of a cruise depends on two major factors: departure date and cabin category. The price printed in a general cruise brochure is like the sticker price of a car: It is established by the manufacturer and is based on such things as the model and the options that are included.

When you are shopping for a car, how often do you pay the sticker price? Very rarely. There are "end-of-year" bargains, trade-in discounts, and lots of other reasons why you rarely pay the full advertised price for a new car. You can say the same thing for cruises. Paying the full advertised price for a cruise is be-

TABLE 8.2 COST COMPARISON: TYPICAL CARIBBEAN CRUISE VACATION (WITH AIR ADD-ON) VERSUS TYPICAL RESORT VACATION[a]

	CRUISE VACATION	LAND-BASED RESORT
Base price	$2,000	$2,008
Air fare	784	1,098
Transfers	included	included
Meals	included	805
Tips	112	200
Sightseeing	230	405
Entertainment	included	160
Beverages	160	264
Miscellaneous	100	100
	$3,386	$5,040
COST per day (per person)	$242	$360

[a]*Based on two adults traveling from St. Louis for seven nights.*

coming more the exception than the rule. Buying cabins at discounted prices is what most clients are looking to do. What types of discounts are available, and who offers them? There are discounts offered by the cruise lines themselves and discounts offered by cruise-only agencies.

Cruise lines offer deals to boost sales on certain cruise departures. Usually, the better discounts are offered during off-peak periods such as during summer in the Caribbean. These discounts can represent a dollar value (as much as several hundred dollars off the price of a one-week cruise) or as much as 50 percent off the regular price. Many lines offer "early-bird" booking programs that encourage people to pay in full within a short period of time after booking. Other incentives offered by cruise lines include free pre- and postcruise land packages, "kids-sail-free" offers, and free cabin upgrades.

A popular type of discount is the passenger alumni program. These are discount cruise rates offered to passengers who have sailed previously with the particular cruise company. Special alumni prices are offered on selected cruise departures. Needless to say, this helps the cruise lines gain customer loyalty and thus increase repeat business.

Travel agents are informed of the many cruise deals being offered through travel trade publications, advertisements sent or faxed to the agency by cruise companies, and through the Internet. It's just a matter of doing some research.

► Cruise-Only Agencies

Within the past several years, *cruise-only agencies* have become a major force in the marketing and selling of cruises. These are companies that have found a niche—they only market and book cruise travel for the traveling public. Since their specialty is the cruise product and because they can guarantee a higher volume of cruise business, these agencies negotiate special discounts with the cruise lines they represent.

Cruise-only agencies usually offer their discounts directly to the general public; as a rule, they don't offer these deals through the all-service travel agencies to sell to their clients. Cruise-only agencies advertise their cruise bargains through ads placed in newspapers, magazines, through direct mail, and on the Internet. Figure 8.17 shows an example of a promotion offered by a major cruise-only agency on some discounted cruise departures through the Panama Canal. As you

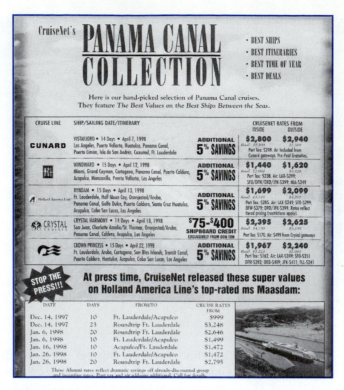

Figure 8.17 *Promotional advertisement.*

can see, these individual sailings offered more than 50 percent discount value on selected cabin categories.

Who's Who on Board

Cruise ships can have anywhere between 250 and 500 crew and staff members (see Table 8.3). The number of crew and staff members depends on the size and type of cruise vessel. Most members of the cruise staff never come into direct contact with passengers; they handle cargo, cleaning and painting, and perform maintenance duties during the cruise.

To understand who works on ships and what they do, think of a cruise ship as a floating hotel or resort. Similar amenities and services are provided for passengers on a cruise ship and guests vacationing at a land-based resort. On most traditional cruise ships, management is organized into two groups. The ship's staff is comprised of the captain, hotel manager, chief engineer, and chief officer. The hotel staff is headed by the hotel manager and is comprised of the cruise director, food service manager, purser, physician, chief housekeeper, and beverage manager. There are about a dozen or so key staff members who interact with passengers. Both you and your future clients should know who they are and what they do.

Tipping Policies

Tipping is a concern for most people who are taking a cruise for the first time. Who to tip, when to tip, and how much to tip are frequent questions asked of the travel professional. Tipping is at the passenger's discretion and should be based

TABLE 8.3   CRUISE SHIP CREW AND STAFF MEMBERS

TITLE	RESPONSIBILITIES	PASSENGER CONTACT
These people don't charge for their services:		
Captain	Serves as master of the ship; in charge of the well-being and safety of all passengers and crew members	Infrequent
Chief engineer	Deals with all technical aspects of running the ship	Infrequent
Chief officer	Responsible for maintaining the physical condition of the ship, inside and out	Infrequent
Hotel manager	Directly responsible for nearly all aspects of the passenger's comfort and guest services; oversees everything except the nautical and technical aspects	Infrequent
Purser	Supports the hotel manager in all matters of administrative management, and supervises the activities of the front offices, such as money-related matters and passenger safety-deposit boxes	Frequent
Chief housekeeper	Oversees the maintenance of all staterooms, public rooms, lounges, and bars	Infrequent
Food service manager	Coordinates and directs the supply and operation of the ship's kitchen, dining room(s), and restaurant(s)	Infrequent
Beverage manager	Responsible for the service in all lounges and bars; also assists passengers in the planning of private parties or functions on board the ship	Infrequent
Cruise director	Supervises all passenger information and entertainment; serves as master of ceremonies during shows, revues, and other entertainment functions; responsible for staff members, including hosts and hostesses, entertainers, and shore excursion staff	Frequent
Cabin steward	Takes care of passengers' accommodations; cleans and makes up cabins	Frequent
Deck steward	Takes care of passengers while they are on deck; serves drinks and distributes pool towels	Frequent/ as needed
Host/male escort	Provides companionship to single women on board by conversing and dancing during day and evening functions (available on certain ships)	As needed
Dining room staff—these people don't charge but you usually have to tip at the end of the cruise:		
Maitre d'	Supervises entire dining room; takes care of any special passenger requests, such as birthday or anniversary cakes and changes in table/seating assignments	As needed
Table waiter	Recommends items on the menu, takes meal orders, and serves food during all formal meals served in the dining room	Frequent
Bus person (assistant waiter)	Serves as a table waiter in training; assists the table waiter by clearing the table, serving meals, and filling water glasses	Frequent
Wine steward	Recommends and serves wine at the table upon request	As needed
These people charge for their services:		
Doctor	Serves as physician on board; may have one or more nursing assistants, depending on the size of the ship	As needed
Beautician	Provides hair and beauty care for all female and male passengers; on larger ships there may be several on staff	As needed
Masseuse	Provides massages upon appointment	As needed
Photographer	Takes pictures of passengers while on the ship and during shore excursions; passengers have the option to purchase the photos	Frequent

on the amount, quality, and level of service provided. Sometimes tips are given at the time that service is rendered; other times the tip is given in one lump sum at the end of the cruise.

- Passengers tip the following staff upon services rendered: bartenders, wine stewards (although they are sometimes tipped at the end), masseuses, and hair stylists or beauticians. The amount of tip would be the same as if you were being provided the same service off the ship—approximately 10 to 15 percent of the cost.

- Passengers tip the following staff at the end of the cruise in one lump sum: cabin stewards, table waiters, buspersons, and the maitre d'.

The most convenient policy is the *no tipping policy*. A few cruise lines do not want or expect tips to be given to any members of the staff; tips have been figured into the cost of the cruise. Some of the cruise lines that have a "no tipping required" policy are Cunard Sea Goddess, Seabourn, and Windstar Cruises, Radisson Seven Seas Cruises, and Holland America Line.

Tipping guidelines are printed in cruise brochures. A standard guideline to follow for a typical seven-day cruise is as follows:

Cabin steward	$ 3 per passenger/per day
Table waiter	$ 3 per passenger/per day
Busperson	$ 2 per passenger/per day
	= $ 8 per passenger/per day
Total	$56 per passenger/$112 per couple

Accommodations

Ship accommodations are called **cabins** or **staterooms.** As a rule, cabins on a cruise ship are much smaller and compact than standard hotel rooms. Cabins come in all varieties, shapes, and sizes and differ from ship to ship. However, you should be familiar with what a typical cabin accommodation is like.

All ships have private bathrooms with shower, air-conditioning, twin beds that can be converted to queen, radio, television, and closets. The more expensive accommodations usually contain bathtub/shower with a lot more space. Although the majority of cabins are designed for two passengers, many ships have accommodations for three or four passengers in the lower categories; these tend to be most popular for families and sell out quickly. On many of the newer ships, each passenger cabin comes equipped with television and VCR. Passengers can help themselves to the ship's video library and view current movies and other performances at any time from the comfort of their cabins.

How to select the best cabin? For the smoothest ride, select a **cabin** located the closest to amidships as possible; this is where the least amount of motion is felt. On some ships, cabins located in the stern may be subject to the noise of the anchor dropping when the ship docks early in the morning. Also to be avoided are cabins located close to elevators and in noisy areas such as below the disco, casino, and entertainment lounges.

Also, some expensive cabins situated on higher decks may have obstructed views. Lifeboats are sometimes mounted on the side of the ship and hang down to the deck below. The lifeboats often obstruct the view from some of the *outside cabins* on that deck. Passengers who pay a higher price for an outside cabin for the view will be unhappy if their view is of the side of a lifeboat. Many cruise lines identify those outside cabins with obscured views in their brochures.

Figure 8.18 shows several types of accommodations on a typical cruise ship, starting with *suites*, which are the most expensive down to standard inside cabins.

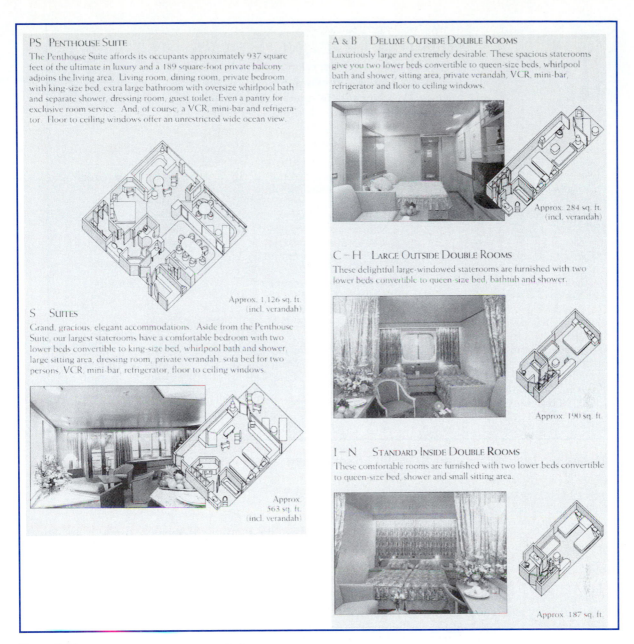

PS PENTHOUSE SUITE

The Penthouse Suite affords its occupants approximately 937 square feet of the ultimate in luxury and a 189 square-foot private balcony adjoins the living area. Living room, dining room, private bedroom with king-size bed, extra large bathroom with oversize whirlpool bath and separate shower, dressing room, guest toilet. Even a pantry for exclusive room service. And, of course, a VCR, mini-bar and refrigerator. Floor to ceiling windows offer an unrestricted wide ocean view.

Approx. 1,126 sq. ft.
(incl. verandah)

S SUITES

Grand, gracious, elegant accommodations. Aside from the Penthouse Suite, our largest staterooms have a comfortable bedroom with two lower beds convertible to king-size bed, whirlpool bath and shower, large sitting area, dressing room, private verandah, sofa bed for two persons, VCR, mini-bar, refrigerator, floor to ceiling windows.

Approx.
563 sq. ft.
(incl. verandah)

A & B DELUXE OUTSIDE DOUBLE ROOMS

Luxuriously large and extremely desirable. These spacious staterooms give you two lower beds convertible to queen-size beds, whirlpool bath and shower, sitting area, private verandah, VCR, mini-bar, refrigerator and floor to ceiling windows.

Approx. 284 sq. ft.
(incl. verandah)

C – H LARGE OUTSIDE DOUBLE ROOMS

These delightful large-windowed staterooms are furnished with two lower beds convertible to queen-size bed, bathtub and shower.

Approx. 190 sq. ft.

I – N STANDARD INSIDE DOUBLE ROOMS

These comfortable rooms are furnished with two lower beds convertible to queen-size bed, shower and small sitting area.

Approx. 187 sq. ft.

Figure 8.18 *Types of cruise accommodations.*

DINING

A major feature of any cruise vacation is dining on board—and there's a lot of it! Passengers are offered several opportunities throughout the day to dine: breakfast, midmorning snack, lunch, afternoon tea or snack, dinner, and a midnight buffet, in addition to 24-hour cabin service (see Figure 8.19).

Formal meals—breakfast, lunch, and dinner—are offered in the ship's dining room. Mealtimes and seating are strictly regulated. Most cruise ships have a more informal, cafeteria-style restaurant or cafe, usually located near the swimming pool area. Here passengers can eat breakfast or lunch more informally and at their leisure. Also, most ships provide self-service coffee and tea round the clock

MONDAY'S DINING HOURS

Tonight's Dress (after 6:00pm): Formal
Ladies: A dressy outfit.
Gentlemen: Dark suit and tie, dinner jacket, or tuxedo.
(Please maintain Formal dress code throughout the evening).

Times	Meal	Location
6:30am – 7:30am	Sunrise Coffee, Tea	Oasis Café
6:30am – 10:00am	Continental Breakfast	In cabin on request
6:30am – 12 Midnight	Coffee available	Oasis Café
		Aft Beverage Station
7:00am – 10:00am	Breakfast Buffet	Oasis Café
7:30am	Main Seating Breakfast	Orion Restaurant
8:45am	Late Seating Breakfast	Orion Restaurant
10:00am – 11:30am	Light Breakfast served continuously	Oasis Grill
10:00am – 12 Noon	Croissants, Danish, Muffins available	Tastings
12 Noon – 2:00pm	**Open Seating Luncheon**	Orion Restaurant
12 Noon – 2:00pm	Hot Dogs & Hamburgers	Ocean & Oasis Grills
12 Noon – 2:00pm	Buffet Luncheon	Oasis Café
3:00pm – 5:00pm	Pastries available	Tastings
3:00pm – 7:00pm	Pizza	Ocean Grill
4:00pm – 5:00pm	Casual Afternoon Tea	Oasis Café
6:00pm	**Captain's Gala Dinner** Main Seating	Orion Restaurant
8:30pm	**Captain's Gala Dinner** Late Seating	Orion Restaurant
10:00pm – 1:00am	Pizza	Ocean Grill
12:00 Midnight – 1:00am	"Gourmet Bites"	Savoy Night Club, Casino, Stratosphere Lounge

Figure 8.19 *Sample dining hours, Celebrity Cruises'* Galaxy.

as well as buffets or pizza parties late at night. However, dinners are always served in the formal dining room. Figure 8.20 shows an example of a dinner menu.

Passengers' special dietary requirements, such as Kosher or no-salt meals, should be requested in advance at the time of booking. In addition, most dining room menus include "lean and light" items for health-conscious passengers who are looking for low-calorie and low-fat meals.

➤ Dining Room Assignments

On most ships, dining hours and seating are strictly regulated. Dining is not typical restaurant style where passengers can eat any time and at any table they want in the formal dining room during mealtimes. Some of the brand-new ships do offer restaurant-style dining; the majority of ships do not. The dining request is made at the time a cruise is booked. The *dining request* consists of two things:

1. *Seating times.* Since the main dining room on most cruise ships can accommodate only half of the passengers at a time, meals are served in two sittings: *main* (or *early*) *seating* and *second* (or *late*) *seating.* Each seating is timed approximately 1½ to 2½ hours apart. Seating times will differ from ship to ship. The times are printed in the cruise brochure for easy reference. On many ships, seating times apply only for dinner. There may be *open seating* during breakfast and lunch, which means that the passenger may sit anywhere at any time during the posted times of the meal. Typical seating times are as follows:

Dinner

Apricot Nectar
Chilled Tomato Juice
Half Grapefruit Maraschino
Eggplant and Mushrooms, Riviera Style
Escargots de Bourgogne · Crab Meat Cocktail · Canapé de Foie Gras

❋ ❋ ❋ ❋ ❋

Cream of Shrimp au Sherry · Chilled Vichysoisse
French Onion Soup (Cheese Crouton)

❋ ❋ ❋ ❋ ❋

PARISIAN COQUILLE ST. JACQUES with Mixed Seafood, au Gratin.

CALF'S SWEETBREADS SAUTÉED GRENOBLOISE, Capers and Lemon.

COQ AU VIN, Chicken Parts, sealed, flamed with Cognac,
simmered with Onions and Mushroom in a hearty Burgundy Wine.

ROAST LOIN OF WESTERN PORK ROBERT, Julienne of Sour Pickles.

ROAST PRIME TENDERLOIN OF BEEF STRASBOURGEOISE, Goose Liver, Madeira Sauce

❋ ❋ ❋ ❋ ❋

Carrots Vichy · Artichoke Heart au Gratin · Petit Pois á la Française
Fondante Potato · Dauphine Potato

❋ ❋ ❋ ❋ ❋

Iceberg Pimiento
Caesar Salad · Health Salad
French · King and I · Thousand Island · Caesar

❋ ❋ ❋ ❋ ❋

Crisp Napoleon · Gâteau Paris Brest
Parfait Parisien · Soufflé Glacé Grand Marnier
Pineapple Sherbet · Cherries Jubilee

❋ ❋ ❋ ❋ ❋

Edam · Swiss · Gorgonzola · Cream
Camembert · Jarlsberg · Cream of Gruyére · Bel Paese
Port Salut · Cheddar

❋ ❋ ❋ ❋ ❋

Compote of Baked Apple
Fresh Fruit

❋ ❋ ❋ ❋ ❋

Sanka · Milk · Postum
Hot Chocolate
Coffee or Tea
Hot or Iced

Figure 8.20 *Dinner menu.*

Meal	Main Seating	Second Seating
Breakfast	7:00 A.M.	8:30 A.M.
Lunch	12:00 noon	1:30 P.M.
Dinner	6:00 P.M.	8:30 P.M.

2. *Table assignments.* There are tables for two, four, six, eight, or ten people. Each passenger is assigned to a specific table number, dependent on the table size requested.

Key Point ➤ Seating times and table assignments are requested at the time of booking. The assignment is confirmed when the passenger boards the ship on the first day. It is also important to note that if passengers are unhappy with the seating time and/or table assignment, the maitre d' can usually change the time or seating if the dining room is not completely full. This should be taken care of on the first day of the cruise, during embarkation.

It should be noted here that the majority of the newer megaships offer restaurant-style or specialty dining as an alternative to the formality of the ship's dining room. Passengers can make a reservation at one of the ship's restaurants on any evening and dine at the time of their choosing. For example, in addition to three main dining rooms on Princess Cruises' *Grand Princess*, the ship offers a Southwest-themed eatery, a casual Italian trattoria, a 24-hour casual dining area in the Horizon Court, a pizzeria near the pool, and a champagne-and-caviar bar.

A Ship's Tour

In this section we take you on a tour of a typical cruise ship: the shops, dining areas, and sports and recreational facilities. A cruise ship is like a recreation center, an entertainment and shopping complex, a grand resort hotel, an art gallery, a health spa, several restaurants, and a seaside resort all rolled into one. A cruise vessel has practically anything for anyone (see Figure 8.21).

To help you visualize what it's like on board a typical cruise ship, the list below will take you on a cruise ship tour using the Royal Caribbean International's super megaship *Voyager of the Seas* (see Figure 8.22).

1. *Sports deck.* This top deck, also called the sun deck, is where many different sports and recreational facilities are located. In addition to one or more pools, this area may include deck sports such as volleyball, paddle tennis, golf driving ranges, shuffleboard, or table tennis. Some ships even offer a basketball court.

2. *Miniature golf.* A nine-hole miniature golf course is a unique feature on several Royal Caribbean International ships.

3. *Spa and health.* Full-service on-board spas offered on most cruise ships include such services as massage therapy, facials, manicures, hairstyling, and such exotic therapies as skin seaweed wraps, and oil and mud bath treatments. Pricing and service vary from ship to ship.

4. *Fitness center.* Fitness centers range from a small room on a lower deck to an airy and sunny, glass-enclosed space on the top deck with a sweeping view of the sea. Standard equipment include low- and high-impact aerobics, a jogging track, treadmills, stair steppers, and stationary bikes. Some ships offer virtual-reality monitors with games on some of their equipment to keep the activity interesting.

CRUISE CAPERS

M.S. ECSTACY   **SATURDAY, DAY 7**

6:20 A.M.	Coffee & Danish	Panorama Grill—Lido
7:00 A.M.–8:00 P.M.	Nautica Spa and Gym Opens	Sports Deck Forward
7:00 A.M.	Walk-A-Mile	Olympic Track—Sun Deck
7:30 A.M.	Stretch & Relaxation	Aerobics Studio
7:45 A.M.	Breakfast—Main Sitting	Both Dining Rooms
8:00 A.M.	Slot Machines Open	Crystal Palace Casino
8:00 A.M.–8:00 P.M.	Nautica Spa Salon Opens	Sports Deck Forward
8:00–10:00 A.M.	Light Deck Breakfast	Panorama Grill—Lido
8:30 A.M.	Low Impact Aerobics	Aerobic Studio
9:00 A.M.	Breakfast—Late Sitting	Both Dining Rooms
9:00 A.M.–8:00 P.M.	Galleria Shopping Mall Opens	Atlantic Deck
9:30 A.M.	Dynaband® Calisthenics	Aerobics Studio
9:30 A.M.–8:00 P.M.	Video Diary Desk Opens	Empress Desk
9:30 A.M.	Bridge Walk-Through	Meet Portside—Lido Deck
10:00–11:00 A.M.	Coffee, Tea & Bouillon	Panorama Grill—Lido
10:00 A.M.	Trapshooting	Promenade Deck Aft
10:00–11:00 A.M.	Library is Open	Explorer's Club
10:00 A.M.	Horse Racing	Blue Sapphire Lounge
10:30 A.M.	Aqua Aerobics	Verandah Deck Aft
11:00 A.M.	Photo Gallery Opens	Empress Deck Grand Atrium
11:00 A.M.	Senior Aerobics	Aerobics Studio
11:30 A.M.–2:30 P.M.	Light Lunch & Salad Bar	Panorama Grill—Lido
11:30 A.M.–2:00 P.M.	Specialty Sandwiches	Lido Deck Poolside
11:50 A.M.	Captain's Bulletin from the Bridge	
12:00 NOON	Lunch—Main Sitting	Both Dining Rooms
12:00 NOON	Full Casino Opens	Crystal Palace Casino
1:00 P.M.	Ice Carving Demonstration	Lido Deck Poolside
1:30 P.M.	Lunch—Main Sitting	Both Dining Rooms
2:00–3:00 P.M.	Library is Open	Explorer's Club
2:00 P.M.	Trapshooting Tournament	Promenade Deck Aft
2:00 P.M.	Ping Pong Tournament	Verandah Deck
2:45 P.M.	Newlywed & Not-So-Newlywed Game	Blue Sapphire Lounge
3:00 P.M.	Bingo	Blue Sapphire Lounge
4:00 P.M.	Multi-Impact Aerobics	Aerobics Studio
4:00–5:00 P.M.	Ice Cream & Cookies	Lido Grill—Outside
4:00–5:00 P.M.	Frozen Yogurt	Lido Grill—Inside
4:00–5:00 P.M.	Tea Time	Society Bar
4:30 P.M.	Masquerade Parade	Blue Sapphire Lounge
5:00–6:00 P.M.	"Fun Ship" Highlight Party (Main)	Metropolis Bar
6:00 P.M.	"American" Dinner Main Sitting	Both Dining Rooms
7:00–8:00 P.M.	"Fun Ship" Highlight Party (Late)	Metropolis Bar
7:30–8:30 P.M.	Farewell Party for Teens & Jr. Cruisers	Stripes Disco
8:00 P.M.	"American" Dinner Late Sitting	Both Dining Rooms
9:00 P.M.	Super Trivia	Blue Sapphire Lounge
9:00 P.M.	Sweet Music	Society Bar
9:30 P.M.	Bingo	Blue Sapphire Lounge
9:30 P.M.	Listen to "Sea Breeze"	Starlight Lounge
9:30 P.M.	Piano Bar Opens with "Scott"	Neon Bar
9:45 P.M.	Music Society Plays	Chinatown
10:00 P.M.	Disco Opens with "Jeff"	Stripes Disco
12:30—1:30 A.M.	Quiche & Salad Buffet	Wind Song Dining Room
1:30—2:00 A.M.	Mini Buffet	City Diner—Promenade Deck

DRESS FOR THE EVENING: Casual. MOVIE: "Regarding Henry" 7:30, 10:00 A.M., 12:30, 3:00, 5:30, 8:00, 10:30 P.M., 1:00, 3:30 A.M.

Figure 8.21 *Sample passenger activity schedule on a typical cruise ship.*

Figure 8.22 *Royal Caribbean International's super megaship* Voyager of the Seas.

5. *Dining room(s).* Many ships offer two or more formal dining rooms on board where fixed sitting times and table seating prevail for dinner. Typically, breakfast and lunch are open seating, where passengers can eat at any time and at any table during the established mealtime. Menus are varied and most ships include low-fat, low-cholesterol selections at every meal.

6. *Solarium.* Located on the top deck is a pool, whirlpools, and bar/dining areas set under a retractable glass canopy.

7. *Viking Crown Lounge.* Unique to Royal Caribbean International ships, a glass-enclosed lounge area perched high above the ocean offers drinks, entertainment, and an almost 360-degree bird's-eye view of the watery surroundings.

8. *Central atrium.* Many large cruise ships built circa 1985 have a central, open area located amidships that serves as the focal point of all activities on board. In many cases, the atrium is measured several decks high and usually surrounded by shops, lounges, and other entertainment and recreational facilities.

9. *Conference and meeting room.* Cruise ships are not only sold to vacation passengers but also serve as business sites for meetings and conferences. Many ships offer state-of-the-art presentation equipment and facilities that accommodate large or small groups.

10. *Library/game rooms.* Most cruise ships offer library facilities; some have a small collection of a few dozen books up to more than 1,500 volumes, consisting of best sellers, reference books, and magazines. Many ship libraries also stock video-tapes. In addition, many vessels offer video arcades and computer learning centers. Check this out: Several of the newer megaships now offer virtual-reality arcades featuring motion-based rides.

11. *Bars and lounges.* Depending on the size and type of cruise ship, there can be anywhere from one to several different bars and lounges scattered throughout the vessel. Prices are comparable to those on land.

12. *Swimming pool(s).* One or more swimming pools is a standard feature on most cruise ships. Some of the larger vessels feature two large pools and a small wading pool for children; some have indoor pools in addition to those that are located on deck. Pools are not large enough for long-distance laps but can be very elaborate, with water slides and retractable roofs. Some of the newer megaships now offer a first in cruising: a swim-against-the-current lap pool.

13. *Shops and boutiques.* Depending on the size of the ship, there may be one or two stores that offer everything from toothpaste to sweatshirts, up to a multi-tiered mall-like shopping center chockfull of specialty stores and boutiques. Stores on ships are duty-free, and in addition to standard personal items, they include fine jewelry, gift items, liquor, and fashionable clothes.

14. *Casino.* Once a cruise ship is in international waters (12 miles offshore), passengers are permitted to gamble. On smaller and older ships, the casino may consist of several slot machines. On the larger and most recently built ships, casinos can accommodate up to 200 passengers with Vegas-style gambling, such as baccarat, blackjack, roulette, craps, electronic slots, and video poker.

15. *Restaurant-style dining and cafes.* As an alternative to the formalities in the ship's dining room(s), many offer casual-style options and "dine-anytime" restaurants. Usually, a ship has a café or restaurant off the main pool area that serves casual breakfasts, lunch buffets, beverages, and snacks throughout the day and night. Some larger ships offer one or more specialty restaurants where passengers can make dinner reservations on a nightly basis.

16. *Youth centers.* Many cruise lines are marketing their ships for the entire family, and children of all ages are welcome. Some ships provide more things for children to do than others; it should be checked out during the ship selection process. Those ships that target families will offer structured activities day and night for children of all ages. To find out if a ship is "family friendly," check out the following services and amenities that indicate that children are welcome: child playrooms and youth centers with professional counselors, structured daily activities, special discos and electronic game rooms, ice-cream and pizza parlors.

17. *Main show lounge/theater.* There is a wide range of nightly entertainment choices on board traditional cruise ships. The variety and sophistication of theater, nightclub revues, stage performances, and variety shows differ from ship to ship. Many of the larger ships feature professional performers and Broadway-style music revues with a lot of razzle-dazzle, such as laser and light effects. During the day this area may serve as a full-size cinema that features recent movies plus other presentations, from port-of-call lectures to cooking demonstrations.

Web Link

A Ship's Virtual Tour on the NET: Holland America Line offers cyber-travelers a virtual tour of their ship *Veendam,* plus other ships that are featured from time to time. It's better than a color brochure since it gives you a 360-degree angle as you walk through the ship's public rooms and cabins. It works like this: Go to HAL's site, go to the virtual-reality tour, download a plug-in, follow instructions (or ask a Net-savvy person), head back to the virtual tour, and click on the area you want to explore. It takes a few minutes but is worth it! To get there, go to *http://www.hollandamerica.com*

Key Point ➤

Money Matters: Cruise ships use the cashless system. Passengers open accounts when they board, settled at the end of the cruise by using a major credit card, cash, and traveler's checks. Some of the newer ships have ATM machines. At the beginning of the cruise, passengers are given an on-board charge card that is used for all purchases while on board the ship. The on-board card is used to purchase drinks in all bars and lounges, items in shops, shore excursions, and so on.

Bells and Whistles

Here are some of the unique and dazzling features available on some newer cruise ships:

- *Wedding bells at sea.* Princess Cruises' 109,000-ton *Grand Princess* was the first ship to offer a wedding chapel on board. Under the authority of the ship's Liberian registry, the ship's captain is able to perform weddings at sea. Wedding cruise packages are available that include music, champagne, bridal bouquet, video of the ceremony, and cake. Many larger ships built circa 1997 have this feature.

- *Ice skating and mountain climbing Caribbean-style.* Royal Caribbean International's 142,000-ton *Voyager of the Seas*, one of the largest cruise ships afloat, comes complete with a skating ice rink complete with a Zamboni machine and an inline skating track. Tired of skating in circles? Passengers can keep in shape by scaling the rock-climbing wall on board.

- *Dancing on Waves.* The disco on the *Grand Princess* is an aluminum structure that juts off the back of the ship and is suspended 155 feet above the water, giving guests a floating-in-space perspective. By day the disco serves as an observation lounge.

✓ Check Your Understanding 8-4

1. For each cruise feature or service listed below, write Y if it is included in the cost on most cruise ships and N if it is available at an extra charge on most cruise ships.

   A. medical services ____ G. all meals ____

   B. spa services ____ H. tips ____

   C. entertainment ____ I. shops ____

   D. accommodations ____ J. air transportation from/to ____
   home city

   E. shore excursions ____ K. alcoholic beverages ____

   F. laundry/dry cleaning ____ L. hair/beauty salon ____

2. Explain why cruise vacations offer a superior value. How would you "prove" this to a client if you were selling cruises?

   _____

   _____

3. Name two cruise staff members who are usually tipped upon services rendered.

   A. _____ B. _____

4. Circle the amount that comes closest to what two people would pay in tips to the following staff members at the end of a four-day cruise: cabin steward and dining room staff.

   A. $95 C. $25

   B. $65 D. $125

5. What is the difference between an inside and an outside cabin?

   _____

6. Match each staff member with his or her main responsibility.

A. cabin steward   ____ 1. Recommends menu items and serves meals in the formal dining room.

B. captain   ____ 2. In charge of passenger entertainment; serves as master of ceremonies at all functions.

C. busperson   ____ 3. Brings towels and drinks at poolside.

D. maitre d'   ____ 4. In charge of all money matters.

E. cruise director   ____ 5. Assists in dining room, clears table, and fills water glasses.

F. purser   ____ 6. Converses and dances with single women on board.

G. deck steward   ____ 7. In charge of the formal dining room.

H. table waiter   ____ 8. In charge of everyone's safety and well-being during the cruise; master of the vessel.

I. host   ____ 9. Takes care of passengers' accommodations.

True or False?

____ 7. Most ships include round-trip air and transfers in the price of the cruise (i.e., air/sea packages).

____ 8. The average cost of a cruise per person based on double occupancy is between $200 and $250 per day.

____ 9. Two types of cruise discounts are "early-bird" and passenger alumni programs.

____ 10. As a rule, cabins on a ship are larger than standard hotel rooms.

____ 11. Cruise-only agencies usually offer their discounts only through other travel agencies, who then sell to their clients.

____ 12. On some ships, outside cabins located on higher decks may have obstructed views.

____ 13. Dining room assignments—seating times and tables—are confirmed only on the cruise departure date.

____ 14. Passengers usually pay for drinks and other purchases on board ship by either cash or traveler's checks during the cruise.

____ 15. Select a cabin as close to amidships as possible for a smoother ride.

ITINERARIES

"Where am I going?" Next to "What is the ship like?" and "How's the food?", this question is likely to be asked. In fact, often the itinerary of the ship is the first factor when selecting a cruise (see Figure 8.23). There are the common or traditional cruise itineraries, such as the Caribbean, Bahamas, and Mexican Riviera. There are the less traditional itineraries, such as trips to Antarctica, Galápagos, or the Far East.

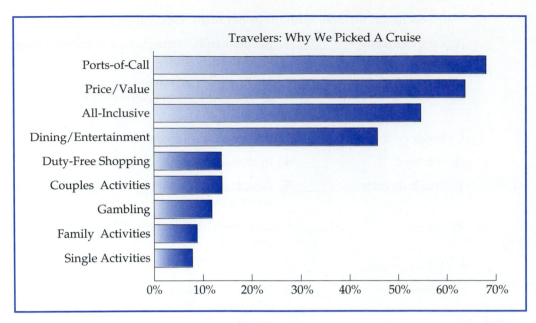

Figure 8.23 *Traveler's reasons for choosing a particular cruise, based on the New York-based Newspaper Association of America survey of 908 adults who had taken at least one cruise in the last three years. Total exceeds 100 percent because of multiple responses.*

You would be amazed to find out to which places on earth you can cruise! First, we will familiarize you with the major cruise itinerary areas of the world. Let's start with a map of the world and see where these areas are located. Figure 8.24 divides our world into the following major cruise areas:

- Southeast Asia
- Orient
- East Indies
- Australia/New Zealand
- South Pacific
- Hawaii
- Alaska
- Mexican Riviera
- Inland Rivers of North America
- Western Caribbean
- Eastern/Southern Caribbean
- Amazon River
- New England and Maritimes
- British Isles
- East Atlantic
- Western Mediterranean
- Eastern Mediterranean
- Black Sea
- InlandWaterways of Europe
- Baltic
- Fjords
- Indian Ocean
- Nile River
- Antarctic Peninsula

And yes, your clients can even take a slow boat to China!

According to a recent survey conducted by the Cruise Lines International Association, the Caribbean ranks as the leading cruise itinerary in regard to number of passengers and available berths. *That is why Miami, Florida is the busiest cruise port in the world.*

➤ Western Hemisphere Cruises

The majority of first-timers cruise to destinations within the western hemisphere: the United States and Canada, West Indies, Mexico, and South America.

National Geographic and Cruise Experts Pick the "World's Best" Sailings

Journalists and veteran cruise-specialist travel agents weigh in on top voyages for couples, families, and singles.

	Alaska	New England and Canada	Northern Europe	Mediterranean	Caribbean	South America
Couples	Princess Cruises Holland America Line Alaska Sightseeing/Cruise West	Princess Cruises Clipper Cruise Lines Seabourn Cruise Line	Cunard Radisson Seven Seas Cruises Crystal Cruises	Cunard Windstar Cruises Star Clippers	Celebrity Cruises Holland America Line Windstar Cruises	Silversea Cruises Princess Cruises Crystal Cruises
Families	Princess Cruises Holland America Line Royal Caribbean International	Princess Cruises Holland America Line Royal Caribbean International Norwegian Cruise Lines	Royal Caribbean International Cunard	Royal Caribbean International Princess Cruises Norwegian Cruise Lines	Princess Cruises Carnival Cruise Line Disney Cruise Line	Princess Cruises Royal Olympic Line
Solo Travelers	Holland America Line Princess Cruises Crystal Cruises	Holland America Line Princess Cruises	Norwegian Cruise Lines Holland America Line Bergen Line	Princess Cruises Holland America Line Costa Cruises	Carnival Cruise Line Holland America Line Royal Caribbean International	Holland America Line Princess Cruises Crystal Cruises

Source: National Geographic Traveler *November/December*.

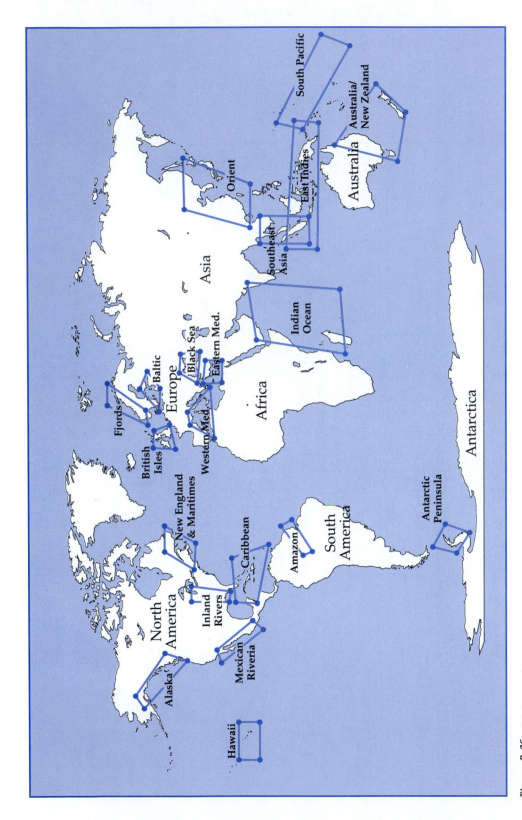

Figure 8.24 *Major cruise areas.*

Hawaii

Alaska
North
America

Fjords

British
Isles

Baltic

Europe

Black Sea

Eastern Med.

Western Med.

New England
& Maritimes

Inland
Rivers

Mexican
Riveria

Caribbean

Amazon

South
America

Antarctic
Peninsula

Antarctica

Africa

Asia

Orient

Southeast
Asia

East Indies

South Pacific

Australia/
New Zealand

Australia

Indian
Ocean

Source: *Cruise Lines International Association, New York. As published in* Travel Weekly, *July, 1998.*

United States and Canada

In the United States, there are two popular itineraries that are offered year-round. Nostalgic riverboat cruises on the Mississippi evoke what it was like to travel on the opulent paddlewheelers of the past. During the warmer summer and fall months, these riverboats concentrate on northern itineraries visiting such ports as Minneapolis/St. Paul and St. Louis. During the cooler months, the southern port cities of New Orleans and Memphis are key gateways used to tour the old southern plantations and antebellum mansions. The Delta Queen Steamboat Co. operates three ships: *Delta Queen, Mississippi Queen,* and the *American Queen,* which is the largest passenger steamboat ever built.

The other year-round cruise destination is Hawaii. The only registered major cruise company in the United States, America Hawaii Cruises, schedules weekly sailings that embark from Honolulu on the island of Oahu, with stopovers in Maui, Kauai, and the big island of Hawaii. These cruises are considered to be port-intensive, since they visit a new port of call each day.

Alaska is the fastest-growing cruise destination in North America. The Alaska cruise season is a short one that begins in May and ends in early October. Many consider this to be a cruise to the last frontier and the ultimate travel experience. Alaskan itineraries combine spectacular scenery of towering fjords and

TABLE 8.4 ALASKA SEVEN-DAY CRUISE ON PRINCESS CRUISES' *REGAL PRINCESS*

Day	Port	Arrive	Depart
Sun.	Vancouver		5:30 P.M.
Mon.	Cruising Inside Passage		
Tues.	Juneau, Alaska	1:00 P.M.	11:00 P.M.
Wed.	Skagway	7:00 A.M.	8:00 P.M.
Thurs.	Cruising Glacier Bay		
Fri.	Sitka	7:00 A.M	1:00 P.M.
Sat.	Cruising Inside Passage		
Sun.	Vancouver	7:00 A.M.	

glaciers, along with historical sites in places such as Juneau, Ketchikan, Skagway, and Sitka (see Table 8.4). Holland America Line, Princess Cruises, and Crystal Cruises operate many ships in this area.

West Indies and Mexico

The most popular cruise destination in the world is the West Indies. This includes seasonal sailings to Bermuda plus year-round cruises to the Bahamas and the Caribbean Islands. The entire Caribbean is divided further into three cruise regions: eastern Caribbean, western Caribbean, and southern or deep Caribbean.

Eastern Caribbean cruises include ports of call in Freeport and Nassau, Bahamas, plus San Juan, Puerto Rico, and St. Thomas, U.S. Virgin Islands. Embarkation is usually from the ports of Miami and Ft. Lauderdale.

Western Caribbean cruises combine visits to Mexico's Yucatán Peninsula and the island of Cozumel, with Caribbean islands such as Grand Cayman and Jamaica. The major ports of embarkation for western Caribbean itineraries are Miami and Tampa, which usually include a short stopover at nearby Key West, Florida.

Southern or deep Caribbean cruise itineraries have more ports of call than do eastern and western Caribbean cruises. They are port intensive since most ships embark from San Juan, Puerto Rico, in the heart of the Caribbean (see Table 8.5). This saves sailing to and from the coast of the United States, which results in fewer days at sea, more days in port. Deep Caribbean itineraries usually reach down to the South American ports of Caracas, Venezuela or Cartagena, Columbia.

Mexican Riviera cruises concentrate on the western or Pacific coast of Mexico. The Pacific coast is generally considered to be the "Riviera" of Mexico, since many popular vacation resorts are located here: Cabo San Lucas, Mazatlán, Puerto Vallarta, Ixtapa, and Acapulco. These are year-round cruises and can be taken either round trip or one way in either a northbound or southbound direction.

Panama Canal cruises allow passengers to experience the best of both worlds—the Caribbean and the Mexican Riviera—and the unique passage between the two oceans. It takes one full day to transit the canal, which is done during daylight hours for maximum effect. Cruises can be taken either in a westbound direction (from the Caribbean to the Pacific) or in an eastbound direction (the Pacific to the Caribbean). These cruises are usually 10 to 14 days in length.

TABLE 8.5   SOUTHERN CARIBBEAN: SEVEN-DAY CRUISE ON CELEBRITY CRUISES' *ZENITH*

Day	Port	Arrive	Depart
Sat.	San Juan		11:30 P.M
Sun.	St. Thomas	7:00 A.M.	5:00 P.M.
Mon.	Guadeloupe	9:00 A.M.	4:30 P.M.
Tues.	Grenada	8:00 A.M.	4:30 P.M
Wed.	La Guaira	10:00 A.M.	6:00 P.M.
Thurs.	Aruba	7:00 A.M.	6:00 P.M.
Fri.	Day at sea		
Sat.	San Juan	9:30 A.M.	

South America

South American cruises offer a wide variety of sights and experiences for both first-time and repeat cruisers. Cruise ships ply along the eastern and western coastlines stopping in such ports as Rio de Janeiro and Buenos Aires or Lima, Peru and Santiago, Chile, respectively. Popular expedition-style itineraries include explorations along the Amazon River, scientific expeditions to the Galápagos Islands, and ice-breaker adventures to the continent of Antarctica.

► Eastern Hemisphere Cruises

The balance of the world or the eastern hemisphere offers many scenic, adventurous, and exotic cruise destinations. This is the part of the world that is more appealing to the repeat or seasoned cruise traveler.

Europe

The continent of Europe, because of its geography, offers some of the greatest opportunities for cruising. Europe is made up of a series of islands and peninsulas that results in a lengthier coastline than most people would expect. Many capitals and major cities are located on or near the European coastline, which makes them easily accessible to cruise ships. Many other cities and points of interest are located on navigable rivers found throughout the continent. European cruises can be placed in the following general categories: Mediterranean (western and eastern; see Table 8.6), Atlantic coast, Scandinavian peninsula, Black Sea, and Baltic Sea.

Growing in popularity are river boat and barge cruises throughout the vast network of Europe's *inland waterways.* This continent offers hundreds of miles of rivers and canals that wind through beautiful scenery passing important archeological and historic sites. Small river boats, deluxe barges, and chartered yachts can take cruise passengers deep into the interior regions of Europe, where the traditional larger cruise ships cannot go.

TABLE 8.6   Mediterranean: Twelve-Day Cruise on Princess Cruises' Grand Princess

Day	Port	Arrive	Depart
Sun.	Barcelona, Spain		1:00 P.M.
Mon.	Monte Carlo, Monaco	7:00 A.M.	7:00 P.M.
Tues.	Livorno (Florence/Pisa), Italy	6:30 A.M.	6:00 P.M.
Wed.	Naples/Capri, Italy	8:00 A.M.	7:00 P.M.
Thurs.	At sea		
Fri.	Venice, Italy	12:00 noon	—
Sat.	Venice		2:00 P.M.
Sun.	At sea		
Mon.	Piraeus (Athens), Greece	7:00 A.M.	5:30 P.M.
Tues.	Kusadasi (Ephasus), Turkey	7:00 A.M.	5:00 P.M.
Wed.	Istanbul, Turkey	12:00 noon	—
Thurs.	Istanbul; Disembark A.M.		

Pacific Rim

Another important cruise area is the Pacific Rim. This huge area includes eastern and southern Asia, Australia, New Zealand, and many of the South Pacific islands. This part of the world is fast becoming a major destination for cruise ships. The most popular itineraries include coastal China and Japan, southeast Asia, East Indian islands, Australia, and South Pacific islands.

Coastal China and Japan cruise itineraries open up one of the most mysterious and exotic regions of the world to the cruise traveler. Cruises to this part of the world usually exceed fourteen days in length and sail as far north as Tokyo, Japan, and Beijing, China to as far south as Hong Kong (see Table 8.7).

Southeast Asia itineraries include visits to the following countries: Vietnam, Thailand, Singapore, and Malaysia. Cruise ships embark from Hong Kong, Singapore, or Bangkok and are usually fourteen days or more in duration. This region is relatively new to cruise travel, which provides easy access to destinations that have been difficult to visit in the past. Some of the unique ports of call include Denang and Ho Chi Minh cities in Vietnam.

East Indies itineraries emphasize the countries of Indonesia and Malaysia, which are made up of thousands of islands and extend from the South Pacific to the Indian Ocean. Major destinations include the island of Bali and Jakarta in Indonesia, and the exotic country of Brunei.

The continent of *Australia* and the many islands of the *South Pacific* afford a vast and ideal area to explore by ship. Itineraries in Australia include ports of Sydney, Brisbane, and Cairns, the latter of which is the gateway to the Great Barrier Reef. Extended cruises from either Australia or New Zealand include visits to some of the more exotic South Pacific islands, such as Fiji, American Samoa, and Tahiti in French Polynesia.

TABLE 8.7 Coastal China and Japan: Fourteen-Day Cruise on Princess Cruises' *Sky Princess*

Day	Port	Arrive	Depart
Thurs.	Osaka/Kyoto, Japan		12:00 midnight
Fri.	At sea		
Sat.	Nagasaki, Japan	8:00 A.M.	6:00 P.M.
Sun.	Pusan, South Korea	7:00 A.M.	5:00 P.M.
Mon.	At sea		
Tue.	Beijing (Tianjin), China (disembark for land package)	8:00 A.M.	
Wed.	Beijing and the Great Wall, China		
Thurs.	Beijing (Tianjin), China		5:00 P.M.
Fri.	Dalian, China	9:00 A.M.	5:00 P.M.
Sat.	At sea		
Sun.	Shanghai, China (overnight on ship)	8:00 A.M.	
Mon.	Shanghai, China		6:00 P.M.
Tues.	At sea		
Wed.	At sea		
Thurs.	Hong Kong	8:00 A.M.	

Repositioning: A Special Way to Cruise: Some cruise ships make seasonal changes in their itineraries during the year. For example, a cruise company may operate a ship in the Caribbean during the winter season and in the Mediterranean during the summer months; the ship is being *repositioned* from the Caribbean to Europe. Or another ship may cruise Alaska during the summer season and reposition to the South Pacific during the winter and spring. Rather than sail without passengers and therefore suffer a loss of revenue, cruise lines market these repositionings as special cruises for passengers. Repositioning cruises often include exotic or interesting ports of call along the way and usually exceed fourteen days in duration. They are especially attractive to travelers who have a lot of time and who are looking for a different and unique experience.

Going Ashore

Now that you have some idea of what happens on board cruise ships and places where they go, let's take a look at what happens when the cruise ship is in port.

➤ Tendering versus Docking

When the cruise ship arrives at a port of call, it either *docks* at the pier or drops anchor offshore. The decision to dock or drop anchor depends on any one or all of these factors:

- Size of ship
- Space available at pier
- Weather conditions

If the ship docks at the pier, it pulls up alongside the dock area. Passengers debark or leave the ship by walking down the gangway, which extends from the side of the ship to ground level. If the ship anchors offshore, the passengers debark or leave the ship by riding small boats or *tenders* to shore. Tenders usually accommodate between 100 and 200 passengers at one time. They will sail back and forth continually between the ship and shore while the ship is at anchor.

➤ A Day on Land

While the cruise ship is in port, passengers have four options:

1. Purchase a **shore excursion**/*land tour*.
2. Arrange own tour.
3. Walk around on own.
4. Do nothing and stay on board the ship.

A popular option for most passengers is to purchase one or more shore excursions. Shore excursions usually include land transportation from the ship, narrated tour, sightseeing by local guides, and sometimes a meal/snack. Some shore excursions may consist only of scheduled transportation to and from the major beach or shopping areas.

Usually, a shore excursion is either a half-day (three to four hours) or a full day (six to eight hours). For lengthy cruises to such places as the Middle East or the Orient, overnight land accommodations may be included in the shore excursion. For example, a popular shore excursion on an eastern Mediterranean cruise is a trip up the Nile River to visit Cairo and points farther south. Because of the distance covered, an overnight in Cairo is included.

Shore excursions are not part of the cruise fare; they are always extra. They usually cannot be purchased before the cruise; shore excursions are confirmed and paid for during the cruise. The exception to this applies to lengthy, international cruises through Europe, the Middle East, or the Far East, for example. Since land options sometimes have to be arranged and confirmed far in advance with the local ground operators in these foreign countries, passengers have the option of reserving and paying for shore excursions before they depart. The best policy is to check with the cruise line regarding its policy on shore excursions.

➤ Pre- and Postcruise Land Tours

Many cruise lines offer extensions to the beginning or end of a cruise called *pre-* and *postcruise land tour* packages, respectively. These packages include accommodations, transfers, and sightseeing at selected hotels at either the beginning or the end of the cruise vacation. Pre- and postcruise land tours must be booked and purchased before the cruise departure.

✓ *Check Your Understanding 8-5*

Multiple Choice

Circle the correct answer.

1. The most popular cruise itinerary in terms of number of passengers and ships operating is:
   A. Alaska
   B. Caribbean
   C. Hawaii
   D. Mexico
   E. Europe

2. The busiest commercial cruise port in the world is:
   A. Tampa
   B. New York
   C. San Juan
   D. Miami
   E. Los Angeles

3. An eastern Caribbean seven-day cruise would not include which of the following ports of call?
   A. St. Thomas
   B. Cancún
   C. Nassau
   D. San Juan
   E. All of the above would be included

4. Which of the following ports would not be included on a seven-day Mexican Riviera cruise?
   A. Cozumel
   B. Acapulco
   C. Puerto Vallarta
   D. Mazatlán
   E. Cabos San Lucas

5. Which of the following cruise itineraries is seasonal (not year round)?
   A. Mexican Riviera
   B. Hawaii
   C. Mississippi River
   D. Alaska
   E. Trans-Panama Canal

6. Which of the following ports would not be included on an eastern Mediterranean cruise?

    A. Haifa, Israel   D. Alexandria, Egypt

    B. Kusadasi, Turkey   E. Venice, Italy

    C. Barcelona, Spain

7. Your clients want to include both the resorts of the Caribbean and a visit to the Mayan ruins in Mexico on their next seven-day cruise. Which itinerary would you suggest?

    A. southern Caribbean   D. Panama Canal

    B. Mexican Riviera   E. western Caribbean

    C. eastern Caribbean

8. If you were visiting the ports of San Juan in Puerto Rico, Caracas in Venezuela, Guadeloupe, and Aruba, what cruise itinerary are you taking?

    A. U.S. inland waterways   D. western Caribbean

    B. southern Caribbean   E. Mexican Riviera

    C. eastern Caribbean

9. Coastal China and Japan cruises can be taken in either direction: north- or southbound. Select the two ports that would serve as the embarkation/debarkation points.

    A. Sydney, Australia and   D. Osaka, Japan and
        Hong Kong, China   Hong Kong

    B. Hong Kong and   E. Ho Chi Minh, Vietnam and
        Bangkok, Thailand   Singapore

    C. Sydney, Australia and
        Singapore

10. The Baltic Sea, Black Sea, and scenic inland waterways are examples of cruise itineraries in what part of the world?

    A. northern Africa   D. Pacific Rim

    B. South America   E. North America

    C. Europe

Short Answers

11. Name three major cruise areas in the United States.

    A. _____

    B. _____

    C. _____

12. Name three major cruise areas in the Pacific Rim.

    A. _____

    B. _____

    C. _____

13. Your clients are repeat cruise travelers and are looking for something more adventurous or unique in their next cruise. They can leave at any time and would like to go to South America. What three cruise itineraries would you suggest?

    A. _____

    B. _____

    C. _____

14. America Hawaii Cruises operates weekly Hawaiian cruises year round. From which port do these cruises embark?

_____

15. Define a repositioning cruise and include the type of traveler it attracts.

_____

16. List three reasons why a ship would drop anchor rather than dock at a port of call.

_____

_____

_____

17. What is the name of the small boat that carries passengers between the ship and shore when the ship is at anchor?

_____

True or False?

_____ 18. Shore excursions are usually included in the cost of a cruise.

_____ 19. Shore excursions are not usually paid for in advance of the departure date.

_____ 20. Pre-cruise and post-cruise land packages are often included in the cost of a cruise.

CRUISE BROCHURES: DECK PLANS AND PRICING

Of all the sales and booking tools available to agents, the cruise brochure is probably number one. The cruise lines realize the importance of the cruise brochure during the selling process. In many cases the client is sold on a particular cruise ship based on the pictures, design, and descriptions contained in a cruise brochure; a poorly designed brochure does little to motivate the client to buy. This is why cruise lines pay a lot of money to produce colorful and dazzling marketing pieces like brochures that are aimed to sell their ships to the general public.

It is important that travel agents learn how to use cruise brochures effectively. All brochures contain the same type of information; style and design are what make each brochure different. Just think of any brochure broken down into these five general sections (refer to Figure 8.25, sample pages from a Costa Cruise Line brochure):

1. Promotion
2. Itineraries and ports of call
3. Ship descriptions and deck plans
4. Cabin categories and cost chart
5. Terms and conditions

➤ Promotion

The first several pages of any cruise brochure usually contain dazzling pictures and descriptions of the company's ships and services. This is for promotional purposes only, not informational. They are designed to intrigue and motivate clients to buy. Not only do these photos convey what it's like on board the ship, but they also hint at something very important. Usually you can tell the average

Figure 8.25 *Cruise brochure.*

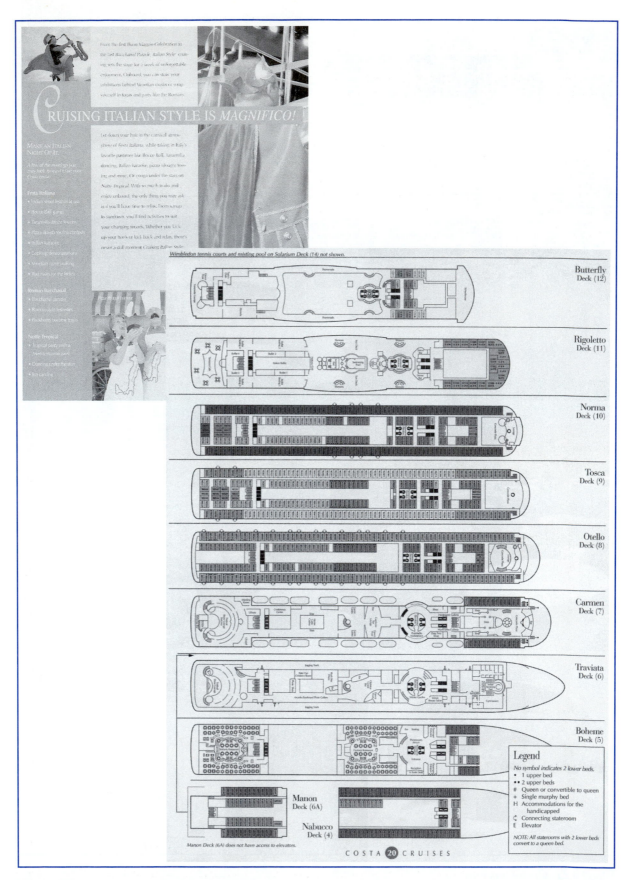

Figure 8.25 *Cruise brochure. (Continued)*

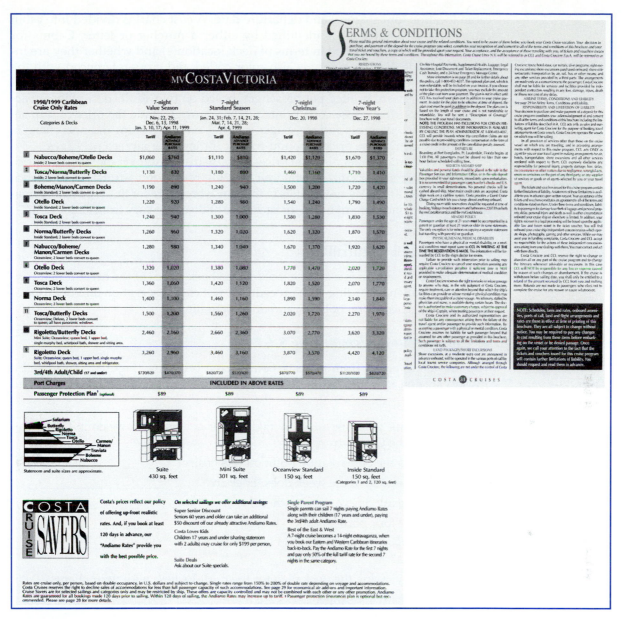

Figure 8.25 *Cruise brochure. (Continued)*

age of the ship's passengers by noting who is posing in the brochure's pictures. It is a subtle, but effective way of telling you if the ship is targeting families, swinging singles, or mature travelers, for example.

► Itineraries and Ports of Call

One of the most important factors in choosing a cruise is the ship's itinerary and ports of call. Cruise lines will always feature itineraries in their brochures, along with detailed descriptions and pictures of all the ports visited.

► Ship Descriptions, Deck Plans, and Cost Charts

In addition to a description of a ship's recreational and service facilities, each brochure will contain a cost chart. Cruise costs are dependent on two factors:

cabin location (or category) and departure date. A cost chart is divided into cabin categories; each category is identified by either a number or letter. Cabins for each category are described in terms of deck location(s) and whether they are inside or outside. Each category is also color-coded and cross-referenced with the deck plan for easy identification.

Cruise costs are printed per passenger, based on two adults occupying an accommodation. Most cruise costs printed in brochures include the price of ship accommodations, all meals and passenger facilities on board ship, and port charges. Some ships include the price of round-trip air if they offer air/sea packages.

Most cruise lines offer discount prices. Typical discounts over the standard price or tariff include senior citizens, children (sharing room with adults), and advance purchase rates. The sales agent refers to the cruise brochure for this type of information since the conditions of travel for each type of discount vary from ship to ship.

➤ Terms and Conditions

This important section is usually placed in the back pages of the brochure. It contains information regarding ship procedures, policies, reservation and deposit requirements, cancellation policies, and documentation.

✔ Check Your Understanding 8-6

You are using pages from a Costa Cruise Line brochure (Figure 8.25) to sell a cruise vacation to your clients. Answer the following questions by referring to Figure 8.25.

1. Your clients are interested in taking the seven-night western Caribbean cruise on the *CostaVictoria.*
   A. What is the embarkation point on this cruise? _____
   B. On what day of the week does it depart? _____
   C. How many days at sea are there? _____
   D. List the four ports of call. _____
   E. How many hours is the ship in port in Jamaica? _____

2. You are reviewing the deck plan for the *CostaVictoria* with your clients.
   A. How many passenger decks are there? _____
   B. Accommodations are on every passenger deck except for: _____
   C. On which deck is the casino located? _____
   D. How many pools are on this ship (outdoor and indoor)? _____
   E. On Boheme Deck, the passenger cabins are located _____ (forward or aft) of the restaurants.

3. You are helping your clients select a cabin from the deck plan and accompanying cost chart.
   A. Cabin categories on this ship are identified by numbers. There are _____ (how many) cabin categories (costs).
   B. Your clients are interested in any of these outside cabins: 10309, 10307, or 10305. They belong in _____ cabin category (by number).
   C. These accommodations are _____ (outside or inside) cabins.
   D. Category 6 cabins are located on two different decks. Name them.
      (1) _____ (2) _____

E. Categories for suite accommodations are identified by letter. On which two decks are the minisuite accommodations located?

(1) _____ (2) _____

4. The cost of a cruise depends on two factors: cabin category and date of travel. This ship has two seasons: value (lesser expensive) and standard (more expensive). In addition to cabin category and departure date, which affect the price of a cruise, many ships offer a discount for advance purchase. In this case, two prices are shown for each category: standard tariff and advance purchase rates. All costs are shown per adult based on double occupancy. What is the cruise cost for each of the following?

A. Standard tariff, cabin in category 3, departure date November 29, is _____ per adult passenger.

B. Standard tariff, outside cabins on Otello deck, departure date March 28, is _____ per adult passenger.

C. Standard tariff, cabin 50115, departure date December 20, is _____ per adult passenger.

5. Cruise ships offer many types of discounts: for example, advance purchase (Andiamo rates), third/fourth adult sharing same cabin, senior citizen, and children rates. What is the cruise cost for each of the following?

A. Standard tariff, outside (oceanview) cabin on Norma deck, departure April 11. Two adults plus a child 12 years old sharing a cabin. Additional adult passenger cost is in front of slash; child cost is after. The total cruise cost for three is _____.

B. Your clients—two adults—purchased their cruise six months (180 days) before departure, so they are eligible for the Andiamo discount. If they are confirmed in cabin 80301, the price per adult if they depart February 14 is _____.

6. You have just sold a cruise on the *Costa Victoria*. Refer to the "Terms and Conditions" to answer these important booking questions.

A. You have booked a seven-night cruise for two adults. What is the total amount of deposit that you are required to send to secure this reservation? _____

B. Your clients booked a cruise for departure on May 30. They canceled on May 5. What is the cancellation charge per person? _____

C. In addition to ocean transportation, accommodations, and all meals on board ship, costs include port charges. What is the total amount of port charges for one passenger on a ten-night cruise? _____

D. Your clients (U.S. citizens) are on a Caribbean cruise. What type of travel document are they required to carry? _____

E. What time does embarkation (boarding) start if the cruise is from Port Everglades? _____

GENERAL CRUISE RESOURCES

The travel professional has a wealth of printed resources on hand to assist in the selling and booking of cruise travel. The cruise brochure is used as an effective sales tool: with deck plans, costs, terms and conditions, and other important information. In addition to brochures, there are three resource books used for more general information: *Official Steamship Guide, Official Cruise Guide,* and *CLIA Manual.*

➤ Official Steamship Guide International

The *Official Steamship Guide International* (see Figure 8.26) is a soft-covered publication issued four times per year on a seasonal basis: winter, spring, summer, and fall. Travel agencies subscribe to this resource, which costs approximately $90 for an annual subscription. This resource should be used as a general directory of cruise ships: what ships are traveling where and when. It won't provide detailed deck plans and rates, but it provides you with enough information to direct you to the specific cruise line and ships that you are trying to find.

Figure 8.27 is a cutaway page from the cruise list section of this resource. It provides a chronological list of departure dates, cruise ships by name, embarkation point, length of cruise, ports of call, and minimum cabin rates by cruise area. This resource also contains many helpful maps of ports of call within each cruise area.

➤ Official Cruise Guide

The *Official Cruise Guide* (see Figure 8.28) is a soft-bound resource book printed annually by *Travel Weekly*, a major travel trade publication. Travel agents can subscribe to this cruise resource at an approximate cost of $95 per year. The intention of this publication is to create a one-stop source for the travel agent when selling cruises. It attempts to provide answers to typical questions regarding the matching of cruise to client, booking a cruise, and ship particulars. The contents include deck plans, port profiles, ship profiles, booking information, sailing schedules, and destination maps.

Figure 8.26 Official Steamship Guide International *cover.*

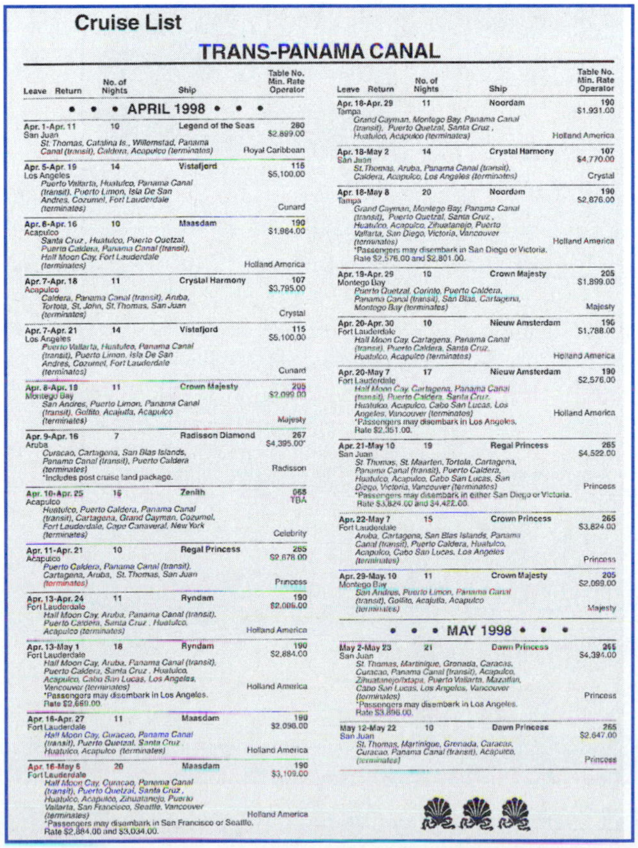

Figure 8.27 *Sample content of* Official Steamship Guide International.
(*Reprinted with permission from Transportation Guides, Inc.*)

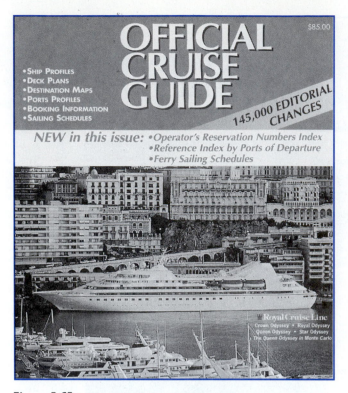

Figure 8.28 Official Cruise Guide *cover.*
(Reprinted with permission from Transportation Guides, Inc.)

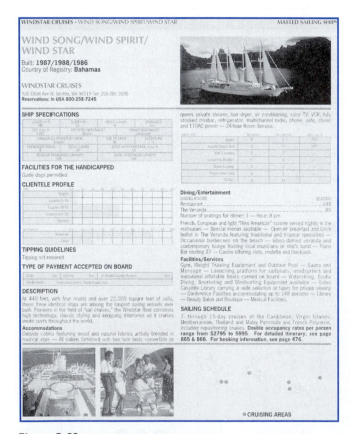

Figure 8.29 *Sample content of* Official Cruise Guide.

A feature section of this resource, Ship Profiles, provides descriptive data on over 375 ships, including information on ship specifications, facilities, services, accommodations, clientele (passenger) breakdown, and sailing schedules. Figure 8.29 is a sample page describing the masted sailing ships of Windstar Cruises.

➤ CLIA Manual

The **Cruise Lines International Association (CLIA)** consists of 33 member cruise lines plus more than 20,000 travel agency affiliates. CLIA's main objective is to market and promote cruise vacations to the traveling public in addition to offering educational and training support to its member travel agencies to assist them in selling cruise travel.

One of the association's major publications is the *CLIA Manual* (see Figure 8.30), which is issued on an annual basis to travel agencies. It is similar to the *Official Cruise Guide* since it contains detailed descriptions of cruise ships. The main difference is that the *CLIA Manual* is more graphic in nature. That is, it contains deck plans, sample menus and wine lists, examples of daily programs, and a lot more. Figure 8.31 is a sample page for the Carnival Cruise Lines' *Holiday*.

SENDING PAYMENTS AND MEETING OPTIONS

When the travel agent books a cruise, the cruise reservation agent places a temporary hold on the cabin of choice. The cabin isn't actually confirmed or secured until the deposit is received by the cruise line. Usually, the deposit is required between seven and ten days after the booking is made. Final payment is due usually 45 to 60 days before departure. Following are some important questions and answers related to the option and payment process when booking cruises.

1. *What is the cruise* **option date?** It is the final date at which time the deposit must be received by the cruise line to secure the cabin of choice. Usually, the option date is seven to ten days after the booking is made.

Figure 8.30 CLIA Cruise Manual *cover.*

PUBLIC ROOM CAPACITIES

NAME	Capacity
FOUR WINDS DINING ROOM	356
SEVEN SEAS DINING ROOM	482
AMERICANA LOUNGE	700
BLUE LAGOON	492
TAHITI LOUNGE	114
REFLECTIONS DISCOTHEQUE	175
RICK'S CAFE AMERICAN	81
CARNEGIE LIBRARY	40
CAPUCCINO'S BAR	45
THE BUS STOP	
THE BUS STOP BAR	
GAMING BAR	60
GAMING CLUB CASINO (standing room)	200+
ELECTRONIC GAME ROOM	
LIDO (Outdoor) PATIO BAR & POOL	150
LIDO (Indoor) THE WHARF	335
CHILDREN'S PLAYROOM	30
CARD AREA	
Times Square/Union Square (each)	32
ENCLOSED PROMENADE-BROADWAY	

NAME: HOLIDAY
COMPANY: CARNIVAL CRUISE LINES
ORIGINALLY BUILT: 1985
COUNTRY OF REGISTRY: PANAMA
SPEED: 21 KNOTS
NORMAL CREW SIZE: 660
NATIONALITY OF CREW
    OFFICERS: ITALIAN
      HOTEL STAFF: INTERNATIONAL
      CRUISE STAFF: INTERNATIONAL

SIZE/CAPACITY

GROSS REGISTERED TONNAGE: 46,052
LENGTH: 728 FEET   BEAM: 92 FEET
TOTAL CAPACITY (incl uppers): 1760
NORMAL CRUISE CAP. (Basis 2): 1452
SPACE RATIO 32

ACCOMMODATIONS

TYPE	No. Outside	No. Inside
SUITES† *	10	
TWINS*	433	250
UPPERS/LOWERS	10	23
TOTAL	453	273
TOTAL CABINS	726	

* All convert to king size beds.
† Include bathtub jacuzzis.

FACILITIES

AIR COND. FULLY	HAIR DRYERS (Allowed)
BARBER SHOP	HOSPITAL
BEAUTY SALON	MASSAGE ROOM
BOUTIQUE	PASSENGER DECKS (9)
CHILD COUNSELLORS	PHOTO GALLERY
(Seasonally)	SAUNA
CHILDREN'S PLAYROOM	SHUFFLEBOARD
CLOSED CIRCUIT TV	SKEET SHOOTING
DRUG STORE	SPAS (2)
DUTY FREE SHOPS	STABILIZERS
ELECTRIC CURRENT	STEREO
(110 AC)	IN CABINS
ELEVATORS (8)	SWIMMING POOLS
FULL CASINO	OUTSIDE (3)
GOLF DRIVING PLAT.	TABLE TENNIS
GYMNASIUM	TELEPHONES
(whirlpool)	TOUR OFFICE

Figure 8.31 *Sample page from* CLIA Cruise Manual.

2. *What happens if the deposit is not received by the option date?* The cruise line has the right to cancel the booking immediately. Whatever cabin they were holding for your client is lost.

3. *What should you do if you know that the deposit won't be received by the option date?* The travel agent should contact the reservation's office immediately to request an extension. The cruise line will usually extend the option by a few days. *Remember:* If the option cannot be met, make sure that you contact reservations on or before the option date to be granted an extension.

4. *Can the client's personal check be sent for deposit or final payment to the cruise line?* No! The deposit and final payment for cruise bookings are issued on the travel agency's check; personal checks from clients are not accepted by the cruise line. Also, most cruise lines will accept an MCO for a credit card transaction.

► Transmitting Payment: Agency Check or MCO

Deposits and final payments for cruise bookings are issued by sending the travel agency's check for the appropriate amount; personal checks from clients are not accepted by the cruise line. For credit card payments, most cruise lines will accept the miscellaneous charges order (MCO). MCO forms are issued by the Airlines Reporting Corporation (ARC). The ARC also prints and distributes to travel agencies other airline-related forms, such as airline tickets and refund notices. The MCO is designed to record a deposit or final payment for a wide variety of air and land services, such as airline tickets, hotel accommodations, land tour packages, and cruises. Figure 8.32 is an example of a completed MCO for a deposit payment on an air/sea cruise package on the Norwegian Cruise Line

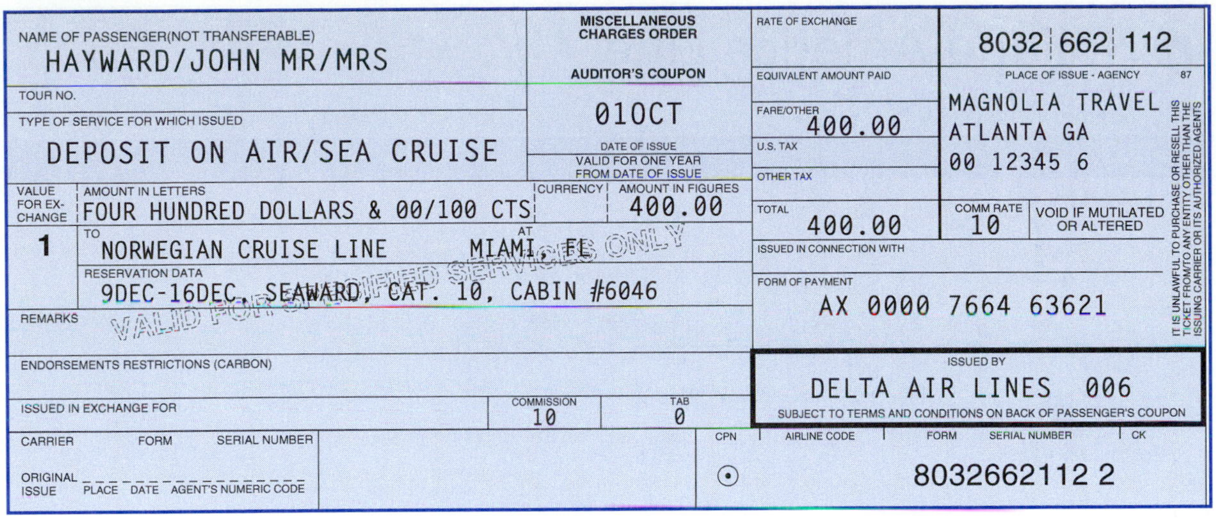

NAME OF PASSENGER(NOT TRANSFERABLE)	MISCELLANEOUS CHARGES ORDER	RATE OF EXCHANGE		8032 662 112

```
NAME OF PASSENGER(NOT TRANSFERABLE)        MISCELLANEOUS          RATE OF EXCHANGE                8032 662 112
  HAYWARD/JOHN MR/MRS                       CHARGES ORDER
                                                               EQUIVALENT AMOUNT PAID      PLACE OF ISSUE - AGENCY   87
TOUR NO.                                   AUDITOR'S COUPON                               MAGNOLIA TRAVEL
TYPE OF SERVICE FOR WHICH ISSUED              01OCT           FARE/OTHER                  ATLANTA GA
  DEPOSIT ON AIR/SEA CRUISE                DATE OF ISSUE            400.00                00 12345 6
                                          VALID FOR ONE YEAR   U.S. TAX
                                          FROM DATE OF ISSUE
VALUE   AMOUNT IN LETTERS        CURRENCY  AMOUNT IN FIGURES   OTHER TAX
FOR EX-  FOUR HUNDRED DOLLARS & 00/100 CTS     400.00
CHANGE                                                        TOTAL                       COMM RATE  VOID IF MUTILATED
  1    TO                             AT            400.00                   10         OR ALTERED
       NORWEGIAN CRUISE LINE       MIAMI FL        ISSUED IN CONNECTION WITH
       RESERVATION DATA
       9DEC-16DEC, SEAWARD, CAT. 10, CABIN #6046   FORM OF PAYMENT
REMARKS                                              AX 0000 7664 63621
ENDORSEMENTS RESTRICTIONS (CARBON)                              ISSUED BY
                                                        DELTA AIR LINES    006
ISSUED IN EXCHANGE FOR         COMMISSION  TAB    SUBJECT TO TERMS AND CONDITIONS ON BACK OF PASSENGER'S COUPON
                                  10        0
CARRIER   FORM   SERIAL NUMBER         CPN   AIRLINE CODE   FORM   SERIAL NUMBER   CK
ORIGINAL                                              8032662112 2
ISSUE    PLACE  DATE  AGENT'S NUMERIC CODE
```

Figure 8.32 *Miscellaneous charges order.*

(NCL). The MCO is being sent to transmit a deposit in the amount of $400 that is being charged to the customer's credit card.

► Cruise Confirmation Notice

The cruise line sends a cruise confirmation or invoice to the travel agency after the booking is made or after the deposit is received. The following information is usually indicated on the invoice: passenger name(s), dining requests, deposit amount/due date, reservation data/cabin assignment, cost breakdown, and final payment due date.

► Cruise Documentation

After the final payment is received by the cruise line, all travel documents are sent to the travel agency. Documents for a cruise are inserted in a cruise line document jacket and usually include the following material:

1. *Cruise ticket.* As you can see in Figure 8.33, the cruise ticket looks different from a standard airline ticket. What it does have in common is the pertinent data regarding the passenger's cruise booking. Read through the sample printed ticket. What types of reservation data appear on it?

2. *Baggage tags.* It is very important to advise your cruise clients to complete the baggage tags (see Figure 8.34) and attach them to each piece of luggage before they depart. On the day of embarkation, the clients surrender their luggage either at the airport upon arrival (if an air/sea package or air add-on supplement) or at dockside (if independent). Baggage is transported automatically to the ship and cabin number indicated on the baggage tags. Each piece of baggage must clearly identify the passenger's name, ship, sailing date, and cabin number.

3. *Immigration questionnaire.* Advise your clients to complete this important document before their departure. It is surrendered along with the cruise ticket before boarding the ship. This form establishes citizenship and allows the passenger to debark from the ship in the non-U.S. ports of call on the itinerary. Advise your clients of all required travel documents, such as passports and proof of citizenship, in plenty of time before departure. This information is explained in the cruise brochure under "Terms and Conditions."

4. *General information.* Helpful information regarding the ship is also included in the client's documentation. Included would be any of the following:

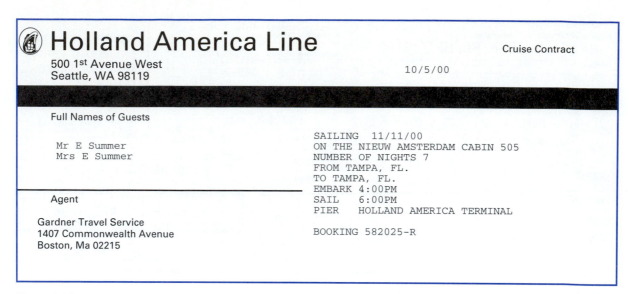

Figure 8.33 *Cruise ticket.*

- Deck plans
- Shore excursions
- Description of ports of call
- Description of ship's facilities and services

5. *Airline tickets.* If the passenger purchases an air/sea package or purchases an air add-on rate, the cruise line company books the air reservation. In most cases the cruise company prepares the airline tickets and sends them along with other

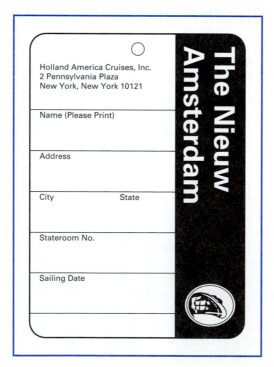

Figure 8.34 *Baggage tag.*

cruise documentation. The sales agent checks the ticketing procedure with each cruise line when booking. For those passengers who are making air reservations independently, the travel agent books the flight and issues airline tickets under normal procedures.

 *Close-Up: Cruise-Related Careers*

Reservations agent	Purser	Sales representative
Reception/hospitality	Shore excursion staff	Cruise specialist

The best starting position with any cruise line is off the ship, where most of the entry-level jobs are. The usual place to start is in the cruise reservation department. A cruise reservation agent acts much like an airline or tour reservations agent: He or she takes calls from travel agents and the general public, books reservations, and provides information about the ships, itineraries, and departures. There are also positions in the sales departments of the cruise companies for representatives. Like their counterparts in the airlines, hotels, and tour companies, cruise sales reps call on travel agencies to promote their cruise ships, resolve problems, and act on special requests.

Another avenue is to become a travel agent who specializes in cruise travel. Many large retail agencies have cruise departments staffed by experts in the field. There are also numerous cruise-only agencies that deal exclusively in this product. These positions require vast knowledge of the cruise product in addition to experience in sales and customer service.

Jobs on board ships are hard to find. They are virtually identical to those of a luxury hotel. Like a hotel, a cruise ship offers positions in food service, housekeeping, front office, and entertainment. Some typical entry-level positions on board follow.

Reception/Hospitality Staff

The reception/hospitality staff members serve as the "front office" of the ship. They take care of passenger's questions and concerns regarding their accommodations and related issues.

Purser

The purser's department consists of a chief purser and purser assistants; the number of assistants increases with the size of the ship and number of passengers. The purser is in charge of the ship's paperwork, clearing the ship while it is in port, and ensuring that the passengers' passports and other required documentation are in order.

Shore Excursion Staff

The shore excursion staff normally consists of a manager plus one or two assistants. They provide passengers with information about the ports of call and frequently give presentations regarding each stop. They also sell the tour excursions for each port of call and ensure the smooth handling of passengers during the tours.

Cruise Staff

The cruise staff consists of the cruise director, an assistant cruise director, and one or more assistants depending on the size of the ship. The large megaships may have a cruise staff of a dozen or more people. This staff is responsible for planning all entertainment and recreational programs and passenger services throughout a voyage.

➤ Key Terms

- aft
- air add-on
- air/sea packages
- amidships
- berth
- boat deck
- bow
- bridge
- cabin
- center of gravity
- Cruise Lines International Association (CLIA)
- debark
- deck
- deck plan
- embark
- forward
- galley
- gross registered tons (GRT)
- hold
- hull
- leeward
- main deck
- manifest
- option date
- per diem
- pitch
- port
- port of call
- porthole
- post-cruise land tour
- pre-cruise land tour
- quay
- registry
- roll
- shore excursion
- stabilizers
- starboard
- stateroom
- stern
- superstructure
- tender
- weather deck
- windward

 Flashback   Years ago anyone could describe what cruising was all about to the proverbial visitor from Mars; traveling by passenger liner was pretty cut and dry. During the 1930s and 1940s, the term *ocean voyage* meant a slow luxury liner between the United States and Europe. Except for dining, dancing, and lounging, just about the only thing that made the cruise experience different from traveler to traveler was the class of service the passenger paid for.

The all-inclusive cruise vacation as we know it today flourished during the 1960s and 1970s with new cruise companies such as Carnival, Norwegian Cruise Line, and Royal Caribbean International operating regularly scheduled cruises to the West Indies and Mexico.

As time went on, cruise products became increasingly sophisticated. Today, so much segmentation exists that it is difficult for any traveler to select the right ship without the assistance of a travel professional. Prospects can select a ship on the basis of price, intimate luxury barges or 130,000-ton megaships, entertainment options available, ships with sails or paddlewheels, relaxing visits to tropical islands or ice-breaking adventures to Antarctica, and so on.

Selling cruises effectively means product knowledge—knowing which ships are targeting what markets—and knowing the tastes, interests, and budget of the traveler. Sales agents have many resources on hand, including the Internet and dazzling cruise brochures.

Why is it so important to know about cruise travel? It is a gold mine that is virtually untapped; only about 10 percent of all leisure travelers have taken a cruise. Another reason is that the cruise industry generates the second-largest revenue source for U.S. travel agencies. In the era of diminishing returns on airline ticket sales, travel companies are seeking to earn higher profits by selling the bigger-ticket items, such as cruises and related leisure products.

CHAPTER REVIEW

True or False?

_____ 1. America Hawaii Cruises is the only major cruise company that is registered in the United States.

_____ 2. Tampa is a popular embarkation port for Mexican Riviera cruises.

_____ 3. Most ships include tipping in the total cost of the cruise vacation.

_____ 4. A major reason why ships anchor rather than dock while visiting a port of call is poor weather conditions.

_____ 5. Most cruise lines offer round-trip discounted air from certain home cities as air add-on options.

_____ 6. Shore excursions are usually reserved in advance and prepaid before cruise departure.

_____ 7. Compared to a traditional seven-day cruise, a repositioning cruise is often longer in duration and visits more exotic ports of call.

_____ 8. The growing number of land tours by motorcoach in the 1960s is the major reason why luxury transatlantic liners lost their popularity.

_____ 9. The trend for traditional cruise vessels in the future will be that they will be built larger and larger—far exceeding 100,000-gross registered tons.

_____ 10. Miami, Florida is the busiest passenger cruise port in the world.

Multiple Choice

Circle the _best_ answer.

11. The leading cruise itinerary in terms of number of ships is:
    A. Mexico
    B. Alaska
    C. Caribbean
    D. western Europe

12. Cunard Sea Goddess, Seabourn Cruises Line, and Silversea Cruises are examples of:
    A. small luxury ships
    B. masted sailing ships
    C. traditional cruise ships
    D. luxury barges

13. Your clients want to sail on a modern-day masted sailing ship with all the comforts and luxury of a land resort; price is no object. Which cruise company would you recommend?
    A. Royal Caribbean International
    B. Windjammer Barefoot Cruises
    C. Windstar Cruises
    D. Renaissance Cruises

14. If you were visiting Jamaica, Grand Cayman, and the Yucatán in Mexico on a week cruise, what itinerary would you be taking?
    A. southern Caribbean
    B. western Caribbean
    C. Trans-Panama Canal
    D. eastern Caribbean

15. Which itinerary below is offered year round?
    A. Hawaii
    B. Antarctica
    C. Alaska
    D. Bermuda

16. When booking cruises, the latest date that deposit payment must be received by the cruise company to secure the reservation is called the:
    A. embarkation date
    C. due date
    B. close date
    D. option date

17. You want to find out which ships are cruising to Alaska during the last week in August: their minimum cruise rates, departure dates, and ports of call. Which one resource is the best for this query?
    A. *Official Steamship Guide International*
    C. *CLIA Manual*
    B. *Official Cruise Guide*
    D. a cruise brochure

18. This cruise resource is very graphical in nature and contains information on all major cruise companies. In addition to pictures and details of individual ships, it contains such helpful sales tools as deck plans, sample menus, and daily programs.
    A. *Official Steamship Guide International*
    C. *CLIA Manual*
    B. *Official Cruise Guide*
    D. a cruise brochure

19. This resource provides promotional material as well as detailed information regarding cabin categories, prices, and terms and conditions of travel about a particular cruise company. It is also the leading sales tool when booking cruises.
    A. *Official Steamship Guide International*
    C. *CLIA Manual*
    B. *Official Cruise Guide*
    D. a cruise brochure

20. This document is sent to the travel agency after the reservation is made and records such things as passenger name(s), deposit required or paid, cabin assignment, and final payment due date.
    A. cruise ticket
    C. immigration questionnaire
    B. miscellaneous charges order (MCO)
    D. confirmation notice

Short Answers

There are common objections voiced by travelers regarding buying a cruise vacation for the first time. If you were the sales agent, how would you handle these common objections? Write what your response to your clients would be.

21. "A cruise is just too expensive."

    _____

    _____

22. "I'm going to get bored."

    _____

    _____

23. "Ships are just too confining; I like my space."

    _____

    _____

24. "I'm on a strict diet and don't want to eat my way through my vacation."

    _____

    _____

25. "We want to vacation with our children and don't think a cruise ship is the best choice for our family."

    _____

    _____

Chapter 9

Car and Rail Travel

A solitary traveler can sleep from state to state, from day to night, from day to day, in the long womb of its controlled interior. It is the cradle that never stops rocking after the lullaby is over.

Lisa St. Aubin de Terán
(b. 1953)

Fast Forward ▼

adventures, coast to coast to practically every corner of the continental United States. . . . 443

➤ Amtrak offers some great promotions and discount deals: Amtrak Explorer Fares to explore the United States by regions and the North American Rail Pass, which combines travel on Amtrak and VIA Rail Canada. . . . 447

➤ From Europe's Venice Simplon-Orient Express to Japan's high-tech bullet trains, here are some of the most unique and fastest trains in the world. . . . 456

➤ As the scenery changes from country to country, so does the atmosphere and the personality of its trains. . . . 465

➤ Rail passes are a convenient and cost-effective way to travel long distances when traveling abroad. . . . 467

INTRODUCTION TO CARS

Car rental bookings may not seem as glamorous or "fun" to do as cruises or adventure expeditions to the Middle East. However, car rental bookings are an important part of the mix in the total revenue generated by travel agencies. In fact, car rental bookings are the fifth-largest source of revenue, after airline, tour, cruise, and hotel bookings. Commission on car rentals is also slightly higher than that on some other products, ranging from 10 to 20 percent, 10 percent being the industry standard. Forgetting to ask a business or vacation traveler for a car rental booking can translate into thousands of dollars in lost revenue every year.

Business and vacation travelers each book car rentals for different reasons. Business travelers are looking for a convenient and reliable form of ground transportation to get them from point A to point B with a minimum amount of fuss and bother. They are much more concerned that the car be in good mechanical condition and that the pickup and drop-off procedures be smooth and efficient. They don't want to spend time waiting in long lines. They have a set agenda; they have meetings to attend and appointments to keep on a strict timetable.

Vacation travelers are looking for a comfortable form of transportation to sightsee along the way. The size of the car is of major concern, due to the number of people traveling together and the amount of luggage and recreational equipment that needs to be transported. The type of vehicle is also a major concern for a family of six on a long-distance sightseeing vacation or the adventure traveler who expects to ride over rough terrain or snow conditions. The two popular states where car rentals are booked for vacation travelers are Florida and California. These destinations are chock full of sightseeing opportunities that are spread over a wide area. They also lack the required level of public transportation to get from one attraction to another in relative ease.

➤ Class/Size of Uehicles

Travelers can rent just about any type of vehicle: small subcompacts that seat no more than four passengers, full-sized sedans, station wagons, sport cars, convertibles, luxury cars, and sport utility vans. What type of vehicle to rent depends on the pickup location, traveler's budget, reason for travel, and personal taste. There

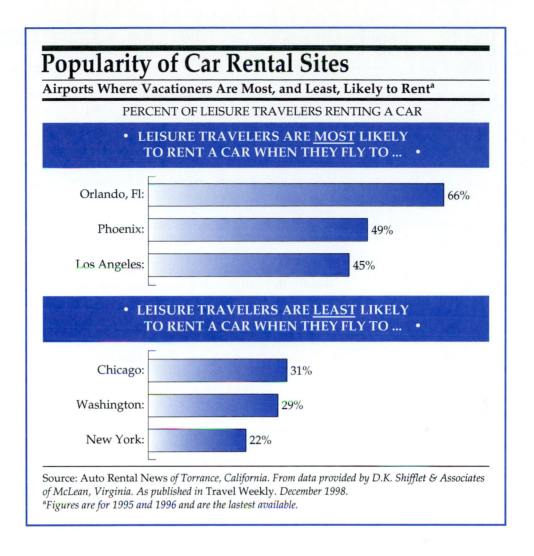

Popularity of Car Rental Sites

Airports Where Vacationers Are Most, and Least, Likely to Rent[a]

PERCENT OF LEISURE TRAVELERS RENTING A CAR

• LEISURE TRAVELERS ARE <u>MOST</u> LIKELY TO RENT A CAR WHEN THEY FLY TO ... •

Orlando, Fl:	66%
Phoenix:	49%
Los Angeles:	45%

• LEISURE TRAVELERS ARE <u>LEAST</u> LIKELY TO RENT A CAR WHEN THEY FLY TO ... •

Chicago:	31%
Washington:	29%
New York:	22%

Source: Auto Rental News *of Torrance, California. From data provided by D.K. Shifflet & Associates of McLean, Virginia. As published in* Travel Weekly. *December 1998.*
[a]*Figures are for 1995 and 1996 and are the lastest available.*

are several basic car categories, from the smallest with basic features (least expensive) to the largest with special features (most expensive) (see Table 9.1).

➤ Special Services and Equipment

Car rental companies are just as competitive as any other travel supplier. In addition to promotions and discounts for special customers, they compete by offering specialized services and equipment. Some are free, while others are at an additional cost. Most car companies offer special equipment such as child safety seats, hand-controlled systems, and skierized and winterized vehicles.

Here are some other examples of special services and equipment offered by various companies. Remember, not all car vendors offer all of the following services and equipment; this should be checked at the time of booking:

- *Satellite guidance systems.* An in-car computer is designed to help the customer pinpoint locations and the best way to get there. These systems are user-friendly, with moving on-screen maps, and highlight the planned route with turn-by-turn directions. Some even have a voice to alert the driver of upcoming turns. This special equipment comes at an extra charge.

- *Concierge service.* The 800 toll-free concierge service offered by Avis is for their customers visiting an unfamiliar city. This service provides information about local restaurants, points of interest, sporting events, shows, and

TABLE 9.1 RENTAL CAR CATEGORIES

CLASS/SIZE	DESCRIPTION	EXAMPLES
Economy or subcompact	Seats two adults and two children with a minimum amount of luggage. When rented in the United States, this type of car usually comes with an automatic transmission; internationally, this type of car comes with manual transmission.	Chevrolet Geo Metro, Ford Escort
Compact	Slightly larger in size than economy or subcompacts. Also, usually automatic and manual transmissions in the domestic United States and internationally, respectively. Either two- or four-door.	Pontiac Sunfire, Chevrolet Cavalier
Intermediate or midsized	Seats four adults comfortably including luggage. Includes four doors, air conditioning, and all standard options. In the United States these cars always have automatic transmission; internationally, they can be rented with either automatic or manual transmission.	Ford Contour, Chevrolet Celebrity, Oldsmobile Achieva
Full-sized (standard)	This vehicle is larger than intermediate and is equipped with automatic transmission both domestically and internationally.	Ford Taurus, Chevrolet Lumina, Chevrolet Monte Carlo
Premium	This type of vehicle is one step above standard full-sized; seats five adults comfortably with luggage; V-8 vehicle includes many extras.	Ford Crown Victoria, Buick LeSabre
Luxury class	These types of cars are available at select locations; not all car rental companies offer them. Accommodates five adults plus luggage comfortably.	Lincoln Town Car, Cadillac Sedan de Ville, Mercedes-Benz
Special	These run the gamut: sleek sports cars, station wagons, convertibles, four-wheel-drive vehicles, and minivans.	Jeep Cherokee, Dodge Caravan, Chevrolet Blazer, Chevrolet Venture

local events. The customer does not pay for this service, only for the services rendered.

- *Touch-screen navigators.* As easy to use as an ATM machine, several major rental companies offer this computer touch-screen map, which provides directions to multiple destinations. Usually, found at car rental locations in major airports.

- *Weatherfax.* Detailed weather forecasts for a specific geographical region are faxed to the car rental pickup location on a daily basis. Usually consisting of one page, the forecast includes a report for that day, for the next day, and a five-day extended forecast. Located at airport and downtown locations.

- *Flight checks.* This service provides real-time information about specific flight departures, flight status, and gate numbers for major airlines. This informational service is provided at car rental return lots and airport counters in selected cities.

- *Emergency roadside service.* Most major rental companies provide 24-hour toll-free emergency roadside service for their customers. Available throughout the United States and in selected countries worldwide.

- *Heads-up displays.* This equipment provides a windshield display of critical driving information, such as low fuel, directional, and speed readings, all projected at eye level. Available in certain types of cars.

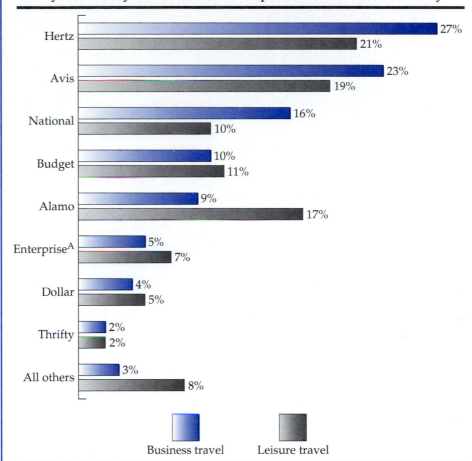

Car Rental Firms' Market Shares[a]

Survey of industry shows Hertz with 27 percent of business rental days.

Firm	Business travel	Leisure travel
Hertz	27%	21%
Avis	23%	19%
National	16%	10%
Budget	10%	11%
Alamo	9%	17%
Enterprise[A]	5%	7%
Dollar	4%	5%
Thrifty	2%	2%
All others	3%	8%

Business travel   Leisure travel

Source: Auto Rental News *(Bobit Publications) of Torrance, California. U.S. market share is based on car rental days. From a survey conducted by D.K. Shifflet & Associates of McLean, Virginia. As published in* Travel Weekly. *August 1998.*
[a]*Data cover the period July 1996 through June 1997.*
[A]*Reflects Enterprise travel transactions and does not include local replacement rentals.*

➤ Requirements to Rent a Car

Practically any traveler can fly on an airplane, ride a train, take a tour, or stay in a hotel room. Not everyone can rent a car. Car rental companies have strict rules with regard to who can and cannot rent their cars. Car rental companies entrust the safety and good condition of their vehicles to the drivers; they have little control over what happens to these cars once they leave their lots. Here are some of the basic rules and requirements when renting cars in the domestic United States and internationally:

1. *License.* The renter must have a valid and current driver's license issued from the country of residence. The license must be valid during the entire rental period and cannot have any erasures or changes. The physical description and signature on the license are matched up with the traveler when picking up the car rental. If the driver's license is in a language other than English and the rental is in the United States, an international driver's permit is recommended.

2. *Age.* The standard minimum age is 25 years. Some rental agencies rent their vehicles to customers between 18 and 24 years in selected corporate locations. Renters must possess a valid license, provide an acceptable form of payment, and be subject to driver's license verification and certification. In many cases, corporate accounts have agreements with certain car agencies which permit employees of those companies between the ages of 21 and 24 to rent for business purposes. A valid corporate identification card must be presented. Most rental companies impose a maximum age limit—either 65 or 70 years of age, depending on the car rental company. Maximum-age limitations are more prevalent internationally.

3. *Credit.* Renters must prove that they are financially responsible in case the car is stolen, lost, or damaged. All rental companies prefer—if not require—a major credit card made out in the renter's name. Another person's credit card is not acceptable. In lieu of a credit card, some rental companies accept a large cash deposit, up to $500. In addition, the rental company may require additional references, such as the traveler's employer or bank.

Key Point ➤ In case of no credit card, most car vendors accept a cash transaction as long as the following can be verified: (1) customer's current employment, minimum one year; (2) address and phone number in renter's name; and (3) bank and/or credit references. A cash deposit equal to or greater than the estimated rental charge is usually required at the time of rental. This should be checked with each company when booking.

➤ Car Rental Costs and Fees

Travelers have choices of renting a car on a daily, weekly, weekend, or monthly basis. If renting on a daily basis or during a weekend, rates are quoted on a 24-hour basis. A weekly rate is based on five to seven 24-hour cycles. Weekly rates are less expensive than a daily rate multiplied by the same number of days.

Rental rates may or may not include mileage. Some rates include *unlimited mileage,* while others require a charge for each mile driven. Other plans allow a maximum number of miles free plus a charge for each mile over the limit. Here are some examples of car rental rate plans:

- $195 per week, including unlimited mileage
- $45 per day plus $0.15 per mile
- $64 per day with 150 free miles, $0.25 per additional mile

Any additional hour(s) above and beyond the rate plan is also an additional charge. Most car vendors give a "grace" period of one or two hours above the agreed time. However, for each additional hour a charge on the average of $15 may be added.

In addition to rental rates and mileage charges, other fees, such as taxes and options, may be added to the total cost. Sales taxes apply when renting cars in the United States and will vary according to location. On international rentals, **value-added taxes (VATs)** or similar taxes are imposed by the laws of some countries. Generally, taxes are not included in any rates quoted at the time of reservation, unless specifically noted. On average, additional taxes range between 5 and 30 percent of the rental charge.

Optional equipment is also at a price. Such things as ski and luggage racks and infant seats may cost anywhere from $5 to $10 per day. Sometimes, rental companies charge an extra few dollars per day for each additional driver.

For one-way rentals a drop charge may apply. This occurs when the car is picked up in one location and dropped off in another. The locations may be two different cities in the same state or in two different states. Drop-off charge policies differ between car vendors and destinations. The exception to this is in the state of Florida. Almost all car vendors do not charge extra for one-way rentals as long as the car is picked up and dropped off in the state of Florida.

Gasoline

Car rental rates generally do not include gasoline unless specified in the published rate. Typically, cars are rented with a full tank of gas and the customer is offered one of three options (may vary slightly between car rental agencies):

1. *Fuel purchase.* Customer purchases a tank of gasoline from the rental agency and therefore is urged to return the car with as little fuel as possible; fuel left in the tank is not credited.
2. *Refill upon return.* Customer refills the car upon return to the car rental agency.
3. *Return with less than full.* Customer returns the car with less than a full tank of gas and the car agency charges a refueling service charge that is applied to the cost of the rental.

Car Insurance

A car rental customer's financial responsibility for loss of/or damage to the rental car varies by country and/or state in the United States. Generally, the customer is liable for an initial amount due to any damages to the car. To avoid this possible charge, car agencies offer insurance at an additional cost. The two basic types of liability protection are **collision damage waiver (CDW)** and **loss damage waiver (LDW).**

The CDW and LDW coverages are optional and when accepted, waive or reduce the customer's responsibility for loss of or damage to the rental car. In simple terms, if the customer purchases the CDW, the car rental agency waives the right to charge for damages in the case of an accident. The LDW releases the renter from paying damages in case the car is either stolen or vandalized. On average, the CDW or LDW costs between $8 and $15 per day and the cost varies according to type of car and location of rental.

Another type of coverage option is **personal accident insurance (PAI).** PAI covers the customer's accidental death or medical expenses resulting from bodily injury. The amount of this type of coverage is minimal and most people are already protected under their own life or health insurance policies. If purchased, the PAI costs on average between $3 and $7 per day.

► Car Discounts and Programs

Car companies want to increase rental sales by offering promotions and special rates for their largest customer base, business travelers. To increase corporate sales, car rental companies offer two types of discounts: *corporate* and *agency negotiated*. They are very similar to the corporate and agency-negotiated rates that hotels offer.

If a particular company rents a lot of cars from one or more car vendors, it negotiates a discounted *corporate rate*. This corporate rate is strictly for travelers from that company while traveling on business. A company may have special corporate rates with more than one vendor. The company is assigned a special corporate identification number that is included in every reservation. Without the ID number, the corporate rate cannot be confirmed.

Travel agencies also negotiate with one or more car rental companies. These discounts, called *agency-negotiated* rates, are only for business travelers who are clients of the travel agency. These clients receive agency-negotiated rates with one or more car vendors through their agencies whether they are traveling on business or pleasure. A travel agency identification number or code is also entered into the traveler's rental booking in order to receive the special rate.

Car rental companies will offer promotional discounts to any traveler during the slower rental periods or off-season. A good example of special promotional rates exist in many major cities. The busy or high period of car rental in these destinations is during the business week; the slower period is during the weekends (Friday, Saturday, and Sunday). Many car vendors offer discounted weekend rates to boost business in certain city locations. Other promotional rates may be offered for a limited period to increase rental bookings in a particular destination.

Car rental agencies inform travel agencies and their clients about rates and special programs through the agency CRS and over the Internet.

➤ Frequent-Renter Programs

Car rental companies are much like airlines and hotels in their attempts to gain customer loyalty. One way of doing that is to offer *frequent-renter programs,* much like the frequent-flyer and frequent-stay award programs offered by airlines and hotels respectively. In fact, car companies have frequent-travel tie-ins with airlines and hotels that service their locations. For example, a traveler can earn extra points by flying on a specific airline, staying at a specific hotel chain, and booking a car with that vendor at a particular destination. Frequent-renter programs enable the customer to earn points for future rental upgrades, free rentals, and other rewards.

Figure 9.1 is a sample description of *Hertz #1 Awards* program. This award program lets customers earn one awards point for each qualifying dollar spent. As you can see, renters can use their earned points toward many types of rewards, such as free car rentals and upgrades. Customers can also exchange their earned points to air miles in frequent-flyer programs of partner airlines. They can even earn golf clubs and tennis rackets.

➤ Car Rental Clubs

While the majority of car companies offer frequent-renter programs where points are earned for rental up-grades, free rentals and other prizes they also offer *car rental clubs* aimed to provide better and more efficient service. Membership in car rental clubs is free. Customers are required to complete an application for membership (see Figure 9.2). Customers can pick up paper applications at most travel agencies or at car rental counters at airports. They can also complete an electronic registration on the Internet at the car rental's Web site.

Frequent-renter clubs (see Table 9.2) offer their members faster and more efficient service when picking up and dropping off cars. Often, preferred service may be more important to the busy business traveler than a free upgrade or something similar. Preferred service awards may enable the renter to bypass regular counter lines when picking up and dropping off the car. In other cases, members are offered courtesy transportation from the airport directly to the traveler's rental car.

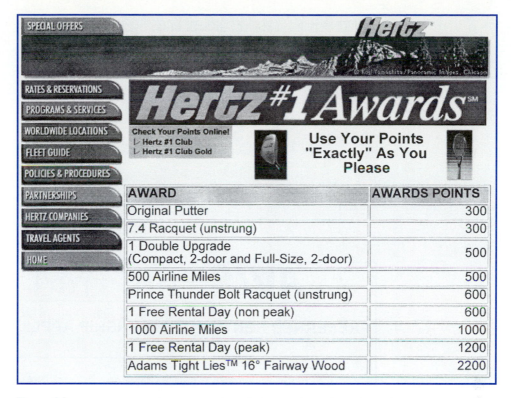

Figure 9.1 *Hertz #1 Awards Program described at Hertz Web site* http://www.hertz.com

► Benefits of Booking Car Rentals

When planning travel for their clients, travel agents must discuss the benefits of purchasing a certain product or service. The same goes for car rentals. If the traveler only intends to stay in one location, where places to visit are easily accessible by public or courtesy transportation or within walking distance, a car rental may be an unnecessary expense. On the other hand, if the traveler plans to cover a lot of ground, is traveling to a location where public transportation is scarce or nonexistent, or is traveling to an area where the places to visit are spread far apart, renting a car may be the best solution.

Here are some important benefits to remember about car rentals:

1. *The more the merrier!* In many cases, renting a car to get from point A to point B is more economical depending on the number of people traveling together. Remember, rental costs are per car; the more people traveling together, the less per person cost incurred. Over long distances the cost of a car rental for three or four people, for example, is far less than buying four airline tickets, four train seats, or four bus rides.

2. *Do your own thing!* You can go practically anywhere, any time, and at your own pace. There are no set departures and arrivals to follow. Business travelers can rearrange schedules and change times for meetings and appointments without worrying about airline or rail timetables. Leisure travelers linger longer in places they really want to see and skip over those of lesser interest.

3. *Suitcase on wheels!* You can pack and transport practically any item—skis, books, large and small suitcases, tennis rackets, golf clubs—without worrying about excess baggage fees, storage, and the inconvenience of carrying them around with you from place to place.

Table 9.2   Frequent-Renter Clubs

Alamo	Alamo Express
Avis	Preferred Renter
Budget	AwardsPlus
Dollar	Corporate Account
Hertz	#1 Club, #1 Club Gold
National	Emerald Club
Payless	Championship Club

AVIS Preferred

PREFERRED RENTER® MEMBERSHIP APPLICATION

As an Avis Preferred customer®, you will be entitled to Preferred service during peak travel periods at more than 900 locations worldwide. No waiting. No paperwork. No delays. Get to your Avis car hassle-free, stress-free. Preferred Service is ideal for frequent travelers like you.

Walk to your car :

At most Preferred service locations, your car will be waiting for you right outside the airport terminal door. Just stop at the special Preferred service counter and show us your driver's license. We'll direct you to your nearby car.

Ride to your car :

At airports where our rental location is away from the main terminal, our courtesy bus will drop you off near your car. No need to stop at any rental counter. Just show your license and rental agreement to the parking attendant as you drive away.

And best of all, it's free!

As this service requires the completion of what we call a Master Rental Agreement, including your signature, we have attached a form to this page which allows you to request the application from us. Fill out the form below and we will snail mail the application to you for your completion and signature.

Please Note - all fields are required information.

YES! Mail me an application for Preferred Service!

We will only send you email in response to this inquiry. We will NOT resell your email address. We value your privacy, too.

Email Address:	
Full Name:	
Address:	
City:	
State/Province | Postal Code:	
Country:	

Figure 9.2   *Avis Preferred Renter Club described at Avis Web site* http://www.avis.com

4. *Where no man has gone before! . . .* Having your own transportation allows you to explore out-of-the-way places that public transportation or guided tours rarely visit. The vacation traveler who wants to stay clear of busy cities and other well-traveled tourist areas can visit small towns and villages tucked away "behind the scenes." It also affords the tourist in foreign countries to do some "life-seeing"—getting to know the people, their customs, and their way of life up close and in their own surroundings.

➤ Qualifying Clients

When booking any type of travel arrangement, you must learn to ask the right questions in order to help your clients make a well-informed decision about their travel plans. The same thing goes for car rentals. After determining the benefits of a car rental for the traveler, here are some key questions and issues to discuss before booking the car:

1. *Where and when will you be picking up the car?* Most car rental companies have facilities at major airports, near airports, in city centers, and in suburban locations. The major car companies, such as Hertz, Avis, National, and Budget, have their service counters situated in the baggage claim areas for easy access. Even though rates are generally higher when renting at an airport, business travelers are willing to pay for the convenience. Car companies that have off-airport facilities usually offer courtesy transportation to and from the rental area.

2. *Where and when will you be dropping off the car?* Rates vary from destination to destination. Also, if the customer plans to pick up and drop off in two different locations, there may be a one-way drop charge. This should be checked beforehand.

3. *What type of car do you want?* Related questions may be: How many are traveling, and what are the reasons for travel? Cars come in all sizes, makes, and models. The business traveler using the car to get from meeting to meeting may be satisfied with a compact or standard-sized car. A couple taking an outdoor vacation through the Rocky Mountains may require a four-wheel drive with a lot of room for luggage, skis, and other outdoor gear. If no special car category is requested at the time of booking, the car rental firm will reserve a standard-sized car. Since not all makes and models are available at all sites, this is important to ask.

4. *When and for how long will you need the car?* Cars are rented on a 24-hour basis. Most rental firms offer daily, weekend, weekly, and monthly rates. However, the rate applies whether or not the car is used. Tell the client to minimize the amount of time the vehicle is sitting in parking lots or garages. If this is the case most of the time, a car rental for a long period of time may not be the best thing to do. Also, blackout dates may apply during vacation and holiday periods, thus making discount or special promotional rates unavailable.

5. *What additional charges might be added on?* There may be additional charges for special services or equipment that the customer is requesting. For example, cellular phones or portable fax machines in the vehicle come at additional costs. Or the family traveling on vacation may require a ski or bike rack, for which there is also an additional charge.

6. *Is the client eligible for discounts or other special promotions?* Car rental firms offer discount rates during off-peak travel times or to certain destinations to promote sales. Also check to see if the rental firm offers standard corporate discounts to qualified companies. Travel agencies also do business with certain preferred car rental suppliers and may have agency-negotiated rates with certain firms. Another important question: Is the traveler a member of any frequent-travel programs either directly with a particular car company or with airlines and hotels that offer tie-in programs?

➤ International Car Rentals

Renting cars in foreign countries is much like renting them for domestic travel in North America. But here are some essential differences and things to watch out for:

1. *Know your right from your left.* In most countries in the world, the law dictates driving as we do in North America, on the right side of the road. However, in the following countries and on the following islands, driving is on the left (not a complete list):

Western Hemisphere	*Eastern Hemisphere*
• Bahamas	• United Kingdom (England, Wales, Scotland, Northern Ireland)
• Barbados	• Republic of Ireland
• British Virgin Islands	• Kenya
• Jamaica	• Tanzania
• U.S. Virgin Islands	• South Africa
• Trinidad and Tobago	• Pakistan
• Turks and Caicos	• India
• Guyana	• Malaysia
• Suriname	• Thailand
	• Hong Kong
	• Australia
	• New Zealand

2. *Don't take this for granted.* Most cars come with automatic transmission and air-conditioning when rented in the United States and Canada; these are standard features in most vehicles and locations. When renting cars internationally, vehicles with automatic transmissions or air-conditioning must be requested specifically at the time of booking; and they cost more. Also, air-conditioning is not available in certain countries and may only be an option in the largest or more expensive vehicles.

3. *Things that cost a little more.* In many foreign countries, gasoline prices are higher than they are in North America. In fact, prices abroad can be three or four times higher. Also, value-added tax (VAT) is usually not quoted in the car rental price. VAT can be anywhere from 10 to 25 percent of the rental charge.

4. *Beware of where you drive.* Certain countries have restrictions that may affect the North American tourist on a self-drive holiday. For example, a special sticker is required when driving on Austria's and Switzerland's autobahns (high-speed highways). Another example is Eastern Europe. Due to car theft problems in this area of the world, many car rental companies do not allow their vehicles to be taken into this part of Europe. Those that do may require that the rental car be parked in locked garages when not in use.

➤ Car Rentals on the CRS

Travel agents book car rentals for their clients by contacting the car rental reservation office on a toll-free 800 number or on the agency's computer reservations system. The majority of car rentals are booked by travel agents through the computer.

The major CRSs can provide current rates and availability for all major rental companies. Figure 9.3 is a sample display of a car shopper's display on American Airlines' *SABRE* system. The travel agent requested a display of car

```
CFPDX/12JUN-15JUN/8A-12N
PORTLAND OR      -WED      12 JUN    8A    PDX          SAT 15 JUN    12N
```

	CAR	COMPANY	S	TYPE	R	USD	DAILY	MI/KM	CHARGE	APT
001	ZT	THRIFTY	S	ECAR	G		23.95X	UNL	.00	OFF
002	ZR	DOLLAR	S	ECAR	G		23.95X	UNL	.00	IN
003	AL	ALAMO	S	ECAR	G		24.95	UNL	.00	OFF
004	ZL	NATIONAL	S	ECAR	G		26.99	UNL	.00	IN
005	ZI	AVIS	S	ECAR	G		33.99X	UNL	.00	IN
006	ZD	BUDGET	S	ECAR	G		34.99	UNL	.00	IN
007	ZE	HERTZ	S	ECAR	G		34.99	UNL	.00	IN
008	ZS	SEARS	S	ECAR	Q		34.99	UNL	.00	IN

Figure 9.3 SABRE *display of car availability and rates.*

rentals available in Portland, Oregon. The specific car category requested is economy car (coded as ECAR). Pickup date and time are June 12 and 8 A.M.; drop-off date and time are June 15 and 12 noon. After selecting the car company from the list, the travel agent can "sell" or make a reservation directly from the display. The columns in the display are described as follows:

1. Line number by car type. The agent identifies the line number when selling a car rental off the display.
2. Car vendor two-letter code.
3. Car vendor's full name.
4. Status of car (S, available for sale; N, request basis only; C, sold out).
5. Car type code (ECAR, economy-sized car).
6. Rate variability (G, rate is guaranteed; Q, rate is subject to change).
7. Rate column (daily, rate per day; weekly, rate per week; weekend, special weekend rate; monthly, rate per month). An "X" following the rate indicates that extra day or extra hour rates may apply.
8. Mileage plan (UNL, unlimited mileage).
9. Charge indicates the cost per mile (if applicable).
10. Location of car rental counter in relation to airport/shuttle availability (OFF, off-airport location or within five miles of airport, a shuttle is required; IN, in-airport location, a shuttle is not required; S-IN, in-airport location, shuttle is required).

✔ *Check Your Understanding 9-1*

1. Identify the six major car classes or categories, not including special vehicles such as sports cars, convertibles, sport utility vehicles, and minivans.

   A. _____   D. _____

   B. _____   E. _____

   C. _____   F. _____

2. What is the standard minimum age required when renting cars?   _____

3. What is the major form of payment for car rentals?   _____

4. What is the difference between CDW and LDW?

_____

5. In addition to renting a car on a daily basis, what are three other types of basic rental plans?

A. _____   C. _____

B. _____

6. You are helping to plan a two-week sightseeing vacation through the United States and into Canada for a family of four. They want to explore new destinations and to see as much as they can during this trip. Give three reasons why renting a car may be the best thing for them.

A. _____

B. _____

C. _____

Introduction to Rail

How about train travel? Have you ever asked yourself *who travels by train anymore when you can get from point A to point B much faster by airplane?* Some people may question the importance of rail travel in the age of supersonic jet travel, high-speed computer communications, and the busy and sometimes frenetic lifestyle in today's society. Believe it or not, there are important markets for rail travel, both domestically and internationally. Who travels by rail? You would be surprised: business people wanting a more comfortable space to work in transit; vacation travelers operating on "low speed"; sightseers who want to see things at ground level; senior citizens, student groups, and others who just love the history and nostalgia associated with rail travel.

U.S. Rail: Amtrak

The most historic benchmark in U.S. rail history took place in Promontory, Utah. This is when two construction gangs were building the first transcontinental track across the United States. One group started on the east coast and the other started on the west coast; they met in Utah on May 1869.

Rail service boomed for many decades. Some private railroads made a profit, but more and more were soon in trouble, due to the duplication of routes and services among several companies. The trend became the merger of railways, which did help some companies.

By the 1970s a decline in railways affected business worldwide. This downturn in passenger rail service was strongly felt in the United States. Many privately owned railroad companies came close to bankruptcy due to duplication of rail service, ruthless competition, and a decreasing demand for passenger rail service. Up until that time, resistance to any type of federal financial support or nationalization of the railroads was strong. But in 1970, by Act of Congress, the *National Railroad Passenger Corporation* (**Amtrak)** was established to support the operation of a network of intercity passenger trains. In general, Amtrak has been a success by ensuring the continued existence of passenger train service by ordering new rail equipment, consolidating service over certain routes, and subsequently winning back passengers to rail transport.

Magans Bay, St. Thomas, U.S.V.I.

Lodging above the Arctic Circle, Lofatan Islands, Norway

The Observatory, Chichen Itza, Yucatan in Mexico

On safari, Kruger National Park, Republic of South Africa

Houseboats on Lake Dal, Kashmir, India

Chinese New Year—Hong Kong harbor

Taj Mahal—Agra, India

Falucca boats—Nile River, Egypt

Pyramids in Giza—Cairo, Egypt

Opera House—Sydney, Australia

Eiffel Tower—Paris, France

Best Rail Trips in the World

From China to Norway to Chicago, here are ten favorites.

1. *South America:* Puno to Machu Picchu, Peru
2. *United States:* Portland, Oregon to San Fracisco
3. *Asia:* Xian to Chengdu, China
4. *South America:* Ferrocarril Austral Fuegino, Argentina
5. *Europe:* Myrdal to Flam, Norway
6. *Europe:* Istanbul to Paris
7. *North America:* Copper Canyon, Mexico
8. *United States:* Los Angeles to Chicago to Washington to Orlando to New Orleans to Los Angeles
9. *Asia:* Siliguri to Darjeeling, India
10. *United States:* The Howard "El," Chicago

Source: *Contributors and editors of America Online's Travel Corner, hosted by Weissmann Travel Reports of Austin, Texas. As published in* Travel Weekly, *September 1998.*

➤ Amtrak Equipment

Amtrak has four types of rail equipment in its fleet: single-level (plus viewliner sleeping cars), superliner, and the special Auto Train. On overnight trains, sleeper cars with accommodations and dining cars are also available.

Single-Level Fleet

The trains in the *single-level fleet* operate primarily in the east and offer three classes of service: coach, custom, and club. Custom class is similar to business class on airplanes; seats are more comfortable than coach with better service. Club class is first class, with the most comfortable and spacious seats plus other amenities.

Viewliner Sleepers

Part of the single-level fleet, the *viewliner sleepers* are available on selected single-level rail service operating in the eastern region, as far west as Chicago in the north and New Orleans in the south. Viewliner cars have been built with the latest technology, for a smoother, quieter ride. Passengers ride in their own private bedrooms, which consist of seating during the day, and folddown berths or beds during evening hours. An additional row of windows brings in more light during the day and provides upper berth passengers their own window at night (see Figure 9.4). Each bedroom also has its own sink and toilet, an electrical outlet, mirror, linens, towels, soap, and in-room audio/video entertainment with first-run movies.

Deluxe bedrooms offer a comfortable sofa and armchair during the day, and convert to an upper and lower berth at night. Deluxe accommodations also have an enclosed shower, along with a sink and toilet. Families or couples traveling together can purchase two deluxe bedrooms, which can be combined into a deluxe suite, which accommodates up to four, with two private bathrooms. Special accessible bedrooms are available for passengers with mobility requirements. Food

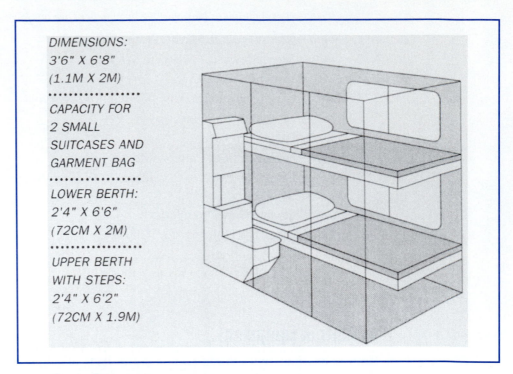

DIMENSIONS:
3'6" X 6'8"
(1.1M X 2M)
....
CAPACITY FOR
2 SMALL
SUITCASES AND
GARMENT BAG
....
LOWER BERTH:
2'4" X 6'6"
(72CM X 2M)
....
UPPER BERTH
WITH STEPS:
2'4" X 6'2"
(72CM X 1.9M)

Figure 9.4 *Viewliner standard bedroom.*
(From Amtrak Travel Planner.)

and beverage service to the room is provided along with in-room audio and video movies. All sleeper accommodations offer complimentary meals.

Superliner Fleet

The *superliner fleet* provides bilevel train service operating on trains west of Chicago and selected trains in the east. The Superliner coaches feature upper-level seating with huge panoramic windows. Each seat reclines with overhead reading lights and a fold-down tray. Each train has a sightseer lounge car, which consists of comfortable seating in front of huge wraparound windows on the upper level, and table booths and an eating café on the lower level. Full-service dining is available in the dining car.

The superliner fleet also has sleeper cars that include standard bedrooms (for one or two passengers without private facilities), deluxe bedrooms (with seating during the day and private facilities). Large family bedrooms, which occupy the entire width of the lower level at one end of a car, have private windows on both sides and come with a long sofa and two seats for daytime viewing. At night, the cabin converts to upper and lower berths for adults and two child-sized berths (see Figure 9.5).

Auto Train

The **Auto Train** provides passenger seating, dining, and entertainment cars in addition to enclosed carriers at the end of the train to transport passengers' cars, vans, and motorcycles. Daily departures leave Lorton, Virginia at 4:30 P.M. and arrive in Sanford, Florida early the next morning. Both coach seating and sleeping car accommodations are available, with breakfast and dinner served in

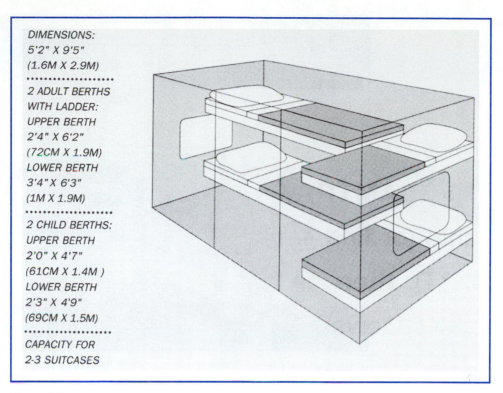

DIMENSIONS:
5'2" X 9'5"
(1.6M X 2.9M)
....
2 ADULT BERTHS
WITH LADDER:
UPPER BERTH
2'4" X 6'2"
(72CM X 1.9M)
LOWER BERTH
3'4" X 6'3"
(1M X 1.9M)
....
2 CHILD BERTHS:
UPPER BERTH
2'0" X 4'7"
(61CM X 1.4M)
LOWER BERTH
2'3" X 4'9"
(69CM X 1.5M)
....
CAPACITY FOR
2-3 SUITCASES

Figure 9.5 *Superliner family bedroom.*
(*From Amtrak* Travel Planner.)

the dining cars and movies and other entertainment features in the lounge cars. The lounge cars are designed on two levels, with audio and video systems and a combination of booth and lounge seating. This is a great way for vacationers to avoid the 900-mile trip by car along route 95 in either or both directions.

➤ Rail Services and Requirements

Traveling by rail has some things in common with air travel: baggage requirements, boarding procedures, first-class and coach cabins, reserved seats, and meals. Unlike air travel, rail service includes unreserved seating plus other amenities, such as entertainment (other than movies) and sleeping accommodations.

Classes of Service

Coach class is the standard class of service on Amtrak. Amtrak's coach seats are more spacious and comfortable than standard coach seats on commercial airlines. Coach seats on trains recline, with fold-down tray tables. Coach rail cars have two-by-two seating with one walking aisle down the middle. Many long-distance coach seats are extraspacious, including leg rests and pillows (for overnight travel; see Figure 9.6).

On selected trains on the Amtrak system, there are two types of upgraded seating from standard coach: custom and club. Custom and club class of service on Amtrak are similar to business and first class on an airplane. They are both more expensive than standard coach, with club class being the most expensive. Both types of seats require a reservation.

Custom class offers a guaranteed seat (due to the advanced reservation requirement), with extra legroom and more comfortable seats. Custom passengers

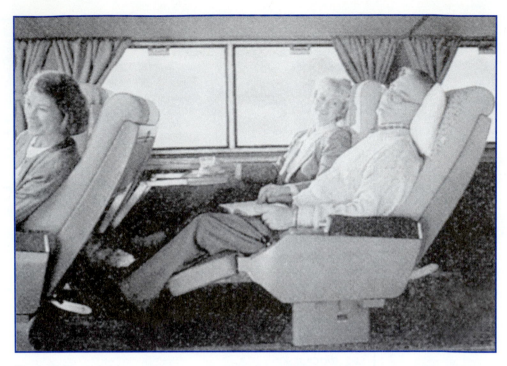

Figure 9.6 *Reclining coach seats with leg rests are available on many overnight trains.*

receive complimentary juice, soft drinks, coffee or tea, plus the latest edition of a major newspaper.

Club class, Amtrak's first-class seats, are located in a separate reserved car. Seats have more legroom and are more deluxe than custom class. For privacy, passengers can reserve single seats as well as the customary double ones. Club class cars feature Railfones as well as a private phone booth. Club passengers receive a choice of hot or cold meals, plus complimentary soft drinks, including wine by the glass. Passengers in club class receive all meals and beverages at-seat service plus extra touches such as mints and hot towels. Club passengers also have first-class Amtrak lounge privileges at major stations, such as New York, Philadelphia, and Washington, DC. Lounges offer amenities such as complimentary beverages, telephones, conference rooms, and PCs.

Unreserved and Reserved Tickets

Amtrak offers both reserved and unreserved tickets. A reserved ticket guarantees a seat or an accommodation. On unreserved trains, seats are available on a first-come, first-served basis. Upon boarding, passengers can choose their own seats or be assisted by an onboard conductor. When all seats are occupied, especially during peak travel times such as holidays or school vacations, passengers may be required to stand until seats become available.

Reservations are *always required* on the following rail services:

- Long-distance overnight coach seats
- Sleeping accommodations
- Wheelchair-accessible seats
- All first-class seats (club and custom class)
- Coach seats on selected trains, such as high-speed rail and other services in the east and midwest corridors

Travel agents can make Amtrak reservations for their clients by contacting Amtrak by telephone or through the agency's computer reservations system. Amtrak can also be booked directly from their Web site. Reservations can be made at any time from eleven months prior to departure date. Once the reservation is made, the Amtrak agent provides a reservation number that identifies the booking and a deadline for purchasing the rail ticket. If the ticket is not purchased by this date, the reservation is canceled.

➤ Examples of Major Routes

Amtrak offers service to practically every major city in the continental United States. What's so special are the names of some of their special routes. Names such as the *Twilight Shoreliner, Lake Shore Limited, Sunset Limited,* and *California Zephyr* evoke romantic rail adventures, coast to coast, to practically every corner of this land. Here are just a few of these special routes that are of particular interest to vacation and business travelers.

High-Speed Rail

The northeast corridor, between Boston and Washington, DC is served by *Acela,* Amtrak's latest technology: high-speed trains that reach speeds of 150 mph that run on overhead electric cables (see Figure 9.7). There are hourly trains between Boston and New York, and two trains each hour between New York and Washington, DC. Travel time between New York and Washington on standard rail service takes approximately four hours; this is reduced to 2¾ hours on this latest high-speed service.

Believe it or not, the time it takes to fly between these city centers takes just as long if you consider the ride to the airport, parking the car, claiming luggage upon arrival, and the ride into town. Many business travelers prefer to take the trip by high-speed rail because of the high-speed service, spacious worktables, and business amenities on board, such as phones and laptop outlets at each seat. Seats are extrawide, with more legroom than first-class seats on most airlines.

Figure 9.7 *Amtrak's high-speed train service along the northeast corridor.*

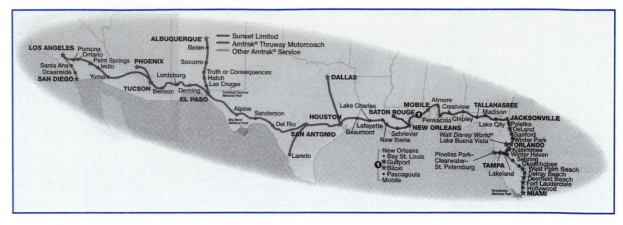

Figure 9.8 *Route of Amtrak's* Sunset Limited.

Sunset Limited

The *Sunset Limited* follows Amtrak's southern and sunny route, from sea to shining sea. The terminal points of the Sunset Limited are in balmy southern California and the palm-lined beaches in Florida (see Figure 9.8). The route takes the passenger through eight states and an exciting cross section of the different scenes and moods of America: the posh desert resort of Palm Springs; Native American culture around Tucson and Phoenix, Arizona; Mexican flavor between San Antonio and Houston, Texas; the bayous and the French Quarter of New Orleans; and the Atlantic beaches of Florida. Last stop is Orlando, Florida.

Coast Starlight

The *Coast Starlight* is Amtrak's exploration of some of the best West Coast destinations. The scenic trip combines gorgeous beaches and coastline panoramas, sophisticated cities, and the mountainous terrain of the Cascades, speeding through 22 tunnels and a countless number of hairpin turns. The terminal points on this adventure route are Seattle, Washington and Los Angeles, California (with convenient rail connections farther south, to San Diego; see Figure 9.9).

Silver Service

The *Silver Service* is Amtrak's link between cosmopolitan New York City and the balmy beaches of Miami, Florida. Passengers travel past historic battlefields of the Civil War in Virginia, rich history surrounds such places as Charleston, South Carolina and Savannah, Georgia. Last stops may include Orlando, land of the Disneyworld theme parks, Tampa along the gulf coast, and such Atlantic beach resorts as West Palm Beach, Fort Lauderdale, and Miami (see Figure 9.10).

California Zephyr

The *California Zephyr* is Amtrak's route through America's natural wonders. As described in Amtrak's literature, the *California Zephyr* takes the passenger from the fertile farmlands of the corn belt to the deep red canyons and western mountains. The terminal points are Chicago and Oakland, with bus transfers to

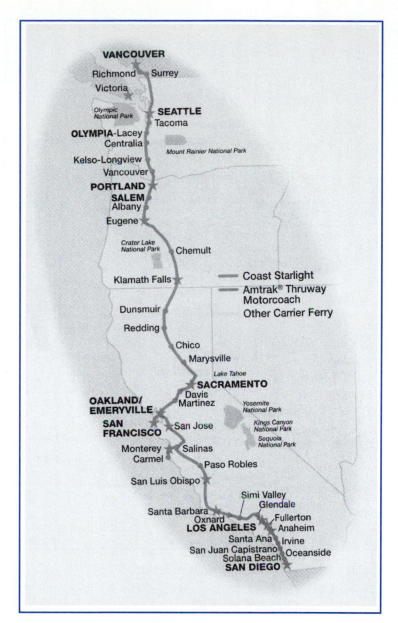

Figure 9.9 *Route of Amtrak's* Coast Starlight.

San Francisco (see Figure 9.11). The route highlights a breathtaking ride through the Front Range of the Rocky Mountains, across the Continental Divide, through Gore Canyon, which is surrounded by sheer rock walls reaching over 1,500 feet. Salt Lake City, which is on the route, serves as a gateway to major ski resorts and the heritage center of the Mormons. In contrast, the glittering casinos of Reno and the natural beauty of Lake Tahoe are some of the last sightseeing features before arriving in San Francisco.

Amtrak on the Web: This site has everything: schedules and prices, reservations and ticketing, discounts and special promotions, route maps, and a lot more. Point your browser to *http://www.amtrak.com*

Web Link

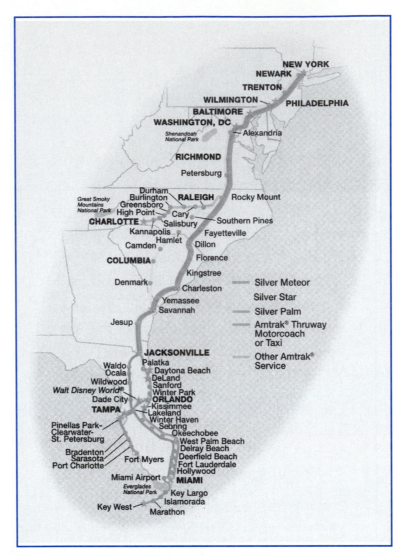

Figure 9.10 *Route of Amtrak's* Silver Service.

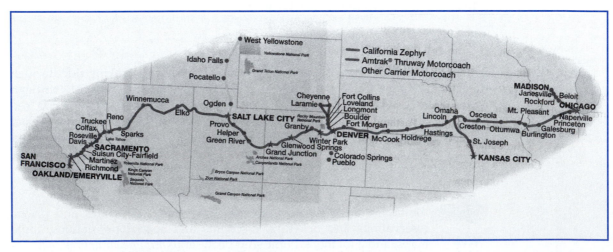

Figure 9.11 *Route of Amtrak's* California Zephyr.

Multiple Choice

Circle the *best* answer.

1. The original name of Amtrak, enacted by Congress in 1970, was:
    A. National Railroad Corporation of America
    B. Passenger Railroad of America
    C. National Railroad Passenger Corporation
    D. National Railroad Company

2. If you were riding on a train between Lorton, Virginia and Sanford, Florida and taking your car along, you would be riding on what train service?
    A. *Silver Star*   C. *Auto Train*
    B. *Twilight Express*   D. superliner

3. Bilevel rail service with upper-level seating and huge picture windows, operating primarily west of Chicago, is the:
    A. high-speed service   C. Auto Train
    B. viewliner   D. superliner

4. Amtrak's first-class service that provides at-your-seat meal service is:
    A. club   C. custom
    B. coach   D. premier

5. Reservations are required on Amtrak for:
    A. sleeping accommodations   C. overnight coach seats
    B. custom seats   D. all of the above

6. Amtrak's sunny route that travels between Florida and southern California through such places as Palm Springs, Phoenix, and New Orleans is:
    A. *Coast Starlight*   C. *Silver Service*
    B. *California Zephyr*   D. *Sunset Limited*

7. The type of sleeping accommodation found on the superliner trains that occupies the full width of a train car and sleeps two adults and two children is:
    A. standard bedroom   C. deluxe bedroom
    B. family bedroom   D. bedroom suite

8. Amtrak's high-speed service called *Acela* between Boston, New York City, and Washington is attractive to business travelers because:
    A. There is comfortable seating with space to work.
    B. There are laptop connections at each seat.
    C. It is almost as fast as airline transportation over the same route.
    D. All of the above.

➤ Amtrak Fares and Discount Travel

Amtrak offers several types of special fares and discount promotions. Here are a few examples.

Amtrak Explorer Fares

Use of Amtrak's *explorer fares* is a good deal for those wanting to travel long distances by rail. These discount fares are based on regions: east, central, west, and Florida (for those just traveling within that state). Choose the destinations and count the number of regions the passenger travels across. For example, Chicago to Dallas is one region; San Diego to Kansas City is two regions; and Washington, DC to San Francisco is three regions (see Figure 9.12). The fare is based on the number of regions traveled and allows three stops within a 45-day period. Discounted fares are usually not available on special trains such as high-speed rail service.

Additional values may be available when purchasing round-trip tickets, travel during off-peak times of the year or during mid-week on certain routes. *Amtrak fares are lowest for travel during these off-peak travel periods:*

- Early January through mid-June
- Late August through mid-December

Auto Train fares are lowest for travel during these periods:

Northbound

- Early January through mid-February
- Mid-June through mid-December

Southbound

- Mid-February through late March
- May through September

Children (ages 2 to 15) ride at half-price when accompanied by a full-fare passenger. Senior citizens 62 years of age and older receive a 15 percent discount on most coach fares. In addition, persons with disabilities receive 15 percent off coach prices, and travelers on military furlough and their families receive 25 percent discounts. Additional restrictions apply.

North American Rail Pass

In 1998, Amtrak and **VIA Rail Canada** joined forces for the first time and developed a rail pass that is valid for domestic and international visitors in both the United States and Canada. With the pass, the traveler has unlimited travel by rail

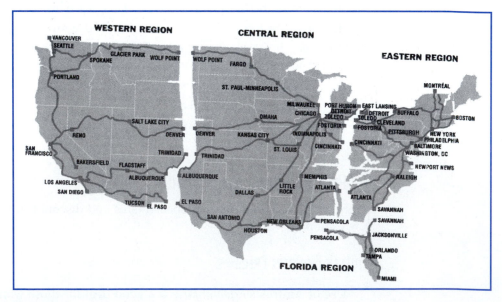

Figure 9.12 *Amtrak's fare regions.*

over 28,000 miles of track. The *North American Rail Pass* is valid for systemwide travel on both Amtrak and VIA during 30 consecutive days. The trip must include travel in both countries. Prices vary according to season. High season is considered to be from June 1 through October 15. The price per adult for high-season travel is approximately $675; during low season or the balance of the year, the price is approximately $475. Prices are subject to change each year.

➤ Reading Amtrak Schedules

There are many ways to find Amtrak schedules. The major computer reservations systems have Amtrak information that include system timetables, availability on reserved trains, pricing, and related information. Similar information is also available at Amtrak's Web site on the Internet.

One printed resource is the *Official Railway Guide (ORG)*, which is printed six times per year. It has a similar format as the *Official Airline Guide (OAG)* for flight information. Amtrak also prints timetables for different geographical regions. Figure 9.13 is a sample Amtrak schedule from the northeast timetable. The Twilight Shoreliner is an overnight train that travels between Boston and Newport News, Virginia. Reading train schedules is easy; read down along the left column for arrival and departure time; read up along the right column for arrival and departure times.

Another resource for Amtrak schedules and prices is on the Internet. The user just enters the departure and arrival cities in a "fill-in-the-blank" mask to display all schedules that operate between the city pair requested. Figure 9.14 is a cutaway example of a train schedule from Amtrak's Web site. It shows the schedule for the Coast Starlight service that operates between Los Angeles and Seattle, Washington. As you can see, it is a lot more user-friendly than the printed resource is.

SPECIAL TRAINS OF NORTH AMERICA

➤ The *American Orient Express*

The *American Orient Express* is a privately owned company that has restored vintage railcars from the 1940s and 1950s. The restoration project cost more than $14 million, and the results have been worth every penny both for historians and for those who love to ride the rails. The interiors of the cars have been restored to the last detail: polished mahogany and brass that glistens, rich fabrics, and custom carpets (see Figure 9.15).

The *American Orient Express* evokes memories of the opulence and luxury of Europe's *Orient Express*. The train includes:

- Two dining carriages where passengers dine at tables set with china, silver, crystal, and linen while feasting on gourmet meals reflecting regional cuisine.
- Sleeping carriages that have twin beds, a large picture window, writing table, built-in wash basin, and private toilet facilities. During the day, the lower berths are converted into comfortable couches. A shower compartment is located at the end of each car. Suites are also available that are larger and accommodate up to three people. The presidential suite even has a private shower. Suites are also available at additional cost.
- Lounge or club cars that are decorated with brass, leather, and ebony, where pianists perform nightly on a baby grand piano.
- An observation car located at the end of the train that offers plush seating and a circular bay window.

TWILIGHT SHORELINER

Boston • New York • Philadelphia • Washington • Richmond • Newport News

67		◀ Train Number ▶		66	76
Daily		◀ Days of Operation ▶		See below	See below
Read Down	**Mile**	▼	▲	**Read Up**	
8 30P	0	Dp Boston, MA–South Sta. (ET)	Ar	⌐ 6 55A	⌐ 6 55A
R 8 37P	1	Boston, MA–Back Bay Sta.		D 6 47A	D 6 47A
R 8 51P	11	Route 128, MA		D 6 30A	D 6 30A
9 26P	43	Providence, RI		6 00A	6 00A
10 01P	70	Kingston, RI		4 46A	5 00A
10 15P	87	Westerly, RI		4 28A	4 43A
10 25P	96	Mystic, CT	Mo-Fr	4 18A	SaSu 4 33A
10 39P	105	New London, CT		4 05A	4 20A
10 56P	123	Old Saybrook, CT		3 43A	3 58A
11 30P	156	Ar New Haven, CT	Dp	3 05A	3 20A
11 50P		Dp	Ar	2 40A	2 55A
12 34A	195	Stamford, CT		1 51A	2 06A
1 19A	231	Ar New York, NY–Penn Sta.	Dp	∟ 1 00A	∟ 1 00A
1 45A		Dp	Ar	12 15A	12 15A
2 10A	241	Newark, NJ–Penn Sta.		⌐ 11 44P	⌐ 11 44P
2 25A	255	Metropark, NJ		11 28P	11 28P
2 49A	289	Trenton, NJ		11 03P	11 03P
3 20A	322	Ar Philadelphia, PA–30th St. Sta.	Dp	10 28P	10 28P
4 05A		Dp	Ar	10 18P	10 18P
4 30A	347	Wilmington, DE		9 55P	9 55P
5 30A	416	Baltimore, MD–Penn Sta.		9 08P	9 08P
5 43A	427	BWI Airport Rail Sta., MD		8 50P	8 50P
5 58A	448	New Carrollton, MD		8 31P	8 31P
6 15A	457	Ar Washington, DC	Dp	Su-Th 8 20P	FrSa 8 20P
6 55A		Dp	Ar	7 55P	7 55P
7 11A	466	Alexandria, VA		7 28P	7 28P
7 39A	492	Quantico, VA		6 58P	6 58P
7 59A	512	Fredericksburg, VA		6 39P	6 39P
8 41A	556	Ashland, VA		5 57P	5 57P
8 58A	566	Ar Richmond, VA	Dp	5 45P	5 45P
9 04A		Dp	Ar	5 37P	5 37P
10 25A	621	Williamsburg, VA		4 23P	4 23P
10 58A	644	Ar Newport News, VA (ET)	Dp	∟ 4 00P	∟ 4 00P

Connecting Services

Amtrak Thruway Connection—Newport News, VA/Virginia Beach, VA

Daily			Days of Operation		Su-Th	FrSa
11 10A	0	Dp	Newport News, VA	Ar	3 15P	3 15P
D 11 55A	22	Ar	Norfolk, VA		R 2 35P	R 2 35P
12 35P	41	Ar	Virginia Beach, VA	Dp	1 50P	1 50P

SERVICES ON THE TWILIGHT SHORELINER

Coaches: Reservations required.
Sleeping Cars: First Class Viewliner Service. Amtrak's Metropolitan Lounge® available in New York and Washington.
Custom Class: Reserved coach seating. Complimentary non-alcoholic beverage.
Twilight Lounge: Open to First Class and Custom Class passengers.
Cafe Car: Sandwiches, snacks and beverages.
No Checked Baggage: Passengers may carry hand baggage on board.

Figure 9.13 *Amtrak schedule.*

The *American Orient Express* offers a variety of rail and tour itineraries spanning the entire continental United States, ranging from five days to ten days in length. Examples of popular rail itineraries include "National Parks of the West," "Antebellum South," "The Rockies and Yellowstone," and the "Jazz and Blues Express." Train lovers can also select from two transcontinental journeys. In the United States, take a nine-day rail trip between Washington, DC and Los Angeles, stopping in such places as New Orleans, San Antonio, Santa Fe, and the Grand Canyon. In Canada, take a nine-day rail trip between Montreal and Vancouver, with sightseeing in such places as Ontario, Winnipeg, Jasper National Park, and through the Canadian Rockies. Prices start at approximately $400 per day per person (double occupancy), which includes accommodations on board the train, meals, and sightseeing.

Train 14 Coast Starlight: 🅡 🅑 ✕ �,
Departs Los Angeles, CA daily

City	Mile	Time*	Connections
Los Angeles, CA (LAX) ✈ ♿	0	9:30 am PT	-
Glendale, CA (GDL) ✈ ♿	5	9:48 am PT	-
Simi Valley, CA (SIM) ♿	37	10:29 am PT	-
Oxnard, CA (OXN) ✈ ♿	67	11:02 am PT	-
Santa Barbara, CA (SBA) ✈ ♿	104	12:03 pm PT	-
San Luis Obispo, CA (SLO) ✈ ♿	223	2:45 pm PT / 2:58 pm PT	-
Paso Robles, CA (PRB) ♿	251	4:00 pm PT	-
Salinas, CA (SNS) ♿	357	5:50 pm PT	
San Jose, CA (SJC) ✈ ♿	424	7:20 pm PT	
Oakland, CA (OKJ) ✈ ♿	464	8:25 pm PT / 8:40 pm PT	🚌
Emeryville, CA (EMY) ✈ ♿	469	9:20 pm PT / 9:30 pm PT	14
Martinez, CA (MTZ) ♿	496	10:12 pm PT	-
Davis, CA (DAV) ♿	540	10:59 pm PT	-
Sacramento, CA (SAC) ✈ ♿	553	11:28 pm PT / 11:38 pm PT	-
Marysville, CA (MRV) ♿	605	12:45 am PT	-
Chico, CA (CIC) ✈ ♿	649	1:28 am PT	-
Redding, CA (RDD) ✈ ♿	723	2:44 am PT	-
Dunsmuir, CA (DUN) ♿	780	4:35 am PT	-
Klamath Falls, OR (KFS) ✈ ♿	885	7:35 am PT / 7:45 am PT	-
Chemult, OR (CMO) ♿	959	9:03 am PT	-
Eugene, OR (EUG) ✈ ♿	1080	12:11 pm PT	-
Albany, OR (ALY) ♿	1124	12:57 pm PT	🚌
Salem, OR (SLM) ♿	1151	1:29 pm PT	-
Portland, OR (PDX) ✈ ♿	1204	3:20 pm PT / 4:00 pm PT	28, 🚌
Vancouver, WA (VAN) ♿	1214	4:23 pm PT	-
Kelso--Longview, WA (KEL) ♿	1253	5:06 pm PT	-
Centralia, WA (CTL) ♿	1296	5:52 pm PT	-
Olympia [Lacey], WA (OLW) ♿	1318	6:14 pm PT	-
Tacoma, WA (TAC) ✈ ♿	1350	7:02 pm PT	-
Seattle, WA (SEA) ✈ ♿	1390	7:55 pm PT	🚌

Figure 9.14 *Train schedule for Amtrak's Web site.*

Web Link — *American Nostalgia on the Net:* Check out the *American Orient Express* Web site for schedules, route maps, photos, and information about the rail company's vintage cars. Go to *www.travelpower.com/aoe*

➤ Canada's *The Canadian*

Since the old Canadian Pacific and Canadian Rail systems merged into the new VIA Rail system, many train buffs have noted that Canada's government-run VIA Rail is a mixed bag. There are high-speed trains (up to 84 mph) in the Montreal–Toronto corridor that compete head to head with air travel in the same region. However, many other rail journeys are slower and are considered to be

Figure 9.15 *Views of the* American Orient Express.
(From American Orient Express *brochure.)*

more like land cruises. This is fine for vacation travelers, since traveling by rail is one of the best ways to see some of the most beautiful and majestic scenery in the world.

One of the most famous of the trains of VIA, *The Canadian*, travels coast to coast on a regularly-scheduled basis. What makes this train unique is that unlike the U.S. railroad, VIA *Canadian's* tracks extend from the Atlantic to the Pacific as a single entity. VIA's *Canadian* departs in the evening of day 1 in both directions every 24 hours and arrives on the morning of day 5. The train has full dining service, a dome car with huge windows, and a lounge car with comfortable single seating, buffet, and drinks (see Figure 9.16). Sleeping accommodations are available from reclining seats, roomettes, and bedrooms with private facilities.

Figure 9.15 *Views of the* American Orient Express. *(Continued)*
(From American Orient Express *brochure.)*

The most top-rated segment of this trip is the run between Toronto and Vancouver, which covers approximately 2,800 miles in under three days. The train averages only 41 mph through some of the most beautiful scenery in the world through the Canadian Rockies, especially the segment between Jasper and Prince Rupert.

➤ Copper Canyon (Barranca del Cobre)

One of the most breathtaking parts of Mexico is located in the north central region in an area referred to as Barranca del Cobre, or Copper Canyon. It is said that a huge volcanic eruption 25 million years ago formed four enormous, interconnected

Figure 9.16 *Observation lounge on* The Canadian.
(From Kemwel's Premier Selection brochure.)

canyons that are four times larger than the Grand Canyon and 240 feet deeper. The most interesting aspect of this region is the rail system, which was begun in 1909 and finished 52 years later. The **Sierra Madre Express** consists of five refurbished railcars, including sleeping, dome, and dining cars (see Figure 9.17).

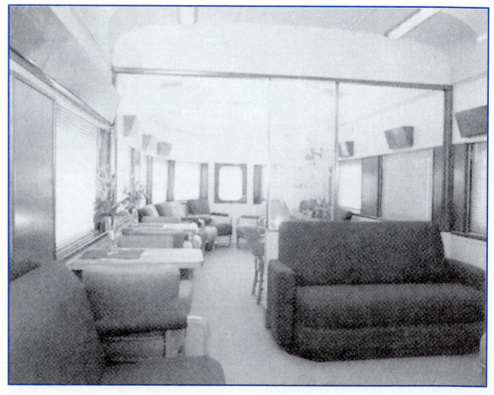

Figure 9.17 *Observation lounge on the* Sierra Madre Express, *Copper Canyon, Mexico.*
(From Kemwel's Premier Selection brochure.)

The thirteen-hour train ride takes passengers through breathtaking landscape which makes this itinerary one of the top ten train rides in the world according to rail connoisseurs and industry professionals. The embarkation points for the rail trip are *Chihuahua*, a desert town in the north, and *Los Mochis*, only one hour from the Gulf of California and close to such beach resorts as Mazatlán, Mexico.

The train winds through eyecatching scenery around mountains, over 39 bridges that sometimes tower high above the canyon floor, and in and out of 68 tunnels through the mountains. It is recommended that passengers make one or more overnight stops along the way for in-depth sightseeing, hiking, or camping. Many tour operators offer excursions and guided tours at the major stops along the route. Passengers can take the train trip independently or by organized tours.

✓ Check Your Understanding 9-3

Multiple Choice

Circle the *best* answer.

1. The name of Amtrak's discounted fare that is based on the number of regions traveled within the continental United States is:
   - A. Amtrak regional fares
   - B. Amtrak explorer fares
   - C. Exploring America fares
   - D. Exploring regional America fares

2. Amtrak fares (not Auto Train) would be highest during what travel period?
   - A. June 1–June 15
   - B. December 10–December 17
   - C. August 15–August 20
   - D. October 20–October 25

3. Children between the ages of 2 and 15 years of age ride at what discount when accompanied by a full-fare passenger?
   - A. one-half
   - B. one-third
   - C. one-fourth
   - D. children ride free

4. The North American Rail Pass, valid for travel on both Amtrak and VIA Rail Canada must include travel in the Untied States and Canada during how many consecutive days?
   - A. 45
   - B. 90
   - C. 7
   - D. 30

5. Which of the following is not a source for Amtrak schedules?
   - A. travel agency CRSs
   - B. *Offical Railway Guide*
   - C. Internet
   - D. *Official Airline Guide*

6. The name of the luxury train with restored vintage railcars from the 1940s and 1950s era which operates rail tours throughout the United States is:
   - A. American Orient Express
   - B. American Queen
   - C. American Empress
   - D. American Rail Express

7. The name of VIA Rail's train that is unique because the tracks extend from the Atlantic to the Pacific as a single entity is:
   - A. *Pacific Express*
   - B. *Canadian Express*
   - C. *The Canadian*
   - D. *Trans-Canadian*

8. The breathtaking and scenic ride on the Copper Canyon rail trip is in:
   - A. southern Mexico
   - B. western Canada
   - C. north central Mexico
   - D. southwestern United States

Great Trains of the World

Rail travel is available in many countries in the world. Some trains are nationally owned and others privately owned. Some are better than others in terms of comfort, amenities, and passenger service. Trains operated in such countries as the United Kingdom, Switzerland, France, Germany, Sweden, and Norway are known for offering the highest levels of passenger rail comfort, speed, and efficiency.

Travel sales agents in North America access information and book tickets and other train-related products in a variety of ways: the Internet, agency CRSs, and through rail distributors located in North America. Two major distributors are Rail Europe, Inc. and DER. These companies and others like them provide full international rail service: general information, schedules, prices in addition to point-to-point tickets, and rail passes. These rail distributors have toll-free 800 numbers for easy access.

In addition to regular scheduled train services, there are some unique and special trains that surpass the standard. Why are they so unique? Some offer the nostalgia and romance of bygone days by recreating the Golden Era of rail travel. Some are the fastest trains and most technologically advanced as they approach speeds of 200 mph. Some travel on many scenic and breathtaking itineraries in certain parts of the world. Here are some of the world's most fascinating and unique trains:

- Europe
  - *Venice Simplon-Orient-Express*
  - *Nostalgic Istanbul Orient Express*
  - *The Royal Scotsman*
  - *The Flying Scotsman*
  - *The Glacier Express*
  - *Bernina Express*
  - *Andalusian Express*
- South Africa
  - *The Blue Train*
  - *Rovos Rail*
- India
  - *Palace on Wheels*
- Japan
  - *Twilight Express*

➤ Europe's *Venice Simplon-Orient Express*

When one thinks of the romance and nostalgia of rail journeys of the past, the name "Orient Express" springs to mind. Books have been written and movies produced revolving around this historic train system. In the past, several trains that operated between the capitals of Europe carried the name Orient Express. Since 1883, princes and film stars, members of royalty and spies, crossed Europe in the lavish luxury of the Orient Express. In 1977, the new owners refurbished the old carriages to their original splendor.

Today there is one *Venice Simplon-Orient Express (VSOE).* It has one main route, London to Paris, Zurich, Innsbruck, and Venice. Sometimes the train does not end in Venice but travels farther east, to Salzburg, Vienna, and Budapest,

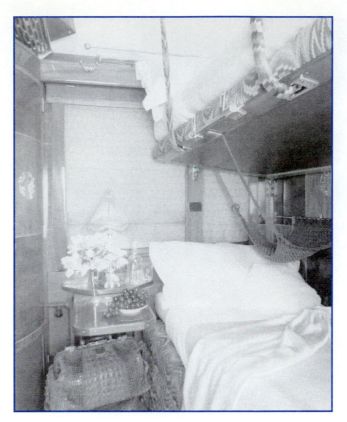

Figure 9.18 *Sleeping accomodations on the luxurious* VSOE.

Hungary. The trips take two days, with an overnight on the train. Passengers starting in London travel to the coast of England in elegant and luxurious Pullman coaches and cross the English Channel by steamer in VSOE's reserved lounge. Upon arrival in France, they board the VSOE once again and travel to Paris, where other passengers board the train.

Passengers dine elegantly on fine cuisine, appreciate impeccable service, and sleep comfortably in cozy cabins which convert into a parlor during the day (see Figures 9.18 and 9.19). One is never overdressed on the VSOE. At dinner, jacket and tie are required dress for men and the equivalent dress for women. Trips are available in segments for approximately $1,000 to $2,500 per person, double occupancy. Also, visitors can get a taste of this luxurious lifestyle by taking a day trip on the VSOE from London, with a champagne lunch or dinner served on board and sightseeing in southern England. Day trips cost approximately $300 per person.

➤ Europe's *Nostalgic Istanbul Orient Express*

The *Nostalgic Istanbul Orient Express* is considered to be the second Orient Express, with a fleet of rail carriages with such famous rail names as the Train Bleu, the Cote d'Azur, Sud Express, and the original Orient Express that was seen in the hit movie *Murder on the Orient Express*. Unlike its sister *Venice Simplon-Orient Express*, this train is based in Zurich, Switzerland and operates only one scheduled trip to Istanbul, Turkey each year. For the rest of the year, the train operates charter trips to such areas as the Burgundy region of France, to Germany, and to Italy. Although most staff and passengers are Swiss, English is widely spoken. Meals are catered and served by a Swiss "Pullman brigade."

Figure 9.19 *Dining car on the luxurious* VSOE.

Key Point ➤ People often get the *Nostalgic Istanbul Orient Express* confused with the *Venice Simplon-Orient Express (VSOE)*. Remember, think of the *Nostalgic Istanbul Orient Express* as a luxury *tour train* and the *VSOE* as equally luxurious *regularly-scheduled* train service.

➤ Scotland's *Royal Scotsman*

Those who have traveled on the **Royal Scotsman** compare it to being like invited guests at an exclusive country house in the highlands of Scotland (see Figures 9.20 and 9.21). The train consists of nine beautifully appointed Edwardian-style carriages that accommodate only 32 passengers. Passengers can sit on an open-air verandah in the observation car to watch the mountainous scenery of the highlands pass by. The *Royal Scotsman* departs from Edinburgh on a six-day round trip, but passengers can choose three- or four-day segments on the West Highland or North Highland lines, respectively.

The rail tour includes transportation by its own liveried motorcoach for visits to private homes, castles, and local places of interest. Passengers remain on board and sleep comfortably on the train, which remains at a station each evening. Six-day rail tours start at approximately $5,800 per person, double occupancy, which includes rail fare, meals and beverages on board, and sightseeing.

➤ Scotland's *Flying Scotsman*

The **Flying Scotsman** is the budget counterpart of the *Royal Scotsman*. The interior of this train is not as lavish as its Royal counterpart, but it is still very comfortable and several notches above many other rail systems in the world in terms of comfort

Figure 9.20 *Dining car set for dinner on the* Royal Scotsman.
(From Abercrombie & Kent, The Royal Scotsman *brochure.)*

and style. The *Flying Scotsman* offers four- and five-day trips over some of the same tracks as the Royal Scotsman and makes many of the same sightseeing stops.

This train tour operates several different itineraries from London on fast Intercity trains to Scotland, where passengers board private restored railcars for touring. During the rail tour, some overnights are in sleeper cars on board, and others are in hotels. Prices start at approximately $1,300 per person, double occupancy, including hotel nights in London and meals.

➤ Switzerland's *Glacier Express*

This rail itinerary has been considered to be one of the most scenic and exhilarating train rides in the world (see Figure 9.22). It is also one of the best ways to see the best of alpine Europe from the comfort of a train. The **Glacier Express** (a mis-

Figure 9.21 *Luxurious lounge car for passengers on the* Royal Scotsman.
(From Abercrombie & Kent, the Royal Scotsman *brochure.)*

Figure 9.22 *The* Glacier Express *over Landwasser Viaduct, Switzerland.*
(From Kemwel's Premier Selection brochure.)

nomer since it doesn't go very fast at all!) takes about seven hours to travel through the heart of the Swiss Alps, between St. Moritz and Zermatt.

The train crosses more than 290 bridges and shoots through 91 tunnels along its panoramic journey through some of the most beautiful mountain scenery in the world. Travelers who are afraid of heights beware: The train climbs up to a dizzying height of 6,670 feet over the Oberalp Pass. A dining car serves lunch during the trip, and passengers can have panoramic and unobstructed views of the breathtaking scenery from the fully air-conditioned Panoramic Car. Rail tour packages available from several tour operators combine overnight stops and sightseeing along the way.

➤ Italy's *Bernina Express*

This bright red narrow-gauge train offers similar spectacular scenery from the comfortable rail cars. The ***Bernina Express*** runs between Chur, Switzerland and Tirano, in northern Italy. The rail tracks hug the side of mountainous terrain as the train follows steep gorges, flies over soaring bridges and through looping tunnels, as it passes by the Morteratsch Glacier and the famous circular viaduct near Brusio, Italy. Extended rail tour packages are also available that include overnight stops in hotels, sightseeing, and some meals along the train route.

➤ Spain's *Andalus Expreso (Andalusian Express)*

The ***Andalusian Express*** is considered to be a five-star hotel on rails, which also boasts the widest rail carriages in Europe. It is a restored vintage train that is fully air-conditioned and restored in the grand Belle Époque style of the Roaring 20s. The train features luxurious interiors with many intricate details restored to their original luster (see Figure 9.23). The train is fully air-conditioned and features restaurant cars, bar and recreation car, and a choice of sleeping accommodations and compartments. It operates a circular itinerary through historic southern

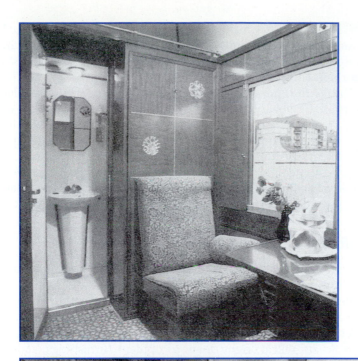

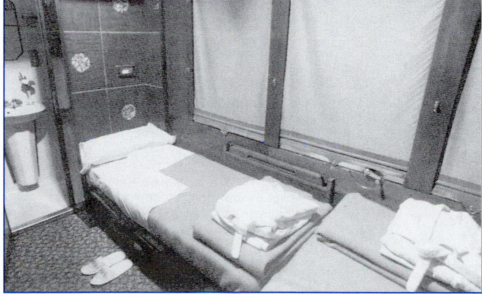

Figure 9.23 *Standard accommodation on the* Andalusian Express. *By day private sitting area; at night a bedroom with folddown berths and adjoining bathroom.*

Spain between Seville, Cordoba, Granada, and Bobadilla, a starting point for a side trip to the Costa del Sol.

➤ South Africa's *Blue Train* and *Rovos Rail*

South Africa boasts two trains, owned by separate companies, that offer different routes but the same high-quality service, comfort, and luxury. The **Blue Train** has been in operation for several decades and is a regularly scheduled train that operates overnight trips between Cape Town and Johannesburg. The *Blue Train* consists of fully air-conditioned sleeping compartments, including suite accommodations, hot and cold water on tap, and shower and private facilities. Several tour operators offer tours built around the *Blue Train's schedule,* including extended sightseeing with hotel accommodations at the terminal points of Cape Town and Pretoria in addition to the overnight train ride.

Unlike the *Blue Train,* **Rovos Rail** is not regularly scheduled rail service but a tour train. The beautiful rail carriages reflect the golden era of steam trains and luxury travel in the heart of the South African bush. The nineteen-coach *Rovos Rail* carries a maximum of 70 guests and travels between Cape Town and Pretoria, with sightseeing through the wine lands of Stellenbosch, the Victorian town at Matjiesfontein, and the quaint Karoo town of Beaufort West. Two nights can also be added at the exclusive Game Reserve of Mabula. Many consider Rovos Rail to be one of the most elegant and luxurious trains in the world.

➤ India's *Palace on Wheels*

The **Palace on Wheels** is a vintage train that was custom-built for the Maharajahs and Viceroys of India. The original train has long since retired, and the current train has been renovated within the past decade. It has fourteen salons (or cars) with four cabins in each and a lounge between with comfortable sofas and glass tables used to serve breakfast and evening tea. Each salon is a beautiful recreation of a Victorian-era railcar, right down to opulent furnishings, stained glass, and dark wood-paneled cabins. Each salon maintains the emblem of the princely state to which it belonged and which served as a miniature traveling palace. Each salon is manned by its own attendants, who are dressed in traditional Rajasthani costume.

Many agree that touring India by train is one of the best ways to explore this country. In fact, India harbors the second-largest rail system in the world, behind Russia. Palace on Wheels offers seven-night tours between September and April (avoiding the monsoon summer months). The itinerary, taking in what's known as the Golden Circle (Delhi, Agra, Jaipur), is a circle trip that begins and ends in New Delhi. This luxury rail tour averages approximately $375 per person per day.

Web Link

Palace on Wheels: This luxury rail service in India is described in detail on the Web. It contains a route map, a list of departure dates and space availability; prices; a virtual tour of the coach, and brief descriptions and photos of points on the itinerary. Get on board at *http://www.travbuzz.com/tour.html*

Key Point ➤

Japan's **Twilight Express:** This ultimate in rail luxury came into service several years ago. Many who have traveled on the railways of the world agree that this is the most deluxe and luxurious train in the world, surpassing even the famed Orient Express. The train travels from one end of the island of Honshu to the other. The entire trip takes one full day plus an overnight. It has bilevel seating that rivals that on any first-class train or jet plane. The Twilight Express includes plush sleeping accommodations plus a magnificent passenger suite that has a wraparound view at the end of the train. Gourmet meals are served on crystal and china in the posh restaurant cars. Recommend to the most discriminating traveler.

HIGH-SPEED TRAINS OF THE WORLD

Now that we have experienced some of the most unique and luxurious trains in the world, let's turn to the fastest passenger trains on record. These rail systems offer the latest in technology, combining energy efficiency with a smoother ride.

They all have one thing in common: They are the fastest forms of passenger land transportation ever known!

► France's *TGV*

The *Train à Grande Vitesse (TGV)* is the French high-speed train (see Figure 9.24). It is a system whereby the train equipment, track, and signaling technologies, when combined, result in one of the fastest trains in the world, with average speeds of 186 mph (300 km/h). It is owned and operated by the French national railroads.

There are several major trunk lines radiating out from Paris. The most frequently traveled is the track connecting Paris and Lyon to the south. The northern line extends to Belgium, the Netherlands, Germany, and Britain through the Channel Tunnel. A third serves points west of Paris. This train has become so successful that it has become a technological symbol associated with France.

► Europe's Eurostar

The *Eurostar* speeds passengers through the **Channel Tunnel,** one of Europe's biggest infrastructure projects in recent history. The Channel Tunnel (referred to as the **Chunnel**) is a ground and underwater link between Great Britain and continental Europe. The tunnel consists of three tunnels or interconnected tubes: one rail track in each direction plus one service tunnel. Each tunnel is 31 miles long, of which 23 miles are underwater. The average depth is 150 feet under the English Channel. It takes only 20 minutes to cross the channel by rail (compared to approximately 1.5 hours by boat).

Eurostar offers rapid service between London, Paris, and Brussels. Running smoothly along special tracks, the *Eurostar* can reach speeds close to 200 mph. London to Paris takes 3 hours; London to Brussels, 3¼ hours; Paris to Brussels, 2¼ hours. At these speeds and frequency of service, it is possible for a passenger to leave London in the morning, lunch, sightsee, and shop in Paris or Brussels,

Figure 9.24 *The* Train à Grande Vitesse (TGV) *is France's high-speed train service that reaches 186 mph.*

Premier Trains of Europe

Europe has the largest system of high-speed trains in the world. Premier trains are European trains that travel 125 mph and up.

- Eurostar: links Paris and London with connections to Brussels, Belgium.

- Artesia: covers routes between France and Italy.

- Ave (Alta Velocidad Española), Talgo 200, and Euromed: high-speed trains that operate within Spain; top operating speed of 186 mph.

- Cisalpino: tilting Italian Pendolino trains travel within Switzerland and between Switzerland and Italy; top operating speeds of 155 mph.

- Eurostar Italia: high-speed train operating within Italy.

- ICE (InterCity Express): German high-speed train that travels 512 miles of track between Hamburg and Munich in six hours; top operating speed of 174 mph.

- TGV: high-speed train that serves more than 150 French cities; top operating speed of 186 mph.

- Thalys: links Paris to Brussels; Cologne and Dusseldorf, Germany, and Amsterdam.

- X2000: high-speed rail serving cities in Sweden; top operating speeds of 124 mph.

European Rail Routes

Source: Rail Europe

Routes Served By Premier Trains
- Artesia
- AVE
- Cisalpino
- Euromed
- Eurostar
- Eurostar Italia
- ICE
- Talgo 200
- TGV
- Thalys
- X2000
- Ferry Lines

and return to London on the same day. First- and second-class seating is available. With a first-class ticket, passengers sit in wide seats that recline, receive daily newspapers, and are served meals at their seats. In second-class or standard seating, clusters of four facing seats with a large table in between are offered.

The one-way first class fare between London and Paris is approximately $200 per adult (all fares are subject to change). Youth, senior-citizen, and round-trip discount fares are available for passengers who qualify.

➤ Japan's *Bullet Train (Shinkansen)*

The New Tokaido line, opened in 1964, has the distinction of being the first railway completely designed and built from scratch as a specifically high-speed passenger railway. It stretches more than 320 miles between Tokyo and Osaka along an area called the Tokaido, the most heavily populated and industrialized area, where more than 40 percent of Japan's dense population lives. The Japanese refer to these trains as *Shinkansen* (which means "new trunk line"). In the United States we refer to them as the **Bullet Trains** because they reach speeds in excess of 150 mph. They can cover the 320 miles between Tokyo and Osaka (with stops) in less than three hours.

This highly efficient and speedy rail system also has the distinction of never having had an accident since its development; all train speeds and directions are controlled through specialized computers. It is also considered to be the most efficient rail system in the world: Arrivals and departures at stations, including debarking and embarking of passengers, are done *within seconds!*

Web Link

Access to Rail Web Sites: Want to access information about rail schedules, train descriptions, prices, and rail pass options about practically any rail system in the world? Try a "one-stop shopping" Web site that provides links to railroads around the world. Point your browser at *http://www.trainweb.com/frames_travel.html*

Seating and Sleeping Accommodations

As the scenery changes from country to country, so does the atmosphere and the personality of its trains. When traveling by rail throughout Europe and other parts of the world, passengers buy passage on either day or night trains. The seating and sleeping accommodations vary from train to train and from country to country.

➤ Day Trains

Day trains usually have either compartment car seating or coach car seating. A compartment is a cabin that opens to a corridor along one side of the car. The compartment can accommodate up to six passengers in first class and up to eight passengers in second class. Coach car seating is available in a car that is open, with a center aisle and seats on either side, like an interior of a narrow-body aircraft. In first-class cars, there are usually two seats on one side and one on the other. In second class, there are two seats on each side of the aisle.

➤ Night Trains

Passengers traveling at night can either sit in standard seats in a compartment car or coach car, or they can consider sleeper accommodations. Sleeper accommodations are on a *reserved basis only* and require an additional fee. There are generally two types of accommodations:

1. Sleepers. This type of accommodation contains berths, with a private washstand, fresh linens, towels, and a pillow. First-class sleepers accommodate one or two people, second-class sleepers accommodate from two to four people. Couples, families, or travelers of the same gender can share this type of accommodation. Charges for sleepers range approximately between $35 and $200 per person and vary according to number of occupants, type of accommodation, distance, and route traveled.

2. Couchettes. This type of accommodation can be described as public sleepers. They are open bunks in a compartment with a pillow and blanket. Couchettes are located in either first or second class and accommodate up to four or six people, respectively. There is no distinction by gender, so passengers can expect to sleep in daytime clothes. Couchette charges are a flat per-night fee of approximately $35, regardless of distance traveled.

➤ Advance Reservations

Seat reservations are required for most high-speed trains (i.e., TGV, AVE, and X2000), all specialty trains (i.e., Glacier Express and Bernina), as well as certain InterCity and ICE trains. All night trains require an advance reservation for sleeper and couchette accommodations. There is a reservation fee for seats and sleeping accommodations even if the passenger holds a ticket or a rail pass.

➤ Thomas Cook Timetables

Primary printed resources for international rail schedules are the *Thomas Cook European Timetable* and the *Overseas Timetable*. The overseas edition is a compilation of rail travel timetables for virtually all countries outside Europe. The two editions have a similar format. Figure 9.25 is an example of a rail schedule from the European edition. This schedule is between Paris and Milan, Italy. As you can see, all times are published in the 24-hour clock, which is standard format in all international transportation schedules. Departure times from Paris to Milan are listed down the left-hand column. The departure times from Milan to Paris are listed down the right-hand column. Train numbers are listed on the top of each column, along with the type of train service. Notice that the TGV, France's high-speed train, is represented in addition to regular train service.

Example: Refer to the Thomas Cook Timetable in Figure 9.25. Find the TGV service—train number 627—that has the second departure listed from Paris. This train departs Paris at 1500 (3:00 P.M.) local time and arrives in Lyon, France at 1700 (5:00 P.M.). It does not go all the

Table 45 PARIS AND LYON - TORINO

	410/1 1,2 🍷		TGV 925 1,2⁄	416/7 1,2 🍷		TGV 627 1,2⁄	218 1,2 🍷B		211 1,2 P	217 2 M
Paris Lyon d.	...	...	1047	...	...	1500	...	...	2056	2222
Lyon Perrache d.	0649	...	|	1231	...	|	1703	...	|	|
Lyon Part Dieu d.	0659	...	|	|	...	1700	1714	...	|	|
Chambéry d.	0830	...	1342	1407	...	...	1838	...	0248	|
Modane 🏛 d.	1004	...	...	1538	...	...	2001	...	0435	0550
Torino Porta Nuova a.	1116	...	...	1700	...	...	2122	...	0610	0706p
Milano Centrale a.	...	...	...	...	...	...	2305	...	...	0845

	214 1,2 🍷B			414 1,2 🍷	TGV 922 1,2⁄		418 1,2 🍷		216 2 M	210 1,2 P
Milano Centrale d.	0710	...	...	...	...	...	...	...	2100	...
Torino Porta Nuova d.	0855	...	...	1225	...	...	1645	...	2240p	0015
Modane 🏛 a.	1025	...	...	1348	...	...	1807	...	0018	0143
Chambéry a.	1147	...	...	1510	1557	...	1925	...	0146	0312
Lyon Part Dieu a.	|	...	...	1637	|	...	2101	...	|	|
Lyon Perrache a.	1326	...	...	1647	|	...	2111	...	|	|
Paris Lyon a.	...	...	...	...	1858	...	...	...	0722	0852

NOTES for Tables **44** and **45**.
A – LUTETIA – [12] and ✕ Paris - Lausanne and v.v.
B – LE MONT CENIS – [12] and 🍷 Lyon - Milano and v.v.
C – CISALPIN – [12] and ✕ Paris - Lausanne and v.v.
E – CHAMPS ELYSEES – [12] and ✕ Paris - Lausanne.
G – PARTHENON – June 24 - Sept. 4: ▬ 2 cl. and [12] Paris - Brindisi and v.v.; 🛏 1,2 cl. (T2), ▬ 2 cl. and [2] Paris - Rimini and v.v.
H – Hellenic Mediterranean Lines, for days of running see Table **1525**.
K – RIALTO – 🛏 1,2 cl., 🛏 1,2 cl. (T2), ▬ 2 cl. and 🍷 Paris - Venezia and v.v.
L – GALILEI – 🛏 1,2 cl., 🛏 1,2 cl. (T2), ▬ 2 cl. and 🍷 Paris - Firenze and v.v.
M – STENDHAL – 🛏 1,2 cl., 🛏 1,2 cl. (T2), ▬ 2 cl. and [2] Paris - Milano and v.v.
N – PALATINO – 🛏 1,2 cl., 🛏 1,2 cl. (T2), ▬ 2 cl. and 🍷 Paris - Roma and v.v.
P – NAPOLI EXPRESS – 🍷 Genova - Napoli and v.v.; 🛏 1,2 cl., ▬ 2 cl. and [12] Paris - Torino - Napoli and v.v.
SC – SeaCat service.
T – May 29 - Sept. 4.
b – Brindisi Centrale.
g – Milano Porta Garibaldi.
p – Torino Porta Susa.
r – Roma Ostiense.
t – Roma Tiburtina.
⁄ – Supplement payable.

Figure 9.25 *Rail schedules from the* Thomas Cook European Timetable.

way to Milan, Italy. Passengers who wish to continue to Milan must change trains. To which train number would you connect to travel to Milan? Right! Train number 218, which departs at 1714 (5:14 P.M.) and arrives in Milan at 2305 (11:05 P.M.).

RAIL PASSES

Rail passes are a convenient and cost-effective way to travel long distances when traveling abroad. There are various types of passes, each with its advantages and disadvantages. Some are available to youths, others are available to travelers older than 65. Some are valid in one country only, others in several countries. Some must be purchased outside the country of use; others must be sold inside that country.

Rail passes are especially popular throughout Europe, due to the vast rail system network and efficiency of service. Not only are major cities linked by rail but there is frequent and convenient service to countryside destinations, sightseeing regions, resort areas, and international airports.

The main function of any type of rail pass is to provide an unlimited number of rail trips for the travel days indicated on the pass. A rail travel day is measured as 24 hours, from midnight to midnight. Passes may also be valid on other forms of ground transportation, such as bus and passenger ferry services.

It is important to remember that a railpass allows the boarding of a train *but does not guarantee a seat*. To reserve a seat, the passenger must purchase a seat reservation at additional cost.

There are several major distributors of European rail passes and train-related services in the United States and Canada. The leading distributor is Rail Europe, Inc., which is appointed by the major railroads of Europe to represent them in North America. In addition to rail-related products, Rail Europe, Inc. handles all premier or high-speed trains in Europe and a variety of specialized rail passes. Other distributors include DER, in Chicago, and CIT which represents Italian rail.

The alternative to traveling by rail with a pass is to pay a *point-to-point ticket*. This type of ticket is valid for a single rail journey between two points along a specific route. A point-to-point ticket does not restrict the traveler to a specific date or time of travel unless a reservation is necessary. A ticket covers most high-speed train supplements and allows the boarding of the train but will not guarantee a seat unless a reservation is made.

➤ Rail Pass Categories

There are three basic categories of rail passes:

1. Flexipasses. Flexipasses are valid for travel during a number of travel days, which can stretch over a longer time period: The travel days *do not have to be consecutive*. This allows the traveler to make stops for a few days at points along the way without losing the allotted number of travel days. For example, a traveler purchases a Flexipass that is valid for fifteen days within a two-month time period. If the traveler begins rail travel on June 1, he or she can travel for any fifteen days until two months later, August 1.

2. Consecutive passes. Consecutive passes allow unlimited rail travel on a certain number of *consecutive* days for the duration of the pass. This type of pass is ideal for the traveler who plans to do a lot of traveling during a certain period. For example, a traveler purchases a consecutive pass that is valid for 21 consecutive days. This means that he or she can take the train for an unlimited number of times within the 21-day period.

3. Rail 'n drive passes. This type of pass combines an unlimited number of rail trips and an unlimited mileage car rental for a certain number of days or weeks indicated on the pass. A certain number of train days and a certain number of car rental days are provided, which the traveler can use in any combination. With a rail 'n drive pass, the traveler can cover long-distance travel in comfort, then pick up a self-drive car at or near the train station to explore the town and countryside at leisure.

➤ Types of Rail Passes

There are many options for unlimited travel on single- or multiple-country passes throughout the world. Here are just a few examples.

Eurailpass

The **Eurailpass** is considered the "crème de la crème" of all rail passes and one of the best buys when traveling long distances through two or more countries in western Europe (see Table 9.3). This pass allows for unlimited travel throughout seventeen European countries on more than 100,000 miles of track. All but one of these countries (Republic of Ireland) are located on the *continent* of Europe:

- Austria
- Belgium
- Denmark
- Finland
- France
- Germany

- Greece
- Hungary
- Republic of Ireland
- Italy
- Luxembourg
- The Netherlands

- Norway
- Portugal
- Spain
- Sweden
- Switzerland

TABLE 9.3 EURAILPASS REFERENCE GUIDE[a]

Pass Type	Class	Validity	Cost per Adult	Restrictions
Eurailpass, adult	First	15 days	$538	Valid for consecutive days in the 17 countries of Europe
		21 days	698	
		1 month	864	
		2 months	1,224	
		3 months	1,512	
Eurail Flexipass, adult	First	10 days	634	Travel any 10 or 15 days (nonconsecutive) within a 2-month period
		15 days	836	
Eurail Saverpass, adult	First	15 days	458	For two up to five people traveling together; Eurail Saver Flexipass also available for any 10 or 15 days within a 2-month period.
		21 days	594	
		1 month	734	
		2 months	1,040	
		3 months	1,286	
Eurail Youthpass, youth	Second	15 days	376	Must be under 26 years of age; Youth Flexipass also available for second-class travel in any 10 or 15 days in a 2-month period.
		21 days	489	
		1 month	605	
		2 months	857	
		3 months	1,059	
Eurail Drivepass, adult	First	7 days	350–400[b]	Includes 4 days of rail, and 3 days of rental car; additional days optional

[a]Note that prices change on a frequent basis. These prices are for illustration purposes only.
[b]Based on car category.

Eurailpasses must be purchased in the United States or outside Europe. Travelers must use the pass for the first time within three months of purchase. The first time it is used, the pass is validated by a railway official, who enters the first and last date of the allowed time period.

This pass includes free or discounted travel on selected international ferry crossings, lake and river steamers, and bus services. Reservations for all sleepers, couchettes, and seats on certain trains are subject to additional fees for pass holders. It is important to remember that the rail pass only allows the passenger to board the train; it does not guarantee a seat.

Europasses

Many travelers don't visit ten countries in one trip. As an alternative to the seventeen-country Eurailpass, many single-, double-, and triple-country passes were developed. A prime example is the **Europass.** The Europass is a flexipass that covers five to fifteen days of travel in France, Germany, Italy, Spain and Switzerland over a two-month period.

For an additional cost ranging from approximately $50 to $70, the traveler can select up to two associate countries. The associate countries/regions that can be added to the Europass include Austria/Hungary; Belgium/Netherlands/Luxembourg; Greece, and Portugal.

The approximate per person cost of a first-class Europass ranges from $325 (five day minimum) to $775 (fifteen-day maximum). Like the Eurailpass, the Europass must be used the first time within three months of purchase.

Table 9.4 is a sampling of other types of individual country and regional rail passes. Remember, in addition to those listed here, there are many others that

TABLE 9.4   RAIL PASSES OTHER THAN EURAILPASSES

Arctic Fjord Pass	Travel in northern Sweden above the Arctic Circle and northern fjord country in Norway.
Balkan Flexipass	Allows travel in such countries as Bulgaria, Greece, former Yugoslav Republic of Macedonia, Romania, Serbia, and Turkey.
Benelux Tourrail Pass	Explore the Benelux countries of Belgium, the Netherlands, and Luxembourg.
Britrail Pass	Allows travel through England, Scotland, Wales, and Northern Ireland (countries not covered under Eurailpass).There are also special passes offered by British Rail that include the Republic of Ireland, British heritage sights, Scotland only, and BritRail Pass + Car plan.
Canrailpass	Unlimited coach-class travel on any 12 days during a 30-day period on the entire Canadian rail system.
Fest-Pass	Allows holder to get into various festivals in Europe.
Indrail Pass	Provides unlimited travel over India's extensive rail system in either first- or second-class seating. Air-conditioned first class is available on some trains but not all.
Italian Rail 'n Drive	A five-day pass that includes first-class rail for three days and an economy-sized car for two days. Travel days must be completed within one month.
Japan Rail Pass	Unlimited travel on most Japan trains, including the very fast Hikari service. Top mainline trains are air-conditioned in both ordinary and green car classes.
ScanRail Pass	Explore Denmark, Finland, Norway, and Sweden in one pass.
Swiss Rail 'n Drive	Travel anywhere in Switzerland by train or car.

represent countries and regions throughout the world which are important to tourism.

Key Point ➤ When is it more economical to pay point-to-point rail tickets versus a rail pass? The basic rule is to consider a rail pass if you plan to cover lots of ground during the trip. If you plan to travel only between two or three cities that are located relatively close together, a point-to-point ticket may make more sense. Here's a good rule of thumb: When covering 1,500 miles or more, it is probably worth purchasing a rail pass.

✓ Check Your Understanding 9-4

1. Match each train with the correct country.

   A. Italy   _____ 1. *Glacier Express*

   B. India   _____ 2. *TGV*

   C. Japan   _____ 3. *Blue Train*

   D. Scotland   _____ 4. *Bernina Express*

   E. France   _____ 5. *Bullet Train*

   F. Spain   _____ 6. *Royal Scotsman*

   G. Switzerland   _____ 7. *Palace on Wheels*

   H. South Africa   _____ 8. *Andalusian Express*

2. Name the high-speed train that carries passengers between Great Britain and Continental Europe through the Channel Tunnel.

   _____

3. Name the rail pass that is valid in seventeen countries on the European continent.

   _____

4. A popular rail pass that is valid in a minimum of five and a maximum of seven countries in western Europe. Price depends on the number of days purchased and the number of countries selected.

   _____

5. Passengers on European trains taveling at night have the option of sitting in standard seats or reserving an accommodation on board. Name the two types of accommodations.

   A. _____   B. _____

6. In addition to the rail 'n drive pass, there are two other basic categories of rail passes. Name them.

   A. _____   B. _____

7. Name the primary printed resource for European rail schedules.

   _____

☀ *Close-Up: Ground Transportation-Related Careers*

Reservation sales representative   Rental agent   Sales manager

There are many types of career opportunities with car rental agencies and rail companies.

Reservation Sales Representative

An excellent entry-level position with car rental companies and Amtrak which requires public contact and customer service skills. Car rental sales agents provide car rental rates, insurance information, and fleet descriptions to travel agents and the public. Amtrak reservation agents check seat and accommodation inventory, accept bookings by phone, and provide pricing information.

Car Rental Agent

Many car rental service areas are counters located at airports. Others are located in downtown office locations. Car rental agents who work in airport or downtown locations deal directly with customers. They complete the paperwork, discuss insurance and other options, and ensure that renters have the correct credentials. Since most of the work is done face to face with customers, most employers look for personality and skills in communications, sales, and customer service.

Sales Manager

The sales manager works closely with airlines, companies, and travel agencies to promote his or her car rental firm. The sales manager is responsible for negotiating discount rates and incentive programs with clients. Employers look for a background in sales and marketing, with excellent written and verbal communication skills.

➤ Key Terms

- *American Orient Express*
- Amtrak
- *Andalusian Express*
- *Auto Train*
- *Bernina Express*
- *Blue Train*
- *Bullet Train*
- Channel Tunnel (Chunnel)
- collision damage waiver (CDW)
- consecutive pass
- couchette

- Eurailpass
- Europass
- *Eurostar*
- flexi-pass
- *Flying Scotsman*
- *Glacier Express*
- loss damage waiver (LDW)
- *Nostalgic Istanbul Orient Express*
- *Palace on Wheels*
- personal accident insurance (PAI)
- rail 'n drive pass

- *Rovos Rail*
- *Royal Scotsman*
- *Sierra Madre Express*
- sleeper
- *Train à Grande Vitesse (TGV)*
- *Twilight Express*
- value added tax (VAT)
- *Venice Simplon-Orient Express (VSOE)*
- VIA Rail Canada

Flashback   When people think of selling the excitement of travel, they do not usually consider car rentals and trains on the top of their list. However, these two very important segments of the travel and tourism industry contribute high revenues to travel agents who know these products and how to sell them.

Renting a car goes hand in hand with selling an airline ticket and a hotel room. A lot of lost revenue results from travel agents simply forgetting to offer this service. Profitable markets for car rentals are both vacation and business travelers. For leisure travelers, transportation and sightseeing in self-drive cars, especially in such popular "self-drive-states" as Florida and California, mean freedom, independence, convenience, and a low-cost option especially for families.

Car companies also compete for their biggest market, business travelers, by offering them upgraded service through car rental club memberships. They also gain customer loyalty by awarding such things as rental upgrades or free car rentals through frequent-renter programs and similar tie-ins with airlines and hotel chains.

How about rail travel as an alternative way to travel? There are good reasons why many people choose to travel by rail. For leisure travelers it is the romance and excitement, sometimes tinged with nostalgia. North American travelers don't have far to go to experience the romance of the rails. Domestic travelers can experience Europe's famous and luxurious Orient Express by riding on America's own American Orient Express train through some of the most scenic and historic places in the United States. To the north, VIA Rail's Canadian is an ideal way to see some of the most spectacular scenery along southern Canada from sea to shining sea. To the south, one of the top ten train rides in the world, the Sierra Madre Express, takes travelers through a breathtaking tour of Copper Canyon, four times larger than the Grand Canyon.

Travelers outside North America can ride some of the most luxurious and scenic trains in the world in such places as Spain, Italy, Switzerland, India, and Japan. They can also experience the fastest way to travel on ground level on such trains as France's TGV, Japan's Bullet Train, or on the Eurostar, the link between London, Paris, and Brussels through the underwater Chunnel.

The real pull of rail travel is basic transportation service coupled with the romance and nostalgia associated with trains, and it is much better than many people and even some travel professionals realize.

CHAPTER REVIEW

True or False?

_____ 1. Most international car rentals have automatic transmission and air-conditioning as standard features.

_____ 2. Car rental rates are generally higher when renting at major airports.

_____ 3. ICE, X2000, and AVE are examples of high-speed trains in Europe.

_____ 4. Europe's *Nostalgic Istanbul Orient Express* operates as a tour train and not a as a regularly-scheduled train.

_____ 5. The standard minimum age to rent a car in North America is 18.

_____ 6. A rail pass does not guarantee a seat on any train.

_____ 7. The Eurailpass can only be purchased in Europe.

_____ 8. Weekly car rental rates are less expensive than a daily rate multiplied by the same number of days.

_____ 9. Value-added tax (VAT) is usually included in the cost of international car rentals.

_____10. Most rail passes in Europe are based on either a flexible or a consecutive-day plan.

Multiple Choice.

Circle the *best* answer.

11. Most car rental agencies do not charge a fee for a one-way car rental between two different cities in which state?

    A. Texas

    B. California

    C. New York

    D. Florida

12. Which country below would not be included on the Eurailpass?

    A. France

    B. Germany

    C. England

    D. Hungary

13. Which liability coverage waives a car rental agency's right to charge a customer for damages in the case of an accident?

    A. VAT

    B. CDW

    C. LDW

    D. PAI

14. In which city would vacation travelers be most likely to rent a car?

    A. Chicago, Illinois

    B. San Francisco, California

    C. New York, New York

    D. Orlando, Florida

15. What is the name of Amtrak's high-speed rail service in the eastern U.S.?

    A. Auto Train

    B. Acela

    C. Ava

    D. turboliner

16. Reservations on Amtrak are always required on:

    A. long-distance overnight coach seats

    B. club seats

    C. sleeping accommodations

    D. all of the above

17. Amtrak high-speed trains that reach speeds up to 150 mph operate between:

    A. Chicago and Los Angeles

    B. Lorton, Virginia and Sanford, Florida

    C. New York and Washington, DC

    D. Miami and New York

18. The North American Rail Pass is valid systemwide on Amtrak and VIA Rail in:

    A. the United States and Mexico

    B. Mexico and Canada

    C. Canada and the United States

    D. the United States, Canada, and Mexico

19. You are riding a train known for its scenic route through the Swiss Alps between Zermatt and St. Moritz. What train are you on?

    A. *Glacier Express*

    B. *Bernina Express*

    C. *Venice Simplon-Orient Express*

    D. *Twilight Express*

20. You are riding on one of the world's most luxurious and scenic tour trains in South Africa. What train are you riding on?

    A. *Bernina Express*

    B. *Palace on Wheels*

    C. *Rovos Rail*

    D. *Andalusian Express*

Short Answers

21. List three types of car rental discount rates or programs.

    A. _____

    B. _____

    C. _____

22. Your client wants to travel by train from Frankfurt, Germany and Paris, France during a three-week business trip in Europe. Would you suggest a one-way ticket or a Eurailpass? Explain your answer.

_____

23. Name the major printed resource for all international rail schedules outside Europe.

_____

24. Name the major rail distributor in North America for European tickets, rail passes, and related information.

_____

25. Identify a minimum of three extra charges that may be added to the basic cost of a car rental.

   A. _____   C. _____

   B. _____

26. Describe the difference between sleepers and couchettes on European trains.

_____

27. What is the name of the major rail pass that is used within the United Kingdom?

_____

28. Can children under 12 years of age ride free on Amtrak with a full-paying passenger?_____

29. List two benefits for business travelers who take Amtrak on short-distance routes (under five hours).

   A. _____

   B. _____

30. Name four destinations where driving is on the left side of the road, opposite to that in the United States and Canada.

   A. _____   C. _____

   B. _____   D. _____

Chapter 10

Corporate Sales and Group Travel

The key difference between leisure and business travelers: Leisure travelers don't have to travel, but they want to travel; business travelers have to travel, but don't necessarily want to travel.

Corporate travel agents everywhere

Fast Forward ▼

➤ Business travel is a prime market that offers travel agencies significant profit potential. . . . 476

➤ Leisure travelers spend discretionary dollars, business travelers spend nondiscretionary dollars; there are other differences between these two markets. . . . 477

➤ Because of the special and unique demands of business travelers, successful corporate agents need to have excellent computer skills, and much more. . . . 478

➤ When a company is actively seeking a travel agency to handle its travel business, it sends out an RFP as part of the bidding process. . . . 480

➤ Corporate agencies do much more than booking travel; they establish travel policy, assist in supplier negotiations, and much more. . . . 480

➤ A travel agency can work with a corporate account in several different ways: everything from full service to an STP on site. . . . 482

➤ Corporate travel departments can choose to be ARC-approved or not; their choice affects the way they do business. . . . 484

➤ Rebating as a practice is on the decline; charging service fees is on the rise. . . . 484

➤ Passenger profiles is a major time management tool used for an agency's frequent travelers. . . . 485

➤ Leisure and business group planning has become a highly sophisticated and profitable venture in the travel business. . . . 490

➤ When booking group travel, the agency may choose to handle it in several different ways: working through a tour wholesale company, working directly with a receptive service operator, or dealing directly with local suppliers. . . . 491

➤ A key resource when booking individual and group tours is the Master-Key WATA Tariff. . . . 493

➤ Tour designing is one of the most creative and challenging aspects of being a travel professional. . . . 496

➤ Meeting planners organize meeting events for a wide variety of sponsors; typical meetings include conferences, conventions, symposiums, trade shows, and workshops. . . . 501

➤ Incentives is a very profitable market segment for group travel that is business or work related. . . . 501

➤ Some of the steps involved in planning meetings include qualifying the client, conducting site inspections, negotiating, and managing the event on site. . . . 504

Big Bucks for Business

Business in North America is booming, and business-related travel is booming right along with it. Business-only and a combination of business and leisure trips average close to $62 billion of travel revenue per year (see Figure 10.1). In terms of number of travel agencies, more than 90 percent of U.S. travel agencies handle business travel to some extent. The number of different corporate accounts varies depending on the size, location, and business mix of each agency. According to a

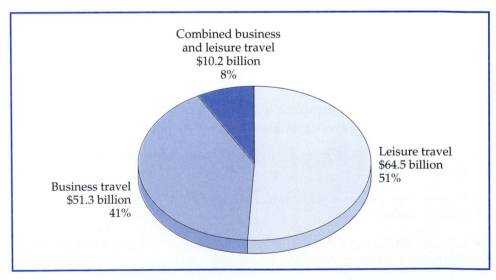

Figure 10.1 *Business versus leisure dollars.*
From U.S. Travel Agency Survey, Travel Weekly, September 1998.

recent survey of U.S. travel agencies, each agency handles on the average 44 different corporate accounts.

Business travel is a prime market that offers travel agencies significant profit potential, quick growth through volume transactions, steady growth through regular travel patterns, and the opportunity to expand into other travel markets through referrals. There are many reasons why business travel is often considered to be the "bread and butter" of many agencies. The volume of business travel varies from one business to another, but each corporate travel account normally represents a significant sales volume achieved through numerous transactions. If a travel agency is successful in recruiting a number of new accounts on a regular basis and is successful in maintaining the ones it currently handles, a travel agency receives a continual stream of revenue and quick growth in sales and revenue.

Most business travel occurs on a regular basis, practically seven days a week on a year-round basis. Except for the months of August and December, when business travel has a tendency of dropping off slightly due to vacation and holiday periods, this market is not subject to seasonal fluctuations. This results in a steady flow of revenue while the agency can achieve a stable and steady growth pattern.

The third reason is that business travel leads to other travel markets, such as vacation planning and group travel. Each corporate account is a prospect for these other markets. The company's employees and their families are vacation prospects, while the company itself may require group travel arrangements, such as business meetings and conventions.

BUSINESS VERSUS LEISURE TRAVELER

The travel industry has always defined leisure and business clients as two very different markets—and they are. Leisure travel is **discretionary travel:** Travelers go on a trip because they want to. They travel to visit friends, family, or to take a hard-earned vacation from work. What they want to do most on these trips is to pursue special interests or hobbies, or just to relax, unwind, and enjoy themselves. The *where* is more important than the how—the destination becomes the major focus, and how they get there is secondary.

Business travel is **nondiscretionary travel:** Travelers go on a trip because they have to. They travel to attend meetings, conventions, or to visit customers. Business travelers must go when and where their business dictates. The *how* is more important than the where—how they get to their destination is more important than the destination itself. They expect to get where they are going in a speedy and efficient manner.

Another difference is price flexibility. Most travelers, both business and leisure, are cost conscious. However, vacation travelers can take advantage of advance-purchase discounts and other special offers since they make plans far in advance of departure. Vacation travelers have more flexibility in adjusting their plans to take advantage of cost savings.

Business travelers usually do not have the luxury of long-range planning and have little choice in terms of scheduling and prices. Last-minute planning and short stays are the standard pattern. Business people usually travel during weekdays and return home by Friday. Since discounted air fares are based on advance purchase and a Saturday-night stay, business travelers are not eligible for discounted fares.

Another difference involves the types of products that are sold to leisure and business travelers. Leisure clients are sold a variety of transportation, from airline tickets to rail passes; stay in a range of accommodations, from bed & breakfasts to ocean-front resorts; and take vacation get-a-ways, from escorted motorcoach tours to cruises. Most corporate travel involves the booking of three main products: air tickets, accommodations, and car rental. Business travelers usually don't have much choice regarding which airline or hotel to stay in. To reduce travel costs, most companies restrict their travelers to flying on certain airlines, paying the lowest price, reserving a room with a preferred hotel chain, and renting a certain size of car.

SELECTING A CORPORATE AGENCY

Business travelers agree that a good travel agent can make the difference between being snowed in at a Denver motel with cardboard walls or a smooth connection through Dallas/Ft. Worth for an on-time arrival. Here are just a few of the important factors that they consider when selecting a corporate agency to handle their business:

1. *Is the agency available 24 hours?* When checking into a hotel in Tokyo, Japan, only to find that there is no record of the reservation, the business traveler doesn't want to call his or her agent and hear an answering machine.

2. *Does the agency have a Web site with an automated booking system?* When a change of travel plans occurs during a trip, the business traveler can whip out his or her notebook computer, link up with the agency on-line, and make a booking for on-going travel. Or at the very least, does the agency have E-mail?

3. *Who are the agency's preferred suppliers?* If the traveler is a frequent flyer with Delta and United and the agency has a relationship with American and Continental, it may not be a good match.

4. *Does the agency have a rate desk?* If the traveler goes on a lot of international trips, the agency that has international rate specialists would be an added bonus.

5. *What is the average length of experience of the agency's corporate agents and representatives?* According to survey results, a minimum of four years of experience is very good.

6. *What is the agency's quality-assurance system?* The agency should have an automated system that scans for lowest fares and better seats. Two popular systems used by agencies are AQUA and ATS.

7. *Does the agency have experience booking to the places where the company's travelers go?* A small agency that handles mostly vacation packages to Florida may not have the technical expertise to handle a multimillion-dollar account whose employees often travel to Asia.

WHAT IT TAKES TO BE A CORPORATE AGENT

Because of the special needs and demands of business travelers, corporate travel agencies and their employees have to provide essential services unique to this profitable market. The basic profile of successful corporate travel agents includes:

1. *Friendly and convenient service.* Corporate agents must have a friendly and enthusiastic voice and attitude because a lot of communication is over the telephone. Since business travelers tend to make many last-minute changes, a positive and patient demeanor is a must. Remember, business travelers use a travel agency to avoid the hassles they would experience in making their own arrangements. Offering convenience means being easy to deal with, friendly and personable. It means being accessible: easy to reach by telephone, in person, or through E-mail.

2. *Computer expertise.* Efficiency and speed on the agency's CRS is essential in the

Special Services Expected from Corporate Travel Agents

Response (%) of business travelers to which of the following their corporate agents had been able to do for them recently:

• Secure a preassigned seat in an emergency-exit row (more legroom)	40
• Block off an empty adjacent seat	25
• Obtain a room in a supposedly sold-out hotel	23
• Offer a free business-class upgrade	21
• Book a consolidator ticket	20
• Obtain a seat on a supposedly sold-out flight	20
• Offer a free upgrade to first class	18
• Waive an airline's advance-purchase restriction	16

Source: Condé Nast, Business Extra, 1998.

corporate travel environment. Because of the volume of bookings and last-minute changes transacted each day, the corporate agent must love to work with computers and be familiar with many of the shortcuts and special entries not generally used for leisure bookings.

3. *Attention to detail.* Because of the special needs of the business traveler, corporate agents must pay attention to details and do it right every time. They must be knowledgeable about travel procedures and technical details. For example, the business traveler attending a convention in midtown Manhattan will be irked to find out that the agent booked accommodations in downtown Manhattan, a good six miles away!

4. *Speed and accuracy.* Business travel is fast-paced, last-minute, and with a lot of changes, with hardly any letup. Corporate agents must respond quickly with fare quotes, routings, time schedules, availability, and confirmations. Corporate accounts expect quick and efficient service on the telephone, speedy handling of last-minute bookings and changes, and prompt delivery of tickets and other travel documents.

ESTABLISHING RELATIONSHIPS

When a company decides how their travel arrangements will be handled, there are three basic options from which a choice can be made. One choice is to select any one of a number of travel agencies in the area to handle its travel arrangements. Another choice may be to deal directly with the airlines, hotels, and car rental companies. A third choice is to establish a travel department within their own organization.

In the majority of cases, companies use the services of a travel agency to handle their business travel. Large companies that do a high-volume of travel may have their own corporate travel departments to handle some travel arrangements, but still rely on a travel agency to process tickets and to handle other specialized services for them.

In most cases, travel agencies win corporate accounts by soliciting their services. In smaller, independently owned agencies this responsibility usually falls under the owner or manager's role. In larger agencies that handle millions of business travel dollars, an employee of the agency called an **account executive** actively solicits new commercial accounts for the company. The account executive's role does not end when a corporate account is won. He or she acts as a liaison between the account and the agency to ensure a smooth-working operation. The account executive also acts as a troubleshooter to handle problems and address complaints for quick and speedy solution.

When a company is actively looking for a travel agency to handle its business travel, it develops a **request for proposal (RFP).** This document is a profile of the company and its business travel needs. It describes in detail who travels, how frequently, for how long, and to what destinations. The RFP also outlines the types of services expected from the travel agency.

The RFP is distributed to those agencies that wish to bid on the business. In response to the company's RFP, the travel agency answers all questions and includes a detailed description of its staff organization, business history, computer capabilities, and other technical and service support systems that it can provide.

CORPORATE SERVICES: MORE THAN JUST ORDER-TAKERS

Nearly all corporate accounts rely on their travel agents to handle the nuts and bolts of reservations and ticketing. However, the role of the travel agency in the corporate arena is much more than that. Many companies expect their travel agencies to assist them with other specialized services, such as developing and monitoring the company travel policies, negotiating with travel vendors, and generating management and expense reports.

➤ Developing and Enforcing Travel Policy

Travel is the second largest controllable expense at most companies and is considered the top candidate when companies see the need to control expenses. A company's travel policy is one of the most important documents used to control its expenses. In many cases the travel agency assists in the development of a company's travel policy. Since business travel is the third highest and controllable expense (after salaries and technology), most companies will complete a thorough study of such things as who travels, how they travel, and where do they travel, for example.

The results are analyzed by the company. The company, with the assistance of the travel agency, will then develop a business travel guideline called a *travel policy*. This formal policy serves as a guideline to all business travelers. It outlines a broad range of business travel requirements, from which airline to fly and in what class of service, to what size car to rent. The policy also serves as a guideline for the travel agency since the corporate agents must adhere to these policies when making reservations for the company's travelers.

Some travel agencies go one step further and monitor the effectiveness of a company's policy. The agency would be sent on a periodic basis, travel reports that show the details of business travel for the preceding month. From these data the agency can monitor the company's travel trends and patterns and monitor for compliance. Are business travelers flying on preselected airlines? Did they fly at the lowest available price? Did the traveler use a hotel chain or car rental company from the preferred supplier list? These types of data and more are used to monitor and enforce corporate travel policies, and as a result, the agency and corporate account work together to control costs.

➤ Vendor Negotiations

Another area where many travel agencies get involved is vendor negotiations. Travel suppliers such as airlines, hotels, and car rental companies offer discount rates to their favorite customers—the frequent business traveler—in order to win their business.

Corporate Airline Negotiations

Survey of corporate travel managers shows most frequently obtained benefits for their business travelers.

Benefit Obtained Through Negotiation	% Citing It
Upgrades to first/business class	79
Premier frequent-flyer status	72
Free tickets	56
Airline club memberships	44
Special wait-list clearance	35
Waiver of advance-purchase restrictions	34
Waiver of Saturday-night-stay restriction	19
Management information reports	18
Ticket coupon books	7
Installation of automation systems	7
Credit terms	4

Source: Survey by Runzheimer International of Rochester, Wisconsin.

Many large companies that generate a large amount of business travel negotiate directly with travel suppliers for *company-negotiated discount* rates. Company-negotiated discounts are special prices that apply only to travelers from a specific company. The travel agency is often asked to assist, since their knowledge of travel suppliers and the industry as a whole are valuable during the negotiation phase. These rates are company-specific.

In some cases the agency itself negotiates directly with suppliers on behalf of all their business clients. These rates, called *agency-contract discounts,* apply to all business travelers who use the services of that travel agency. These rates are agency-specific, not company-specific.

In addition to discount rates, companies also negotiate for certain benefits, such as upgrades, free tickets, and airline club memberships for their business travelers. The box above shows a recent survey of corporate travel managers and the types of benefits negotiated and obtained for their company's travelers.

➤ Travel Management Reports

Management reports also play a key role in cost control. **Travel management reports** are vehicles to demonstrate to a company how much money it is spending on travel and entertainment (T&E) expenses. Some companies use automated software systems to generate their own reports. However, approximately 23 percent have their travel agencies do it for them (see Figure 10.2).

These reports can track travel spending by department or by an individual employee. They can also track how much money was spent on each airline, hotel chain, and car rental company. In fact, most systems can calculate the cost for each airline segment flown. Most management software can provide a year-to-date total travel expenditure and a comparison with previous years to track trends over a long period of time. Most travel management reports can also serve as the "police" in identifying policy violations and who made them.

Depending on the size of the company's management and the level of sophistication needed, an agency's back-office accounting system can handle the more simplified reports. However, most companies and agencies use more sophisticated travel management automated systems.

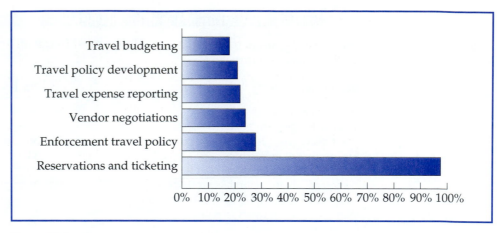

Figure 10.2 *Percentage of business travelers receiving each service.*
Source: U.S. Travel Agency Survey.

How Business Is Handled

A travel agency can work with a corporate account in several different ways: as a full-service agency, with a satellite ticket printer (STP), as a corporate on-site, or in conjunction with the company's corporate travel department.

➤ Full-Service Travel Agencies

The majority of corporate accounts are handled in a full-service manner. The travel agency is a separate facility and operates independently from the corporate account. The full-service agency probably handles a number of different corporate accounts. Some agencies specialize in business-related travel only; others handle a mix of leisure and corporate travel. Depending on the size of the corporate account, one or more travel agents may be assigned to handle the travel for that company. These agency employees who handle all the business travel for one or more specific accounts are called *dedicated* corporate agents. This is usually the case since a company becomes familiar with a particular travel agent and feels comfortable dealing with that person.

➤ Satellite Ticket Printers

For those corporate accounts whose employees do a great deal of traveling, some travel agencies install a **satellite ticket printer (STP).** The STP is owned and operated by the travel agency and installed in the corporate account's office building. This is a form of speedy electronic ticket delivery. The agency's computers are linked to the STP. The travel agent books the reservation on the agency's CRS and transmits the passenger record data directly to the company's STP. The company's STP then prints the airline ticket and other necessary documentation, such as boarding passes, itineraries, and invoices for the traveler.

STPs cost travel agencies a lot of money to install and operate. Also, the travel agency is responsible for the security of all tickets generated at STP sites. Because of these cost and security concerns, STPs are usually installed only for high-volume corporate accounts or in corporate locations a long distance from the agency.

➤ Corporate On-Site Agencies

A corporate **on-site agency** is a dedicated travel agency that is located physically inside the corporate account's business premises. The primary purpose of an on-site location is to serve all the business and leisure travel of the employees of that particular corporate account. An on-site is actually a branch office of the travel agency, and the agents who work there are employees of the travel agency, not of the corporation. The only difference is that they work on the premises of the account rather than in the agency location. Depending on the amount of travel business a company generates, an on-site office can be staffed from one to several agents.

➤ Corporate Travel Departments

Many large companies that generate millions of dollars worth of travel business have their own **corporate travel departments.** Staff members who work in corporate travel departments are employees of the company, not a travel agency. The number of staff will vary depending on the amount of business travel the company generates. Usually, the corporate travel department is supervised by a *travel manager*, whose primary responsibility is to control travel expenses. This includes a broad range of job duties, from developing travel policy to planning company meetings (see Figure 10.3).

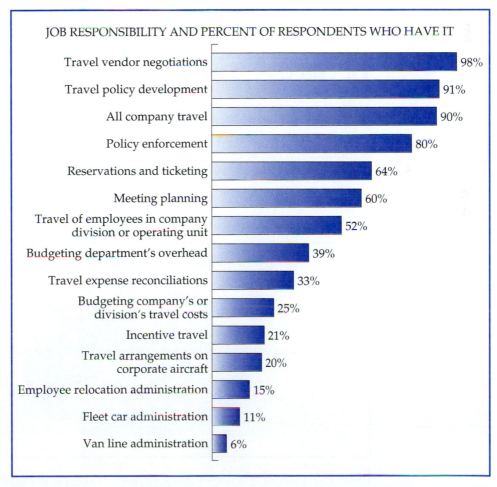

JOB RESPONSIBILITY AND PERCENT OF RESPONDENTS WHO HAVE IT

Job Responsibility	Percent
Travel vendor negotiations	98%
Travel policy development	91%
All company travel	90%
Policy enforcement	80%
Reservations and ticketing	64%
Meeting planning	60%
Travel of employees in company division or operating unit	52%
Budgeting department's overhead	39%
Travel expense reconciliations	33%
Budgeting company's or division's travel costs	25%
Incentive travel	21%
Travel arrangements on corporate aircraft	20%
Employee relocation administration	15%
Fleet car administration	11%
Van line administration	6%

Figure 10.3 *Job responsibilities of corporate travel managers, based on a survey of 195 corporate travel managers.*
Source: Runzheimer International of Rochester, Wisconsin.

Prior to 1998, corporate travel departments were not able to gain ARC approval or accreditation. They either had to work with a travel agency or become a travel agency open to the general public to obtain ARC accreditation and be able to issue their own tickets.

In 1998, ARC began granting accreditation to corporate travel departments for the first time. Those that have ARC approval are able to issue tickets for company travel. Under the rules established for ARC accreditation as a corporate travel department, the department cannot sell travel at retail, be open to the public, or solicit customers from the general public. The departments with ARC approval are permitted to outsource to a travel agency functions such as staffing, fulfillment, and 24-hour service.

Those corporate travel departments that are not ARC approved will have the same CRS as that of the travel agency that services the account. In that way, employees who work in the corporate travel department serve as reservation agents, booking airline, car, and hotel reservations on their computer. Their reservations are then routed electronically to their partner travel agency for ticketing and other documentation.

Web Link

The Web of Culture: This site gives the business traveler a guide to appropriate (and inappropriate) gestures in various European countries. Many travel professionals recommend this site since it provides useful tips for corporate travel agents to pass on to their international travelers. For more do's and don't when traveling far from home, point your browser to *www.webofculture.com/edu/gestures.html*

THE PRICE OF DOING BUSINESS: REBATES AND FEES

Most of a corporate travel agency's revenue is generated through airline ticket sales. Since the airline commission caps of 1995 and other negative influences, many travel agencies are looking at the way they do business with their corporate accounts. As a result, many corporate agencies are charging fees and reducing or eliminating rebating of ticket commissions (see Figure 10.4).

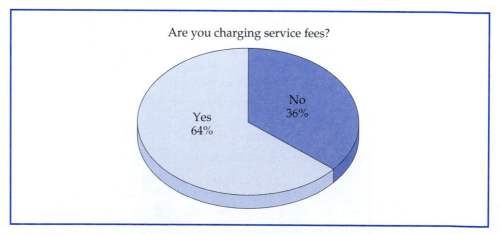

Figure 10.4 *Percent of corporate travel agencies charging a service fee, from a survey of 506 agencies.*
Source: ASTA, based in Alexandria, Virginia.

► Rebating: A Dirty Word?

First, let's take a look at the practice of rebating, which has been a controversial issue in the travel industry. **Rebating** is the practice of a travel agency to return a portion of its earned commission to the corporate client. So what does the travel agency get in return? The corporate account promises its business travel to that agency. In the past, more agencies were involved in rebating. Winning corporate accounts is highly competitive. Some travel agencies believe that the practice of rebating will give them the competitive edge that they need to win the account over their competitors.

Rebating might have made more sense before the days of the commission cap restriction on domestic airline tickets. Before commission caps, the agency earned a standard 10 percent commission on each ticket it sold. For example, a round-trip ticket that cost $1,200 earned $120. With the commission cap, the same ticket earned only a $50 commission. Rebating further erodes the profit realized on the sale of that airline ticket. As a result, the number of agencies that practice rebating is growing smaller.

► Service Fees: One Solution

On the other side of the scale, a majority of travel agencies have determined that charging service fees is a necessity in the current business climate. The problem is not deciding whether or not to charge service fees, but how much and when to charge.

There are essentially two general types of service fees: transactional- and management-based. A **transactional fee** is a set charge for a specific item or service, such as issuing an airline ticket or booking a hotel. A **management fee** is a flat charge that may include a per transaction fee plus the cost of other services the agency may provide, such as monitoring the company's travel policy and providing management reports. Other agencies impose a fee for specific transactions, such as ticket changes and cancellations (see Figure 10.5). According to a recent survey conducted by ASTA, the majority of travel agencies levy a transactional fee, and the average service fee charged is $10.37.

► Passenger and Company Profiles

Business travelers are frequent travelers; some average one trip per month, whereas others may travel several times in one month. Some of the special products and services that target this lucrative market are frequent-travel awards programs sponsored by suppliers and airline clubs, all designed to win customer loyalty.

Electronic or paperless tickets were also introduced with the busy corporate traveler in mind. As discussed elsewhere, electronic tickets are designed to make traveling more convenient and to reduce the chance of losing a paper ticket on the way to the airport.

Corporate travel agents also have many timesaving techniques in place when handling their business clientele. When booking a reservation in the computer for a repeat traveler (business or leisure), some of the booking information remains the same from trip to trip. Data such as passenger's name, phone contacts, form of payment, preferred seat assignment, and in-flight meal service will probably remain the same.

During a normal workday a travel agent can be responsible for more than sixty passenger reservations and almost the same number of last-minute changes!

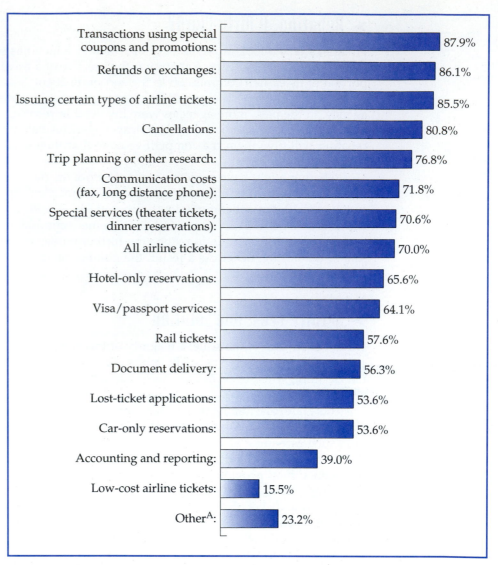

Figure 10.5 *Services for which travel agencies charge fees. Based on a survey of 506 agencies. ([A]Includes after-hours service, airport delivery, frequent-flyer tickets, upgrades, copies of tickets, issuance of foreign checks, foreign currency drafts, handwritten tickets, Internet bookings, noncommissionable hotels, returned checks, and voids.)*
Source: ASTA, based in Alexandria, Virginia, as published in Travel Weekly, *August 1998.*

Time management is very important in the busy office to ensure a smooth work flow during the day and accurate and timely completion of client bookings.

The computer reservations systems have a time management tool called passenger **profiles.** A passenger profile is an electronic file in which the travel agent can store any data that relate to a particular traveler. The travel agent can retrieve and move these data directly into the passenger's record at the time it is being created in the computer. For example, when entering a special meal request in the standard way, the agent makes approximately 14 keystrokes. If the special meal preference is stored in the profile, the agent makes only two or three keystrokes to "move" the information into the traveler's record. As you can see, profiles are excellent timesavers.

Figure 10.6 is an example of a passenger profile in American Airlines' SABRE system. A profile in SABRE is called a STAR. Notice that each line of a STAR is

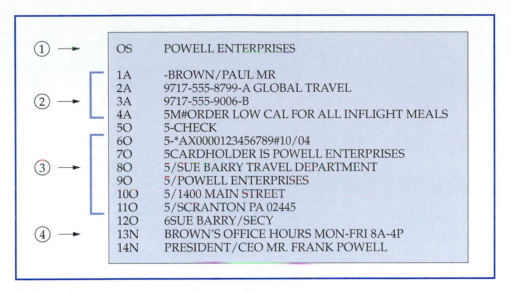

① →	OS	POWELL ENTERPRISES
② →	1A	-BROWN/PAUL MR
	2A	9717-555-8799-A GLOBAL TRAVEL
	3A	9717-555-9006-B
	4A	5M#ORDER LOW CAL FOR ALL INFLIGHT MEALS
	5O	5-CHECK
	6O	5-*AX0000123456789#10/04
	7O	5CARDHOLDER IS POWELL ENTERPRISES
③ →	8O	5/SUE BARRY TRAVEL DEPARTMENT
	9O	5/POWELL ENTERPRISES
	10O	5/1400 MAIN STREET
	11O	5/SCRANTON PA 02445
	12O	6SUE BARRY/SECY
④ →	13N	BROWN'S OFFICE HOURS MON-FRI 8A-4P
	14N	PRESIDENT/CEO MR. FRANK POWELL

Figure 10.6 *SABRE system passenger profile.*

numbered. These numbers are used to move the individual lines as needed into the client's reservation record when the booking is being created. The lines are described as follows:

1. *OS Powell Enterprises.* The top line of a profile identifies the name of the client. In some cases it is the name of the individual traveler, in others the company's name.

2. *A (always move) lines.* A lines indicate data elements that are *always* moved into the passenger's booking record. Examples of common A-line data are the passenger's name, phone contact, and travel preferences.

3. *O (optionally move) lines.* O lines indicate data elements that are sometimes or *optionally* moved into the passenger's booking record. Examples of common O-line data are form of payment, mailing address, and "received from" information.

4. *N (never move) lines.* N lines indicate data elements that are *never* moved into the passenger's record; they are used for informational purposes only. Examples of common N-line data are office hours and company executive names.

Let's take a look at an example of a booking using STAR information.

Example: Brenda Miller, a corporate agent from Global Travel, is on the phone with Sue Barry from Powell Enterprises. She wants to book flights for a company employee, Paul Brown. Since this is a repeat client, the agency has created a profile for this company.

1. Brenda begins to create a passenger name record in the agency's SABRE computer reservations system. First, she books round-trip flights on United Airlines between Chicago O'Hare (ORD) and Los Angeles (LAX). She also enters the date the ticket will be prepared, July 10. All other data elements, such as the passenger's name, phone contacts, and form of payment, will be moved from the company profile. The partial passenger name record, which includes only the booked flight segments and ticket information, appears in the following box:

```
1UA   101B   13JUL   M   ORDLAX   SS1   700A    921A
2UA   818B   15JUL   W   LAXORD   SS1   1200N   545P
TKT/TIME LIMIT
   TAW10JUL/DELIVER TKT
```

2. The agent displays the profile or STAR for the corporate account, Powell Enterprises:

```
OS      POWELL ENTERPRISES

1A      -BROWN/PAUL MR
2A      9717-555-8799-A GLOBAL TRAVEL
3A      9717-555-9006-B
4A      5M#ORDER LOW CAL FOR ALL INFLIGHT MEALS
5O      5-CHECK
6O      5-*AX0000123456789#10/04
7O      5CARDHOLDER IS POWELL ENTERPRISES
8O      5/SUE BARRY TRAVEL DEPARTMENT
9O      5/POWELL ENTERPRISES
10O     5/1400 MAIN STREET
11O     5/SCRANTON PA 02445
12O     6SUE BARRY/SECY
13N     BROWN'S OFFICE HOURS MON-FRI 8A-4P
14N     PRESIDENT/CEO MR. FRANK POWELL
```

3. To save time, the agent moves all A lines from this STAR into the passenger record: passenger name, agency phone, passenger's business phone, and a reminder to book a low-calorie meal on his flights. Also she wants to include that the form of payment is by check (optional line 5) and that Sue Barry is the contact (optional line 12). The entry she makes is easy. To move all A lines plus optional lines 5 and 12 from a STAR, the entry is: NM5‡12 (the NM entry automatically moves all A lines in addition to the optional line numbers shown in the entry). When this entry is made, the data from the STAR are moved automatically into the PNR and displayed in the correct sequence:

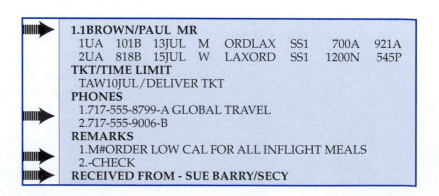

```
1.1BROWN/PAUL MR
   1UA   101B   13JUL   M   ORDLAX   SS1   700A    921A
   2UA   818B   15JUL   W   LAXORD   SS1   1200N   545P
TKT/TIME LIMIT
   TAW10JUL/DELIVER TKT
PHONES
   1.717-555-8799-A GLOBAL TRAVEL
   2.717-555-9006-B
REMARKS
   1.M#ORDER LOW CAL FOR ALL INFLIGHT MEALS
   2.-CHECK
RECEIVED FROM - SUE BARRY/SECY
```

✓ Check Your Understanding 10-1

Multiple Choice

Circle the *best* answer.

1. Which would not be a major factor when a company selects a travel agency to handle its business travel?
    A. agency's expertise in destinations
    B. agency's 24-hour reservation service
    C. agency's preferred cruise lines
    D. agency's quality assurance programs

2. The function of a company's request for proposal (RFP) is:
    A. a request for a lower fare from an airline
    B. the company's profile and its travel needs
    C. frequent-traveler program application
    D. a request to issue airline tickets

3. A function in which a corporate travel department is least likely to be involved is to:
    A. issue airline tickets
    B. make hotel reservations
    C. negotiate with suppliers for lower prices
    D. develop company travel policies

4. An automated passenger profile is a time-management tool used to:
    A. search quickly for names and addresses of corporate clients
    B. enhance the travel agent's knowledge of a traveler's needs
    C. speed up the process of booking flights for repeat travelers
    D. contact business travelers anywhere in the world

5. *STP* stands for:
    A. standard ticket printer
    B. satellite transmission process
    C. standard ticketing procedure
    D. satellite ticket printer

6. A travel office that is located physically inside the corporate account's business premises but whose agents are employed by the travel agency is called a:
    A. branch office
    B. corporate on-site
    C. full-service agency
    D. corporate travel department

7. The practice of returning part of the agency's commission to a corporate account is called:
    A. repayment
    B. transmitting fees
    C. time management
    D. rebating

8. For which service below would a travel agency typically charge a transactional fee?
    A. booking a cruise
    B. changing a ticket
    C. sending a fax
    D. developing travel policy

9. Many corporate agencies generate travel management reports for their corporate accounts. The main purpose of these reports is to:
    A. evaluate the job performance of the corporate travel department's manager and staff
    B. allow the travel department at the company to issue airline tickets

C. record the amount of service fees the company owes the travel agency

D. track and analyze the company's travel and entertainment expenses

10. A special discount rate that applies only to the travelers of a specific company is called a(n):

A. agency contract rate   C. company-negotiated rate

B. corporate rebate   D. contract rate

GROUP TRAVEL

Group travel does not mean a swarm of people who have come together to be shuttled from one destination to the next. It has become a highly sophisticated and profitable venture in the travel business. Group travel is a highly diversified field that has become more than traditional motorcoach tours. It ranges from business meetings to ballooning adventures over the Serengeti; from trade missions to mountain trekking; from study programs on board an expedition ship to a wine-tasting odyssey through Burgundy, France.

In the past, group travel was regulated strictly by those who specialized in group travel planning: tour operators, the airlines, meeting planners, and motorcoach companies, for example. Even though this is a highly sophisticated field that requires specialized skills and know-how, many experienced travel agents are acquiring those skills through experience, training, and study.

Why is group business so attractive? One reason is the promise of volume business and profits. If the product is priced correctly, an agency can expect to make approximately 20 to 40 percent profit margin on the groups it sells. Group business is a way to break free of the rigid commission structures established by airlines, hotels, cruise lines, and tour operators. Basically, an agency can shop around for the lowest **net prices**—base cost without commission built into it—from each supplier when putting together a group event. Through volume discounts, agents can obtain much lower prices for airline seats, hotel rooms, meals, and ground transportation for each traveler in the group. The agency then determines its profit margin by marking up the total net cost to get the selling price.

Who travels in groups? Generally speaking, anyone who travels for practically any reason is a potential group client. Rather than marketing across the entire traveling population, many agencies have found their specialized niche and direct their expertise, products, and marketing efforts to a specific segment of the market. Some areas of specialization are customer-driven: senior citizens, students and teachers, upscale, ethnic, and business markets, for example. Other areas of specialization are product-driven: cruise-only, adventure tours, ecotourism, and rail trips, for example.

HOW THE GROUP TRAVEL BUSINESS WORKS

We can simplify matters by dividing the group business into two general categories: leisure and business. Both group categories essentially work the same way. The group travel business can appear very confusing at first. There seems to be many different types of companies involved with too many middlemen and choices. How does the travel agency interact with the airline, hotels, motorcoach company, and transfer companies? Where does the traveler or sponsoring group fit in? Who deals with whom?

It usually starts when a person who belongs to a club, organization, or company contacts the travel agency to arrange a trip for the entire group. This person, called the *trip organizer*, works closely with the travel agent throughout the trip planning process. The trip organizer is also referred to as the **"pied piper"** since he or she is the person who motivates the group members to travel.

The club, organization, or company is called an *affinity* or *preformed group*. An affinity is a group of people who share a common interest or reason for travel. An affinity group may be comprised of members of a club, school, church, civic organization, special-interest club, or company. This is a group that already exists, that formed for purposes other than travel.

Depending on the group's complexity, their interests, budget, and other factors, the travel agent may choose to handle the group booking in a number of ways. The three most prevalent methods of handling groups are to (1) work through a "middleman" or tour wholesaler, (2) work directly with receptive service operators, or (3) work directly with each supplier.

➤ Working through a Tour Operator/Wholesaler

Working through a tour operator or wholesaler is the method usually employed if the travel agency does not have the staff and expertise to handle custom-designed group bookings. This method is the standard scenario when an individual client contacts his or her travel agency to book a tour. The travel agency works as a broker between the traveler or sponsoring group and a wholesale tour operator.

The group organizer consults only with the travel agency, not with the wholesaler. The organizer and travel agent discuss various aspects of the group event, including reasons for travel, preferred destinations and hotels, desired activities and sightseeing, and budget considerations. After determining the needs of the group or *qualifying*, the travel agent researches the best tour product for the client. In this way the retail travel agent acts as a *broker* or matchmaker by searching for a company that has the tour product that best fits the group's interests and needs.

The tour operator offers the package to the travel agency at a selling price. The selling price already includes the agency's commission (the standard is 10 percent). The travel agency then sells the package to the group at no additional cost and receives its commission from the selling price (Figure 10.7).

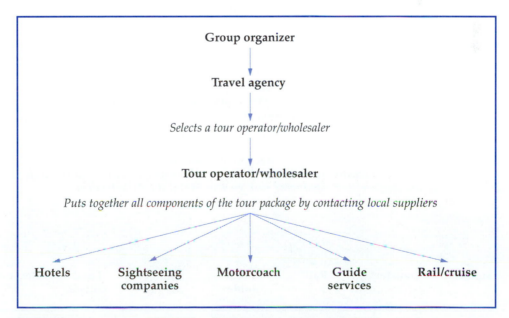

Figure 10.7 *Standard scenario when booking individual tour clients as well as some groups. The chain of events starts with the group organizer, to retail travel agency, to a tour company who has a packaged tour developed that suits the group's needs and interests.*

➤ Working Directly With RSOs

A retail agency that has group travel experience and agents who are savvy in this type of booking process may go a slightly different and more aggressive route. The agency may handle the specific aspects of the tour for the organization. First, it would research and select all the different elements of the group trip, such as hotels, transfers, sightseeing, local guides, and special activities. The travel agency in turn uses the services of a local or U.S.-based tour wholesaler, who in turn contacts a **receptive service operator (RSO)** at each destination.

A receptive service operator is a local company that receives group travelers who visit and tour the region. When working in conjunction with the retail travel agency, the RSO coordinates and books each supplier that is located at the destination. Receptive service operators are also called *ground operators* or *inbound operators* since they handle land arrangements for travelers arriving at the destination.

When a group booking is made by this method, the travel agency can be compensated in one of two ways: a set commission percentage or on a net per-client basis. The *set commission* is similar to booking individual clients. The tour operator sells the group tour at a selling price that includes the agency's commission. The *net per-client basis* allows the travel agency to mark up or increase the price by a certain percentage in order to make a profit. The **markup** amount is added to the net amount to obtain the **selling price.** The average percentage of markups for group tours average between 25 and 40 percent (Figure 10.8).

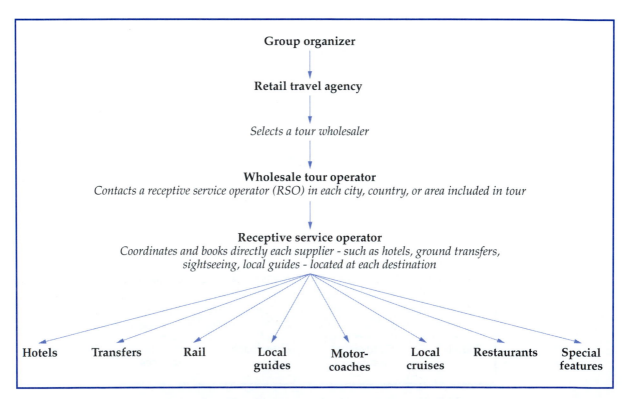

Group organizer

↓

Retail travel agency

↓

Selects a tour wholesaler

↓

Wholesale tour operator
Contacts a receptive service operator (RSO) in each city, country, or area included in tour

↓

Receptive service operator
Coordinates and books directly each supplier - such as hotels, ground transfers, sightseeing, local guides - located at each destination

| Hotels | Transfers | Rail | Local guides | Motor-coaches | Local cruises | Restaurants | Special features |

Figure 10.8 *The chain of events starts with the group organizer, to retail travel agency, to a U.S.-based tour wholesale operator, to one or more receptive service operators, who then book each individual supplier.*

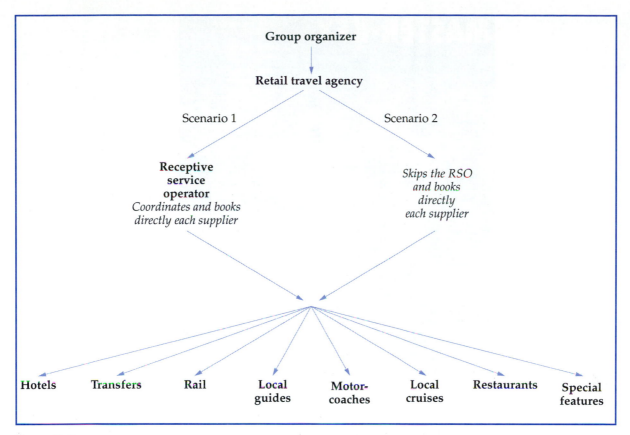

Figure 10.9 *The tour wholesaler/operator is bypassed entirely. Scenario 1: The group organizer, to retail travel agency, to RSO, who books each supplier. Scenario 2: The group organizer, to retail travel agency, who books each supplier directly.*

► Working Directly with Suppliers

This method of conducting group business can be called "skipping the middleman." In this scenario the travel agency chooses to be both the wholesaler and the retailer. The agency does one of two things: (1) works directly with the receptive services operator or ground operator in each destination, or (2) bypasses the receptive services operators altogether and deals directly with individual suppliers, such as hotels, motorcoach sightseeing, guide services, and transfer companies in each destination.

This more direct booking method is usually done by larger travel agencies, which operate group departments. Group managers and coordinators in these specialized departments have experience and expertise in coordinating custom-designed group tours in both domestic and international destinations. In addition, they have the clout and know-how necessary to negotiate with suppliers to obtain the best group rates. When a group booking is done this way, the travel agency obtains *net* prices for most (if not all) land arrangements and applies a markup to cover direct expenses, time, and commission (Figure 10.9).

► WATA: Resource for Tour Planners

An important resource that travel agents use when designing tours for either individual or group clients is the *Master-Key WATA* **(World Association of Travel Agencies)** *tariff* (see Figure 10.10). **WATA** is a nonprofit organization created by

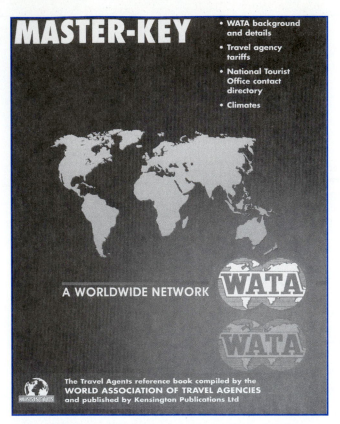

Figure 10.10 Master-Key *cover.*

independent travel agencies around the world. WATA is comprised of more than 200 members located in more than eighty countries.

The WATA tariff is published annually and contains a list of services and rates for a number of overseas inbound operators. Rates are published net (selling price minus commission) for a variety of ground arrangements, such as transfers, sightseeing, motorcoach hire, official guides, entrance fees to attractions, and rail reservations. The WATA is called a *confidential tariff* since it is not for public use; it is only used by travel agencies since the rates in this resource are published net.

This is a major resource used to obtain net prices for land arrangements such as transfers, motorcoach hire, sightseeing, excursions, and guide services. All prices in the WATA tariff are published in the currency of the country and net (without commission). The travel agency obtains the selling price by adding up all the net prices and adding a markup. The total selling price is converted to U.S. dollars according to the exchange rate at the time.

Figure 10.11 is an excerpt from the WATA tariff for Madrid, Spain. Notice that prices are shown for both individual and group bookings for most ground arrangements.

✔ Check Your Understanding 10-2

Short Answers

1. Define the "pied piper" and describe briefly his or her role in the group travel field.

   _____

   _____

Founded: 1944
Staff number: 120
Branch offices: 25
Professional Organisations: AEDAVE, GEBTA
Activities: 1, 2, 3, 4, 6, 7, 8, 9, 13, 14, 15, 16

WATA — VIAJES VINCIT

TORRE DE MADRID, PLANTA 10, PLAZA DE ESPAÑA 18 - 28008 MADRID (SPAIN)
PHONE: 5594518 — FAX: 5593426/5592502 — NEW DIRECT FAX: 542 12 48
TLX: 47766 — E-mail: vinvec37@medusa.es
Office open from 9.00 a.m. to 1.30 p.m. and from 4.30 p.m. to 7.30 p.m.
On Saturday, from 9.30 a.m. to 1.30 p.m.

General Manager: José Manuel MACIÑEIRAS
Manager of the Incoming Department: José RAMON ARNAL
Incoming Department: Assistant Manager: Felisa VELA — Maria José SANCHEZ

Who are we

VIAJES VINCIT was founded in 1944 and employs 250 staff working in 25 branches in the main Spanish cities.
The Company has more than 40 years experience in business travel with very important volume of incoming and outgoing tourism from all over the world.

What we offer

VIAJES VINCIT's main aim is to provide quality travel-related service driven by clients' needs. With a very personalised and efficient service we take care of your FIT clients, incentive travel and special interest groups.
Our professional team offers to you many years of experience in meeting and convention events.

LOCAL ARRANGEMENTS - 1998   CURRENCY: PESETAS

CONFIDENTIAL TARIFF FOR TRAVEL AGENCIES

1. TRANSFERS
Including interpreter meeting and assistance, accompanying clients, porterage and transportation of two pieces hand luggage per person between hotels and points indicated below or vice versa. Tip to driver included. (Tip to hotel porters not included).

1. Individual clients: per person

	1	2	3
a) Station, bus, air terminal or pier			
Bytaxicab	.6500	3500	2450
By private car	.6500	3500	2450
b) Airport			
Bytaxicab	.6500	3500	2450
By private car	.6500	3500	2450

2. Groups: per person

	10-14	15-19	20-30	31 and up
a) Station, bus or air terminal, pier				
By motorcoach	3200	2500	2100	1450
b) Airport				
By motorcoach	3200	2500	2100	1450

One person free per 25 paying participants.

2. RESERVATIONS
Reserved seats on trains (tickets and agency fee)
Agency fee only for:

	Individuals per person	Party of 15 or more per person
couchettes	.500	400
sleepers	.500	400
boat	.500	400
hotels (see also the page "General Information")		

Take note that possible telephone calls or cables will be charged in addition.

3. OFFICIAL GUIDE — Max. 30 pers. per Guide

	up to 5 persons	Any add. person
Half day	.18500	250
Full day (lunch included)	.26500	250
Night	.21000	250
Holiday supplement in addition		

4. ENTRANCE FEES (for parties using own car or coach)

	Per person
Half day (Artistic Tour)	.1800
Full day (Artistic + Modern Museums Tour)	.3300

5. SIGHTSEEING (within city limit)
Terminal: Plaza de Oriente, 8
Artistic tour (morning): whole year, daily at 8.45 a.m. Main streets and avenues and inside visit of Prado Museum and Royal Palace.
Panoramic tour (afternoon): whole year, daily at 3.30 p.m. (from September 16 to March 31 at 3.00 p.m.). University City, main streets and avenues of the old and new quarters, Retiro Park and Bullring.
Bullfight tour (afternoon): in season - usually from mid-March to mid-October - every Sunday, also holidays featuring a bullfight. Depart 90 minutes before bullfight's starting time. Short drive in the city and then attend a "corrida" on reserved seats. Note: Special rates in force during San Isidro corridas (May) and other occasional dates.
Night tour: whole year except January 1, 5, Holy Week, Sundays, December 24, 25, 31. At 10.00 p.m. (if dinner included 8.30 p.m.). Drive through the streets of Old Madrid. Attend flamenco show.

	By rg. mlcoach	Individuals: by private car 1	2	3	15-19	Groups: by private coach 20-30	31-40	41-50
Artistic tour (Daily except Monday)	.4600	38000	20400	14600	4050	3650	3300	2900
Panoramic tour	.2600	34600	18000	12000	2650	2250	1850	1500
Bullfight tour (Sundays only)	.7700	38900	22000	16000	7200	6600	6000	5700
Night tour - Flamenco show plus 1 drink	.6100	38500	22000	16000	7500	7100	6600	6300
Night with dinner and Flamenco show	.11200	42500	25000	19000	11000	10300	9800	9500

Figure 10.11 *Sample page from* Master-Key WATA tariff.

2. What does RSO stand for?

_____

3. What are two other terms for RSO?
   A. _____   B. _____

4. What is the term used to describe a preformed group of people who share a common interest, whose group has been formed for purposes other than travel?

_____

5. Why is the retail travel agency's role like that of a broker when handling group bookings?

_____

6. If a retail travel agency is quoted a per-client net cost for a tour, how does the agency make its profit?

_____

7. What does the term *confidential tariff* mean?

_____

8. What does *WATA* stand for?

_____

Multiple Choice

Circle the *best* answer.

9. A retail travel agency that has a specialized group department with group specialists on staff will probably handle groups by:

    A. purchasing a tour developed by a tour operator

    B. allowing a receptive service operator to book with each supplier

    C. bypassing the RSO and book each supplier directly

    D. working through a U.S.-based tour wholesaler

10. The Master-Key WATA tariff shows prices for many of its land arrangements by way of:

    A. net rates   C. individual and group

    B. local currency of the country   D. all of the above

TOUR PLANNING

Itinerary planning or tour designing is one of the most creative and challenging aspects of being a travel professional. Whether you are designing a tour for individual clients or a group, the basic process is practically the same. Imagine that you are sitting in your office and a client contacts you to put together a tour through Europe for a group of students and teachers from a local college. What do you do first? Who do you contact?

The step-by-step process of planning a tour will be different according to the type of client, destination, budget considerations, and the travel agency's expertise in handling this type of arrangement. After you have qualified the group and conducted research, the following is a brief overview of the general steps involved in designing, pricing, and packaging a group tour.

➤ Step 1: Obtaining Air Transportation

If air transportation is involved, this should be completed as the first step since it defines the conditions and restrictions of the itinerary. Some of the things the agent checks include (1) blackout periods of the air fare, (2) stopover provisions, (3) minimum and/or maximum stay restrictions, (4) complimentary seat(s) for tour escort, and (5) deposit and payment regulations.

The type of airfare selected often drives the design of the entire tour. For example, if the fare restricts passengers to travel on-line or on a specific carrier, you may be forced to plan the entire itinerary around that airline's schedule. Or you may have to alter the tour's departure and return dates to avoid fare blackouts, which are usually time periods over holidays or vacations when the air fare is not in effect. Minimum and maximum stay restrictions can also affect the scheduling of the land tour portion.

➤ Step 2: Resolving Scheduling Problems

After establishing the type of airfare, the tour planner outlines a rough itinerary based around all transportation and land arrangements that are dependent on schedules. This would include all transportation segments, such as air flights, rail trips, short cruises, and ferry services. It also includes attractions, sightseeing trips, and special events that also depend on set schedules.

This step usually takes some juggling and compromise. If the tour includes a short cruise or a rail trip, you must make sure that space is available on the desired date. It takes a lot of planning to make sure that all the pieces fit: planning a visit to an open-air market that is open only on Saturday mornings, not scheduling a tour of the Louvre in Paris on a Tuesday when the museums are closed, or planning a dramatic sunrise visit to such places as Ayers Rock in Australia or Haleakala Crater in Hawaii.

If the travel agent is booking everything directly, this stage takes a lot of research and time. If the travel agent is booking through a wholesaler, all of these time-sensitive arrangements are taken into consideration and the itinerary is planned by the tour wholesaler to work around local schedules and other time constraints.

➤ Step 3: Designing an Itinerary

After making sure that all scheduled transportation and activities fit, it is time for the real creative work of designing the day-to-day itinerary to match the interests and goals of the group. Decide if the tour is to be full escorted; not all groups have to be. If you are providing a nonescorted tour, you should consider the following guidelines:

1. The group should be an affinity or preformed group and have an established leader who knows the destination(s) well.

2. The tour itinerary incorporates enough free time.

3. Hire step-on guides or local guides who "step on and off" the motorcoach who are specialists in the particular destination or locale being visited.

A lot goes into planning itineraries that work. Here are some important considerations when designing itineraries for either individual or group travelers:

- *Keep a comfortable pace.* Don't schedule too much traveling or sightseeing in one day.

- *Include some R&R.* Allow time for rest, relaxation, shopping, etc.

- *Begin and end the tour with a bang.* Begin and end the tour with an interesting attraction or special activity. At the beginning of the trip it serves as motivation; at the end it leaves a last impression of a good time.

- *Remember that variety is the spice of life.* Offer a variety of features and activities: Vary each day—don't cram all the art museums into one day. Also, balance each day with some "serious" sightseeing along with some fun or entertainment, such as a night on the town or at the theater.

- *Provide formal introductions.* When first arriving at a new destination, book a general one-half-day sightseeing tour, which serves as an introduction to the major sights, attractions, shopping, and entertainment areas. This allows travelers to get their bearings and know what sights and attractions to visit in greater depth later.

- *Keep hotel changes to a minimum.* Change is good; too much change is bad: Try to book at least two nights at each stopover on the itinerary. This affords time to see the local sights, to relax, and it also serves as a home-base for excursions into the surrounding countryside. Anyway, travelers don't want to pack and unpack each day of their trip!

- *Break up lengthy motoring segments.* Whether it is booking a motorcoach for a group of travelers or planning a self-drive itinerary, make sure that rest stops, coffee breaks, and quick stopovers to see important attractions are included.

- *Know your geography and terrain.* Knowledge of physical geography and local topography is a must when planning surface transportation: What may appear to be a short 50-mile drive measured on a map may take several hours over rugged mountainous terrain.

➤ Step 4: Pricing the Tour

The next step is to price the tour. When pricing tours, both the variable and fixed costs are included on a per person basis. A **variable cost** is any item that is priced on a *per passenger* basis. Some examples of variable costs include air fare, meals, sightseeing tours, taxes, tips, and admission fees. A **fixed cost** is related to the entire project and *does not vary with the number of passengers*. Some examples of fixed costs include advertising (printing brochures or flyers), direct mail, and the charter of vehicles such as motorcoach, plane, or ship.

The tour planner identifies the variable and fixed tour costs on a pricing sheet. This is a good way for the planner to "walk" through the entire tour to ensure that all requested arrangements have been included. The costs on the pricing sheet are shown net and per person. Table 10.1 is an example of a two-day/one-night tour pricing sheet.

➤ Step 5: Applying a Markup

Remember that the markup is a certain percentage *of the selling price.* It represents the amount of profit the travel agency made on the group tour. There is no set amount; it is determined by the travel agency. The amount of markup depends on several factors, such as (1) the amount of time it took to plan the trip; (2) complexity of planning and operations of the tour; and (3) expenses such as long-distance phone calls, overnight mail deliveries, and so on.

For our example, let us say that the travel agent has determined that a 25 percent markup is fair and will provide the appropriate amount of profit. Applying

TABLE 10.1

Day and Time	Itinerary/Items	Variable Cost per Person	Fixed Cost per Person (20 Participants)
Day 1			
8:30 A.M.	Motorcoach departure ($400 per day/20-passenger minimum)		$20
10:30 A.M.	Museum tour, $10 per passenger	$10	
12:30 P.M.	Lunch, $14 inclusive of tax/tip	14	
2:00 P.M.	Shopping	—	—
5:00 P.M.	Hotel arrival; welcome reception, $15 per person inclusive of tax/tip	15	
	Rooms: $100 (net per room); add per person 10% tax + $2 baggage handling	57[a]	
Day 2			
7:00 A.M.	Breakfast (continental), $9 inclusive	9	
9:00 A.M.	Step-on guide; $200 for 1/2 day, inclusive		10
11:00 A.M.	Boat ride	45	
12:30 P.M.	Lunch, on board included		
2:00 P.M.	Departure		
	Subtotals	150	30

Total net: $150 + $30 = **$180 per person**

[a]double occupancy

the markup can be tricky! Remember, you want to mark up the price so that the travel agency earns the percentage *from the selling price.*

In our example, the net price per person for the two-day, one-night tour was $180. You wish to apply a 25 percent markup. A common mistake made by most first-time trip planners is to shortchange their markup earnings by applying the percentage to the *net price, not the selling price.* The example below shows a total net price of $180 for a tour. If you increase $180 by 25 percent, the amount is $225.

This is incorrect: $180 \times 25\% = \$45$
$\$180 + \$45 = \$225$ selling price

Why is this incorrect? The passenger pays the travel agency the selling price of $225. Out of that amount the travel agency pays $180 for the land services (hotel, meals, sightseeing, step-on guide, etc.). This means that the travel agency is left with $45 [$225 − $180 = $45]; *$45 is only 20 percent of the selling price.* In other words, the agency earned only 20 percent, not 25 percent, of the selling price!

To calculate the correct amount of markup, you must calculate backward. The mathematics is: $180 (net) divided by 75% (take 100 minus 0.25).

This is correct: $\$180 \div 0.75 = \$240$ selling price

This works since the agency is left with $60 after paying the net amounts for land services ($240 − $180 = $60); $60 commission is 25 percent of $240, the selling price.

➤ Final Steps

Some final steps to the tour planning process include the following.

1. *Creating a tour brochure.* This is the most effective way of presenting a tour product. The brochure serves two purposes: It serves as a legal contract or agreement between the travel agency and travelers since it outlines clearly the terms and conditions of travel. It also serves as an attractive marketing piece in order to promote interest and sales.

2. *Handling clients.* The travel agency handles the group from the time of the first inquiry to the last date of the trip. The agency handles reservations and deposits, sends letters of confirmation or acknowledgment, creates and sends information bulletins on such topics as passports, visas, customs, travel insurance options, and so on. Effective handling keeps the group travelers motivated and enthusiastic and gives them confidence in your company. It also sets the stage for a successful tour later on.

3. *Managing the tour enroute.* Any company that sponsors group tours is keenly aware that the ultimate success of the tour experience and the reputation of the company depends on the leadership of the *tour manager.*

The tour manager may be an employee from the travel agency. Often, when the agency books a group tour, free transportation and accommodations may be available for one or more tour escorts. Many travel agencies send a regular staff employee on the tour to make sure that the tour is conducted in a manner that builds goodwill for the agency.

In other cases the tour manager may be a freelance professional hired by companies under a contractual basis, an officer of the sponsoring group or organization, or someone who is acting as a "one-time" tour leader since he or she has an area of expertise that relates to the group's interest.

A tour manager's job is not an easy one. It is his or her responsibility to handle all aspects while on tour: flight check-ins, hotel arrivals and departures, and host to all tour activities and social events. The successful tour manager must be prepared thoroughly by studying the itinerary of the tour, including geography, customs, and climate of the areas being visited.

The tour manager also must know how to deal with the carriers, suppliers, ground operators, hotel personnel, local guides, and others involved in the execution of the tour. Most important, he or she must be prepared to deal with all the various personalities and temperaments of the tour participants: from the habitual worriers and chronic late arrivers to the complainers and compulsive talkers!

✓ Check Your Understanding 10-3

Short Answers

1. Why is it important to plan air transportation as a first step in the tour planning process?

   _____

2. Briefly describe at least four important considerations when designing a tour itinerary.

   A. _____

   B. _____

   C. _____

   D. _____

3. List two examples of fixed costs.

   A. _____   B. _____

4. List two examples of variable costs.

   A. _____   B. _____

5. What are the markup and selling price amounts for a tour that is priced at $350 net, per person, with a 30 percent markup of the selling price?

   A. selling price $ _____

   B. markup amount $ _____

6. What are the two main purposes of designing a tour brochure?

   A. _____

   B. _____

7. Why is the tour manager a key player in the success of a group tour?

   _____

BUSINESS GROUPS: MEETINGS AND INCENTIVE TRAVEL

Some of the more lucrative—and creative—types of trip planning for many agencies today are meetings and incentives.

➤ Types of Meetings

First let's define what a *meeting* is. The simplest definition is: a planned event with two or more people who come together for a common goal or to accomplish one or more established objectives. The size and duration of the gathering varies. The term *meeting* encompasses a broad spectrum of organized events, ranging from a small session of a few people to a huge convention or trade show with thousands of participants. Meetings can be classified into several categories. The **Professional Convention Management Association (PCMA),** a travel organization involved in meeting planning, classifies meetings into several different categories. Some of the most common types of meetings include:

- *Conference:* a formal meeting for discussion and interchange of views on a particular subject. Conferences are usually comprised of general sessions (for all participants as a group) and smaller group meetings or "breakout" sessions to plan, fact-find, and solve problems related to a specific topic or issue.

- *Convention:* a large gathering of delegates or representatives of an association to meet established goals and/or to exchange views, ideas, and information about subjects relevant to all participants. The term **congress** is a commonly used European designation for a convention which is mainly international in scope.

- *Symposium:* an event in which several speakers deliver short lectures or demonstrations on related topics and where opinions are gathered. All topics discussed are usually based on various aspects of the same topic.

- *Trade Show or Exposition:* a public showing, display, or show where the displays or exhibits themselves are the central focus. The exhibitors are using the trade show to promote future sales of their products or services. Trade shows can be limited to one or two tables with various brochures or as many as hundreds of exhibitors. Trade shows are classified either as *consumer* (open to the public) or *private* (limited to those involved in a particular industry or profession).

- *Workshop:* a short course or training session that is geared to enhance skills or develop knowledge in a specific topic. It is generally led by a trainer or presenter who encourages a free exchange of ideas and who demonstrates methods and procedures. Workshops are usually intended as hands-on learning experiences for participants.

➤ Incentive Travel

This is a very profitable market segment for group travel that is business- or work-related. It may or may not include a type of formal meeting. **Incentive travel** is planned by a company as a reward for outstanding service, productivity, or sales performance. Some incentive trips are not designed as rewards but to stimulate or motivate performance. These are probably best known as motivational trips. Incentive travelers from a particular company sometimes travel independently or, in most cases, travel in groups on scheduled departure dates. Quite often, family members accompany the tour participants. Scheduled activities, special events, dining, and sightseeing are included for standard features of an incentive tour.

Since incentives are used as either a reward or a motivation, they usually take place in lovely resort destinations that offer a wide range of planned activities, high-quality service, friendliness, good weather, and convenient geographic location. The majority of incentives are planned in the United States and the Caribbean. Incentive trip planning is highly specialized and in most cases is done by incentive houses, companies that offer a wide range of travel-related services designed especially for incentive travelers.

SEGMENTS OF THE MEETING INDUSTRY

All types of meetings are a result of many types of people and companies working together to achieve a common goal: to plan and create a successful group event, whether it is a one-day corporate meeting of twelve participants in a local downtown location or a week-long congress of more than 1,000 physicians in

London. The key players of any type of meeting consist of *meeting sponsors, meeting planners, meeting facility suppliers,* and *meeting service suppliers.*

➤ Meeting Sponsors

Many different types of groups plan meetings: educational institutions, fraternal organizations, special-interest clubs, religious groups, and political groups, for example. However, the two major sponsors of meetings are:

1. *Corporations.* Any company that has a need to sponsor any type of meeting event comprises the corporate meeting market. It is not limited to size. Corporations that sponsor meetings range from several workers to thousands of employees.

Corporate events comprise the lion's share of the meeting market. More than 800,000 corporate meetings are held each year. This represents approximately 79 percent of the total corporate and association meeting market. A survey conducted by *Meetings and Conventions* magazine shows that most corporate meetings are small: nearly two-thirds have fewer than 50 attendees, and 82 percent have less than 100.

Corporate meetings are held for various reasons: training employees, discussing sales techniques, building morale, and introducing new products. Meetings are held on the management level for executives, company stockholders, and employees on all levels. Corporate planners spend most of their time planning management and training meetings.

2. *Associations.* Corporations may conduct a larger number of meetings than any other type of sponsor, but associations are the most visible and spend almost two-and-a-half times more on their meetings. An **association** is defined as a group of people who share similar interests. Members of associations come from all backgrounds and areas of interest. There are associations for college educators, medical workers, sport enthusiasts, computer "tekkies," and travel professionals.

There are two common types of association meetings. Conventions are the most common type of meeting event for this market. Conventions are usually huge events with hundreds or thousands of attendees. They also tend to be longer than business meetings—from three to five days in duration. After conventions, shorter educational and training seminars are the most popular types of meetings planned by associations.

There are some common characteristics of meetings conducted by corporations and associations. There are also many differences. Some of the major features that are different include scheduling, attendance, and destination. Business sponsors conduct meetings at any time throughout the year, for a wide variety of reasons. They are often planned spontaneously or as the need for a meeting event occurs. On the other hand, most association meetings are conducted like clockwork each year, for the same reasons. When one annual convention is coming to a close, the meeting planners have already started putting together the next one.

Attendance at corporate and association meetings is also different. Attendance at business meetings is usually required except for such events as stockholder meetings or new product introductions. Since attendance is required, the company pays for most, if not all of the attendees' expenses, such as accommodations, meals, and transportation to and from the meeting site. Attendance at association events is usually on a voluntary basis. Members attend to increase their knowledge, to network and interact with other attendees, and to take advantage of scheduled recreation and social events. All meeting expenses are the responsibility of each member.

The third difference is the location of the meeting or site selection. Meeting planners conduct site selection on two levels: destination and facility. When selecting a destination for corporate meetings the two most important considerations are meeting facilities and transportation. Often, a destination is selected based on the availability of hotels and meeting facilities. Another important consideration is the ease and cost of transporting participants, who are often traveling from different cities. This is of particular interest since the company usually pays for time and travel costs.

Since attendance at association events is voluntary, the site selected should be attractive to the delegates. Availability of recreational and sports facilities become just as important as the size of meeting facilities required to fit the event's needs. Since attendees are paying the costs of the trip, the meeting planner must also be sensitive to select a hotel with rooms that are both attractive and within the majority of the participants' financial standards.

Key Point ➤ What's a **SMERF?** In the meetings industry, a SMERF is a social, military, educational, religious, or fraternal organization. The SMERF market alone is estimated to represent close to 25 percent of the entire meeting market.

➤ The Meeting Planner

With the increasing importance of the meeting industry, the role of the meeting professional has become more complex and sophisticated. Simply defined, a **meeting planner** is someone who plans, coordinates, and produces a meeting, from start to finish. According to the Professional Convention Management Association, there are more than 230,000 full- and part-time meeting planners in the United States alone, and many more throughout the world.

Meeting planners work in a variety of ways. Corporate planners organize meetings for a corporate (private business) sponsor. Huge corporations that plan many meetings throughout the year may employ one or more meeting planners to devote 100 percent of their time in planning these events for their company. Other corporate planners may have other responsibilities, in administration, sales, or marketing with the company. Planning meetings for them is only one function of their job role for the organization.

Other meeting planners organize meeting events for an association (a group of people with similar interests). Some association meeting planners are independent; they are hired on a contractual basis to plan an event. Other association planners may hold an officer's position in the organization in addition to organizing all meeting events for the group.

So far you have discovered that meeting planners work in a variety of ways. Some work as independent planners on a contractual basis. They are hired by companies and associations that do not have a meeting planner in their employ. Companies or associations that plan many meeting events will usually have a meeting planner who organizes all meetings and similar events. Depending on the number of meeting events to plan each year, these "in-house" planners may spend some or all of their time planning meetings for the organization.

Other players in this growing group market are travel agencies. More and more travel agencies are jumping on the meetings and incentive bandwagon. Why? They are highly profitable: The average commission markup ranges between 15 and 30 percent. They require creativity: Meetings are becoming less serious and more fun. They offer the satisfaction of developing something from A to Z: The planner does everything from arranging speakers to thinking up theme parties.

One major difference between a travel agency meeting planner and a corporate or association meeting planner is that corporate or association meeting planners do not get involved with the travel part of the program; their sole function is to plan the meeting. They usually do not have any interaction with the meeting attendees until they are on site.

The travel agency meeting planner not only gets involved with the planning of the meeting but is also involved with travel arrangements to and from the meeting. They can make airline reservations, negotiate discount fares, and generate airline tickets for the attendees.

The best potential meeting customers are the corporate accounts of the agency. The travel agency as meeting planner may handle all aspects of the meeting, from transportation of all attendees, to hiring entertainment, to planning dinner menus. Or the travel agency may work with the organization's meeting planner in planning some of the aspects of the event, such as site selection and transportation.

Key Point ➤ **Meeting Professionals International (MPI)** is a professional society for all meeting planners, including full-time meeting consultants, and suppliers of goods and services to meeting planners. The group publishes a monthly magazine, *Meeting Manager*, and has established an on-line computer service, MPINet. Other meeting planning organizations include the *American Society of Association Executives*, *International Association for Exposition Management*, and *Professional Convention Management Association*.

➤ Meeting Facility Suppliers

Another major component of the meeting industry is *facility suppliers*. These are firms that provide facilities for meeting events. In addition to hotels, the other major meeting and trade show site is convention centers. The number of convention centers in major cities have increased more than 200 percent in the last two decades. Centers are increasing in size and number, and along with this growth is their ability to serve a wider segment of the meeting market. In addition to huge convention and trade shows with thousands of attendees, many convention centers are set up to host the small meeting market.

➤ Meeting Service Suppliers

The final major component of the meeting industry is service suppliers. These are firms such as convention service contractors, audiovisual firms, and exhibit design companies that supply services for meetings. An important meeting service supplier is the **convention and visitors bureau (CVB).** All CVBs are nonprofit organizations with one goal in mind: to increase the number of visitors to the area. The major function of the CVB in the meeting industry is to serve as the middleman in the process of selecting a meeting site and promoting the meeting. The CVB can present a list of possible meeting sites that meet the planner's needs.

Steps Involved in Planning Meetings

You won't hear any meeting planner say: "You've planned one meeting, you've planned them all!" Nothing is further from the truth. Every group is different; every meeting is different. Planning a meeting for company A will be a totally different experience from company B. However, there are some basic steps that planners follow for just about any type of meeting event. Here's a brief overview of what it is like to plan a meeting.

➤ Step 1: Qualifying the Meeting

To qualify the business means to develop a history of the company or group with which you are working. You must get an idea of what the group has done before and what it is looking to do for this meeting event. Some questions to ask about the company's profile and history may include:

- What is the company's business?
- How many years in business?
- How many locations or offices?
- How many employees?
- What is the company's past meeting history; have they ever had meetings?
- What kind of meetings in the past: trade show, workshop, seminar, and so on?
- On which location(s) have past meetings been held?

Once the meeting planner has a company profile, it is time to find out what the company wants for the next meeting event. Some questions to ask about the current meeting include:

- What type of meeting will it be: Incentive? Trade show? Symposium? Seminar?
- Where will the meeting be held: city versus resort, domestic versus foreign?
- When will the meeting be held?
- How many attendees?
- Where will they be coming from?
- What kind of budget?
- Will the meeting have a theme?
- Will they need: speakers, entertainment, spouse programs, breakout sessions?

➤ Step 2: Selecting the Site

This is probably one of the most important functions of the meeting planner. Guiding the client to make the right decision about where to hold the meeting can result in an event being a total success or a total failure.

The first item is to find out if the client wants to hold the event in a city or resort, or is the meeting event to be held at a conference and convention center? Do they want to hold the meeting in a domestic or international destination? Many factors come into play when determining the site: budget considerations, objectives of meeting, who will be attending and from where, and so on.

Once the location has been decided on, the meeting planner begins the task of selecting a hotel property. The selection is based on the facilities, amenities, and pricing. The meeting planner conducts a site selection. A site selection allows the planner to view, firsthand, all facilities that will be used by the attendees. In addition to guest rooms, the planner inspects meeting facilities, function areas for cocktail receptions and dinners, public areas, and recreational facilities. A site inspection form like the one shown in Figure 10.12 is completed and reviewed by the meeting planner.

➤ Step 3: Negotiating

In meeting planning, negotiation is the process by which two parties reach an agreement on various items important to both sides. The ability to negotiate is high on the list of desired skills of a meeting planner. With whom does the meeting planner negotiate? If the planner is involved in airline transportation, there may be negotiations with this supplier in terms of discount fares based on volume and other services. The planner negotiates primarily with a representative from the hotel or conference site.

At this stage the meeting planner has a **meeting résumé** or *outline* developed. The résumé is very important during the negotiating process because it serves as a guideline for the planner and meeting facility from this point on. The résumé is almost an hour-by-hour rundown of scheduled meetings, activities, meals, workshops, and refreshment breaks throughout each day of the event. Figure 10.13 is an example of a meeting résumé.

Three major items of negotiation include facilities, service, and costs. Facilities include the number and type of guest rooms, meeting and exhibit rooms, and other facilities, such as recreation and sports areas for organized events which are available. Items regarding service include the number of food and beverage staff, the type of service available (buffet, full service, etc.), provision for audiovisual equipment and room setup, registration procedure upon check-in, and other categories, such as housekeeping services, shuttle service, and baggage storage. Once the planner understands the facilities and services the meeting site can and cannot provide, costs associated with guest rooms, food and beverage, gratuities, function rooms, and recreation are discussed.

The final phase of the negotiation process is the preparation and signing of the contract or letter of agreement. This contract spells out in detail all items and costs that were negotiated and agreed upon by both parties.

➤ Step 4: On-Site Management

The meeting planner's administrative and organization skills come into play at this stage. What does the planner do while the meeting is taking place? He or she *plans, organizes, directs,* and *controls* the meeting event behind the scenes. Most of the planning and organizing have occurred leading up to the meeting. Planning is establishing objectives and determining the methods to use to achieve these goals. Organizing is determining what activities and jobs need to be done and who will perform them.

During the meeting event the abilities to direct and control become more important. Directing is the ability to guide, train and lead others in order for them to

SITE INSPECTION FORM

Hotel name: _____

Address: _____

Contact: _____ Phone: _____ E-mail: _____

Meeting date: _____ Expected no. of attendees: _____

Length of meeting: _____ Seating arrangement: _____

General comments _____
_____
_____

Inspected by: _____ Date: _____

Classification: ☐ city commercial ☐ resort ☐ airport ☐ conference ☐ other

Accommodations

1. Location to meeting rooms _____
2. Comfort _____ 3. Cleanliness _____
4. Noise level _____ 5. Size _____
6. Rates: Single _____ Double _____
   Triple _____ Quad _____ Xtras _____
7. Phone/fax/computer _____
8. Security _____
9. Guarantee policy _____
10. Other _____

Meeting Facilities

[1 = Excellent; 2 = Average; 3 = Unacceptable]   Meeting Room Dimensions: _____

	1	2	3
1. Seating capacity			
2. Appearance			
3. Entrance exit locations and number			
4. Noise level			
5. Lighting/lighting controls			
6. Heating/air conditioning			
7. Furniture/ergonomics			
8. Electrical outlets/capacity			
9. Secure storage areas			
10. Services			

Equipment available

[1 = Excellent; 2 = Average; 3 = Unacceptable]

1. Blackboard ____ | 3. Screens ____ | 5. Projector(s) ____ | 7. Other ____
2. Lectern   ____ | 4. Easel   ____ | 6. P.A. system ____ | ____

Food and Beverage (menu attached)

1. Variety _____
2. Special considerations _____
3. Schedules - flexibility _____
   Breakfast _____ Lunch _____
   Dinner _____ Break _____
4. Seating arrangement; capacity _____
5. Guarantee _____
6. Menu planning - timing _____
7. Other _____

Other Services

1. Parking _____
2. Messages _____
3. Business services: Phone _____ Fax _____
   Computer _____
4. Medical facility _____
5. Other _____

Site Personnel List

Name	Function(s)	Phone/Email

Equipment and Supplies

Item	Supplied by	Responsibility

Figure 10.12 *Site inspection form.*

MEETING RÉSUMÉ		
Start Time	**Activity**	**Arrangements**
7:00 – 8:00 AM	Continental breakfast	Reception area outside general session room: coffee, tea, and assorted pastries. Number of attendees: 200
8:00 – 10:00 AM	General session	Theater-style seating, stage, lectern, overhead projector and screen. Number of attendees: 200
10:00 – 10:15 AM	Refreshment break	Reception area outside general session room: coffee, tea, and assorted fresh fruit pieces. Number of attendees: 200
10:15 – 12:30 PM	Breakout workshops: four concurrent workshops Workshop A—70 attendees Workshop B—70 attendees Workshop C—70 attendees Workshop D—70 attendees	Schoolroom setup, 22-inch tables, water and glasses, floor lectern and lavalier microphone, slide projector with remote control and screen.
12:30 – 2:00 PM	Luncheon	60-inch round tables, 10 to a table. Set up for award ceremony 1:30–2:00 PM; stage in front of room, setting for six, floor lectern in middle of stage table, lectern with lavalier microphone. Number of attendees: 200
2:00 – 3:00 PM	Panel discussion	Theater-style seating. Stage seating for 8 panel members, each with table microphone. Each table draped. Number of attendees: 200
3:00 – 3:15 PM	Refreshment break	Coffee, tea, soft drinks, assortment of cookies.
3:15 – 5:00 PM	Breakout workshops	Same setting as for 10:15 AM–12:30 PM

Figure 10.13 *Meeting résumé.*

do their jobs efficiently. Meeting planners hold premeeting briefings and training sessions with key staff members, such as convention service managers and staff, exhibit contractors, suppliers, and others involved with the meeting.

Other important skills required onsite are solving problems and handling emergencies. There is no such thing as a hassle-free meeting. Problems arise and emergencies occur even during the best-organized event. However, a lot of preparation and forethought can reduce the impact of emergencies and problems.

Typical problems include bad weather, which can disrupt planned events, and mechanical problems, which range from a nonoperating microphone system to the lack of air conditioning, labor disputes, and medical emergencies. The professional meeting planner anticipates these types of problems and plans solutions before they occur.

✓ Check Your Understanding 10-4

Matching

A. association   ____ 1. Trip planned by a company as a reward for outstanding performance or achieving sales goals.

B. convention   ____ 2. Large gathering of delegates from an association to exchange ideas; usually held on an annual basis.

C. incentive   ____ 3. Detailed timetable of a meeting event.

D. symposium   ____ 4. One of the major categories of meeting sponsors, a group of people who share common interests.

E. CVB   ____ 5. Public or private exposition event.

F. workshop   ____ 6. Social, military, educational, religious, or fraternal organization.

G. SMERF   ____ 7. Event at which two or more speakers deliver short presentations on related topics.

H. conference   ____ 8. Type of meeting service supplier that recommends possible meeting sites at a destination.

I. meeting résumé   ____ 9. Short course or training session.

J. trade show   ____ 10. Formal meeting comprised of general sessions and small breakout sessions to exchange ideas on a subject.

 Close-Up: Group-Related Careers

Group coordinator	Tour manager	Tour designer
Sales representative	Reservations agent	Convention and visitors bureau positions

Careers in Group Departments, Tour Operators, and Wholesale Companies

There are career positions in group travel with tour operators and wholesale companies. However, remember that not all positions are available with each type of company since staffing requirements and descriptions depend on the size and internal organization. Similar positions can also be found in specialized group tour departments of large travel agencies.

Tour Reservations Agent

A tour reservations agent's job is similar to that of any reservations position with airlines, car rental, and other travel providers. The tour reservation agent handles telephone calls from travel agents, airlines, or the general public (if the company handles retail sales). After checking availability, the agent either confirms a reservation or suggests alternative date(s) or package(s).

Reservation agents must also be highly knowledgeable about all the tour products being offered. They are asked direct questions about the components of each tour, such as prices, schedules, hotels, and meals. They are also asked to provide destinations information such as sightseeing, attractions, weather, and the society of the places visited.

Candidates are hired based on their personality, telephone manner, initiative, and skill on a computer. Many companies seek reservation agents who have had prior customer service and sales background in any type of business.

Sales Representative

Just like the airlines and other travel suppliers, tour sales reps are responsible for a region of travel agencies and other customers. Their primary concern is to encourage them to sell the company's tours and packages through educating them about the various products. They are often called upon to help travel agencies with their marketing efforts to sell tour products by giving a talk and showing a video or film to the agency's potential groups and individual clients.

Group Coordinator

Group coordinators are involved in a variety of functions, depending on the size and type of company in which they are working. Typically, they are involved in all of the processing of group movements: selling special tours, taking reservations, maintaining inventory of airline seats and hotel rooms sold, and completing travel documentation. This type of position is also available with large travel agencies that operate a group or tour division. In many cases, group coordinators may also serve as a group escort.

Tour Designer

Tour designer is usually not an entry-level position and requires in-depth destination knowledge, research, and writing skills. This person may be a retail travel agency employee, a tour operator, or a consultant or independent contractor with these specialized skills. The tour designer puts together all the elements of a tour: airline transportation, planning the day-to-day itinerary, sightseeing and attractions, special events, hotels, land and/or water transportation, meals, and so on.

Many tour designers are hired as DIT or FIT specialists with large travel agencies that specialize in this type of travel. They are usually experienced travel professionals who bring to the table a knowledge of the company's clients, travel industry skills, good business sense, and marketing and costing of travel products.

Tour Manager

The position of tour manager is also called tour escort or tour conductor. The tour manager is many things rolled into one. Tour managers must be very versatile, since they have multiple functions during a tour: They serve as "housemothers," business managers, social directors, psychologists, and teachers. The tour manager provides continuity from city to city and country to country but does not serve as a tour narrator at each destination. This is handled by local city guides who join the group for any length of time. Local guides may be with the group for just a few hours for a narrated city sightseeing tour, or two or more days for a guided tour of a broader region.

Careers with Convention and Visitors Bureaus

Almost every city or community has a convention and visitors bureau (CVB). In general terms the CVB is a sales and marketing organization that serves a city's entire meetings and visitor industry. Every CVB is staffed differently; however, most CVBs operate four primary areas or departments: (1) convention sales and service, (2) tourism sales and service, (3) marketing and communications, and (4) finance and administration.

Convention Sales and Service

This area is usually the largest department and the main focus of a CVB. Employees first identify companies, clubs, and other types of organizations that hold meetings, determine their needs, and put together sales presentations to show them how the city or destination can serve their needs. The emphasis is on selling what the city has to offer. Entry-level positions include sales trainees, sales assistants, convention registrars, and convention cashiers.

Tourism Sales and Service

The tourism sales and service department focuses on leisure individual and group travelers. The staff solicits tour organizers by convincing them to include the city or destination in their itineraries.

Marketing and Communications

Anything and everything that has to do with advertising and marketing the city to individual and group travelers and tour organizers is the focus of the marketing and communications department. Responsibilities include developing and implementing sales promotions, creating and producing ads and brochures, writing and distributing newsletters, and planning and executing public relations and publicity for the city. This department employs people who are writers and artists in addition to managers, secretaries, and researchers.

Finance and Administration

Employees in the financial and administration area perform the same types of functions that are found in any company. Responsibilities include accounting, planning, budgeting, personnel, and payroll. This department employs people with experience or education in the area of finance and/or administration.

➤ KEY TERMS

- account executive
- association
- conference
- congress
- convention
- convention and visitor's bureau (CVB)
- corporate travel department
- discretionary travel
- exposition
- fixed cost
- incentive travel
- management fee
- markup
- meeting planner

- Meeting Professionals International (MPI)
- meeting résumé
- net price
- non-discretionary travel
- on-site agency
- "pied piper"
- Professional Convention Management Association (PCMA)
- profile
- rebating
- receptive service operator (RSO)

- request for proposal (RFP)
- satellite ticket printer (STP)
- selling price
- SMERF
- symposium
- trade show
- transactional fee
- travel management report
- variable cost
- World Association of Travel Agencies (WATA)
- workshop

Flashback   Business travel is booming and most travel agencies are taking advantage of it. More than 90 percent of U.S. agencies handle corporate travel exclusively or in combination with leisure sales. This market offers agencies significant profit potential, quick growth through volume transactions, steady growth through regular travel patterns, and the opportunity to expand into other markets, such as leisure and group travel.

Corporate agents today are much more than just order-takers. They are involved in providing a wide range of management tools and services to their corporate clients, such as developing and enforcing travel policy, assisting in vendor negotiations, and generating travel management reports.

Group travel is another market that provides special benefits to the travel industry. It stimulates new business on a large scale by providing a higher profit due to volume business. Group travel and its benefits affect not only retail travel agencies but the many suppliers and service companies, such as receptive service operators, tour wholesale companies, and ground operators.

The two major categories of group travel are leisure and corporate. Planning tours for the leisure market entails creating exciting itineraries, timing scheduled events, pricing and costing all air and land arrangements, marketing, and managing the tour enroute.

Group travel also involves planning meeting events and incentives for such sponsors as corporations, associations, and representatives from SMERF (social, military, educational, religious, and fraternal groups). In addition to sponsors, other components of the meetings industry include meeting planners, facility providers, and service providers. These segments of the meeting industry work together to produce a successful meeting event, whether it is a small one-day workshop of twelve businesspeople or a huge week-long convention with thousands of participants.

Chapter Review

True or False?

_____ 1. The main responsibility of a corporate account executive is to serve as a front-line reservation agent.

_____ 2. Rebating is the practice of returning part of the agency's commission to guarantee business from a corporate account.

_____ 3. Corporate travel is discretionary and leisure travel is nondiscretionary in nature.

_____ 4. A corporate on-site travel office is managed and staffed by employees of the company and not the agency.

_____ 5. Corporate travel departments are allowed to apply for ARC approval.

_____ 6. A net-per-client cost allows the travel agent to mark up the price of a tour in order to make a profit.

_____ 7. A travel agency with a specialized group department is more likely to skip the services of a wholesaler or RSO and book directly with suppliers.

_____ 8. Corporate meetings outnumber meeting events held by associations but more money is spent for association meetings.

_____ 9. Convention and visitor bureaus are an example of a meeting facility supplier.

_____ 10. A meeting résumé is a timetable of the planned events and activities during a meeting and is helpful during the negotiation process.

Multiple Choice

Circle the *best* answer.

11. The document that is distributed to travel agencies that wish to bid on a new corporate account is the:

A. MCO
B. RFP
C. STP
D. SRO

12. The service that most business travelers receive from their travel agents is:

A. enforcement of travel policy
B. travel expense reporting
C. assisting in vendor negotiations
D. reservations and ticketing

13. A type of process that allows a travel agency to make a reservation and transmit the information to a corporate account's office premises for ticketing is a(n):

A. prepaid ticket
B. electronic ticket
C. satellite ticket
D. manual ticket

14. Which task would not be an example of a transactional service fee charged by a travel agency?

A. ticket refund
B. monitor travel policy
C. hotel-only booking
D. visa service

15. A time-management tool that is an electronic passenger data file used to build a passenger name record in an agency's CRS is a:

A. queue file
B. passenger profile
C. record locator
D. data form

16. The Master-Key WATA tariff is called a confidential tariff because its information:

A. is only for clients of the travel agency
B. is only made available to corporations
C. is only for public use
D. is only made available to travel agencies

17. The step that is usually completed first when planning a group air and land tour is to:

A. reserve hotel space
B. book air flights
C. check scheduled events
D. create the itinerary

18. The percentage of markup on a group tour averages between:

A. 10 and 25 percent
B. 50 and 75 percent
C. 80 and 100 percent
D. 25 and 40 percent

19. All of the following are characteristics of association meetings except:

A. Attendance is on a voluntary basis.
B. Paying expenses is the responsibility of each attendee.
C. Conventions tend to be short: one or two days at the most.
D. Most conventions are held on an annual basis.

20. The main purpose of organizing an incentive travel program is to:

    A. promote team camaraderie

    B. release tension and relax

    C. reward performance

    D. introduce a new product

Pricing

21. Below is a list of the itinerary items and their net prices for a one-day tour you are planning. Complete the pricing sheet below by filling in the cost of each item under either the variable or fixed column. At the end obtain the final price by applying a 20 percent markup of the selling price.

Day and Time	Itinerary/Items	Variable Cost per Person	Fixed Cost per Person (30 participants)
7:30 A.M.	Motorcoach departure ($600 per day/ based on 30)		
7:30 A.M.	Daily guide service, ($90 per day/based on 30), includes lunch for guide		
8:00 A.M.	Breakfast, $7 per person, includes tax and tip		
10:00 A.M.	Attraction: Hearst Castle, $15 per person, inclusive		
12:30 P.M.	Lunch, $15, add 20% tip per person		
2:00 P.M.	Shopping	—	—
5:00 P.M.	Return		
	Subtotals		

    A. total *variable cost* per person   _____

    B. total *fixed cost* per person   _____

    C. total net (variable + fixed) per person   _____

    D. total *selling price per person* (*with* 20% markup)   _____

    E. markup amount   _____

Chapter 11

Sales and Communications

*Nothing happens until some-
one sells something.*

Garber Travel Service, Inc.
slogan

Fast Forward ▼

➤ Follow-up and customer service after the sale is made are crucial to build customer loyalty and repeat business. . . . 533

➤ Approximately 68 percent of all client interactions are over the telephone: Learn to use it wisely. . . . 535

➤ The trend away from general sales and toward niche marketing started gaining momentum in the 1990s. Niche marketing involves focusing your sales efforts on a specific product, destination or customer base. . . . 542

➤ The practices of up-selling and cross-selling are closely related: They both aim to increase the agency's bottom line and customer satisfaction at the same time. . . . 544

➤ When selling any type of trip, don't forget to recommend travel insurance: it provides peace of mind for the traveler and some of the largest commissions. . . . 544

➤ After the sale is made, some basic office procedures and record keeping need to be done. . . . 546

➤ There are all sorts of reasons why you have to write business letters to suppliers, clients, and colleagues—now learn to write them. . . . 552

➤ Electronic communication such as E-mail has its own set of rules, just like traditional business letters and other types of paper correspondence. . . . 557

INTRODUCTION

Picture yourself on a hot, sunny beach. You want something cold. In the distance you see an ice cream vendor selling exactly what you want—ice cream cones. You walk up to the counter. The ice cream vendor doesn't ask you if you want ice cream, but asks you what flavor.

So what does selling ice cream have to do with selling travel? At first glance, absolutely nothing at all. After all, an ice cream cone and a European tour don't have very much in common. What is important is *how the sale was made*. You weren't asked if you *wanted* to buy ice cream, but what flavor you wanted. The assumption was already made that you wanted to make a purchase; the salesperson had to determine what type of product you wanted that would best suit your needs.

Do you get it? The first step toward being a successful salesperson—whether you are selling ice cream cones, computers, refrigerators, or travel—is to assume that the customer wants to buy what you are selling. When it comes to selling leisure or business travel, very little "hard-selling" is involved. You don't have to convince the client that he or she needs to travel, but what type of travel product to buy. It is up to you to be a matchmaker: to investigate, select, and recommend the best travel product based on the client's needs.

Remember, unless you are selling travel door to door, your customers will come to *you* to buy travel. Once you get over that first psychological hurdle, you are ready to do your thing: to guide and counsel your clients to make the right choice for them based on their needs and expectations.

The Myths of Selling

Believe it or not, many people dislike selling, even travel agents! To some travel professionals, being called a salesperson is somehow demeaning, not very professional, and "beneath" them. Nothing could be further from the truth. In any sector of the travel industry—whether it is working in a travel agency, on a cruise ship, in a hotel, or with a tour company—all professionals are involved in selling. They sell themselves, their companies, and the products they represent.

Certainly, a good part of the travel agent's job is to conduct travel research and counsel their clients on where to go and what to do once they get there. Imparting your travel wisdom and knowledge of the world is important. But travel agents are not working for non-profit organizations—they are in business to make money. And *no one makes money unless someone sells something!*

The first thing to do is to get rid of any misconceptions that you may have about the role of the travel professional and sales. Here are some common myths that must be dispelled before you can open yourself up to the challenging and exciting job of selling travel and servicing your clients.

➤ Myth 1: Selling is pushy and manipulative.

Response: "Sell" has four letters, but it isn't a dirty word.

You may think that to be successful in sales you have to be fast-talking, manipulative, and pushy: someone like a used-car salesman who uses "strong-arm" tactics to practically force people to buy cars. Nothing is further from the truth. Think about your own personal experiences as a consumer; think back to the *best* and *worst* salespeople you have encountered. Let's start with the worst. Being ignored when wanting to buy something is probably top on your list. Or a pushy salesperson who just wanted to make a sale and couldn't care less what you really wanted is probably another bad memory!

How about the best? You probably felt comfortable with salespeople who were confident, professional, and above all, showed that they were concerned about what was best for you. You probably did buy what the person was selling because he or she asked the right questions and made wise recommendations based on your tastes and needs.

Keep in mind that as a travel agent, you are fulfilling a *need* of your customer. The customer has contacted you because he or she wants to buy travel—the only question is exactly what? You didn't make the first move—the customer did. The good salesperson never has to pressure his or her clients.

➤ Myth 2: The travel agent's first priority is to provide information and service.

Response: Travel agencies are not information bureaus; there's no money in it.

Don't get confused between sales and service. *Sales comes first.* Service starts after the trip has been sold, not before! Many agents make the mistake of offering too much information at first—without selling anything. For example, a client walks into your office and requests information about cruises next winter. What would you do: give as many cruise brochures as the client can carry out of your office? Or how about the caller who wants to know about inexpensive packages to Disneyworld? Do you go over all of the options over the telephone, providing as much information as you can before even getting the caller's name?

Remember: A travel agency is *not* an information bureau. It is in business to sell travel. Travel agents first need to discover who the client is, what he or she wants, and make sound recommendations based on the client's needs. This is called **qualifying** the client and is a very important step in the sales cycle.

Remember: The travel agent's first priority is *to sell travel.* Travel agents inform, advise, and counsel their clients only *in the context of selling.* Providing customer service occurs after the sale is made. Service then takes top priority in order to ensure repeat business and additional clients through recommendations.

➤ Myth 3: Selling is repetitive and boring.

Response: As a travel agent you are a "dealer in dreams": travel products and destinations that are exciting to your clients.

As a travel agent you are a "dealer in dreams." You have chosen an industry where the products you sell are, for the most part, exciting and positive. There is nothing boring about selling travel because of the variety of products you deal with: leisure trips, cruises, tours, independent trip planning, world destinations, and so on. Also, your customers are different from one another. Customers have different needs and expectations. The way you meet those needs during the sales encounter will be different each time. You handle the first-time traveler one way and the well-traveled customer who "knows the ropes" in another. Remember, the successful salesperson is able to identify the needs and expectations of the client and to adapt the sales process to suit those needs.

CHARTING YOUR COURSE: THE SALES PROCESS

One of the reasons that travel sales is so challenging and so much fun is that there is very little repetition; you won't be bored doing the same thing over and over again. Why? No matter how many times you sell a trip to Disneyworld, for example, everything will be different: different clients, preferences, budgets, departure dates, hotels, packages, and so on. You will never sell exactly the same product to the same client under the same conditions more than once. Every sale is different and a challenge!

There is no magic formula that works every time on every client. Every client is different in temperament, wants, needs, and desires. What will satisfy one client simply won't do for another. You must learn to adapt your selling skills and techniques to the client.

However, there is a basic *sales cycle,* a series of events that every successful agent follows when selling any product, whether it is an airline ticket to Cleveland, a honeymoon cruise to Mexico, or a luxury safari to east Africa. Stick with this process—remember it each time the phone rings or someone walks in the door—and chances are that you will make the sale and win your clients back for their next trip!

The Seven Steps of Selling

Step 1	Sell yourself.	It's a cliché, but true: First impressions are established quickly and last a long time (people *do* judge a book by its cover).
Step 2	Identify the client.	Determine the client's personality type and adapt your approach.
Step 3	Qualify the client.	Ask the right questions and listen: Selling is 80 percent listening and 20 percent speaking.
Step 4	Recommend.	Play the matchmaker: Limit choices and don't confuse!

Step 5	Overcome objections.	The ones to fear are the unspoken ones: Deal with them upfront and honestly.
Step 6	Close the sale.	Know when and how to ask for the business.
Step 7	Follow up.	Turn every client into a repeat customer by providing service and follow-up on details.

✔ *Check Your Understanding 11-1*

1. Explain how selling travel is different from selling other types of products or services.

   _____

   _____

2. List and briefly describe three common myths in selling travel.

   A. _____

   B. _____

   C. _____

3. List the seven steps of the sales cycle in order.

   A. _____

   B. _____

   C. _____

   D. _____

   E. _____

   F. _____

   G. _____

➤ Step 1: Sell Yourself (and Your Company)

Did you know that it takes only about 10 seconds for a person to decide whether or not he or she likes another person? Think about when you meet someone for the first time. How long does it take you to form that first impression, either positive or negative? Probably not very long.

When prospective clients visit your agency for the first time, they instantly form an impression about your company and the people who work there. If the office is clean, organized, and comfortable and the people who work there dress and act professionally, clients will feel at ease and more open to talk and—hopefully—to buy travel from you. Remember, you and your surroundings set the tone. Here are some important tips to remember:

1. *Keep it clean.* The office and particularly your work area should be clean and organized. Keep stray papers, Post-its, and other odds-and-ends off your desk and out of sight. No half-eaten donuts, morning coffee from the day before, or coffee cup stains on the desktop, please!

2. *Look the part.* This may sound obvious, but it must be said. Dress appropriately—that is business attire—and keep yourself (like your desk) well arranged and tidy. Keep flashy jewelry and similar attire at home—they just serve to distract. Even though we don't really want to believe this, most people do judge others by how they look. If you had a choice, would you seek professional advice and entrust your hard-earned money to someone who is sloppy and disheveled or someone neatly attired in professional clothes?

3. *Get out from behind your desk.* Has this ever happened to you: You walk into a place of business seeking advice or to buy something and no one pays any attention to you? Believe it or not, this happens too often in retail travel agencies.

Agents may be busy working at their computers or at their desks and don't even lift their heads to see who walked in the front door. This may not be an issue in large agencies that have a front-entrance receptionist screening who walks in, or in a corporate agency which does very little or no walk-in business. This does become important in small to medium-sized retail agencies, where agents take turns in answering phones and taking care of walk-in clients.

When a prospective client walks into the office, remember: Look up, smile, stand up, say hello first, come around your desk, and introduce yourself. At the very least, stand up, smile, and shake hands. Walking to the client and offering your hand shows that you are on equal terms. Don't ever leave a walk-in client waiting for more than a few seconds.

➤ Step 2: Identify the Client

Before a client walks into your office or calls on the phone, something has motivated that person to do so. The travel agent needs to determine the client's motivations and needs and match them with the right travel plans to satisfy those needs.

It is important to remember that all clients are not alike! Having said that, we can also place most travelers into general categories or segments of the population which describe various aspects of their lives, such as age, income, location, attitudes, values, and personality. This type of information can provide useful insight into a client's interests and motivations. We can study the population of travelers according to demographic, geographic, psychographic, and behavioristic *travel profiles* (see Table 11.1):

Let's study one aspect of the psychographic segment: personality. Part of understanding what is best for clients is to learn to identify their personality types. Understanding your own personality and that of your client makes it easier for you to adapt your sales approach to be compatible with the needs of each client.

For our purposes in terms of providing an overview of sales techniques, we can study four basic personality types. You can use these types to help identify who your clients are and the best approach to take with them during the sales process. Each personality type is described in Table 11.2 together with several key selling tips for each type. Use these selling tips as a *general guide only* and modify as appropriate according to each situation.

First Encounters

How many times have you introduced people? Introduced a peer to a business associate? Introduced a business partner to a senior executive of another company? Introduced a younger person to an older person? Making proper introductions is as much part of the social scene as it is crucial in the business world. At a seminar for business people, Lannon Communications, a public relations and marketing consulting firm in Chicago, presented the way to make proper introductions in various circumstances:

- Introduce a younger person to an older person.
- Introduce a peer in your own company to a peer in another company.
- Introduce a nonofficial person to an official person.
- Introduce a junior executive to a senior executive.
- Introduce a fellow executive to a customer or client.

TABLE 11.1   THE CLIENT POPULATION

Demographic: who they are	**Psychographic:** how they think
• Age	• Values
• Income	• Attitudes
• Occupation	• Lifestyles
• Family size	• Interests
• Education	• Activities
Geographic: where they live	• Personalities
• Climate	**Behavioristic:** what they do
• Region of country	• Habits and preferences
• Urban/rural	• Purpose
	• Benefits sought

Source: *F. Burke and B. Resnick, Selling Tours: Basic Sales Techniques, in* Travel Agent, *September 1998.*

TABLE 11.2   SELLING TIPS RELATED TO PERSONALITY TYPES

PERSONALITY TYPE	TRAITS	SELLING TIPS
DOMINANT	• Commanding and ambitious • Strong ego • Manages time correctly • Has leadership qualities	• Don't get bogged down in minor details. • Don't spend too much time in idle chatter; give direct answers. • Be precise in explanation. • Be businesslike and efficient.
INFLUENTIAL	• Sociable and outgoing • Persuasive • Friendly and socially concerned • Knows a lot of people • Likes to try new products/ new experiences	• Be sociable and outgoing. • Match smile-for-smile. • Let clients talk • Support their dreams and wishes. • Give testimonials—what peers or other clients have said about a product/destination. • Be enthusiastic and friendly but maintain control of sales situation.
STEADY	• More shy or reticent • Follows traditional and proven concepts • Family-oriented • Conventional and patriotic • Takes responsibility for themselves and others • Wants to make friends • Needs to be convinced	• Slow down pace. • Set relaxing tone/atmosphere. • Develop trust. • Give proof and statistics to back up statements/recommendations. • Emphasize product(s) that are proven. • Point out all that is included in product. • When selling provide a complete and organized plan.
SUBMISSIVE	• Suspicious of new things/experiences • Needs reassurance and solid things to rely on • Faithful once trust is established	• Set tone of trust (you are on their side). • Explain fully with details. • Stress how they can benefit from product. • Be patient and reassuring. • Emphasize no risk and reliability of product. • Don't hard-sell or act forceful when clients are resisting. • Don't give short or pat answers; provide full explanations when questioned.

➤ Step 3: Qualify the Client

This is the fact-finding step in the cycle. After you have made a positive first impression and have identified who your client is, the next step is to determine the needs and wants of your client. This is an important step in the sales cycle in order to recommend the best product to satisfy those needs. You have to go on a fact-finding mission, discover what your clients want, and steer them into making the right decision for them.

We call this qualifying clients; you are trying to match them with the best products or service. Qualifying is knowing how to ask the right questions and listening effectively to the answers. Sound easy? Well, it is—as long as you know what *types of questions* to ask at different stages of the sales cycle and how *to listen closely* to their responses and *to hear* what they are saying to you.

How important is it to ask the right questions, listen to your clients, and respond to their questions and concerns in the beginning? Very! If you don't qualify your client right away or too late in the process, any one of the following pitfalls may occur:

Pitfall 1: The Road Leading Nowhere

Client: What's the cheapest fare to Seattle?

Agent: I can get you there for as low as $300!

Client: Sounds great, I'll take it!

Agent: Great, when do you want to depart?

Client: Tomorrow for a last-minute meeting.

Agent: Oops, sorry. We will need at least 14 days advance purchase on that fare. . . .

What questions should have been asked right away?

Pitfall 2: A Waste of Time

Client: My wife and I want to go to Mexico on our next vacation. What do you have?

Agent: I'll go and look . . . (agent pulls out about six or seven brochures). Here we are . . . these packages include some of the most beautiful resorts in Mexico, such as Acapulco and Puerto Vallarta.

Client: Oh no, we aren't interested in a beach vacation. We are both interested in history and archeology and would just love to visit the major Mayan ruins in the Yucatán.

What questions should have been asked right away?

Pitfall 3: Taking the Wrong Turn

Client: Do you sell cruises here?

Agent: We sure do . . . in fact, we are offering a special value on the Carnival Cruise Line ships to the Caribbean. Here are some brochures that can help.

Client: Oh no, we want to go to Alaska this time and wanted to try Princess Cruises since we've heard so much about it . . .

What questions should have been asked right away?

Questioning Techniques

First, let's take a look at how to ask questions. What happens next in the sales process—whether or not the customer makes a purchase—depends on asking the right questions in order to match the best product with your client's needs. There are five functions of questions that you should keep in mind when selling:

1. *Cause Attention.* This starts the other person thinking by responding: *"How are you today?"*

2. *Get information.* Gather necessary information about client's needs in order to make the correct recommendation: *"What type of tour are you looking for?"*

3. *Give information.* Provide clients with the type of information they need to make the right decision: *"Did you know that the price of the cruise includes practically everything?"*

4. *Start thinking.* Cause the client to start thinking about how the product will benefit him or her: *"How about the Sheraton resort, which is located near the beach and centrally located to all downtown restaurants and attractions?"*

5. *Bring to conclusion.* Bring the client's thinking to a conclusion: *"Why don't we call the reservation office to see if this tour is still available on the date you requested?"*

Believe it or not, there are many different ways to ask a question. When selling travel, the three general types of questions are *open, directive,* and *reflective.* The one you use depends on where you are in the sales process and what type of response you want.

1. Open questions do just that: they "open up" your clients so they will feel at ease and bring out a good deal of information. Open questions do not allow for a simple yes or no response but will get clients talking about such things as past vacation experiences and their interests and hobbies. Open questions are preferred during the fact-finding or qualifying stage because you are trying to gather as much information as possible about your clients. Here are some samples of open questions:

"Where did you go on your last vacation? What did you like/not like about it?"

"What do you like to do during your spare time?"

" Describe your most ideal vacation, money is no object!"

2. Directive questions will require a more focused answer. These questions are used by newspaper reporters when investigating a story; they usually start with *who, what, where, when, why,* and *how.* The client will reply with a short answer, a choice, or a simple yes or no. This questioning technique should be used after you have gained a lot of information about your client and now wish to narrow the qualifying process. Here are some examples of directive questions:

"When do you want to travel?"

"What is your preference: more days at sea or more ports of call?"

" Who is traveling with you?"

3. Reflective questions will provide you with more information based on an answer already provided by the client. These questions are also called feedback

> ## Tips for Effective Listening
>
> - Do less talking: Ask a lot of questions and listen to what clients are saying.
> - Pay attention: Focus 100 percent on the client.
> - Don't be rude and interrupt when the client is talking.
> - Remember the important points discussed by taking notes.
> - Adjust your tone and inflection to match your client's.
> - Reserve judgment until all facts are known.
> - Learn to interpret nonverbal signals and modify your approach accordingly.

since they confirm or clarify something that has been said. Reflective or feedback probes may ask the client to expand or clarify an answer already provided, or they may "mirror" a response. Here are some examples of reflective questions:

Client: We went to Nassau last year on our vacation.

Agent: Oh, tell me more about it.

Client: My wife and I enjoy going to fine restaurants.

Agent: Good! Tell me which kinds.

Listening Techniques

While qualifying clients, not only do you want to ask the right questions, but you have to know how to listen to what your clients are saying. Too often we are concerned with what we are saying and how we are saying it, and forget to listen. To employ effective listening techniques, just remember this familiar warning:

Stop–Look–Listen!

1. Stop talking and start listening. All too often, we are so concerned with what we want to say next in the conversation and our sales pitch that we tune out what the client is saying. Try not to interrupt at any time. If you have to interrupt to keep the conversation on the right track, do it politely by asking another question or repeating back what the client has said to avoid misunderstandings. Remember, the agent should always be in control of the conversation but remain polite and respectful of the client at all times.

2. Look to see how your clients are reacting. Don't just listen to what they are saying, but pay attention to *how* they are saying it and to the nonverbal signals, or *body language,* that they are expressing. According to sales experts, only 7 percent of our client's message is conveyed through words; 38 percent through tone of voice; and 55 percent through body language. This means that *93 percent of what we want to say is not through the words we use but how we say them and how we act.*

This means that you have to recognize body language. If you are talking to clients and they lean forward, maintain eye contact with you, and nod and smile at what you are saying, this probably means that they are interested and willing to listen to you. On the other hand, if your clients are leaning back, crossing their arms, not maintaining eye contact, or yawning, this probably means that you have lost their interest or that they feel frustrated or defensive with you.

Your body language is also important when speaking with clients. A good part of this is to feel positive about your role. Project the image of someone who is confident and assured; customers will feel more positive about trusting your suggestions and recommendations. Have an upbeat style of selling. Give all of your attention to a client by all of the following: (1) lean forward when speaking to the client; (2) maintain eye contact (don't look down or over his or her shoulder); (3) smile often and offer verbal encouragement.

Finally, focus all of your attention on the client. No paying customer will be satisfied with an agent who constantly interrupts the conversation to answer phone calls, talk with others in the office, or just daydreams.

3. Listen and tune in to what is being said. The more you listen, the more opportunity you have to discover what your clients want. Tune in to your clients and block out any distractions that are going on around you. This means tuning out ringing phones, other conversations buzzing around you, and other typical distractions that occur in a busy office. You want to make each client feel that he or she is your most important concern at the moment. Demonstrate that you care by giving your undivided attention and listening closely to your clients. According to Dean Rusk, best-selling author: "The best way to persuade people is with our ears—by listening to them."

✓ *Check Your Understanding 11-2*

Identify each question below as Open (O), Directive (D), or Reflective (R) in the space provided.

1. "What are some of the things you like to do on vacation?" _____
2. "Do you like to play golf?" _____
3. "What price range do you have in mind?" _____
4. "You told me that you enjoyed your last trip to Bermuda. Tell me why." _____
5. "Have you ever thought before of taking an escorted tour?" _____
6. "Are you looking to relax in the sun or to discover new and exciting places?" _____
7. "Do you want to take a cruise on your next vacation?" _____
8. "Would you prefer a more independent lifestyle on your next vacation? _____
9. "So, you prefer a cruise to Mexico rather than to the Caribbean?" _____
10. "What else would you like to know about this beach resort in Cancún?" _____

The following are directive (yes/no) questions. Many times you want to ask questions that will provide more information during the qualifying process. Rewrite each question below so that the client provides as much information as possible.

11. "Did you like your last cruise on Princess Cruises?"

_____

12. "Do you enjoy a lot of nightlife?"

_____

13. "Have you thought about where you would like to go on your vacation next summer?"

_____

14. "Have you ever been to Europe?"

_____

15. "Do you think you would like to try more of an adventurous vacation experience, such as white-water rafting down the Colorado?"

_____

➤ Step 4: Present and Recommend

One of the first steps in the sales process is getting to know your client. You have learned that asking the right questions and listening to your clients will help you in the initial fact-finding stage. During qualifying, you keep your ideas to yourself! In the next stage, presenting and recommending, you start sharing your ideas with the client.

Presentation Tips

It is important to present a travel product in a way that is both exciting and informative. And it should be presented in a manner that will enable the customer to remember your sales points within two or three days after the meeting, when final decisions are usually made. The customer reacts in a more positive way and will remember what you have said if you combine a discussion of your sales points along with pictures and graphics.

Remember that the length of time customers retain information depends on how it is presented. Studies in consumer behavior have demonstrated that information received only through *hearing* results in a low 19 percent retention rate after three days. When hearing is combined with seeing and demonstration, retention of the information increases to 80 percent after three days. This means that sales agents must learn to use effective and colorful marketing tools when presenting products. These include color brochures along with videos or graphic presentations on the Internet.

Another important point to remember is not to confuse the customer with too many choices. If you have done a good job qualifying and if you know your travel products, you should be able to select one or two products that best suit the client's needs. Don't offer any more than three choices—any more will complicate the process and the client will tend to take a longer time to think about buying.

When selecting a product to present, don't start with an extremely low or high price if no price preference has been established by the customer. Many travel agents make the mistake of underestimating what a person will pay for the right travel product. The leisure traveler may not mind paying extra for the extra comfort and peace of mind of first-class or deluxe hotels on a tour. Or the business traveler may not mind paying extra for a seat in business class on a long flight if it means a more comfortable trip and room to work during the trip. If you have not established the client as either a high or low spender, start in the middle and work up (or down) from there.

Features versus Benefits

In this step, you present and recommend a product by stressing both features and benefits in response to the client's stated needs. To make the greatest impact on your clients, focus on what is important to them. This is accomplished by selling *benefits* of the travel product in addition to its *features*.

What is the difference between features and benefits? **Features** are *tangible*—they are the objective and factual aspects of the product. Examples of features are round-trip transfers, transportation on a 747 wide-body jet, centrally located downtown hotel, and a secluded beach on Maui.

Benefits are *intangible*—they describe how the client gains or benefits from the product or feature. Benefits are expressed as statements that explain how a product or feature solves a problem, meets a need, or satisfies a desire. The best way to think of a benefit is to put yourself in your client's position and ask yourself, "So what?" or "What's in it for me?" For example, a tour vacation includes the following benefit statements:

Features ("What do I get?")	Benefits ("What's in it for me?")
Round-trip transfers included.	"Having round-trip transfers will free you from worrying about carrying all your luggage and driving to your hotel . . . all that is taken care of for you the minute you step off the plane."
Transportation on a 747	"You will be traveling on a wide-body 747, which is called a jumbo jet. It gives you a lot more room to move around and more comfortable seating during your long flight."
Centrally located hotel	"You will be staying at the Sheraton Hotel Downtown, which is centrally located. All major shops and sightseeing attractions are within easy walking distance . . . you won't have the added expense of paying for parking and the hassle of finding a space in such a busy location."
Secluded beach on Maui	"Imagine miles of white sand beach right outside your door on Maui . . . your beach is protected by a reef with clear blue water that is ideal for what you want to do: swimming and snorkeling."

If you just use features to sell a travel product, it starts sounding like a laundry list: "This tour package features three meals per day, ground transportation, local guide service, and first class accommodations." What is important is how each feature will benefit the client. Remember, to turn a feature into a benefit statement, put yourself in the client's place and ask yourself, "So what?" or "What's in it for me?"

✔ Check Your Understanding 11-3

For each feature listed, write a benefit statement you would give to a client in order to focus on his or her needs.

1. Feature: Resort hotel has three restaurants.
   Benefit: _____

   _____

2. Feature: The land package in China is fully escorted.
   Benefit: _____

   _____

3. Feature: The Caribbean cruise vacation includes six ports of call in seven days.
   Benefit: _____

   _____

4. Feature: The Disneyworld package in Orlando, Florida includes the use of a car rental.
   Benefit: _____

   _____

5. Feature: The cruise ship has indoor and outdoor pools.
   Benefit: _____

   _____

6. Feature: Car rental includes unlimited mileage.
   Benefit: _____
   _____

7. Feature: Hotel includes full American plan.
   Benefit: _____
   _____

8. Feature: After-hours rental car drop-off.
   Benefit: _____
   _____

➤ Step 5: Overcome Objections

No matter how great a salesperson you are, clients will voice some concerns or objections about what you are trying to sell them. Concerns are nothing to be afraid of. In fact, you should welcome concerns when you hear them so that you can deal with them at once. The type of objection or concern that you should dread is the one the client hides from you! That's the one that will hurt you the most.

A client can have concerns or objections at any point in the sales process. Don't make a list of them and promise to get back to the client with the answers at a future date. They won't go away. In fact, if you don't deal with concerns on the spot, they will cause a prolonged version or a complete breakdown of the sales cycle.

Void versus Valid Concerns

There are two types of concerns or objections: the *void* and *valid concern.* Which type is being expressed determines the best way to handle the situation.

The **void concern** is a misconception that the client has about the product. It is called a void concern because it is not based on anything that is valid or true. Here are some typical void concerns:

"We're in our thirties and too young to go on a cruise!"

"I don't think I want to be restricted by taking an escorted bus tour."

"Isn't it too cold in Bermuda in May?"

The best way to deal with a void concern is with *correct information.* This clears up the client's misconception. For example:

"People in all age groups cruise. In fact, according to this ship's passenger profile, more than 40 percent are under the age of 40."

"There is a lot of free time to do your own thing during the ten-day tour; let's revisit the itinerary and I will show you how many free mornings and afternoons you have."

"It is simply beautiful in Bermuda in May—right before the crowds arrive for the summer but warm enough for relaxing and swimming at the beach."

The **valid concern** exists because the product does not have a feature that supplies a benefit to the client. Or there may be a disadvantage offered by the product or feature. Here are some typical valid concerns about cruise travel:

"Too much sun is not good for you; I shouldn't be out in the sun so much."

"I'm afraid of getting seasick."

The best way to deal with valid concerns is by stating other benefits. This minimizes and outweighs a disadvantage. For example:

> "There are a lot of planned activities and things to do inside the ship during days at sea. There is even an indoor pool. Let's take another look at what the ship offers."

> "I can understand your fears but I don't believe you should be overly concerned with this. The ship's itinerary is port-intensive; you are only at sea for one day out of a full week. Also, these large ships are fully stabilized; you will hardly feel any movement while at sea."

The Biggest Objection: Price

Unless you are selling for the upscale market, price is quite often the number one objection or stumbling block. It shouldn't be. Practically every buyer will object to the price of a product. The secret is to sell **value,** not price. The value of a product is what the client will be getting for his or her money. A good example is selling cruises. Since the cost of a cruise is almost totally inclusive, the price appears to be high at first glance. A good way to handle this concern is to stress the value of a cruise vacation by comparing it to a comparable land-resort package (as was shown in Chapter 7). In other words, the client is getting a lot of features for his or her money. Another approach to soften the "sticker price" of a cruise or an inclusive tour is to quote the per diem rate: "For only $200 a day you will be getting accommodations, all meals, entertainment, and transportation."

If the client says "That's too much money," or "I can't afford it" at any time during the presentation, here are some suggestions as to how to handle it:

1. Qualify the client more thoroughly by asking exactly how much he or she expects to spend.
2. Present the value of one plan over another in terms of benefits: "Let me show you what you will be getting for an additional $200."
3. Suggest saving so much per month extra until the time of the trip.
4. Stress that the same trip may not be operating next year or may cost more.

If the client does not mention budget considerations, should you mention price right off the bat or wait to mention it at the end of your sales presentation? There are arguments for both sides. If you wait to talk price until the end of your sales presentation, the clients may find it easier to accept the price. Also, the client will have already learned the value of the product that he or she would be getting.

On the other hand, price is always in the back of everyone's mind. Remember, the silent concern or objection not voiced is the one you should be afraid of. This unspoken concern may diminish the impact of your sales presentation. It may be better to confront the principal objection at the beginning and get it out of the way. Then build your sales presentation by showing the value of the product.

What is the right answer? It is hard to say. Each client and each sales situation is different. Ideally, the travel agent should introduce price before it becomes an objection. However, if the subject of money is introduced too early, it may get the client in a "confrontational" mode of thinking. The true answer is to try to understand who your client is at the beginning. That is why the meeting and qualifying phases are so important. If you feel that price is probably going to be a major decision maker, you may want to introduce it in the beginning and go from there.

If you feel that price is not the primary objection, it may be better to introduce it toward the end. Time and experience in selling will make it easier for you to determine when the time is right in each situation.

How to Deal with Concerns

A client can express a concern or objection at any time. Deal with it immediately so that you can continue with the sales cycle. Follow these steps when dealing with concerns:

1. *Listen actively.* As part of the qualifying state, asking questions and listening closely to the client's response are very important. If you hear a concern, establish if it is a void or valid one. Also, repeat back to the client in order to clear up any misunderstanding:

> "Are you saying that the price of the cruise is a concern?"

2. *Show understanding.* Don't become defensive, and certainly don't take a voiced objection personally! Stay in touch with your clients' feelings. Show that you have paid attention, and that you certainly understand their concern.

> "I understand how you feel . . . "
>
> "I can see why that is important to you . . . "

3. *Dispel the concern.* Respond to the void concern with education and information; respond to the valid concern with other benefits. Try to back up all that you say with brochures, pictures, videos, or other types of support.

> "I can understand your concern about bringing your children on
> board the ship. This ship has fulltime youth counselors that structure
> activities for children of all ages. "
>
> "I can see why location is important to you. Let me show you a map
> of the city and where your hotel is located. You will see that it is
> within walking distance of the convention center plus at the heart of
> the shopping and theater district as well."

4. *Confirm and move on.* Make sure that the concern has been cleared up. Look for signs of agreement and acceptance. Always ask to ensure that you have overcome the objection.

> "Do you feel better knowing that this escorted tour visits the places
> you are mostly interested in rather than an independent tour?"

✓ Check Your Understanding 11-4

Below is a major concern or misconception about several travel products/destinations. For each client concern below, write the response you would make to handle it.

1. "Cruises are too confining and stuffy."

   _____

   _____

   _____

2. "You can't drink the water in Mexico."

   _____

   _____

   _____

3. "Train travel is slow and uncomfortable."

   _____

   _____

   _____

4. "Airline travel is unsafe."

_____

_____

_____

5. "Escorted bus tours are for old people."

_____

_____

_____

➤ Step 6: Close the Sale

All of your qualifying, presenting, and overcoming objections are leading to one point—closing the sale. The effective salesperson is also a motivator, gently leading and prodding the client to make a purchase. How do you know when to close the sale? There is no magic moment that will go off like an alarm clock, telling you that your client is ready to make a commitment.

When should you ask for the sale? Feel comfortable in winding up the discussion when any of the following has occurred:

- The client has agreed to a key benefit.
- The client starts asking specific questions about particulars, such as departure dates, or what to pack.
- You have answered and resolved all concerns.
- You have justified the cost: You have demonstrated the value of the travel product.
- You recognize strong buying signals from the client.

The last item, buying signals, can happen at any time during the sales cycle and the agent should respond to them promptly. A typical buying signal is when the client shows signs of approval and agreement to what you are saying: " This cruise sounds great to me!" or "Do you think there are any cabins available in our price range?"

Another clear signal is when the client is not asking questions or voicing concerns. If the client starts making plans by "thinking aloud"—"If we were to take the tour to Europe next month, I'd better see about buying a new camera!"—this may also prompt you to close the sale.

When you know the time is right to close, you may wonder what to say or how to say it. After all, you want to make the client feel comfortable with making a decision, not pressured or bullied into it. Remember, these are the steps that lead up to the closing:

1. Qualify client.
2. Recommend and present.
3. Overcome objections.
4. Recap arrangements and key points.

If these steps have been completed, it is time to close!

There are many different ways of asking for business. Here we describe four types of closes that work well: _assumptive, direct, summary,_ and _choice._

Assumptive Close

The **assumptive close** is used when you are sure that your client is ready to buy. This means that you need to read your client's buying signals. If you have done it correctly, you shouldn't receive any resistance. Here's an example:

Client: This cruise sounds like a perfect way to relax!

Agent: Let's go ahead and check availability for an outside cabin on that departure date.

You have recognized that the client is ready to commit, and assume that a booking is in order. In this case you are *recommending a course of action*.

Direct Close

The **direct close** is similar to an assumptive close. In both cases, the client has displayed a willingness to buy. The difference is that you ask for the booking directly and suggest how to handle some of the details of the booking at the same time. Here's an example:

Client: This ecotour to Ecuador is looking better and better to me all the time!

Agent: I suggest that we contact reservations now since space is limited on this tour, and send a deposit to secure your reservation for the time you want to go.

The direct close is similar to the assumptive close; however, it is a little more forceful and suggests details of how the booking should be handled.

Summary Close

The **summary close** is another method to end the sales cycle. Review the features and benefits that were previously discussed, then wrap it up by asking for the sale. Here's an example:

Client: This cruise sounds like a good deal.

Agent: You really get value for your money on this cruise. Remember, everything is included—accommodations, transfers, all meals, entertainment, and a wide range of activities day and night. This is a great way for both you and your wife to relax completely and not worry about anything for two full weeks! I am sure the cabin you want is available; all we need to do is to send a deposit to secure it for you.

Choice Close

The **choice close** is similar to the assumptive close; you offer to book based on the assumption that the client wants to buy. In this case you give the client a choice, assuming that the client will choose one product or feature over the other. Here's an example:

Client: I like the idea of a one-week cruise that includes ports in Mexico.

Agent: Would you prefer that I book an outside or an inside cabin on the cruise to Mexico departing April 21?

✔ *Check Your Understanding 11-5*

For each client in the following list, identify the type of close that would be the most appropriate and write what you would say.

1. Your clients, Mr. and Mrs. Amesworth, seem happy about taking a hosted city tour to London and Paris next September. You have answered all of their questions and concerns.

   What type of close? _____

   What would you say? _____

   _____

2. Your client, Susan Smith, can't make up her mind between a resort package in Cancún or Cozumel next winter.

   What type of close? _____

   What would you say? _____

   _____

3. Your clients, Mr. and Mrs. Plunkett, have never cruised before. You have discussed everything with them, especially their concerns about taking their two young children along, the ports of call, and the variety of activities on board ship. They have no more questions or concerns at this time, but seem to be hesitating.

   What type of close? _____

   What would you say? _____

   _____

► Step 7: Follow Up

This is usually the forgotten step in selling; not doing it may result in a higher percentage of canceled trips or a loss of repeat business. Think of each new and repeat client as an opportunity for a long-term relationship. It costs the typical travel agency almost five times as much to get a new customer through advertising and other marketing than to keep an existing one. All it takes to maintain satisfied clients and thus build repeat business is to take care of the important details after the sale is made. Show clients that you really care that they are wholly satisfied with their trip and the services of your company.

Once your clients have made a commitment, don't forget about them! If a trip is booked far in advance—thus allowing time for second thoughts—call them periodically right up to the time of departure to keep them interested. Send them brochures, maps, or videos about the trip they are taking. If they have a computer at home and are linked to the Internet, send them a list of interesting travel Web sites that are helpful to them. A simple calendar is the agent's handiest tool. Write reminders periodically to follow up on your clients—don't forget to keep the momentum going!

Another tip is to deliver or mail tickets and documents in a timely manner. If a complex document package is involved—airline tickets, personal itinerary, hotel and sightseeing vouchers, and so on—the travel agent should meet with the client in person to review all the documentation. For trips that are less complex—a simple airline ticket, for example—ask if the client would like to schedule to come in to the office to pick up the ticket or wants it delivered or mailed. If that is the case, make sure that the tickets and related documents are in order and correct and that they are mailed or delivered in a timely manner—not at the last minute!

After the client has returned home, other follow-up activities can be put in place. Remember that each sale you make represents future business; you want each client to contact you for his or her next trip, whether it is for business or pleasure. Don't ignore any client, no matter how much the trip cost. The single person who purchases a budget hotel package may come back to you next year to purchase a deluxe honeymoon in the south of France!

Make it a point to contact the client about one week after a trip to see how it went. This can be done either by telephone or with a simple thank-you card. Don't be afraid to use the telephone because you fear something went wrong on the trip! If something did go wrong, you will probably hear about it anyway, and it is better if you have that first contact. If clients have had a bad experience, they want to be acknowledged. If it is a valid complaint and you do everything you can to rectify it, your clients will remember that you went to bat for them. They will also remember that they didn't have to seek you out—that you took the initiative to contact them because you cared.

An excellent way to stay in touch is to mail simple thank-you cards—with the company name or your business card tucked inside—to each client after they return from their trip. These cards are the same size and shape as a standard invitation or thank-you card. Inside can be a simple message, "Thank you for traveling with us," along with your business card (see Figure 11.1). The agency can print them up in bulk and each agent can be in charge of sending cards out to his or her clients at set times each week.

Another good idea is to maintain a reminder file or a "tickler" file that lists your clients and their past travel history, likes, and dislikes. These tickler files can be filed by clients' names and cross-referenced by destination or travel product of interest. For example, let's say that you contacted clients after their recent Caribbean cruise. They tell you that they enjoyed it and would love to consider another cruise—perhaps to Europe—next summer.

On a printed file card or database record in your computer, write down personal data such as names, addresses, and even important dates, such as birthdays and anniversaries. Also include their travel history, likes and dislikes, and future travel plans. File them under "future cruise prospects" with a date to contact. Start sending cruise brochures and other promotional materials to those clients in your tickler file to get them ready for their next trip. Better yet, give them a friendly call. They will be flattered that you have not only remembered their names but their travel plans and interests!

Another great way to solidify long-term relationships with your clients is to remember important dates such as birthdays and anniversaries. Include those in your clients' tickler files. Send them a simple card or a telephone card to offer congratulations. These simple gestures go a long way to ensure long-term and rewarding relationships with your clients. These follow-up contacts can also be used to gain valuable feedback from your clients about the destinations visited,

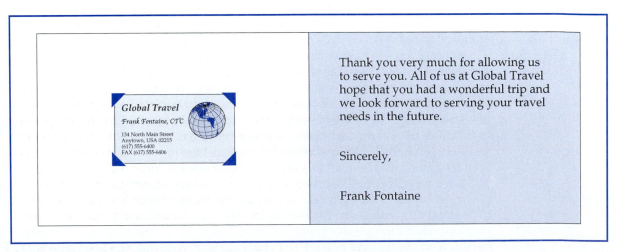

Figure 11.1 *Thank-you card.*

Eight Marketing Tips for Travel Agents

1. *Keep a database.* Maintain client records by including past trips, personal preferences, frequent-flyer affiliations, children's ages, and so on. Include anything that might help you serve them better and keep them coming back to you in the future.

2. *Keep in touch.* Call your clients after each trip to find out if everything went all right and where they want to go in the future, and use this information to update your database entry.

3. *Use the mails.* Create a newsletter to be sent out periodically to your repeat clients, highlighting any specials the agency is offering, perhaps with a handwritten note in the margin next to anything (cruise, specialty tour) that they usually like to do.

4. *Use your windows.* Not the one in your computer—the ones in your agency (assuming that you are working in a storefront location). Update the display frequently. Contact suppliers for posters and other exciting visuals—an easy and inexpensive way to attract customers.

5. *Get attractive business cards.* Are your business cards eye-catching? It's easy and inexpensive nowadays to put color graphics, even color photos, on business cards. Make sure that your E-mail address (if you have one) is there.

6. *Stay open longer.* Does your agency stick to the traditional 9 to 5 Monday through Friday schedule? Depending on your location, you might be well advised to maintain longer—or at least different—hours of service, since many leisure travelers only have time to "shop" after 5 P.M. or on weekends.

7. *Learn public relations.* Want to become recognized as a travel expert in your community? Write to the editor of a newspaper travel section offering to submit stories on trips you've recently taken; offer to be a guest speaker for local organizations' meetings; and network in the community.

8. *Host consumer nights.* Open the doors of your agency to potential customers with a special event, promoted locally, that will focus on a particular product type or destination—cruises, tours, Hawaii, or whatever you want to sell. Suppliers will be eager to provide you with films or videos to show or maybe even a sales rep to talk to your customers. Advertise in the local paper, and tack up flyers on supermarket bulletin boards and other places around the community to get the word out.

Source: *Building Business Supplement, from* TravelAge Supplement, *October 9, 1995.*

accommodations, transportation, and other suppliers for future clients. Figure 11.2 is an example of a client profile or tickler file that can be stored as a paper file or in a computer database program.

TELEPHONE SALES SKILLS

More travel business and sales is conducted over the telephone than face to face with clients. The telephone is a major sales tool, and techniques on how to use it effectively in sales should not be overlooked in any sales training course. A recent study of more than 1,000 travel agents by the Institute of Certified Travel Agents

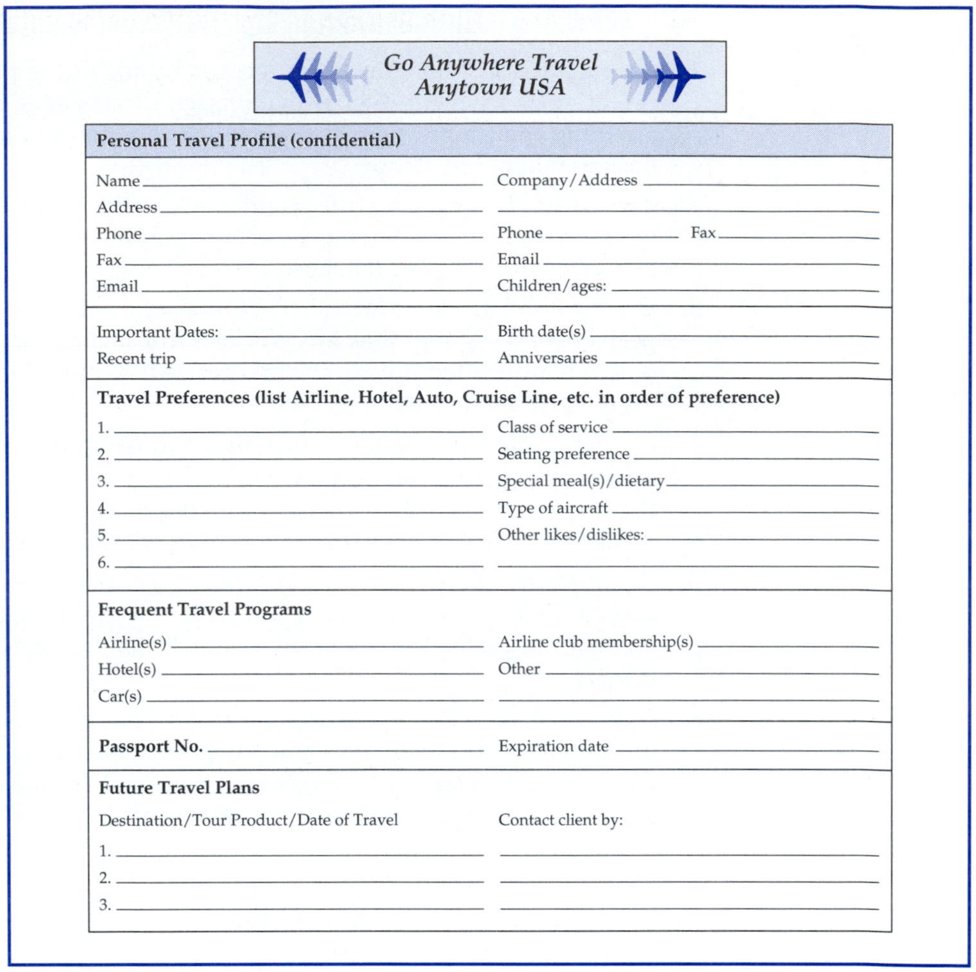
Go Anywhere Travel
Anytown USA

Personal Travel Profile (confidential)

Name ______ Company/Address ______
Address ______ ______
Phone ______ Phone ______ Fax ______
Fax ______ Email ______
Email ______ Children/ages: ______

Important Dates: ______ Birth date(s) ______
Recent trip ______ Anniversaries ______

Travel Preferences (list Airline, Hotel, Auto, Cruise Line, etc. in order of preference)

1. ______ Class of service ______
2. ______ Seating preference ______
3. ______ Special meal(s)/dietary ______
4. ______ Type of aircraft ______
5. ______ Other likes/dislikes: ______
6. ______ ______

Frequent Travel Programs

Airline(s) ______ Airline club membership(s) ______
Hotel(s) ______ Other ______
Car(s) ______ ______

Passport No. ______ Expiration date ______

Future Travel Plans

Destination/Tour Product/Date of Travel | Contact client by:

1. ______ ______
2. ______ ______
3. ______ ______

Figure 11.2 *Client tickler file.*

shows that most client interactions, 68 percent, are by telephone. The rest are face to face.

Remember, unless the caller is an automatic booking, it is more effective to sell face to face. Your ultimate goal in any telephone sale is to get the caller to come into the agency. Especially for leisure travelers, most sales are made during a face-to-face meeting, not over the telephone. However, you will have to be flexible.

How large or complicated the trip is, the time available, and the client's schedule will determine if you can effectively close a sale on the telephone or if a face-to-face meeting is required. A good response is: "We have so many options that would interest you. If you can come into the office, you can get a much better picture of your choices. When would you like to come in?" If the client states that he or she will have to think about a good time, say you will call back. Be specific and mention a time and date of your call-back. Most important, do it!

There are many reasons why customers and potential customers contact a travel agency. Here are some reasons:

1. Shopping around for the best price
2. Request for schedule, price, and trip information
3. A cancellation or change of a previously booked reservation
4. An automatic booking (primarily from corporate accounts)

Each call is important and should be considered a sales opportunity. What's so different about conducting business over the telephone rather than face to face? You can't "read" the caller's facial expressions or body language. As you learned earlier, nonverbal signals are important during the sales process. Also, the caller cannot see *your* nonverbal signals, such as your smile, your nod, and other body language that you use to make the client feel comfortable and to discuss openly what he or she wants.

To have effective telephone sales skills is the ability to project all of these nonverbal positive signals into your voice. What you say and how you say it are direct reflections of how you feel about yourself and the importance of that phone call. A monotone with no inflection doesn't project interest in what the caller has to say; a pleasant tone of voice with inflection does. Next, we give a quick telephone primer—from the first ring to the final hang-up.

➤ Mind Your Phone Manners

Don't forget the Golden Rule of telephone sales: Don't ever let the phone ring more than two or three times; the caller will hang up and call the next agency on the list. Think of every unanswered ring as hundreds of dollars of lost revenue.

Most travel agency business involves calls from potential customers requesting information. Remember that the first step in the sales process is to leave a positive first impression. Answer each phone call in a warm and friendly tone. Most agencies have a standard style of answering the phone. If that is the case, stick to it each time you answer; callers like consistency in their business dealings.

Phone calls should be answered with these four components:

1. Greeting: "Good morning!"
2. Identify Agency: "Global Travel."
3. Give Agent Name: "This is Susan."
4. Offer assistance: "How may I help you?"

One of the first questions after your four-part greeting is to ask for the caller's name and phone number. This is extremely important to do early in the call. If the call is disconnected by mistake, you have a name and number to call back. Also, it is very important to use the person's name throughout the phone conversation. Try to use the caller's name at least twice during the conversation. That serves to make the caller feel more comfortable and starts building trust between you and the customer.

Some people may refuse to give you their names—let alone phone numbers. There is nothing you can do to force it out of them. Asking for a name and number can serve as part of qualifying. If callers refuse to give you their names, it is probably because they are not serious about buying from you at this time.

How to handle it graciously? Provide some information over the phone, but urge them to schedule a visit to the agency, where you can give them the time and attention they deserve when planning their next trip. If they are still unwilling to give their name or schedule a visit, be gracious, thank them for the call, and hang up. If they are serious buyers, they will call you back. In the meantime, give your attention to those clients who want to do business with you.

Another "no-no" is to *tell* a client you have to put him or her on hold. If you are on another line and all other agents in the office are busy, what do you do? Just *ask* the client if you may put him on hold. By *asking* for his permission, the caller does not feel defensive or ignored.

Keep a caller on hold for no more than 30 to 45 seconds. If you or someone else in the office is still unavailable, get back to the caller and thank her for holding. Indicate that it may be a little longer and ask if she would like to continue to hold or, if you can have the name and number so that you call right back. Try to get the name and number; don't have the caller promise that he or she will get back to you—they rarely do!

➤ Qualifying over the Phone

There are many clients who are willing to buy, and feel quite comfortable buying, over the telephone. In fact, many clients are calling their agent to save time. They probably work, so it is difficult for them to get to your agency after hours or on a Saturday morning when there are other personal tasks they have to take care of. This trend toward a higher percentage of telephone sales is seen in the increase of catalog operations and the success of the big 800-line travel agencies and suppliers.

Ask Lots of Questions

When the client doesn't have time or is unwilling to come to your agency, you need a lot of questions to qualify that client. When someone walks into your office, you make some assumptions about that person based on his or her appearance and mannerisms. A woman in a mink coat may be a prospect for a Seabourn luxury cruise or a deluxe FIT. A young couple in sweaters and jeans may be considered prospects for a Carnival Cruise or a budget fly/drive package. Of course, you may be entirely wrong!

On the phone and without these visual clues, you have to ask a lot more questions in order to qualify. You don't see the first client's mink coat. It may turn out that she is a grandmother who wants to take her grandchildren on the Disney Cruise line. You don't see the second client in jeans and a sweatshirt. It turns out that he is planning his honeymoon, for which his parents are paying. They want something quiet and low-key and price is not a major concern. This client is the better prospect for an expensive Seabourn cruise!

Be Specific

To build a more accurate profile of the caller, you need to ask very pointed questions: What kind of hotels do they usually stay in? Do they want to travel with other people or are they more independent? What kind of restaurants do they frequent? Where did they go on their last trip—what did they like best and least about it? If the clients tell you the Ritz rather than a Days Inn, that they would rather travel independently and dine in only the finest restaurants, you have started to build an accurate profile.

Control the Conversation

Not only do you need to ask the right questions, but also need to control the conversation throughout the discussion. The key to successful telephone sales is to get information quickly and not to prolong it unnecessarily with a lot of idle chitchat. The agent should make sure to ask the pertinent questions and not simply respond to questions. If the client controls the conversation, the travel agent is not getting the right information.

Not only control the conversation, but keep it moving. Remember, the person who is calling on the phone is trying to save time. Some travel agents are very pleasant, likable, and popular with the agency's customers, but may also have the poorest sales records. They may talk too much and give out too much information all at once. Remember, to be effective in telephone sales you need to answer questions and move on.

Don't Just Recite: Use Visual Images

Just don't recite dry facts about a product by listing all its features over the telephone. Remember, the client is not sitting with you looking at an exciting brochure or pictures. A good salesperson paints word pictures. This involves using verbal images of the benefits of a trip. To get ideas about good "visual" words to use, check out the professional brochures printed by cruise lines, tour companies, and hotels. Use words like the following:

- Elegant
- Stately
- Quaint
- Brilliantly-colored

- Jewel-like
- Majestic
- Exhilarating
- Picturesque

- Towering
- Gourmet
- Spectacular
- Glittering

What of the following sounds better? "The ship is 74,000 gross registered tons, the price includes an outside cabin, all meals in the dining room, plus entertainment each night" or "The ship is a towering floating resort! I can get you a room with a spectacular ocean view where you can have breakfast in bed each morning. You'll be dining in the elegant two-story dining room with enormous floor-to-ceiling windows. After a gourmet dinner you can watch Las Vegas–style entertainment or a full Broadway production in any of the ship's enormous entertainment theaters."

If you sell cruises—or any other travel product—with enthusiasm coupled with vivid imagery and a "can-you-just-see-yourself?" attitude, selling the trip can be a cinch.

➤ Telephone Body Language

The sales process is energized by the nonverbal language and cues that your physical mannerisms and facial expressions provide. Body language is also very important—and still possible—over the telephone. The only thing you can use to demonstrate your concern, confidence, and high level of professionalism is your *voice*. Clients can *hear* the agent who is bored; can *hear* the agent who is slouching at his or her desk, and can *hear* the agent who is not really paying attention to them.

When talking to clients over the telephone, it is often *how* you say something rather than the words you use that is more important. According to a recent industry survey regarding telephone communications, voice tone contributes *87 percent* toward telephone effectiveness; the words that are used account for only 13 percent. Follow these basic rules in telephone body language:

1. *Sound warm and friendly.* No matter how busy or stressed you are on the job, part of being a professional is never letting on how you really feel when speaking to a client! Translate warmth and friendliness through the tone of your voice. Try smiling when you speak over the phone; it is a proven fact that a person's voice quality improves if he or she is speaking with a smile. Believe it or not, *your smile can be heard*!

2. *Develop voice personality.* Treat each call with special attention rather than routine. Speak directly into the phone. Picture the caller in your mind, as though he or she is seated right across from you. Talk with the client, not at him. Talk personally and easily. Give your full attention to the caller. Don't carry on conversations with others in the office while on the phone with a client; covering the mouthpiece doesn't work!

Your Telephone Personality

It is easy to remember these do's and don'ts of phone body language, but for many people it doesn't come easily. You have to practice to create and maintain a pleasant and professional telephone manner. Check out *your* phone personality. Tape your voice on a recorder or telephone answering machine; listen to it carefully. Check off the following desirable and undesirable phone traits.

Desirable Traits		*Undesirable Traits*	
is pleasant sounding	_____	is nasal	_____
has pitch variations	_____	sounds throaty	_____
has a normal rate	_____	is raspy	_____
varies in volume	_____	sometimes squeaks	_____
has distinct articulation	_____	is a boring monotone	_____
sounds like "I am smiling"	_____	is too weak	_____
has ample force	_____	is too loud	_____
stresses proper accents	_____	has too many pauses	_____

Source: *Lloyd C. Finch Telephone Courtesy & Customer Service, (Menlo Park, CA: Crisp Publications, Inc., 1990).*

3. *Improve voice mechanics.* All the caller "sees" is your voice, so let it sound pleasant, relaxed, and confident. Don't speak in a monotone. Highlight certain words by pausing before you say them, and again afterward. Raise and lower the pitch and volume of your voice to emphasize what you are saying. Relax and talk at normal speed, and never shout or speak loudly.

4. *Be courteous.* When receiving calls, try to answer the phone on the first or second ring. Return calls promptly. Make a note of each promise to call back, and do it when you said you would! When closing a call, review details or the main purpose of the call. Say "Thank you for calling" and hang up gently (it is a good idea for the caller to hang up first). Last but not least, the time to have a cup of coffee, a snack, or lunch is not while you are on the telephone. That goes for chewing gum also.

✔ Check Your Understanding 11-6

Check your comprehension of effective telephone sales techniques by evaluating the following phone conversation.

Agent: Hi, can I help you?

Client: Is this Global Travel?

Agent: Yes it is.

Client: Do you have information about Disneyworld?

Agent: We have a lot of information about that destination.

Client: Well, can you help me?

Agent: Excuse me, there goes the other phone. I will be right back, please hold.

How would you rate the phone skills of this agent? Excellent, good, fair, poor? List at least four ways that you would improve on this performance.

1. _____

2. _____

3. _____

4. _____

DIRECTED SALES: PREFERRED SUPPLIERS

The inventory of travel products on the market is mind-boggling! There are literally thousands of airlines, cruise ships, destinations, tour packages, and other products on the market. In addition, the inventory changes all the time: new destinations, new resorts, new prices, and so on. How can you be an expert on absolutely everything on the market? You really can't. However, you can become expert on a selection of these products. We call this selection of products **preferred suppliers.**

Due to this huge inventory of products in addition to other factors, many travel agencies have decided to focus their sales efforts on a select number of products or preferred suppliers, which is called **directed selling.** Which airlines, cruise ships, or tour products to sell is not a decision made by front-line agents; these are management decisions. There are many factors that determine how an agency selects its preferred suppliers. Some of the important ones include:

- *Reputation and dependability.* How long has the company been in business; how dependable is the company; have there been any complaints from past clients or business peers?
- *Financial confidence.* How financially strong is the company? How long has the supplier been in business?
- *Product match.* Does the product match the needs of the agency's client population?
- *Reliable documents.* Does the supplier have timely delivery of documents with a neat and professional appearance?
- *Commission structure.* Does the supplier pay an override (higher or incentive commissions)?

The last factor—override commissions—is often one of the more important factors when considering preferred suppliers. The difference between the standard commission of 10 percent and override commissions, which can reach as high as 25 percent, can determine if the agency makes a profit or not. Take, for example, a typical cruise booking. If you sell a $4,000 cruise at a standard commission of 10 percent, your agency makes $400. However, a preferred supplier may pay at the rate of 20 percent, which increases commission earnings to $800. A difference of $400 on one booking may not seem like much, but it certainly adds up when booking preferred suppliers every day over a long period of time.

In addition to making more money, there are other benefits to selling preferred products. Your clients will benefit from your in-depth knowledge of the products you sell: It is better to have expert knowledge about a select number of products rather than some knowledge about many.

Another benefit of working with preferred suppliers is the greater "clout" agencies have. Preferred suppliers such as airlines, cruise companies, and tour operators can solve problems or grant special requests that are not usually done through normal channels. Special requests and services, such as last-minute bookings, waiving of cancellation or change penalties, or clearing space when the product is sold out, are typical of things that preferred suppliers can do for their associated agencies and their clients.

Now that you understand the importance of selling preferred products, how do you alter or change your sales process? You don't really. You still qualify your clients and resolve any concerns they may have. The difference is that you first recommend the product of your preferred supplier that would best meet the needs of that client.

Remember, management selects its preferred suppliers based on the company's reputation, dependability and other factors that benefit the client directly. And since you are highly knowledgeable in these selected products, you are able to make accurate recommendations to your clients.

You will get some clients who just don't match up with any of your agency's preferred suppliers. Or they may insist on buying a product that you have not recommended. In that case you would certainly sell the other product to your customer, assuming that your agency handles it. If for some reason the agency is not representing a certain company's products, due to a lack of dependability or financial stability, you should be upfront with the customer and explain the reasons of the decision. It is better to be honest in the beginning rather than selling the product to make a quick commission with the result of creating an unhappy client who won't return to do business with you.

SPECIALIZED SALES: FINDING YOUR NICHE

Being able to sell every product and destination equally effectively used to be the general—if the only—trend in retail travel agency sales. Most travel agents were considered to be **generalists** since their sales and marketing efforts were across the board.

The trend away from general sales and toward **niche marketing** started gaining momentum in the 1990s. Niche marketing means focusing your sales efforts on a specific product, destination, or customer base. According to travel forecasters, niche marketing will continue to grow and become a dominant force in the retail travel industry.

How about today? Are the majority of travel agents generalists or specialists? According to a recent survey conducted by the Institute of Certified Travel Agents, approximately 57 percent of agents surveyed were specialists in one particular segment or combined general sales with one or more specialties (see Figure 11.3).

How many specialties or niches are there? Probably hundreds. For every hobby, interest, sport, destination, travel product, or customer type that you can think of, there is a niche for it. To simplify matters we can categorize travel specialties into two main groups: product-driven and customer driven.

A *product-driven niche* focuses on a specific travel product such as cruises, tours, or a destination. The travel agent who focuses on one or more product-driven niches has an interest in and in-depth knowledge of that particular product and all the different customer bases that are drawn to that product. For example, cruises target a broad range of customer types: upscale, family, adventure, and senior markets, for example.

A *customer-driven niche* focuses on a particular customer base or segment of the traveling population. The travel agent who has a customer-driven niche has to know all the products and destinations that are relevant to that segment of the traveling population. For example, the travel agent who specializes in the mature or senior market has to be knowledgeable in what motivates and interests this type of traveler. In addition, the specialist must also know in depth all the products and destinations that are relevant to those customers, such as specific cruise companies, motorcoach tour companies, and so on.

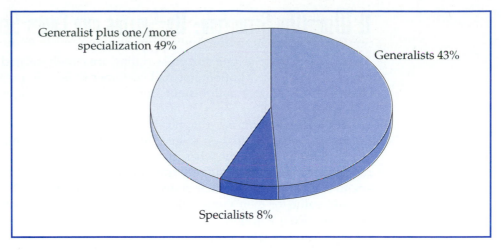

Generalist plus one/more specialization 49%

Generalists 43%

Specialists 8%

Figure 11.3 *General versus specialized sales survey conducted by the Institute of Certified Travel Agents.*

ICTA conducted a related survey of a number of travel agencies that specialize in one or more niches. The survey (Table 11.3) shows the top thirteen niches and the percentage of agencies surveyed that handled each as their area of specialization. Notice that the first four areas of specialization are product-driven: cruises, a particular destination or region, package tours, and FITs. The remainder are customer-driven, such as upscale, family, business, and mature travelers.

....
Key Point ➤
....

What does it take to make it in niche marketing? Expert travel specialists were asked what it takes to succeed in this type of sales. The number one response is that you have to love it! For example, if adventure travel is your niche, you have to believe that it is the most exciting and interesting segment of the industry. You have to be willing to commit yourself to educate yourself about the product or destination by reading, research, and firsthand experience. If your chosen specialty is *customer-driven*, you need to know what motivates these travelers in addition to what turns them on and off when it comes to the sales process. There's a lot of psychology associated with niche sales.

TABLE 11.3   TRAVEL AGENCY SURVEY: WHAT ARE YOUR AREAS OF SPECIALIZATION?

1. Cruises	51%	8. Family travel	22%
2. A destination	41%	9. Mature travel	14%
3. Package tours	36%	10. Adventure travel	17%
4. FITs	36%	11. Incentive travel	9%
5. Upscale travel	35%	12. Ecotourism	8%
6. Leisure groups	30%	13. Conferences	7%
7. Business travel	26%		

A Win-Win Situation: Up-Selling and Cross-Selling

The practices of up-selling and cross-selling are closely related: They both aim to increase the agency's bottom line and customer satisfaction at the same time. The client and the agency both benefit from these sales techniques if they are done correctly and wisely.

Up-selling is offering a higher-priced product or level of service to a client during the recommendation stage. This doesn't mean recommending a room at the Ritz for $500 a night when the client's budget is more in the Holiday Inn range. Keep the client's budget firmly in mind while up-selling. Most people will spend a little more over their stated budget if they feel that they are getting increased value for their money. Be wise: Don't recommend a higher-priced product or service if you don't feel it is worth it for the client. You don't want an unhappy customer who won't use your services in the future at the price of the extra commission. Up-sell only when the upgraded product or service will benefit the traveler. Some examples of up-selling include:

- Inside to outside cabin on a cruise ship
- Outside cabin with a private verandah
- Standard room to oceanfront room
- Compact to full-size car rental
- Coach to business class on a long flight

Cross-selling means offering additional products or services before closing the sale. These are things that the client may never have considered during the planning stages. A good example is to suggest a car rental along with buying an airline ticket. Some travelers get in the habit of reserving something as simple as a car rental on their own. It may never have occurred to them to ask their travel agent to do it for them. Other examples of cross-selling include:

- Travel insurance
- Hotel room
- Theater tickets
- Round-trip transfers
- City tour

Remember, it never hurts to ask when up-selling or cross-selling. Don't hesitate to recommend an upgraded service or additional product if you are convinced that it will enhance the client's trip. It's a win-win situation: The client is happier and the agency earns additional revenue.

Travel Insurance

What product pays travel agencies one of the highest commissions in the industry and gives the customer peace of mind for just a few extra dollars? If you said *travel insurance,* you would be right! Unfortunately, this source of easy revenue is overlooked by many travel agents. It's easy to sell since insurance costs the client a few extra dollars to protect an investment that can be worth thousands of dollars. The peace of mind that comes with it is worth it. Also, agencies can earn up to 30 percent commission, which is much higher than the industry standard of 10 percent.

Selling insurance to clients is not the hard part; deciding what type of insurance can be more tricky. It is important for travel agents to understand the ins and outs of the various policies so that the traveler can collect in case of trip cancellation, departure delay, medical evacuation, and loss of baggage and valuables. Every policy comes with a lot of fine print that spells out under what strict conditions the traveler can or cannot collect. It is up to travel agents to understand these exclusions and to educate their clients, to avoid problems later.

➤ Cancellation Insurance

This is probably the most popular form of travel insurance since it is used the most frequently. Every policy is different but most include the total amount of deposit or payment already made for the trip before cancellation date. The agent and traveler must be clear on what types of situations most travel insurance policies will and will not cover. Most cancellation policies cover claims due to the following situations:

- Illness of the traveler, family member, or traveling companion that requires medical treatment (documentation from a doctor is required)
- Financial default of the travel supplier—tour operator, airline, or cruise line, for example—resulting in the complete cessation of service (not just a simple closing or disappearance of its owners!)
- Strike or other "disaster" resulting in total cessation of the transportation or tour company's operations
- Layoff or firing of the traveler from his or her place of business
- Jury duty or other required court-appointed appearances
- Traveler's home is destroyed by fire or flood
- Traveler's home is burglarized
- Terrorist incident in a foreign destination prior to arrival
- Traveler, family member, or traveling companion directly involved in a car accident while en route to a departure

Most cancellation policies will not cover claims due to these situations:

- Voluntary change of travel plans
- Traveler cannot obtain passport or visa by the time of departure
- Business or family obligations
- Airline or carrier delay if it is the fault of the airline/carrier, including bad weather
- Being detained by a Customs official
- Giving birth

➤ Emergency Evacuation Insurance

After cancellation insurance, *emergency evacuation insurance* is the next type of policy most frequently purchased by consumers. This policy covers costs incurred if the traveler needs to be moved or evacuated due to severe illness or other medical emergency. The majority of insurance companies will pay on this only if a qualified physician documents that the evacuation was necessary. This coverage is certainly worth it if needed, since some policies cover up to $50,000 for this service. Some policies pay upfront all expenses incurred due to the evacuation; others require the traveler to pay upfront and then be reimbursed upon settlement from the insurance company. This should be checked on a case-by-case basis.

➤ Delay Insurance

Delay insurance is similar to cancellation insurance since the policy pays the traveler for missing part of a trip due to a delay. Acceptable reasons for travel delay are: the traveler, family member, or travel companion being delayed by, but not directly involved in, a traffic accident while en route to a departure; carrier delays due to bad weather; lost or stolen passports, tickets, or money; hijacking; unannounced strikes; natural disasters or riots. Exclusions are similar to those for trip cancellation.

➤ Medical Coverage Insurance

To collect on medical expenses incurred while traveling, the client must visit a doctor and have the visit, cause, and treatment documented. Most travelers have their own personal health insurance which must be used first to cover medical expenses. Most trip *medical coverage insurance* policies will then cover the difference. If the traveler's personal health insurance does not extend overseas, the trip medical policy will pay the total bill. There are exclusions. Medical policies don't pay if the traveler is participating in certain types of team sports or personal adventures such as skydiving, hang gliding, bungee jumping, or scuba diving. Childbirth, alcohol, substance abuse, or mental disorders are additional examples of exclusions under this type of coverage.

➤ Lost Baggage Insurance

Lost baggage insurance is the type of coverage that is purchased the least by consumers since most policies exclude costly items. Things such as eyeglasses, contact lenses, hearing aids, money, credit cards, tickets, and documents are usually not covered. Also, there is a maximum coverage of $500 to $1,000 for jewelry, watches, computers, and cameras lost with the baggage.

Key Point ➤ **It pays to buy direct** is the recommendation by most travel professionals (see Figure 11.4). It is better for travel agents to buy directly from the insurance company rather than from the travel supplier when buying coverage on behalf of their clients. Why? Travel agencies make a higher commission when dealing directly with the insurance company. Suppliers pay the standard 10 percent commission on the policies that they handle; most insurance companies pay 30 percent. Also, if the cruise line or tour operator from which you purchased the insurance goes out of business, your client is out of luck when trying to collect! Almost every policy excludes coverage if there is a "default of the organization from which you purchased the coverage."

AFTER THE SALE: PROCEDURES AND RECORD KEEPING

This section is about how travel agencies process sales and maintain records pertaining to how business is conducted on a day-to-day basis. Every agency should have a well-planned system to manage all the information that it handles (see Figure 11.5). A lot of these data are maintained in the computer; some is maintained in paper files.

Even though we live in an electronic environment, a wholly paperless travel agency does not exist. In fact, many agents maintain paper files and forms just to be on the safe side or to supplement what is stored in the agency's computer.

All you have to do to secure a worry free vacation is fill out the simple application or call us for immediate enrollment.

Traveling with GlobalCare is like traveling with a trusted friend and travel expert.

GLOBALCARE CRUISE AND TOUR PROTECTION - PLAN C211

CRUISE AND TOUR PROTECTION PLAN BENEFITS

INSURANCE COVERAGES	MAXIMUM BENEFIT PER PERSON
Trip Cancellation	Trip Cost Per Person
Trip Interruption/ Travel Delay	150% of the Trip Cost Per Person
Baggage Loss	$500
Baggage Delay	$100
Medical/Dental Coverage	$10,000
Collision Loss/ Damage Coverage	$25,000 (Policy Maximum)
Travel Accident	$25,000

NON-INSURANCE SERVICES

24-HOUR EMERGENCY HOTLINE

- Medical Referral
- Emergency Cash Transfer
- Legal Assistance
- Lost Ticket and Passport Assistance
- Emergency Medical Transportation

GlobalCare's Cruise and Tour Protection Plan can protect your vacation investment.

Questions? (800) 779-1017

CRUISE AND TOUR PROTECTION PLAN PRICING

PREMIUM RATES

TRIP COST PER PERSON	AGE BAND		
	AGE 55 & UNDER	AGE 56 - 70	AGE 71 & OVER
$ 0 - $ 500	$ 31	$ 40	$ 48
501 - 1,000	41	59	73
1,001 - 1,500	52	78	98
1,501 - 2,000	62	96	123
2,001 - 2,500	73	115	149
2,501 - 3,000	83	140	177
3,001 - 3,500	93	165	205
3,501 - 4,000	104	190	235
4,001 - 4,500	117	218	275
4,501 - 5,000	133	248	315
5,001 - 6,000	162	303	390
6,001 - 7,000	191	358	465
7,001 - 8,000	218	413	535
8,001 - 9,000	245	463	605
9,001 - 10,000	272	513	675

OVER $10,000 or TRIPS OVER 31 DAYS — **CALL GLOBALCARE (800) 779-1017**

YOUR SATISFACTION IS GUARANTEED

If you're not completely satisfied, simply return your Certificate or Policy of Insurance and Description of 24-Hour Emergency Hotline Services within 10 days of receipt and include a letter indicating your desire to cancel.

If you haven't already left on your trip, you'll receive a full refund.

2   3

Figure 11.4 *Sample travel insurance exemplifying typical trip cancellation and emergancy medical protection policies.*
(Reprinted by permission from Edmund A. Cocco, President, GlobalCare Insurance Services, Inc.)

Some of the basic paper forms and/or computer files that are used and maintained for client trip files include:

- Reservation record/booking form
- Itinerary
- Invoice
- Receipt

➤ Reservation Record/Booking Forms

Whether you are handling a $95 airline ticket or a $35,000 luxury cruise, you are obligated to maintain and keep accurate records of what you did for your client. Before computers hit the travel agency scene, all of this information was recorded on paper. Simple airline/car/hotel bookings were maintained on what was called a reservation or booking form.

Today, the majority of full-service agencies are computerized with one or more airline computer reservations systems and most booking data are maintained electronically. However, we do not live in a totally paperless age; many travel agencies maintain a duplicate "hard copy" of each reservation just to be on the safe side, which allows easy access to client information during those times that the agency's computers experience "downtime." Figure 11.6 is a sample paper reservation or *booking form* used for this purpose.

Whether in written or electronic form, every client reservation record should contain, at a minimum, the following types of data:

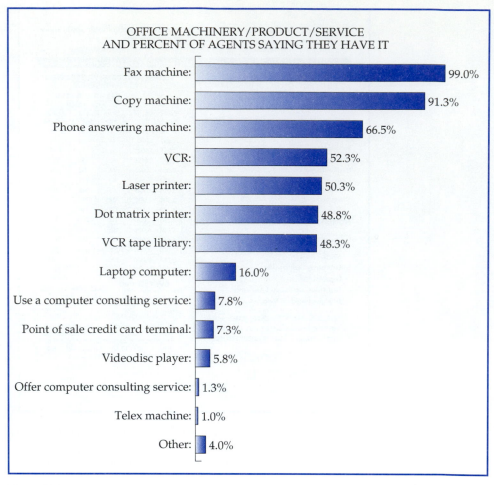

Figure 11.5 *Equipment used in a travel agency, based on responses from 404 mostly smaller agencies.*
(From ASTA Agency Automation Survey, Travel Weekly, *June 1998.)*

- Passenger name(s)
- Address
- Home and/or office telephone contact
- Fax number and/or E-mail address
- Complete itinerary
- Date ticket(s) to be written/delivered; ticket option date(s)
- Confirmation number(s) of nonair segments (car rentals, hotels, etc.)
- Name or insignia of the reservation agent with whom agency booked
- Form of payment
- Notes relating to land arrangements, such as deposit/payment requirements and cancellation policies
- Name or insignia of the travel agent who made the booking/date of booking

➤ Invoice/Itinerary Forms

An **invoice** is an important document that records a sale and/or a credit (e.g., in the form of a deposit already paid) to a client's account. Most travel agencies issue invoices that are generated by the CRS. This electronic version combines

1344 Main Street
Anytown, USA
(617) 555-1400 FAX (617) 555-1435

GLOBAL TRAVEL
Serving all your travel needs

Date: ______
Client Name(s) ______
Address ______
Telephone Bus. ______ Home ______ Fax ______

AIR

FROM	TO	DEP.	ARR.	AIRLINE/FLIGHT	CLASS	MEAL(S)

Frequent Flyer(s): ______ Airport Club(s) ______
Special Request: Seat(s) ______ Meal(s) ______
Other: ______ Form of Payment: ______

CAR

CITY	TYPE	NO. DAYS	RATE	P.U./D.O. DATE	CONF. NO.	SPECIAL REQ.

Frequent Renter(s): ______
Special Requests/Rate ______ Form of Payment: ______

HOTEL

CITY	HOTEL	NO. NIGHTS	RATE	ARR DATE	DEP DATE	CONF NO.

Frequent Stay(s): ______
Special Requests/Rate ______ Form of Payment: ______
Guaranteed by: ______

Remarks/Comments: ______

Agent ______ Trip No. ______

Figure 11.6 *Paper reservation/booking form.*

both invoice and **itinerary** data on the same form. That is why the automated version is called the invoice/itinerary document. Sometimes a paper invoice is used. This is usually the case for long and complex trips that include a combination of air and land services, such as cruises, tour packages, or FIT arrangements. All information is neatly typed and not handwritten on paper invoices.

Invoices are accountable documents that are numbered and used in order. If an invoice is not used due to an error, it is voided and sent to the accounting office of the agency. Figure 11.7 is an example of an automated invoice/itinerary form.

Whether in written or electronic form, an invoice should contain, at a minimum, the following types of data:

- Name and address of the client. If the customer is a corporate client, the name and address of the company.

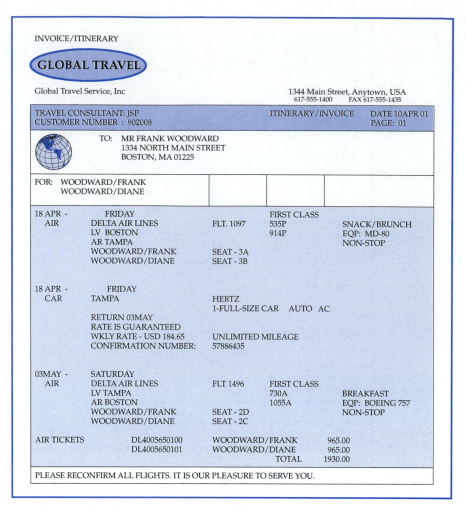

Figure 11.7 *Automated invoice/itinerary form.*

- Name of the passenger(s).
- A brief description of what was purchased. The automated invoice/itinerary document shows air and land arrangements in detail.
- Any due date or payment deadline date if a copy of the invoice is sent to the customer as a request for payment.
- Ticket number(s) if the sale involves an airline ticket or other related document (such as a PTA, MCO, etc.) that has already been issued.
- The name or initials of the travel agent in charge of the booking.

An invoice form should be printed in four parts, to be distributed as follows:

- *Top copy:* to the client as a receipt or notice that payment is due.
- *Second copy:* duplicate copy for the client. This copy usually remains with the completed ticket documents if the first copy was already sent as a request for payment. Otherwise, both are kept together.
- *Third copy:* advice of payment, sent to the agency's accounts receivable department.
- *Fourth copy:* numerical file copy. Procedure varies between agencies. A standard process is to remove the fourth copy immediately, attach to the

```
+-----------------------------------------------------------------------+
|                                                                       |
|   RECEIPT   1022                           GLOBAL TRAVEL              |
|                                                                       |
|   To: __FRANK BENSON____   Address: _123 MAIN STREET, ANYTOWN, USA_   |
|                                                                       |
|   Payment Amount _$400.00_  Form of Payment: _PERSONAL CHECK #1044_   |
|                                                                       |
|   For: _DEPOSIT CRUISE-VOYAGER OF THE SEAS, DEP11NOV2001 CAT. C_      |
|                                                                       |
|-----------------------------------------------------------------------|
|   Total:      $4500.00                     Agent: Susan Howard       |
|   Payment:    $400.00                                                 |
|   Balance Due: $4100.00   Due By: September 5, 2001  Date: May 17, 2001|
+-----------------------------------------------------------------------+
```

Figure 11.8 *Receipt for deposit.*

accounting copies of tickets, and place in the accounting office "in" basket. If payment is received before or at the time of ticketing, this copy is usually bundled with the third copy (advice of payment) and attached with ticket copies and applicable check or credit card draft.

➤ Receipts

A **receipt** is a document that is completed every time a client's payment is made. It records the amount paid and, if applicable, the balance due. A receipt also indicates the form of payment, whether cash, personal check, or credit card. If the form of payment is by credit card, the credit card name and account number are recorded on the receipt. A copy of the receipt is given to the client, one copy provided to the accounting office, and a third copy should be maintained in the client's file. Figure 11.8 is a sample receipt that has been completed for a deposit payment toward a cruise.

✓ *Check Your Understanding 11-7*

Multiple Choice

Circle the *best* answer.

1. Selling products of preferred suppliers is called:
   A. niche marketing
   B. directed selling
   C. up-selling
   D. target marketing

2. A factor that probably would be least considered when a travel agency selects preferred suppliers is:
   A. financial stability of company
   B. dependability of company
   C. location or proximity of company to agency
   D. override commission program

3. Recommending a car rental or hotel room after booking an airline ticket for a client is an example of:
   A. closing
   B. cross-selling
   C. qualifying
   D. up-selling

4. Which would be considered a customer-driven niche?

    A. deluxe FIT to Orient   C. business meeting in Honolulu

    B. senior citizen escorted tour   D. cruise to Alaska

5. The majority of travel agencies are:

    A. specialists   C. generalists

    B. combination generalist with   D. none of the above
       one/two specialties

6. The leading area of specialization in terms of number of travel agencies is:

    A. a destination   C. cruises

    B. senior citizens   D. business travel

7. The most popular type of travel insurance purchased by clients is:

    A. medical coverage   C. trip delay

    B. baggage loss   D. trip cancellation

8. A situation that would not be covered in a trip cancellation policy that was purchased directly from the insurance company would be:

    A. illness of the traveler's family member or traveling companion

    B. traveler's need to serve jury duty

    C. traveler's inability to obtain required passport in time

    D. travel supplier's cessation of operation due to financial default

9. An office document that records a sale or credit to a client's account and which also may be combined with a detailed itinerary if automated is a(n):

    A. invoice   C. passenger name record

    B. receipt   D. booking form

10. An office document that records a payment and is completed each time a payment is made by a client is a(n):

    A. invoice   C. itinerary

    B. receipt   D. booking form

Business Communications

➤ Business Letters

As a travel professional you write letters to many people during a typical work-day: to clients, suppliers, and business associates. You write letters to clients confirming reservations or welcoming them home from a trip. You write letters to suppliers requesting brochures or seeking refunds on behalf of your clients. You write letters to associates regarding meetings and business proposals. There are all sorts of reasons to write business letters, and unless you have your own private secretary, you will be writing them all by yourself!

All business letters have one thing in common: They should be clearly written, direct, and courteous in tone. Keep words and sentences short and sweet: The reader should not have to dig through a lot of useless words and lengthy sentences to get to the meaning of your letter.

Letters should also be conversational in tone. Stay away from very formal and stilted language. Phrasing should be businesslike but still sound comfortable. Pretend that you are speaking your message out loud to help you choose the right words. This helps to keep the tone of your letter less stilted and smoother.

Writing well takes practice. Have others in your office proofread for grammatical mistakes and misspellings. If typing a letter, use a dictionary. If you are using a word processing application, use the spell check function. With all these resources to help you there is no excuse for a poorly worded and misspelled document. See Table 11.4 for a list of words you should know how to spell.

Three basic formats are used when writing business letters: *block, modified block,* and *simplified.* There are no set rules as to when to use which format. The decision is up to you or your company. For all formats, most business letters include these parts in the order presented:

- Return or heading address (*letterhead*)
- Date
- Inside address (recipient's name, title, company name, mailing address)
- Attention line (optional)
- Salutation (not used in simplified format)
- Subject line (used primarily in simplified format)
- Body of letter
- Complimentary close (not used in simplified format)
- Company name (can be omitted when letterhead is used)
- Signature block (signature, writer's typed name and title)
- Reference initials (if typed by other than writer)
- Enclosure notation (if used)
- Copy notation (if used)

TABLE 11.4 WORDS OFTEN MISSPELLED IN BUSINESS WRITING

abbreviate	environment	miscellaneous	recipient
accidentally	etiquette	misspell	reciprocate
accommodation	exaggerate	necessary	recommendation
accrued	exorbitant	negotiate	registration
accumulate	facsimile	noticeable	reimbursement
advantageous	February	oblige	schedule
analysis	formatting	obsolete	separate
analyze	fulfill	occasion	serviceable
beneficiary	grateful	occupancy	similar
budget	grievance	occurrence	sufficient
calendar	guarantee	omission	susceptible
capability	illegible	ordinarily	tariff
changeable	initiative	peripheral	technique
conceivable	intention	permanent	terminal
convenient	intercede	permissible	thorough
correspondence	irrelevant	persevere	traceable
courtesy	itinerary	personnel	transferable
deductible	judgment	precede	turnaround
definite	knowledgeable	preferable	undoubtedly
definitely	leisure	privilege	usage
describe	liaison	proceed	valuable
desirable	license	processor	variety
desperate	lien	programming	weight
develop	likable	pursue	yield
disbursement	manageable	questionnaire	
efficient	merchandise	receipt	
eligible	mileage	receivable	

Block Letter Format

When the *block format* is used, all lines of the letter begin at the left margin. Single space within the body of the letter, double space between paragraphs. The signature block (signature, typed name with or without title) should be four spaces below the complimentary close (Sincerely, Yours truly, and so on). An option is to include the name of your company two lines below the complimentary close and the signature four lines below that. Figure 11.9 is a sample letter written by a travel agency to a client confirming a speaking engagement. The letter is in block format.

GLOBAL TRAVEL
DETROIT, MICHIGAN 10456
(312) 55506734

August 22, 2001

Mr. Allan Cooper
President
Allendale Outdoor Club
1344 West Terrace Drive
Northfield, MI 48044

Dear Mr. Cooper:

I am writing in response to your request for a guest speaker during your next club meeting. We would be happy to conduct a presentation next Wednesday at 7:30PM. You had suggested a 45-minute presentation regarding adventure tours in South America.

Our senior travel counselor, Ms. Miriam Johnson, is our specialist on ecotourism and adventure tours at Global Travel. Ms. Johnson has traveled extensively throughout Central and South America and has prepared an intriguing 30-minute slide presentation regarding her trip to Patagonia last winter. The last fifteen minutes can be devoted to questions and answers.

Miriam Johnson will contact you on Monday to go over last-minute details and answer any questions which you may have.

Thank you very much for contacting Global Travel. We look forward to assisting you and your club members with your future travel plans.

Sincerely,

Global Travel

Jeanne Sunberg, CTA
Manager

JS:gw

Figure 11.9 *Block letter format.*

Modified Block Format

A letter written in *modified block format* is similar to block format with one exception: Start all lines at the left margin except for the date, complimentary close, company name (if applicable), and signature block. The date line can begin at the center of the page or be typed so that it is flush or ends at the right margin. The complimentary close, signature block, and company name begin at the center of the page. The same spacing is used. Figure 11.10 is a letter accompanying a brochure to clients and an invitation to schedule a visit to discuss their next vacation. The letter is in modified block form.

ROCKY TRAVEL
45 Hilltop Avenue
Denver, Colorado 67443
(818) 555- 8622

February 21, 2001

Mr. & Mrs. Wendell Bland
86 Westerly Drive
Denver, CO 89665

Dear Mr. & Mrs. Bland:

With summer vacation only a few months away, you are probably already planning your next trip. When we last spoke you expressed an interest in taking a cruise through the Panama Canal. I just wanted to let you know that I have just returned from a delightful two-week cruise that included a transit through the Canal plus stops in the Caribbean and Mexico. It was a fascinating cruise and I would love to share my experiences with you.

Holland America is offering ten- and fourteen-day cruises this summer which your whole family can enjoy. I am enclosing their latest brochure, which features Caribbean/Mexico/Panama Canal adventure cruises.

Let's schedule a time to discuss your future vacation plans and how I can assist you in finding the right cruise for you and your family! I will call you next Thursday so that we can arrange a convenient time to visit together.

In the meantime, enjoy the brochure!

Sincerely,

Robert Townsend, CTA
Travel Consultant

RT:hr

Enclosure

cc: Sharon Long, Manager

Figure 11.10 *Modified block letter format.*

Simplified Format

Many companies use the *simplified format* variation of the more formal block format. All lines begin at the left margin. The major difference is a subject line—usually typed in capital letters—that is inserted in place of a salutation. This subject line begins three lines below the address. Then the body of the letter begins three lines below the subject line. Another major difference is that the complimentary close is not used. Some companies include the company name two lines below the body of the letter. The signature block follows and is inserted four lines below the company name. This format is effective when writing request letters to other travel companies and suppliers. Figure 11.11 is a letter to a supplier requesting a refund on behalf of the agency's clients. The letter is in simplified form.

ABACUS TRAVEL SERVICES
1334 California Street
San Francisco, CA 12234
(401) 555–7800

September 2, 2001

Amazon Tours
1334 Berkeley Avenue
Seattle, Washington 13324

RE: Refund Request: Sutherland/George Confirmation No. 1445B

This letter is to request a deposit refund in the amount of $400.00 for our client Mr. George Sutherland who was confirmed on the *Amazon Discovery Tour* departing October 23.

Unfortunately he is unable to travel at this time. We canceled this trip with your reservation office on August 17, well in advance to avoid cancellation penalties. I am enclosing a copy of the reservation acknowledgment.

Thank you very much for your prompt attention to this matter.

Mary McEachern - Office Supervisor

MM:rp

Enclosure

cc: Accounting Department

Figure 11.11 *Simplified letter format.*

➤ E-mail Etiquette

For those connected, **electronic mail** or **E-mail** is replacing typed memos, letters, and telephone messages. "Talking" to people on-line really means "typing" to them. Electronic communications has its own set of rules, procedures, and guidelines, just like business letters and other formal "paper" correspondence. Remember, when typing E-mail, no one can hear or see you! Sending E-mail is pure message: no voice and no visual signals. According to the publication *America Online for Dummies,* E-mail is considered *WYTIWYS* (What You Type Is What You Say) messaging at its best.

To type clear and understandable messages to clients and colleagues, America Online offers these rules of the road when sending electronic communications:

- *Rule 1: Type your message the way you talk.* Don't use any long words or flowery language when sending E-mail. The best way to do this is to talk out loud and type what you say.

- *Rule 2: "Spel Wrds Rite."* Nothing is more annoying then receiving a message with misspelled words. Just as you would in standard business letters, reports, and other paper communications, pay close attention to spelling and grammar.

- *Rule 3: Don't shout.* Typing in capital letters is very bad form. It means that you are shouting at the reader. Type your E-mail message with normal upper- and lowercase lettering.

- *Rule 4: "Dnt typ lk ths."* There was once a rumor going around in E-mail circles that you should abbreviate messages by dropping out vowels. The rea-

E-mail Emoticons and Shorthand

How do you show someone you are smiling, frowning, happy, or confused in the "faceless" medium of E-mail, discussion groups, and chat rooms? One way is by typing emotion icons or *emoticons.* You use different letter keys and punctuation marks, such as the colon : , hyphen -, and parentheses ( ) . Tilt your head to the left to read them. Another way is to type in shorthand. Here are a few to start you off.

Emoticons

: -)	Smile
: - (	Frown
; -)	Wink
: - /)	Big smile/laugh
: - /	Confused/befuddled

Shorthand

LOL	Laughing out loud
ROTF	Rolling on the floor (laughing)
AFK	Away from keyboard
BAK	Back at keyboard
BRB	Be right back
BTW	By the way
IMHO	In my humble opinion

son? You can type more quickly. To use abbreviated language or not is up to you. There are some situations when you should spell it out and not abbreviate: for example, when sending E-mail to your boss or a company executive. If you want to use an abbreviation or two, just make sure that the reader will get the meaning. It is a good idea to introduce a new abbreviation in your message by writing out the phrase the first time you use it, with the abbreviation next to it in parentheses.

✔ Check Your Understanding 11-8

1. The letter shown in Figure 11.12 is being sent to a client. Can you spot the mistakes? Look for content, format, and spelling errors. Circle and correct them.

TRAVELER'S WORLD
1334 Jasmine Way
Portland, OR 12345

Ms. Mary Juniper

134 Lambert Way
Eugene, OR 14355

Dear Mr. Juniper:
We are pleased to receive your deposit for the western Mediteranean cruise departing Febuary 24. Your outside cabin in catagory D is confirmed and I have put in a request for your dining room assignment: second seating and a table for four.

You are also confirmed at the Sheraton Palace for your pre-cruise tour in Athens. The price of the package is $116.00 per person based on double occupancy. This price also includes courtisy transportation from the airport plus two meals per day.

I have also received correspondance from the cruise line and a list of shore excursions that you can prepay. I am enclosing this list with this letter. My recommendation is to select and prepay the excursions you wish to take since they sell out very quickly.

Thank you for using Traveler's World for your vacation plans. If you have any questions, please contact me at any time.
Sincerely,

Janice Paige
Travel Consultant

Figure 11.12

➤ Key Terms

- assumptive close
- behavioristic
- benefit
- choice close
- cross-selling
- demographics
- direct close
- directed selling
- directive question
- electronic mail (e-mail)

- feature
- generalist
- geographic
- invoice
- itinerary
- niche marketing
- objection
- open question
- preferred supplier

- psychographic
- qualifying
- receipt
- reflective question
- summary close
- up-selling
- valid concern
- value
- void concern

Flashback The three ingredients of travel success are to acquire a wealth of product knowledge, work on people skills, and understand the sales process. It's the last ingredient—sales ability—which spells either gloom or glory for a travel company. Travel professionals who see themselves as simple order-takers and informational providers just won't cut it in today's competitive workplace. Companies don't earn profits, salaries don't increase, and promotional ladders become all too rare unless people sell. Remember, nothing happens until someone sells something. These are good words to live by.

As a travel industry professional you need to understand and apply these seven steps in the sales cycle when working with your clients: Sell yourself, identify the client, qualify, recommend, overcome objections, close the sale, and follow up.

Since a majority of client contact is over the telephone, you must also develop a different set of sales skills. Because the telephone is a nonvisual medium, the agent must use his or her voice to establish rapport and provide nonverbal signals to the caller. More in-depth qualifying and the use of visual imagery are two important aspects of this type of selling.

There are other important aspects of selling which play a large role in the success of any travel company. The concept of directed selling benefits both the agency and the consumer. The agency carefully selects a number of preferred suppliers to promote and sell to their customers. The agent becomes highly knowledgeable, with a select number of suppliers, and is able to recommend their products and services with confidence.

Another trend is that many agencies are moving away from general sales and toward focused selling or niche marketing. The majority of travel agencies today handle one or more specialty markets. There are literally hundreds of specialties. The more popular product-driven niches include cruises, a destination, package tours, and FITs. Popular customer-driven niches include upscale travel, leisure groups, family travel, and the mature market.

Other methods that result in higher sales and customer satisfaction are up-selling and cross-selling, travel agents offering additional products or services to their clients. If handled correctly, these practices increase customer satisfaction and commission earnings for the agency. Offering products such as travel insurance, round-trip transfers, and a car rental with an airline ticket are examples of cross-selling. Upgrades such as an oceanfront hotel room, business-class air ticket, and a cabin with a verandah on a cruise are examples of up-selling. These practices result in a win–win situation: The client is happier with the increased value of his or her trip, and the agency earns higher revenue.

Finally, after the sale is made, the travel agent concentrates on providing necessary follow-up and customer service. These practices ensure that clients will return and recommend you to their friends and business associates.

CHAPTER REVIEW

True or False?

_____ 1. Features are the objective, inherent characteristics of products.

_____ 2. Loss of baggage is the most popular type of travel insurance purchased by travelers.

_____ 3. When listening to a customer, concentrate on what your reply will be.

_____ 4. Close-ended questions will require a lot more than just a yes or no response.

_____ 5. About 93 percent of what we want to say is not through words but through how we say them and our behavior.

_____ 6. Client invoices and itineraries are generated usually as separate documents when printed by the computer.

_____ 7. The fact-finding step in the sales cycle is qualifying the client.

_____ 8. The best way to deal with a void concern is with correct information.

_____ 9. Price should always be discussed after you recommend a product.

_____ 10. Cruise sales is the leading niche in terms of number of travel agencies who specialize.

Multiple Choice.

Circle the *best* answer.

11. Service, an integral part of the entire selling process, refers to:
    A. finding out what the customer wants during the sales cycle
    B. begins only after the sale is made
    C. is provided before any recommendation is made
    D. takes priority over selling

12. The job of a travel salesperson is to:
    A. make the sale no matter what
    B. recommend the high-profit items first and sell down from there
    C. identify the needs of the client and make recommendations based on those needs
    D. provide as much information about many different products so that the client can make an informed decision

13. Which of the following statements best describes a benefit?
    A. A hotel has 600 rooms.
    B. There is no unpacking and repacking since your cruise ship is your hotel.
    C. The resort has indoor and outdoor pools.
    D. A car rental desk is in the lobby.

14. The traditional who, what, where, when, why, and how queries are examples of:
    A. directive questions
    C. open questions
    B. reflective questions
    D. feedback questions

15. What is the best way to go about determining customer needs?
    A. Ask probing, open-ended questions.
    B. Offer to make a reservation.
    C. Make immediate recommendations.
    D. Give out brochures and watch for reactions.

16. What is the best way to motivate a customer to action?
    A. Keep telling the customer about the features and benefits of the product.
    B. Tell the customer to book now or miss out on the trip.
    C. Tell the customer to call you back when a decision has been made.
    D. Recap your recommendation, stress benefits, and offer to make the reservation.

17. After you have responded to a client's objection or concern, you should:
    A. Go back and requalify.
    B. Confirm and move on.
    C. Ask if the clients have any more objections.
    D. Recommend another product.

18. Recommending the products and services of preferred suppliers is called:
    A. directed selling
    C. specialized selling
    B. cross-selling
    D. up-selling

19. "Should I book an outside or an inside cabin for you?" is an example of a:
    A. direct close
    C. choice close
    B. assumptive close
    D. summary close

20. If the client says "That's too much money," you should:
    A. Present the value of the product in terms of its benefits.
    B. Stress that the same trip may cost more or not be operating next year.
    C. Qualify the client more thoroughly by asking questions about budget.
    D. All of the above

21. Which of the following would be considered a way to divide the population in terms of demographics?
    A. values
    C. interests
    B. age
    D. habits and preferences

22. Which of the following would be considered negative body language?
    A. leaning forward when you speak
    B. crossing your arms in front of you
    C. smiling and nodding
    D. looking clients straight in the eye

23. What is the most important part of the sales process?
    A. presenting and recommending products and services
    B. talking about your travel experiences
    C. using visuals
    D. listening

24. What is the ultimate goal of any telephone call?
    A. to recommend a product as fast as possible
    B. to get the client into the agency
    C. to provide visual imagery
    D. to provide information

25. During a telephone call, what is the first thing you should do after you identify yourself and ask how you can assist the caller?
    A. Ask the caller where he or she wants to go.
    B. Get the caller's name and phone number.
    C. Make the caller feel comfortable by chatting informally.
    D. Provide information about the best deals and bargains the agency is offering.

Short Answers

26. Read through the following conversation between agent and client and answer the question that follows.

    Agent: "Well, I think we covered everything about cruises, Mr. Smythe. Is there anything else I can do for you?"

    Client: "No, you have been so helpful. We love the idea of a cruise and really appreciate you taking the time to answer our questions and send us all those brochures."

    Agent: "It's my pleasure, that's what I am here for. When you make a final decision, just let me know."

    Client: "Well, I sure will call you. Thanks again for all your help. Good-bye."

    Did this agent do a good job? _____ If not, what did the agent do wrong, and how would you have handled it?

    _____

    _____

27. Use the skills in overcoming objections you have learned about in this chapter to close the sale in the following examples (either write responses or act out during a role-play demonstration).
    A. After remaining silent throughout your presentation about a seven-day Caribbean cruise, your client says that she likes the idea but feels that it may be too much money for such a short period of time. You would:

    _____

    _____

    _____

    B. Your clients—who have always traveled independently—like the idea of an escorted tour for their next vacation to the Orient. The price is right, but somehow they are unsure of the whole idea since they are in their

30s and don't want to be cooped up in a bus with people a lot older than they are. You would:

_____

_____

_____

C. Your client is making arrangements to travel to Bermuda with his family over the holidays. He seems very interested in the Sonesta Beach Hotel since it is right on the beach and has children's programs and facilities. But midway through your presentation, he tells you that maybe it would be better if he waited and consulted his wife. You would:

_____

_____

_____

28. On a separate sheet of paper type a business letter using either block or modified block letter format. Use your name and today's date in the letter.

Your agency:	Voyager Travel, 1134 Pacific Beach Drive, San Diego, CA 92108 Phone: 619–555–7800
Recipient:	Your client: Mrs. Frieda Thompson Address: 67 Mission Bay Drive, San Diego, CA 92213
Subject:	She is planning a surprise cruise for her husband on their twenty-fifth wedding anniversary. She asked you for any information you have on Alaskan cruises for next summer. You are sending her one or two brochures in the mail. You also want to invite her to a "Cruise Night" that your agency is having next month. She booked her last trip to Europe with you, so she is a repeat client.

Role-Play Exercises

Role-play can be informative and fun. For each of the two situations below, place yourself in the role of travel agent. If possible, act out the scenerio with either the instructor or another student in the class serving as the "client." In these role-plays, you should concentrate on identifying the client's needs (qualifying), recommending, overcoming concerns, and closing the sale. Don't forget the additional practices of cross- and up-selling when possible. A very general description of each client is provided, including the client's opening question to you. If role-play is not possible, describe these clients in more detail, their responses during the qualifying state, and then write out an explanation of how you would handle each sale.

29. Background:

Who:	Jeanne and Bob Cameroon
How many:	Two
Where:	Somewhere in the Caribbean—have never been before. This is their first vacation together since they put their last child through college.
When:	Next winter
How long:	They have one week.
Kind/class:	They haven't traveled very much in the past, only short weekends here and there. Money is important but they are willing to pay a little more for this long-overdue vacation.

The client's opening statement as they walk into your agency: "Do you have some brochures on the Caribbean?" How would you handle these clients through the sales cycle?

30. Background:

Who:	A caller on the phone
How many:	Not determined
Where:	Wants information about your best deals to Disneyworld
When:	Sometime next summer
How long:	One or two weeks
Kind/class:	Caller has expressed the least expensive

The client's opening statement on the phone is: "What deals do you have to Disneyworld?" How would you handle this caller through the sales cycle?

Chapter 12

Career Development

"People who are afraid to fail can never experience the joys of success."

Pete Zafra
California

Fast Forward ▼

➤ Tourism is the second-largest employer, and employment opportunities are predicted to increase over the next decade. . . . 565

➤ Find out what it takes to succeed as a travel professional. . . . 568

➤ There are lots of choices: different types of travel agencies and job functions. . . . 568

➤ Today's technology has changed radically what it now takes to start up and operate a home-based travel company. . . . 569

➤ How are agents paid, and how much do they earn? . . . 570

➤ There are many factors that have a significant impact on your earning power. . . . 572

➤ Your travel education doesn't stop here; professional development opportunities are offered by various trade organizations and suppliers. . . . 573

➤ The résumé is the most important job search tool; which one is right for you? . . . 575

➤ The cover letter's main purpose is to enhance your résumé. . . . 584

➤ Interviewing is a lot like public speaking; you have butterflies before going on but you remain confident because you know your subject— yourself! . . . 586

➤ Don't forget to follow up after the interview; getting the job may depend on it. . . . 591

INTRODUCTION

Did you know that tourism is North America's second-largest employer? (The largest is health services.) This translates into more than 14 million people in the United States alone who are employed in tourism. These numbers also translate into a total payroll in excess of $110 billion.

Table 12.1   World Travel Employment

Year	Tourism Employees (millions)	Percent of Total Employees
1990	185.9	10.2
1992	192.1	10.5
1995	212.2	10.7
2005 (projected)	337.9	11.8

Source: Travel Weekly, *March 18, 1996.*

According to current indicators, opportunities in the travel and hospitality field are expected to increase substantially in the decades ahead. According to the World Travel & Tourism Council, the number of tourism employees will reach over 337 million in the year 2005. This represents close to 12 percent of all world employees (see Table 12.1 and Figure 12.1).

For many people the travel industry means the excitement of travel, discovering new destinations, and experiencing new things. Some are attracted to this dynamic industry for that reason alone. Travel professionals do have access to numerous travel benefits, including discounted air travel, cruises, hotel rooms, car rentals, and other services and products that they actively promote and sell. Travel suppliers such as tour operators and cruise lines offer discounted trips for agents for educational purposes. Suppliers offer these educational trips or *famil-*

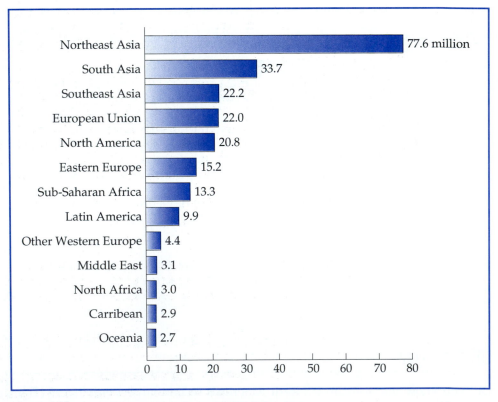

Figure 12.1 *Travel and tourism jobs worldwide.*
(From World Travel & Tourism Council Annual Report, Travel Weekly, *August 1998.)*

iarization trips ("*fams*") to encourage and educate travel agents to actively promote and sell their products to their clients.

For others, the appeal of the travel industry is not the time away from the office, but the time spent in the office with clients and colleagues. Every day brings new challenges and new opportunities to learn, grow, and succeed. People who work in this dynamic industry are well traveled. They are interesting people. They are energized and motivated to learn as much as they can about their specialty—the world's destinations, different cultures, and societies.

Finally, everyone recognizes that the travel industry is an incredible center for profit and business opportunities. It offers a huge interlocking web of careers and networking possibilities. Very few people, especially the real go-getters, remain at their first travel job for very long. This industry provides a lot of opportunity for growth and advancement within a relatively short period of time. For example, top management positions in the retail travel industry can be achieved after only four or five years of industry experience; in other industries, similar advancement may take as long as ten or fifteen years to achieve! The major ingredients in the formula for success in the travel industry are hard work, motivation, and continuing education.

This chapter is divided into two major sections. The first section focuses on what it is like to work in the retail and corporate travel agency arena. Emphasis is placed on this sector of the industry for two reasons: (1) the majority of entry-level positions are with travel agencies; and (2) travel agency experience is the perfect springboard for career advancement with other segments in the industry, such as airlines, tour operators, cruise lines, sales and marketing, informational management systems, and so on.

Finding Fulfillment

What Part of Your Job Is Most Satisfying?[a]

MOST SATISFYING

1.	Helping clients get the best value for their money	65%
2.	Helping clients make travel decisions	63%
3.	Interacting with different customers	59%
4.	Variety of the workday	53%
5.	Generating new sales for the agency	49%
6.	Accomplishing detail work quickly and accurately	48%
7.	The opportunity for personal travel	46%
8.	Participating in educational activities and events	39%

LEAST SATISFYING

1.	Handling reservations and ticketing	53%
2.	Working in a highly competitive industry	51%
3.	Working in a rapidly changing industry	48%
4.	The opportunity for personal travel	32%

[a]*Most satisfying figures show the percentage of respondents who answered "very satisfying." Least satisfying figures show the percentage of respondents who answered "slightly satisfying" or "not at all satisfying."*
Source: *A survey of travel agent professionals conducted by Institute of Certified Travel Agents, printed in the Travel Counselor, August, 1998.*

The second section prepares you for the job search. How to prepare your résumé and cover letters, as well as interview and follow-up techniques, are covered in detail. If you are a career changer, you will have to revise and update your job search skills to suit this new industry. If you have not conducted a job search before, this is the best time to start the process.

CAREERS IN TRAVEL AGENCIES

The day-to-day responsibilities of a travel agent varies from agency to agency. Needless to say, there are many different tasks waiting to be performed in today's busy travel office: counseling and advising clients, selling and providing customer service, booking and ticketing, researching destinations, and performing administrative tasks (see Figure 12.2).

What skills do you need to keep pace with this ever-changing and fast-paced industry? You'll need business skills, the sensitivity and empathy of a counselor, and the knowledge of a seasoned traveler. It is also important to have a background or training in geography, communications (both verbal and written), world history, and computers.

What's it like? Typically, travel agents work in an office behind a desk for most of the time. The exception are outside salespeople, sales representatives, independent contractors, and others who are not bound to a desk. Much of the work they do is detail-oriented, so organizational skills are extremely important. Travel agents must be skilled at multitasking because their typical days include handling new bookings over the computer and telephone, counseling clients face to face or over the telephone, conducting research for trip planning, and completing the many administrative duties that are part of the job.

This is a career chock full of deadlines, option dates, and last-minute purchasing. Travel agents must be patient and be able to work under pressure. Working with most clients is a pleasure since you are dealing with a positive and uplifting product—travel! However, working with some people can be difficult, especially clients with complaints or those who are very demanding.

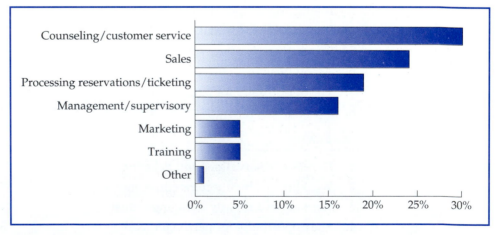

Figure 12.2 *Question to travel agents surveyed: How much of your day is devoted to the following tasks?*
(From Institute of Certified Travel Agents Survey, Travel Counselor, *August 1998.)*

➤ Full-Service Agencies

Let's take a look at the various categories or types of travel agencies. Some of these are formal categories established by the Airlines Reporting Corporation (ARC) for approval purposes. The majority of travel agencies fall under the full-service category. According to the ARC, a **full-service agency** must be open, freely accessible, and clearly identified to the public. Most travel agencies fall under this category. There are three general types of full-service agencies:

1. *General sales agencies.* These agencies can also be called "general stores" since they handle a mix of business: leisure, corporate, group, special interest, and so on. These travel agents are considered generalists since they are equally adept at selling a full range of products, such as a simple air ticket between Cleveland and Atlanta, booking a safari in east Africa, or organizing a small meeting in Hawaii for a business group. General sales means that the agency handles all types of travel—business and leisure—and all types of products and services. *The majority of full-service agencies are involved in general sales.*

2. *Leisure sales agencies.* These agencies only service the needs of vacation or leisure travelers. Leisure agents serve as counselors and advisors and develop long-term relationships with their clients. Most of the selling in the leisure environment is face to face and requires a lot of people-oriented skills. The successful leisure agent must be knowledge in destination geography, sales techniques, and product knowledge such as cruises, tours and resorts. Since leisure agents must be versatile and have a full range of knowledge, they must know how to use the full array of resources available to recommend the best leisure products for their clients. The leisure agent is not merely an order-taker but a counselor, advisor, planner, researcher, and above all, a salesperson.

3. *Corporate sales agencies.* These agencies only service the needs of business travelers. Corporate agencies are not identified prominently as travel agencies since they do not handle walk-in business or handle telephone inquiries regarding leisure-oriented trips (except from their business travelers). Corporate agents must be highly proficient on the computer; accuracy and speed are essential. The agent must have patience, a head for detail, and the ability to work under pressure in a very fast-paced environment. The typical business day of a corporate agent is often hectic and busy; there is no such thing as a slow period in the corporate arena; business people travel all the time throughout the year.

There is a lot of pressure in this line of work since business travelers tend to travel last-minute and make changes right up until boarding time. The corporate agent usually conducts business over the telephone and seldom meets the traveler face to face. In fact, most of the travel planning is done through the company's travel coordinator or secretary.

➤ Home-Based Travel Agencies (Independent Contractors)

Before the 1990s, operating a home-based travel business was impractical; very few people were willing to face the challenges of booking travel, accessing resources, and marketing their services without the office equipment and resources that a traditional office provided. Today's modern technology has radically changed what it now takes to start up and operate a business from home. With personal computers, modems, voice mail, E-mail, the Internet, and other advances, operating a *home-based agency* is becoming a reality for a growing number of **independent contractors.**

In the formal sense an independent contractor is someone who works from home under his or her own business name. Many of them are incorporated. A typical independent contractor will have at a minimum an extra telephone line installed at home, a personal computer, and a contractual agreement with a nearby travel agency for ticketing purposes.

The agent at home can do practically everything an in-office travel agent can do except issue airline tickets; a home-based agency is not an ARC- or IATA-approved location. The independent contractor selects an agency to generate airline tickets with some sort of shared commission arrangement. Another option for the independent contractor is to purchase the bulk of their airline tickets through consolidators, who issue tickets from their offices.

There are also support companies that assist independent agents by providing a range of services, such as training, marketing and business services, and access to a pool of preferred suppliers to earn higher commissions. In addition, these support networks can provide software that links the home-based agent to a major CRS database, with airline ticket delivery options.

Most independent contractors specialize in a particular segment or niche of the travel industry which yields higher profits; just selling airline tickets at 8 percent commission is not very profitable. Many home-based agents concentrate in such areas of specialization as cruise-only, group travel, special-interest travel, senior travel, and meeting planning.

Web Link

The Independent Travel Agent Network: This site offers resources to the small and home-based travel agent, with information about starting and operating your home agency, suppliers, and links to other useful sites. Point your browser to *http://members.tripod.com/aitc/index.html*

➤ Outside Sales

Many travel agencies are building outside sales networks to increase revenue and profits. Major reasons to establish a network of outside salespeople are to increase the agency's market base and to control costs. Since the outside sales agent is not pinned to a desk in the office, he or she can make contacts that extend beyond the normal scope of the in-house staff. The agency can also extend its business hours. Outside agents work primarily from home, with flexible hours. They can conduct business during those times that the agency is closed: evenings, weekends, or holidays.

Hiring outside sales agents makes sense since they are paid only when they sell something. They are usually compensated by splitting the earned commissions with the agency that hires them. The normal split is 50–50. In many cases, commission earnings can be as high as 60 to 75 percent for experienced agents who specialize in such markets as groups and upscale travel. The downside? The outside agent is usually not hired as a full employee of the agency. This means that benefits such as vacation, holiday and sick pay, and health insurance are usually not provided.

Web Link

Positive Space, a huge resource for travel professionals, includes a comprehensive list of companies and support networks for home-based travel agencies. Visitors to this site are required to enroll in this free service. Point your browser at *http://www.positivespace.com*

➤ How Are Agents Paid?

Travel agents are paid either by straight salary, straight commission, or a combination. According to a survey conducted by *Travel Weekly* and published in the 1998 U.S. Travel Agency Survey, the great majority of agents are paid by

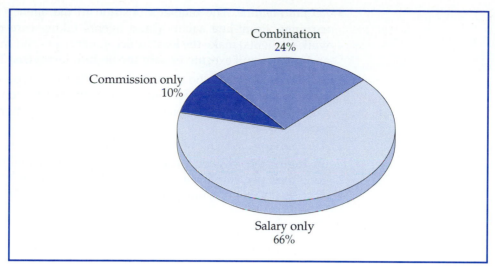

Figure 12.3 *How travel agents are paid.*
(*From U.S. Travel Agency Survey,* Travel Weekly Focus, *November 1998.*)

straight salary followed by a combination salary/commission/bonus package (see Figure 12.3).

➤ How Much Do Agents Earn?

To quote average annual earnings of travel agents is tricky to do. The level of compensation depends on many factors. Two major factors are agency location and types of sales. Agencies located in areas with a higher-than-average cost of living pay accordingly. Cities such as New York City, Boston, San Francisco, and Washington, DC fall into that category. The second major factor is the type of sales. On the average, corporate agents and managers earn slightly more than their leisure counterparts earn. Table 12.2 is a travel industry survey showing annual salary ranges in major U.S. cities.

In addition to agency location and type of sales, there are other factors that may have a significant impact on earning power. Chief among these are the following:

TABLE 12.2 TRAVEL AGENCY ANNUAL SALARY RANGES IN MAJOR CITIES[a]

	CORPORATE AGENTS	LEISURE AGENTS
Atlanta	$29,000–$36,000	$22,000–$26,000
Boston	$35,000–$42,000	$25,000–$28,000
Chicago	$30,000–$36,000	$24,000–$29,000
Dallas	$28,000–$35,000	$22,000–$25,000
Los Angeles	$32,000–$36,000	$22,000–$26,000
Miami	$25,000–$30,000	$19,000–$23,000
New York	$38,000–$45,000	$25,000–$31,000
Phoenix	$32,000–$40,000	$25,000–$30,000
San Francisco	$35,000–$38,000	$26,000–$30,000
Seattle	$27,000–$32,000	$24,000–$28,000
Washington	$33,000–$38,000	$24,000–$28,000

[a]*Numbers reflect a minimum of two to three year's experience, with CRS skills.*
Source: *Yours in Travel Personnel,* Travel Weekly, *May 1998.*

- *Job function/title.* The retailer's position in the agency determines annual earnings. Front-line agents (sales agents taking care of phone calls and walk-in clients) make the least; office supervisors and managers earn more; and owners and executives earn the highest levels (see Table 12.3).
- *Sales focus.* Agents who specialize in selling one type of travel (incentive travel, leisure groups, ecotourism, family travel, etc.) earn more than a sales generalist or someone who is a combined generalist and specialist (see Table 12.4).
- *Sales performance.* The higher amount of personally booked annual sales, the higher the paycheck. The average agency revenue that is expected to be generated per employee is $579,000. Revenue levels that are higher than this usually result in higher paychecks (see Table 12.5).

TABLE 12.3   AVERAGE PAY BY JOB FUNCTION

Front-line agent (53%)[a]	$26,100
Manager (18%)	33,400
Owner/executive (29%)	34,800

Source: Travel Counselor, *August 1998. Institute of Certi-fied Travel Agents.*
[a]*Percentage of respondents who are in that position.*

TABLE 12.4   AVERAGE PAY BY SALES FOCUS

Specialist in selling one area/type of travel	$32,500
Combination generalist and specialist	29,600
Sales generalist	29,300

Source: Travel Counselor, *August 1998. Institute of Certified Travel Agents.*

TABLE 12.5   AVERAGE PAY BY ANNUAL SALES

Personally booked annual sales of:	
$200,000–$299,000	$24,000
$300,000–$399,000	26,000
$400,000–$499,000	26,500
$500,000–$599,000	27,400
$600,000–$699,000	29,800
$700,000–$799,000	32,700
$800,000–$899,000	33,800
$900,000–$999,000	34,500
$1,000,000–$1,490,000	37,000
More than $1,500,000	40,600

Source: Travel Counselor, *August 1998. Institute of Certi-fied Travel Agents.*

PROFESSIONAL DEVELOPMENT

Your training and education do not end after you start working in the travel industry. There are many options open to you to keep current with the latest in technology, destination markets, travel products, and services. Following are some recommendations of ways to ensure continuing *professional development*.

➤ Suppliers

Industry suppliers offer informational seminars, workshops, and trade shows periodically each year. Most of these presentations are at no cost and can be an excellent way to learn about new products and services, exchange ideas with your industry peers, and build a professional network of contacts.

Suppliers also offer educational opportunities called familiarization (fam) trips. There is nothing like firsthand experience of a destination, a new resort, or a cruise ship to increase your sales effectiveness. Suppliers such as airlines, tour operators, hotels, cruise lines, and local governments operate fam trips to popular destinations so that agents can inspect hotels, restaurants, sample attractions, and experience the local culture.

Fam trips do not mean all play and no work! Agents invited on a fam trip are required to participate in all planned activities and tours. Often, this means getting up at dawn, having an early breakfast, inspecting several hotel properties, going on sightseeing tours, attending functions and seminars—all day, practically every day of the trip. Fam trips can be a quick weekender to a domestic resort, or a lengthy escorted foreign tour, including all transportation, transfers, sightseeing, most meals, and evening functions sponsored by hotels.

Seminars, workshops, and fam trips are opportunities that should be considered part of your job. They provide you with increased knowledge and confidence, which translates into becoming a more effective and professional salesperson.

➤ Trade Publications

Travel publications such as directories, magazines, and newsletters provide essential information on all aspects of the travel industry. Trade periodicals are indispensable for keeping current with industry news and issues. A selection of major trade periodicals and publications is listed in Table 12.6)

➤ Professional Education

There are many opportunities to build your credentials as a travel professional by completing training courses sponsored by professional organizations (see Table 12.7). In most cases you will earn a certificate or some other professional credential after completing the program.

➤ Institute of Certified Travel Agents

The Institute of Certified Travel Agents (ICTA) is the industry's primary educational organization, offering a pyramid of professional training, from entry level through advanced industry experience.

ICTA's Ladder of Professional Education Accomplishment

Entry level	Foundation level	Expert level
TAP ⟶	CTA ⟶	CTC

TABLE 12.6   TRAVEL INDUSTRY TRADE PUBLICATIONS

PERIODICAL	AUDIENCE	MEDIA	DESCRIPTION	SPECIAL FEATURES
Business Travel News (BTN)	Corporate travel managers and corporate travel agents	Web and print	News regarding corporate travel and travel management	Bulletin board, current issues, archives, calendar, subscription form
Cruise Industry News	Companies involved in the cruise industry	Web and print	Industry news, new ships, and features	Job board
Fam Connection	Travel agents	Web and E-mail	Announcement of latest fam trips	
Interactive Travel Report	Travel sales and marketing executives	Print and E-mail	News and trends in interactive travel	Free three issue trial subscription
Jax Fax Travel Marketing Magazine	Leisure travel agents	Print and Web	Product listings and travel intelligence	Charter and consolidator fares and departures
Leisure Travel News	Leisure travel agents	Print and Web	Product and destination news.	
Meetings and Conventions	Meeting planners	Print and Web	Industry news, destination reports, and how-to information	
Travel Agent	Travel agents	Print	Product and destination news, trends, and issues	
Travel Trade and Cruise Trade	Leisure and cruise-only travel agents	Print and Web	Product and destination news	
Travel Weekly	All travel agents and suppliers	Print and Web	Industry news, destination reports, current events and issues, editorials, job listings	Published twice per week
Travel Weekly Crossroads	Travel agents and travel industry personnel	Web	Articles from Travel Weekly, listings and bulletin boards	
Weissmann Travel Reports	Travel agents	Print and software	Destination information	

Source: *www.positivespace.com*

► Level 1: TAP

The Travel Agent Proficiency (TAP) examination is your first step to a rewarding career as a travel professional. The TAP is a basic competency evaluation that measures entry-level skills expected of new travel agents. This exam is recommended for a student or graduate of a travel certificate or degree program and can be taken at any time. Your course work combined with the *Travel Vision* textbook can prepare you for this important first step.

► Level 2: CTA

The Certified Travel Associate level of certification focuses on the basic skills required during the first few years of your career. The CTA program consists of core courses in communication and technology, geography, sales and service, and the *Travel Industry* trends and issues. CTA candidates must also complete a

Table 12.7 Professional Education Courses

Organization	Course Overview	Description	Requirements
Cruise Lines International Association (CLIA)	Accredited Cruise Counselor (ACC) Master Cruise Counselor (MCC)	Formal classroom training with options for additional study through industry seminars, ship inspections, exams, and cruises	Members of the travel industry
American Hotel & Motel Association (AH&MA)	Short-term certificate courses	Courses in all phases of hospitality sponsored by AH&MA's training division, *Educational Institute*	
American Society of Travel Agents (ASTA)	Certified Specialist certificate program	Training courses that focus on niche sales and marketing in any of the following areas: senior travel, family travel, special-interest travel	Members of the travel industry
National Tour Association (NTA)	Certified Tour Professional (CTP)	Earn a required number of credits by attending workshops and seminars sponsored or endorsed by NTA	Minimum five years' experience in travel industry
Institute of Certified Travel Agents (ICTA)	Destination Specialist (DS) Industry Skills courses TAP, CTA and CTC designations	Offers a wide variety of certificate courses in either a formal classroom setting, discussion groups, or independent	From entry level to experienced

number of elective courses in addition to the core curriculum. The CTA designation signifies a minimum of eighteen months' industry experience and a foundation level of professional competence

➤ Level 3 CTC

The Certified Travel Counselor is the culmination of the TAP and CTA certification process. This level is for experienced professionals wishing to build on the foundation of the CTA program. The CTC program consists of three core skill areas: business development, contemporary issues, and professional development. CTC candidates must also complete two electives from each skill area. The CTC designation signifies a minimum of five years of full-time travel industry experience with the highest level of accomplishment.

Preparing a Résumé

The **résumé** is the most important written tool that you have to market yourself during your job search. It is where you have to sell yourself—your skills, accomplishments, and ability to do the job—all on one sheet of paper. Not only that— the average time the prospective employer will spend reading your résumé is about 45 seconds! How do you maximize your abilities in such a short time?

The main objective of your résumé is not to tell your life history; it is to summarize briefly the most important facts about yourself that *pertain directly to the position you are seeking*—no more and no less. A résumé has done its job if the prospective employer grants you an interview; the rest will be up to you to sell yourself face to face later.

Also, the résumé is not a static document; it never remains the same because you will need to change and modify it each time you conduct a job search. Keep it updated with new jobs, new skills, and new objectives that evolve over the years.

▶ Your Résumé Checklist

Where to start? Let's take a look at this checklist when creating a professional résumé. Don't ever send one out before it passes this crucial test!

1. *Focus on what's important.* Since the average employer spends less than a minute scanning résumés, make sure that skills and abilities that pertain directly to the job are emphasized or highlighted.

2. *Know what you're doing.* Your résumé is a personal billboard of accomplishments; use specific terms to communicate your worth to a prospective employer. Remember that less is better than more; be concise and direct.

3. *Show some action.* Keep your language action-oriented; the tone of your résumé should be in "power mode" and not "passive mode." Sentences should start out with power words: *coordinated, planned, directed,* or *managed* are a lot more dramatic than the "My responsibilities included. . . ."

4. *Be persuasive and prove it.* In those sections of the résumé that allow you the freedom to do so, don't hesitate to communicate your abilities in strong language. Back up a *qualitative* statement ("effective in sales") with a *quantitative* statement ("exceeded the department's sales goal by 150 percent").

5. *Find a good editor.* Every good writer needs one and you are no exception when writing your résumé. Don't send it out with any typos, grammatical errors, or misspellings. This turns an otherwise great résumé (and an equally great job candidate) into a failure. Ask a family member, a teacher, another student, or a friend to help you. It may needs several "reads" before all the kinks are worked out.

6. *Don't be cheap or gaudy.* Don't hesitate to spend a few extra dollars necessary to present a professional-looking résumé. Stay away from superthin paper and mismatched pages. Also, your résumé will get the wrong attention if you print on oversized paper and in bright gaudy colors.

7. *Be brief.* Prospective employers do not have time to wade through several pages of a lengthy résumé; remember that their attention spans are limited to under 60 seconds! Try to keep it short, compact, and powerful; one page is best but two pages are okay.

8. *Choose what works for you.* There are dozens and dozens of résumé formats. The three that are recommended are chronological, functional, or a combination. Create a résumé in a style that you feel is right for you and presents you in the best light.

▶ What to Keep, What to Throw Out?

One of the most difficult things to do is to include all the pertinent things about yourself in a short one- or two-page résumé. Most people tend to write too much because they are afraid of leaving out something important. There are a lot of options about what to include and leave out in your résumé. Some data should always be included, some are optional, and others should never show up on your résumé.

You should *always* include the following:

- Your name, mailing address, and telephone number (fax and E-mail address, if applicable)
- Pertinent educational history
- Pertinent work history

- Membership in organizations
- Personal travel experience
- Related skills, such as foreign languages

You have the *option* of including the following:

- Career objective
- Personal data (e.g., age, marital status)
- Hobbies and interests
- Summary of qualifications

You should *never* include the following:

- Photograph (unless one is required)
- Why you left your previous job
- References (not with the résumé!)
- Salary history or requirements (if asked, then include in the cover letter)

Key Point ➤ There is definitely a school of thought that discourages any mention of personal data: marital status, health, age, and so on. The choice is yours to include or not. Keep in mind that these factors about your life are not necessary (and should not be examined) when someone is making a decision regarding your candidacy for a typical office job. Our suggestion is to omit! Only if this information directly affects the work you will be doing—for example, the state of your health if you are seeking a job as a commercial jet pilot—should you include it.

➤ Maximizing the Form and Substance

You already know to limit your résumé to a single page, if possible, two at the most. When you are laying out your résumé, try to leave a lot of "white space" with generous margins all around and spacing between entries. A résumé that is loaded with a lot of text will only confuse and frustrate the busy employer, who has to read through dozens of résumés at a time.

Your résumé should be printed on standard paper that measures 8½ by 11 inches. Remember, it should always be in a typed format (never handwritten), and do not photocopy it unless it is professionally done. If you don't want to use standard white, use soft-tone colors such as cream, ivory, or light gray. Don't scrimp on paper quality; use the best bond or weight you can afford. When asking for assistance at the store, ask to see paper stock used for résumé purposes. The ink should be black or, at most, royal blue.

References: How Do You Handle Them?

References should be listed on a separate sheet. Do not include them in your résumé and do not send references with your résumé unless you are asked to do so. You should have a minimum of three references: one personal and two business (if recent school grad, make one reference an instructor or advisor, for example). For each reference include full name, title/position, name of company, address, and telephone number. Bring the reference list with you on interviews. P.S.: Contact the people you wish to serve as references and ask for their permission first!

TABLE 12.8   POWER WORDS

accelerated	communicated	instituted	regulated
accomplished	completed	instructed	reorganized
achieved	computed	introduced	researched
administered	coordinated	issued	reviewed
advised	critiqued	launched	revised
analyzed	delegated	managed	scheduled
applied	determined	negotiated	selected
approved	developed	operated	solved
arranged	devised	organized	supervised
budgeted	formulated	planned	systematized
directed	generated	prepared	taught
established	guided	presented	tested
evaluated	implemented	presided	trained
calculated	improved	promoted	updated
classified	initiated	recommended	utilized

➤ Power Words

For many people writing anything—a business letter, term paper, an article, or a résumé—is an agonizing endeavor. To write clearly and effectively takes practice and skill. You don't have to be a Pulitzer prize winner to write a professional résumé. All it takes is some guidance and a little common sense.

The secret of a powerful résumé is to write short statements and not long sentences. In fact, you don't have to write in complete sentences at all (contrary to what you have learned in English classes!). Another secret is to use *power words* or action verbs at the beginning of each short statement. Choose your power words carefully: *developed* is more powerful than *put together; launched* is more powerful than *began; communicated* is more powerful than *wrote reports and memos.*

Table 12.8 is a list of some power words for résumés. Look them over and select those that will help you.

➤ Stating Your Accomplishments

In addition to using power words, include short statements that describe accomplishments. Accomplishments are the best way to write about your qualifications and work history. Remember to back up every accomplishment that you include. It is one thing to tell people how great you are, but if you cannot back it up with a specific accomplishment, it won't have much impact.

Following are some examples of *accomplishment statements.* As you read through them, think about your own work history and experiences and how you can turn them into a series of positive accomplishment statements.

- Awarded Employee of the Month for three consecutive years: 1997, 1998, and 1999
- Developed a new employee training program that resulted in a 50 percent decrease of employee turnover rate
- Directed a fund-raising committee that raised approximately $500,000 for underprivileged families in my local community
- Managed a sales force of fifteen people whose total revenue exceeded other departments by 75 percent

- Created and implemented a marketing plan that resulted in $2 million profitable sales in one year
- Reorganized a purchasing department that realized a 35 percent decrease in spending

► Chronological versus Functional Résumés

There is no such thing as a right or wrong résumé. A résumé should reflect each person's experience, career objectives, and background. You should use whatever format that suits you best. However, there are two general types of résumé formats that are used by most people: the chronological and functional. Depending on who you are and your background, one format may be better than the other.

The *chronological résumé* is best used by people who have had one or more jobs or have been in the same field for a long period of time. This type of résumé does not serve recent school or college graduates very well, since part-time or summer jobs may not relate directly to the travel and hospitality industry. The chronological résumé is the more familiar in format and used most often. This résumé organizes your life and work history by date, starting with the most recent.

The *functional résumé* is best used by career changers, frequent job changers, and those with limited or no work experience. This type of résumé can be used by recent school graduates or people returning to the workforce after a long period of time. This résumé organizes experience in terms of skills and accomplishments.

Many people choose to combine the best elements of both types. It is up to you to decide which format or combination will put you in first place.

The Chronological Résumé

The chronological résumé is the most widely used since it probably is the easiest to write and is traditionally accepted everywhere. Employers are accustomed to seeing it. The advantage of a chronological résumé is that it presents your background and experiences in a very precise and clear-cut manner. This is an easy-to-read format that enables the reader to quickly size up your qualifications.

This is the best format if your employment history shows a graduating progression of jobs in fields directly or indirectly related to the field that you are seeking. In travel and hospitality this includes positions in sales, marketing, and administration; anything involving sales, people skills, and office work will do. Remember, list your employment and education history in reverse order; the most recent first. Figure 12.4 is a sample chronological résumé.

The Functional Résumé

Unlike the chronological résumé, the functional résumé concentrates on your skills, abilities, qualifications, and accomplishments. A *summary of qualifications* or list of *key credentials* should be placed at the beginning of the résumé.

This format is excellent for those who lack an extensive and progressive work history, such as recent graduates or adults returning to the workplace. The advantage of a functional résumé is to mention all your good points without emphasizing where and when you received these qualifications.

Figure 12.5 is a sample functional résumé of a recent school graduate who has a limited work history. Her summary of qualifications and her course work that related directly to travel and tourism are highlighted first.

Jeffrey Knowles, CTC
431 Tremont Street
Boston, Massachusetts 02216
(617) 555–9055

CAREER
OBJECTIVE

A career position with a progressive travel company that involves both corporate and leisure sales opportunities in a challenging and fast-paced environment.

WORK HISTORY

1992–1997   **Sales Coordinator,** ABC Travel Services, Boston, Massachusetts.
Supervised a telephone sales force of 45 travel agents—Generated leads and
conducted sales training courses that resulted in a 45% increase of travel sales
over the previous year—Developed a publicity campaign for a new land-tour
product that exceeded sales projections by 35% during the first year.

1989–1992   **Travel Consultant,** Worldwide Travel, Hartford, Connecticut.
Promoted and sold corporate and leisure travel for all agency clients—Orga-
nized, booked, and served as tour director for three local school groups to
Mexico, California, and Canada—Developed and conducted a series of
Cruise Travel Nights for the general public that resulted in a 75% increase
of revenue from cruise sales over the previous year.

1987–1989   **Front Desk Clerk,** Holiday Inn, Hartford, Connecticut.
Registered all guest arrivals—Coordinated activities of the bell service and
the housekeeping departments—Maintained guest bills by posting charges
and credits to guest accounts—Responded to all guest inquiries and provided travel information and related services. Promoted to *Front Desk Supervisor in June, 1988.*

FORMAL EDUCATION

1994–1997   **Certified Travel Consultant (CTC)** awarded. Institute of Certified Travel
Agents, Wellesley, Massachusetts.

1983–1988   **Bachelor of Science,** University of Hartford, Connecticut.
Major: Hotel and Travel Management. Dean's List: 1984–1988.

1980–1983   **Associate of Science,** Bunker Hill Community College, Boston, Massachu-
settes. Major: Business Administration.

RELATED EXPERIENCES

Personal Travel: Extensive through Western Europe; South Africa; and Latin
America with an emphasis on Brazil and Peru; Resided in Germany and Italy
for a total of 12 months.

Train Buff: Traveled on the following special rail trips: Venice Simplon-
Orient Express, Europe; Blue Train, South Africa; and Andalusian Express,
Spain.

References available upon request

Figure 12.4 *Chronological résumé.*

Susan Stone
431 Norton Road, Westerville, Ohio 43081
(614) 555–6722

CAREER OBJECTIVE	A career position with a travel agency that involves both corporate and leisure sales responsibilities and which offers challenge and growth potential.

SUMMARY OF QUALIFICATIONS

Sales Experience
- Worked with adult and adolescent clients in business and retail settings.
- Provided product knowledge information for clients.
- Assisted business associates and friends in organizing and planning personal trips.

Administrative Skills and Organization
- Organized and directed social and campus activities during college.
- Hired and supervised staff of 12 at a clothing store.

Leadership and Supervision
- Developed a successful "Smiles Are Contagious" program at work. Received employee of the month as a result.
- Designed, organized, and recruited more than 50 volunteers to work on a fund-raising campaign for the Heart Fund; amount raised exceeded the previous year by 50%.

PROFESSIONAL EDUCATION

Travel Training Institute, Columbus, OH. CERTIFICATE AWARDED, TRAVEL INDUSTRY SALES AND MANAGEMENT, JUNE, 1999. GRADE AVERAGE: A

An intensive 300-hour career preparation program included -

- American Airlines' SABRE
- Fares & Ticketing
- Cruise Travel and Tours
- Office Procedures
- Hospitality
- Tourism Geography
- Travel Sales & Customer Service
- Corporate Travel and Services
- Business Communications
- 4-week Internship in Travel Sales

FORMAL EDUCATION

Associate in Science, Brevard College, Columbus, OH. Major: Computer Applications - June, 1998.

EMPLOYMENT HISTORY

Customer Sales and Service. Computerland, Columbus, OH. 1984–1988. Summer employment: Served walk-in customers—Generated leads and conducted sales follow-up within local area—Supervised telephone "help-desk" for customer service—Received employee of the month for a total of 4 months.

SPECIAL SKILLS/ EXPERIENCE

Languages: Fluent in Spanish, conversational in French.
Personal Travel: Extensive travel throughout United States; Cruise travel: Eastern Caribbean on *Dreamward*, Norwegian Caribbean Line and Southern Caribbean on *Sovereign of the Seas*, Royal Caribbean International.

Figure 12.5 *Functional résumé.*

Combined: The Best of Both

Your third, and perhaps best alternative is to use the best features of both: chronological and functional. It uses the summary of qualifications/key credentials section, which can be very impressive and catches the reader's eye immediately. It also uses the chronological approach when listing employment history, which is an organized and clear format. This format is recommended for its versatility and its impact on employers by matching your skills to their specific needs.

Figure 12.6 shows an example of a combined résumé. Again, there is no definite format to follow; it is up to you to create the combined résumé that will put you in the best light.

Web Link

Using the Internet Like a Help Wanted Section: The following Web sites offer on-line job services and/or job seekers in the travel and hospitality industry. In most of them, candidates can post and edit their résumés on line, search for positions, and submit applications for jobs listed, free of charge. Point your browser to any of the following sites:
1. *TravelManagement:* www.travelmanagement.com
2. *ASTA Employment forum:* www.astanet.com/www/asta/pub/for/employment.htmlx
3. *Job site with travel sections:* www.4work.com/

✔ *Check Your Understanding 12-1*

1. What is the primary purpose of a résumé?

   _____

2. In addition to basic personal data such as name, address, and phone contact, list five other sections that always should be included in the résumé.

   A. _____

   B. _____

   C. _____

   D. _____

   E. _____

3. List at least three types of information about yourself that are optional on a résumé.

   A. _____

   B. _____

   C. _____

4. List at least three type of information that should never be included on a résumé.

   A. _____

   B. _____

   C. _____

5. For each person below, select which résumé would be the best: chronological or functional.

   A. a recent school graduate who worked part-time a few summers   _____

   B. a person who has had two jobs: five years in one and seven years in the other   _____

C. a person who is entering the workforce after a fifteen-year absence _____

D. a person who has had six jobs in as many years _____

E. a person who has had the same job for more than fifteen years _____

6. Why is a combined résumé a better choice for some people?

_____

JAMES CALDWELL

784 North Main Street • Edgewood, Maryland 21286 • Phone (410) 555–0964 • Email JCALL@AOL.COM

KEY CREDENTIALS

Sales and Customer Service
- Top salesman at Webster Realty, 1994, 1995, and 1997.
- Promoted to Customer Service Manager within two years with a major retail outlet.
- Responsible for generating an increase of 50 percent of revenue from previous year.

Organizational Ability
- Reorganized advertising department of college newsletter and doubled advertising sales.
- Implemented new inventory procedures at a major clothing retail store.

Working with People/Team Skills
- Worked with individuals to help them buy homes and secure mortgages for first-time buyers.
- Assisted business associates and friends in organizing and planning trips for both business and leisure.
- Trained and supervised a team of ten salespeople in a retail environment.

EXPERIENCE

1993–Present   Webster Realty, Baltimore, Maryland
Real Estate Broker
- Assisted customers with all of their realty needs.
- Earned top salesperson award for three years.
- Counseled first-time home buyers in regards to process and securing mortgages.

1990–1993   Michaud's Clothing Store, Baltimore, Maryland
Sales Associate/Customer Service Manager
- Generated leads and conducted sales follow-up within established region.
- Winner of "Best Part-Time Salesperson of the Year" award.
- Trained and supervised a sales staff of ten members.
- Promoted to Customer Service Manager within one year.

EDUCATION

1990   Goldey-Beacom College, Wilmington, Delaware
- Associate of Science, Travel and Hospitality Management

1991–1994   Harding University, Baltimore, Maryland
- Completed course work in the following -
  Business Administration, Computer Information Systems, Desktop Publishing

References Available Upon Request

Figure 12.6 *Combined résumé.*

Preparing a Cover Letter

The **cover letter** is the second most important document in your job search portfolio. In fact, it probably equals that of the résumé since this is the first document that the prospective employer reads—before scanning your résumé. The cover letter is always included with résumés preprinted on the same paper as the résumé. The cover letter's main purpose is to enhance your résumé by emphasizing your strengths and relating your qualifications more directly to the job.

The cover letter is your introduction to a specific person who will have a say in the hiring decision. The cover letter should be very brief and grab the reader's attention right away; if not, it and the accompanying résumé may very well be ignored.

Before writing the cover letter, find out as much as you can about the company and the person to whom you are writing if possible. Showing the reader that you know something about the company beforehand will show that you are motivated, earnest, and thorough as a worker.

Since each cover letter will be a little different, and to save time, try to create one or two basic cover letters in a word processing program and save them. All you then have to do is to insert the new information before sending it off. It sure beats creating an entirely new cover letter with each résumé!

Here are some very important guidelines to follow when writing a cover letter:

1. *Always type, never write.* Would you send a handwritten business letter? Same thing goes for a cover letter; it should always be typed.

2. *Perfect grammar and spelling are a must.* Grammar and spelling should be flawless (just like your résumé).

3. *Never send a copy.* Don't send a cover letter that is obviously a photocopy; it means that you are blanketing the entire city with your résumé! Print each cover letter on a decent printer (a laser printer is the best quality).

4. *Don't mix, but match.* Use the same paper color and bond (weight or type) that you used for the accompanying résumé; they should match perfectly. Remember to use standard size: 8½ by 11 inches.

5. *No one by that name works here!* Don't ever address your cover letter to *"To Whom It May Concern"*—no one with that name works there! Always address your cover letter (and the outside of the envelope) to a specific person's name and title. If you are answering an ad in the paper and no name is identified, call the company and indicate that you are sending correspondence and need the name of the personnel director or manager.

6. *Keep it short.* Two or three paragraphs at the most is your limit! Within that short space you must convince the reader that you have the qualifications for the job—all he or she has to do is to scan your résumé and schedule an interview!

Being able to sell yourself in a few short paragraphs is a difficult task for many. To help you collect your thoughts before putting "pen to paper," remember to include these three sections in your cover letter:

- The first paragraph explains why you are writing. Are you responding to a job position posted at your school? Or are you just sending your résumé not knowing if there is a position at this time (sending a "cold" cover letter). Whatever is the case, state your objective in writing the cover letter: *"I am sending my résumé in response to the position as Corporate Travel Agent which appeared in the Chicago Tribune on November 11."*

- The second or middle paragraphs include a brief synopsis of your qualifications for the job and examples of your experience. Use action verbs and complete sentences that are brief and specific. Include why you feel that you are perfect for the job with that particular company.

- The closing paragraph has another positive statement and tells the reader when you will call as a follow-up to set up an interview.

Figures 12.7 and 12.8 are examples of cover letters. The first is in response to a known opening or ad, and the second is an inquiry; no known opening.

Mr. William Tanner   June 21, 2001
Manager
Tanner Travel Service
1345 Main Street
Burlington, Kentucky 14339

Dear Mr. Tanner:

I am eager to begin a challenging and rewarding career in leisure and corporate sales with a company like Tanner Travel Service. This letter and accompanying résumé is in response to your newspaper ad in the Lexington Times on May 12.

A recent graduate of an intensive travel industry training program in Lexington, I have received intensive training and practical application on System One in addition to courses in geography, sales techniques, and travel product knowledge.

In addition to my professional training, I have worked in the retail industry rising to the level of sales manager for a major clothing store chain.

I believe my strong professional training and previous work experience in customer service and sales can be of great value to Tanner Travel Service.

I would appreciate the opportunity to meet with you to explore my qualifications and my contributions to your company. I will call early next week to arrange an appointment.

Thank you very much for your consideration.

                                          Sincerely,

                                          Jeanne Browning

                                          Jeanne Browning

enclosure

Figure 12.7 *Cover letter in response to a known opening or an ad.*

1008 Clarks Lane
Brighton, MA 02116
(617) 555–0955
March 22, 2001

Ms. Florence Wrenn
Manager
Odyssey Travel
1156 Bristol Road
Wrentham, MA 02554

Dear Ms. Wrenn:

Having completed formal training with academic honors in travel management, I am interested in learning whether there is a career position available at Odyssey Travel for someone with my talents and accomplishments.

In addition to my qualifications stated on the enclosed résumé, I bring with me a history of conscientious and honest effort, a consummate attention to detail, and a congenial approach to working closely with others as a team member.

Perhaps your schedule would permit us to meet briefly to discuss mutual interests. I will call your office next week to see if such a meeting can be arranged.

I appreciate your consideration.

Sincerely yours,

Janet Wilson

Janet Wilson

Enclosure

Figure 12.8 *Cover letter for an inquiry.*

Preparing for an Interview

Remember the last few job *interviews* you went on? Did you go to them hoping to get lucky? Or were you full of self-confidence? Would you describe yourself as being a nervous wreck or a cool cookie? If you are like the majority of us, you were probably not full of self-confidence and definitely not calm, cool, and collected!

Interviewing is a lot like public speaking; you will always have the butterflies before going on but you remain confident because you know your subject. This can't be more true when talking about job interviews since the subject is your-self—and who knows this subject better than you do?

Preparing for an interview is a process; don't show up without doing research and preparing what you are going to say. Preparation is vital since it affords you an edge over your competition. Most people will call in response to an ad, set up an interview, and show up. No research, no thought about what they can do to benefit the company, no knowledge of the science of how to get hired!

That is why candidates who do get hired are sometimes *not necessarily the best skilled or best qualified*. However, they are often adept at *selling themselves in the interview.*

Thirty Most Frequently Asked Interview Questions

1. Why do you want to work for this company?
2. Describe your ideal job.
3. What can you offer us?
4. Where do you see yourself in five years? Ten years?
5. What did you enjoy the most about your last job?
6. What did you enjoy the least about your last job?
7. Have you ever quit a job? Why?
8. What do you consider your greatest strengths?
9. What do you consider your greatest weaknesses?
10. Do you enjoy working under supervision or on your own?
11. Would you be successful working as part of a team?
12. Name the one accomplishment during your previous work experience of which you are most proud.
13. Do you like to take risks?
14. What do you know about our company (products)?
15. Did you receive a good education at . . . ?
16. Do your grades accurately reflect your ability?
17. Have you worked under deadline pressure? How do you rate your performance?
18. Are you able to work on several projects at once?
19. What are your hobbies and interests?
20. What jobs have you held, and why did you leave them?
21. What are your career goals?
22. Why did you choose the travel (hospitality) industry?
23. Why were you out of work for such a long time?
24. Why do you think you will be successful in this business?
25. Why do you want to change careers?
26. Describe your ideal boss.
27. Where have you traveled?
28. Define success. Define failure.
29. What classes in school/college did you like the most? The least?
30. Tell me about yourself.

What if you were sitting in an interview and you were asked, "If I interview ten people today for this position, all of whom have on paper credentials equal to yours, why should I hire you?" In other words, *what makes you so special?* If your answer is to mumble something, just shake your head, or say "I don't know!", you failed in the most important respect: You did not sell yourself or convince them that you are special.

Just having paper credentials alone doesn't slice it—you have to convince the prospective employer that you indeed are the means to solve his or her problems and the one that can help the company grow and be successful. If you emphasize what *you can do for them,* chances are you will be hired almost on the spot.

Here are some very important tips to follow when preparing for the interview and during the interview itself:

1. *Smile, be happy.* You are studying about a career in the travel and hospitality industry, which is extremely *customer-service oriented.* The way you project your personality and enthusiasm often persuades the employer that you are just the type of person who will fit in and will be able to handle the clientele of the company in a pleasant and professional manner.

Most employers in this industry recognize the value of a happy work environment; just one sourpuss on the staff can cause dissension, animosity, and tension on the job. It is a fact that unhappy people just don't produce. A person with charm, a good sense of humor, and a pleasant and agreeable smile will get hired before someone with better credentials who doesn't crack a smile, mumbles, and shows no interest.

Remember, to get hired, the interviewer must like you as a person. The interviewer must also be able to imagine you as part of the team and able to get along with others. Be warm, friendly, be yourself, and try to relax! To show a little nervousness during the interview is to be expected; just don't let it get in the way of a bright and cheerful face.

2. *Dress for success.* Appearance is vital to your success in business and it says a great deal about who you are. Psychologists have determined that 60 percent of the impression you leave with others is based on visual contact. Make sure that you dress with care and that your attire won't offend anyone.

Men, in some ways, are easier to dress for success! Wear suits or a well-coordinated sport jacket, with a light-colored shirt (white is always good), conservative tie, and long, dark socks. If you are going to buy a new suit, dark blues and grays are your best bet. Avoid loud colors when you choose your tie and shirt, and make sure that the style is being worn currently.

Women have a lot more choices. Most experts agree that a dark-skirted suit and a light-colored blouse or top is preferable for an interview. The jacket should be full cut, the skirt—just below or at the knee, the blouse—long sleeved. Pantsuits are okay but not advisable. A dress can be worn but be careful; don't wear anything flashy, short-short, or overbearing. Nothing low-cut, please!

Good advise for both men and women: Go easy on the jewelry, colognes, and makeup. Fingernails clean, cut, and/or polished. Hair washed, shoes neat and polished. Remember, the first impression is made within 30 seconds after meeting!

3. *Don't be fashionably late.* It may be okay for a party, but there is no such thing as being fashionably late for an interview. Plan to arrive ten to fifteen minutes before the scheduled appointment time. If you are in an unfamiliar city or have a long drive to the appointment, allow extra time for the unexpected delays that always seem to occur at the wrong times! Arriving late does not make a sterling first impression. Especially in the travel and hospitality industry which places an emphasis on deadlines and timetables—being on time is of paramount importance!

4. *The eyes have it.* Did you know that the interviewer's mind is 50 percent made up within 30 seconds of meeting you? The first impression is as important as the rest of the interview! When you meet the interviewer, shake hands firmly. People notice handshakes and often form that important first impression based on them! Also, maintain eye contact with the interviewer during the conversation. Failure to make eye contact is a common error; many good candidates failed to get a job simply because they were unable to look the interviewer straight in the eye. Maintaining eye contact indicates that you are interested and focused on what the other person is saying.

5. *Be attentive, but relaxed.* Sit straight in the chair. Don't go overboard and sit like a frozen stick; on the other hand, don't make yourself at home by slouching or putting your feet up. Legs and feet should be together on the floor (don't cross foot over knee), and sit a little bit forward in the chair to show that you are attentive. Hands should be in the lap, but do not fold your arms. That is body language that says: "I am not comfortable with you and I am resisting what you are saying."

6. *Speak up, don't mumble.* Keep your voice at a comfortable level, and try to sound enthusiastic without going overboard like a cheerleader at a football game. On the other end of the scale, don't mumble or speak in a monotone. Be confident, poised, smile, and provide direct and honest answers. Also, if you are offered coffee or tea, you may accept only if the interviewer is joining you.

7. *Prove it.* You sell yourself during the interview by providing relevant qualification statements: you are organized, a hard worker, work well under pressure, and are a great salesperson, for example. However, only identifying all your sterling qualities will just sound like anyone's grocery list. They don't mean very much unless you can back them up with actual *examples and situations.* When you respond with, "I am a successful salesperson," back it up with a verifiable example: "When I was employed at ABC Company, I increased my department's annual sales by 150 percent over the previous year." Prepare by making a list of all your qualifications and abilities. Next to each, write a valid example or situation that occurred that strengthens your claim. If you say that you can work well under pressure, talk about a project at work or school that you completed after long hours of work to get it done ahead of schedule. Be as specific as you can; the more examples you can point to, the better.

8. *The last impression counts, too.* We all know by now the things during an interview that won't get you a job: street language, complete lack of eye contact, insufficient or vague answers, lack of energy and enthusiasm, and poor interpersonal skills. Every impression counts at the beginning and during the interview. The very last impression may outweigh everything that came before it. Before you allow an interview to end, summarize why you want the job, why you are qualified, and what, in particular, you can offer the company. Impress on the interviewer again that you are now, more than ever, eager to join their team.

► What Interviewers Cannot Ask You

The laws today are very specific as to what can be asked by an employer in an interview or on an application. It is illegal to ask you any of the following questions:

- Your gender (on the application)
- Your marital status
- If you have ever been separated or divorced
- If you live with someone
- Physical information (weight, height, physical and/or mental handicaps)

(These questions are okay if specific physical or health requirements are necessary for the job)

- If you have ever been arrested, jailed, or convicted of a crime (unless a security clearance is a requirement of the job)
- If in the military, what branch of the service you were in, or if you received an honorable discharge
- Any reference to age other than, "Are you over 18?"
- Whether you own a home, rent, live in an apartment, etc.
- Any questions pertaining to your religious beliefs

How do you handle it when the interviewer asks you one of the types of questions noted above? In many cases, the interviewer may not be aware that a particular question is not allowed, especially if the person is not a professional interviewer from the human resource department of a large company. If you feel that the interviewer has no ulterior motive than to find the best candidate and you don't feel an honest answer can hurt your chances of being hired, answer the question anyway.

If you can see that an honest answer may hurt your chances, you may want to turn the situation around and ask the interviewer tactfully (not in an accusing tone), "Just out of curiosity, why would you ask me that?" It is not a good idea to get huffy and tell the interviewer you have no intention of answering the questions. Here's a hypothetical situation:

Interviewer: Do you have any young children at home?

Candidate: Just out of curiosity, why are you asking me that question?

Interviewer: Oh, in the past we have hired women with young children and they often had to interrupt work to take care of any problems at home or school.

Candidate: I assure you that I will give 100 percent to this job if I am hired, and by no means will I allow my personal life to affect my work performance.

As you can see, the candidate never answered the question directly but has answered the concerns of the interviewer—that of missing work and being late.

➤ Now It's Your Turn

After you have been properly grilled and bombarded with questions, usually the interviewer will then turn it over to you: *"Do you have any questions about the position or the company?"* Preparing for the interview means more than just having the right answers; it also means having the right questions. No matter how thorough the interview went, you should always ask at least a few questions. If your response is, "No, not at this time," it leaves the interview on a cool note; it implies that you really aren't interested and can't wait to get out of there.

Key Point ➤ *Remember:* The interview process is not only a chance for the company to find out if you are right for the job, but an opportunity to find out if the *company is right for you!* Don't take a defensive attitude about the experience; be just as curious about the company as they are about you. After all, this is *your* career we're talking about!

Here's a list of ten excellent questions to ask. *Beware:* Only ask those questions that have not already been discussed during the interview! If you draw an absolute blank, are nervous, and can't remember one question to ask, remember to ask the last one on this list. The author can speak from personal experience that it is a sure-fire winner!

1. What will my typical day be like?

2. How often has this position been filled in the past five to ten years?

3. What have been the primary reasons for persons leaving the company?

4. What are some of the objectives that you would like accomplished in this job?

5. What are some of the more difficult problems or tasks that one would face in this position? How do you think these could best be handled?

6. Where could a person go who is successful in this position, and within what time frame?

7. How is one judged or evaluated? What accounts for success?

8. How do you characterize the management philosophy of your firm?

9. What characteristics do the travel professionals at your company have in common?

10. Describe the most ideal candidate for this position.

INTERVIEW FOLLOW-UP TECHNIQUES

Now that your interview is over, you can sit back, relax, and wait for the phone to ring! Right? Wrong! What follows after the interview can make or break your chances of getting a job offer. It is surprising that more job candidates don't realize the importance of taking the appropriate steps after the job interview. Many people's reaction may be: "So what else do they want from me? I've sent my résumé, I got through the interview okay, so what else can I do?"

Remember what we said about leaving a lasting impression? The first thing that you should do right after the interview is to write a thank-you follow-up letter to the interviewer. It is a nice touch and it also reinforces your interest and enthusiasm about the job. The interview follow-up letter is essentially a thank-you letter, thanking the prospective employer for the interview. This letter is fast becoming an expected courtesy, so join the crowd!

Timing is important! Write the letter right away; don't sit on it. If your interviewer has talked to a number of candidates, a decision is probably in the making. If it comes down to you and one or two equally-qualified people, your thank-you may tip the scales in your favor.

Your follow-up letter should contain three elements: (1) thank the recipient for the interview; (2) make reference to one or two specific things that were said or learned during the interview, and (3) emphasize again one or two of your sterling qualifications for the job.

By the way, it is perfectly correct to handwrite the thank you; in fact, it is preferred. It is best to use a folded thank-you card—very simple, no cute flowers or kittens on the front, please! Figure 12.9 is a sample of a follow-up letter. Notice that the three required elements are included in this letter.

FINAL WORDS TO LIVE BY

If you don't get the job, don't take it as a personal rejection. There are many reasons why you won't get the job you wanted—perhaps you didn't fit the pattern the employer was looking for; you may not have liked the job if they had hired you.

2153 Grand Avenue
Everett, Michigan 11433

June 26, 1999

Ms. Pauline Brown
Manager
Marchand Travel Services
1345 Crosstown Parkway
Everett, Michigan 11344

Dear Ms. Brown:

Thank you for the opportunity to interview yesterday for the group travel coordinator position at Marchand Travel Services. I enjoyed meeting you and your assistant, George Hillman, and learning more about your exciting company.

Your company appears to be growing in a direction that parallels my interests and goals. The interview with you and your staff confirmed my initial positive impressions of Marchand Travel Services, and I want to reiterate my strong interest in working for you.

My prior experience in retail sales, extensive volunteer and committee work in the local area, and my recent completion of my travel industry studies would enable me to progress steadily through your orientation training program and become a productive member of your team.

Again, thank you for your consideration. If you need additional information from me, please feel free to call.

Cordially,

Hillary Dexter

Hillary Dexter

Figure 12.9 *Sample thank-you interview letter.*

If you feel that you had the necessary qualifications and you did very well in the interview but still didn't get the job, contact the person who interviewed you and ask if he or she can give you some suggestions for the next time you go out on an interview. Don't be defensive or confrontational and don't say, "What did I do wrong?" Chances are you didn't do anything wrong; someone else had more experience, an extra qualification, or in some way fit better for that particular position.

This happens to everyone, so do not be disappointed or angry if you don't get the job of your dreams. Recognize that few people get the first job for which they interview. Most people have to go on many interviews before they come to the job that is right for them. Treat each interview as a learning experience; analyze what occurred and make changes if you think that will help the next time around.

✓ Check Your Understanding 12-2

Preparing for an interview: Below is a list of concerns that many employers in the travel and hospitality field have when hiring new employees. For each, think about how you would respond to the concern if you were asked during an interview. There is a description of how you may want to phrase your response. You will then be asked to fill in, using your own words, how you would respond to that concern during an actual interview. Remember, try to back up each qualification statement ("I am a successful salesperson") with a back up statement ("During my employment with ABC Company, I increased my department's annual sales total by 150 percent over the previous year.").

1. *Concern:* Are you responsible?
   Employers want to know if you are the type of person who is going to be on the job every day and on time. Are you reliable? You may respond with, "Oh, I am very reliable. If I get this job, rest assured that I will be at work on time, every day." These may sound great, but always back up statements with something from your experience or background. On the lines below, how would you respond to this concern during the interview?

   _____

   _____

   _____

   _____

2. *Concern:* Will you put company business first during the workday?
   Some employees take very little interest in the growth of the company or the quality of product or service; they are just interested in punching a clock and getting a paycheck. Travel employers want to know what types of contributions you can make that would benefit the entire company. Your answer may be, "I intend to give 100 percent and I expect others to do the same for the company. That is the only way that companies can compete effectively." In your own words, write a statement that you feel comfortable with that lets the prospective employer know that you truly care about the company.

   _____

   _____

   _____

   _____

3. *Concern:* Why did you select this industry?
   Your answers to this question reveal a lot about you, your work ethic, interests, and motivation. An answer like "I like the travel benefits" won't do! Using your knowledge and understanding of the tourism industry, explain why you find the industry exciting and where and how you see yourself fitting in.

   _____

   _____

   _____

   _____

4. *Concern:* What are your strengths?
   This is often asked during interviews. A good answer to this question is one that the interviewer can identify as benefiting the company. When you answer

this question, think about all the skills and abilities necessary for the job. Think about what you do well that relates to those skills, and back up your statements. How would you describe your strengths in an interview?

_____

_____

_____

_____

5. *Concern:* What are your weaknesses?

Well, you knew this question was coming. Whatever you do, don't provide a laundry list of what you consider to be your faults! On the other hand, don't claim you don't have any; everyone has a fault or two. There are two approaches. The first is to admit to a weakness that is relatively unimportant to the job. For example, to admit that higher mathematics and physics were not your strong points in school won't do much harm! The second approach, which make more sense, is to turn the weakness into strength. For example, "In my last job as office supervisor, I found it difficult to delegate work to my employees. I knew I could probably get the job done faster myself; I tend to take on too much responsibility." Now, you try it. Think about your background and past experiences. How would you answer this question in an interview?

_____

_____

_____

_____

➤ Key Terms

- cover letter
- full-service agency
- independent contractor
- résumé

Flashback The travel and hospitality field is one of the fastest-growing industries in the world. It encompasses a variety of specialized areas and functions. The two sectors that offer a vast number of entry-level positions and opportunities for growth are with travel agencies and hotels. In addition to these tourism segments, there are additional career opportunities with airlines, tour operators, cruise lines, ground transportation companies, inbound tourism services, and many others. This industry is so vast that one out of every three people who are employed is working in tourism.

Travel offers many benefits to hardworking people. It is demanding work and requires people who not only have a love of travel and the world around them, but who have the skills to handle both the technical and people-oriented skills that this industry demands.

The majority of travel professionals are paid by straight salary, but an increasing number of travel companies are compensating their employees with combined salary, bonus, and commission packages. There are many factors that affect a person's earning power: agency location, experience, title, sales focus, and individual sales earnings are a few examples.

Beginning your career in tourism should be accomplished in a professional and businesslike manner. The most important tool you have to market yourself is the résumé. When preparing the résumé, use the format and style that you feel will put you in the best light. Other job search documents, such as the cover letter, are also essential.

Going on job interviews is a lot like public speaking. You will probably get a little nervous before going on, but you should feel confident because you know the subject so well—that is, your personal background, work experience, and accomplishments. After the interview, appropriate follow-up is a must; it can make the difference between getting the job you want or missing out. Follow the rules and recommendations that will put yourself in the best light, and chances are that you will achieve success in your new and challenging career in tourism!

CHAPTER REVIEW

Preparing Your Résumé

Decide which résumé format will put you in the best light: chronological, functional, or a combination of both. Start the process now by filling in the following templates. The first is for a chronological résumé, and the second is for a functional résumé. Use the appropriate sections from each if you want to design a combination résumé. After you have compiled all of your information, put the information in an attractive format.

Chronological Résumé Template

NAME [no nicknames please!] _____

ADDRESS [current and complete mailing address] _____
_____
_____

PHONE NUMBER _____

EMAIL ADDRESS [if applicable] _____

CAREER OBJECTIVE [This is optional. If you include it, keep it as general as possible.] _____
_____

WORK HISTORY [Start with most recent] Just show position/title, name of employer, location by city and state, and years of work. If your work experience is either directly or indirectly related to travel or hospitality, briefly describe your duties. Remember: Use power words or verbs at the beginning of each statement.

1 Position/title: _____
    Name of company/employer:_____
    City/state:
List 2 or 3 major duties (try to make them relate to your career objective)
Duties _____
_____
_____
Year(s) of work:_____

2 Position/title: _____
    Name of company/employer:_____
    City/state:
List 2 or 3 major duties (try to make them relate to your career objective)
Duties _____
_____
_____
Year(s) of work:_____

3 Position/title: _____
    Name of company/employer:
    City/state:
List 2 or 3 major duties (try to make them relate to your career objective)
Duties _____
_____
_____
Year(s) of work:_____

EDUCATION [Start with most recent]
Hints: If you have earned a college degree, you do not need to show high school history. If you attended college but did not complete, simply write "Attended" plus the pertinent information.

Highlight or emphasize your professional training in travel and tourism.

College: _____
Location [city/state]:_____
Type of degree awarded: _____
Major course of study: _____
Year degree awarded (or years attended if no degree): _____
Grade point average [optional] _____
Any awards/honors: _____

Post-secondary (certificate program): _____
Type of certificate awarded:_____
Major course of study: _____
Year degree awarded (or years attended if no degree): _____
Grade point average [optional] _____
Any awards/honors: _____

High school (if no degree earned): _____
Location [city/state]:_____
Type of program (i.e., college preparation, business, etc): _____
Year of graduation:_____
Any awards/honors: _____

SPECIAL SKILLS/EXPERIENCE
This is where you list any additional qualifications or experiences that do not appear elsewhere in the résumé. Include such things as other languages, computer skills, typing (words per minute if you're fast!), personal or business travel experience, and those hobbies and interests that relate to the tourism and hospitality field.

_____
_____
_____
_____
_____
_____
_____

Functional Résumé Template

NAME [no nicknames please!] _____

ADDRESS [current and complete mailing address] _____
_____
_____

PHONE NUMBER _____

EMAIL ADDRESS [if applicable] _____

CAREER OBJECTIVE [This is optional. If you include it, keep it as general as possible.] _____
_____

SUMMARY OF QUALIFICATIONS (or Key Credentials) This is where you describe any transferable skills and abilities that pertain to the type of job position you are seeking. First, draw up a list of three or four competencies required for work in the travel field. Such headings as sales, organizational, leadership, administrative, people-related skills, or human relations are good examples. Under each heading, list a few action statements that demonstrate your competency. Try to include not only what you did but any results.

Competency heading 1: _____
Statement 1: _____
Statement 2: _____
Statement 3: _____
Competency heading 2: _____
Statement 1: _____
Statement 2: _____
Statement 3: _____
Competency heading 3: _____
Statement 1: _____
Statement 2: _____
Statement 3: _____

WORK HISTORY [Start with most recent] Just show position/title, name of employer, location by city and state, and years of work. If your work experience is either directly or indirectly related to travel or hospitality, briefly describe your duties. Remember: Use power words or verbs at the beginning of each statement.

#1 Position/title: _____
Name of company/employer: _____
City/state:
List 2 or 3 major duties (try to make them relate to your career objective)
Duties _____
_____
Year(s) of work: _____

#2 Position/title: _____
Name of company/employer: _____
City/state:
List 2 or 3 major duties (try to make them relate to your career objective)
Duties _____
_____
Year(s) of work: _____

#3 Position/title: _____
Name of company/employer: _____
City/state:
List 2 or 3 major duties (try to make them relate to your career objective)
Duties _____
_____
Year(s) of work: _____

EDUCATION [Start with most recent] Hints: If you have earned a college degree, you do not need to show high school history. If you attended college but did not complete, simply write "Attended" plus the pertinent information.

Highlight or emphasize your professional training in travel and tourism.

College: _____
Location [city/state]: _____
Type of degree awarded: _____
Major course of study: _____
Year degree awarded (or years attended if no degree): _____
Grade point average [optional] _____
Any awards/honors: _____

Post-secondary (certificate program): _____
Type of certificate awarded: _____
Major course of study: _____
Year degree awarded (or years attended if no degree): _____
Grade point average [optional] _____
Any awards/honors: _____

High school (if no degree earned): _____
Location [city/state]: _____
Type of program (i.e., college preparation, business, etc): _____
Year of graduation: _____
Any awards/honors: _____

SPECIAL SKILLS/EXPERIENCE This is where you list any additional qualifications or experiences that do not appear elsewhere in the résumé. Include such things as other languages, computer skills, typing (words per minute if you're fast!), personal or business travel experience, and those hobbies and interests that relate to the tourism and hospitality field.

_____
_____
_____
_____
_____

Travel Industry ABC's

AAA	American Automobile Association
ABTA	Association of British Travel Agents
A/C	Air-conditioning
AGT	Agent
AH&MA	American Hotel and Motel Association
AP	American Plan
APEX	Advance-purchase excursion
APHIS	Animal and plant health inspection
APT	Air passenger tariff
ARINC	Aeronautical Radio Incorporated
ARNK	Arrival unknown (in "computer" language)
ARR	Arrival
ARTA	Association of Retail Travel Agents
ASI	American Sightseeing International
ASTA	American Society of Travel Agents
ATA	Air Transport Association
ATB	Automated ticket/boarding pass
ATC	Air Traffic Conference
B & B	Bed & breakfast
BBR	Banker's buying rate
BP	Bermuda plan
BTA	British Tourist Authority
CAB	Civil Aeronautics Board
CDW	Collision damage waiver
CLIA	Cruise Lines International Association
CP	Continental breakfast plan
CPU	Central processing unit
CRS	Computer reservations system
CT	Circle trip
CTA	Certified travel associate (ICTA designation)
CTC	Certified travel counselor (ICTA designation)
CTM	Circle-trip minimum
CTO	City ticket office
DDWB	Double-double room with bath
DET	Domestic escorted tour
DIT	Domestic independent tour
DLX	Deluxe
DLY	Daily
DOS	Disk operating system
DOT	U.S. Department of Tourism
DP	Demi-pension
DS	Destination specialist (ICTA designation)
DSM	District sales manager
DWB	Double room with bath
EAP	Each additional person
EB	Eastbound
EMA	Extra mileage allowance
EMS	Extra mileage surcharge
EP	European plan

ETA	Estimated time of arrival
ETC	European Travel Commission
ETD	Estimated time of departure
FAA	Federal Aviation Administration
FAP	Full American plan
FET	Foreign escorted tour
FIT	Foreign independent tour
FLIFO	Flight information
FOP	Form of payment
FP	Full pension
GI	Global indicator code
GIT	Group inclusive tour
GMT	Greenwich Mean Time
GRT	Gross registered ton
GTD	Guaranteed
HIP	Higher intermediate point
HK	Holds confirmed
IACVB	International Association of Convention and Visitors Bureaus
IATA	International Air Transport Association
IATAN	International Airlines Travel Agent Network
ICAO	International Civil Aviation Organization
ICC	Interstate Commerce Commission
ICTA	Institute of Certified Travel Agents
IDP	International driver's permit
INS	Immigration and Naturalization Service
IT	Inclusive tour
LAN	Local-area network
MAP	Modified American plan
MCO	Miscellaneous charges order
MPI	Meeting Professionals International
MPM	Maximum permitted mileage
MS	Motor ship
MV	Motor vessel
NACOA	National Association of Cruise Only Agents
NBTA	National Business Travel Association
NPTA	National Passenger Traffic Association
NTA	National Tour Association
NTO	National Tourist Office
NTSB	National Transportation Safety Board
NUC	Neutral unit of construction
OAG	*Official Airline Guide*
OHG	*Official Hotel Guide*
OJ	Open jaw
OK	Confirmed
OW	One way
PAI	Personal accident insurance
PATA	Pacific Asia Travel Association
PAX	Passenger(s)
PCMA	Professional Convention Management Association
PFC	Passenger facility charge
PNR	Passenger name record
PP	Per person
PSGR	Passenger
PTA	Prepaid ticket advice

PUP	Pick up
QSS	Quadruple screw steamship
RFP	Request for proposal
RMS	Royal mail ship
ROE	Rate of exchange
ROH	Run-of-the-house
RQ	On request
RT	Round trip
RTG	Routing
SATH	Society for the Advancement of Travel for the Handicapped
SGL	Single
SS	Steamship
SST	Supersonic transport
STAG	Society of Travel Agents in Government
STE	Suite
STP	Satellite ticket printer
STTE	Society of Travel and Tourism Educators
SUP	Superior
SWB	Single room with bath
SWOB	Single room without bath
TA	Travel agent
TAP	Travel agent proficiency
TIAA	Travel Industry Association of America
TIAC	Tourism Industry Association of Canada
TIX	Tickets
TPM	Ticketing point mileage
TRPL	Triple
TS	Turbine ship
TSS	Turbine steamship
TTL	Total
TTRA	Travel and Tourism Research Association
TV	Turbo vessel
TWB	Twin room with bath
TWOB	Twin room without bath
UFTAA	United Federation of Travel Agents Association
UM	Unaccompanied minor
USD	U.S. dollar
USTDC	U.S. Travel Data Center
USTOA	United States Tour Operators Association
VAT	Value-added tax
VFR	Visiting friends and relatives
WATA	World Association of Travel Agents
WB	Westbound
WCHR	Wheelchair
WHO	World Health Organization
WK	Week
WKLY	Weekly
WKND	Weekend
WL	Waitlist
WTTC	World Travel and Tourism Council
WWW	World Wide Web

Appendix B

Travel Trade Associations and Agencies

Acronym	Name	Members	Head Office	Contacts
ABA	American Bus Association	Motorcoach and tour companies, travel industry companies, manufacturers and suppliers of bus products and services	1100 New York Avenue Suite 1050 Washington, DC 20005	Tel: (800) 283-2877 Fax: (202) 842-0850 E-mail: abainfo@buses.org
ACTA	Association of Canadian Travel Agents	Travel agencies, tour operators, national and international travel service suppliers in Canada	201-1729 Rue Bank Street Ottawa, ONT K1V-7Z5 Canada	Tel: (613) 521-0474 Fax: (613) 521-0805
ACTE	Association of Corporate Travel Executives	Companies involved in corporate travel, including corporate travel managers, travel service suppliers, and travel management companies	515 King Street Suite 330 Alexandria, VA 22314	Tel: (800) ACTE-NOW Fax: (703) 683-2720 E-mail: info@acte.org
AH&MA	American Hotel and Motel Association	Companies in the lodging industry	1201 New York Avenue, N.W. Washington, DC 20005-3931	Tel: (202) 289-3100 Fax: (202) 289-3199 E-mail: info@ahma.com
ARC	Airlines Reporting Corporation	Airlines and travel agencies operating in the United States	1530 Wilson Boulevard Suite 800 Arlington, VA 22209	Tel: (703) 816-8000 E-mail: tbrady@tampa. arccorp.com
ARTA	Association of Retail Travel Agents	Retail travel agents	501 Darby Creek Road, Suite 47 Lexington, KY 40509	Tel: (606) 263-1194 Fax: (606) 264-0368 E-mail: ARTAHDQ@aol. com
ASI	American Sightseeing International	Sightseeing, tour, and charter companies	490 Post Street, #1701 San Francisco, CA 94102	Tel: (415) 986-2082 Fax: (415) 986-2703
ASTA	American Society of Travel Agents	Travel agents, travel service suppliers, and other companies involved in travel sales and promotion	1101 King Street Suite 200 Alexandria, VA 22314	Tel: (703) 739-2782 Fax: (703) 684-8319 E-mail: online form
ATA	Air Transport Association of America	Airlines	1301 Pennsylvania Avenue, N.W. Suite 1100 Washington, DC 20004-1707	Tel: (202) 626-4000
CLIA	Cruise Lines International Association	Cruise-oriented travel agencies and cruise lines	500 Fifth Avenue Suite 1407 New York, NY 10110	Tel: (212) 921-0066 Fax: (212) 921-0549
FAA	Federal Aviation Administration	Federal government agency	800 Independence Avenue, S.W. Washington, DC 20591	
IACVB	International Association of Convention and Visitors Bureaus	Convention and Visitors Bureaus	2000 L Street, N.W. Suite 702 Washington, DC 20036-4990	Tel: (202) 296-7888 Fax: (202) 296-7889 E-mail: info@iacvb.org
IATA	International Air Transport Association	Airlines, government, general public, and other companies involved in the airline industry.	IATA Centre route de l' Aeroport 33 P.O. Box 416 15-Airport CH-12125 Geneva Switzerland	Tel: +41(22) 799-2525 Fax: +41(22) 798-3553

Acronym	Name	Members	Head Office	Contacts
IATAN	International Airlines Travel Agent Network	Travel agents	800 Place Victoria, Suti 800 P.O. Box 123 Montreal, Quebec H4Z 1C3 Canada	Tel: (514) 868-8800 Fax: (514) 868-8858
ICTA	Institute of Certified Travel Agents	Travel professionals	148 Linden Street P.O. Box 812059 Wellesley, MA 02181-0012	Tel: (800) 542-4282
IFWTO	International Federation of Women's Travel Organizations	Organizations serving women involved in the sale and promotion of travel.	13901 North 73rd Street #210B Scottsdale, AZ 85260-3125	Tel: (602) 596-6640 Fax: (602) 596-6638 E-mail: ifwtohq@ primenet.com
ITSA	Interactive Travel Services Association	On-line travel service providers and other companies related to providing on-line travel services	1001 G Street, N.W. Suite 900 East Washington, DC 20001	Tel: (202) 879-9305 Fax: (202) 393-5510 E-mail: detchon@inter activetravel.org
ITSA	International Travel Services Association	Inbound/receptive tour operators, destination management companies, and sellers of travel	7200 Lake Ellenor Drive Suite 150 Orlando, FL 32809	Tel: (407) 888-3351 Fax: (407) 888-3329 E-mail: ista@tish.net
MPI	Meeting Professionals International	Meeting planners and suppliers to the meeting industry	4455 LBJ Freeway Suite 1200 Dallas, TX 75244-5903	Tel: (972) 702-3000 Fax: (972) 702-3070
NACOA	National Association of Cruise Oriented Agencies	Cruise oriented agents and the cruise industry as a whole	7600 Red Road Suite 128 South Miami, FL 33143	Tel: (305) 663-5626 Fax: (305) 663-5625 E-mail: nacoasl@aol.com
NACTA	National Association of Commissioned Travel Agents	Outside sales agents/ independent contractors	P.O. Box 2398 Valley Center, CA 92082-2398	Tel: (760) 751-1197 Fax: (760) 751-1309 E-mail: NACTA@aol.com
NBTA	National Business Travelers Association	Corporate travel managers and travel service suppliers	1650 King Street Suite 401 Alexandria, VA 22314	Tel: (703) 684-0836 Fax: (703) 684-0263 E-mail: info@nbta.org
NTA	National Tour Association	Tour operators, destination management organizations, and suppliers	546 East Main Street Lexington, KY 40508	Tel: (606) 226-4444 Fax: (606) 226-4404
OSSN	Outside Sales Support Network	Outside sales agents/ independent contractors	1340 U.S. Highway One Suite 102 Jupiter, FL 33469	Tel: (561) 743-1900 Fax: (561) 575-4371 E-mail: ossn@ossn.com
PATA	Pacific Asia Travel Association	Government, state, and city tourism bodies, airlines, cruise lines, and industry members serving the Pacific Asia region	One Montgomery Street Telesis Tower, Suite 1000 San Francisco, CA 94104-4539	Tel: (415) 986-4646 Fax: (415) 986-3458 E-mail: patahq@pata.org
STAG	Society of Travel Agents in Government	Travel agencies providing travel services to government bodies	6935 Wisconsin Avenue Suite 200 Bethesda, MD 20815	Tel: (301) 654-8595 Fax: (301) 654-6663 E-mail: govtvlmkt@ aol.com
TIA	Travel Industry Association	Travel industry associations, travel service suppliers, and other travel industry companies	1100 New York Avenue, N.W. Suite 450 Washington, DC 20005-3934	Tel: (202) 408-8422 Fax: (202) 408-1255
TTA	Travel Technology Association	Companies that provide computerized technology to the travel industry	910 Charles Street Fredericksburg, VA 22401	Tel: (540) 370-4894 Fax: (540) 370-0015 E-mail: tta@traveltech.org

Acronym	Name	Members	Head Office	Contacts
USACA	United States Air Consolidators Association	Air consolidator businesses that provide travel agency customers	925 L Street, Suite 220 Sacramento, CA 95814	Tel: (916) 441-4166 Fax: (916) 441-3520 E-mail: webmaster@ usaca.com
USTOA	United States Tour Operators Association	Tour operators that conduct business in the United States	342 Madison Avenue Suite 1522 New York, NY 10173	Tel: (212) 599-6599 Fax: (212) 599-6744 E-mail: ustoa@aol.com
WTO	World Tourism Organization		Capitan Haya 42 28020 Madrid Spain	Tel +34 (1) 567 81 00/20 Fax +34 (1) 571 07 57 E-mail: omtweb@ world-tourism.org
WTTC	World Travel and Tourism Council	Chief executives from all sectors of the travel and tourism industry	Chaussee de la Hulpe 181 Box 10 1170 Brussels Belgium	Tel: +1 (301) 656 0414 Fax +1 (301) 656 9128 E-mail: JulieKutner@ compuserve.com

Source: *PositiveSpace.com.*

Practice TAP Test

Circle the *best* answer for each question.

1. A U.S. citizen, traveling alone, is returning to the United States with $1,200 of custom-free merchandise purchased during the trip. From which destination is this traveler returning?
   A. Bermuda
   B. Nassau, Bahamas
   C. St. Thomas, U.S.V.I.
   D. Montreal, Canada

2. Which pair do not belong together?
   A. LH–Lufthansa
   B. VA–Varig
   C. AZ–Alitalia
   D. SR–Swissair

3. A flight departs Los Angeles at 7:00 A.M. local time and arrives New York at 3:30 P.M. local time. How long did the flight take?
   A. 8½ hours
   B. 7½ hours
   C. 5½ hours
   D. 10½ hours

4. A U.S. passport for an adult is valid for how many years?
   A. 10 years
   B. 5 years
   C. 15 years
   D. 1 year

5. You want to find a list of airline consolidators who offer discounted flights between New York and Amsterdam. Where would you go for this information?
   A. *Travel Planner*
   B. *Jax Fax*
   C. *Official Airline Guide*
   D. *Air Tariff*

6. You have purchased a room with breakfast and dinner included. What plan are you on?
   A. American plan
   B. Continental plan
   C. modified American plan
   D. European plan

7. Which factor would be least likely to affect the cost of a cabin on board a cruise ship?
   A. cabin located on upper deck
   B. cabin with a window
   C. cabin with color TV and air-conditioning
   D. cabin with a verandah

8. Clients are looking to sail luxury class, where price is no object. Which cruise company would you recommend?
   A. Seabourn Cruises
   B. Princess Cruises
   C. Premier Cruise Line
   D. Royal Caribbean International

9. Which pair do not belong together?
   A. Cote d'Azur–France
   B. Algarve–Spain
   C. Turquoise Coast–Turkey
   D. Costa del Sol–Spain

10. Where would you look to find the schedule for the Eurostar between England and France?
    A. *Thomas Cook Timetable*
    B. *Official Steamship Guide*
    C. *Travel Planner*
    D. *Official Airline Guide*

11. Clients are traveling on a luxury train in South Africa. They are probably riding on:
    A. Venice Simplon-Orient Express
    B. Rovos Rail
    C. TGV
    D. Glacier Express

12. The regulatory agency whose main functions is to appoint and regulate travel agencies to sell airline tickets on international airlines that serve the United States is:
    A. ARC
    B. FAA
    C. IATAN
    D. DOT

13. Which is not a required field in a CRS's passenger name record?
    A. passenger name
    C. ticketing date
    B. itinerary
    D. seat preference
14. Which code below does not identify a wide-body aircraft?
    A. 777
    C. M11
    B. 747
    D. 757
15. A traveler purchases two discounted round-trip tickets and uses the first coupon of one and the return coupon of the other to avoid a Saturday night stay. This ticketing practice, which is banned by the airlines, is called:
    A. hidden city
    C. back-haul
    B. back to back
    D. circle trip minimum
16. Which service would be included in the cost of a cruise at no extra charge?
    A. a massage
    C. a ship's photo
    B. a haircut
    D. room service
17. A train is scheduled to depart London's Waterloo station at 1930. What time does it leave?
    A. 6:30 P.M.
    C. 7:30 P.M.
    B. 5:30 A.M.
    D. 8:30 A.M.
18. Which is not a name of a major airline CRS?
    A. SABRE
    C. Apollo
    B. Amadeus
    D. Neptune
19. The maximum amount of commission that can be earned on most round-trip domestic U.S. tickets is:
    A. $25
    C. $50
    B. $100
    D. $75

Answer questions 20 to 25 from this availability display.

```
121APRBOSDEN7A
 21APR      FRI      BOS/EST      DEN/MST-2
1UA    201   F4  Y3  B3  M0  Q4  H2  BOSDEN 7   838A  1110A  M11 BS   0  XS
2CO    129   F2  C0  Y7  H1  K2  B3  BOSDEN 8   855A  1140A  737 B/S  0
3CO    215   F5  C1  Y2  H2  K2  B2  BOSDEN 7   125P   432P  M11 S/   0
4UA    291   F0  Y3  B0  M0  Q0  H4  BOSDEN 9   520P   749P  D10 D    0
5CO    765   F5  C2  Y0  H3  K3  B5  BOSDEN 8   640P   933P  767 D    0  XJ
6UA    445   F1  Y4  B2  M0  Q1  H0  BOSDEN 5   915A   205P  757 BL   1
```

20. Which airline and flight number is direct service?
    A. CO 129
    C. UA 445
    B. UA 291
    D. all are direct
21. Which airline and flight number offers breakfast in first class and snack in coach?
    A. UA 201
    C. CO 129
    B. UA 445
    D. UA 201
22. Which airline and flight number is sold out in standard coach class?
    A. CO 765
    C. CO 129
    B. UA 291
    D. UA 201
23. Which departure does not operate every day?
    A. 125P
    C. 855A
    B. 520P
    D. 640P
24. What is the earliest departure that you can book for four passengers traveling together in B class service?
    A. CO 129
    C. UA 201
    B. UA 291
    D. CO 765

25. Which flight has the highest rate of on-time performance?
    A. CO 129   C. CO 215
    B. UA 291   D. UA 201

26. Which is not a city code in Europe?
    A. MIL   C. TYO
    B. GVA   D. ATH

27. In the Middle East, what city is the home of three religions where the traveler can visit such places as the Church of the Holy Sepulcher, Dome of the Rock, and Western Wall?
    A. Cairo, Egypt   C. Ankara, Turkey
    B. Jerusalem, Israel   D. Beirut, Lebanon

28. After airline flights, the typical travel agency uses the CRS to book what product for its clients?
    A. cruises   C. car rentals
    B. tour packages   D. theater tickets

29. Airlines and other suppliers communicate with travel agencies through the CRS in regard to schedule changes, updates, and current industry news broadcasts by way of:
    A. profiles   C. fare quotes
    B. queues   D. availability

30. Airline passengers originating travel in New York, Washington, DC, and Miami all travel on direct flights on American Airlines to Dallas/Ft. Worth. From Dallas they each connect on a continuing American flight to a different destination. This is an example of what type of system?
    A. interline connecting   C. passenger-controlled capacity
    B. hub-and-spoke   D. regional airlines

31. The term *code sharing* most closely means:
    A. the choice between two airlines in an availability display on an airline's computer reservations system
    B. a cooperative agreement between two or more airlines to share the sales of seats on one airline's aircraft
    C. a connecting service between two different airlines through a connecting city
    D. a fare agreed upon by two different airlines for the same route

32. The continent of Australia is bordered by what two major oceans?
    A. Pacific and Atlantic   C. Pacific and Indian
    B. Indian and Atlantic   D. Arctic and Pacific

33. You are visiting Tiananmen Square, the Forbidden City, and the Summer Palace. Where are you?
    A. Hong Kong, China   C. Beijing, China
    B. Sydney, Australia   D. Tokyo, Japan

34. Your client wants to scuba and snorkel in one of the world's best places for underwater tropical viewing in the eastern hemisphere. Where would you suggest?
    A. Grand Cayman, Cayman   C. Waikiki Beach, Hawaii
       Islands   D. Inside Passage, Alaska
    B. Great Barrier Reef, Australia

35. An airline program that allows passengers to earn awards such as free airline tickets and upgrades based on the amount of airline travel they purchase is:
    A. airline clubs   C. run-of-the-house
    B. negotiated discounts   D. frequent flyer

36. The African river that is considered to be the longest in the world is the:
    A. Yangtze   C. Amazon
    B. Nile   D. Volga

37. Which computer application would you use to track sales revenue that your agency earns from different suppliers and create a chart that shows the results?
    A. word processing   C. communications
    B. database management   D. spreadsheet
38. The free baggage allowance for economy-class travel on the majority of international carriers is:
    A. 88 pounds (40 kilograms)   C. 44 pounds (20 kilograms)
    B. two check-in, one carry-on D. three check-in, one carry-on
39. The method to send electronic messages instantaneously from your computer to the computer of another person located anywhere in the world is:
    A. fax transmission   C. E-mail
    B. telegram   D. telex
40. Visitors to Gettysburg, the Alamo, and Harper's Ferry are probably interested in:
    A. ecotourism   C. historical sightseeing
    B. health and fitness   D. amusement/theme parks
41. The main reason why most travel agents use the Internet is:
    A. to play games   C. to do travel research
    B. to write letters   D. to do office accounting
42. The process by which travel agencies report and settle ticket transactions with the ARC carrier participants on a weekly basis is:
    A. weekly revenue reporting C. airline compensation plan
    B. area settlement plan   D. agreement settlement report
43. If you were visiting such famous museums as the Prado and Queen Sophia along the "Kilometer of Art," you are in what European city?
    A. Rome, Italy   C. Madrid, Spain
    B. Athens, Greece   D. London, England
44. Which pair is not correct?
    A. Los Angeles–LAS   C. Reno–RNO
    B. Daytona Beach–DAB   D. Dayton–DAY
45. Which factor would least affect the price of a hotel room?
    A. hotel location   C. room location
    B. nonsmoking/smoking room D. time of stay
46. The type of accommodation that is the largest category of transient properties and located close to their markets—business and financial districts, shopping and entertainment centers—is:
    A. city commercial   C. resort
    B. spa   D. motel/motor inn
47. Super Clubs, Sandals, and Couples in the Caribbean are examples of what type of accommodation?
    A. bed & breakfasts   C. all-inclusives
    B. spas   D. pensions
48. Which sightseeing region below does not belong in England?
    A. Cotswalds   C. Amalfi Drive
    B. Salisbury   D. Yorkshire
49. What do Baja in Mexico, Italy, and the state of Florida have in common?
    A. they are all islands   C. they are all peninsulas
    B. they are all in the western D. they are all in the tropics
       hemisphere
50. Which pair do not belong together?
    A. ryokan–Mexico   C. Relais & Chateaux–France
    B. paradores–Spain   D. Romantik Hotels–Germany
51. The three countries in Africa known for safaris are:
    A. Morocco, Algeria, Tunisia   C. Egypt, Sudan, Ethiopia
    B. Tanzania, Kenya, South Africa D. Senegal, Ivory Coast, Ghana

52. The Mississippi valley region is the home of many forms of American music. Nashville for country music and Memphis for rhythm and blues are located in what state?
    A. Kentucky
    C. Georgia
    B. Louisianna
    D. Tennessee

53. A major reason why many business travelers prefer staying at chain hotel properties is that:
    A. all are conveniently located in downtown locations
    B. you can expect the similar level of service and amenities
    C. prices are less expensive
    D. all offer courtesy transportation to and from airports

54. A common practice of airlines to minimize the loss of revenue due to last-minute cancellations or no-shows at the airport is:
    A. upgrades
    C. trip cancellation insurance
    B. seat swap
    D. overbooking

55. The travel agent who wants to research the correct way to complete entries on a prepaid ticket advice (PTA) would consult the:
    A. *Travel Planner*
    C. *Official Airline Guide*
    B. *Industry Agents' Handbook*
    D. *Airline Tariff*

56. The requirement that the partner, owner, or manager of a new travel office must have at least two years of full-time experience selling travel is called:
    A. agency appointer
    C. agency designate
    B. agency qualifier
    D. agency nominee

57. The line of latitude that circles the globe and is located halfway between the North and South Poles is the:
    A. equator
    C. Prime Meridian
    B. Tropic of Capricorn
    D. International Date Line

58. To visit the famous Mayan ruins of Chichén Itzá, Tulum, and Uxmal, you would travel to:
    A. Central America
    C. South America
    B. Mexico
    D. southern United States

59. A passenger is flying from Chicago to Los Angeles. He rents a car and drives to San Francisco. The return flight is from San Francisco back to Chicago. This is an example of a(n):
    A. round trip
    C. circle trip
    B. open jaw
    D. one way

60. A location on the globe that is located a short distance north of the equator and south of India has an absolute measurement of:
    A. 5 degrees north latitude, 80 degrees east longitude
    B. 80 degrees south latitude, 5 degrees west longitude
    C. 5 degrees north latitude, 80 degrees west longitude
    D. 80 degrees south latitude, 5 degrees east longitude

61. Which pair do not belong together?
    A. Grand Canyon–Arizona
    C. Zion National Park–Utah
    B. Yosemite–Wyoming
    D. Glacier National Park–Montana

62. A hotel room with housekeeping facilities, usually including a stove, refrigerator, and sink, is a:
    A. suite
    C. efficiency
    B. cabana
    D. duplex

63. The climate of the British Isles is mostly influenced by:
    A. the Gulf Stream
    C. location above sea level
    B. proximity to mountains
    D. the jet stream

64. A nonstop transpacific flight departs Los Angeles at 9:30 A.M. on Wednesday and arrives in Tokyo, Japan at 1:30 P.M. On what day does it arrive?
    A. same day
    C. Thursday

B. Tuesday   D. Friday

65. The least expensive cabin on board a ship is probably located:
    A. upper deck forward   C. upper deck stern
    B. lower deck amidships   D. lower deck stern

66. Which island is not located in the Caribbean?
    A. Jamaica   C. Bermuda
    B. Trinidad   D. Antigua

67. If you wanted to take a warm and sunny beach vacation in the United States during February, you would want to travel to:
    A. Waikiki Beach, Hawaii   C. San Francisco, California
    B. Virginia Beach, Virgina   D. Hilton Head, South Carolina

68. The Canadian provinces that are best known for their natural beauty and where such popular destinations as Jasper, Banff, and cosmopolitan Toronto are located are:
    A. Ontario and British Columbia C. Quebec and Newfoundland
    B. Alberta and Ontario   D. Saskatchewan and Northwest Territories

69. A hotel in Europe offers a *full-pension* plan. A hotel in the United States that includes a room with the same meal plan would be called:
    A. modified American plan   C. European plan
    B. Bermuda plan   D. American plan

70. The national carrier of Israel is:
    A. All Israel   C. Israeli Air
    B. El Al   D. Air Israel

71. Cathay Pacific is the flag carrier for which of the following?
    A. Singapore   C. Hong Kong
    B. Thailand   D. Taiwan

72. The leading cruise area in the world is:
    A. the Mediterranean Sea   C. the South Pacific
    B. Alaska   D. the Caribbean

73. The ARC document that uses a different coupon for each service included on a land package is a:
    A. miscellaneous charges order   C. prepaid ticket advice
    B. tour order   D. automated ticket/boarding pass

74. All computer reservations systems located in travel agencies are affiliated with:
    A. railroads   C. airlines
    B. tour operators   D. cruise lines

75. *CRT* stands for:
    A. computer reservation terminal C. computer recording tape
    B. cathode ray tube   D. cathode reservation transmission

76. Which of the following cannot be booked by an airline reservation system?
    A. hotels   C. tours
    B. cruises   D. restaurants

77. Mr John Smith
    R - Vickie
    Tel - 717–555–9088-H
    TAW27MAR
    The data above represent required elements of a:
    A. profile   C. client account
    B. PNR   D. Web site

78. If you were visiting Glacier Bay National Park, Juneau, and Sitka, you are probably on a:
    A. cruise to the Norwegian fjords C. cruise to Alaska
    B. motorcoach trip through   D. rail tour through northern Russia
       northern Canada

79. A company that plans, arranges, and markets packages to travel agencies and directly to the traveling public is a:
   A. ground operator
   B. wholesaler
   C. tour operator
   D. regulatory agency
80. A Europass is used primarily for:
   A. car rentals
   B. rail
   C. boat and ferry services
   D. motorcoach
81. If a client wanted to travel only within Great Britain, which rail pass would you recommend?
   A. Britrail Pass
   B. Europass
   C. UK Pass
   D. Eurailpass
82. A tour that includes most meals, motorcoach transportation, and the services of the same guide who accompanies the group throughout the itinerary is called a(n):
   A. foreign independent tour
   B. hosted tour
   C. fly/drive tour
   D. escorted tour
83. Qantas is the airline of:
   A. Quebec
   B. Kenya
   C. Cuba
   D. none of the above
84. The principal airline of Switzerland is:
   A. Sabena
   B. Swissair
   C. KLM
   D. Olympic
85. You would suggest places like Costa Rica and Belize in Central America and the Galápagos Islands to someone who is interested in:
   A. shopping
   B. beach resorts
   C. sporting events
   D. ecotourism
86. In which hemisphere are all of the following destinations located: Mexico City, Mexico; Paris, France; Tokyo, Japan?
   A. western hemisphere
   B. northern hemisphere
   C. southern hemisphere
   D. eastern hemisphere
87. What hotel category defines the following chain properties: Days Inns, Comfort Inns, Motel 6, and Hampton Inns?
   A. first class
   B. luxury
   C. economy
   D. midprice
88. Which type of hotel rate represents the greatest discount?
   A. standard corporate
   B. convention and meetings
   C. weekend specials
   D. rack
89. You want the most detailed, comprehensive, and objective description of a particular hotel in Paris for your client. Which resource would you use?
   A. *Official Hotel Guide*
   B. *Star Report*
   C. *Travel Planner*
   D. *Hotel & Travel Index*
90. Which factor would be the least consideration when a business traveler selects a hotel?
   A. location
   B. airline mileage tie-in
   C. price/discounts
   D. fitness center
91. The standard commission travel agencies earn when booking hotels is:
   A. 8 percent
   B. $25 per booking
   C. 10 percent
   D. 15 percent
92. Your client is planning a late arrival at the hotel after the hold time. To secure the reservation you would probably request:
   A. a deposit payment to send to the hotel
   B. a payment for the full amount to send to the hotel
   C. the client's credit card information to guarantee the reservation
   D. any of the above
93. A local tour guide who specializes in a specific area or region and serves as a

guide for a specific segment—lasting from a few hours to a few days—of an escorted motorcoach tour is a:

A. host
B. escort

C. group leader
D. step-on guide

94. The term *net prices* is most commonly associated with which of the following?

A. car rentals
B. consolidator tickets

C. cruise travel
D. designing a Web site

95. You have booked clients on a "soft-adventure" trip. What activity will they experience?

A. mountain climbing
B. scuba diving

C. bird/animal watching
D. white-water rafting

Answer questions 96 to 100 by referring to Figure C.1.

96. What letter represents Scotland?

A. H
B. I

C. F
D. G

97. What body of water is represented by *AA*?

A. Black Sea
B. Mediterranean Sea

C. Baltic Sea
D. Norwegian Sea

98. Four major mountain ranges are indicated by *number* on the map. Which number represents the Ural Mountains?

A. 1
B. 2

C. 3
D. 4

99. You are visiting the cities of Berlin, Munich, and Copenhagen. What two countries—by letter combination—are on your itinerary?

A. E and C
B. A and C

C. J and A
D. B and A

100. You are taking the Eurostar between London and Paris through the Channel Tunnel. Between what two countries, by letter, are you traveling?

A. A and J
B. F and A

C. F and E
D. F and C

Figure C.1

Glossary

....

account executive Employee of a corporate agency who actively solicits new commercial accounts for the company and serves as a liaison between the account and the agency to ensure a smooth-working operation.

adjoining rooms Two or more rooms or units located side by side but without private connecting doors; access between rooms is through the outside hall.

adventure tour Special interest tour that is more strenuous and active than traditional packages. See also soft-adventure and hard-adventure.

aft Toward or in the rear (stern) of the ship.

air add-on Air transportation sold separately from a cruise package; passengers have a choice of purchasing the air transportation from the cruise line or on their own.

Air Traffic Conference (ATC) Airline regulatory agency prior to the Airline Deregulation Act of 1978, which controlled major aspects of commercial passenger air service such as establishing air routes and setting prices.

airline clubs Private and enclosed lounge areas located in major airports worldwide which are operated by specific airlines. Passengers are required to pay a fee to become members in order to take advantage of certain amenities between flights, such as beverage and snack services, private check-in, business facilities, television, and periodicals.

Airline Deregulation Act of 1978 Ensured a decrease and an eventual cessation of US federal government control over the airline industry. The act which was signed in 1978 allowed airlines to control most aspects of their operations, such as establishing routes, setting air fare prices, and setting agency commission levels.

Airlines Reporting Corporation (ARC) Independent corporation that consists of the majority of U.S. airline carriers on a voluntary membership basis. Among its principal functions are (1) to establish standard practices regarding passenger airline service and the sale of airline tickets, (2) to approve authorized travel agencies to sell air transportation on behalf of member airlines, and (3) to serve as a clearinghouse to distribute monies to individual airlines for travel agency ticket sales transactions.

airport codes Three letter abbreviations used to identify specific airport when a city is served by more than one.

air/sea package Cruise package that includes the basic cruise plus round-trip airfare, transfers, and baggage handling.

all-inclusive resort Type of resort that offers complete vacation packages at one price. Price includes accommodations, all meals, full use of sports and recreation facilities, entertainment and transfers. Examples are Club Med properties located throughout the world, and Sandals and Couples in the Caribbean.

allocentric Type of personality defined by the social scientist Stanley C. Plog that is typified by being adventurous and questing knowledge of new ideas and exotic cultures.

American Hotel and Motel Association (AH&MA)   Trade federation of regional and state associations composed of hotel and motel properties throughout the western hemisphere.

American Orient Express   Luxury rail service operating in the United States that offers a variety of rail tours on restored vintage cars.

American plan (AP)   Room rate that includes three meals per day. Also called full American plan (FAP). See also full pension.

American Society of Travel Agents (ASTA)   Trade organization whose principal membership is comprised of travel agencies located primarily in the United States and Canada, in addition to allied members from other travel suppliers such as airlines, tour operators, car rental agencies and motorcoach companies. A primary function of ASTA is to recommend ethical standards and practices within the travel industry.

amidships   In or toward the middle of the ship. Also called *midships.*

Amtrak   National Railroad Passenger Corporation established in 1970 to support the operation of a network of intercity passenger trains in the United States.

Andalusian Express   Luxury train that operates restored vintage cars on scenic routes through historic southern Spain.

archipelago   Group of geologically related islands.

area settlement plan   Process by which travel agencies report and settle ticket transactions to the Airlines Reporting Corporation on a weekly basis.

ARINC (Aeronautical Radio Incorporated)   Intermediary switching system through which computers of all airlines and suppliers communicate with each other.

association   Group of people who share similar interests.

Association of Retail Travel Agents (ARTA)   Trade organization whose membership is open exclusively to retail travel agents. Its primary focus is to help legislation that benefits directly the retail travel agency community.

assumptive close   Type of sales close that is used when the client is ready to buy.

Auto Train   Amtrak's scheduled service between Lorton, Virginia and Sanford, Florida, which carries both passengers and cars.

automated ticket/boarding pass (ATB)   Type of airline ticket generated from the CRS that combines both the airline ticket and the boarding pass.

base fare   Published fare without tax(es).

bay   Part of a lake, sea, or ocean that is partly surrounded by land.

benefit   Item included in a travel product that is intangible—it describes how the client gains or benefits from the product or feature.

Bermuda Plan (BP)   Room rate that includes a full American-style breakfast.

Bernina Express   Popular scenic train that operates rail service between Chur, Switzerland and Tirano in northern Italy.

Berth   Bed in a ship's cabin; the location at a pier where a ship docks.

Blue Train   Luxury train that operates scheduled overnight trips between Cape Town and Johannesburg, South Africa.

boat deck   Deck of a ship where the lifeboats are located.

bow   Front part of a ship.

bridge   Navigational and command center of a ship.

broadcast (burst) faxing   Method that enables the sender to send a fax transmission to any number of pre-programmed fax numbers at one time.

Bullet Train   Scheduled high-speed rail service in Japan. Also called *Shinkansen*.

bumping   Practice of displacing a confirmed airline passenger due to the practice of over-booking or for a passenger with a higher priority.

cabana   Hotel room located on the beach or pool area, usually separated from the main building.

cabin   A passenger's accommodation on board the ship. Also called *stateroom*.

canyon   Deep, narrow valley having high, steep sides or cliffs.

cape   Narrow part of land along a shore that usually curves out into the water.

cathode ray tube (CRT)   Display monitor of a computer.

center of gravity   Balancing point or exact center of a ship; located at the point where a vertical and a horizontal line are each drawn through the middle of the ship.

central processing unit (CPU)   Piece of hardware in a computer where most processing takes place; it interprets data, performs calculations, and stores and receives information. Also called a *microprocessor*.

certified carrier   Major commercial airline carrier that flies medium- to long-distance routes. Examples are American Airlines, United Airlines, TWA, and Delta Airlines. Also called a *trunk carrier*.

Channel Tunnel (Chunnel)   Ground and underwater link between Great Britain and continental Europe.

charter flights   Airline passenger services which do not travel on a set schedule and do not have predetermined fare structures.

choice close   Method used in sales when the agent offers to book a reservation by providing the client a choice of one product or feature over another.

circle-trip   Journey over a continuous route that returns to the same city as the origin but does not qualify as a round trip; a different routing, airline, and/or fare amounts are assigned for each segment of travel.

city code   Three-letter abbreviation used to identify a city that is served by one or more airports.

city pair availability (CPA) display   Display from a CRS when an agent requests what flights are available for a given city pair, travel date, and time.

Civil Aeronautics Board (CAB)   Until the Airline Deregulation Act of 1978, this federal government agency regulated every facet of the commercial airline industry in the United States. See also Airline Deregulation Act of 1978.

classes of service   Compartments or cabins on an aircraft that distinguish the level of service and ticket price.

climate   General pattern or cycle of weather conditions over a large area and averaged over many years.

coast   Land along the shore of a sea, ocean, or lake.

code-sharing   Practice of one carrier using the code of another carrier for a specific flight segment or route. Also called dual-designated carriers.

collision damage waiver (CDW)   Optional insurance coverage that waives the right of a car rental agency to charge for damages in the case of an accident.

commercial flights   Airlines which serve airports on a routine basis with published timetables and fares.

commission cap   Maximum amount of commission that can be earned by travel agencies when selling airline and related travel.

commuter airline   Carrier that operates short-haul routes of less then 400 miles. Most commuters operate small propeller or turbo-prop airplanes that seat from 12 to 40 passengers.

compact disk (CD-ROM)   Disk storage device that holds more information than a floppy or hard disk. A major difference is that a CD-ROM can play video, animation, and sound presentations, in addition to display text and graphics.

computer reservations system (CRS)   Term used in the travel industry for the main computer database of an airline company that contains travel-related information such as fares, flight schedules, seat numbers, and special meals, and allows travel agents to make reservations, print tickets, and other documents for their clients.

conference   Formal meeting for discussion and interchange of views on a particular subject.

configuration   Seating arrangement on an aircraft.

congress   Commonly used European designation for a convention that is mainly international in scope.

connecting city   City on the routing where the passenger is required to transfer flights with no more than four hours between flights on domestic trips, no more than 24 hours on international trips.

connecting flight   Flight itinerary that requires a physical change of aircraft and a change of flight number at a designated connecting city.

connecting rooms   Two rooms or units located side by side with a private connecting door which enables guests to move between rooms without going through an outside hall area.

consecutive-pass   Type of European rail pass that allows unlimited rail travel on a certain number of consecutive days for the duration of the pass.

consolidators   Companies which contract with airlines and other travel suppliers to buy airline seats or space in bulk and sell them at a discount to the general public and/or travel agencies.

continent   Major land mass surrounded by water.

Continental plan (CP)   Room rate that includes a small breakfast consisting of coffee, tea, juice, and rolls.

controlled-inventory basis   Method used by an airline to sell a certain number of seats in coach or economy class of service for each type of discounted fare that it offers.

convention   Large gathering of delegates or representatives of an association to exchange views, ideas, and information about subjects relevant to all participants.

Convention and Visitors Bureau (CVB)   Nonprofit organization whose main goal is to increase the number of visitors to the area.

corporate travel department   Department in a company that handles travel arrangements, usually in conjunction with an outside travel agency; staff members are employees of the company, not of a travel agency.

couchette   Public sleeping accommodation on European trains; usually open bunks in a compartment with pillow and blanket.

cover letter   Typed document that is sent along with the résumé and which emphasizes the candidate's strengths by relating his or her qualifications more directly to the job.

cross-selling   Method used in sales by offering additional products or services to a client.

Cruise Lines International Association (CLIA)   Trade organization that consists of representative cruise line companies and travel agency affiliates. Primary functions of CLIA include the following: (1) to market and promote cruise travel to the traveling public, and (2) to educate and provide sales support to its member travel agencies.

custom allowance   Limit of the value and kinds of items and goods that travelers can bring back into the country of origin.

database   Type of software or computer application that allows you to manage data and produce reports and charts from those data. A database program is also used to sort and access lists of data, such as names, addresses, phone contacts, and so on.

debark   To get off or exit the ship.

deck   Any floor on a ship, inside or out.

deck plan   Blueprint or a floor plan of a ship's design to locate passenger areas, such as cabins, suites, dining areas, recreational facilities, and other services.

delta   Land formed by soil deposited at the mouth of a river.

demi-pension   In Europe, a room rate that includes two meals per day (breakfast and lunch or dinner); also called modified American plan in North America.

demographics   Study of the interests and motivations of a group or population of people by defining who they are in terms of such things as age, income, occupation, family size, and education.

denied boarding compensation   Amount of money or other form of compensation a passenger is paid by an airline as a result of being bumped from a flight.

desert   Portion of land area in which there is little or no rainfall every year; a desert can be a land, water, or polar region.

destination   Final or ultimate stopping place on an air or land itinerary.

direct close   Method used in sales when the agent asks for the booking directly and suggests how to handle some of the details of the booking at the same time.

direct flight   Flight between two cities that has one or more intermediate stop(s) along the route. Similar to nonstop flights since there is no change of flight number.

directed selling   Policy of an agency focusing its sales efforts on a select number of products or preferred suppliers.

directive question   During the sales process, a type of question that requires a focused answer; usually starts with who, what, where, when, or how.

discretionary travel   Segment of the tourism market that is comprised of people who go on trips because they want to travel, such as leisure or vacation travelers.

disk operating system (DOS)   Operating system of a computer which handles all the mechanics, such as starting the computer, regulating hardware components, and shuffling information between different parts of the equipment. This was the major operating system of most PCs before Windows.

Domestic Independent Tour (DIT)   Custom-designed tour for an individual traveler or group of travelers that includes destinations within the home country.

double   Any accommodation occupied by two people.

dual-designated carriers   See code-sharing.

duplex   Two-story suite accommodation that is connected by a private stairway.

eastern hemisphere   Part of the world that consists of Europe, Asia, Africa, Australia, one-half of Antarctica, and the majority of the islands in the Pacific Ocean.

ecotourism   Travel arrangements that combine people's interest in nature along with their concern about the health of the world's environment.

efficiency   Hotel room with housekeeping facilities, usually including a stove, refrigerator, and sink.

electronic fare rules   Detailed descriptions of the terms and travel restrictions governing a particular type of air fare that is programmed and continuously updated in the computer reservations system.

electronic mail (E-mail)   Method to send messages instantaneously to the computer of another person or group of people through the Internet, a local-area network (LAN), or an online service provider.

electronic ticket   Process when a flight reservation is stored in the computer but no passenger ticket flight coupons are issued.

embark   To get on board a ship.

equator   Line of latitude that circles the globe and is located halfway between the North and South poles.

escorted tour   Most structured and organized type of package which generally includes transfers, sightseeing, most meals, and the service of a tour escort or manager throughout the trip.

estancias   Privately owned cattle ranches located in the grasslands of Argentina where guests participate in many recreational activities, such as horseback riding and hiking. Price includes room and all home-cooked meals.

Eurailpass   Rail pass that allows unlimited first-class travel through seventeen European countries during limited time periods.

Europass   European rail pass that covers five to fifteen days of travel in France, Germany, Italy, Spain and Switzerland over a two-month period; other countries are available at additional cost.

European plan (EP)   Room rate that includes no meals.

Eurostar   High-speed train that operates scheduled service between London, England and Paris, France and Brussels, Belgium on the continent of Europe through the *Channel Tunnel*.

exposition   See trade show.

facsimile (fax)   Transmission of any hard copy, such as text, graphics, or photos over telephone lines between fax machines or a PC equipped with a fax/modem.

fare-type code   Code that identifies a type of air fare; the code is comprised of one character or a combination of alpha or numeric characters.

feature   Item included in a travel product that is tangible—it is an objective and factual aspect of the product.

Federal Aviation Administration (FAA)   Agency of the U.S. federal government that is responsible for commercial aviation. Some of its primary functions include airport regulations, air-traffic control, aircraft safety, and maintenance.

feeder airlines   See regional airlines.

fixed cost   Cost related to an entire tour that does not vary with the number of passengers.

fjord   Deep, narrow inlet of the sea, between high, steep cliffs.

flexipass   Type of European rail pass that is valid during a set number of travel days, which can be used over a longer period of time; travel days do not have to be consecutive.

floppy disk   Computer storage device that is a thin, rounded piece of plastic on which information is stored magnetically. Most floppy disks are 3 inches in diameter. Use to copy information to and from a computer's hard disk.

Flying Scotsman   First class rail service in Scotland that offers four- and five-day rail tours through Scotland; the budget counterpart of the *Royal Scotsman*.

foreign independent tour (FIT)   Custom-designed tour for an individual traveler or group of travelers that includes destinations in foreign countries.

forest   Large area of land where many trees grow.

forward Toward or in the front (bow) of a ship.

frequent-flyer program Promotional programs sponsored by airlines which allow passengers to accumulate mileage flown that can be traded in for awards such as class upgrades or free tickets for future travel.

full-pension Price of a room that includes three meals per day. This term is used for accommodations in Europe. Also called *full board*.

full-service agency Travel agency that is open, freely accessible, and clearly identified to the public.

galley Kitchen area on board a ship.

generalist Travel professional whose sales and marketing efforts are diverse and not focused on a particular client or product market.

glacier Thick, large mass of ice that forms in mountains and moves slowly downhill.

Glacier Express Popular scenic rail journey through the heart of the Swiss Alps between St. Moritz and Zermatt.

globe Spherical representation of the earth in three dimensions; it is the most accurate representation of the earth.

Goode's interrupted projection Type of map that interrupts or cuts the globe to minimize distortion of shape; commonly used for large world-thematic map projections.

Greenwich Mean Time (GMT) Prime meridian located at zero degrees longitude that serves as the basis of all the world's time zones.

gross registered tons (GRT) Ship's measurement of size. One GRT is equal to 100 cubic feet of enclosed passenger space within the ship.

ground operator Coordinating company that provide land arrangements and services for travelers arriving at a destination. Examples of ground operators include transfers, sightseeing, and guide services.

guarantee Term used primarily when booking hotels, which means that payment for a reservation is secured even if the guest fails to arrive or cancel in time. Some methods of guaranteeing include deposit, full payment, and credit card.

gulf Large area of the ocean or sea that lies within a curved coastline.

harbor Sheltered body of water where ships anchor and are safe from the winds and waves of storms at sea.

hard disk Storage device that is built inside the computer and works like a floppy disk; it reads and copies information.

hold Interior space below the main deck for storage or cargo and where passengers are not allowed.

hold time Time that a hotel will hold a room reservation without a guarantee. See also *guarantee*.

hospitality suite Room in a hotel used for entertaining, usually at conventions or meetings.

hosted tour   Tour package that includes a local host who is available to assist travelers at each destination with sightseeing recommendations or planning additional tours and entertainment.

hub   Major city airport through which an airline schedules most of its flights to arrive and depart for passenger connecting services.

hull   Frame and body of a ship; that part of a vessel that rests in the water.

inbound sector   A term used in flight or travel itineraries to describe the portion of a trip measured from the outward destination (farthest point), to and including the final destination. This is also called the *return sector.*

incentive travel   Trip that is planned by a company as a reward for outstanding service, productivity, or sales performance.

independent contractor   Someone who works from home under his or her own business name; may or may not be incorporated.

independent tour   Package tour that includes the minimum amount of structure and prepaid features and the maximum amount of freedom and flexibility for the traveler.

intermediate city   Any ticketed point of travel on an airline ticket that is between the origin and final destination.

intermodal tour   Tour that combines two or more types of transportation.

International Air Transport Association (IATA)   Worldwide regulatory agency comprised of the majority of international airline carriers on a voluntary basis. Its primary function is to promote a standard and unified system of worldwide air travel by establishing routes and setting safety and service standards for passenger air transportation.

International Airlines Travel Agent Network (IATAN)   Not-for-profit corporation which is a subsidiary of IATA. Its main function is to appoint and regulate travel agencies to sell airline transportation on international carriers that serve the United States.

international certificate of vaccination   Document issued by the World Health Organization (WHO), used to record immunizations or other preventative measures required of travelers visiting certain countries threatened by disease. Also called the shot card.

International Date Line (IDL)   Boundary that extends from the North to the South Pole across the Pacific and which follows closely the 180th meridian; the IDL designates a calendar date change.

international driver's permit (IDP)   Document that serves as an international driver's license and is required for travelers driving a car in specified foreign countries. The document is written in nine languages and is valid for one full year from the date of issue but is not valid in the country of issue. The IDP is obtained from the American Automobile Association (AAA).

International Standards Organization (ISO)   Standard codes created by IATA to identify countries, local currencies, and taxes.

Internet   Giant computer network that links thousands of commercial, government, and education organizations and millions of users throughout the world.

intranet   Internal, private communication link within a company or organization that uses Internet and Web technologies. An intranet, unlike the Internet, which is available to anyone, is only accessible to people within the organization and other people authorized to use it.

invoice   Document that records a sale and/or a credit to a client's account.

island   Land that is surrounded completely by water.

isthmus   Narrow piece of land that joins two larger land bodies.

itinerary   Complete and detailed schedule of trip.

jet streams   Bands of high-altitude winds about 33,000 to 64,000 feet above the earth; these are the winds that produce a bumpy ride on a jet aircraft.

joint fare   Airline fare that is agreed to by two airlines via a specific connecting city along the route. A joint fare is charged when a passenger is traveling on an off-line (or inter-line) connection between two airlines with such an agreement.

junior suite   Large accommodation with a partitioned sitting area and bedroom.

keyboard   Input device that allows you to type information into a computer.

lagoon   Pool of shallow water linked to the sea by an inlet.

lake   Body of water, usually fresh water, that is surrounded by land.

lanai   Room with a balcony or patio overlooking water or garden, usually in a resort-style hotel.

latitude   Measurement of distance north and south of the equator.

local-area network (LAN)   Network that connects computers in a limited or small area, such as within an office or building.

longitude   Measurement east and west of the prime meridian. Also called *meridians*.

loss damage waiver (LDW)   Optional insurance that releases a renter from paying damages in case a rented car is either stolen or vandalized.

main deck   Longest deck on a ship; separates the hull and the superstructure.

management-fee   Type of service fee that is a flat charge that covers two or more services such as monitoring a corporate account's travel policy and providing management reports.

manifest   Official list of passenger names on a cruise, air flight, or tour.

mark-up   Percentage by which a net total amount is increased to cover direct expenses and commission earnings for such services as DIT and FIT planning.

market exchange rate   Amount of local dollars needed to exchange for other currencies. These rates change periodically and can be obtained through such resources as airline computer reservations systems, major banks, and the *Wall Street Journal*.

maximum permitted mileage (MPM)   The highest number of air miles an airline passenger can travel between two cities at the published fare.

meeting planner   Someone who plans, coordinates, and produces a meeting event.

Meeting Professionals International (MPI)   Professional society for all meeting planners, including full-time consultants, and suppliers of goods and services to meeting planners.

meeting résumé   Guideline that is a detailed schedule of all planned activities during a meeting which includes presentations, workshops, meals, refreshment breaks, and other activities related to an event.

Mercator projection   Common type of map that provides accurate land shapes but with increasing distortion of area located farther from the equator.

meridian   See longitude.

midships   See amidships.

miscellaneous charges order (MCO)   Accountable ticket form issued by the Airlines Reporting Corporation that is used for a variety of payment transactions such as payments for car rentals, accommodations, surface transportation, and cruise deposits.

modem   Device that serves as a computer translator because it changes the data you enter into a computer into a form that can be transmitted over telephone lines and back again. *Modem* stands for *modulator-demodulator*.

modified American plan (MAP)   In North America, a room rate that includes two meals per day (breakfast and lunch or dinner); also called *demi-pension* in Europe.

mountain   Land that rises very high; much higher than the land at its base.

mountain range   Row of mountains that are joined together.

mouse   Optional hardware device that is used along with a keyboard to communicate with a computer; provides a "point-and-click" method of communication.

narrow-body aircraft   Any aircraft that is configured with one walking aisle.

National Tour Association (NTA)   Trade association of tour operators and tour wholesalers located in the United States and Canada.

net price   Price for a product or service that is quoted without commission. Group arrangements, such as hotels and charter air and tours are often quoted net or noncommissionable by the supplier.

neutral unit of construction (NUC)   Basic counting unit, used in international fare construction, that is changed mathematically to become equivalent to a currency.

niche tour (marketing)   Travel arrangement or tour that targets a specific segment of the traveling population or a particular interest or hobby.

non-discretionary travel   Segment of the tourism market that is comprised of people who go on trips because they have to travel, such as commercial or business travelers.

nonstop flight   Flight that has no intermediate stops along the route; there is no change of flight number from the origin to the final destination.

northern hemisphere   Top half of the world, measuring from the equator up to and including the North pole.

Nostalgic Istanbul Orient Express   Luxury tour train that operates only one scheduled trip each year from Zurich, Switzerland to Istanbul, Turkey; the rest of the time the train operates charter trips.

oasis   Place in a desert where water is available from underground springs or irrigation.

Official Railway Guide (ORG)   Amtrak's publication of rail schedules and other related information.

Official Tour Directory   A publication subscribed to by travel agencies that provides information related to the selling and booking of vacation packages.

on-site agency   Dedicated travel agency that is located physically inside the corporate account's business premises.

one way   Continuous trip from the origin to a different final destination, without a return to the city of origin.

open jaw   Journey that is an incomplete round or circle trip, which is not completely closed because of a surface or nonair segment within the itinerary.

open question   During the sales process a type of question that does not allow for a simple yes or no response but tries to elicit as much information as possible from the client.

option   Final date on which a deposit or payment must be received by a supplier to secure a reservation.

origin   Term used in flight or travel itineraries to describe the city where a trip begins.

outbound sector   Term used in flight or travel itineraries to describe that portion of a trip measured from the origin, to and including the outward destination (or farthest point).

outbound services   Companies that provide travel arrangements and services for travelers who are traveling from the home community to a destination (outbound service providers). Examples are travel agencies and tour operators.

outward destination   Term used in flight or travel itineraries to describe a city that is located farthest from the origin.

overbooking   Common practice among airlines to overbook by a projected number of seats on a flight to avoid lost revenue due to no-shows and last-minute cancellations.

override commission   Commission earned by a travel agency that is higher than the standard level, as a bonus or incentive to increase productivity.

Palace on Wheels   Luxury tour train that operates seven-night trips on the route called the Golden Circle of India, with stops in Delhi, Agra, and Jaipur.

paradores   Network of government-owned lodgings in Spain that have been converted from old, historic buildings such as castles, convents, and monasteries.

passenger name record (PNR)   All required and important information regarding a passenger's reservation in a CRS such as passenger name(s), phone contacts, ticketing information, and flight itinerary.

passport   Federal government document which proves that the bearer is a citizen of the country of issue; it authorizes the bearer to travel outside, and return to, the country of origin.

peninsula   Land area with a narrow link to a larger land area; it is almost totally surrounded by water.

per diem   Priced on a per-day basis.

personal accident insurance (PAI)   Optional insurance coverage offered by car rental firms which covers the renter's accidental death or medical expenses resulting from bodily injury during an accident.

"Pied Piper"   Person from an association or organization who motivates the group members to travel and organizes the trip during the planning stages with the travel agency.

pitch   Front-to-back (bow-to-stern) motion of a ship; distance between seats on an airplane.

plain   Large, flat area of land.

plateau   Large land area that is high and generally very flat.

point-to-point fare   Fare calculation term meaning that a fare is charged to each stopover city on the routing.

political map   Representation of the earth or part of the earth that identifies by name, and separates by boundaries, countries, states, cities, provinces, and other geographical regions.

port   Left side of a ship when facing toward the bow or front end; the place where ships dock.

port-of-call   Scheduled visit to a destinations or port during a cruise.

porthole   Round window or opening on the side of a ship.

post-cruise land tour   Hotel land package offered at the end of a cruise; includes accommodations, transfers, and sightseeing.

pousadas   Network of government-owned lodgings in Portugal that have been converted from old, historic buildings such as castles, convents, and palaces.

pre-cruise land tour   Hotel land package offered at the beginning of a cruise; includes accommodations, transfers, and sightseeing.

preferred supplier   Travel company whose products a travel agency chooses to sell above others.

prime meridian   Line of longitude that runs through Greenwich, England and represents zero degrees longitude. Also called *Greenwich Mean Time (GMT)*.

printer   Piece of hardware hooked up to one or more computers that generates hard copies of documents, airline tickets, invoices, or anything else that is created in the computer. The three major types of printers in the order of average to best quality are dot matrix, ink jet, and laser.

Professional Convention Management Association (PCMA)   Trade organization whose members are involved in meeting planning in the medical, engineering, scientific, and educational fields.

profile   Electronic file in which the travel agent can store any data that relate to a particular traveler or corporate account.

psychocentric   Type of personality defined by the social scientist Stanley C. Plog that is typified by someone who is more comfortable in familiar surroundings and conforming socially.

quad   Any accommodation occupied by four people.

qualifying   Fact-finding stage during the sales cycle used to gather as much information as possible about the client.

quay   Berth, dock, or pier (pronounced *key*).

rack rate   Full, published room rate without a discount.

rail 'n drive pass   Type of European rail pass that combines an unlimited number of rail trips and an unlimited mileage car rental for a certain number of days; this type of rail pass is available in various countries.

random access memory (RAM)   Temporary storage area located inside a computer's central processor unit that holds the programs and files with which you are currently working. RAM is also called *read/write memory* since you can retrieve or *read* information stored there and also record or *write* information to it.

rebating   Practice of a travel agency to return a portion of its earned commission to a corporate account to guarantee its business.

receipt   Document that records the amount paid and, if applicable, the balance due; also indicates the form of payment, whether cash, personal check, or credit card.

receptive service operator (RSO)   Company that provides receptive services for inbound travelers; also called *ground operators.*

receptive services   Companies that provide services and facilities for travelers when they arrive at a destination (inbound travelers). Examples are lodging, food service, meet and greet services, hosts and guides, attractions, and tourist offices.

reef   Chain of rocks or ridges of sand at or near the surface of the water.

reflective question   During the sales process a type of question which confirms or clarifies something that has already been said. Also called a *feedback question.*

regional airline   Domestic or local airline carrier that provides air service within a defined geographical area. Offers short- to medium-distance routes between small cities and connects these communities with high-density air traffic centers. Also called *feeder airline.*

registry   Country whose laws the ship and its crew are obliged to comply.

relief map   Representation of the earth or part of the earth that shows natural features of the land including mountains, valleys, rivers, and hills; land elevations and shapes are indicated by different colors or shading.

request for proposal (RFP)   Document that is sent out to travel companies for bidding purposes; serves as a profile of the company and its business travel needs.

resort   Hotel that is considered to be a destination by itself due to the full range of services and leisure amenities for guests.

résumé   Summary of the important facts about a person which pertain directly to the position that he or she is seeking.

river   Large, moving body of fresh water that starts at a source in higher land.

Robinson projection   Map projection that maintains overall shape and area relationships without extreme distortion; widely used in textbooks, atlases, and classrooms.

roll   Side-to-side motion of a ship.

round trip   Journey via a continuously charged route that returns to the same city as the point of origin. Each direction of travel will have the same routing and/or fare charged.

route map   Representation of the earth or part of the earth that shows major routes of airlines, trains, and cruise ships through drawn lines and curves on political or relief maps.

Rovos Rail   Luxurious and elegant tour train that operates over scenic routes between Cape Town and Pretoria, South Africa.

Royal Scotsman   Luxury train appointed in the Edwardian style that operates between Edinburgh and other points in Scotland.

run-of-the-house (ROH)   Type of discount and automatic upgrade program found in hotels where the guest pays a flat minimum rate and receives the best available accommodation at check-in.

ryokans   Typical Japanese inns and accommodations that offer all facilities and amenities in Japanese style. Guests sleep on tatami mats, with other services that include Japanese-style baths and food served in the traditional way.

satellite ticket printer (STP)   Ticket printer owned and operated by a travel agency which is installed at the corporate account's office premises.

scanner   Type of computer hardware that works like a copy machine; takes an electronic image of a picture, text, or illustration and stores it in the computer.

sea   Large body of salt water nearly or partly surrounded by land; a sea is much smaller than an ocean.

search engine   Type of index for web sites; it helps the user to find one or more specific sites after entering key words or phrases. Examples of popular search engines are AltaVista, Excite, HotBot, Yahoo!, and Webcrawler. Also called *search directories*.

seat map   Diagram showing the seating configuration of an aircraft.

selling price   Total cost of a tour or other product that includes tax (if applicable) and an agency's commission.

service provider   Mostly for-profit-company that offers computer users a method of sending and receiving information to and from other computers linked to the Internet. Popular commercial service providers include America Online, Microsoft Net, and Prodigy.

shore excursion   Organized sightseeing land tour for passengers while a cruise ship is visiting a port of call; shore excursions are at an additional price.

Sierra Madre Express   Scenic rail ride through the Copper Canyon region in north central Mexico.

single   Any accommodation occupied by one person.

sleeper   Sleeping accommodation on European trains; contains berths with private washstand, linens, towels, and pillow.

SMERF   Market for meeting events including any type of social, military, education, religious, or fraternal organization.

southern hemisphere   Bottom half of the world measuring from the equator down to and including the South Pole.

spa   Health resort that specializes in diet and fitness programs. Price includes all standard resort services and amenities with the emphasis on health, fitness, and diet.

spreadsheet   Type of software or computer application that allows you to enter numbers and formulas to instruct a computer to make a variety of calculations, such as add, subtract, multiply, divide, or obtain averages and percentages.

stabilizers   Finlike devices that extend from both sides of a ship below the waterline to provide a smoother ride.

starboard   Right side of a ship when facing toward the bow or front.

step-on guide   Local specialist or guide who joins a motorcoach tour to provide a local sightseeing tour for a short period of time. Also called a *local* or *city guide*.

stern   Back end of a ship.

stopover city   City on a routing where the passenger makes a deliberate or voluntary stop of more than four hours on domestic trips; 24 hours on international trips.

strait   Passageway of water that connects two large bodies of water.

studio   Room with couches for daytime use that convert into beds for sleeping.

subscriber   Travel agency that buys and uses a particular CRS.

suite   Large accommodation with a separate sitting area that is connected to one or more bedrooms.

summary close   A method used in sales when the agent reviews the features and benefits of the product before finalizing or asking for the sale.

superstructure   Part of a ship above the hull.

symposium   Meeting event in which several speakers deliver short lectures or demonstrations on related topics and where opinions are gathered.

tariff   Compilation of fares, rules, and related information in a published volume.

tender   Small vessel used to carry passengers to shore when a ship is at anchor.

through fare   Air fare calculation term that indicates a published fare between two stopover cities over an intermediate connecting city; a fare is *not* charged to or from the connecting city.

ticketed point mileage (TPM)   The most direct air mileage measured between two cities; used in international fare calculation.

time zone   Slice of the earth equivalent to 15 degrees of longitude or 15 degrees wide; there are 24 times zones that divide the earth.

tour operator   Company that plans, arranges, and markets vacation packages. Most tour operators sell directly to the public and through travel agencies.

tour order   Accountable ticket form issued by the Airlines Reporting Corporation that is used to transmit payments for tours.

tour package   Opportunity to purchase two or more different travel components that otherwise would be purchased separately from different suppliers.

tour wholesaler   Company that plans, arranges, and markets tours through travel agencies. As a rule, tour wholesalers do not sell directly to the public.

tourist card   Government document that serves as permission to enter a foreign country and indicates the name of the traveler and the purpose of traveling to that country.

trade show   Public exhibit, display, or show where the displays or exhibits themselves are the central focus. Also called *exposition*.

trade winds   Global winds that blow steadily toward the equator from the northeast or southeast; responsible for weather conditions at the surface.

traffic conference areas   IATA's three geographical divisions of the world used for international faring and ticketing purposes.

Train à Grande Vitesse (TGV)   High-speed rail service in France.

transactional fee   Type of service fee that is a set charge for a specific item or service, such as issuing an airline ticket or booking a hotel.

transient hotel   Category of accommodations that is designed for short-term stays. Four examples of transient lodging include city commercial, airport, all-suite, and motels or motor inns.

travel management report   Accounting of how much a company is spending on travel and entertainment (T&E) expenses.

tributary   Stream or small river that flows into another river or stream.

trunk carriers   See certified carrier.

Twilight Express   Deluxe and luxurious train in Japan that operates scheduled service from one end of the island of Honshu to the other.

twin   Any accommodation occupied by two people.

United States Tour Operators Association (USTOA)   National organization of tour operators, hotels, airlines, car rental companies, tourist boards, and other travel service providers worldwide. Its primary goals are to inform the industry and traveling public about tour operators' activities and maintain a high level of professionalism within the tour operator community.

up-selling   Practice of offering a higher-priced product or level of service to a client during the recommendation stage of a sales cycle.

valid concern   During the sales cycle, an objection due to a product not having a feature that supplies a benefit to the client; or a perceived disadvantage offered by the product or feature.

valley   Lower land between hills or mountains.

value   What the client will be getting for his or her money when buying a travel product or service.

value-added tax (VAT)   Taxes charged by various countries which are built into the purchase price of goods purchased in those countries. VAT taxes vary from 2.9 to 20 percent.

A VAT refund is a privilege extended to U.S. residents when shopping in certain foreign countries.

variable cost   Any item of a tour that is priced on a per-passenger basis.

Venice-Simplon-Orient Express (VSOE)   Luxury train that evokes the romance and nostalgia of rail journeys of the past which operates scheduled service over one main route between London, England and Venice, Italy.

VIA Rail Canada   Rail system operating in Canada.

visa   Endorsement or stamp in a passport that is placed by a government official or in the form of a separate document that is obtained in advance of a trip. A visa is required by some, but not all countries, and indicates the conditions under which a traveler may enter the country.

void concern   Misconception that a client has about a product because it is not based on anything that is valid or true.

volcano   Vent in the earth's crust where molten or hot rock and steam are ejected from the earth's interior. Three types are: active, dormant and extinct.

weather   Expression of day-to-day conditions.

weather deck   Any deck on a ship open to the outside.

western hemisphere   Part of the world that consists of the North and South American continents, Iceland, one-half of Antarctica, plus all of the adjacent islands, including Hawaii.

wide-body   Any aircraft that is configured with two walking aisles.

windward   Side of a mountain, ship, or coastline that is facing into the wind.

word processing   Software program or application that allows you to compose letters, memos, reports, proposals, or any other text document.

workshop   Meeting event that is a short course or training session geared to enhance skills or develop knowledge in a specific topic.

World Association of Travel Agencies (WATA)   Non-profit organization created by independent travel agencies around the world.

World Health Organization (WHO)   International agency that establishes regulations regarding immunizations and other preventive measures for travelers to certain countries of the world which are threatened by such diseases as cholera and yellow fever.

World Wide Web (WWW)   Menu-based software program that links millions of information and research resources on the Internet. The WWW creates a user-friendly interface with the Internet, which allows companies to advertise and promote their products through web sites.

Index